D1416972

PRENTICE-HALL SERIES
IN INDUSTRIAL RELATIONS AND PERSONNEL

Dale Yoder, Editor

Compensation
Administration

DAVID W. BELCHER

San Diego State University

PRENTICE-HALL, INC., *Englewood Cliffs, New Jersey*

Library of Congress Cataloging in Publication Data

BELCHER, DAVID W
    Compensation administration.

    (Prentice-Hall industrial relations & personnel series)
    Published in 1955 and 1962 under title: Wage and salary administration.
    Includes bibliographical references.
    1. Wages.   I. Title.
HD4909.B43 1974   658.32   73-11068
ISBN 0-13-154161-7

Printed in the United States of America.

10   9   8   7   6   5   4   3

Prentice-Hall International, Inc., *London*
Prentice-Hall of Australia, Pty. Ltd., *Sydney*
Prentice-Hall of Canada, Ltd., *Toronto*
Prentice-Hall of India Private Limited, *New Delhi*
Prentice-Hall of Japan, Inc., *Tokyo*

To

B. A. B.

Contents

II Contributions

||| Rewards

IV The Comparison Process

V Compensation Problems of Special Employee Groups

VI System Integration and Control

Preface

Compensation management presents real and continuing problems to most organizations, and solutions tend to be temporary and imperfect. These problems arise from: (1) the changing nature of compensation, (2) the changing nature of the labor force, (3) rising expectations of employees.

Compensation, for most employees, includes not only money but numerous and varied benefits and many nonfinancial rewards. One of the problems flows from the differing definitions of compensation by different employee groups. Some employee groups recognize only money as a reward for work. Most employee groups increasingly value benefits as part of their compensation. Many employee groups recognize and value numerous nonfinancial rewards, some of which the organization may not be aware of providing.

Because the resources of all organizations are limited, compensation systems must be designed to meet the requirements of all employee groups and to achieve optimum returns to the organization for the resources it spends. When compensation consists of a number of different elements, coordination become a problem. Unless all forms of compensation are reasonably well integrated for each employee group, the reward system may be giving conflicting signals to employees.

Quite different employees groups continue to emerge. Most organizations are employing more professional employees of various kinds. Organizations involved in rapidly changing technologies are employing more managers, and many organizations are restructuring jobs to assign managerial tasks at lower levels. More women at all levels are being employed, as are members of minority groups. Separate compensation systems are required to the extent that organizations expect different work behaviors from different groups and to the extent that different employee groups have different definitions of compensation.

Perhaps the only common denominator of all employee groups is rising expectations. The guaranteed annual raise has become an almost universal expectation of employees, at least during periods of rising prices. Employees appear to have become more sophisticated about the relationship between their pay and the cost of living. Rising expectations also appear to apply to the other forms of compensation. At least certain employee groups expect more interesting and challenging jobs and more control over their life at work. The young (even among middle management) are questioning organizational restrictions and rules.

Given these changing forces, it is surprising that compensation management works as well as it does. Part of the reason, perhaps, is the almost universal acceptance of certain compensation practices and the pragmatic adjustments that have been made in them. In the face of change and imperfect knowledge, an understandable human tendency is to do nothing or, if forced to do something, to do what others are doing.

Although we know quite a bit about managing compensation, there is much we do not know. Although economists have studied wages for years their primary concern has been with wage determination and only secondarily with pay decisions within organizations. Because economists define wages as prices for labor services, organizations have understandably accepted this definition, with the result that other forms of compensation largely have been ignored. Very little thought has been given to what organizations should expect in return for compensation.

In recent years, psychologists have devoted a good deal of study to pay. Their emphasis has been on behavior elicited by pay within organizations and the way in which pay was administered. Psychologists and sociologists also have studied other rewards that employees receive within organizations and the conditions under which they do so. Sociologists and psychologists have also studied human behavior as an exchange transaction.

The latter approach seems to be a useful way of bringing together the findings of economists, psychologists, and sociologists on managing compensation in organizations. Looking at employment as an exchange between the organization and the employee, in which each gets something and gives something, seems to be a fruitful way of seeing what is going on in compensation management. This approach is used in this book to analyze compensation problems and common compensation policies and practices as applied to different employee groups. If it has been successful, students will have a clearer picture of compensation management and compensation administrators will know more about fitting compensation policies and practices to the requirements of the organization and the desires of employees.

Although this book is a result of over twenty years of studying compensation, it also reflects comments and suggestions from the users of the first and second editions of *Wage and Salary Administration.* Although I am deeply indebted to those who provided these suggestions, I fully accept the responsibility for their interpretation.

A special debt is due my colleague, Professor T. J. Atchison, who via a long-term dialogue greatly influenced the plan of the book. Our debates on compensation issues, his suggestions and criticisms of some of the chapters, and his contributions to the basic model are all deeply appreciated. Appreciation is also expressed to the authors, editors, and publishers whose materials contributed to the ideas in this book. Every effort has been made to give full credit; any omission is unintentional. Finally, deepest appreciation is expressed to Betty Ann Belcher who assumed responsibility for transforming crude drafts into a finished manuscript. My debt to her can be fully appreciated only by another author fortunate enough to acquire by marriage his own librarian, editor, artist, typist, and friendly critic.

The author was gratified to find the first and second editions of *Wage and Salary Administration* used by graduate and undergraduate schools of business, in economics courses both at the graduate and undergraduate levels, by schools of engineering, and by numerous practitioners. I hope that these groups find this book equally useful.

D. W. Belcher

Compensation Models

Compensation is interpreted in this book as involving an exchange between employees and organizations in which each is getting something in return for giving something. Because economists, psychologists, and sociologists have studied compensation from different vantage points, this part of the book summarizes the theory and research in these disciplines that seem to bear upon compensation. Chapter 1 examines a number of possible views of the employment relationship and develops an employment exchange model, which is the framework for the book. Chapter 2 examines the considerable contribution of economics to understanding compensation. Chapter 3 summarizes the behavioral science theory and research and develops two motivation models that are used in the book as submodels to the employment exchange model.

1

The Employment
Exchange Model

Compensation represents a transaction between man and organization involving the employment contract. Although the transaction may be variously considered as an economic, psychological, sociological, political, or ethical exchange, it is all of these and more than any one of them.

AN ECONOMIC TRANSACTION

Compensation does represent an economic transaction. Pay is the price the organization pays for employing a factor of production. In this sense, payment for employee services is an economic transaction governed by the same logic as any other purchase in which the purchaser attempts to obtain the greatest quantity and the highest quality for his money. In this sense, also, the worker is selling his services to obtain income and he holds out for the highest price he is able to command. These transactions are supposed to set the price in terms of the demands of purchasers and the supplies of the sellers and to allocate the scarce economic resource (labor) to the employment wherein it has most value. These results would accrue if labor were a commodity.

Unfortunately for the potential employee, however, his labor is perishable in that if today's labor is not purchased today it has no value tomorrow. Also, labor is not a commodity like an ingot of aluminum that can be bought according to size, weight, and strength specifications and chemical composition, all of which can be tested before purchase and will remain stable after purchase. In addition to being perishable, labor

3

varies with the ability of the individual to work, it may differ from day to day and hour to hour, and it is affected by the conditions of work.

In this way, the quantity of labor supplied is a variable that is influenced only partially by factors controllable by the purchaser. In fact, the attitude of the supplier is a major element in the labor supplied, and the supplier cannot be separated from his labor and can change it if he so desires.

This variability of supply has both advantages and disadvantages for the purchaser. Because the supply purchased is variable and capable of being employed in many ways, the purchaser may be able to influence the quantity and quality purchased. He may, for example, through developmental efforts, upgrade the quality of his purchase. Likewise, when the needs of the organization change, the labor supplier can quickly fill the changed needs. In this way the variable nature of the supply permits the purchaser's demands to be variable.

And these demands *are* variable. The purchaser is not buying labor service for his own use but to produce goods or services for sale. The employer's demand for labor is derived from the demands for these goods and services, and a change in these demands may call for a change in his needs for labor service. Equally important are the various kinds of demands for labor service the employer has at any one time —from janitors to vice-presidents—and the needs of the organization may require labor suppliers to shift from one type of work to another.

But the variability of both demands and supplies makes it difficult for the purchaser to quote a price. The real cost of labor to the employer is the cost per unit of output. The seller, however, requires that a price be quoted before he sells. Hence, the purchaser must offer a price before the bargain is made. He must quote a price that represents what an average unit of labor is worth to him, and he must derive this price from his cost per unit.

The supplier of labor services likewise experiences difficulty in determining what price to accept. His knowledge is even more imperfect than the employer's. At best, he can only know what range of prices other employers are paying. Furthermore, he cannot know the conditions of employment in the organization in advance, but nevertheless must somehow translate all the unknowns into monetary terms. Also, the labor supplier may have chosen to be represented by a sales representative (his union) possessing motives beyond his own.

The labor market is assigned the task of making sense of this wide array of forces. It must bring together the purchasers and sellers of labor services, it must set prices, and it must seek to maintain a balance between demands and supplies. A multiplicity of labor markets exist corresponding to the different types and grades of labor. But perfect balance in which one price exists for each grade seldom occurs. Wide differences prevail in rates paid by employers for equivalent labor on similar jobs.

If such wage diversity does not exist, it is because of market restrictions, not because of market operations. In some highly unionized markets, for example, one price is set for the market—not by market forces, but by union contract.

If compensation for labor services were influenced only by economic considerations, pay for similar work would be equal in all employment, and differences in pay among occupations would reflect only scarcities that the market has not had time to adjust or actual differences in ability. Although it is feasible to explain the diversity that actually exists in terms of frictions that attenuate market forces, it appears much more realistic to recognize the noneconomic forces that affect compensation decisions.

In our society, the total income of most of our adult population comes from the sale of their labor services. These payments are extremely important in the operation of the economy. In the aggregate, compensation makes up the largest single type of income. In our system, pay is important not only because it represents the largest single source of income, but also because of the part it is expected to play in the operation of our economy. Compensation is expected to play a major role in creating both an efficient allocation of human resources and their careful utilization. At the same time, aggregate compensation plays a major part in maintaining a satisfactory level of purchasing power. This purchasing power should be balanced with our aggregate output of goods and services to ensure the smooth functioning and stability of our economy.

Although it is useful to view the transaction involving compensation as an economic exchange, a number of dysfunctions result from this perspective. One is the focus on the organization and the economy rather than on the individual. Because the organization is the purchaser of labor services, it is assumed to be the active decision-maker, with the individual assigned a passive role. Unions are assumed to influence the transaction but nonrepresented employees are not.

Another dysfunction stems from the assumption that compensation is limited to economic rewards. Organizations extend a wide variety of rewards. Many noneconomic rewards are involved in the transaction, often without being recognized by either party. To the extent that the economic perspective ignores noneconomic rewards, the transaction is incompletely analyzed.

Another dysfunction appears to result from two assumptions: that labor services are what organizations purchase, and that individuals are passive instruments in the transaction. As already mentioned, organizations appear to realize that the major advantage of human beings to organizations is their flexibility. But the economic perspective serves to conceal the contributions organizations actually require from employees. Including, for example, concern for quality, cooperation with other organization members and units, and willingness to accept change under labor services tends to ignore important parts of the transaction.

Still another dysfunction of the economic perspective is the emphasis it encourages on looking to labor markets rather than the other party to the transaction—the individual—to evaluate the transaction. If the organization looks outward and the individual looks inward, neither party to the transaction may be satisfied.

A PSYCHOLOGICAL TRANSACTION

Compensation also represents a psychological transaction. In fact, employment represents a psychological contract between man and organization in which the individual exchanges certain desired types of behavior for pay and other sources of job satisfaction.

The situation and the needs, perceptions, and attitudes of the individual determine behavior. But the situation and the individual are not independent because the situation is that perceived by the individual. Needs are invisible even to the individual. Means for satisfying needs are those perceived by individuals and interpreted as such through attitudes (categories of past experiences). It is quite possible for one need to be satisfied by a number of means and one means to satisfy a number of needs.

The psychological contract between the individual and the organization attains reality through the eye of the beholder. Rewards offered by the organization enter the contract only if the individual perceives them as relevant. The same applies to behavior sought by the organization.

Pay is perceived by most individuals as a means of satisfying many kinds of needs, and thus is a relevant reward in the contract. But many other sources of job satisfaction (interesting jobs, congenial associates, competent supervision, and security, for example) may also be perceived as rewards. In fact, employees do not regard pay as their most important reward, at least not employees in the United States.

Rewards are offered to individuals by organizations to motivate certain types of behavior. But which rewards motivate what kinds of behavior and how they operate are functions of perceptions and attitudes. Motivation is an exceedingly complex phenomenon and only partially understood. All rewards appear to follow the law of diminishing returns, requiring a determination of whether or not a particular reward motivates and within what range.

Organizations do not consciously use rewards other than money to motivate employees, and employees speak and often act as if they believe that they only work for money. But even carefully controlled laboratory investigations of simple employment contracts show that many other rewards are operating.

Organization pay practices typically seem oblivious to the perceptual nature of the psychological contract. Pay does serve to motivate behavior in organizations, but the kind of behavior motivated and the conditions under which these results are obtained are more complex than organizations assume.

Unlike the economic perspective, which views the employment transaction from the eyes of the organization, the psychological contract exists only in the eyes of the individual. Organization reward practices and behavior demands have consequences only through this contract. This emphasis on the individual would seem to encourage introspection or comparing situations with other individuals in order to evaluate the transaction.

A SOCIOLOGICAL TRANSACTION

Compensation also represents a sociological transaction, because organizations are associations of persons and employment is an important relationship to both individuals and organizations.

The compensation the individual receives from his employment serves as a symbol of status both within organizations and in society. In a small and relatively immobile community, the status of individuals is a product of many standards of judgment: their families, friends, occupations, education, religious and political affiliations, and so on. In a large and mobile community, however, many of these standards become harder to measure and tend to lose their significance. Income as a symbol of status does not present this problem.

Organizations create status structures of jobs, and status differences are measured by both individuals and organizations by compensation differences. In fact, individuals with experience in organizations have learned to place associates in the status structure by finding out how much they are paid.

Because compensation is such a ubiquitous measure of status in organizations, it is easy to understand why even small differences in pay assume great significance and why methods of payment and frequency of payment have symbolic value without reference to amount. "Salary" may imply a status different from "wage" and yearly salary may indicate a higher status than monthly or weekly salary. This symbolic significance of compensation adds another dimension to its importance to individuals. As it acquires more meanings and utilities, its importance to individuals increases.

Understanding compensation as a status measure helps to explain the force of custom and tradition in compensation determination. The protection of present status and the desire to improve status appear to be universal human values. Protection of present status gives force to custom, defined as "what is right." Custom and tradition require that change be justified. The force of custom is conservative. Changes must not be made unless justified, and when made they call forth numerous other changes based on traditional relationships.

These values operate within an organization as well as in society. The organization is influenced by and also influences the values of society. The organization, in designing the status structure of jobs and pay, is influenced not only by organization needs, but by also what the job paid in the past and by what other organizations are presently paying. The force of outside influences varies with the kinds of people hired, their attachment to the organization, and the extent to which the jobs of the organization are similar to those found elsewhere. If the organization can differentiate its jobs from those found elsewhere, hire only for beginning jobs, and do its own training for all higher-level jobs, it is relatively isolated from outside influences. But customary relationships that are equally conservative soon arise inside the organization. Groups within the organization struggling for status and pay bring forces to bear at least as powerful as traditional forces from outside the organization.

Unions are as subject to these forces as are employing organizations. In fact, unions tend to serve as channels through which customary relationships are made or restored. Furthermore, they may be as unable to restrain group pressures or to bring them into line with union goals as are employing organizations. Both unions and employing organizations hesitate to violate customary relationships.

Viewing the employment transaction from the sociological perspective focuses neither on organizations nor individuals but on the relationship between them. The requirements and mutual influence of individuals and organizations as well as groups internal to the organization and groups representing other units in society seem to provide all the requisite criteria for evaluating the transaction. If it were necessary to restrict our study of compensation to the tools of a single discipline, the most balanced view would seem to flow from sociological concepts.

A POLITICAL TRANSACTION

Compensation also represents a political transaction involving the use of power and influence. Organizations, unions, groups, and individual employees all exert power to influence or change the transaction. Unions exert influence at the time the contract is bargained and during the life of the contract through the grievance procedure. Similarly, the transaction in unionized organizations influences those in nonunion organizations.

Organizations exert power in the same situations. In addition, some choose to be "wage leaders" and thus become major forces in labor markets. Within organizations, groups exert power to obtain a more favorable transaction for themselves. As organizations acquire more differentiated but interdependent units, more and more individuals acquire power to influence the employment transaction. Highly skilled individuals in demand by other organizations may have great power to influence the transaction.

Viewing the employment transaction from a political perspective indicates that it does not require that the parties to the transaction have equal power. Nor does all the power reside on the side of the organization, as the economic perspective appears to suggest. The political perspective, like the sociological view, stresses that evaluation of the transaction involves accommodating the influence of all the parties.

AN ETHICAL TRANSACTION

Compensation also represents an ethical transaction. Few discussions of compensation are conducted without repeated appeals to fairness. Phrases such as "a fair day's pay," "the just wage," and "gross inequities" are commonly used. But opinions differ widely on what justice, fairness, and equity mean in matters of compensation. There are no absolute, objective, universally accepted standards of equity.

The fact that equity is viewed from the eyes of the beholder means that one party to a transaction cannot define what is equitable for the other. Each must decide for himself. This in turn means that although equity can exist for both parties to a transaction, this situation is unlikely unless it results from bargaining and a relatively complete specification of the terms. In situations wherein the transaction cannot be specified completely, equity for both parties can be achieved only if both parties are free to change the terms to achieve it.

From an ethical perspective, the transaction must be analyzed from both sides. Organizations cannot determine what is equitable for individuals, and vice versa.

A MULTIPLE TRANSACTION

The employment transaction has been studied selectively, perhaps because it involves all of these different kinds of exchanges. Economists have focused on the price (wage) of a factor of production and thus emphasized the organization and de-emphasized the individual and the behavior required by organizations. Psychologists have focused on the needs of individuals and the means by which they may be met by organizations, with less emphasis on needs of the organization. Political scientists and philosophers have been quite uninterested in the employment transaction. Sociologists have only recently begun to employ concepts developed for other purposes to examine the employment transaction.

This book takes the position that understanding compensation requires an analysis of the employment transaction from the perspectives of all of these disciplines and equally from the perspectives of both individuals and organizations. But equally as important as the needs of both individuals and organizations is their mutual influence and the reciprocal effects of the transaction on other units in society.

THE EXCHANGE MODEL

To provide the broad perspective required to study compensation, employment is viewed as an exchange in which the parties provide something and receive something and in which the balance of these values actuates the process. This perspective focuses on the parties to the exchange, what each gives and receives, and the decision to make or to continue the employment exchange.

The exchange model is especially useful because economists, psychologists, and sociologists are using the concept of exchange to view behavior. Hence, it may provide the means of integrating theory and research findings in the three disciplines. Economists treat employment as the exchange of time, effort, and ability for payment in money or in kind. Psychologists view employment as the exchange of behavior and attitudes for money and other sources of satisfaction. Sociologists approach employment as a broad exchange of tangible and intangible inputs and outputs among people whose behavior influences one another and in turn influences and is influenced by other segments of society.

THE PARTIES

The parties to the exchange may be two individuals, an individual and a group, or two groups. Ordinarily the employment exchange is a relationship between an individual and a group—the organization. If a union is involved, the exchange involves two groups—the union and the organization.

The parties to the exchange need not be equal. Indeed, in most situations one or the other party has more power. However, both parties must be able to influence the other party to some degree. Each party to the exchange must be giving and receiving something of value to him. Unless both parties so view the exchange, it does not take place.

Exchange is thus a double input-output system. Each party is contributing something to the exchange in return for which he receives something of value to him—for a given input on his part he receives some output. It is a double input-output system because the input for one party is the output of the other, and vice versa.

The exchange process works because it is perceptual. Each party to the exchange views what he considers to be his and the other party's contributions to and outcomes from the exchange. Because of this dual perception, the two parties may not view the exchange in the same manner. There can be a considerable difference in perception, however, and the exchange will still take place.

This disparity in perceptions is what makes the exchange possible. If both parties were to place the same value on a particular input or output, there would be no exchange. An exchange can take place because the two parties place different values on the same item.

An exchange also can be transacted if either party to the exchange sees something in the exchange that the other does not. In order for an input or output to enter the exchange, at least one party must recognize its presence and consider it relevant. The closer the two parties come to considering the same inputs and outputs as relevant, the higher the probability that the exchange will be regarded as fair by both parties. But the different perceptual orientations of the organization and its managers on the one hand and its employees and the union on the other suggest that the inputs and outputs in the employment exchange are likely to be regarded quite differently unless special efforts are made to specify and agree on them.

Individuals enter the employment exchange because they perceive the outputs from the employment exchange as greater than their inputs. Organizations enter the employment exchange in turn because they perceive that the outputs the organization receives from the exchange are greater than organization inputs. Unions enter the employment exchange because they perceive that the outputs they receive from the exchange from members and from organizations exceed the inputs the union and its members make to the exchange.

Other institutions in society influence and are influenced by the employment exchange along the same lines. Households receive more from organizations (outputs) than they contribute to organizations (inputs). The economic system receives outputs from organizations and organization members greater than inputs to organizations and organization members. Governments receive outputs from organizations and individuals greater than inputs to organizations and individuals.

SPECIFICITY AND CONTINUITY IN EXCHANGE

Exchanges intended to be short-term tend to be carefully specified whereas continuing exchanges tend to be ill-defined. Most employment exchanges fall into the second category. Although hours of work and sometimes production standards on one side of the exchange and pay rates and benefits on the other may be specified for some types of employees, no attempt is made to specify the noneconomic aspects of the exchange. Organization expectations of loyalty and commitment and individual expectations of status, achievement, and recognition, for example, are not stated and the discrepancy between them may be great.

Nor is the time perspective in the employment exchange carefully defined. There is some tendency to make clear the economic variables. People are paid at specific intervals for specific time periods. Pensions are awarded for a certain time period of association with the organization. In some instances—in the construction industry—for example, people are hired for certain projects, at the end of which their employment is terminated. Usually, however, the employment exchange is expected to continue as long as both parties are reasonably satisfied. Also, it is unclear at what point the scales balance in the employment exchange. If the employment exchange involved only economic terms, it might be assumed that on each payday the scales are balanced, except for deferred benefits. In a few employment exchanges, such as those involving casual labor, this may be the case. But in most employment exchanges there are long-range expectations by both parties that extra inputs today will result in extra outputs sometime in the future. Certainly such long-term perspectives of the employment exchange are held by managers and professionals and probably by increasing proportions of employees in most organizations.

PARTS OF THE MODEL

Up to this point, the employment exchange has been characterized as a double input-output exchange. More formally, the exchange model consists of a number of parts: contributions, rewards, the comparison process, and results. The individual engages in the employment exchange by making contributions to the organization for which he receives some rewards. In making and continuing the employment exchange, he compares these contributions and rewards, which affects his attitudes and behavior. Similarly, the organization engages in the employment exchange by making contributions to the individual for which the organization receives some rewards. In making and continuing the employment exchange, the organization compares rewards and contributions and the resulting feedback is used to implement decisions concerning the employment exchange. For convenience, the parts of the model are viewed from the standpoint of the individual. The reader should remember that rewards to the individual are contributions of the organization and contributions of the individual are rewards to the organization.

Contributions.   Contributions are what the individual provides in the exchange—his investments and costs. Many kinds of contributions to organizations are possible—from beauty (a decorative receptionist) to total commitment (top management). But to qualify as a contribution, the input must be recognized and considered relevant by the individual. Contributions are the price the individual pays for participating in the exchange.

The employment exchange always involves a commitment of the individual's time and effort and certain of his abilities. But organizations usually require many more kinds of contributions than they recognize as required. Also, individuals have convictions about the abilities they wish to contribute to the exchange.

Because organizations have assumed that the contribution required was work and because employees have assumed that their contribution consisted of work, the actual contributions required in the employment exchange have not been carefully studied. Even a cursory examination of organizations shows that many kinds of contributions are required and different contributions are expected from different employee groups. Also, the variety of employee groups in organizations suggests that different employee groups have different ideas about the contributions they wish to make in the employment exchange.

Rewards.   Rewards are what the individual receives from the exchange. The importance of the exchange to him depends on the degree to which he wants or needs the rewards available to him in the exchange. Almost any item the individual needs or desires can be a reward—the single requirement is that he recognize the reward as relevant. The employment exchange may involve only one reward or it may involve many. The more rewards available, the more likely the exchange will be binding and important to the individual.

Most employment exchanges entail many important rewards. Besides money, a few of the other possibilities are challenging work, congenial associates, and security. In particular, the employment exchange provides the way in which the individual finds his place in society.

The Comparison Process.   The comparison process involves relating contributions and rewards to each other and to some criterion. It is a crucial part of the employment exchange and has both behavioral and attitudinal consequences in that the comparisons determine whether the exchange will be made or continued and also its fairness.

The comparison process involves a number of complexities. The time lag between rewards and contributions and the lack of specificity of both complicate comparisons. Power differentials between the parties may permit one party to take advantage of the other. Expectations, in ill-defined situations, may be quite different for both parties and both may diverge from reality.

Equally troublesome is the problem of units. Neither rewards nor contributions reduce to common units, and a direct comparison between rewards and contributions is difficult. In some situations, such as one involving a wage incentive plan, a specific reward is apparently associated with a particular contribution. But even in this situation the association is illusory, and in the typical employment exchange direct associations are absent.

Another problem faced in the comparison process is the lack of a common standard of fairness. Equity seems to be derived from expectations that are determined partially by social norms and partially by previous experience in other exchanges.

The lack of a definite standard suggests that the two parties to the employment exchange may be using different criteria. There may be a tendency for organizations to compare themselves to other organizations and for employees to compare themselves with other employees, which means that organizations are making external comparisons and employees are making internal comparisons. But both parties in an unstructured situation could be expected to select the criterion most advantageous to themselves.

The availability, quality, and amount of information should be important variables in the comparison process and criteria selection.

Results of the Exchange Process.   The final part of the model focuses on the behavioral and attitudinal results. The exchange is made or continued and adjudged as fair or unfair.

The primary result is likely to consist of behavior. If both parties value the rewards to be obtained from the exchange more than the contributions they must make, the exchange will take place. If the exchange is perceived as unfair, either party may search for a better one, attempt to change the terms in his favor by increasing rewards or decreasing contributions, perceptually increase rewards or reduce contributions, or change to more acceptable criteria of equity. The more choices are perceived to be limited, the more likely the last procedure will be followed. If, however, the exchange is perceived as fair, the individual is more likely to be committed to the organization, to define contributions in the broadest possible manner, and to seek opportunities to make contributions beyond the minimum requirements of the exchange.

The behavioral and attitudinal results of the exchange process are usually assumed to be interdependent and equivalent. But because some employment exchanges are made that one party perceives as unfair and other exchanges are not made although both parties regard them as fair, the assumed equivalence between behavior and attitudes needs further study.

ASSUMED GOALS

Although the exchange model of the employment exchange is sufficiently broad to permit analysis of compensation for all levels of employees in all types of employing organizations, the author's assumptions about employee and organization goals concerning the employment exchange should be made clear. It is not assumed that employees at all levels of the organization have the same goals. Some employees will think of the employment exchange merely as a means to a livelihood and will want to limit the terms of the exchange to specified economic rewards and contributions. Other employees will regard the employment exchange as an opportunity for a career and will seek to expand both rewards and contributions to make such a career possible within the organization. Still other employees will perceive the employment exchange as synonymous with their professional life and will tend to define their contributions and rewards as those coming from their present stage of development.

But it is assumed that all organizations have the same goals concerning the employment exchange. These goals are (1) to obtain and keep employees, and (2) to obtain the kind of employee performance that will permit the organization to survive and achieve its goals. Although the distinction between these two goals is deferred until Chapter 3, they are considered to be separate. Organizations are assumed to require both, but not from all employees, at least as a direct result of the employment exchange; and the routes to the separate goals are assumed to be quite different.

PLAN OF THE BOOK

The exchange model provides the outline of the book. Chapters 2 and 3, which present theory and research findings from economics, psychology, and sociology, complete Part I. Part II examines job, performance, and personal contributions. Part III examines economic and noneconomic rewards for the job, for performance, and for membership in the organization. Part IV analyzes the comparison process utilizing public policy, social forces, and economic criteria as standards. Part V analyzes the employment exchange of some particular employee groups. Part VI discusses system integration and control.

2

Compensation Theory—Economic

The multiple facets of the employment exchange described in Chapter 1 suggest that compensation theorists face a huge task. This task is to specify the factors that determine compensation, the manner in which they do so, and the relative and absolute importance of each factor. Although theorists have not yet attained this goal, they have made a great deal of progress in the last few years. Economists have continued their study of wage determination with fruitful results. Psychologists have achieved a number of significant breakthroughs in the study of pay. Sociologists have developed new methods of analyzing compensation practices in organizations. Sociologists and psychologists in their study of human behavior in organizations have produced findings that have important implications for compensation.

Compensation policies and practices are based on theory regarding compensation determinants and relationships, whether or not those who make policy or design techniques are aware of it. Compensation techniques have been shown on analysis to be based on numerous untested assumptions regarding human behavior in organizations.[1] As these assumptions are tested and either verified or negated, compensation policies and practices can be improved. Compensation theory and research designed to test and improve theories thus are shortcuts to improving understanding and practice. If we knew precisely just what conditions or factors determine compensation, it would be far easier to

[1]Marvin D. Dunnette, "Compensation: Some Obvious Answers to Unanswered Questions," *Compensation Review* (First Quarter, 1969), pp. 8–15; David W. Belcher, "Ominous Trends in Wage and Salary Administration," *Personnel* (September–October, 1964), pp. 42–50.

agree on the means of solving compensation issues. Such understanding would indicate the relative usefulness of various policies and practices and the relative advantages and disadvantages of each alternative.

Economists, perhaps because they have always perceived employment as involving an exchange of labor services for payment in money or in kind, have long been concerned with compensation theory. Wage theories designed to explain the determinants of wages and wage relationships have been developed over two centuries. Wage theory has changed with changes in the economy, with changes in pertinent wage issues, and with improvements in our knowledge and understanding. The major changes in wage theory came from the understanding that different kinds of wage theory were required for different types and levels of wage problems. Quite different theories are required, for example, to explain the general level of wages in the economy, the average wage in a firm, wage rates for particular jobs, and wage structures or relationships.

Wage theorists have customarily employed economic variables as explanatory factors, although labor economists point to the influence of noneconomic variables. The review of noneconomic influences on compensation in Chapter 1 suggests that an explanation in purely economic terms is impossible. As mentioned previously, psychologists and sociologists have made a number of recent contributions to compensation theory. But attempts to integrate the contributions of the separate disciplines to compensation are overdue.[2]

This chapter and the next attempt to set out theory and research findings of economists, psychologists, and sociologists that in the author's view provide some explanation of compensation determinants and effects. First, historical wage theory is reviewed. Then macro-economic theories of the general wage level are examined, together with their implications for national income policies. Next, economic theories of particular wages and wage relationships are reviewed including the significant insights and theory developed by labor economists. In Chapter 3 the contributions of the behavioral scientists (primarily psychologists and sociologists) to compensation theory and research are presented. The substantial work on the psychology of pay and on motivation and job satisfaction are interpreted as highly supportive of two complementary models—a membership motivation model and a performance motivation model. Some sociological contributions to explanation of compensation and the theoretical foundations of the exchange model described in Chapter 1 also are reviewed in Chapter 3.

---

[2]For an attempt to do so, see D. W. Belcher and T. J. Atchison, "Compensation for Work," in Robert Dubin (ed.), *Handbook of Work, Organization and Society* (Chicago: Rand McNally, in press).

the observation that most workers were paid during the production period. Also, applying the residual-claimant idea to wages seemed less logical to most economists than applying it to profits. Walker, however —perhaps as a result of American experience—held that if labor increased its productivity without the use of more capital or land, the added production would increase the residual going to labor. This suggestion that labor could improve its position through increased efficiency contains the germ of a productivity theory of wages.

The economic and social climate that fostered classical wage theory with its dismal predictions of labor's lot perhaps inevitably produced *Marxian wage theory.* Karl Marx substantially accepted the subsistence and wages-fund theories. He accepted from Smith and Ricardo the labor theory of value, which is that the true value of all commodities is their labor cost. To Marx this meant that labor is the sole source of economic value. His explanation of the wage-setting process was that the entrepreneur collects the value created by labor but pays labor only the cost of subsistence. The difference is surplus value, roughly equivalent to profit. Since all value is created by labor, the existence of surplus value means exploitation of labor. Competition among capitalists results in the accumulation of labor-saving capital that, because capital is substituted for labor, results in technological unemployment and the reserve army of the unemployed. The substitution of capital for labor, because labor is the sole source of surplus value, results in a falling rate of profits. Thus, as capitalists spend relatively more on capital and relatively less on labor, surplus value can be maintained only by further exploitation of labor. This combination of forces and the resulting class conflict would, according to Marx, result in the demise of capitalism. Marx's assumptions and predictions were faulty. Land and capital, as well as labor, produce value. Labor's absolute share has continually increased and real wages have risen. Many of Marx's objectives have been realized without revolution.

This brief review of historical wage theories yields little of current value in explaining compensation in industrialized countries. Most of the early theorists were concerned with the general level of wages rather than particular wages. Although the general level of wages still requires explanation, many other compensation questions are equally important, and it is quite unlikely that a single theory is applicable to today's complex compensation issues. But even though it is apparent that the questions that historical wage theorists sought to answer are not today's questions, it is instructive that neither theories that emphasized labor supply nor labor demand were sufficient to answer the questions that were attacked. In fact, the theories emphasizing noneconomic variables seem to have a more modern ring. The just-price theory, with its sociological explanation of wages, and the Marxian implications of the influence of the social system on wages, may have more to say about current compensation issues than the early economic wage theories.

But the values that flow from classical and Marxian wage theory appear to continue to influence current thought. For example, beliefs that improving the lot of the worker is self-defeating and that unions aid their members at the expense of nonunion workers seem to be an intellectual legacy of classical wage theory. Also, the fear of "exploitation of labor" may be a bequest from Marx.

CONTEMPORARY WAGE THEORIES

Wage theory is one of the least settled segments of economic analysis. A generally accepted theory of wage determination does not exist. A plausible reason for the difficulties facing a theory of wages is the "perplexing combination of circumstances—ranging from the inherent properties of labor services and the derived nature of labor demand to the institutional and sociopolitical forces which come to bear on the labor market."[3]

Perhaps even more plausible is Reynolds' suggestion that the many different kinds of wage questions require different theories.[4] For example, determining wages in the long run may involve different variables from those that are involved in short-run questions. Likewise, determinants of the wage level in the economy may be different from those at the industry level and still different from those involved in determining the wage level in the firm. Similarly, questions concerning wage level are different from questions of wage structure—wage relationships between geographic areas, industries, and occupations. Finally, questions concerning wage determinants are different from questions about the effects of wage decisions.

The discussion of economic wage theory and research findings that follows focuses first on the theory applicable to the economy (the macro level). Then attention is directed to micro theory—those theories applicable to the level of the industry and the firm. Applicability of the theory to questions of wage level, wage structure, and the effects of wage decisions are considered at both macro and micro levels.

MACRO THEORY

The determinants of the wage level of the economy and the effects of changes in the wage level on economic variables are the subject matter of macro theory. Although the determinants of the general wage

---

[3]Campbell R. McConnell, *Perspectives on Wage Determination* (New York: McGraw-Hill Book Company, 1970), p. 1.

[4]Lloyd G. Reynolds, "The State of Wage Theory," IRRA, *Proceedings of the Sixth Annual Meeting* (Washington, D.C., December 28–30, 1953), p. 235.

level remain a serious research interest of economists, there is perhaps more agreement on the applicable wage theory at the macro than at the micro level.

Marginal Productivity Theory.   Long-run changes in the general level of wages, it is usually agreed,[5] are best explained by the *marginal productivity theory.* The marginal productivity theory postulates a relationship among wages, productivity, and employment. An early rendition of the theory by John Bates Clark[6] employed the device of the stationary state and assumed (1) perfect markets (including perfect information and perfect mobility), (2) constant population, (3) a constant amount of available capital (in a fund with an infinite variety of forms), (4) unchanging productive technology, (5) a given amount of labor reduced to labor units of unskilled labor, and (6) diminishing returns (the addition of labor units to a fixed quantity of capital results in a decline in the marginal product of labor as the number of labor units applied is increased). Figure 1 depicts the results. The general level of wages is *AE* given the quantity of labor *AD.* Labor's share is *AECD* and capital's share is *BEC.*

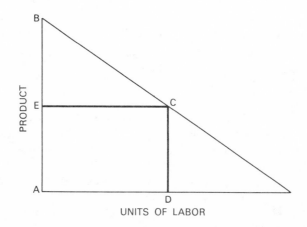

FIGURE 1

Employment is AD and the wage AE(=DC) is precisely equal to the marginal product of labor.

[5]Frank C. Pierson, "An Evaluation of Wage Theory," in George W. Taylor and Frank C. Pierson (eds.), *New Concepts in Wage Determination* (New York: McGraw-Hill Book Company, 1957), p. 29; Melvin Reder, "Wage Determination in Theory and Practice," in Neil W. Chamberlain, Frank C. Pierson, and Theresa Wolfson (eds.), *A Decade of Industrial Relations Research—1946–1956* (New York: Harper and Brothers, 1958), pp. 64–97.

[6]John Bates Clark, *Distribution of Wealth* (New York: The Macmillan Company, 1899).

At the level of the economy, supplies of the factors are fixed and the marginal product of the given quantity of labor determines the wage level. The marginal product attributable to differing quantities of labor units is the schedule of the aggregate demand for labor. A supply schedule is not included because the assumption of a constant, unvarying population provides a fixed supply of labor.

The theory is expressed in real terms—*i.e.,* the marginal physical product (the added product attributable to each added unit of labor) at a given level of employment is the wage. Translating marginal physical product into money terms under perfect competition merely requires multiplying this quantity by product price, which is assumed to be constant regardless of output.

The marginal productivity theory explains long-term changes in the level of real wages (money wages divided by cost of living) quite well. A careful study of real wage changes in five countries from 1860–1960 showed that these changes were based primarily on increased productivity.[7]

National Income Theory.   Short-run changes in the general level of wages may be partially explained by *national income theory.* Sometimes called "full employment wage theory," it deals with aggregate levels of income and employment. Actually, it is more a theory of employment because it was originally offered as a solution to widespread unemployment in the great depression of the 1930s. John Maynard Keynes, the spokesman for the theory,[8] explained that the price system could fail to maintain full employment even in a country with a well-trained labor force, an elaborate money and credit structure, a large stock of capital equipment, and a highly competitive business system. National income theory postulates the relevant variables associated with full employment, their relationships, and the manner in which they may be manipulated to restore full employment.

According to the theory, full employment requires planned total spending sufficient to buy the full employment output. Total spending or aggregate demand equals the total of consumption spending plus private and public investment spending. Whenever a nation's output or income falls below the full employment level, one or more of the spending variables must be manipulated to achieve full employment once more—that is, expansion in consumption, private investment, and/or public investment must be brought about by increased spending in such a way as to ensure that expansion in one of the three variables does not result in contraction in another. A major policy implication of the

[7]E. H. Phelps Brown and Margaret Browne, *A Century of Pay* (New York: St. Martin's Press, 1968).

[8]John Maynard Keynes, *The General Theory of Employment, Interest, and Money* (New York: Harcourt, Brace and Company, Inc., 1936).

theory is that through fiscal and monetary planning by government, spending can be maintained at a level that will result in full employment. The three main governmental policies available for attaining this level of aggregate spending are (1) monetary policies (control interest rates and the money supply), (2) fiscal policy (adjust levels and forms of government taxing and spending), and (3) direct controls (over prices, wages, investment, production, and consumption).

National income theory, although primarily an employment theory, is also a wage theory. The manipulations outlined above are determinants of aggregate wages through full employment. But it is also a psychological theory in that major determinants of aggregate wages are the anticipations of consumers and business leaders. These anticipations are attitudes that create propensities to consume, to save, to invest, to expand or contract, to venture or not. These propensities determine what happens in all markets in the pricing and employment of resources. Maintaining or increasing the propensity to consume and to invest is essential to maintaining national income and full employment.

The theory implies that wages may remain stable or increase but not decrease, because decreasing wages would reduce the propensity to consume and, through expectations, perhaps decrease propensity to invest. Thus national income theory specifies a stable or increasing general wage level as a prerequisite to full employment, and presumably shows how we can get both.

Thus the theory purports to show the way to two important national economic goals—full employment and higher wages. But because it emphasizes aggregate demand, it tends to ignore cost-price relationships, thus raising the possibility that another important national economic goal—price stability—may be overlooked. In fact, although national income analysis may involve either real or money terms, it usually involves money terms, with the result that effects on real wages are ignored. Thus prescriptions based on national income theory could produce conflicts among these three goals.

As formulated, national income theory is applicable only to full employment. Once full employment is attained, the important considerations become those used in explaining long-run changes in real wages. But the difficulties encountered by national income theorists in bridging the gap between money values and real values make the shift difficult. Also, the theory ignores labor supply just as does marginal productivity theory.

Neo-Keynesian Distribution Theory. The *Neo-Keynesian theory* of distribution can be interpreted as a method of extending the concepts of national income theory to full employment conditions without producing conflict among rising standards of living, full employment, and stable prices.[9] As so interpreted it becomes a theory of the general wage level for both the long and short run in both real and money terms.

According to the theory, in the long run the general wage level is determined by economic growth determinants such as the rate of saving, technological progress, and availability of labor. But the major determinant of economic growth is assumed to be investment by capitalists, and economic growth determines profits. In this two-sector (capitalists and consumers) model, profits and wages represent the two shares.

In the short run, the general level of wages is determined by entrepreneurial decisions with respect to prices, including wages. With a given productive capacity, entrepreneurial decisions are influenced by degree of monopoly, the strength of unions, and the rate of investment. The general wage level in the short run is a function of the level of output and employment. Money wage rates within limits are determined by bargaining between capitalists and unions. Because at full employment bargaining can result in a depressed rate of growth through pressures on profits, an "incomes policy" to control price and wage decisions is suggested.

It is significant that in the model the general wage level in neither the long nor short run is determined by pure economic forces but by decisions of men. In this it differs substantially from marginal productivity theory, wherein economic forces determine.

The real wage level in Neo-Keynesian theory is determined by the money wage level (influenced in part by collective bargaining) and average pricing policies of firms. Thus the real wage level as well as the money wage level is determined by human decisions.

The emphasis on decisions made by capitalists and bargainers suggests that Neo-Keynesian distribution theory is more a behavioral science theory of wages than an economic one. It does, however, appear to hold some solutions to the dilemmas of national income theory at full employment. Furthermore, labor supply, although not an important variable, is at least given some consideration.

Empirical Studies—Macro Level. Theories are tentative explanations of phenomena. As such, they involve some abstraction from the real world and attempt to cut through the underbrush and seek out one or a few explanatory variables. Thus, few theories purport to provide complete explanations. Consequently, the pertinent question to apply to competing theories is, given their level of abstraction, which one

---

[9]Marjorie S. Turner, "Wages in the Cambridge Theory of Distribution," *Industrial and Labor Relations Review* (April, 1966), pp. 390–401.

provides the most complete explanation and leads to the most accurate predictions.

A great deal of empirical work has been conducted by economists to ferret out the determinants of the general wage level and to establish whether one or another theory offers an acceptable explanation.[10] Already cited is the finding that real wage increases in five countries over the past century were based primarily on increased labor productivity.[11] The authors of this study believe that the favorable real wage record may have been significantly influenced by the strength of unions in these countries, especially in the United States. A study of real wages in the United States agrees on the influence of productivity.[12] Another study of one company's records from 1860 to 1960 and the close parallel between this company's wages and earnings in manufacturing appear to support the influence that unions exert on real wages.[13]

But the evidence does *not* show that the share of national income going to labor has increased. Labor's share was found to approximate 75 per cent in a study[14] of five countries over the past century. Further evidence is supplied by the stability in the production worker payroll compared to value added in manufacturing over time in the United States.[15] It appears that unions have only a limited effect on labor's share in the long run.[16] There is, however, cyclical variation in labor's share related to short-term changes in productivity[17] and to the influence of union practices such as three-year labor agreements and virtual elimination of wage reductions,[18] although the ratchet under wages existed before unions became a potent force.

[10]For an excellent report on wage research in the past ten years, see E. Robert Livernash, "Wages and Benefits," in Woodrow L. Ginsburg, E. Robert Livernash, Herbert S. Parnes, and George Strauss, *A Review of Industrial Relations Research, Vol. I* (Madison, Wisconsin: IRRA, 1970), pp. 79–144.

[11]Brown and Browne, *A Century of Pay.*

[12]Albert Rees, assisted by Donald P. Jacobs, *Real Wages in Manufacturing* (Princeton, N.J.: Princeton University Press, 1961).

[13]Robert Ozanne, *Wages in Practice and Theory* (Madison: The University of Wisconsin Press, 1968).

[14]Brown and Browne, *A Century of Pay.* See, however, R. M. Solow, "A Skeptical Note on the Constancy of Relative Shares," *American Economic Review* (September, 1958), pp. 618–631.

[15]Allan W. Rucker, "Gearing Wages to Productivity," (Cambridge, Mass.: The Eddy-Rucker-Nickels Company, 1962).

[16]George H. Hildebrand, "The Economic Effects of Unionism," in Chamberlain et al., *A Decade of IR Research,* pp. 98–145; Norman J. Simler, *The Impact of Unionism on Wage-Income Ratios in the Economy* (Minneapolis: The University of Minnesota Press, 1961).

[17]Charles L. Schultze, "Short-Run Movements in Income Shares," in Charles L. Schultze and Louis Weiner (eds.), *The Behavior of Income Shares, Studies in Income and Wealth, Vol. 27* (Princeton: Princeton University Press, 1964).

[18]Livernash, in Ginsburg et al., *A Review of IR Research,* p. 87.

Thus, research on real wages and income shares appears to lend major support to the marginal productivity theory. Although there is some evidence of the influence of unions and presumably also other decision making units, they affect real wage levels far less than do changes in productivity.

Research on the level of money wages, however, has isolated many more variables. One classic study, for example, attributed changes in money wage rates to (1) unions, (2) product markets, (3) labor markets, (4) profits, (5) unemployment rates, (6) certain heavy industries, and (7) wage rounds.[19] Profits and unemployment were found to be very highly correlated with changes in earnings.

Much wage research has been focused on the so-called Phillips curve. Phillips found that the rate of change in money wage rates in the United Kingdom from 1861–1957 could be explained quite well by the level of unemployment and the rate of change in unemployment.[20] From this basis Phillips reasoned that increased demand (less unemployment) drives up prices and that the rate of change in prices affects the rate of change in money wages. The Phillips curve has come to represent the unemployment-inflation problem—*i.e.,* how low unemployment is associated with a high rate of money wage increase and vice versa. Other investigations have supported Phillips' findings.[21]

The Eckstein-Wilson study cited above confirms the existence of a Phillips curve in the United States. A statistical study of hourly earnings in manufacturing in the United States from 1948 to 1960 found that a rate of unemployment higher than 6 per cent, at average profit rates, was required to keep money wage changes equal to changes in productivity.[22] The trade-off between unemployment and inflation may have worsened in the past fifteen years so that, for any given level of unemployment, inflation has been 1 percentage point higher than it was in the 1950s.[23]

But it seems important to emphasize that empirical wage research, although substantiating the existence of the Phillips curve, also shows that other variables besides unemployment are involved in the

---

[19]Otto Eckstein and Thomas A. Wilson, "The Determination of Money Wages in American Industry," *Quarterly Journal of Economics* (August, 1962), pp. 379–414.

[20]A. W. Phillips, "The Relationship Between Unemployment and the Rate of Change of Money Wage Rates in the United Kingdom, 1861–1957," *Economica* (November, 1958), pp. 283–299.

[21]Richard Lipsey, "The Relation Between Unemployment and the Rate of Change of Money Wage Rates in the United Kingdom, 1861–1957: A Further Analysis," *Economica* (February, 1960), pp. 1–31.

[22]George L. Perry, *Unemployment, Money Wage Rates and Inflation* (Cambridge, Mass.: The MIT Press, 1966).

[23]"Why Unemployment Will Be So Stubborn," *Business Week* (April 17, 1971), pp. 90–92.

determination of money wages. In a study[24] of the 1953–1966 period, it was found that union strength was a factor, but not profits. A 1968 review[25] found that "with one exception,[26] all successful explanations of money wages have employed variables both reflecting the state of the labor market and the state of the product market." Productivity has been found in one study[27] to explain more of the variance in wages than unemployment and profits. Another study[28] found money wages determined by conditions in both product and labor markets.

The previously cited longitudinal study[29] of wages in five countries found that money wages were determined by wage claims; the state of the demand for and the supply of labor; the unit wage costs after taking productivity into account; and the readiness of employers to cover a rise in unit costs by higher prices, in the current state of price trends, government policy, and expectations. The historical record shows that it is quite improbable that unemployment alone can explain changes in money wages. It also shows that competitive forces operate as international constraints so that an international trend in unit wage costs and changes in a particular country's productivity together provide a good explanation of changes in money wages.

Whether unions have an identifiable effect on the general level of money wages is still controversial. The authors of the five-country longitudinal study[30] believe that unions have had an impact, but found that impact hidden in the record. The already cited study of one U.S. company's records for a century[31] suggests that unions have influenced both money and real wages, especially since 1947. Opinions concerning union influence on the general level of money wages vary from almost complete[32] to relatively weak.[33] A comprehensive review of statistical studies found that the union-nonunion differential in the U.S. has varied

[24]Gail Pierson, "The Effect of Union Strength on the U.S. 'Phillips Curve'," *American Economic Review* (June, 1968), pp. 456–467.
[25]Otto Eckstein, "Money Wage Determination Revisited," *Review of Economic Studies* (April, 1968), pp. 133–143.
[26]Sarah Behman, "Wage Determination Process in U.S. Manufacturing," *Quarterly Journal of Economics* (February, 1968), pp. 117–142, explains money wage rates in terms of supply of skilled workers.
[27]Edwin Kuh, "A Productivity Theory of Wage Levels—An Alternative to the Phillips Curve," *Review of Economic Studies* (October, 1967), pp. 333–360.
[28]J. Simler and Alfred Tella, "Labor Reserves and the Phillips Curve," *Review of Economics and Statistics* (February, 1968), pp. 32–49.
[29]Brown and Browne, *A Century of Pay.*
[30]*Ibid.*
[31]Ozanne, *Wages in Practice and Theory.*
[32]Sidney Weintraub, *Some Aspects of Wage Theory and Policy* (Philadelphia: Chilton Books, 1963).
[33]Albert Rees, *The Economics of Trade Unions* (Chicago: The University of Chicago Press, 1962).

over time from as little as zero to over 25 per cent.[34] Such studies, however, do not show that unions have increased the general wage level because higher union wages may have been offset by lower nonunion wages. The union-nonunion differential has varied over time, rising in recession and falling during inflation[35] but this varying differential does not show whether unions affect the general wage level or only the wage structure.

Much of the empirical work on general wage level determinants has been concerned with the relationship between the general wage level and inflation. The Phillips curve, for example, implies that large wage increases and strong inflationary forces accompany full employment and that a trade-off exists between full employment and price stability. The effect of the trend of international prices on the money wage level found in the five-country longitudinal study also implies an inflationary force through unit wage costs. Excess demand and excessive negotiated wage increases have been identified as *two independent causes* of international inflation.[36]

There is a lack of consensus among economists about the explanation of inflation.[37] Cost-push and demand-pull inflation, for example, interact in a complex manner.[38] Also, cost-push does not derive solely from increases in money wages but from increases in other costs and from profit push.

In any case, one of the results of rising general wage levels in many countries has been the adoption of national incomes policies. The effectiveness of such policies and the conditions under which they do and do not work have been studied by economists. For example, the effectiveness of the wage guideposts of the early 1960s in the U.S. produced a lively controversy. A statistical study of wage increases between 1962 and 1965 found them lower than those of the 1946–1960 period, especially in visible industries, and adjudged the guideposts effective.[39] Other economists do not believe that the guideposts were responsible for any wage restraint.[40] It seems significant that those most familiar

[34]H. Gregg Lewis, *Unionism and Relative Wages in the United States* (Chicago: The University of Chicago Press, 1963).

[35]M. W. Reder, "Unionism and Wages: The Problems of Measurement," *Journal of Political Economy* (April, 1965), pp. 188–196.

[36]William Fellner *et al., The Problem of Rising Prices* (Paris: The Organization for European Economic Cooperation, 1961).

[37]Martin Bronfenbrenner and Franklin D. Holzman, "Survey of Inflation Theory," *American Economic Review* (September, 1963), pp. 593–601.

[38]William G. Bowen, *The Wage-Price Issue* (Princeton: Princeton University Press, 1960).

[39]G. L. Perry, "Wages and the Guideposts," *American Economic Review* (September, 1967), pp. 897–904.

[40]George P. Shultz and Robert Z. Aliber (eds.), *Guidelines, Informal Controls, and the Market Place* (Chicago: The University of Chicago Press, 1966) is an excellent compilation of the pro and con arguments.

with union-management negotiations do not believe that the guide-posts provided much constraint.

The wage and price controls inaugurated in the U.S. in 1971 have proved to be no less controversial. Economists have questioned the need for controls, their intent, and the possibility of their achieving positive results.[41] For example, some point out that inflationary forces were abating at the very time that controls were installed and that in any case, the inflation was due to government actions rather than to decisions of economic units. Furthermore, there is no agreement that inflationary expectations (which the controls were installed to reduce) existed in the economy or that controls can reduce them. In fact, some economists believe that controls may increase inflationary expectations by alerting economic units to raise prices to the permitted limits and by signaling that the government plans further inflationary policies. Finally, some authorities argue that the experience with wage and price controls during World War II and the Korean War showed that such controls appear to mask but not control inflation. At least some economists believe that the controls were designed to convince the public that something was being done about inflation in order to permit the government to pursue expansionary policies in order to expand employment.

The case for an incomes policy if it is based on monetary and fiscal rules rather than political discretion has been well made by Bronfenbrenner.[42] He argues that no society can achieve more than three of these four goals: a full-employment policy or guarantee (independent of wage behavior), price stability, strong economic pressure groups (not merely trade unions), and freedom from direct controls (over wages and prices, often extending to rationing and allocations). Given the adoption of sound monetary and fiscal rules, he argues that policy guidelines can moderate the actions of pressure groups by advising them what the government wishes them to do. His suggestions call for enforcement sanctions but not direct controls. But he rejects an incomes policy under which monetary and fiscal policy remain political decisions.

Although they have not been notably successful, incomes policies have been followed by advanced industrial economies in efforts to achieve reasonably full employment without incurring unacceptable inflation. A strong case can be made that they represent political rather than economic policy in that they are more shaped by political pres-

[41]See the following articles in *The American Economic Review* (September, 1972) analyzing the 1972 Report of the President's Council of Economic Advisers: Edgar L. Feige, "The 1972 Report of the President's Council of Economic Advisers: Inflation and Unemployment," pp. 509–516; Reuben A. Kessel, "Inflation and Controls," pp. 527–532; Edmund S. Phelps, "Economics and Government," pp. 533–539.

[42]Martin Bronfenbrenner, "A Guidepost-Mortem," *Industrial and Labor Relations Review* (July, 1967), pp. 637–649.

sures than economic analysis.[43] Studies of the effects of such policies[44] have shown that they often result in substantial costs. Often cited is the lack of due process, although a study of British experience shows the required stages in the voluntary acceptance of an incomes policy by labor and management.[45] The target effect, wherein economic units increase prices to policy limits, thereby increasing inflationary pressure, is another cost usually encountered. But the heaviest cost appears to stem from the delusion that monetary and fiscal policies can be highly expansionary without having adverse effects while income policies are in force.

MICRO THEORY

Particular wages and wage relationships are the subject of micro wage theory. Thus, explanations of wages in particular regions, industries, labor markets, firms, and occupations and wage relationships (structures) at these levels are the subject matter of this section.

Marginal Productivity Theory. Marginal productivity theory has already been discussed as a useful explanation of long-run changes in the general level of wages. At the micro level, its usefulness is somewhat controversial. Although it remains at the heart of distribution theory and is widely used to explain changes in prices of other factors of production, even in the short run, economists are divided about its effectiveness in explaining short-run changes in either general or particular wages.

Labor economists, especially, question the abstract nature of the theory (all labor services are reduced to common units, for example), the stringent assumptions employed, and how the theory fits with real-world labor markets.[46] In spite of these limitations, however, marginal productivity theory has been found useful in specifying the economic limits to particular wage movements and the relationship between wage and employment decisions. For example, what is called the competitive hypothesis[47] (assuming that the relevant variables behave as though they were determined by a purely competitive system) can

[43]Murray Edelman and R. W. Fleming, *The Politics of Wage-Price Decisions* (Urbana: University of Illinois Press, 1965).

[44]H. A. Turner and H. Zocteweij, *Prices, Wages, and Income Policies in Industrialized Market Economies* (Geneva: International Labor Organization, 1966); Lloyd Ulman, "Wage-Price Policies: Some Lessons from Abroad," *Industrial Relations* (May, 1969), pp. 195–213.

[45]Derek Robinson, "Implementing an Incomes Policy," *Industrial Relations* (October, 1968), pp. 73–90.

[46]Pierson, in Taylor and Pierson, *New Concepts in Wage Determination.*

[47]Reder, in Chamberlain *et al., A Decade of IR Research,* pp. 64–97.

usefully explain interfirm wage differentials and wage-determined labor mobility. It is also useful in tracing the wage and employment effects of changes in labor demand and supply and their components as well as the probable effect of policy decisions such as paying above the market rate and lowering standards of employability.

Some authors, accepting abstraction from the real world as a necessity in uncovering the relevant variables and relationships, use marginal productivity theory to explain the forces that operate on firms and unions in determining wages and employment. Cartter,[48] for example, uses marginal productivity theory and the knowledge of labor markets and collective bargaining to construct a series of static models of wage determination at the level of the firm.

Cartter's analysis makes use of the formulation of marginal productivity theory shown in Figure 1 as a wage theory at the level of the economy and an employment theory at the level of the firm. Although Figure 1 postulates long-term results, Cartter accepts Marshall's assertion[49] that the marginal productivity principle (the premise that a rational employer, in attempting to maximize profits, is guided by the marginal productivity of a factor of production in determining the relationship between the return of the factor and its employment) is useful for analysis in short-run situations and in cases in which competition is perfect and less than perfect. From this premise, Cartter develops models of the wage-employment relationship of a firm under conditions of perfect competition in labor and product markets and under various conditions of imperfect competition.[50] For example, after analyzing the effect of imperfect competition in the product market on a firm's demand for labor and justifying his assumption of an upward-sloping labor supply curve, he develops models of monopsony (one buyer of labor) in the labor market, monopoly in the labor market (assuming that the union acts as a monopolistic seller of labor), and bilateral monopoly (assuming that both employers and unions have monopoly power). But his most interesting models are based on knowledge of collective bargaining behavior. He develops a union wage-employment preference path based on the assumption that unions prefer increased wages to increased employment when labor demand increases and reduced employment rather than wage reductions when labor demand decreases, and that the present contract represents the base point in union preferences. He postulates that unions follow this

[48]Allan M. Cartter, *Theory of Wages and Employment* (Homewood, Illinois: Richard D. Irwin, Inc., 1959).
[49]Alfred Marshall, *Principles of Economics* (London: Macmillan and Co., Ltd., 1947).
[50]Cartter, *Theory of Wages and Employment*, chapters 7 and 8.

path in negotiations rather than a labor supply curve if they have the power to do so. He also shows that the labor demand curve is the employer's profit preference path and why the employer prefers to move down this assumed path. Using both preference paths as well as the assumed actual labor supply schedule, he develops models of perfect bargaining conditions (mutual knowledge of the preference paths and desire to reach agreement) and imperfect bargaining conditions (dropping both assumptions).

Although these models involve static analysis (changing one variable at a time while holding others constant), the assumptions employed are realistic and the predictions carry a good deal of face validity. For example, in the imperfect bargaining model, if the union forecasts a greater increase in demand than actually occurs and has the power to obtain a wage increase based on this estimate, the subsequent employment consequences predicted by the model not only seem realistic but may explain some union demands for employment security along with wage demands. On the other hand, the results predicted by the models under all assumptions other than perfect competition are indeterminate—i.e., they establish a range within which the actual wage decision will presumably be set under the assumed conditions.

Bargaining Theory.   This indeterminate range within which the wage rate will be set by marginal productivity analysis has long bothered economists. Attempts to explain the behavior of unions and employers in determining the wage rate within this range are called bargaining theory.

A number of bargaining theories have been offered. They all attempt to explain bargaining strategy and attempt to conceptualize the forces that influence strategy in wage negotiations. Unfortunately, the forces identified by the models are virtually impossible to make operational.

An example is the model developed by Pen.[51] Pen attributes bargaining power to interdependence of the parties. Given some degree of interdependence, a contract zone exists and within this zone agreement is possible. The model consists of a pair of equations, one reflecting the position of the union leader, and the other that of the employer. Agreement is reached when both equations are satisfied at the same time. The union equation specifies that the union will be willing to agree at some wage rate if the cost of agreeing (as represented by the difference between the rate sought and the rate under consideration) divided by the cost of disagreeing (as represented by the differ-

[51]J. Pen, *The Wage Rate Under Collective Bargaining* (Cambridge, Mass.: Harvard University Press, 1959).

ence between the desired rate and the rate that would be gained in the case of actual conflict) multiplied by a risk evaluation function, minus an estimate of the employer's will to resist, is equal to zero. A similar equation must be satisfied for the employer if agreement is to be reached. The wage agreed to must satisfy for both parties the conditions that its utility just equals the risk (disutility) involved in fighting for it rather than accepting a less favorable wage.

Unfortunately, the "fighting functions" and the "risk functions" are subjective and impossible to measure. Moreover, the essence of bargaining is the process by which these functions are made to shift. Although the model helps to clarify the concept of bargaining power, it does not predict a wage rate.

Cartter[52] has developed a less complex bargaining model based on the costs of agreeing and disagreeing. Either party's bargaining attitude is assumed to consist of the cost of disagreeing with the other party divided by the cost of agreeing on the other party's terms. Conditions for agreement are unfavorable when this equation is less than 1. The cost of disagreeing is the cost of lost income resulting from a work stoppage (actual anticipated loss in any time period multiplied by the probable length of the stoppage). The cost of agreeing is the difference between the income if one party settles on the other party's terms and the income that would accrue if the first party's offer were substituted, capitalized.

As bargaining proceeds, each party's bargaining attitude becomes more favorable because anticipated costs become actual costs, thus increasing the cost of disagreeing. As one party's bargaining attitude approaches unity, he may offer a compromise settlement. A compromise improves the bargaining attitude of the party offering to compromise by reducing his cost of disagreeing (reducing the expected length of the stoppage) while not affecting his cost of agreeing. The new offer, in turn, reduces the other party's cost of agreeing. The compromise offer may be sufficient for settlement because the other party's cost of disagreement has been rising over time. If not, the other party may make a compromise offer. The process continues until settlement is reached. In Cartter's model, bargaining skill consists of the ability to raise the other party's cost of disagreeing by convincing him of your ability to hold out and to lower the other party's cost of agreeing by convincing him that he has overestimated this cost.

This model, although useful in explaining some important aspects of bargaining behavior, is still based on subjective variables that impede measurement. Also, it is no more predictive than Pen's model.

[52]Cartter, *Theory of Wages and Employment,* Chapter 9.

Other formal bargaining theories range from the application of game theory and conflict theory to bargaining strategy to the formalization of pain and pleasure functions.[53] All of them represent attempts to explain the *process* of wage determination under collective bargaining within the range of indeterminacy rather than the wage rate.

If, as seems apparent, bargaining theory does not seek to narrow the range of indeterminacy in wage determination but to explain the process by which indeterminacy is reduced, Chamberlain's explanation of bargaining power and the costs of disagreeing and agreeing, although less formal, seems most useful.[54] Chamberlain defines a union's bargaining power as management's willingness to agree to the union's demands. The willingness of management to accept the union's terms depends in turn on how costly disagreeing will be relative to how costly agreeing will be. Thus union bargaining power is management's cost of disagreeing to the union's terms divided by management's cost of agreeing to the union's terms. No agreement can be reached until, for either union or management, the cost of agreeing on the other's terms is less than the cost of disagreeing.

An interesting implication of this definition of bargaining power is that one party's bargaining power is relative to the demands he makes. The lower his demands, the higher his effective bargaining power. Furthermore, since one party's bargaining power is based on his estimate of the costs of disagreeing and agreeing on the other party's terms, bargaining consists largely of convincing the other party that the costs of agreeing are lower and the costs of disagreeing higher than he had estimated.

Chamberlain traces the source of each party's costs of agreeing and disagreeing back to aspirations and alternatives. Thus costs become sacrificed aspirations and foregone alternatives. In this way, bargaining strategy includes attempts to alter *apparent* as well as real sacrifices of aspirations or foregone alternatives. If one party offers something that appears to be a concession but does not constitute a sacrifice of aspiration to the other party, it has raised its bargaining power.

Institutional Wage Theory. Labor economists have long complained of the myopia of traditional economic theory when applied to

[53]R. L. Bishop, "Game Theoretic Analyses of Bargaining," *Quarterly Journal of Economics* (November, 1963), pp. 559–602; J. C. Harsanyi, "Bargaining and Conflict Situations in the Light of a New Approach to Game Theory," *American Economic Review* (May, 1965), pp. 447–457; C. Stevens, "On the Theory of Negotiations," *Quarterly Journal of Economics* (February, 1958), pp. 77–79; J. G. Cross, "A Theory of the Bargaining Process," *American Economic Review* (March, 1965), pp. 67–94; B. D. Mabry, "The Pure Theory of Bargaining," *Industrial and Labor Relations Review* (July, 1965), pp. 479–502.

[54]Neil W. Chamberlain, *The Labor Sector* (New York: McGraw-Hill Book Company, 1965), pp. 231–237.

buying and selling labor services. Their observations of wage determination in the real world, with numerous sizes and types of employing organizations and unions, have convinced them that wage theory was attempting to answer the wrong questions and was neglecting important variables. Thus labor economists, or industrial relations scholars as many of them prefer to be called, stress the range of variables—political, psychological, social, and ethical, as well as economic—that impinge on wage determination. Their concern has been with particular wages and wage relationships (structures) as the questions that most need answering. Industrial relations scholars, like their progenitors—the institutional[55] economists—have been more interested in learning more about the behavior of unions and employers than in developing theories. They have, however, devised a number of theories, chiefly of wage structure.[56]

The institutional approach is· heavily empirical. The details of wage experience, the variability of wage relationships, the latitude available to wage decision-makers, the dimensions added to wage determination by collective bargaining, all are regarded as important matters requiring explanation. All of these issues add to the variables that must be encompassed by theories of wage determination. The wage rate in this approach is seen as inseparable from considerations such as when, how much, how distributed, union recognition, labor efficiency, other wage bargains, lower wage competitors, recruitment problems, company reputation, strikes, control over discharge, and job prospects. Although such considerations may be involved in marginal productivity analysis, they are either treated as separate rather than interacting variables or subsumed under abstract concepts. As such, institutional economists approach wage decisions as involving a variety of choices that depend on weights assigned to varying and perhaps conflicting considerations. The alternatives available to the decision-makers are as important to study as the determinants of wages and wage relationships. The effects of wage changes also must be considered because the parties can alter the wage by administration.

The institutional approach questions the usefulness of static analysis wherein changes are studied singly while other considerations are held constant on the grounds that the interrelationships among changes (dynamic analysis) are the more important issues. Observation of wage

[55]The term "institutional" is employed here in part because of its descriptive nature and in part because of its use in Britain to describe interdisciplinary study of the industrial relations system. See Alan Fox, *A Sociology of Work in Industry* (London: Collier-Macmillan Limited, 1971), p. v.

[56]Taylor and Pierson, *New Concepts in Wage Determination;* John T. Dunlop (ed.), *Theory of Wage Determination* (New York: St. Martin's Press, 1957).

decision-making suggests that in wage matters (1) a variety of results is possible, (2) the system of relationships is itself changing, and (3) results may be cumulative rather than self-correcting. Furthermore, analysis limited to a point in time may hide forces that change and interact with one another over time and the influence of past decisions and future expectations.

Of considerable importance in institutional analysis is the definition of wages. Conceptually, the wage agreement under collective bargaining not only includes the wage rate and benefits, but also clauses that affect wages through (1) the effect on labor costs, (2) the present and ultimate costs of benefits, (3) tactical considerations involving how and when wage increases are granted, (4) continuing bargaining over wages in the grievance procedure, and (5) the way in which the various clauses in the agreement are administered. Thus wages may be defined as all the clauses in the agreement that hold cost implications or limited to wage rates and benefits.

The latter definition is usually employed because of measurement problems in the former. As mentioned previously, institutional analysis, although interested in wage levels, is more concerned with wage structures. In considering wage structures, interest is focused on both equalities and differentials. All types of wage structures are subjected to analysis—interpersonal, interfirm, interarea, interoccupational, and interindustry—and the relationships among them. Within each type of structure, the range of choice and the wage determinants are subjects of study.

But institutional analysts have not neglected measurement problems involving wages. Wage movements, for example, are considered as significant as wage levels. Wage differentials are examined in both percentage and absolute terms, and the purpose of the analysis determines the measure used. The question of equivalence of wages and benefits has been analyzed. For example, it appears that, in principle, wages and benefits are substitutes for each other and wage negotiations include both in the total package. But, in practice, the components are subject to separate comparisons based on employee reactions, tactical considerations, and both their actual and apparent value to employees.

Also of importance in institutional analysis are the influences exerted by institutions and the leadership of these institutions. Institutional forces are seen to modify, and at times possibly even to overshadow, economic forces. Unions, for example, are observed to have a wage philosophy with strong ethical overtones that may stress certain standards of health, safety, and decency, and that may call for improvements in these standards regardless of cost. Also observed is the union conviction that wage pressures energize the economic system on the cost side by forcing employers to increase efficiency, and on the income side by expanding consumer markets. Union leaders typically do not regard cost relationships as static and unchanging and are skeptical about predicted economic effects of wage increases. But unions differ in philosophy and type of leadership, and explaining these differences appears to involve psychological, sociological, and political variables as well as economic ones. For example, the force of tradition on labor markets and the psychological makeup of union leaders are regarded as just as pertinent in explaining differences as are the economic differences in product and labor markets.

Employers are also observed to be influenced by forces other than economic. The large employer is probably just as concerned with the status of his organization as a dependable supplier, a conscientious employer, and a wage leader, as he is with economic necessity. Management may treat wages and prices as institutional decisions rather than as reactions to economic forces. Wage and price decisions appear to be based at least in part on company convenience. In large organizations, organizational slack permits wage increases to be absorbed until prices or efficiency can be increased. Observation suggests that wage rates and benefits are paid because other organizations pay an equal amount or because they were settled by agreement rather than determined by cost considerations. Employers as well as unions differ in philosophy and types of leadership and many of the differences can be explained in sociological, psychological, and political terms. Perhaps differences associated with size of organization come closest to requiring an economic explanation.

Institutional analysis, in addition to identifying both economic and noneconomic forces, is concerned with the relative weight of each factor in wage determination in general and in each type of wage relationship. Economic forces, institutional analysis tends to show, set rather broad limits on wages, leaving a range of discretion. But the amount of discretion varies with the type of wage rate or wage relationship under analysis. For example, the internal wage structure of a company is largely under the control of the decision-makers, the external wage structure is only partially under their control, and the general level of wages in the economy is beyond their control.[57] Wage uniformity where it appears usually results from conscious decisions rather than market forces. One of the strongest forces on wages is custom.

The observation that a wide latitude exists for wage decisions has prompted study of the effects of wage changes based on the reasoning that anticipated and actual effects influence wage decisions. These

---

[57]Arthur M. Ross, "The External Wage Structure," in Taylor and Pierson, *New Concepts in Wage Determination*, pp. 173–205.

effects depend on such *noneconomic* considerations as (1) organization goals, (2) union-management relations and labor agreements, (3) the influence of personnel programs on employee attitudes and productivity, (4) the influence of wage administration on costs, (5) the skill with which the wage change is presented to employees, (6) the way the wage change is distributed among employees, (7) management's perception of its alternatives, (8) the extent to which seniority and hiring policies have insulated the firm from external labor markets, (9) employee opinions of equity, (10) management's ability to adjust to conditions or to create new ones, and on *economic* considerations such as (1) size of firm, (2) product market competition, (3) the proportion of labor cost to total cost, (4) the rate of growth of the industry, and (5) general economic conditions. A useful by-product of this analysis calls attention to the distinction between wage costs and labor cost per unit, and the fact that labor costs may be affected by changes in (1) hiring specifications; (2) administration of incentive plans, merit increases, and promotions; (3) the classification of jobs; and (4) amount of overtime, without a change in wage rates.

Much of institutional analysis comes from studies of collective bargaining and of labor market behavior. As such, the results represent hypotheses concerning wage determinants and wage relationships. Some results of tests of these hypotheses are presented later in this chapter.

A particularly interesting set of institutional analysis hypotheses concerns the effects of collective bargaining on wages. Collective bargaining is assumed to raise wage rates for jobs, alter intraplant differentials, and change the wage level of particular employers and to create more logical internal wage structure policies and administrative practices. But above the level of the firm, the effect of collective bargaining becomes more controversial. Whether the movement of the general wage level of the economy under collective bargaining differs significantly from its movement under nonunion conditions and whether increases secured through collective bargaining are substantially larger than could be accounted for on economic grounds remain hypotheses. So is the question of whether or not unions have increased the relative share of national income going to labor, although analysis suggests that it is impossible for them to do so unless they acquire much more decision-making power from employers or governments.[58] But the absolute share going to labor has increased as a result of full employment and growth of the economy.

[58]Clark Kerr, "Trade-Unionism and Distributive Shares," *American Economic Review* (May, 1954), pp. 279–292.

Quite probably, institutional analysis has generated few theories because it has uncovered such a wide range of forces that affect wage rates and wage relationships. Attempts to develop wage theory encompassing this wide range of variables require courage.

A number of wage theories have been developed that attempt to incorporate the conclusions of institutional analysis with respect to collective bargaining and labor markets. Most of the theories attempt to explain wage structures (relationships) as the pertinent question. But some are applicable to both wage structures and wage levels.

A *range theory* of wage differentials was developed by Lester,[59] employing what he calls anticompetitive, impeditive, and competitive variables. The anticompetitive factors include institutional and ethical considerations used to restrict or prevent competition for jobs. The impeditive factors include historical, psychological, and institutional considerations that present obstacles to market adjustment by creating frictions and personal preferences of workers. The competitive forces are those that operate with respect to hiring and pay. The range theory represents a useful attempt to encompass much of the rich detail of collective bargaining and labor market behavior along with market forces in explaining wage differentials.

Taylor's[60] analysis of wage determination processes attempts to explain wage determination in all sizes and types of organization in terms of the *consequences of nonagreement.* The upper and lower limits of the negotiating area are the points at which the employer and the employee or his representative consider the costs of settlement prohibitive. Although these limits are set by economic forces, they are not precise; they are variously conceived at the start of negotiation; they change at critical points during negotiations; and they are influenced by bargaining tactics and skills of the parties. Using only the one variable—consequences of nonagreement—Taylor is able to explain wage determination in situations involving individual bargaining, management-administered wage determination involving both craft and semiskilled jobs, and wage determination under collective bargaining involving different relative power positions of employers and unions.

Taylor's explanation of wage determination processes seems to involve both compensation theory and a theory of collective bargaining. It is compensation theory rather than wage theory in that wages are defined as all clauses in a contract affecting labor costs. Further-

---

[59]Richard A. Lester, "A Range Theory of Wage Differentials," *Industrial and Labor Relations Review* (July, 1952), pp. 483–500.

[60]George W. Taylor, in Taylor and Pierson, *New Concepts in Wage Determinations,* Chapter 4.

more, it recognizes that these clauses are affected by what goes on in preparation for negotiation, the bargaining, and the effectuation of the agreement. As collective bargaining theory, it serves to explain that although employees are never without power in wage determination, collective bargaining enhances that power by operating on the premise that individual employees have no right to work at employment terms rejected by the union. Also, distinguishing wage determination processes in individual bargaining and in collective bargaining for semi-skilled workers and craftsmen accords with research findings concerning labor markets.

Another conceptual scheme sets forth the existence, for each employer, of a *hiring preference function* that relates the number of man-hours of labor employed (labor suppliers possess certain specified characteristics) to the hourly wage rates and/or marginal expenditures for these labor quantities.[61] The firm's employment decisions are conceived as involving a mutual adjustment of jobs, personnel, and wage rates in such a way that a change in the labor market will be met by a change in jobs, hiring requirements, wage rates, or all three. Thus the employer, in meeting a change in the labor market, may adjust jobs to people or people to jobs, as well as, or instead of, changing wage rates within the limits set by technology and other constraints. These changes involve time and cost considerations as well as employee, union, and management preferences. This formulation accords with conclusions from empirical research into employee, union, and employer behavior in labor markets and includes both economic and noneconomic considerations. Although it is a useful explanation of the wage determination process for particular employee groups within a firm and of the wage relationships among different types of employees, it is also a theory of hiring policy and job design.

A theory of wage structure offered by Dunlop[62] accords with knowledge of labor markets and collective bargaining but confines itself to an explanation of wage rates. The structure of wage rates within a company, within an industry, and among different industries and regions is assumed to be a system. The elements in the system are: (1) A *job cluster*—a stable group of jobs within a company linked together by technology, administrative organization, and social custom. Wage rates of jobs in a cluster are more closely related to one another than to rates for jobs elsewhere in the firm. The structure of wage rates within a cluster consists of one or more *key rates* and a group of associated rates. The wage structure of a firm (or installation in the multiplant firm) is

[61]Reder, in Chamberlain *et al., A Decade of IR Research,* pp. 69–70.
[62]John T. Dunlop, in Taylor and Pierson, *New Concepts in Wage Determination,* Chapter 5.

made up of a number of clusters, and rates of key jobs in each cluster are related to one another through technology, organization, and custom. (2) A *wage contour*—a stable group of companies linked together by a common product market, labor market, or custom so that they have common wage-making characteristics. The wage rates of particular occupations in a company are more closely related to the wage rates of some firms than of others. A contour for particular occupations is defined in terms of both the product market and the labor market. A wage contour has three dimensions—occupational, industrial, and geographic. The firms that comprise a contour belong to a particular product market and may be located either in one labor market or be broadly dispersed geographically. The contour does not have sharp boundary lines, however. The product market of a company may place it in several wage contours. The contour is often composed of a wage leader and a group of associated firms. The wage contour operates through wage comparisons that usually result in one or more key bargains.

Wage-making forces operate on key rates in job clusters. These rates spread externally through the operation of wage contours and internally through the relation of key job rates to one another and to associated rates. A company's internal wage structure is related to the market through a limited number of key job rates and key wage settlements or bargains. The particular rates selected for comparison are determined, at least in the short run, by the technology and administrative practices of firms, product market competition, and sources of labor supply. Long-run forces affecting technology and competitive conditions may change both job clusters and wage contours.

The concepts of job clusters and wage contours not only accord with research findings concerning labor markets and collective bargaining, but also should strike a note of familiarity with wage practitioners. These concepts seem to provide some theoretical underpinning for two common techniques of compensation administration—wage surveys and job evaluation.

In fact, Livernash's[63] refinement of the job cluster concept serves to define boundaries of job clusters and to clarify their operation. Within a firm there are broad job clusters containing narrower clusters, and relationships within and among clusters vary. Within narrow clusters, wage relationships are based on job content comparisons. Comparison of key jobs in separate clusters is less precise and emphasizes established internal relationships and external market relationships rather then job content, especially as job content differences increase.

[63]E. Robert Livernash, in Taylor and Pierson, *New Concepts in Wage Determination*, Chapter 6.

Internal relationships among job clusters are typically based in part on the relative cost significance of jobs. Also, Ross[64] has further operationalized the wage contour concept by emphasizing that comparisons are matters of decision by the parties, that under union conditions industry comparisons predominate, and that custom influences wage contours through traditional differentials.

An *investment theory* of wages has been developed by Gitelman[65] that proposes that labor input is the proper route to explaining wages. Workers' investment in their productivity consists of several varieties of education, training, and experience. These investments vary in scope and scope determines the mobility potential of the individual. In the same manner, labor markets vary in the scope of worker investments required. The wider the labor market, the higher the wage. The worker investment associated with the widest labor market determines his wage.

The theory recognizes that individuals vary in their desire to maximize income relative to other goals and that employing organizations vary in their capital-worker ratios and breadth of job assignment. Thus the wage in any particular employment is determined by the rate of return on the worker's investments adjusted for the scope of his assignment. But all occupational wages are associated with worker investments except those rare ones in which the return is based solely on talent. Organization requirements control wage decisions more than external labor markets but organizations become aware of mistakes in wage-setting by analyzing labor turnover.

The investment theory of wages accords with research findings concerning labor market behavior by individuals and organizations. It offers an explanation of both wage levels and wage structures in employing organizations. Perhaps its most significant feature is its concentration on labor input rather than demand.

Other attempts to build wage theory applicable to particular wages and wage relationships have included more wage determinants and are more tentative about their operation. Salkever,[66] for example, after reviewing the economic literature on wage structure, offered an explanation of the emergence and persistence of wage differentials. Social inertia resulting from employment consciousness, rather than wage consciousness of employees and resistance to change, is one variable. Another is employer creation of occupational differentials based on judgments of the relative importance of tasks and the learning curve

---

[64]Ross, *ibid.,* Chapter 7.

[65]H. M. Gitelman, "An Investment Theory of Wages," *Industrial and Labor Relations Review* (April, 1968), pp. 323–352.

[66]L. R. Salkever, *Wage Structure Theory* (New York: Humanities Press, 1964).

associated with these tasks. Once created, differentials persist because employees reinforce the judgments. A third determinant is the cost to workers of acquiring skills. A fourth is the immobility resulting from the social reality of noncompeting groups and the nature of labor reserves associated with these groups. Product markets influence differentials chiefly through the extent to which the employer is insulated from market pressures. Economic fluctuations also affect wage differentials through their effects on worker willingness to undergo training, employer ability to take advantage of the learning curve, and differential pressures of occupational groups amplified by the nature of the labor reserve. Governments and quasi-governments (unions and employer associations) influence wage differentials primarily by transmitting pressures originating elsewhere.

Other explanations of wage structures have focused attention on differences between labor markets and the forces operating within them. Kerr,[67] for example, showed that in some labor markets economic forces are powerful in determining wages, whereas in others they are attenuated or absent. Hildebrand,[68] in an effort to explain the forces operating on the internal wage structure, categorized internal wage structures as primarily (1) union-oriented, (2) market-oriented, (3) internally determined, and (4) union- and product-market-oriented. Although he found the job cluster-wage contour theory and the hiring preference function useful in explaining wage-determining forces in the different markets, they were neither sufficient to suggest the forces operating nor to assign relative weights to market and nonmarket forces. Interestingly, Hildebrand's analysis led him to conclude that attention to nonmarket forces has served to conceal the influence of the product market as an environmental force on wage structures.

Empirical Studies—Micro Level. The empirical work of economists at the micro level has been directed at seeking out the actual determinants of particular wages and wage relationships. As such, much of it may be interpreted as tests of wage theory.

For example, the question of the relationship between changes in wages and changes in employment is a partial test of the marginal productivity theory. One large international study concluded that employment changes among industries were related to job vacancies but not to relative wages.[69] Only at the extremes were employment and

[67]Clark Kerr, "Labor Markets: Their Character and Consequences," *American Economic Review Papers and Proceedings* (May, 1950), pp. 278–291.

[68]George H. Hildebrand, "External Influence and the Determination of the Internal Wage Structure," in J. L. Meij (ed.), *Internal Wage Structure* (Amsterdam: North-Holland Publishing Company, 1963), pp. 260–299.

[69]P. de Wolff, Chairman, *Wages and Labor Mobility* (Paris: Organization for Economic Cooperation and Development, 1965).

wage changes associated, and then only imperfectly. The same study found a high degree of stability in industrial, occupational, and regional wage differentials over time.

Interpreting these findings is difficult because of imperfections in wage statistics. Industry and regional wage data usually involve different occupational groups, and if the data were adjusted for skill level different conclusions might result. A long-term narrowing of occupational differentials seems to have occurred[70] and some narrowing of regional differentials,[71] primarily in industries dominated by multi-plant firms and operating in national product markets.

One method of determining the effect of collective bargaining on wage rates has been the study of pattern bargaining. The Organization for Economic Co-operation and Development (OECD) study concluded that wage patterns were largely responsible for the uniformity of wage changes.[72] Studies in the United States, however, have found that the strength of wage patterns varies greatly over time and that the influence of a pattern loses its clarity beyond the particular industry, the jurisdiction of the particular union, and national product markets.[73] In fact, such studies serve to emphasize the influence of competitive forces. A study that sought to determine the effect of blue-collar unionism on white-collar earnings found no spillover and concluded that competitive forces account for the interindustry salary structure of nonproduction workers.[74]

Numerous statistical studies of the effect of unions on industry wage levels have been made. A comprehensive analysis of twenty of these studies reached the conclusion that unionism served to raise union wages over nonunion wages, but that this union impact varied greatly over time and among industries.[75]

But studies of the effect of unionism on industry wage levels have been complicated by inadequate attention to differences between product and labor markets in poorly organized, highly competitive

[70]Paul G. Keat, "Long-run Changes in Occupational Wage Structure, 1900–1956," *Journal of Political Economy* (December, 1960), pp. 584–600.

[71]Martin Segal, "Regional Wage Differences in Manufacturing in the Postwar Period," *Review of Economics and Statistics* (May, 1961), pp. 148–155.

[72]de Wolff, *Wages and Labor Mobility.*

[73]George Seltzer, "The United Steelworkers and Unionwide Bargaining," *Monthly Labor Review* (February, 1961), pp. 129–136; Walter H. Carpenter, Jr., and Edward Handler, *Small Business and Pattern Bargaining* (Babson Park, Mass.: Babson Institute Press, 1961).

[74]Robert L. Raimon and Vladimer Stoikov, "The Effect of Blue-Collar Unionism on White-Collar Earnings," *Industrial and Labor Relations Review* (April, 1969), pp. 358–374.

[75]Lewis, *Unionism and Relative Wages.*

industries and in highly organized industries with little price competition. The former are strongly influenced by competitive forces, the latter are not.[76]

Wage changes have been similar in highly concentrated, highly organized industries. There apparently is a strong pattern influence within this group.[77] The idea of a pattern influence gains support from the finding that profit is the only economic variable apparently associated with industry wage changes.[78] But interindustry wage dispersion has been found to be associated with the rate of price level change.[79]

Within industries, a size-of-establishment differential on the order of 20 per cent has been found by Lester.[80] Lester finds it paradoxical that firms with monopoly power do not use it. He also rejects the usual explanations. Conant, although not able to explain such large differences, found that clerical workers in higher-wage firms are more proficient than clerical workers in lower-wage firms.[81]

An interesting finding of the OECD study was that similar industries in all countries studied experience similar wage and employment changes. In all countries, commonly known competitive industries exhibited below-average earnings and employment increases. Levinson studied wage changes in six industries in the U.S. and found (1) a great deal of individuality in each of the industries, and (2) that explanation required economic variables, political variables, and "pure power" (collective bargaining) variables.[82]

The OECD study also found that institutional differences among countries were unimportant in wage determination. Johnson's study of collective bargaining in Sweden found that the market rather than unions narrowed wage differentials.[83]

Some evidence of the effects of decision-making by the parties on

[76]Albert Rees and Mary T. Hamilton, "Postwar Movements in Wage Levels and Unit Labor Costs," *Journal of Law and Economics* (October, 1963), pp. 41–68.

[77]H. M. Levinson, *Postwar Movement of Prices and Wages in Manufacturing Industries* (Washington, D.C.: Joint Economic Committee, 1960); John E. Maher, "The Wage Pattern in the United States," *Industrial and Labor Relations Review* (October, 1961), pp. 3–20.

[78]de Wolff, *Wages and Labor Mobility*.

[79]Rees and Hamilton, in *Journal of Law and Ecnomics* (October, 1963), pp. 41–68.

[80]Richard Lester, "Pay Differentials by Size of Establishment," *Industrial Relations* (October, 1967), pp. 57–67.

[81]Eaton H. Conant, "Worker Efficiency and Wage Differentials in a Clerical Labor Market," *Industrial and Labor Relations Review* (April, 1963), pp. 428–433.

[82]Harold W. Levinson, *Determining Forces in Collective Wage Bargaining* (New York: John Wiley and Sons, Inc., 1966).

[83]T. L. Johnson, *Collective Bargaining in Sweden* (Cambridge, Mass.: Harvard University Press, 1962).

wages is available from a study of job evaluation in various countries by the British National Board for Prices and Incomes.[84]   Industrywide applications in Sweden provided both stability and flexibility. Denmark's countrywide application has been relaxed and now provides for industry differences.

Wage determination in employing organizations has not been the subject of much empirical research by economists. The major exception is the study by Slichter, Healy, and Livernash.[85] This penetrating study included an examination of wage decisions within organizations under collective bargaining and the effects on wage administration. Job evaluation, seniority and merit increase plans, incentive plans, and selected benefits were studied. The influence of decisions by the parties on wage levels and wage structures and the effects of these decisions were analyzed. Interestingly, reasonable accommodation between the parties is the rule on job evaluation, wage structure administration, and benefit plans. But incentive plans often caused problems.

The British study previously mentioned analyzed the application of job evaluation to organizations. Marriott[86]   has confirmed the Slichter, Healy, Livernash study's less than positive conclusions with respect to incentive plans. A British study[87]   concludes that incentive plans are responsible for a good part of wage drift.

Benefit determination and administration have been studied by economists. The influence of collective bargaining seems to be shown in the advantage of union workers over nonunion workers in benefits.[88] Another influence is firm size. In large firms benefit costs apparently are double those in small firms.[89]   Most students of labor relations appear to feel that unions have had a wage structure impact in enlarging the benefit package (the total package has risen at about double the rate for wages).[90]   The influence of benefit plan decisions seems especially important in the U.S., where, unlike other western countries, benefit decisions are made primarily by the parties to the employment exchange.

[84]National Board for Prices and Incomes, "Job Evaluation," *Report No. 83* (London: Her Majesty's Stationery Office, 1968).

[85]Sumner H. Slichter, James J. Healy, and E. Robert Livernash, *The Impact of Collective Bargaining on Management* (Washington, D.C.: The Brookings Institution, 1960).

[86]R. Marriott, *Incentive Payment Systems*, 3rd ed. (London: Staples Press, 1968).

[87]National Board for Prices and Incomes, "Payment by Results Systems," *Report No. 65* (London: Her Majesty's Stationery Office, 1968).

[88]William Davis and Lily Mary David, "Pattern of Wage and Benefit Changes in Manufacturing," *Monthly Labor Review* (February, 1968), pp. 40–48.

[89]Lester, in *Industrial Relations* (October, 1967), pp. 57–67.

[90]Livernash, in Ginsburg *et al.*, *A Review of IR Research*, pp. 79–144.

SUMMARY

This chapter has reviewed the theory-building and empirical work of economists in their efforts to explain wages. Economists have been studying wages longer than anybody else, and they have made some significant contributions to our understanding of the problem. For example, it is well established that economic forces strongly influence wage determination. It is quite well settled that the primary influence on long-term changes in real wages is productivity. But money wage levels are affected by a number of other economic variables. Although economic forces are the main element affecting the general wage level, implementing policies that this explanation suggests is complicated by political factors, as the study of incomes policies indicates.

The marginal productivity theory or competitive hypothesis also explains a significant portion of particular wages and wage structures. But here noneconomic forces assume a larger role, as institutional analysis suggests.

Thus, although economists have contributed a great deal to our understanding of wages, economic theory provides only a partial explanation, and the explanation becomes less useful the closer one comes to the level at which wage decisions are actually made. Perhaps at this point in our analysis the most useful conclusion is that of Barbara Wootton: "The contemporary wage and salary structure . . . (is) the accumulated deposit laid down by a rich mixture of economic and social forces . . . [these forces] act and react upon one another to produce a result which is quite inexplicable if either is left out of the reckoning."[91]

[91]Barbara Wootton, *The Social Foundation of Wage Policy* (London: Allen and Unwin, 1955).

3

Behavioral Science Compensation Theory and Research

In recent years behavioral scientists have added greatly to our understanding of compensation. Psychologists have devoted a great deal of research effort to pay and pay plans and to motivation and job satisfaction. Although American sociologists have not devoted a great deal of attention to compensation, some of their research in other areas speaks to compensation problems; and European industrial sociologists, are giving considerable attention to compensation.

Although the micro-macro dichotomy is not so descriptive of behavioral theory and research as it is of economic wage theory, it is used in this chapter as in the preceding one. Micro theory emphasizes the individual but gives some attention to organizations. Most of micro theory is the work of psychologists who are concerned with the behavior of individuals. Macro theory emphasizes organizations but gives some attention to forces acting on the organization from without and within (including the behavior of individuals as members). Thus although micro theory and research is chiefly the work of the psychologists and macro theory chiefly the work of the sociologists, both disciplines have made contributions to both areas.

MICRO THEORY AND RESEARCH

The most visible contribution of behavioral scientists to compensation theory and practice has been motivation theory and research. Such work represents attempts to explain the forces that activate behavior and the process by which these forces work. Psychological motivation theory seeks to explain all kinds of motivated behavior in all kinds of situations, including behavior in organizations, although many psychologists are more interested in explaining individual behavior than in the kinds of behavior relevant to organizations.

Organizations, of course, must be concerned with many different kinds of individual behavior. For example, organizations require that individuals (1) join the organization and remain with the organization (membership), (2) carry out job assignments dependably, (3) achieve organization objectives beyond role expectations through innovative and spontaneous activity, (4) cooperate with others, (5) protect the organization against disaster, (6) make creative suggestions, (7) carry out self-training, (8) create a favorable climate.[1] Psychologists in developing motivation theory have not typically distinguished the forces making for these different types of behavior. Nor, unfortunately, have organizations. Organizations act as if one set of motivating forces induces all types of required behavior.

Perhaps the most explicit statement of the distinction between two of these types of behavior required by organizations and the quite different sources of these behaviors was made by March and Simon.[2] They carefully distinguish the motivation to acquire and keep organization membership (their phrase is motivation to participate) and motivation to produce. Membership motivation results from a favorable inducements-contributions balance—*i.e.,* applicants must perceive that what they get from the organization at least balances what they must give to the organization, and employees must perceive a continuing favorable balance if they are to remain members. Motivation to produce represents a much more complex psychological contract between man and organization involving perceived alternatives, perceived consequences of these alternatives, and individual goals.

Organizations have no choice but to provide membership motivation if they wish to remain organizations. But if motivation to produce is too costly or too much trouble, the organization may choose other routes to organization goals such as designing jobs so that prescribed job performance is sufficient.

The discussion of motivation theory and research that follows distinguishes these two types of motivation. Although recognizing that motivation is complex and that much remains to be learned, the position taken here is that membership motivation and motivation to produce must be distinguished in compensation theory.

[1]Daniel Katz, "The Motivational Basis of Organizational Behavior," *Behavioral Science* (April, 1964), pp. 131–146.

[2]James G. March and Herbert A. Simon, *Organizations* (New York: John Wiley and Sons, Inc., 1958), chapters 3 and 4.

Accordingly, the two psychological theories most relevant to compensation issues—equity theory and expectancy theory—attempt to explain quite different kinds of motivation. Equity theory because it is conceptually similar to the inducements-contributions balance is concerned with motivation to participate (membership). Expectancy theory is primarily concerned with the variables and relationships involved in motivation to perform.

As mentioned previously, the proponents of these theories do not make a distinction between the two types of motivation. Equity theorists propose that motivation in organizations can be obtained by manipulating inputs and outcomes. Expectancy theorists postulate a broader set of variables as necessary to explain motivation in organizations but include those used in equity theory.

But because organizations believe that they require both kinds of motivation and because obtaining these different kinds of behavior requires different actions by the organization, they are distinguished in this book. In fact, the author believes that many of the issues faced in compensation are clarified by carefully distinguishing membership motivation from motivation to perform.

MEMBERSHIP MOTIVATION THEORY AND RESEARCH

What we are calling membership motivation theory is called *equity theory* by psychologists and involves a convergence of two streams. The first involves the work of Elliott Jaques in Great Britain and the second, the work of J. S. Adams and others in the United States.

Jaques' theory of equitable payment holds that individuals have an intuitive knowledge of their capacity, the level of their work, and the propriety of their pay, and when their capacity is properly utilized in their work and when their pay matches their level of work they achieve psychological equilibrium.[3] When, however, pay is less than or more than that justified by the level of their work, individuals perceive inequity and react to it.

Jaques believes that level of work can be measured by determining an individual's time-span of discretion on his job (the maximum period of time during which the use of discretion is authorized and expected without a review of that discretion by a superior). He reports measuring time-span of discretion at all levels of work and has published a handbook[4] describing his methods. Jaques also reports success in measuring "felt fair pay," the amount of pay the individual perceives

[3]Elliott Jaques, *Equitable Payment* (New York: John Wiley and Sons, Inc., 1961).
[4]Elliott Jaques, *Time Span Handbook* (London: Heinemann, 1964).

as fair for his level of work. Thus operationalizing Jaques' theory of equitable payment consists of measuring the level of an individual's work and providing the proper pay for that level of work. Equity is assured when "felt fair pay" equals actual pay or deviates from it by less than minus 10 per cent or plus 20 per cent.

Notice that although equity or inequity is perceived by the individual, it is keyed to the level of his work for the organization as well as functioning as a pay standard for him. Thus it is conceivable that equity as perceived by the individual would accord with equity as perceived by the organization.

Unfortunately, in spite of Jaques' elaborate explanations, neither time-span nor felt-fair pay has proved easy to measure by others. Atchison[5] was able to measure time span by asking supervisors the duration of the most extended task assigned to subordinates and felt-fair pay by submitting an elaborate distance scale to subordinates. Richardson[6] reports measuring by interview both time span and felt-fair pay in a large organization and finding high correlations between them. Goodman,[7] however, found that time spans of 141 managers were not necessarily greater at higher levels of the organization and that abilities of individuals did not correlate highly with job level. Milkovich and Campbell found little agreement among individuals on norms of felt-fair pay.[8] Others question whether time span is the principal or sole measuring stick used by organization members in determining the equity of their pay.[9] Whether time span itself can be reliably measured is still controversial[10] and application of the time-span approach has been limited.[11]

The other stream of equity theory is based on the work of a number of American behavioral scientists. From Festinger's[12] theories of

[5]Thomas Atchison and Wendell French, "Pay Systems for Scientists and Engineers," *Industrial Relations* (October, 1967), pp. 44–56.

[6]Roy Richardson, *Fair Pay and Work* (Carbondale and Edwardsville: Southern Illinois University Press, 1971).

[7]Paul S. Goodman, "An Empirical Examination of Elliott Jaques' Concept of Time-Span," *Human Relations* (May, 1967), pp. 155–170.

[8]George T. Milkovich and Keith Campbell, "A Study of Jaques' Norms of Equitable Payment," *Industrial Relations* (May, 1972), pp. 267–271.

[9]Don Hellriegel and Wendell French, "A Critique of Jaques' Equitable Payment System," *Industrial Relations* (May, 1969), pp. 269–279.

[10]George Strauss, "Organization Behavior and Personnel Relations," in Woodrow L. Ginsburg, E. Robert Livernash, Herbert S. Parnes, and George Strauss (eds.), *A Review of Industrial Relations Research, Vol. I* (Madison, Wisconsin: Industrial Relations Research Association, 1970), p. 197.

[11]National Board for Prices and Incomes, "Job Evaluation," *Report No. 83* (London: Her Majesty's Stationery Office, 1966).

[12]L. Festinger, "A Theory of Social Comparison Processes," *Human Relations* (May, 1954), pp. 117–140; Leon Festinger, *A Theory of Cognitive Dissonance* (Evanston, Ill.: Row Peterson, 1957).

social comparison processes and cognitive dissonance and Homan's[13] theory of distributive justice, Adams[14] postulated that individuals determine equity by comparing their inputs (contributions) and outcomes (rewards) to inputs and outcomes of some "other" and that if inequity is perceived as a result of the comparison, there are behavioral and attitudinal consequences. Equity theory focuses on inputs, outcomes, the comparison process, and the results of the comparison. The entire process is perceptual. Only those inputs and outcomes recognized by the individual and perceived as relevant are pertinent in determining equity. The comparison process and comparison standards are those employed by the individual. The existence of equity or inequity is determined by the individual and reaction to inequity is made by the individual. Although the organization can conceivably influence the equity determination process, it can only do so by influencing the perception of individuals.

Adams' formulation of potential inputs includes education, intelligence, experience, training, skill, seniority, age, sex, ethnic background, social status, effort, appearance, health, even the characteristics of the individual's spouse.[15] Presumably any of these or any other input the individual considers relevant may be used in determining equity. Outcomes, according to equity theory, include all the rewards that the individual recognizes and considers relevant in equity determination. Of course they include pay and other extrinsic rewards but they also include intrinsic rewards. In fact, the list of potential outcomes is probably much longer than the list of potential inputs. Because the individual determines the relevance of these outcomes, it is quite possible that the individual perceives that he is receiving rewards that the organization is not aware of providing. It is equally possible that the organization is providing rewards that the individual does not consider relevant.

In Adams' formulation of equity theory the comparison process is assumed to consist of the individual's comparing his inputs and outcomes with those of another individual or group. Vroom[16] suggests that the individual may employ his self-concept as a comparison standard. Weick[17] suggests that the individual uses an internal standard when

[13]George Caspar Homans, *Social Behavior: Its Elementary Forms* (New York: Harcourt, Brace, and World, Inc., 1961).

[14]J. S. Adams, "Inequity in Social Exchange," in L. Berkowitz (ed.), *Advances in Experimental Social Psychology, Vol. 2* (New York: Academic Press, Inc., 1965), pp. 267–299.

[15]*Ibid.*

[16]Victor H. Vroom, *Work and Motivation* (New York: John Wiley and Sons, Inc., 1964).

[17]K. E. Weick, "The Concept of Equity in the Perception of Pay," *Administrative Science Quarterly* (December, 1966), pp. 414–439.

objective reality is not available as a standard. Actually, Festinger's theory of social comparison processes (one of the bases of equity theory) holds that people have a drive to evaluate themselves, that when objective means are not available people compare with other people, that objective standards are preferred, and that subjective evaluations are based on perceived similarity of comparison persons. Because comparison standards as well as inputs and outcomes are determined by the individual, presumably objective reality, the self-concept, or another individual or group may serve as the comparison standard. It is quite possible for an individual to use all three standards and to change his comparison standard as information becomes available. Organizations may influence the comparison process by providing information and by emphasizing the relevancy of particular standards but only if they succeed in influencing the individual in his determination of a comparison standard.

Adams' conception of equity theory postulates results of perceived inequity that lean heavily on the theory of cognitive dissonance. Because inequity is a situation involving dissonance, the individual will seek to change the situation. One possibility is that the individual will change his inputs or outcomes. Another is that he will change the inputs and outcomes of others to whom he compares himself. Still another possibility is that the individual will perceptually distort his own or others' inputs and outcomes. A fourth possibility is that the individual will change his comparison standard to one that yields equity. A final possibility is that the individual will withdraw from the situation.

Adams' conception of responses to inequity suggests that an individual chooses responses in the order given. Notice that his first response is to change behavior. If behavior changes are blocked, he changes attitudes. Finally, if efforts to change his or others' inputs and outcomes both actually and perceptually are insufficient, he resorts to another behavioral response—he withdraws.

A large number of experimental studies have been made to test the predictions of equity theory.[18] Most of them involve attempts to manipulate the subject's perception of his qualifications (inputs) in order to determine whether or not the subject reacts as predicted. A lesser number of studies have attempted to manipulate outcomes. Adams, for example, sought to make some subjects feel overpaid by denigrating their qualifications while informing them that in spite of their underqualification they would be paid the same as fully qualified

[18]For reviews of equity research see E. E. Lawler, "Equity Theory as a Predictor of Productivity and Work Quality," *Psychological Bulletin* (December, 1968), pp. 596–610; and R. D. Pritchard, "Equity Theory: A Review and Critique," *Organization Behavior and Human Performance* (May, 1969), pp. 176–211.

subjects. Subjects who were made in this way to feel underqualified (overpaid) increased their efforts to achieve improved quantity when paid by the hour and improved the quality of their work but produced less when paid by the piece. Other studies designed to replicate these findings have found that subjects tend to change their perceptions of their qualifications over time to bring them into line with their rewards. They have also found that other inputs and outcomes not recognized by Adams were operating. For example, the higher quality result under piecework may be explained by insecurity (lower outcomes) resulting from attacks on the subjects' qualifications. A number of studies have explained the apparent increased effort by underqualified subjects in terms of an assault on the subjects' self-esteem (lowered outcomes). In fact, overpaid subjects who were not made to feel underqualified produced no more than equitably paid subjects.

A few studies have attempted to determine the effects of underpayment. According to equity theory, underpaid subjects (low outcomes) should attempt to restrict their inputs. Two studies of underpaid subjects paid by the piece produced a large number of low-quality pieces that increased their outcomes without demanding greater inputs. Two studies of underpaid subjects paid by the hour found no differences in either productivity or quality between underpaid and equitably paid subjects.

These carefully designed laboratory studies tend to show the validity of equity theory. People do tend to increase or decrease both inputs and outcomes both actually and perceptually to achieve equity. But even in simple laboratory experiments there are many inputs and outcomes perceptually present, and we know surprisingly little about how they operate and change.

A number of equity studies in operating organizations have been conducted by the author and a colleague. One series of studies attempted to determine the inputs and outcomes perceived as important by four occupational groups in one organization and the discrepancy between what employees perceived themselves to be getting from (outcomes) and giving to (inputs) the organization and what they believed they should be receiving and contributing.[19] A rather large number (19) of possible rewards and contributions were included, and although there were differences in adjudged importance all were considered important by the respondents. But there were significant differ-

[19]D. W. Belcher and T. J. Atchison, "Equity Theory and Compensation Policy," *Personnel Administration* (July–August, 1970), pp. 22–33; T. J. Atchison and D. W. Belcher, "Equity, Rewards and Compensation Administration," *Personnel Administration* (March–April, 1971), pp. 32–36.

ences in the importance of both inputs and outcomes to different occupational groups. One of the surprising findings was the large number of rewards and the equally large number of contributions that all groups considered important.

The discrepancy findings were also revealing. There were strong indications that compensation practices geared to what employees wanted to receive and to contribute would differ more by occupational group than is usually the case. A highly tentative analysis that classified the inputs and outcomes by both importance and discrepancy (between what employees perceived as existing and what they believed should exist) appears to carry implications for designing compensation programs.

A number of other studies have been made in widely varying organizations and among varying occupational and demographic groups. As much as it is possible by survey research, the results support equity theory. People do perceive a rather large number of outcomes as relevant to the employment situation, and they are also able to compare what they are getting and what they think they should get in each reward. The same is true for inputs. Some rewards are highly valued by some occupational groups but not by others. Other rewards are highly valued by some demographic groups but not others. The inputs that employees expect to contribute to organizations and to be rewarded for appear to be culturally based. But although a common core seems to exist, the inputs also vary by occupational and perhaps by demographic groups. There seems to be some variation between the inputs people want to make to organizations and the inputs that organizations appear to expect from employees.

So far at least, it seems useful to classify outcomes into (1) extrinsic rewards, (2) intrinsic rewards, and (3) rewards provided by organizations that the organization is not aware of providing. Likewise, inputs seem to be usefully classified into (1) job-related contributions, (2) performance-related contributions, and (3) personal inputs—those contributions not obviously required by the job but which individuals believe relevant as a contribution to the organization.

Some studies of comparison standards have been made. Patchen[20] found that a comparison person could be identified and that he was somewhat similar to the comparing individual. The comparison person varied, however, with the situation of the comparing individual and the weight the comparer placed on the results of the comparison. Managers

[20]Martin Patchen, *The Choice of Wage Comparisons* (Englewood Cliffs, N.J.: Prentice-Hall, Inc., 1961).

at different levels have been found to vary about whether their choice of comparison person is from within the organization or from without.[21] Different occupational groups appear to vary in terms of whether standards internal to the person or comparison persons are employed, and there is a tendency by managers to compare their present situation with a previous one.[22] The choice of comparison standard has been found to vary with the result of the comparison, so that when inequity is perceived as inevitable, remote comparisons are preferable.[23]

The laboratory studies cited previously show that individuals do react to perceived inequity as suggested by Adams' formulation of equity theory. They do change inputs and outcomes both actually and perceptually and those of others in the same ways. But which outcomes and inputs (or comparison standards) will be changed in a given situation and whether the change will show up in behavior or be limited to a change in attitude has not been determined. Continuing studies by the author and a colleague are attempting to determine which of the methods of inequity resolution are preferred by different occupational and demographic groups.

Equity theory is assumed to explain membership motivation, because if individuals perceive the situation as equitable they are likely to continue in the situation. An individual's decision that equity exists seems to be the attitudinal counterpart of the inducements-contributions decision that March and Simon postulate as sufficient to explain membership motivation.

Thus when individuals perceive the employment situation as fair, they will accept it or continue it. Organizations get and keep members. Improvements in the inducements-contributions balance exist only in the eye of the beholder. If the organization is able to provide each employee group with a reward-contribution balance that each group considers fair, the organization reaps the benefit—continued membership. However, only membership is guaranteed.

PERFORMANCE MOTIVATION THEORY AND RESEARCH

Psychologists often explain motivation to perform in terms of *expectancy theory,* which postulates the variables and how they operate,

---

[21]I. R. Andrews and Mildred M. Henry, "Management Attitudes Toward Pay," *Industrial Relations* (October, 1963), pp. 29–39; Mary Jo Hamilton, "A Study of Public Management Attitude Toward Pay," unpublished master's thesis (San Diego State, 1966).

[22]Unpublished study, T. J. Atchison and D. W. Belcher.

[23]K. E. Weick and B. Nesset, "Preferences Among Forms of Equity," *Organization Behavior and Human Performance* (November, 1968), pp. 400–416.

or by content theories, which postulate the motivational strength of a variable but not how it operates. Although it has been established that expectancy theory encompasses the content theories,[24] some attention will be given to them later in this section.

Expectancy theory postulates that to motivate good performance the following conditions must exist: (1) employees must want the rewards the organization offers; (2) employees must believe that good performance does in fact lead to more of these rewards; (3) employees must believe that their performance reflects their efforts; (4) employees must see more positive consequences from good performance than negative consequences; (5) employees must see good performance as the most attractive of all possible behaviors. More formally, a recent formulation of expectancy theory[25] states that (1) the sum of perceived probabilities that effort results in performance multiplied by (2) the sum of the perceived probabilities that performance results in certain outcomes times the perceived desirability of these outcomes leads to (3) effort; effort multiplied by (4) abilities and (5) proper role perceptions results in (6) performance; and finally, performance leads to (7) rewards.

Both of the above statements show the difficulties facing organizations intent on securing performance motivation. For example, employees may not want more of the rewards offered by the organization. Or employees may believe that in order to get more of one reward (pay) they must give up another reward (security or pleasant social relationships). Again, employees may not believe that good performance does in fact lead to more desired rewards and convincing them may require more changes than the organization is prepared to make. For example, it is becoming increasingly clear that employees cannot be expected to believe in the performance-reward relationship if pay rates are secret or if employee appraisal is tied to other factors besides performance or if employees do not accept performance appraisals as correct.

Or employees may not believe that performance always reflects their efforts. Many factors beyond employee control may affect performance. Notice that the formal model combines effort, abilities, and role perceptions multiplicatively. This means that mistakes in selection (low ability) or training (improper role perceptions), even with maximum effort, result in poor performance. Any example of low effort-performance relationships can be expected to interfere with the belief that performance reflects effort.

---

[24]Edward E. Lawler, *Pay and Organizational Effectiveness: A Psychological View* (New York: McGraw-Hill Book Company, 1971). This excellent work uses expectancy theory as a framework for interpreting psychological research on pay. This section leans heavily on Lawler's analysis.
[25]*Ibid.*, pp. 107–114.

The requirements that employees (1) see more positive consequences from good performance than negative consequences and (2)
see good performance as the most attractive of all possible behaviors
emphasize the importance of the second variable in the formal model.
Anything that lowers the desirability of a particular reward or anything
that lowers the belief that good performance leads to a reward combines multiplicatively to lower performance. Both the possibility of
always meeting these requirements and their fragility in most organizations should be apparent.

The difficulties facing organizations seeking to provide performance motivation have been emphasized for a number of reasons. If
the reader had any question about the distinction between membership
motivation and motivation to perform, the requirements for securing
motivation to perform should provide the answer. More money or more
of any other reward does not automatically ensure motivation to perform. Assuming that the employee wants more of the reward, a system
of beliefs regarding the relationship between effort and performance
and performance and rewards must be fostered and nurtured. And
these beliefs may be fragile.

It should also be apparent that the possibility of securing performance motivation varies by employee group and the technology of the
organization. Although most employees want more money, there may
be some who don't and who want other rewards the organization
doesn't want to provide (autonomy to a file clerk). In some jobs, the
relationship between effort and performance is attenuated by factors
beyond the control of the employee. For many types of employees (and
in many organizations) the relationship between performance and reward is in fact very low, and it is thus impossible to convince employees
that high performance leads to high rewards.

But fortunately for organizations, there are some employee
groups that do want the rewards the organization has to offer, do want
to believe that greater effort results in improved performance, and do
want to believe that better performance leads to greater rewards. For
such employee groups, the requirements that the organization must
meet to secure performance motivation are less stringent. These employees may need only occasional positive signals to confirm their beliefs and may be able to tolerate some negative signals. But even with
such groups it is useful to remember that expectations are somewhat
fragile.

There is a good deal of research evidence to support expectancy
theory. For example, psychological studies of job satisfaction show that
people place importance on a number of rewards that organizations
provide. Cited above under equity theory were studies by Atchison and

Belcher that showed that employees consider a surprisingly large number of rewards to be important.

A comprehensive review of the importance of pay to employees has been recently made by Lawler.[26] Pay varies in importance to an individual and there are individual differences in the importance of pay. Organization pay policies may influence the importance of pay to its members. A compilation of forty-nine studies of the relative importance of pay shows that it ranked from first to ninth position, with an average rank of three. Herzberg and his associates,[27] on the other hand, reviewed sixteen studies and found pay in sixth position. Actually, no strong conclusions should be reached from such studies inasmuch as the number of items ranked varied from five to thirty-six. Also it has been pointed out that social desirability, the unreality of self-reports, and the fact that people are poor judges of what they really want all affect the results.[28]

Much more reliance may be placed upon studies concerning the importance of pay to specific groups. For example, pay is more important to men than to women.[29] But no differences have been found for different levels of intelligence or different age groups.[30] Personality traits and family background, however, seem to affect the importance of pay such that individuals with low self-assurance and high neuroticism who come from small towns or a farm are likely to value pay highly.[31]

It also appears that the less pay people receive the more important it is to them, and vice versa. But the relationships are so weak that it is not correct to say that pay is unimportant to highly paid people. It is more correct to conclude that pay is likely to be less important to highly paid people than to people paid somewhat less.[32]

Much larger dollar raises are needed to be meaningful to higher paid employees, however.[33] Although this suggests percentage increases, a meaningful raise constitutes a smaller percentage as salary

[26]Lawler, *Pay and Organizational Effectiveness,* Chapter 3.

[27]F. Herzberg, B. Mausner, R. O. Peterson, and D. F. Capwell, *Job Attitudes: Review of Research and Opinion* (Pittsburgh: Psychological Service of Pittsburgh, 1957).

[28]Robert L. Opsahl and Marvin D. Dunnette, "The Role of Financial Compensation in Industrial Motivation," *Psychological Bulletin* (August, 1966), pp. 94–118.

[29]R. Centers and D. E. Bugental, "Intrinsic and Extrinsic Job Motivation Among Different Segments of the Working Population," *Journal of Applied Psychology* (June, 1966), pp. 193–197.

[30]Lawler, *Pay and Organizational Effectiveness,* pp. 47–48.

[31]*Ibid.,* pp. 49–50.

[32]E. E. Lawler and L. M. Porter, "Perceptions Regarding Management Compensation," *Industrial Relations* (October, 1963), pp. 41–49.

[33]S. Zedeck and P. C. Smith, "A Psychophysical Determination of Equitable Payment: A Methodological Study," *Journal of Applied Psychology* (October, 1968), pp. 343–347.

increases.[34]   There is evidence that pay becomes less important at higher levels of the organization, that skilled blue-collar workers consider pay less important than unskilled workers, that blue-collar workers place more importance on pay than white-collar workers, that managers say that pay is less important than workers, and that pay becomes less important at each ascending management level.[35]

Members of different kinds of organizations place different values on pay. Employees of industrial organizations consider pay more important than government employees, who, in turn, place more importance on pay than employees of hospital and of social service organizations.[36] It seems likely that self-selection is operating so that people who value money highly choose business careers.

Somewhat surprisingly, union membership appears unrelated to the importance attached to pay. Promotion has not been shown to change the importance of pay. But the limited evidence available suggests that how pay is determined affects its importance, so that money worked for and earned is more highly valued than money not worked for.[37]

In summary, the research evidence shows that although there are individual differences in the importance individuals attach to pay, pay is sufficiently important to employees to qualify as a valued reward in the performance motivation model. Obviously the individual differences become especially important if the organization seeks to assign employees who had a minimal interest in pay to jobs paid on an incentive plan.

Since some individuals value money more than others, organizations seeking employees who value money highly could try to select such individuals. These organizations might also increase the importance of pay to their current employees by insuring that pay raises are tied to achievement and by seeing that employees know who gets the largest raises. In this way pay is tied to status measured by achievement.

Unfortunately, perhaps the most efficient method that organizations could use to increase the importance of pay to employees isn't available. This method—keeping employees underpaid—represents one of the dilemmas of compensation administration. It would increase

[34]J. F. Hinrichs, "Correlates of Employee Evaluations of Pay Increases," *Journal of Applied Psychology* (December, 1969), pp. 481–489.

[35]Centers and Bugental, in *Journal of Applied Psychology* (June, 1966), pp. 193–197; W. W. Ronan, "Individual and Situational Variables Relating to Job Satisfaction," *Journal of Applied Psychology Monograph* (February, 1970), pp. 1–31; Lawler and Porter, in *Industrial Relations* (October, 1963), pp. 41–49.

[36]E. E. Lawler, "The Mythology of Management Compensation," *California Management Review* (Fall, 1966), pp. 11–22.

[37]Lawler, *Pay and Organizational Effectiveness,* pp. 57–58.

the importance of money to employees and meet one of the requirements of performance motivation. But at the same time, the organization is reducing membership motivation.

Other research evidence also appears to support expectancy theory. For example, studies have consistently found a positive relationship
between job performance and employee beliefs concerning the degree
to which pay is related to performance. Georgopoulos, Mahoney, and
Jones[38] found that 38 per cent of those who perceived that productivity
would lead to high pay in the long run were high producers as measured
by self-reports, whereas only 21 per cent of those who felt it would not
were high producers. Lawler[39] and Porter and Lawler[40] found stronger
beliefs that performance influences pay are associated with both higher
performance as measured by both self-ratings and superiors' ratings and
higher effort. In fact, the relationship between effort and the belief that
performance influences pay was stronger than the relationship between performance and this belief, further substantiating the model
inasmuch as ability and role perceptions stand between effort and performance.

A number of other studies have been made to test the predictions
of expectancy theory.[41] The studies produced data that support the
model. Expectancy theory studies tend to be made in organizations
rather than in laboratories, where most equity theory studies have been
made. Consequently it has been difficult to design studies that carefully
separate importance of pay, effort-performance probability, performance-reward probability, and abilities and role perceptions. In organizations there is a tendency to equate effort and performance, and
obtaining good measures of abilities and role perception has been difficult. Also, organizations provide many rewards besides pay, whether
they realize it or not, and testing the predictions of expectancy theory
with regard to pay alone may lower its predictive power.

Some of the studies have shown that the importance attached to
pay is related to performance in cases wherein good performance does
in fact lead to improved pay.[42] On this conclusion laboratory studies
and studies in organizations agree. Almost all the studies show that the

---

[38]B. S. Georgopoulos, G. M. Mahoney, and N. Jones, "A Path-Goal Approach to
Productivity," *Journal of Applied Psychology* (December, 1957), pp. 345–353.
    [39]E. E. Lawler, "Managers' Job Performance and their Attitudes toward their Pay,"
unpublished doctoral dissertation (University of California, Berkeley, 1964).
    [40]L. W. Porter and E. E. Lawler, *Managerial Attitudes and Performance* (Home-
wood, Ill.: Irwin-Dorsey, 1968).
    [41]See Herbert G. Heneman, III, and Donald P. Schwab, "An Evaluation of Re-
search on Expectancy Theory Predictions of Employee Performance," *Psychological
Bulletin* (July, 1972), pp. 1–9.
    [42]Lawler, *Pay and Organizational Effectiveness*, pp. 137–139.

relationship between pay and performance increases when pay importance and performance-reward beliefs are combined multiplicatively,
as the model specifies. Both ability and role perceptions have been
found to increase the effort-performance relationship, but not in every
study. One study related performance-reward beliefs and present performance and performance one year later.[43] The fact that these beliefs
better predicted future performance suggests that they cause performance rather than the reverse.

Expectancy studies, although much more carefully designed,
agree with earlier studies that tying pay to performance tends to increase performance. Even the most conservative of these earlier studies
suggest that individual incentive plans can increase productivity by 10
to 20 per cent.[44] But, in addition, expectancy studies help explain why
some incentive plans encourage restriction of output. Fear of rate cuts
and other negative consequences can reduce performance-reward beliefs because either pay or other rewards may fail to increase or even
may decrease with improved performance.

Although expectancy theory calls for much more research, the
evidence to date carries many suggestions for organizations concerned
with performance motivation. The requirement that organizations
must have employees who want more of the rewards the organization
has to offer has already been discussed. The requirement that employees hold strong beliefs that improved performance leads to higher
rewards obviously depends on the signals from experience in the organization. If it is clear that rewards in this organization do not depend
on performance, creating beliefs that they do is difficult.

Unfortunately, it appears that pay is not very closely related to
performance in many organizations that have pay plans that imply that
they are. Many studies show a lack of relationship between pay and
performance, or even a negative relationship.[45] This is true even of
managers. Fortunately for organizations, however, managers require
only some positive indications of the relationship to believe that pay is
based on performance.[46]

[43]E. E. Lawler, "A Correlational-Causal Analysis of the Relationship between Expectancy Attitudes and Job Performance," *Journal of Applied Psychology* (December,
1968), pp. 462–468.

[44]Lawler, *Pay and Organizational Effectiveness*, p. 124.

[45]B. Svetlik, E. Prien, and G. Barrett, "Relationships between Job Difficulty, Employee's Attitudes Toward His Job, and Supervisory Ratings of the Employee's Effectiveness," *Journal of Applied Psychology* (October, 1964), pp. 320–324; M. Haire, E. E.
Ghiselli, and M. E. Gordon, "A Psychological Study of Pay," *Journal of Applied Psychology
Monograph* (August, 1967), pp. 1–24; M. H. Brenner and H. C. Lockwood, "Salary as a
Predictor of Salary: A 20-Year Study," *Journal of Applied Psychology* (August, 1965), pp.
295–298.

[46]E. E. Lawler, "The Multitrait-Multirater Approach to Measuring Managerial Job
Performance," *Journal of Applied Psychology* (October, 1967), pp. 369–381.

Managers, according to the same study, believe that performance should be the most important determinant of their pay, but feel that in fact it is not. Other studies show that managers and salesmen prefer to have their pay based on performance. Blue-collar workers are less favorable to merit-based pay plans, although workers on incentive plans usually favor them. It should be obvious that performance motivation cannot be induced if either workers or their managers are opposed to basing rewards on performance.

The kind of pay plans used by the organization can do much to influence employee beliefs in the performance-reward relationship. Individual incentive plans based on objective standards are the strongest signal; merit increases based on subjective judgments are less clear.

Performance measures that do not accord with employee perceptions of performance or that measure factors over which the employee has little control lower employee beliefs regarding the effort-performance relationship. Remembering the expectancy model, a low effort-performance probability combines multiplicatively with the other variables.

In organizations, secrecy with respect to pay rates is accepted practice. Lawler[47] has found that one of the effects of secrecy is that managers make incorrect estimates of the pay of other managers and that managers overestimate the pay of other managers around them and underestimate the pay of superiors. These findings suggest that secrecy lowers the performance-reward probability. It also destroys pay as a feedback to managers to guide their behavior.

The requirements for performance motivation specified by expectancy theory suggest that pay should not be used to motivate performance in some organizations and perhaps among some employees in many organizations. Clearly, if the requirements cannot be met, giving employees more money for no additional performance is a waste of organization resources. Fortunately, as discussed previously, there are other routes to organization effectiveness and the organization can concentrate on membership motivation.

Although the author leans toward expectancy theory as the most useful explanation of performance motivation, some other motivation theories have received wide publicity and deserve some attention. As mentioned earlier, they may be regarded as content theories that postulate the motivational power of one or more variables but not how it or they operate. Expectancy theory appears to encompass these theories.

[47]E. E. Lawler, "Managers' Perceptions of Their Subordinates' Pay and of Their Superiors' Pay," *Personnel Psychology* (Winter, 1965), pp. 413–422; E. E. Lawler, "Secrecy about Management Compensation: Are There Hidden Costs?" *Organizational Behavior and Human Performance* (May, 1967), pp. 182–189.

McClelland[48] and Atkinson[49] postulate three needs to explain behavior: (1) the need for achievement, (2) the need for affiliation, and (3) the need for power. The achievement need, which has been given the most emphasis, is viewed as a relatively stable behavioral tendency to strive for achievement or success. It is not assumed to operate until aroused by a situation or incentive that signals the individual that certain behaviors will lead to feelings of achievement. Thus the need for achievement is actually a label for a class of incentives that the individual has learned.

Need for achievement is usually measured by using the Thematic Apperception Test, which asks respondents to relate what they see in some simple pictures. A number of experiments have been conducted to determine other differences between individual high and low in achievement motivation. Individuals high in need for achievement prefer moderate risks (a 50-50 chance of success), rather than high or low risks. Those with very high achievement needs will work under longer odds than others. Although financial incentives increase performance over achievement motivation alone, it does so particularly among those low in achievement motivation. Need for achievement has been found to be high in middle-class people and lower among both upper and lower classes.[50]

An implication of need for achievement is that any reward that signals the possibility of achievement will be important to those high in achievement motivation. With those lower in need for achievement, money is likely to be an important reward. Thus the major message involves the rewards that can work to achieve performance motivation. However, the fact that individuals with high need for achievement prefer situations wherein the effort-performance probability is approximately 50-50 and at this level tie accomplishment and growth to performance suggests that organizations assign these people to jobs in which success is possible but far from assured.

Maslow's[51] hierarchy of needs is so well known as to require little discussion. Maslow postulated a hierarchy of needs (physiological, safety, social, esteem, and self-actualization) such that needs at a particular level must be largely satisfied before needs at the next higher level become operative. Although needs at more than one level may be

[48]D. C. McClelland, *The Achieving Society* (Princeton, N.J.: Van Nostrand, 1961).

[49]J. W. Atkinson, (ed.), *Motives in Fantasy, Action, and in Society* (Princeton, N.J.: Van Nostrand, 1958).

[50]B. C. Rosen, "Race, Ethnicity, and the Achievement Syndrome," *American Sociological Review* (February, 1959), pp. 47–60.

[51]A. H. Maslow, *Motivation and Personality* (New York: Harper and Brothers, 1954).

operative at one time, the lower-level need takes precedence. Satisfied needs do not motivate and all but self-actualization needs are capable of being satisfied.

The theory is based on existentialism and psychoanalysis and on Maslow's clinical experience. Empirical evidence for it is lacking. It may be pointed out, however, that social needs are similar to need for affiliation and that self-actualization needs are similar to need for achievement, except that need for achievement has a standard definition and self-actualization is defined by each individual.

Maslow's need hierarchy implies that means to satisfy needs operative within an individual are highly important to him and are rewards that have a high potential for motivating performance. But because any given need may be satisfied by a number of means, the theory implies that a large number of rewards of various kinds are important to individuals.

The theory is often interpreted as showing that when lower-order needs (physiological and safety) are satisfied, money cannot motivate. Such an interpretation seems quite illogical in that money can help an individual satisfy social needs, esteem needs, and even self-actualization needs. Maslow has disputed this interpretation of the meaning of his need hierarchy by insisting that "money can mean practically anything in the motivation hierarchy."[52]

Perhaps the best known of the content motivation theories is Herzberg's[53] two-factor theory. Herzberg, from his well-known study involving interviews with engineers and accountants, postulates the existence of two classes of work motivators—extrinsic and intrinsic factors. The extrinsic factors are pay, technical supervision, interpersonal relations with supervision, company policy and administration, working conditions, and job security. The intrinsic factors are achievement, recognition, responsibility, and advancement.

According to the theory, only the intrinsic factors are motivators. Extrinsic rewards may prevent dissatisfaction but do not motivate. Herzberg's theory has generated a great deal of empirical research[54] and whether or not the studies support the theory depends primarily on the method used. Both Herzberg's data and data from other studies show that both extrinsic and intrinsic factors can be satisfying or dissatis-

---

[52]A. H. Maslow, *Eupsychian Management* (Homewood, Ill.: Irwin-Dorsey, 1965), p. 241.

[53]Frederick Herzberg, *Work and the Nature of Man* (New York: The World Publishing Company, 1966).

[54]Perhaps the most complete review of these studies to date is R. J. House and L. A. Wigdor, "Herzberg's Dual Factor Theory of Job Satisfaction and Motivation," *Personnel Psychology* (Winter, 1967), pp. 369–390.

fying. Actually, however, the research evidence has spoken to the question of job satisfaction and dissatisfaction rather than to job behavior.

Thus, perhaps the greatest contribution of the two-factor theory to performance motivation is its reiteration that there is a long list of rewards that may be important to employees and thus may be potential sources of performance motivation. Intrinsic rewards are as important as extrinsic rewards, and perhaps more so to some people. This emphasis on the importance of intrinsic rewards to employees has served to broaden the definition of compensation and has given impetus to the job enrichment movement. There is no question but that intrinsic rewards are important to many employees, especially to managers and professionals. In fact, to some of these employees intrinsic rewards may be more important than extrinsic rewards.

This discussion of motivation theory has included a large part but only a part of psychological studies of pay. For a complete review of psychological studies of pay, the reader is referred to a recent book by Lawler[55] and a review article by Opsahl and Dunnette.[56] Where appropriate, some of this research will be cited in following chapters.

MACRO THEORY AND RESEARCH

Macro theory is also concerned with the forces that activate behavior, but emphasize the forces outside the individual. Sociologists, for example, study the relationships between individuals and how these relationships channel behavior. Unlike psychologists, sociologists have made only a limited number of studies of pay, but many of their studies of other phenomena have implications for pay practices.

For example, sociologists have studied the process by which individuals learn which rewards to expect from work and expected behavior at work. Individuals learn what rewards to expect from work as a result of the socialization process that occurs in the family and in school. Thus, individuals enter employing organizations with a reasonably good idea of what rewards to expect. When they join a particular organization, they learn the rewards offered by that organization.[57] Pay is only one of a long list of rewards available in organizations, however. Dubin has delineated over 100 separate sources of attachment to work that individuals regard as important.[58]

[55]Lawler, *Pay and Organizational Effectiveness.*
[56]Opsahl and Dunnette, in *Psychological Bulletin* (August, 1966), pp. 94–118.
[57]Robert Dubin, *The World of Work* (Englewood Cliffs, N.J.: Prentice-Hall, Inc., 1958).
[58]R. Dubin, "Attachment to Work," unpublished paper (1968).

MOTIVATION

Motivation, to sociologists, is built into the social system. We learn that it is highly appropriate to earn a living, "get ahead," and provide financial and other security for one's family. By the time an individual goes to work, he carries with him these fundamental motivations appropriate to being an employee. Thus, every employee comes to the organization perceiving the appropriate channels of motivation along which his behavior can be directed. These motivations learned from society are given specific form in the organization. Labor unions operate within the motivational system of society and their goals are not concerned with changing it but with influencing management policy in effecting specific rewards for workers.[59]

But many factors outside the organization shape work conduct and the pattern of social relationships inside the organization. To get at the meanings people assign to their work, it is necessary to know their group identifications—the groups from whose norms and controls they take their cues. Different groups have different cultural values about the significance of work.[60]

Apparently, most men in our culture will work even if they have no need for money—they work for self-expression, for social relationships, to give meaning to life. There are, however, differences among occupational groups in reasons for working. Professional men cite interest in their field or a sense of achievement. Managers and sales people cite keeping occupied and active. To blue-collar workers, work becomes important as mere activity.[61]

Sociological self-theory helps explain these group differences. Man lives in a universe of events and objects endowed with meanings by man himself through social definitions couched in language. He learns these meanings along with language and solidifies them through associations in groups important to him. The individual derives his plans of action from the roles he plays and the statuses he occupies in the groups with which he feels identified—his reference groups. Motivation, according to sociological self-theory, is embedded in the attitudes, values, and roles of individuals in various groups.[62]

[59]Robert Dubin, *Working Union-Management Relations* (Englewood Cliffs, N.J.: Prentice-Hall, Inc., 1958), p. 16.
[60]Harold L. Wilensky, in Conrad M. Arensberg *et al.* (eds.), *Research in Industrial Human Relations* (New York: Harper and Brothers, 1957), p. 45.
[61]Nancy C. Morse and Robert S. Weiss, "The Function and Meaning of Work and the Job," *American Sociological Review* (April, 1955), pp. 191–198.
[62]C. Addison Hickman and Manford H. Kuhn, *Individuals, Groups, and Economic Behavior* (New York: The Dryden Press, 1956).

SOCIOLOGY OF LABOR MARKETS

Studies of the sociology of occupations have revealed the different expectations of different occupational groups and have traced the social forces making for these diverse expectations. Caplow's[63] pioneering work emphasized that different occupational groups represent different sociological labor markets with dissimilar expectations regarding rewards and orientations toward work and organizations and analyzed the forces making for these variations. The fact that a typical organization is drawing members from several or all of these different labor markets helps to explain the difficulties that organizations face in maintaining consistent internal pay relationships.

In Caplow's analysis, the *bureaucratic labor market* is used as a benchmark in comparing sociological labor markets. This device is especially useful because organizations often act as if the organization designs and fills its jobs with little regard for the division of labor in society. Although it is true that organizations design their jobs and that the division of labor in the organization may differ from the division of labor in society, few organizations are in a position to train for all jobs in the organization and are thus dependent on the social division of labor.

A bureaucracy is a rationally organized hierarchy of positions designed without reference to the individuals who occupy the positions. The bureaucracy is largely insulated from economic considerations in the labor market in that its labor supply is recruited at the bottom of the hierarchy and moved up to positions structured in terms of qualifications. Promotions are made from within and the labor supply is provided for promotion through training and experience in lower-level positions. The primary labor supply problems in bureaucracies involve the individuals that the bureaucracy cannot train itself—professionals, for example. Labor demand is largely restricted to lower-level positions. In both demand and supply, the closed bureaucracy is primarily a self-regulating system.

In theory, wage determination in a bureaucracy is an administrative decision based on the rational principle that the wage rank order follows the rank order of training and experience required by positions. Status and wage must correlate perfectly. Both qualifications and pay for positions with similar work and responsibility must be equal. Nonfinancial rewards, such as tenure, are further rewards for membership.

In practice, of course, few bureaucracies are sufficiently closed to fit the theory. Some occupational groups cannot be trained by the

[63]Theodore Caplow, *The Sociology of Work* (Minneapolis: University of Minnesota Press, 1954).

bureaucracy and must be brought in from the outside. In these cases, the bureaucracy is at the mercy of the labor market and may be forced to pay the new entrant at a rate that varies from the rational calculation of the worth of his qualifications. Furthermore, unless rewards are comparable with those of other organizations, members may leave. But rewards in other organizations may be affected by historical accidents, occupational monopolies, and political pressure rather than by pure rationality. Even the requirement that differences in qualifications be reflected by differences in pay may be difficult to follow consistently in large complex organizations with many occupational groupings.

Once it becomes apparent that few organizations can operate as closed bureaucracies, the characteristics of labor markets from which the organization must recruit members become important. Perhaps the labor market that differs most from the bureaucratic labor market is the *market for professional services.* In theory, each professional is perfectly noninterchangeable and the value of his unique services is unmeasurable. The supply of professionals is fixed in the short run and may even decrease with increased demand because professional associations tighten their admission standards. Demand for professionals, however, is widely variable. The fixed supply and the varying demand permit professionals to fix the price and to determine its bases. Historically, the client's ability to pay rather than the value of the service (because it is unmeasurable) has been the basis of remuneration, but more recently professional associations have adopted a policy of standard minimum prices and restricted price competition. Finally, the work of professionals is determined by professional training and professional norms rather than by the organization.

The professional labor market has probably been studied more intensively than any of the other labor markets.[64] As a result, a professional model has been developed that purports to distinguish professionals from nonprofessionals. Because, however, some professionals are independent practitioners and some are employees in all sizes and types of organizations, the model is not achieved in reality.[65] Perhaps the theoretical, practical, research-based attributes and the strong control over the professional exercised by the profession itself are the most pertinent points of the model.

Next to the professional, the labor market least within the control of the organization is the *craft labor market.* In theory, the labor supply of a craft is fixed and the demand is variable. Identification is with the

[64]See Edward Gross, *Work and Society* (New York: Thomas Y. Crowell Co., 1958); Ernest Greenwood, "Attitudes of a Profession," *Social Work* (July, 1957), pp. 45–55.

[65]Richard H. Hall, *Occupations and the Social Structure* (Englewood Cliffs, N.J.: Prentice-Hall, Inc., 1969), p. 136.

craft rather than with the employer. Because fluctuating labor demand and fixed labor supply would mean fluctuating wages and cutthroat competition, the craft union operates as a monopolist selling a standardized product. The wage in prosperity tends to be the highest price consistent with full employment of the craft. The lowest wage in depression seeks to assure subsistence of all active craftsmen. Craft control over distribution of work serves as an effective control of labor supply.

Craft control over conditions of sale of craft labor serves to preserve the system of selling labor in standardized units and to prevent the employer from modifying either the system or the attractiveness of work. Not only do crafts rather than employing organizations determine the contents of craft work, but also craftsmen typically collect a standard rate for all levels of craft work.

Craft markets are essentially local and craft controls operate locally. This feature of the craft labor market is probably the most dependable distinction of this market and that of the professional.

The craft labor market probably best fits the building trades, which maintain the tradition of apprenticeship and which were typically highly homogeneous in terms of the ethnic, racial, and religious backgrounds of their membership. Whether such new crafts as television and automobile repairmen will meet the craft model is an unsettled question.[66] The lack of apprenticeship tradition and the greater heterogeneity of membership may mean that their fit with the craft model is as loose as that between the new professions and the professional model.

The *market for semiskilled labor,* in theory, is a close fit with the bureaucratic model. Labor supply depends on the local labor force and competition for workers and demand is determined by the employer who designs the jobs, provides training, and promotes from within. In practice, however, many semiskilled workers are represented by unions and thus labor supply and wage determinants are determined by collective bargaining. Actual wage rates may vary from the legal minimum to the prevailing wage set by collective bargaining.

As in bureaucracies, jobs are designed by the organization and employees are affiliated with the organization. But wage rates are determined by bargaining guided by many considerations, of which employee qualifications are only one. Transfers and often promotions are based on seniority rather than skill.

Custom strongly affects semiskilled wages in that wage changes are determined with reference to wages previously paid and to wages paid by other employers in the industry or area. Wage differentials among jobs in an organization are also influenced by custom and al-

[66] *Ibid.,* p. 217.

though assumed to be related to skill required are at least as likely to be correlated with skill once required by the job, group power struggles, and seniority of the job incumbent.

Unions of semiskilled workers are found primarily in the mass-production industries. Thus many semiskilled jobs exist in nonunion organizations. Perhaps the most important characteristic of semiskilled work is that the job is designed by the employer. Thus the worker is typically not hired for a specific job but is assumed to be trainable for the jobs that exist in the organization. Also, semiskilled jobs are extremely diverse, depending on the technology of the industry and the policies and practices of the employing organization. Probably the exact number of specific occupations that could be included in the semiskilled category is limited only by the number of job titles used by employing organizations.[67] The range of semiskilled jobs is indicated by the fact that fry cooks and cabdrivers as well as chemical operators who monitor automatic processes all fall into this category.

Even if semiskilled workers are not represented by unions it is well to recognize that the conditions of the bureaucratic labor market seldom prevail. As will be seen later, work groups that emerge as soon as people are brought together not only make impersonal decisions unrealistic, but also influence organization decisions. Also, in very small organizations, semiskilled workers (in fact all workers) become key employees.

The *market for unskilled labor* is disappearing as jobs require more in the way of technology and as entry requirements increase. Unskilled labor is perhaps most usefully defined as requiring no skill or training, although the term also is often attached to casual labor.

The supply of unskilled labor is highly variable. Demand is fairly constant in the long run but highly variable in the short run. Although these conditions appear to approach the classical economic model, they do not. Minimum wage laws and public opinion prohibit the continuous price range that the conditions permit. Nonmonetary considerations often are a factor, as in the case of domestic service and farm labor on small farms.

In practice, the unskilled range from those with steady employment in manual or service work to the most marginal members of the labor force.[68] Unionism must be considered even in the case of janitors and construction laborers.

The *market for white-collar workers* is a closer fit with the bureau-

---

[67] *Ibid.,* p. 240.

[68] See Peter B. Doeringer, "Manpower Programs for Ghetto Labor Markets," in Gerald S. Somers (ed.), *IRRA Proceedings of the Twenty-First Annual Winter Meeting* (Chicago, Illinois, December 29–30, 1968), pp. 257–267, and later literature on the "dual labor market."

cratic labor market. The organization designs the jobs, hires at the bottom, and promotes from within. White-collar workers are affiliated with the employer.

But the requirement for impersonal and organizationally rational behavior is no more likely than with semiskilled workers. In fact, white-collar work tends to consist of two types—those, like salesmen and receptionists, who are at the boundary of the organziation and have contacts with customers and clients; and those whose contact is only with other members of the organization performing the same function. The second types of jobs are becoming difficult to distinguish from semiskilled workers, especially in large organizations. But it is the first type that is expanding and may be expected to expand in the future. Because social interaction is a large part of those jobs and success or failure depends on the manner in which the interaction is handled, the job is difficult to standardize and is defined in part by the incumbent rather than by the organization.

The *market for managers* is the most diverse of the sociological labor markets. In some ways, it is a close fit with the bureaucratic labor market. Affiliation is with the organization and success is defined by the organization. There is a strong tendency to hire at the bottom and to promote from within. Pay is geared to status in the organization.

But the rational-impersonal dimension of the bureaucratic model is not met, especially at higher levels of the organization. Although the organization designs lower-level management jobs, above this level the manager is expected to have a voice. Like the boundary white-collar workers, managers must interact with various publics. Interactions with superiors, peers, and subordinates influence the definition of managerial work. Staff managers often have external affiliations not unlike professionals. In Great Britain some levels of management are unionized,[69] and there appears to be some pro-union sentiment among middle managers in the U.S.[70]

Although there is a strong tendency to fill management positions by hiring at the bottom and promoting from within, higher levels of management may be treated as a *market for unique services*—the supply is one individual and the value of the service is difficult to measure. Although the market for unique services is like the professional market, it is only partially so in that in the market for unique services the price is speculative and set by individual bargaining. In spite of the diversity in the market for managers, elements of similarity to the

[69]Joe Kelly, *Organizational Behavior* (Homewood, Ill.: The Dorsey Press, 1969), p. 194.

[70]Alfred T. DeMaria, Dale Tarnowieski, and Richard Gurman, *Manager Unions* (New York: American Management Association, 1972).

bureaucratic labor market are suggested by Galbraith's lumping of white-collar workers, professionals, and managers into a *technostructure* wherein members are affiliated with the organization and accept organizational rationality as long as they believe that their interests are considered in designing organization goals.[71]

Sociological analysis of various types of labor markets serves to emphasize the different forces operating in each. The typical large employer must reconcile the various forces operating in all or most of these markets in designing his reward structure.

SOCIAL STRATIFICATION

Studies of the social stratification process—the means of locating an individual within the social system—have much to say about who gets what rewards. Status differences have been found to rest primarily on occupations.[72] The occupation is not only the most meaningful indicator of status, but also is indicative of and closely related to other status indicators such as education and income.

A number of characteristics of occupations have been found to contribute to their position in the status ranking. One based on the nature of work performed differentiates occupations according to whether they involve manipulating physical objects, symbols, or other people. In general, manipulation of physical objects provides the least status and manipulation of symbols provides the most. But occupations involving social manipulation (managers) also carry high status. Individuals involved solely in symbol manipulation, such as artists and scientists, generally have lower status than those whose occupations involve both symbols and other people. An idea of the utility of this status indicator is reflected in the fact that the latest edition of the *Dictionary of Occupational Titles* is based on this method of distinguishing occupations.

Another indicator of occupational status is prerequisites for entry —the amount of education or training and experience. Another is whether the task is performed on an individual or group basis, with the former carrying higher status. Occupations involving supervision have higher status than those that are supervised. Occupations of higher responsibility have higher status, and responsibility for social and symbolic activities yields higher status than responsibility for physical objects. Work situations are also status indicators, with factories carrying lower status than an office or a research laboratory. Within a commu-

---

[71]John Kenneth Galbraith, *The New Industrial State* (New York: Houghton-Mifflin Co., 1967).

[72]Hall, *Occupations and the Social Structure,* p. 259.

nity, business organizations in different industries carry different statuses, as do business and nonbusiness organizations. Even public, private, and self-employment are status indicators, with self-employment highest, private employment next, and public employment lowest.[73]

The concept of *situs* offers an additional approach to occupational status. An occupation situs or family is a set of occupations whose status system may be viewed as a unit. One study employed ten situses (legal authority, finance and records, manufacturing, transportation, extraction, building and maintenance, commerce, aesthetics and entertainment, education and research, and health and welfare).[74] Each situs is assumed to have its own status system and movement is likely to occur within a situs.

Because the status of an occupation determines the rewards of the incumbent, it is important to determine why occupations occupy different status positions. One explanation is the functional theory of stratification,[75] which involves the differential importance of positions in society, variations in the requirements of the positions, and differences in the kinds of abilities necessary to fill the positions. Another explanation is that the status distribution represents the wishes of those in power to remain in power.[76]

Sociological work on the social stratification process would seem to be useful in developing and testing reward structures in organizations. It would seem that the theory of social stratification is not unrelated to the job and reward hierarchy in organizations.

WORK GROUPS

Much work by behavioral scientists has been devoted to the study of work groups in organizations.[77] Work groups form as a result of the organization of work, develop attitudes and norms, and influence the behavior of group members and the reward structure of organizations. Studies have found that it is the semiskilled jobs that are most susceptible to successful group actions. Uncertainty about the value of the job

[73]Albert J. Reiss, Jr., *Occupations and Social Status* (New York: The Free Press of Glencoe, Inc., 1961).

[74]Richard T. Morris and Raymond J. Murphy, "The Situs Dimension in Occupational Structure," *American Sociological Review* (April, 1959), pp. 231–239.

[75]Kingsley Davis and Wilbert Moore, "Some Principles of Stratification," *American Sociological Review* (April, 1945), pp. 242–249.

[76]Melvin Tumin, "Some Principles of Stratification: A Critical Analysis," *American Sociological Review* (August, 1953), pp. 387–394.

[77]Leonard R. Sayles, *Behavior of Industrial Work Groups* (New York: John Wiley and Sons, Inc., 1958).

because these jobs are not well defined in the labor market and ambiguity of status and skill requirements make for successful group pressures.

These group pressures are an important force affecting the rewards and the status of jobs. It has been found that the worker is occupationally oriented in spite of the ambiguity of semiskilled work and behaves as if he belonged to a highly specific occupational group. Work groups rank certain jobs as more important or desirable and expect these jobs to carry higher pay. Over a period of time the actions of groups perfect the correlation. The union as well as management is forced by group pressures.

REFERENCE GROUPS

The process by which individuals evaluate their situation has also been studied. Reference group theory is concerned with the "determinants and consequences of those processes of evaluation and self-appraisal in which the individual takes the values or standards of other individuals and groups as a comparative frame of reference."[78] The "coercive comparisons" that labor economists have pointed out in collective bargaining have been analyzed in terms of reference group theory.[79] The results show that the choice of reference groups is influenced by rationality and tradition and that comparisons take on a moral tone, yielding "what is right." They also suggest a number of hypotheses. For example, individuals or groups subordinate to the same authority seem likely to use one another as reference groups, but workers in a large "membership" structure like a union are likely to use abstract status reference groups such as skilled workers or steel workers. In an open society, such as the United States, the choice of reference groups is broader and more likely to yield discontent than a more rigid society in which intragroup comparisons are more likely. Unions and presumably employing organizations can modify the choice of reference groups but only in the direction of perceived legitimacy, and the consequences that follow efforts to change reference groups may or may not coincide with intentions. It may be possible to generate new patterns of comparison but impossible to stop their use.

[78]Robert K. Merton and Alice Kitt, "Contributions to the Theory of Reference Group Behavior," in R. K. Merton and P. F. Lazarsfeld (eds.), *Continuities in Social Research* (Glencoe, Ill.: The Free Press, 1950).
[79]Seymour Lipset and Martin Trow, "Reference Group Theory and Trade Union Wage Policy," in Mirra Kamarovsky, *Common Frontiers of the Social Sciences* (Glencoe, Ill.: The Free Press, 1957), pp. 391–411.

PAY STUDIES

Sociologists also have studied pay systems in organizations. Most of them have been concerned with the operation of incentive plans. These studies have served to show the unintended consequences of such plans, such as restriction of output. But they have also shown how the other rewards in organizations may be unintentionally altered by incentive plans.[80]

An especially interesting study sought to determine the factors that individuals believe should determine salaries of jobs in organizations. The method used was to ask respondents (students) to place appropriate salaries in an organization chart in which only one box had an assigned salary. The results indicated strong agreement on the importance of indirect over direct supervision and number of subordinates as contributions to organizations.[81] This study triggered another one by the author and a colleague that extends the method by asking respondents to complete a number of organization charts on each of which material on one possible contribution has been entered—education, job title, performance, job-related factors (experience, etc.), and certain personal characteristics (age, health, life style). One-hundred students and forty managers (second level and above, with salary determination experience) were the respondents. Preliminary analysis shows that although students are quite consistent in their views of relevant contributions, managers are much more so. Students appear to believe that education, job title, performance, job factors, and personal characteristics should be recognized and paid for, in the order given. Managers reversed the first two ranks. The results suggest that there are cultural values concerning the contributions of individuals that organizations should pay for and that these values are held before employment and confirmed during employment.

In Europe, industrial sociologists have studied rewards from work from a broader perspective than has been used in the United States. One concern has been with developing and testing a model for evaluating payment systems in organizations using sociological as well as psychological and economic variables.[82] Another has involved showing how reward systems in organizations must respond to social pressures

[80]W. F. Whyte, *Money and Motivation* (New York: Harper and Brothers, 1955).

[81]James L. Kuethe and Bernard Levenson, "Conceptions of Organizational Worth," *American Journal of Sociology* (November, 1964), pp. 342–348.

[82]Tom Lupton, "The Management of Earnings and Productivity Drift," in Nigel Farrow (ed.), *Progress of Management Research* (Baltimore: Penguin Books, 1969), pp. 92–105; T. Lupton, *Part I, Introduction,* Supplement to the Final Report (O.E.C.D., 1970).

as well as to economic ones and concludes that even the formulations of wage theory by labor economists are too narrow.[83]

EXCHANGE THEORY

The most significant contribution of the behavioral sciences to compensation theory, however, would seem to be the resurgence of interest in behavior as exchange. Both sociologists and psychologists have become interested in the concept of exchange and in viewing behavior as exchange. Homans'[84] concept of distributive justice involving A comparing the ratio of his rewards to his investments and costs to that of B suggests that both are in an exchange relationship. Adams' conception of equity theory involves an individual comparing his inputs and outcomes with those of another wherein both are in an exchange relationship with each other or with a third party.[85] Gergen[86] has re-analyzed many of the findings of social psychologists regarding motivation, social approval, and bargaining in terms of behavior exchange.

Actually, the concept of exchange has been around for some time.[87] Most discussions of it distinguish several kinds of exchange. Polanyi *et al.,*[88] for example, distinguish reciprocative exchange (gift-giving), redistributive exchange (charity), and exchange (the market). Whyte[89] uses the term "transaction" and distinguishes seven varieties: (1) positive exchange, (2) trading, (3) joint payoff, (4) competitive, (5) negative exchange, (6) open conflict, and (7) bargaining. Both formulations distinguish economic from other kinds of exchanges.

In a comprehensive analysis of exchange processes, Blau[90] distinguished exchanges involving purely intrinsic rewards (love relationships), exchanges involving extrinsic rewards (purely economic transactions), and social exchange involving both extrinsic and intrinsic values. Social exchange is defined as consisting of reciprocal transac-

[83]John Corina, *Forms of Wage and Salary Payment for High Productivity* (Paris: Organisation for Economic Co-operation and Development, 1970).

[84]Homans, *Social Behavior.*

[85]J. S. Adams, "Toward an Understanding of Inequity," *Journal of Abnormal and Social Psychology* (November, 1963), pp. 422–436.

[86]Kenneth J. Gergen, *The Psychology of Behavior Exchange* (Reading, Mass.: Addison-Wesley Publishing Company, 1969).

[87]Marcel Mauss, *The Gift* (Glencoe, Ill.: The Free Press, 1954); Alvin Gouldner, "The Norm of Reciprocity," *American Sociological Review* (April, 1960), pp. 161–178.

[88]Karl Polanyi, Conrad Arensberg, and Harry Pearson, *Trade and Market in the Early Empires* (Glencoe, Ill.: The Free Press, 1957).

[89]William Foote Whyte, *Organizational Behavior* (Homewood, Ill.: Irwin-Dorsey, 1969).

[90]Peter M. Blau, *Exchange and Power in Social Life* (New York: John Wiley and Sons, Inc., 1967).

tions oriented largely toward extrinsic rewards but also toward intrinsic rewards because the recurrent reciprocal exchanges result in mutual trust. In this rigorous analysis Blau did not attempt to define the employment exchange; attempting to classify it as either economic exchange or social exchange presented analytical difficulties. For example, Blau states that economic transactions involving services are closer to social exchange than to pure economic exchanges involving commodities.[91] He also shows that the wage bargain differs fundamentally from other economic exchanges because of the great investment people have in their occupations and their jobs. He further points out that only impersonal economic exchanges are focused exclusively on specific extrinsic benefits, whereas social exchange always involves some intrinsic significance that results from the association. Thus, Blau obviously encounters difficulty in classifying the employment relationship as an economic exchange.

On the other hand, Blau's analysis of social exchange yields qualities that equally well describe the employment exchange. For example, social exchange is shown to be oriented toward ends that can only be achieved through interaction with other persons and to employ means to further the achievement of these ends. The same thing must be said of the employment exchange. Blau also shows that social exchange is a positive-sum game in that individuals associate with one another because they all profit from the exchange. This characteristic of the employment exchange was described in Chapter 1. Blau's assumption that in social exchange people choose among alternative potential associates or courses of action by evaluating experiences or expected experiences and then selecting the best alternative is also an assumption regarding the employment exchange. The voluntary quality of social exchange motivated by the returns expected and received is also true of the employment transaction. Social exchange's characteristic of yielding benefits that do not have an exact price in terms of a single quantitative method of exchange is also a characteristic of all employment exchanges except for a very few temporary ones usually involving casual labor. Social exchange is also shown to always involve investments that constitute commitments to the other party. This seems to be equivalent to the characteristic of the employment exchange of always involving contributions and rewards. Although social exchange is shown to focus on extrinsic benefits and on, at least, implicit bargaining, it also contains intrinsic benefits. In the author's view, the employment exchange also entails both extrinsic and intrinsic rewards. Social exchange, Blau

[91] *Ibid.,* p. 93 fn.

shows, involves unspecified obligations, trust that these obligations will be fulfilled, and the absence of an enforceable binding contract. The employment exchange also includes unspecified obligations and at least some trust between the parties; and, as is well known, even when contracts exist, specific performance is unenforceable. Social exchange and employment exchanges are evaluated by comparing expectations of return relative to investment. These expectations come from social norms defining fair rates of return and fairness of the exchange process. In social exchange reference groups serve as standards of comparison to evaluate the exchange. This is also true of the employment exchange.

In social exchange, each party advances his own interests by promoting the interests of others. This is equally a characteristic of the employment exchange. In complex organizations, Blau shows that there are long chains of social transactions involving conformity to official obligations on the part of members in exchange for rewards received from the organization. This quality of social exchanges in organizations appears equally applicable to the employment exchange. Finally, Blau shows that the anticipation that an association will be a rewarding experience is what initially attracts individuals to it, and the exchange of various rewarding services cements the bonds. It would be difficult to more succinctly describe a continuing employment exchange.

It thus appears that the characteristics of social exchange are also qualities of the employment exchange, as outlined in Chapter 1. In the employment exchange both parties are making contributions and receiving rewards. Although the rewards are largely extrinsic, intrinsic values enter the employment exchange whether or not the parties always realize it. The employment exchange is a positive-sum game— both parties benefit. The employment exchange is made or continued because it is adjudged by the parties to be fair, and fairness is largely determined by social norms.

SUMMARY

The theory and studies presented in this chapter and the preceding one show that a great deal is known about rewards, but primarily about pay and other economic rewards. Focusing on the employment exchange suggests that rewards from employment are of several kinds. It also suggests that organizations may be providing a greater variety of rewards than they are typically aware of. Organizations are, of course, aware that they are providing economic rewards and that economic rewards are limited by organization resources. They may or may not be aware that they are providing many other kinds of rewards, and that not all of them are limited by organization resources.

But both the theory and research studies have been much less concerned about contributions. Organizations assume that employee contributions consist of labor service or work. Although aware that the organization requires many different kinds of labor services, organizations assume that contributions are limited to work and that more contributions mean more and better work. Because organizations make these assumptions (while presenting the public with a highly decorative receptionist and attempting to secure total commitment from managers), little attempt is made to specify the contributions when the employment exchange is initiated. Nor is any attempt typically made to determine what contributions the employee wants to make.

Studies in equity theory have served to emphasize how little attention has been given to contributions. As will be seen, organization practices attempt to measure contributions. But, perhaps because of economic reasoning, organizations have not thought through the different kinds of contributions they want from different employee groups nor how employee groups differ in the contributions they want to make. It seems significant that a recent review of psychological research on pay observed that management never really looks at what organizations get in return for pay.[92]

Very little of the theory and research has been concerned with the comparison process. One psychological study established the existence of a comparison person and his characteristics.[93] Reference group theory and equity theory contain suggestions about the process but there are little hard data. When organization practice is compared to what is known about the comparison process employed by individuals, however, an interesting schism appears. Organizations compare economic rewards with other organizations whereas individuals compare both rewards and contributions with other individuals, often within the organization, and with members of reference groups.

We need to know more about comparison standards, the factors compared, and the decision rules employed in comparisons. Comparison criteria would seem to differ for different employee groups. If comparisons are made on the basis of available information, increasing the quality and quantity of information should broaden comparisons, logically to the advantage of both employees and organizations. Lawler's

[92]Lawler, *Pay and Organizational Effectiveness,* p. 12.
[93]Patchen, *The Choice of Wage Comparisons.*

findings on the dysfunctional consequences of secrecy seem apropos here.

Much of the theory and research carries implications for the results of the employment exchange. The desired result is that the exchange is made or continued with interdependent behavior and attitude consequences.

But the research suggests that the actual results are often different from the assumptions held by organizations. Because organizations have approached the employment exchange as an economic transaction involving purchase of a productive resource, they have assumed that the amount of the resource supplied is determined by the price paid. Organizations have also assumed that they want as many units of labor services as are available for the price paid—that they want maximum performance on every job and will get it for the price paid, and if more performance is needed it will be available for a higher price.

Organizations have been aware, of course, that human beings are a unique resource—not at all passive. They have also been intuitively aware that the major advantage to organizations of human resources is their flexibility. They have also shown awareness of the influence of attitudes, but they have assumed that attitudes and performance were highly and positively correlated despite the negative empirical evidence.

These beliefs have largely prevented organizations from perceiving that they require two quite different types of behavior from the employment exchange—membership and performance. But the sources of these quite different types of behavior are not the same. Also, the organization may not require nor be able to obtain both types of behavior from all employees.

The theory and research results in this chapter show that the organization must think of two separate employment exchanges—one for membership and one for performance. The membership employment exchange is unavoidable if the organization is to survive. Equity theory and research show that to obtain and keep the membership of each employee group, the groups must perceive that their relevant rewards at least balance their relevant contributions on a continuing basis. They also show that this balance exists in the eye of the beholder and is dynamic.

Organizations desiring performance have two choices: (1) they can build it into the organization by specifying the contributions they require in the membership employment exchange as in collective bargaining, or (2) they can make a supplemental employment exchange for performance following expectancy theory. But the research on expectancy theory shows that the second alternative may apply only to certain groups, and the organization requirements are stringent.

Fortunately for the organization, individuals perceive only the membership employment exchange. If the reward-contribution balance is perceived to be in their favor, they will want to continue the employment exchange. But employee groups differ. Some groups want to continue the employment exchange with the same balance of rewards and contributions as the initial one. Other groups want to broaden and deepen the employment exchange and search for ways to do so.

Contributions

Contributions represent outputs from employees to the organization in exchange for inputs from the organization in the form of rewards. To the organization, contributions represent inputs from employees in exchange for outputs to employees in the form of rewards. This view of contributions suggests that employee contributions to organizations may be of many kinds (from physical attractiveness to professional skills), of many levels (from mere physical presence to total commitment), and either positive or negative (sabotage). In Chapter 3 it was suggested that employee contributions to organizations could be usefully categorized into job, performance, and personal contributions.

In organizations, the first measure of contribution is the content of the job to which the employee is assigned. Job evaluation is the term usually employed to determine the position of the job in the organization hierarchy by comparing job content. The second measure of contribution in most organizations involves factors assumed to measure performance on the job assigned and in the organization. Personal contributions as separate from job and performance contributions have not often been specifically recognized by organizations. But the insistence of certain employee groups that members be paid for accumulated experience (maturity curves) and the growing emphasis on careers may well force such attention in the future. The theory and research presented in Chapter 3 suggest that employees are providing and organizations are receiving a greater variety of contributions than organizations are typically aware of.

This part of the book examines organization practice in recognition of contributions. Chapters 4 through 7 look at job evaluation as measures of job-related contributions. Chapter 8 gives attention to performance-related contributions. Chapter 9 scrutinizes personal contributions.

4

Job—Related Contributions

Organizations implicitly recognize job-related contributions by assigning pay in accordance with the difficulty and importance of jobs. In fact, two often-cited principles of compensation administration are (1) equal pay for equal work, and (2) more pay for more important work. Both imply that employees are to be paid for contributions required by jobs.

Apparently most organizations, at least in the United States, utilize job assignment as a major determinant of employee contributions. The Bureau of Labor Statistics, in a study in 1953, found formalized wage structures becoming majority practice for office workers in thirty-two out of forty major labor markets, and for time-rated plant workers in all forty labor markets.[1] Formal wage structures were defined as a rate or rate range established for each job classification by job evaluation or collective bargaining. A Brookings Institution study published in 1960 found that rational wage structures based on formal or informal comparisons of job content were employed extensively by management and unions.[2] Job evaluation was found in use in almost all complex wage structures. Labor grade job classification was the rule in complex wage structures not employing job evaluation. Individual job rate comparison was found in less complex structures and in the skilled trades. Thus, formal job evaluation or informal comparisons of job content were found to be major bases of wage rates.

[1] Otto Hallberg, "Wage Formalization in Major Labor Markets, 1951–1952," *Monthly Labor Review* (January, 1953), pp. 22–26.

[2] Sumner H. Slichter, James J. Healy, and E. Robert Livernash, *The Impact of Collective Bargaining on Management* (Washington, D.C.: The Brookings Institution, 1960), chapters 19–20.

Although both formal job evaluation and informal job comparisons imply job-related contributions, these contributions are not typically specified in informal job comparisons. For this reason, this chapter emphasizes formal job evaluation.

JOB EVALUATION

Job evaluation may be defined as an attempt to determine and compare the demands that the normal performance of particular jobs makes on normal workers without taking account of the individual abilities or performance of the workers concerned.[3] As used here, it means the comparison of jobs by the use of formal and systematic procedures in order to determine the relative position of one job to another in a wage or salary hierarchy.

The real object of investigation and comparison is the content of the job, not the rather imprecise notion of its "value" to the organization. Although job evaluation is normally used as an aid in determining relatives wages, its results may be only one of the factors in wage determination, and job evaluation and the internal wage structure may be separated conceptually.

Job evaluation is concerned with jobs, not individuals. Although the next chapter provides careful definitions, it is important at this point to recognize the distinction. A job is a grouping of work tasks. It is an arbitrary concept requiring careful definition in the organization. Job evaluation determines the relative position of the job in the organization hierarchy. It is assumed that as long as job content remains unchanged, it may be performed by individuals of various levels of ability and proficiency. This concept permits separate appraisal of the performance of individuals on the same job.

THE JOB EVALUATION PROCESS

The process employed in evaluating jobs shows how job-related contributions emerge and are employed to compare jobs. Although there are several basic methods of comparing jobs, as well as modifications of the basic methods, the essential components are similar. They may be thought of as requisite steps in establishing the relative position

[3]International Labor Organization, "Job Evaluation," *Studies and Reports, New Series, No. 56* (Geneva, 1960).

of jobs. The first step is a study of jobs in the organization. Through the process of job analysis, information regarding the duties, responsibilities, and relationships are obtained, together with appreciation of worker requirements for successful performance of the job. These data are obtained, analyzed, and recorded in precise, consistent language.

The next step in job evaluation is deciding what the organization "is paying for"—that is, determining what factor or factors place one job at a higher level in the job hierarchy than another. These compensable factors are the yardsticks that are used to determine the relative position of jobs. They are also presumably the job-related contributions considered to be sufficiently pertinent to be used to compare jobs.

Because these factors become the bases on which jobs are compared, choosing compensable factors would seem to be the heart of job evaluation. Not only do these factors determine a job's position in the organization hierarchy, but also they inform job incumbents which contributions are rewarded.

The third step in job evaluation involves either developing or choosing a system for appraising the jobs in the organization according to the factor or factors selected in step two. This system should permit jobs involving more of a factor or factors to be consistently placed at a higher level in the job hierarchy than those involving lesser amounts. Developing this system can assure that the factors chosen are used to compare jobs, whereas choosing a ready-made system involves using the compensable factors built into the system. Thus, applicability of a ready-made system depends on whether the compensable factors in the system correspond to those selected for the organization.

The basic methods of comparing jobs are: (1) the ranking method, (2) the classification method, (3) the factor-comparison method, and (4) the point method. Several modifications of these primary methods have been developed, as well as various combinations.

The fourth step in the process is making use of the system to evaluate jobs. It involves following through the operations specified by the system—choosing and assigning decision-makers, reaching and recording decisions, setting up the job hierarchy.

When the job hierarchy or structure has been established, the final step is pricing the job structure to arrive at a wage structure. Strictly speaking, this step is not a part of the job evaluation process but nevertheless is essential in making the process operational. It is useful to separate the processes conceptually in that the job structure is often not the only consideration in wage structure determination. Unions, for example, may insist on bargaining the wage structure and thus temper the findings of job evaluation to union needs. Organizations may find that labor market considerations force a less than perfect fit between job structure and wage structure.

JOB-RELATED CONTRIBUTIONS

This picture of the job evaluation process serves to show that job evaluation is amenable to inclusion of the job-related contributions that the organization requires and that employees want to make in the employment exchange. There is no apparent reason why the compensable factors could not consist of the variety of job-related contributions that were described in the preceding chapter as required by organizations and that organization members want to make.

In practice, however, as our examination of job evaluation practices in subsequent chapters will show, most job evaluation plans employ responsibility, skill, effort, and working conditions as compensable factors. Items grouped under these major contributions number about 100. Skill, for example, is often measured by education and experience; mental effort is often differentiated from physical effort; responsibility of various kinds is delineated. An implication is that the typical organization recognizes responsibility, skill, effort, and willingness to accept certain working conditions as contributions of employees to the employment exchange.

It may be that because organizations tend to think of the employment exchange as an economic transaction, job evaluation has developed as a method of simulating economic forces. But it has been shown that the employment exchange includes many forces other than economic, and compensable factors should represent these other values.

One approach to measuring employee contributions places the focus on definitions of contributions held by organization members rather than on economic forces. This extreme viewpoint is represented in the Jaques' approach,[4] which essentially ignores economic considerations and concentrates on the norms of equity internal to the individual. Jaques developed a global measure of job level—time-span of discretion (the longest period of time an employee is permitted to exercise discretion without a review of his actions by his supervisor). Time-span of discretion centers on the decision-making aspects of jobs and undoubtedly includes quite a number of contributions that individuals consider relevant.

Application of the time-span approach has been limited. One difficulty has been that operationalizing Jaques' instructions on how to measure time-span is unclear.[5] Atchison was able to measure the time-

[4]Elliott Jaques, *Equitable Payment* (New York: John Wiley and Sons, Inc., 1961).
[5]Elliott Jaques, *Time-Span Handbook* (London: Heinemann, 1964); Eliott Jaques, *Equitable Payment,* revised edition (Harmondsworth: Penguin Books, Ltd., 1967).

span of engineers and scientists.[6] Richardson[7] reports measuring both time-span and "felt-fair pay" (amount of pay individuals believe is equitable for their job) in a large organization and finding very high correlations between them, indicating that time-span includes many of the contributions employees use in determining equity. But other attempts[8] to measure time-span of discretion and felt-fair pay dispute Jaques' conclusions, and whether time-span can be reliably measured is still controversial.[9]

Not all job evaluation plans, of course, are limited to the usual factors nor to single-factor explanations. An example of a plan that appears to be based on thinking through the actually required job-related contributions is that developed for the managerial and professional employees of the British Broadcasting Corporation.[10] The compensable factors included were (1) decisions (on money, staff, public relations, and facilities), (2) specialized knowledge and experience, (3) judgment, (4) creative thought, and (5) man management (ability to obtain cooperation). Other examples could be provided, of course, of plans (especially those developed for management jobs) that appear to encompass the broad range of job-related contributions known by both organizations and members to exist in the employment exchange. The point is that job evaluation in practice often appears to fail to specify job-related contributions to the employment exchange.

OBJECTIVES OF JOB EVALUATION

The general purpose of job evaluation in compensation administration is to provide a measuring instrument that sets forth the relative position of jobs in the organization hierarchy based on job-related contributions agreed to by the parties. From this general purpose a number of more specific goals can be derived.

1. To provide a more workable internal wage structure in order to simplify and make rational the relatively chaotic wage structure re-

[6]Thomas Atchison and Wendell French, "Pay Systems for Scientists and Engineers," *Industrial Relations* (October, 1967), pp. 44–56.

[7]Roy Richardson, "An Empirical Study of Fair Pay Perceptions and the Time Span of Discretion," unpublished doctoral dissertation (University of Minnesota, 1969).

[8]Paul S. Goodman, "An Empirical Examination of Elliott Jaques' Concept of Time-Span," *Human Relations* (May, 1967), pp. 155–170; George T. Milkovich and Keith Campbell, "A Study of Jaques' Norms of Equitable Payment," *Industrial Relations* (May, 1972), pp. 267–271.

[9]George Strauss, "Organization Behavior and Personnel Relations," in Ginsburg *et al., A Review of Industrial Relations Research* (Madison: Industrial Relations Research Association, 1970).

[10]Joan Doulton and David Hay, *Managerial and Professional Staff Grading* (London: George Allen and Unwin, Ltd., 1962).

sulting from chance, custom, and such individual factors as favoritism or aggressive tendencies.

2. To provide an agreed-on device for setting rates for new or changed jobs.

3. To provide a means whereby realistic comparisons may be made of the wage and salary rates of employing organizations.

4. To provide a base from which individual performance may be measured if so desired.

5. To reduce grievances over wage and salary rates by reducing the scope of grievances and providing an agreed-on means of solving disputes.

6. To provide incentive values to employees to strive for higher-level jobs.

7. To provide facts for wage negotiations.

8. To provide facts on job relationships for use in selection, training, transfers, and promotion.

DEVELOPMENT OF JOB EVALUATION

Historically, job evaluation developed out of (1) civil service classification, (2) job analysis applied to time study and selection, (3) early employer wage and salary classification practices as part of personnel programs, and (4) U.S. government regulation of wages during World War II. Requests for job classification by government employees can be traced back to the nineteenth century. Classification of services on the basis of duties performed has been used in the federal service for over fifty years. Frederick W. Taylor's work involved job analysis as a basis for time study. Job analysis as a basis for selection and placement grew with the expansion of the employee relations function in the 1920s and 1930s. In 1925, Merrill R. Lott devised the first point method of job evaluation.[11] The American Management Association and Industrial Relations Counselors influenced the spread of job evaluation. The National Metal Trades Association took the lead in encouraging the introduction of job evaluation. The spread of unionism since the mid-30s influenced job evaluation installation in that employers gave more attention to rationalized wage structures and improved wage administration as unionism advanced. Perhaps the greatest impetus to job evaluation in the United States, however, was wage control regulation during World War II. The War Labor Board, through its concern with wage inequities, its assent to wage increases through the introduction of job evaluation, and its approval of rate ranges encouraged job evaluation programs.

[11]Merrill R. Lott, *Wage Scales and Job Evaluation* (New York: Ronald Press Co., 1926).

PREVALENCE OF JOB EVALUATION

Job evaluation is used in determining compensation throughout the world. Evidence suggests that although job evaluation is much more prevalent in the United States than elsewhere, its use is increasing in other countries. The evidence from the United States consists of surveys made at different times and locations and are thus somewhat noncomparable. The evidence regarding other countries is contained in a large-scale survey of practice in Great Britain together with interviews conducted in other countries.[12]

In the United States, job evaluation is used in organizations employing approximately two-thirds of the employed labor force. The Bureau of Labor Statistics in 1956 found that nine-tenths of the production workers in the machinery industries in Milwaukee and one-half to two-thirds in Baltimore, Chicago, Houston, and three New England areas were covered by job evaluation.[13] Lanham, in a series of studies between 1950 and 1954, found that out of 1,265 firms, 322 had job evaluation plans, 56 were installing one at the time of the survey, and 181 were considering installing a plan.[14] A Bureau of National Affairs survey in 1955 found formal job evaluation plans in six out of every seven firms.[15] A survey by the same organization in 1957 found that all but one-seventh of larger firms (over 1,000 employees) and one-quarter of smaller ones use job evaluation plans.[16] A 1960 survey by George Fry and Associates found that 65 per cent of the employees of over 500 responding companies were covered by job evaluation programs.[17] A national survey of job analysis practices in 1970 found 75.8 per cent of organizations maintaining job analysis programs and over 95 per cent of these programs were used in job evaluation.[18] Larger organizations (200 or more employees) are somewhat more likely to use job evaluation than smaller ones, but job evaluation plans are found even in very small organizations. Job evaluation in the United States is applied primarily at the plant or company level but a few industrywide plans have appeared (steel is the best example). Blue-collar, white-collar, and managerial plans are in use.

[12]National Board for Prices and Incomes, "Job Evaluation," *Report No. 83 and Supplement* (London: Her Majesty's Stationery Office, September, 1968).
[13]Louis E. Badenhoop and A. N. Jarrell, "Wages and Related Practices in the Machinery Industries, 1955–56," *Monthly Labor Review* (August, 1956), pp. 908–916.
[14]E. Lanham, *Job Evaluation* (New York: McGraw-Hill Book Co., 1955), pp. 10–11.
[15]Bureau of National Affairs, *Personnel Policies Forum Survey Number 28* (November, 1954).
[16]Bureau of National Affairs, *Personnel Policies Forum Survey Number 40* (1957).
[17]John A. Patton, "Job Evaluation in Practice: Some Survey Findings," *AMA Management Report Number 54* (New York: AMA, 1961), pp. 73–77.
[18]C. Harold Stone and Dale Yoder, *Job Analysis, 1970* (Long Beach, California: California State College, June, 1970), pp. 18–19.

Great Britain makes less use of job evaluation than the United States but its use is growing. The NBPI survey found only 23 per cent of over 6 million employees covered, but 30 per cent of organizations with over 500 employees and 54 per cent of organizations with over 5,000 employees used job evaluation. Like the United States, job evaluation in Britain is applied at the plant or company level, but industry-wide plans may be growing. Very interestingly, managerial and white-collar employees are more likely to work under job evaluation plans than blue-collar workers.

Sweden has a number of industrywide job evaluation plans covering at least 20 per cent of blue-collar workers and coverage is growing. One of the reasons for the development of job evaluation in Sweden was to maintain skill differentials that had narrowed because of the upgrading of lower-paid jobs. Most of the industrywide schemes operate on a decentralized basis but the breweries plan is compulsory and is installed and administered by a central authority. West Germany has both industrywide and regional job evaluation plans.

Holland has had a national job evaluation plan since 1948 for blue-collar workers. The plan was installed to implement national wage policy and the original plan included a national wage line set by the national government linking job levels to pay. Several revisions of the job evaluation plan have been made and the link between the job structure and the wage structure under present policy is largely left to negotiation between the parties. The plan as originally conceived represented an interesting attempt to base wages entirely on equity without regard for economic forces.

Russia has had an interindustry grading scheme since 1955. The system is based first on "Tariff-qualification" manuals and second on common occupational and industrywide wage scales. The former determine the degree of factors such as knowledge and skill required to qualify a worker for a given trade. Each worker is assigned an occupation and carries that designation until regraded. Thus the Russian plan may be adjudged as a job evaluation-employee classification system.

RESPONSIBILITY FOR JOB EVALUATION

The installation and operation of job evaluation requires personnel, because the various responsibilities outlined in the job evaluation process must be assigned. Several possibilities are apparent. One or more committees may be selected, a department may be specifically set up or an existing one assigned the responsibility, or a consulting organization may be brought in. Actually these possibilities are not mutually exclusive, and all three may be employed at various stages.

Committees. Support for the program is essential because installation of job evaluation involves commitment of time, effort, and money. Such support is usually obtained by securing top management approval and the collaboration of other managers and organization members. The medium through which this approval is attained is usually a committee, which may be set up for the purpose at hand or may already exist. This committee is given an explanation of job evaluation, the purposes it may be expected to accomplish, a rough time schedule, and an estimate of the cost of the program. The committee makes the decision to install job evaluation, decides on the scope of the project, and assigns responsibility for the work. As will be seen later, in joint union-management job evaluation these decisions may be made in collective bargaining negotiations.

The actual work of job evaluation is usually done in committee in both large and small organizations whether the task is accomplished by organization members alone or with the help of a consultant. Committees have the advantage of pooling the judgment of several individuals and serve the even more important function of communication and sustaining member confidence. The committee selects the compensable factors, determines the weighting, determines the method of comparing jobs, evaluates jobs, and in nonunion installations prices the job structure to arrive at a wage structure. Job evaluation committee membership is time consuming and it is important that committee members recognize that it is a primary aspect of their jobs.

Committee Membership. The chairman of the job evaluation committee is typically the compensation administrator, although if a consultant is employed he may assume chairmanship for parts of the work. Other members are typically other managers selected for their analytical ability, fairness, and commitment to the project. Representation of broad areas of the organization aids in communication and sustaining confidence. But job evaluation committees should be kept small to facilitate decision-making—five members may be optimum, ten seems too many. A common procedure is to ask supervisors to sit in on committee meetings when jobs in their department are under study.

In joint installations, one or more union members are regular members of the committee. Employee representation in the typical installation where the union is not involved is often on a rotating basis —an employee from the department whose jobs are being evaluated is asked to sit in.

Regular employee membership on job evaluation committees is becoming more common. In fact, the model of the employment exchange used in this book would suggest that employees be assigned the task of evaluating their jobs. One organization confines membership on job evaluation committees to employees.[19] Some consultants suggest an equal number of management and employee representatives.[20]

The emphasis on perceptions in the model suggests that employee perceptions are the single most important input in job evaluation programs. This implies that employee representation on job evaluation committees is essential if they are to understand and accept the program. Although organizations may avoid employee participation in job evaluation out of a fear that employees are motivated to get the highest pay rate they can for their own job, there is some evidence that employees are less prone to overpay for jobs than are managers.[21]

Committee ratings on jobs are the result of pooled judgment, which means that ratings are made individually and are either averaged or a solution is agreed on as a result of discussion. It is not a matter of majority rule, but of minorities being sufficiently convinced to permit them to go along with the majority.

Committee members must be trained. If the steps outlined in the job evaluation process have been followed, however, committee members already will have received much training in building or choosing a job evaluation system. It only remains to teach them to guard against personal bias and the common rating errors such as the halo effect, in which the rating on one factor influences the ratings of others and constant errors, in which members are consistently too lenient or too severe in rating or having a tendency to rate average. Committee decisions plus good job information tend to reduce the incidence of rating error.

Consultants.   In the discussion of job evaluation committees, it was pointed out that consultants are sometimes employed to install job evaluation plans. Successful consultants are careful to ensure that organization members are deeply involved in installing the plan and are able to operate the plan when the consultant leaves.

Consultants are most likely to be employed in small organizations in which no present organization member possesses the necessary expertise. They are also more likely to be employed when a complex rather than a simple plan is to be installed. Consultants often have their own ready-made plans. In some joint installations, consultants are employed to ensure objectivity, often at the insistence of the union. It is

---

[19]Lee A. Chambliss, "Our Employees Evaluate Their Own Jobs," *Personnel Journal* (September, 1950), pp. 141–142.

[20]"Computer-Assisted Job Evaluation," *The Executive* (Wellington, New Zealand, March 1, 1970), pp. 15–16.

[21]E. E. Lawler and J. R. Hackman, "The Impact of Employee Participation in the Development of Pay Incentive Plans: A Field Experiment," *Journal of Applied Psychology* (December, 1969), pp. 467–471.

also usual practice to hire consultants to evaluate managerial jobs, because the objectivity of committee members rating jobs at higher levels than their own may be questioned.

Information on the proportion of job evaluation plans in the United States installed with the aid of consultants is unknown. But the NBPI study, previously cited, found that about 23 per cent of the plans in Great Britain reflected consultant participation and that consultants were often used to install industrywide plans in other countries. A limited U.S. study made in 1965 found that the use of consultants had dropped from about one-half of installations in 1956 to one-quarter in 1965.[22]

Departments.   It is quite possible, of course, for the organization to delegate the job evaluation process (both installation and operation) to a department. Sometimes the compensation administration section is assigned the task and the department head and a number of job analysts carry it out.

Those who favor this approach are focusing on the technical nature of the task and the difficulty of getting managers at any level to devote the time that the program requires. They may recognize the communication and educational advantages of the committee approach, but take the view that although communication can be provided in other ways, job evaluation is a technical task that requires expertise, time, and energy. They may also doubt the ability of those who are not specialists to make unbiased judgments.

It is doubtful that this position can be justified. The model of the employment exchange shows that employee input is essential in job evaluation if it is to acceptably reflect job-related contributions. Once installation is completed, however, there seems to be no reason why a department cannot operate the program with proper provisions for adjudicating grievances.

UNION PARTICIPATION IN JOB EVALUATION

Union participation in job evaluation installation ranges from formal job evaluation studies conducted independently by the union, through joint union-management job evaluation and through reviews of management job evaluation installations, to complete indifference toward the existence or lack of a job evaluation plan in the organization. It is difficult to determine which form of union participation is typical,

[22]K. O. Mann, "Characteristics of Job Evaluation Programs," *Personnel Administration* (September–October, 1965), pp. 45–47.

although a 1966 survey by Prentice-Hall, Inc., found that four out of five unionized firms involved the union during installation in some way and 48 per cent of union contracts have job evaluation provisions.[23] Also, the NBPI study found that industrywide job evaluation and national job evaluation plans were joint installations.

Some unions profess to evaluate formally all jobs in an organization independently, according to one study,[24] and to use the information as an aid in collective bargaining. Although this is not surprising in view of Gomberg's statement that ". . . any collective agreement is but the result of the use of the ranking and classification methods of job evaluation,"[25] it conflicts sharply with some unions' official position on job evaluation.

Some job evaluation plans have been installed and maintained as a joint venture. Some managements are convinced of the value of a joint approach, and some unions will accept job evaluation only if their interests are adequately protected by joint administrative arrangements. Sometimes such a plan results from union demands for job evaluation, and sometimes the company desires to install a job evaluation plan and asks the union to participate.

A good deal of variety in degree of participation exists. In some cases, unions and management representatives work together from the point of inception of the program. In others, union participation is limited to consultation in classifying new or changed jobs. A well-known joint union-management installation and operation of job evaluation exists in the basic steel industry.[26] Less well known is the plan in the West Coast paper industry. A Princeton study in 1947 found that in nineteen out of fifty-six plans the union had participated in installation of the plan.[27] A study by the Bureau of Labor Statistics in 1956 found union participation in less than 50 per cent of the plans.

If there is joint participation, there is also a great variety in administrative arrangements. In some cases, a consultant, who keeps the parties advised as installation proceeds and calls the parties into conference when their help is needed, is employed to install the plan. This method is probably usual if job evaluation is installed at the request of the union, as Cohen found in eighteen out of sixty-six firms in his

[23]Prentice-Hall, Inc., *Personnel Management—Policies and Practices* (11/1/66), 15, 107.

[24]L. Cohen, "Unions and Job Evaluation," *Personnel Journal* (May, 1948), pp. 7–12.

[25]William Gomberg, "A Collective Bargaining Approach to Job Evaluation," *Labor and Nation* (November and December, 1946), p. 52.

[26]Jack Stieber, *The Steel Industry Wage Structure* (Cambridge, Mass.: Harvard University Press, 1959).

[27]Helen Baker and John M. True, *The Operation of Job Evaluation Plans* (Princeton, N.J.: Princeton University, IR Section, 1947), p. 72.

study.[28] In some cases, committees and other procedures are spelled out in detail in the contract; in most, simple reference is made to the plan in the contract.

Joint union-management participation would seem desirable in assuring union interest and understanding. Also, the not inconsiderable task of explaining the plan to employees may be taken over by the union. Both the Princeton and Brookings Institution studies found some evidence that joint plans are more successful than unilateral plans. This, of course, is not always the case, for the Brookings study found some instances wherein management was extremely dissatisfied with joint committees and was trying to eliminate them. Also some unions, although they accepted job evaluation, wanted no part of joint responsibility.

Perhaps most unions in organizations using job evaluation plans have adopted a policy of reviewing the findings after management has completed its study and, in many cases, installation. This review may range from simple use of the grievance procedure if a union member objects to his rate to collective bargaining on the job hierarchy developed. In the first case, the position the union takes is very similar to complete indifference. The union recognizes the existence of a job evaluation plan only if and when it effects adversely the pay of an employee. In the second case, the union reviews the results of the plan. If the plan results in a different job hierarchy from the one that the union believes is correct, a compromise may be bargained.

Many job evaluation installations are unilateral—made solely by the employer. Although some employers prefer this arrangement, many others invite union participation, realizing the advantages of such practices in promoting employee understanding and acceptance of the plan. Some unions, however, refuse to participate in or even to recognize the existence of an operating plan.

In such instances, the employer installs the plan unilaterally, recognizing the necessity of a logical hierarchy of jobs in administering wages and salaries. The findings of the plan are used in negotiations. If the wage structure developed through bargaining differs from the job hierarchy developed through job evaluation, such deviations may be recognized as exceptions and an effort made to correct them in future negotiations.

It seems useful at this point to recognize that collective bargaining represents a method of specifying contributions as well as rewards. Labor agreements appear to imply at least the following employee

[28]L. Cohen, "Management and Job Evaluation," *Personnel Journal* (June, 1948), pp. 55–61.

contributions: willingness to work under specified conditions, acceptance of jobs and job assignments, work rules, organization policies and practices, willingness to follow specified dispute settlement procedures, acceptance of technological change, and (sometimes) willingness to cooperate in solving organization problems. But if the position taken in this chapter that job evaluation is a method of specifying job-related contributions is accepted, then joint union-management job evaluation should further serve to specify the employment contract to the advantage of all the parties. Organizations with one union representing all employees will, of course, find obtaining such agreement easier than organizations that deal with several unions, but joint union-management job evaluation is equally possible in the second case.

Official union position in the U.S. on job evaluation, with a few exceptions, such as the steelworkers, has been at least in the past one of opposition. Official union position, however, has not been correlated with practice. Union leaders may oppose job evaluation in their official capacity but approve it as individuals in many situations. It was seen in the discussion of union participation in job evaluation that a number of union leaders approve of job evaluation and that many unions have requested that it be installed. Although the UAW, the Packinghouse Workers, and a few other unions have refused to accept it, the majority of unions go along with management proposals for job evaluation.

It must not be thought, however, that even official union opinion is unanimous. Boris Shiskin, writing in the *American Federationist,* states that job evaluation, under certain conditions, has a place in wage administration.[29] Gomberg, a former official of the ladies garment workers, takes this position:

> It is no more possible to pass judgment on the merits of job evaluation, as such, than to pass judgment on the weather, as such. Job evaluation may be good or bad, depending on the nature of the industry, the background of industrial relations, the skill with which an installation is made, the way it is administered, and many other factors.[30]

In reporting results of a conference of labor officials, Gomberg found: (1) unanimous agreement that ranking and classification methods had been used for a long time by trade unions in negotiating; (2) agreement that under no circumstances could the job evaluation plan be used as the sole determinant of the relative wage structure; (3) some agreement that the union may find the need for a common measuring stick that

[29]Boris Shiskin, "Job Evaluation: What It Is and How It Works," *American Federationist* (July–September, 1947).

[30]William Gomberg, *A Labor Union Manual On Job Evaluation* (Chicago: Roosevelt College, Labor Education Division, 1947), p. 7.

will provide the means of resolving disputes among its members; (4) some unions favor joint participation because they lack any other criterion on which to base arguments on relative job worth.[31]

Unions have criticized job evaluation on the following grounds: (1) it is not scientific; (2) it is too rigid; (3) it seeks to base wages solely on job content; (4) employees may measure job importance differently from management; (5) supply and demand should determine wages; (6) it tends to limit collective bargaining; (7) it is too complicated; and (8) it is a management technique. On the other hand, unions typically accept the idea of a job hierarchy and the idea of job rates rather than personal rates.

Most of these objections make the point that the job structure is not the only determinant of wage structure. As the study of job evaluation by the International Labor Organization points out, wage determination is a separate matter from job evaluation. Also as mentioned previously in this chapter, this is the view taken in this book.

The other objections refer to the job evaluation process—the choice of factors, overcomplexity, and so on. One way to meet such objections would be for unions to demand participation in job evaluation. As unions train more members in job evaluation techniques, the unions may be expected to attempt to secure the advantages of a rational job hierarchy and job rates by participating in job evaluation. There is general agreement that one of the fallouts from job evaluation is an increase in the information available to negotiators.[32]

Perhaps one lesson to be learned from the spread of job evaluation around the world is that it can be a useful method for establishing acceptable criteria for wage determination. This is the position taken by both national and local trade union officials in Sweden. Their attitude has been that they must learn enough about job evaluation schemes to influence their application. They employ wage system experts who act as full-time advisers to local union officials.[33]

The NBPI study cited several times in this chapter found a number of benefits from job evaluation accruing to workers as well as to organizations. The gain to workers includes reduced inequity in earnings and in workplace and personal frictions, and where unions take part in the job evaluation process, an extension of joint regulation of workplace conditions; prevention of arbitrary management decisions,

[31]William Gomberg, "Trade Unions and Industrial Engineering," in William Grant Ireson and Eugene L. Grant (eds.), *Handbook of Industrial Engineering and Management* (Englewood Cliffs, N.J.: Prentice-Hall, Inc., 1955).

[32]NBPI, *Report No. 83,* p. 16; John Corina, *Forms of Wage and Salary Payment for High Productivity* (Paris: Organisation for Economic Co-operation and Development, 1970), p. 84.

[33]NBPI, *Report No. 83 Supplement,* p. 26.

and recognition of the hierarchy of skills and responsibilities in the organization. The last benefit, of course, emphasizes the point of view of this chapter that job evaluation is a method of delineating job-related contributions to the employment exchange.

SUCCESS OF JOB EVALUATION

The usual approach to testing the success of job evaluation is to appraise employee, union, and organization satisfaction with it. Patton reports a 1960 survey in which 93 per cent of organized companies and 86 per cent of unorganized companies reported their programs from "rather successful" to "highly successful."[34] The NBPI study found that 88 per cent of organizations in Great Britain with job evaluation plans considered them to be "largely, very largely, and completely success-ful," with only 8 per cent reporting partial success.[35]

Growing union involvement in job evaluation both in the United States and abroad suggests growing union acceptance of job evaluation. Presumably, in joint union-management job evaluation, union accep-tance is achieved as installation proceeds.

Employee acceptance is the primary criterion of organizations in determining the success of the plan. Both increasing use of employees on job evaluation committees and the communication steps accompa-nying job evaluation installations suggest that employing organizations are taking steps to achieve it.

COMMUNICATION

Organizations installing job evaluation plans employ elaborate communications programs to ensure that employees, supervisors and managers will understand and accept the plan. These programs involve communicating to employees at all levels the purpose of the program and how this aim is to be achieved. Employees, supervisors, and manag-ers are helped to understand what is being done, what the objectives of the program are, and what is expected of them.

As soon as job evaluation has been approved, common practice is to disseminate information on objectives, policies, and procedures to be followed. Meetings are often held at which managers and supervisors receive information on what job evaluation is, what steps are involved,

[34]Patton, *AMA Management Report Number 54,* pp. 73–77.
[35]NBPI, *Report No. 83 Supplement,* p. 7.

and what the program and its results will mean to managers and their employees. Some organizations at this point begin regular training programs for supervisors to ensure that they understand the job evaluation program and can answer employee questions regarding it. Written material is given to managers and supervisors to supplement oral communication in meetings.

Employees also are typically given the information both orally and in writing. Supervisors may be encouraged to hold meetings of employees in which the job evaluation program is explained and questions are answered. Job evaluation policies and procedures, together with typical questions and answers about them, may be posted on bulletin boards. Letters from the top executive may be sent to employees containing information such as the following: (1) an announcement that a job evaluation plan will be installed, (2) an explanation of what job evaluation is and what it is expected to achieve for employees and the organization, (3) information on what steps are involved in carrying out the program and who will perform them, (4) assurance that no one will get a pay cut or be laid off or fired because of the program, and (5) the availability of their supervisors to answer any questions.

Union involvement in job evaluation provides another information channel in that unions explain the plan to their members. Management, union, and employee members of the job evaluation committee also explain the workings of the installation to their constituents.

Obviously, the more simple the job evaluation plan the easier it is to explain. Because the success of job evaluation is measured by its acceptance, one of the considerations in design or choice of the plan is its explainability.

COST OF INSTALLING JOB EVALUATION

The costs of a job evaluation plan are of two types: (1) the costs of determining the job hierarchy, and (2) effects on payroll when the job structure is priced out to arrive at the wage structure. It must not be assumed, however, that job evaluation costs exceed the gains derived. The Prentice-Hall survey cited previously found that more than half of the surveyed organizations reported that job evaluation had saved money and another 30 per cent reported that other benefits more than compensated for the expense.

The costs of determining the job hierarchy consist of the time spent on the project by organization members and may also include the fee of a consultant. The time spent by organization members varies greatly from one installation to another because the type of plan adopted, the amount of preliminary training considered necessary, peculiarities of company organization, the level of jobs being evaluated, size and makeup of committees, and whether or not the plan is a joint union-management venture all affect the costs. It has been estimated that about 0.5 per cent of annual payroll or $65 to $100 per job (not per employee) is required for job evaluation. Cost of operating the program following installation has been estimated by the same author to be about 0.1 per cent of annual payroll.[36] Fry Consultants estimates that a complete job evaluation program can normally be accomplished in four engineering hours times the number of jobs studied and evaluated, but that joint union-management job evaluation takes somewhat longer.[37] The Employers' Association of Milwaukee is reported to estimate approximately two hours for factory, office, and technical classifications. The same source reports the cost of evaluating the job of first-line supervisor at $65.[38] It is more expensive to evaluate managerial and professional jobs than lower-level jobs.

Payroll effects also vary greatly. The National Industrial Conference Board found that one-third of reporting organizations experienced an increase of less than 1 per cent and almost two-thirds of them reported 2 per cent or less.[39] Kress reports that the cost of adopting the new pay schedule is typically from 3 to 6 per cent of the existing payroll for white-collar workers.[40] The NBPI study cited previously found few companies able to give the actual percentage increases in the wage bill, but only two companies reported no increase and the average increase was from 2 to 12 per cent.

As mentioned previously, the meaning of both types of cost figures is difficult to interpret because of the variables affecting them. Also, the benefits to the organization of employee agreement to the job-related contributions desired by the organization and a rational job hierarchy, and to employees in perceived equity of job-related contributions, must be balanced against these costs. A true cost of job evaluation to an organization can only be obtained by subtracting from the direct costs of installing and maintaining a plan the indirect costs of doing without its potential benefits.

[36]Charles W. Lytle, *Job Evaluation Methods,* second edition (New York: Ronald Press, Co., 1954), pp. 34–35.

[37]Reported in Prentice-Hall, Inc., *Personnel Management—Policies and Practices,* 15, 029.

[38]Herbert G. Zollitsch and Adolph Langsner, *Wage and Salary Administration,* 2nd ed. (Cincinnati: South-Western Publishing Co., 1970), pp. 161–162.

[39]Herbert S. Briggs, "Cost of Installing a Job Evaluation Plan," *Management Record* (December, 1951), pp. 422–423.

[40]A. L. Kress, "Job Evaluation for White-Collar Workers in Private Sector Employment in the United States," *International Labour Review* (October, 1969), pp. 341–357.

SUMMARY

This chapter has been concerned with job evaluation as a method of measuring the job-related contributions of employees. The definition of job evaluation, the job evaluation process, job evaluation's potential for measuring job-related contributions, objectives of job evaluation, the development and prevalence of job evaluation plans, responsibility for job evaluation, union participation in job evaluation, measures of success of job evaluation, communication and job evaluation, and the costs of installing job evaluation plans were examined.

The next three chapters continue the examination of job evaluation as a process of measuring job-related contributions following the steps in the job evaluation process. Chapter 5 focuses on analyzing jobs and determining compensable factors. Chapter 6 examines nonquantitative job evaluation methods. Chapter 7 considers quantitative job evaluation methods, new methods of job evaluation, and research on job evaluation methods. Following the model outlined in Chapter 1, pricing the job structure and other wage structure considerations are deferred to Part III.

5

Collecting Job Information and Determining Compensable Factors

COLLECTING JOB INFORMATION

The job evaluation process begins with securing facts about jobs. Failure to secure complete job facts has been cited as a primary reason for job evaluation failure.[1] In addition, carrying out later steps in job evaluation procedure is virtually impossible without these facts. Information about jobs obviously contains the job-related contributions that are the compensable factors in job evaluation plans. Moreover, an applicable system of job evaluation cannot be developed or chosen without complete job information.

Job information is obtained through a process known as job analysis, which is defined as a systematic procedure for gathering information about jobs. It notes and records what jobholders do; how they get it done; the proximate and ultimate objectives of their work; the demands that the job makes of the jobholder; relationships among jobs; and environmental conditions.

Job analysis has many uses, of which job evaluation is only one. For example, organizations use information obtained in the job analysis process for such personnel programs as recruitment, selection, and placement; organization planning and job redesign; training; grievance settlement; and job evaluation and other compensation programs. Job analysis is, however, sharply distinguished from time and motion study and methods analysis. As the titles imply, much more detailed information is obtained from these procedures.

[1]John A. Patton, C. L. Littlefield, and Stanley Allen Self, *Job Evaluation* (Chicago: Richard D. Irwin, Inc., 1964), p. 65. See also Jay L. Otis and Richard H. Leukart, *Job Evaluation,* 2nd ed. (Englewood Cliffs, N.J.: Prentice-Hall, Inc., 1954), p. 212.

A national survey found that the major use of job analysis is in job evaluation—98.0 per cent of job analysis programs involving salaried jobs and 94.9 per cent of job analysis programs for hourly rated jobs used the results for job evaluation.[2] Because job information used for job evaluation typically may differ somewhat from that used for other personnel programs, and since these other programs may each involve different information, some organizations make a specialized job study for each specific use. Shartle has criticized such specialized job studies as wasted effort and has suggested that the required job information be obtained at one time and disseminated from this core as needed.[3] Certainly with the trend toward computerized job information this suggestion is even more logical.

But the different uses of job information may require specialized job descriptions. Job evaluation requires information that distinguishes jobs in terms of job-related contributions and this information would seem to include information on the work performed and the demands that the job makes of the jobholder. Recruitment and selection require information on the human attributes a successful jobholder must bring to the job. Training requires information on the knowledge and skills that the successful jobholder must evidence. Although there is overlap between the different requirements, the reason for the move toward separate job analyses is understandable.

The major work on the job analysis process has been performed by the U.S. Department of Labor, formerly through its Bureau of Employment Security and more recently through its Manpower Administration, including the United States Training and Employment Services (UST & ES). The procedures in current use by the department to analyze jobs and the instruments used to record analyses have been published[4] and probably represent the strongest single influence on job analysis practice in the U.S. Because of the department's broad people- and job-matching responsibilities and its responsibilities for publishing the *Dictionary of Occupational Titles (DOT)*, it is quite natural that the approach used is sufficiently broad to obtain job information for all possible personnel uses. The department has experimented with a variety of approaches to job analysis and job classification in the *DOT*. An example of the latter is its "data-people-things" approach to differentiating jobs in terms of worker requirements in the latest revision of the *DOT*.

[2]C. Harold Stone and Dale Yoder, *Job Analysis, 1970* (Long Beach, California State College, June, 1970, mimeographed), p. 19.

[3]Carrol L. Shartle, *Occupational Information, Its Development and Application,* 3rd ed. (Englewood Cliffs, N.J.: Prentice-Hall, Inc., 1959).

[4]U.S. Department of Labor, *Handbook for Analyzing Jobs* (Washington, D.C.: United States Government Printing Office, 1972).

Apparently, job analysis practice closely follows the UST and ES approach. The national survey cited previously found that at least 50 percent and often over 90 per cent of job analyses obtained the following information: what the incumbent does; required qualifications; tools, equipment, materials; purpose of job; supervision received; how job is performed; hazards; relationships with people; comfort; responsibility; relationship to other jobs. Clearly, the responding organizations adhere closely to the basic *does, uses, knows,* and *working conditions* categories long emphasized by UST and ES. These responses may suggest that job analysis must answer questions about what the jobholder does, why he does it, what he uses to do it, what he must know, what responsibilities he must assume, and what working conditions necessitate special personal qualifications.

Although apparently not yet affecting organization practice to any great degree, a number of new approaches to job analysis have been developed in recent years. Kirchner and Dunnette[5] have applied the critical incident technique to determining the behavioral requirements of jobs. Dunnette makes a strong case that critical incident job analysis is superior to conventional job analysis in uncovering the important job requirements and job differences.[6]

The U.S. Air Force has developed what it calls a "job inventory" approach[7] that uses standardized lists of job tasks to describe jobs. Computers are used to produce job descriptions and such variables as difficulty of task performance, training required, and frequency of task occurrence.

The U.S. Naval Personnel Research Activity in San Diego is developing a job analysis tool somewhat similar to that of the Air Force.[8] Variables in the system include duties, responsibilities, classification, knowledge and skills required, training received and required, and work hazards. A taxonomy of work verbs has been developed to describe work performed on naval jobs.

The Bureau of Business Service and Research at California State University, Long Beach, has developed a Job Information Matrix System (JIMS).[9] The system involves a checklist focused on what people

[5]W. K. Kirchner and M. D. Dunnette, "Identifying the Critical Factors in Successful Salesmanship," *Personnel* (September–October, 1957), pp. 54–59.

[6]Marvin D. Dunnette, *Personnel Selection and Placement* (Belmont, California: Wadsworth Publishing Company, Inc., 1966).

[7]Joseph E. Marsh, Joseph M. Madden, and Raymond E. Christal, *Job Analysis in the United States Air Force,* WADD-TR-61-113 (Lackland Air Force Base, Texas: Personnel Laboratory, Wright Air Development, Air Research and Development Command, February, 1961).

[8]Gordon M. Campbell and Robert C. Megling, *Preliminary Data Elements for New Systems Personnel Requirements Data System,* Research Memorandum SRM 69-6 (San Diego, California: U.S. Naval Personnel Research Activity, 1968).

[9]Stone and Yoder, *Job Analysis, 1970.*

do in their jobs, what they *use,* what they have to *know,* their *responsibilities,* and the *working conditions* under which their jobs are performed. It assumes that within an occupational family, certain tasks are common and that description of these tasks can be standardized using activity verbs. A JIMS checklist has been developed and tested for machinist jobs.

Most of the approaches rely on the task and worker requirements concepts pioneered by UST and ES. Some other approaches, however, are based on different concepts of what to look for in job analysis. One such approach, called multidimensional scaling, permits the analyst to evaluate work without restrictions on the way he perceives it. In multidimensional scaling, a set of scale values is first obtained, then the factors represented by these values are established by statistical techniques. Two studies applied the approach to a job analysis situation in the Navy.[10] Another applied it to the position of management analyst in the federal government.[11]

The "Position Analysis Questionnaire" (PAQ) developed by McCormick at Purdue University[12] organizes job information into the following six categories: information input, mediation processes, work output, interpersonal activities, work situation and job context, and miscellaneous aspects. The PAQ seeks to identify worker and job information through the use of standardized check lists and was developed to identify behavioral job requirements in all types of jobs.

An approach based largely on sociological concepts has been reported by Carr.[13] On the assumptions that job analysis must examine the broad structural determinants of work behavior in order to portray adequately the nature of work performed and that interaction patterns, organization location, and technical processes are interdependent determinants of work patterns, a method called Systematic Approach to Multidimensional Occupational Analysis (SAMOA) was developed. The system identifies technical, organizational, and communication dimensions of jobs. The technical dimension is measured by complexity and variety. The organizational dimension is gauged through organiza-

---

[10]D. G. Schultz and A. I. Siegal, "The Analysis of Job Performance by Multidimensional Scaling Techniques," *Journal of Applied Psychology* (October, 1964), pp. 329–335; A. I. Siegal and M. G. Pfeiffer, "Factorial Congruence in Criterion Development," *Personnel Psychology* (Autumn, 1965), pp. 267–279.

[11]Kenneth R. Brown, "Job Analysis by Multidimensional Scaling," *Journal of Applied Psychology* (December, 1967), pp. 469–475.

[12]Ernest J. McCormick, *The Development, Analysis, and Experimental Application of Worker-Oriented Job Variables,* Report No. 8, Contract No. Nonr-1100(19), prepared for the Office of Naval Research (Lafayette, Indiana: Occupational Research Center, Purdue University, July, 1964).

[13]Malcolm J. Carr, "Technical, Organizational, and Communicational Dimensions in Modeling for Job Analysis," *IEEE Transactions on Engineering Management* (September, 1968), pp. 94–99.

tion position and supervision exercised and received. The communication dimension is appraised by assessing volume, scope, status level, and complexity of interpersonal contacts. The approach was developed from data obtained from Navy enlisted personnel.

Actually, SAMOA may be considered to be a combination of job analysis-job evaluation method. As a job analysis method it provides new definitions of tasks involved in jobs. Another feature of the approach is the use of cluster analysis as a method of grouping similar jobs. Although the other approaches examined also employ the computer, use of the computer to conduct cluster analysis of job dimensions is novel. It will be examined in the chapter on quantitative job evaluation.

Although these new approaches may be expected to affect job analysis in the future, present practice emphasizes three types of job information: (1) the identity of the job, (2) a complete and accurate description of the tasks involved in the job, and (3) a specification of the demands that the job makes of the worker. This is the basic information needed for all personnel uses, but especially for job evaluation.

The information obtained and reported has been formalized into a measurement device designated as the "Job Analysis Formula" by UST and ES.[14] The "formula" includes four categories of information: (1) what the worker does, (2) how he does it, (3) why he does it, and (4) the skill involved in the doing.

In most uses of job information, there is need for an indication of the exact nature and scope of the tasks involved in a job and a definition of the level of difficulty of those tasks. The first three parts of the formula, the "what," "how," and "why," bring out the nature and scope of the tasks. The last part, the "skill involved," is concerned with the degree of difficulty of the tasks and with defining the nature of the required skills in order to indicate their difficulty.

JOBS

In order to study a job, it is necessary to know what a job is. The term has so many meanings in lay language that it needs careful definition before it can be used here. Also, its meaning will be clearer if two other terms are explained first and if this information is used in the definition of the word *job.* The other terms are *task* and *position.*

A *task* exists whenever human effort must be exerted for a specific purpose. When sufficient tasks accumulate to justify the employment of a worker, a *position* exists. Thus, a *position* is *an aggregation of duties,*

---

[14]U.S. Department of Labor, *Training and Reference Manual for Job Analysis* (Washington, D.C.: United States Government Printing Office, May, 1965), p. 3.

tasks, and responsibilities requiring the services of one individual.[15] It is seen from the definition that in any organization there are as many positions as workers.

If it were necessary to study every position in an organization, the task involved would be tremendous and probably impractical for many organizations. Fortunately, it is not necessary that every position be studied. Because many positions are identical, it is possible to study jobs.

Thus, a *job* may be defined as *a group of positions that are identical* with respect to their major or significant tasks.[16] An example will perhaps make the distinction between position and job more apparent. A local retail store employs eighteen people—the manager; two office employees; ten sales people; three people involved in receiving, marking, and stocking merchandise; and two people involved in delivery. Let us assume that the tasks are so aligned that the positions involved in each of the functions are identical. Thus the store contains eighteen positions, but only five jobs. The five jobs might be titled (1) manager, (2) bookkeeper, (3) salesman, (4) stockkeeper, (5) deliveryman. It is seen from this example that analyzing each position would be uneconomical. All that is necessary is to analyze the five separate jobs. At higher levels in the organization, however, each position tends to differ from other positions. In this case, each position is also a job.

Before job study is undertaken in an organization, it is necessary to determine what jobs exist in the organization. An organization chart may be of use in this connection. Likewise, listing existing positions by departments provides a useful beginning point. To determine the number of jobs, it is often necessary to go into a department and analyze a group of positions to find the basic units and to discover the exact nature of the jobs in the department. Careful questioning of supervisors may also aid in determining the jobs that exist in the organization.

As an example, suppose an establishment employs ten workers who operate drill presses. Each of these workers occupies a position. Although there may be minor differences among the ten positions with respect to operations performed, materials worked on, and types of machine setup required, all ten workers are operating the same kind of machine, performing operations of a comparable difficulty. Thus these ten positions have identical major tasks and constitute one job. If, on the other hand, five of the workers set up their own machines and do complex work whereas the other five have their machines set up for them and do only routine work, there are two jobs involved.

Jobs should be studied *as they exist* at the time of the analysis in

---

[15]*Ibid.,* p. 7.

[16]Government organizations tend to use "class" or "class of positions" instead of "job."

the organization under study. Although jobs change, job analysis is concerned with the job as it is performed at the time of the study.

Before analysis begins it is useful to prepare an inventory of jobs. This is a listing of jobs by department, indicating the number of employees on each job. It not only indicates the scope of the project, but also tends to eliminate duplication.

Once it has been determined what jobs exist in the organization, a job analysis is made of each job. In individual cases, however, there are complicating situations that may occur and that must be handled in a consistent manner. For example, a situation may exist wherein workers are interchangeable and frequently change from one set of tasks to another. In some organizations this is done to relieve monotony. The essential point here is that all workers can and do perform all the tasks. In such a case, the tasks may be considered *one job* and analyzed collectively.

Another situation involves workers who are interchangeable and who change to another set of tasks in an *emergency*. Here, it is necessary to analyze the separate jobs. If there is any doubt whether one or more than one job is involved, it is better to make separate analyses rather than a combined one.

JOB ANALYZERS

Obviously, job study requires people. On this matter there is much variation in practice. Some employers delegate the task to employees by furnishing them with a questionnaire that they are asked to fill out. Some assign the work to supervisors, whereas others have the preliminary work done by employees and ask supervisors to check the information furnished.

Most organizations, however, employ job analysts. Such job analysts are individuals who have been trained in the process of job analysis and know what to look for and what questions to ask.

Persons with various educational background have been trained as job analysts. Most organizations train their own job analysts by having them work closely with experienced analysts. Job analysis is learned by doing. Although studying the purpose and procedures of job analysis precedes actual analysis, the job analyst's basic training is obtained through analyzing jobs and going over the results with his supervisor or trainer.

Trained job analysts know what to look for and what questions to ask, but when brought in from outside, they must spend time learning the organization. Employees and supervisors, on the other hand, know a good deal about the organization but lack training in how to analyze jobs. An organization starting a program will probably find that the best procedure is to hire a trained job analyst who possesses the attributes of a trainer. Such an individual will be able to train analysts from among an organization's employees and supervisors.

There is some evidence that the work of job analysts is changing and becoming more specialized. Large organizations at least find it expedient to specify different education and experience requirements for job analysts assigned to factory work and those assigned to professional and administrative work. Also, job analysts may be further specialized according to the use to be made of their efforts. Although the same basic job data are employed for personnel uses, job analysts writing job descriptions for use in selection, training, and organization analysis are more concerned with job relationships, whereas job analysts writing job descriptions for use in compensation administration are concerned with distinctions among jobs.

METHODS OF OBTAINING JOB INFORMATION

The methods used in obtaining information about jobs are interviews, observation, combined observations and interviews, questionnaires, supervisory conferences, and checklists. Frequency of use of the methods is in the order given.[17] The interview is employed in about 85 per cent of job analyses, although many organizations interview supervisors rather than job incumbents. Although a combination of interview and observation would seem preferable, less than 40 per cent of organizations use it.

Questionnaires are used by 43.4 per cent of organizations in conducting job analyses of salaried jobs but by only 29.7 per cent of organizations for hourly rated jobs. The tendency for wider use of questionnaires for clerical and managerial job analysis is understandable because of the greater verbal facility of these employees, and limiting its use may represent a saving in time but only at the expense of effectiveness. No one knows more about a job than its incumbent. Also, employees are much more likely to accept the program if they have an opportunity to state the duties and requirements of their job and if they are shown the results of the job analysis. For an example of such a questionnaire, see Figure 2.

Actual observation of the work would also seem to be necessary if all job facts are to be ascertained. Probably only in this way can the relative importance of the various tasks be properly gauged.

[17]Stone and Yoder, *Job Analysis, 1970,* p. 20.

Employee Questionnaire

Employee questionnaire[1]

JOB DESCRIPTION QUESTIONNAIRE

Date _____

Company _____   Present Job Title and Grade _____

Dep't _____   Section or Group _____   Supervisor's Name _____

Home Office ☐   Branch or Area Service Office _____

---

1. Describe major duties of your job: _____

_____

_____

_____

_____

_____

_____

_____

_____

_____

_____

_____

_____

_____

_____

(Attach additional sheets if needed)

---

2. Other, less important job duties: _____

_____

_____

_____

_____

_____

_____

(Attach additional sheets if needed)

FIGURE 2

Source: Prentice-Hall, Inc., *Personnel Management: Policies and Practices* (1966). Reprinted by permission.

3. List machines or equipment you use:

	Continually	Frequently	Occasionally

4. How much formal education is necessary to do this job (check one):
   - ☐ Less than High School
   - ☐ High School
   - ☐ High School plus 1 yr. of other schooling
   - ☐ High School plus 2-3 yrs of other schooling
   - ☐ College Degree (4 yrs) Major _____
   - ☐ College Degree plus other schooling

List additional specialized courses, subjects or training which are **necessary** but which are **NOT** easily available in High School or College: _____

5. How much previous similar or related work experience is necessary for a person starting this job?
   - ☐ None
   - ☐ Less than 3 months
   - ☐ 3 months to 1 year
   - ☐ 1 to 3 years
   - ☐ 3 to 5 years
   - ☐ 5 to 10 years
   - ☐ _____

6. How long should it take an employee with the necessary education and previous experience (as shown above) to become generally familiar with details and to do this job reasonably well?
   - ☐ Two weeks or less
   - ☐ Three months
   - ☐ Six months
   - ☐ One year
   - ☐ Two years
   - ☐ _____

7. What amount of supervision does this job ordinarily require? Check one:

   ☐ Frequent; all but minor variations are referred to supervisor.

   ☐ Several times daily, to report or to get advice and/or assignments. Follow established methods and procedures; refer exceptions.

   ☐ Occasional, since most duties are repetitive and related, with standard instructions and procedures as guides. Unusual problems are referred, frequently with suggestions for correction.

   ☐ Limited supervision. The nature of the work is such that it is performed to a large extent on own responsibility after assignment, with some choice of method. Occasionally develop own methods.

   ☐ Broad objectives are outlined. Work is judged primarily on overall results with much choice of method. Frequently develop methods to achieve desired results.

   ☐ Little or no direct supervision. Have wide choice in selection, development and coordination of methods within broad framework of general policies.

8. What are the nature and scope of any independent decisions you make? _____

Are your decisions to approve usually reviewed before becoming effective? ____ If so, by whom? _____

Are your decisions to reject usually reviewed before becoming effective? ____ If so, by whom? _____

FIGURE 2 (Cont.)

9. In what ways does this job require resourcefulness, originality and/or initiative? Examples: _____

_____

10. What kinds of errors are likely to occur on this job? _____

_____

How are such errors ordinarily checked or discovered? _____

_____

What would be the effect of such errors, if not caught? _____

_____

11. Check the extent of contacts you have regarding Company business:

	Continually	Frequently	Occasionally	Never	Method (Phone, Letter, in Person)
Employees in other units of the the Company					
Policyholders and/or Agents					
General public; community or trade and professional assns.					
Federal and State Govt Agencies					
Other (specify) _____					

Example and purpose of such contacts: _____

_____

12. If the mental and visual alertness required is more than normal: check one in each column:

☐ Occasional; periods of short duration
☐ Close   ☐ Frequent, but with occasional "breaks"
☐ Highly concentrated   ☐ Steady and sustained

13. Describe any muscular action, body movement, working positions or posture changes occuring while performing duties which result in unusual fatigue. Estimate percentage of time in each: _____

14. Indicate any disagreeable job conditions to which you are exposed, such as dirt, noise, water, fumes, heat, outside weather, monotony, accident hazards, etc. _____

If you travel over night on the job, indicate approximate times per month and method:_____

Approximately how many miles per month do you drive in doing this job? _____

FIGURE 2 (Cont.)

ANSWER ONLY IF YOU ARE RESPONSIBLE FOR THE WORK OF OTHERS

15. Check below those supervisory responsibilities which are a part of this job:

☐ Instructing   ☐ Allocating personnel

☐ Assigning work   ☐ Acting on employee problems

☐ Reviewing work   ☐ Selecting new employees

☐ Planning work of others   ☐ Transferring/promoting
                                    (Recommend?__ Approve?__)
☐ Maintaining standards   ☐ Disciplining
                                    (Recommend?__ Approve?__)
☐ Coordinating activities   ☐ Discharge
                                    (Recommend?__ Approve?__)
                ☐ Salary Increases (Recommend?__ Approve?__)

List job titles which are under your <u>direct</u> supervision and the number of employees in each:

_____   _____

_____   _____

_____   _____

_____   _____

_____   _____

Show TOTAL number of employees (including those just above) over which you have **supervisory**

authority: _____

COMMENTS: (Attach additional sheets if needed):

_____

_____

_____

_____

_____

_____

_____

                    Form completed by: _____

NOTE TO SUPERVISOR: Your signature below indicates that you have reviewed the above job description. If you desire to make revisions, please enter them in RED pencil in the appropriate spaces. If needed, use additional sheets, numbering your comments to match the items in question. These items will be reviewed with you before a final job description is prepared.

How many employees under your supervision   Reviewed by _____

do the job described above?_____   Title _____

FIGURE 2 (Cont.)

Likewise, an interview with the employee and with his supervisor appears essential to complete information. Often the importance of tasks can be determined only after knowing where a task fits into the work of the unit. Such information is best obtained by interview.

INFORMATION TO BE OBTAINED

Essentially, the information to be obtained by job analysis fits into three categories: (1) identification, (2) work performed or duties, and (3) performance requirements. This information is entered on a job analysis report or schedule and is later transferred to one or more job descriptions designed for specific uses.

The job analysis report is merely a form for recording job information that is obtained through job analysis. As such, it may take any number of forms and may be extremely detailed. Probably the most inclusive form is the job analysis schedule worked out by the United States Department of Labor and reproduced in Figure 3. The *Physical Demands and Environmental Conditions Form* is part of the total schedule.

Because the emphasis of Manpower Administration is on job analysis sufficiently flexible to encompass job restructuring and job development rather than on personnel practices of specific organizations,[18] Figure 3 includes portions that may or may not be used by organizations. For example, the work-performed ratings and worker-trait ratings[19] represent methods of classifying and determining the level of work based on data, people, and things, and the level of worker traits required, and are in effect job evaluation rather than job analysis. Whether or not organizations use these ratings presumably depends on their decision about the applicability of the rating methods to the organization. But the description of the tasks is the basic job information used in all methods of rating jobs. In the following discussion it is assumed that the job analysis schedule calls for three broad categories of information: (1) identification, (2) work performed, (3) performance requirements.

Identification.   Here, such information will be provided as will serve to identify the job under study. The job title as actually used on the job is employed—that is, the title that would be used by the employer in requesting referral of an applicant, or one used by the workers in referring to the job. If more than one title is used, the alternate titles are listed. Also, the number of personnel employed on the job is usually

---

[18]U.S. Department of Labor, *Handbook for Analyzing Jobs,* p. iii.
[19]Described in detail in the *Handbook for Analyzing Jobs.*

U.S. Department of Labor
Manpower Administration

OMB 44–R0722

Estab. & Sched. No. _____

JOB ANALYSIS SCHEDULE

1. Estab. Job Title _____

2. Ind. Assign. _____

3. SIC Code(s) and Title(s) _____

Code

4. JOB SUMMARY:

5. WORK PERFORMED RATINGS:

	D	P	T
Worker Functions	Data	People	Things

Work Field _____

M.P.S.M.S. _____

WTA Group

6. WORKER TRAITS RATINGS:

GED   1   2   3   4   5   6

SVP   1   2   3   4   5   6   7   8   9

Aptitudes   G__ V__ N__ S__ P__ Q__ K__ F__ M__ E__ C__

Temperaments   D   F   I   J   M   P   R   S   T   V

Interests   1a   1b   2a   2b   3a   3b   4a   4b   5a   5b

Phys. Demands   S   L   M   H   V   2   3   4   5   6

Environ. Cond.   I   O   B   2   3   4   5   6   7

DOT Title

Ind. Desig.

MA 7–36

FIGURE 3

7.   General Education

    a.   Elementary_____High School_____Courses_____

    b.   College_____Courses_____

8.   Vocational Preparation

    a.   College_____Courses_____

    _____

    b.   Vocational Education_____Courses_____

    _____

    c.   Apprenticeship_____

    _____

    d.   Inplant Training_____

    e.   On-the-Job Training_____

    f.   Performance on Other Jobs_____

9.   Experience_____

10. Orientation_____

11. Licenses, etc._____

12. Relation to Other Jobs and Workers

    Promotion: From_____To_____

    Transfers: From_____To_____

    Supervision Received_____

    Supervision Given_____

    _____

13. Machines, Tools, Equipment, and Work Aids

14. Materials and Products

FIGURE 3 (Cont.)

15.   Description of Tasks:

FIGURE 3 (Cont.)

16. Definition of Terms

17. General Comments

18. Analyst_____ Date_____ Editor_____ Date_____

    Reviewed By_____ Title, Org._____

    National Office Reviewer_____

FIGURE 3 (Cont.)

44–R0722

U.S. DEPARTMENT OF LABOR
MANPOWER ADMINISTRATION

Physical Demands and Environmental Conditions

ESTAB. JOB TITLE _____ ESTAB. & SCHED. NO. _____

DOT TITLE AND CODE _____

PHYSICAL DEMANDS	COMMENTS

1. STRENGTH

    a. Standing _____ %
       Walking _____ %
       Sitting _____ %

    b.   Weight
       Lifting _____ | _____
       Carrying _____ | _____
       Pushing _____ | _____
       Pulling _____ | _____

2. CLIMBING
    BALANCING
3. STOOPING
    KNEELING
    CROUCHING
    CRAWLING
4. REACHING
    HANDLING
    FINGERING
    FEELING
5. TALKING
    Ordinary
    Other
    HEARING
    Ordinary Conversation
    Other Sounds
6. SEEING
    Acuity, Near
    Acuity, Far
    Depth Perception
    Accommodation
    Color Vision
    Field of Vision

RATINGS: P. D.:   S L M H VH 2 3 4 5 6

Analyst _____ Date _____ | Estab. Reviewer _____

E.S. Reviewer _____ Date _____ | Title _____ Date _____

MA 7–35

FIGURE 3 (Cont.)

ENVIRONMENTAL CONDITIONS	COMMENTS

1. ENVIRONMENT
 	
   Inside _____ %
 	
   Outside _____ %	

2. EXTREME COLD WITH OR WITHOUT TEMPERATURE CHANGES	
3. EXTREME HEAT WITH OR WITHOUT TEMPERATURE CHANGES	
4. WET AND/OR HUMID	

5. NOISE
   Estimated maximum
   number of decibels
 	
   VIBRATION	

6. HAZARDS
   Mechanical
   Electrical
   Burns
   Explosives
   Radiant Energy
   Other	

7. ATMOSPHERIC CONDITIONS
   Fumes
   Odors
   Dusts
   Mists
   Gases
   Poor Ventilation
   Other	

RATINGS: E. C.:   I O B 2 3 4 5 6 7

PROTECTIVE CLOTHING OR PERSONAL DEVICES

FIGURE 3 (Cont.)

recorded; this record may be pertinent in determining the importance of the job to the organization. If a numbering system is used by the organization to identify jobs, the job number is noted, along with the department in which the job is performed.

Finally, if the job being analyzed can be identified in the *Dictionary of Occupational Titles,*[20] the dictionary title may be entered. Such an entry can be made, however, only if the job under analysis is identical in all significant respects to the job defined in the dictionary. Because such information may be extremely useful in making comparisons among jobs, it should be recorded wherever possible.

Work Performed.   This section is intended to present a clear, concise, accurate statement regarding the tasks performed by a worker in accomplishing the purpose of his job. To define the scope of the job, the work-performed section describes what the worker does, how he does it, and why he does it.

This section gives a correct portrayal of the purpose, content, and requirements of each job. It consists of a summary statement that gives an overall identification to the job in as few words as possible, followed by an orderly series of statements that describe each step of the job. Job analysts tend to write the summary statement after completing the work-performed section. They find that a sentence composed from the flag statements that delineate each task provides much of the material needed for the summary statement.

The function of the summary statement is to give the reader an overall concept of the purpose, nature, and extent of the tasks performed and how the job differs generally from all other jobs. The selection of words is most important. Such vague terms as "designs," "lays out," and "adjusts" are not sufficiently precise to point up the important aspects of the job nor to distinguish one job from others.

The rest of the work-performed section expands on the summary statement and explains the important details of the job so logically, concisely, and specifically that an uninformed reader can visualize the tasks and understand the job. In describing the duties of the job, it is desirable to record the information in either chronological or functional order. Functional order means according to similarity of work. The organization of the tasks will vary with the job, but they are set up in such a way as to provide all the information on one phase of the job in one place. The primary consideration in organization is to present the material so that the uninformed reader can obtain a clear picture of the work performed on the job. The number of tasks into which the work-

[20]U.S. Department of Labor, *Dictionary of Occupational Titles,* 3rd ed. (Washington, D.C.: United States Government Printing Office, 1965).

performed section is broken down must, of course, vary from job to job. There is room, however, for decision on the part of the analyst. The tasks may be grouped into a small number of major tasks with relatively long narrative statements under each, or a larger number of tasks may be delineated with less elaboration. It has been found, however, that three to eight tasks suffice for most jobs.[21]

Especially important in giving a clear concept of the work performed is the style used. The presentation is a concise, well-worded, easily read, informative narrative built on the organization plan. In such a narrative, the job is constructed as it is analyzed. The conciseness desired comes from well-chosen words with specific meanings and not from a "telegraphic" style. The information given is specific and in sufficient detail to give the "what," "how," and "why," but not a mass of unimportant facts.

To ensure clarity in writing the body of the work-performed section, the job is divided into its major tasks and one numbered statement devoted to each. Each task is introduced with a "flag" statement that shows generally what is being done, followed by a detailed account of how and why it is done. (See Figure 4.)

---

1. Job title *Color Matcher*
3. Number employed M *3* F *0*
   (*See Comments*)
5. Date
   Number of sheets *1/6*

7. Dictionary Title and Code *0-50*

2. Number
4. Establishment No.
6. Alternate titles *Colorist*
8. Industry *Plastic Materials*
9. Branch *Production*
10. Department *Color Laboratory*

---

11. WORK PERFORMED

Develops colors for plastic sheet materials and molding powders to customer specifications and verifies color of first lots of plastics in production.

1. Develops colors according to customer specifications: Receives from the Sales Department, and studies, customers' requests for desired colors in the form of samples of material, such as paper, glass, or another plastic, in the form of a written description of the effect desired, or in the form of spectrophotometric terms. Submits requests iin spectrophotometric terms to SPECTROPHOTO-METRIST for conversion to standard color formulas. (See Comments.) Draws up specifications for the shade or tint, and value of the color desired, applying to the problem a consideration of the physical and chemical properties of the materials to be colored, such as phenol formaldehyde, cellulose acetate, or

FIGURE 4

Job Analysis Schedule

[21]Otis and Leukart, *Job Evaluation,* p. 270.

styrene. Considers various dye agents, such as sulphur dyes, oil soluble dyes, or inorganic pigments, and their effect with regard to such factors as density, rate of flow and the known affinities of certain categories of dyes for specific varieties of blenders. Likewise considers the properties of coloring materials, such as melting point, dispersion, and solubility, and the degree to which these properties will affect the end product. Estimates the effect on color stability of the use of the product and the conditions to which it will be subjected, such as heat, dry cleaning, fluids, abrasion, perspiration, or contact with strong acids or alkalies. (10%)

2. Prepares dyes according to specifications: Weighs out pigments on a scale or on a chemical balance according to the amounts involved. Grinds pigments to powder by hand with a mortar and pestle for small quantities or with a *Ball Mill* for large quantities. Reduces ground pigment to uniform fineness by sifting it by hand through fine (300-400 mesh) screens. Dissolves the powdered pigments in appropriate solvents, filters them as necessary to remove impurities, and boils, distills, or otherwise treats them according to required chemical or physical analysis procedures, Determines color reactions on fillers to be combined with basic materials in order to establish correct procedures (see Comments). Composes formulas and procedures to be followed by COLOR WEIGHER in preparing quantities of dyes for production purposes and for introducing the dyes into batches of plastic. (5%)

3. Matches the developed color against specifications: Pours dye into a sample batch of plastic being worked by department workers under his supervision. Visually compares the resulting colored material against specifications, employing a highly developed color sensitiveness and knowledge gained by experience, and by identifying subtle component tints and shades not detectible by an untrained observer. Distinguishes between colors, compensating for conditions that distort perception, such as moisture, thickness, finish of material, adjacent colors, and light under which the comparison is made (see Comments). Revises formula as necessary to correct colors that prove unsatisfactory. Sends suitably colored samples through the Sales Department to the customer for approval. Has a sample tested for color permanency and recommends uses for material on a knowledge of the effect of use on color. (15%)

4. Verifies a specified color and other properties, such as transparency and thickness, of first lots of orders in production: Visually compares colors of samples from Production Department against *sample standards* or *approved standards,* distinguishing between colors and compensating for conditions that distort actual perception, taking into consideration the effect of further processing on the color. Gages the thickness of plastic sheets, using a *Pocket Gage.* Stamps dates and numbers on approved samples with a rubber stamp and notifies the Production Department to continue production. (30%)

5. Supervises workers engaged in miniature production of plastic sheets and molding powders: Orally assigns daily work to ASSISTANTS (COLOR LABORATORY) as outlined generally by SUPERVISOR (COLOR LABORATORY). Helps assistants whenever necessary, answering questions and assisting with the work where most needed, such as polishing samples for spectrophotometric study, using a small *Polish Press.* Contacts Production Department, concerning duplicate orders or improper specifications for color called to his attention by COLOR WEIGHER. Keeps record of personnel attendance. (40%)

6. May originate colors, mottles, and various configurations (intricate designs involving several colors) requiring considerable ingenuity and knowledge of colors and plastic materials. (percentage of time negligible)

FIGURE 4 (Cont.)

The style to be followed conforms to four basic rules of writing:

1. A terse, direct style is employed.
2. Each sentence begins with a functional verb.
3. The present tense is employed throughout.
4. All words that do not impart necessary information are omitted.

The tasks of the job are thus presented as consecutively numbered and paragraphed statements. At the end of each paragraph is a notation giving the approximate percentage of time involved in the performance of the task described.

Performance Requirements. The job analysis report typically also includes information on performance requirements. It is this section that rounds out an explanation of the difficulty of the job.

This portion of job analysis requires that the analyst be more than an observer. Although some judgment is employed in the other two sections of the job analysis schedule, more judgment is involved here. In arriving at and reporting these judgments, the analyst makes a detailed analysis and interpretation of the traits required of the worker for successful performance of the job.[22]

In arriving at these decisions, the job analyst reviews carefully each task recorded in the work-performed section. Careful review of each task suggests attributes the worker must possess. Analysis and interpretation permit a decision not only on presence or absence of the factor, but also on the degree to which it is present. As mentioned previously, Manpower Administration has developed a careful method of evaluating the worker traits required by the job. Organizations may use this method or develop their own.

JOB DESCRIPTIONS

The job analysis report or schedule contains the information secured in the job analysis process. As suggested previously, such information finds many uses in personnel. But to make such information most useful for the various programs, it may be desirable to prepare job descriptions specifically designed for the purpose at hand. For example, those assigned responsibility for training activities may wish to prepare a specialized job description for training, called a job breakdown, which follows the chronological order in which the job is performed and care-

[22]U.S. Department of Labor, *Handbook for Analyzing Jobs.*

fully sets out the steps to be performed and the knowledge and skills required to perform these steps. A job breakdown is quite detailed, making use of almost all of the information contained in the job analysis report. Again, the employment department may wish to prepare a specialized job description consisting of the qualifications a worker must possess in order to adequately perform the job. This information is extracted from the worker-requirements section of the job analysis report. The specialized job description for employment is called a job specification. This term is also used, unfortunately, to describe what is often a somewhat different form often employed in job evaluation and described below. Other specialized job descriptions may be prepared for other personnel uses from information extracted from the job analysis report. As mentioned previously, job analysts are becoming more specialized. It is not unusual for the training department, employment department, or the compensation department to employ their own analysts to prepare their job descriptions. They may, of course, each conduct their own separate job analysis rather than make use of a job analysis schedule prepared by another.

The purpose of writing the specialized job descriptions detailed below is to record the job information in a standard form preparatory to job evaluation. To accomplish this purpose, the information is presented in the most accurate, meaningful, and readable fashion. More important, the organization is standardized so that the information is comparable. In such forms the concern is with information that serves to distinguish one job from another.

Job evaluation may be based on job descriptions, job specifications, or both. Job descriptions normally include identifying data and job content and scope. Job specifications customarily contain job requirements and worker qualifications.

Job descriptions for wage purposes include a standard job title for each job. As a result of the job analysis process, it should be possible to adopt a standardized nomenclature and a single title for each job. The title selected should be (1) similar or identical to one applied previously, (2) set up in natural (not inverted) form, (3) brief, (4) descriptive, (5) conversational, (6) indicative of skill and supervisory level, (7) capable of consistent usage. Many job analysts insist that job titles be consistent with job level and never use the similar sounding titles at different levels.

When used in job evaluation, job descriptions identify, define, and describe jobs. A clear picture of the duties and responsibilities of the job is provided. If job descriptions alone are used as a basis for evaluating jobs, they should provide sufficient detail to permit evaluators to judge the level of difficulty of the job. However, no more detail should be furnished than is necessary to determine the level of difficulty.

In form, the job description includes three parts: (1) identification, (2) summary statement, and (3) work performed. These sections correspond with the identification and work-performed sections of the job analysis report. The work-performed section of the job description may quite possibly include less detail than the job analysis report. In writing the work-performed section of job evaluation job descriptions, however, sufficient detail is provided to permit clear recognition of differences in importance and difficulty of jobs. The reader is able to distinguish this job from other jobs in level and scope. On the other hand, job descriptions are written as concisely as possible. Long descriptions imply variety and difficulty of work.

Careful attention to wording is called for. It is especially important in job evaluation job descriptions that precise language be employed. Words used should have only one possible connotation and must accurately describe just what is being done. Terms should not only be specific, but also should employ language that is as simple as possible. Not only understanding, but also attitudes are involved and long words may suggest duties that are difficult.

Writers of job evaluation job descriptions must be aware of the relationships among jobs within a department and how the work is related to jobs in other departments. Only with this awareness can they see that the job descriptions express the actual differences among jobs. It may occasionally be necessary to go back to jobs and supervision in which overlapping or duplication of work appears.

Obviously, when job evaluation job descriptions are written by different analysts, coordination and consistency are essential. This is usually provided by having some central agency edit the job descriptions to assure consistent language.

Many organizations follow the practice of showing the job description to one or more employees performing the job, the supervisor, and the union representative. This practice ensures that the job description provides a fair and accurate picture of the job.

In addition, in joint union-management job evaluation, job descriptions are tentative until accepted by both parties. Both precision of language and understandability are, if possible, even more important here. Carefully written job descriptions do not limit employer discretion in making job changes or assigning work to employees.

Figures 5 and 6 are examples of job descriptions for job evaluation. Figures 7 and 8 illustrate useful approaches to distinguishing similar jobs.

General Office Clerk	*1 M 2 F*	*114*
Job Title	Number Employed	Job Number

WORK PERFORMED:

Summary: Performs a variety of stenographic, clerical, bookkeeping and cashier duties in the general office.

Details of Operation

1. *Operates bookkeeping machine to post accounts payable and to prepare accounts receivable invoices: places selected form of record on the flat writing surface of machine; depresses keys to type descriptive data, unit costs, and to calculate totals and net amounts; uses hand-operated adding machine to compute totals required on various records and reports. 40%*
2. *Performs stenographic duties: takes correspondence dictation from Office Manager and department buyers in shorthand and transcribes on the typewriter. 10%*
3. *Performs usual duties of cashier: receives sales slips from salesclerks via Lawson vacuum tube system; verifies customer's charge account status and returns duplicate sales slip via same system, and enters charge purchases on customer's account card; operates cash register and makes change when necessary; makes refunds when proper slips are submitted; maintains 3" x 5" file of COD sales slips and credit refunds. 20%*
4. *Performs variety of general office duties; answers telephone; files correspondence, records and reports; prepares monthly statements and places same in envelopes, using envelope sealer, affixes stamps, and mails; assists Office Manager process applications for charge accounts. 30%*

FIGURE 5

Office Job Description

1. Job Title *Chief Maintenance Man*	2. Job Number *13.01*
3. Number employed: Male *1* Female _____	4. Date of Analysis _____
5. Alternate Titles _____	6. Department *Rec. & Maint.*
7. Base Rate _____ Incentive? _____	8. Analyst _____

9. WORK PERFORMED

Summary: Supervises housekeeping of building and does general repair, carpentry and electrical maintenance work.

Details of Operation– % of time

Does general repairs involving carpentry, plastering and masonry: builds partitions; hangs doors; makes and installs wooden machine guards; patches plaster; lays brick. (60%)

Performs various electrical maintenance duties: cleans and changes fluorescent tubes; re-wires work tables with heating elements; installs additional lights and fixtures. (25%)

Supervises housekeeping of building to maintain cleanliness and sanitary standards: checks janitor's work and tests sprinkling and air systems daily; during winter, supervises firing and maintenance of plant boiler and heating systems. (15%)

FIGURE 6

Shop Job Description

OCCUPATIONAL SUMMARY

Operates IBM data processing punched card machines. Performs control panel wiring tasks and sets up and conducts data processing machine tests to determine accuracy of operations.

WORK PERFORMED

Operates all IBM data processing punched card machines. Feeds and removes punched cards and/or paper. Makes adjustments as required in the continuous processing of a complete report through successive machine operations in accordance with established job instructions, procedures, and verbal instructions.

Sets up and tests all types of IBM punched card data processing machines using wired and pre-wired control panels and established job instructions and procedures.

Performs control panel wiring tasks and control panel machine tests from verbal or written instructions on machines indicated, at a level of difficulty described below:

A. Performs control panel wiring tasks for the Tabulator 407 series, including selective control circuitry, addition, subtraction, listing and group totaling.

B. Collator. Performs control panel wiring tasks, including selective control circuitry, merging, sequencing and matching.

C. Calculator. Performs control panel wiring tasks, which must include selective control circuitry, and calculating operations.

D. Reproducer. Performs control panel wiring tasks, which must include selective control circuitry, reproducing, comparing, gang punching, emitting and end printing.

E. Interpreter. Performs all control panel wiring tasks, including selective control circuitry.

Performs control panel wiring on other machines as they become available where the tasks are at the level of difficulty described.

Exercises knowledge and understanding of source documents and related operations as performed by requestors of data processing services to accomplish the following:

A. Verify and reconcile data processing against independent controls.

B. Audit punch cards and/or reports against summaries of basic cards or reports and/or source documents to insure accuracy of and resolve errors in final balances.

Audits procedures and machines throughout operations to insure accuracy of reporting. Initiates action required to correct discrepancies found by audit.

Provides guidance to those lesser classified employees assigned to assist.

FIGURE 7

Standard Job Description

Data Processing Machine Operator "B"

WORK PERFORMED

Operates one or more data processing machines such as sorter, interpreter, collator, reproducing punch, or calculating punch to insure continuous process of data. Feeds and removes punch cards and paper according to a prearranged sequence. Removes card jams from data processing machines, restores the equipment to operating condition. Duplicates damaged cards and submits them for verification by a second operator.

Performs tests of data processing machine accuracy and procedure by verifying and reconciling sample totals and subtotals from established procedures, which indicate sequence of operations to be performed. Reports machine, control panel, operator or procedural failure to higher rated personnel.

Changes control panels and makes machine adjustments according to written and verbal instructions.

Performs control panel wiring tasks where circuitry is copied from established diagrams. Disassembles control panels no longer required. Sorts and returns wires to proper location.

Maintains equipment and area in a clean and orderly manner.

FIGURE 8

Standard Job Description

JOB EVALUATION JOB SPECIFICATIONS

Many job evaluation programs work with job specifications as a substitute for or in addition to job descriptions. Job specifications are written in terms of the compensable factors employed in the job evaluation plan. Hence, they are written after compensable factors have been chosen. Determining compensable factors is examined in the final section of this chapter.

Job specifications determine the extent to which each compensable factor exists in a job and the particular level of the factor found in that job. For example, if experience is one of the factors, job specifications indicate not only the amount of experience required, but also the level or type of experience. This example illustrates the need for very specific information in the job specification. Such specificity is essential because it is this information that becomes the basis and the justification of job values assigned in the job evaluation process. Those charged with evaluating jobs form their judgments from the amount and level of compensable factors reported in job specifications as existing in jobs.

The performance requirements section of the job analysis report is a basic source of information for job specifications. This section is carefully analyzed and translated into terms of the compensable factors. In addition, job descriptions are carefully scrutinized for further information. Materials used, stage of precision, and tools employed all suggest factors present in jobs. It may also be necessary to go back to the job when writing job specifications to make sure that no information was missed that might suggest the presence or absence of a given factor or that might indicate the level of a factor adjudged to be present. Additional observation and further discussion with workers and supervisors may thus aid in the translation of job information into terms that indicate amounts and levels of compensable factors present in or absent from jobs.

The translation of job information into compensable factor terms calls for certain attributes on the part of the writer of job specifications, because more than the ability to discover and record facts is required. Inferences from and judgments concerning the facts are the data for job specifications. Actually, the writer of job specifications is beginning the evaluation of jobs by making these judgments for the evaluators. It is essential, therefore, that such individuals be impressed with the importance of their task, the need for careful analysis, and the necessity to guard against personal bias. Best results are obtained if job specification writers back up their judgments with specific reasons for their decisions.

The style of writing job specifications is not so rigid and formal as that in job descriptions. Certain suggestions, however, may be made: complicated sentences and unnecessary detail should be avoided; terms indicating quantity, degree, or duration of a factor should be the most precise available; devices, tools, and equipment should be carefully identified and the manner of use specified; and judgments must be backed up with justification.

After job specifications have been written in first-draft form, it is wise to submit them to workers assigned to the job and to the supervisor for approval. This step not only helps to insure accuracy, but also helps to convince the readers that a sincere attempt has been made to be accurate.

Although the particular form and organization of job specifications are dictated largely by the compensable factors chosen for use, an example (Figure 9) will assist the reader to perceive the general form.

DETERMINING COMPENSABLE FACTORS

After jobs have been studied and job information obtained, the next step in the job evaluation process is determining what factor or factors are to be used to determine the position of a job in the job hierarchy. These are the compensable factors or job-related contributions. Because these compensable factors are the yardsticks used to compare jobs to establish their position in the job hierarchy, they are

Job Title _____ *Pattern Maker–Wood* _____

Dictionary Title _____ Code No. _____ *540–* _____

Department _____ *1521* _____

Education

This job involves the use of decimals, fractions, and geometry. The incumbent must work from complex drawings. He must have a thorough knowledge of the pattern-making trade, including basic design and construction of pattern equipment, use of hand and power woodworking tools, knowledge of foundry and machine shop practice.

Experience

Up to 9 years are required to become familiar with the design and construction of large and complicated pattern equipment.

Initiative–Ingenuity

This job involves highly diversified work. The employee must construct, alter and repair wooden pattern equipment that is used to produce large castings of complicated design. He must possess a high degree of judgment, initiative, and ingenuity to convert engineers' casting specifications into layouts and models, make allowances for coremaking, molding, cleaning and machining operations, construct all pattern, core box and related equipment necessary to produce a rough casting of desired size and shape.

Physical

Light physical effort is required to use hand tools. Power woodworking operations may involve handling of average weight boards or pattern sections for short periods of time.

Mental–Visual

This job requires concentrated mental and visual attention necessary to work out problems involving the design construction, alteration, and repairing of complicated pattern equipment. The employee must be able to visualize pattern construction, core assembly, mold construction, and casting.

Equipment–Process

The equipment used consists of power saws, planers, joiners, shapers, hole shooter, drill press, lathe, and a wide variety of hand tools. Probable damage is seldom over $50.

Material–Product

Probable damage to materials due to errors in construction seldom over $100. Pattern-checkers follow the job from start to finish.

Safety of Others

Compliance with standard safety precautions necessary as careless use of hand or power tools, improper handling or positioning of patterns or lumber may result in injury to others.

Work of Others

The employee is responsible only for his own work.

Working Conditions

Some wood dust while performing sanding or turning operations. Infrequent job assignments may involve working in foundry for brief periods.

Unavoidable Hazards

There is a possibility of hand or arm injury while using power woodworking equipment or sharp edged hand tools. Improper handling or positioning of lumber or patterns by others may result in injury.

FIGURE 9

Job Specification—Pattern Maker—Wood

also the job-related contributions recognized and rewarded by the organization.

The model presented in Chapter 1 and the discussions of membership motivation theory and social stratification in Chapter 3 carry strong implications for determining compensable factors. Both the model and membership motivation theory show that contributions are perceived and evaluated by individuals. Individuals learn the contributions required by organizations and may have definite ideas about contributions they want to make. Presumably in the case of job-related contributions, individuals accept the fact that organizations require certain kinds of contributions and that different jobs require differing amounts of some contributions and different kinds of contributions. Presumably also, individuals accept the notion that the actual behavior required on jobs should determine the job-related contributions. The discussion of social stratification pointed out that occupation is the greatest single measure of status and that occupational status is determined by functional importance and by certain necessary attributes of members of the occupation.

These ideas suggest that determining compensable factors or job-related contributions is extremely important in securing membership motivation. They also suggest that the decision on compensable factors be a joint one. Although individuals evaluate their contributions to the employment exchange, they recognize that the employer must have certain contributions. But they also expect that the job-related contributions employed to determine the job hierarchy will be those actually required by the organization's jobs.

FACTORS

Before examining methods of determining compensable factors, it is desirable to attend to some technical considerations that the decision must satisfy. For example, to be useful in comparing jobs, factors must possess certain characteristics. (1) They must be present in different amounts in the various jobs. It is apparent that an attribute found in equal amounts in all jobs would be worthless in comparing jobs. (2) If more than one factor is chosen, they must not overlap in meaning. To the extent that two factors overlap, double weight may be given to one factor. (3) Employer, employee, and union viewpoints should be reflected in the factors chosen. (4) Factors selected must be found in all jobs or at least the jobs under study. Difficult job comparisons result when the factor does not apply to some of the jobs.

Entire Organization Versus Job Clusters. The last point involves the consideration of whether one factor or set of factors can be found that is applicable to all jobs in the organization, or whether the jobs must be divided into groups or clusters to which different factors apply. Thus, when the question "What job-related contributions is this organization paying for?" is raised, the immediate answer may be, "That depends on the type of job being considered." If it is decided that no one factor or set of factors applies to all jobs in the organization, the problem becomes one of determining the factor(s) for groups of jobs. On the other hand, it is possible that a decision be reached that one factor or one set of factors encompasses the job-related contributions on all jobs. It may be decided, for example, that job difficulty or the importance of the job to the organization is sufficient. Similarly, it may be decided that the compensable factors applicable to all of the jobs in the organization are skill, responsibility, effort, and working conditions. Or, factors such as job monotony or fatigue potential may be chosen. The important consideration is that the factor or factors selected come from a conscious, careful judgment made in full possession of job facts.

It is apparent that this decision-making process requires thought and analysis. It may happen that a long list of factors suggests itself at first but that careful analysis will reveal that one or a limited number of factors will suffice.

Key Jobs. At least in large organizations, key jobs are important reference points. Since key jobs are related to non-key jobs and to one another, economy of effort suggests employing key jobs rather than all jobs as a source of data for compensable factors. Because key jobs provide the channel of relationships among job groups, they furnish guides to whether given compensable factors are useful for job comparisons within and between job groups.

Job Clusters. Perhaps more frequently than not, the conclusion will be reached early in the process that no one compensable factor or set of factors applies to all the jobs in the organization. In this case, it will be necessary to classify the jobs into groups or clusters.[23] Thus, for example, an organization's jobs may be divided into shop jobs, clerical jobs, sales jobs, engineering jobs, supervisory jobs, and executive jobs. Within each of these larger clusters, smaller groups exist, such as the inspection group or maintenance group in factory jobs. Departments, skill families, or work crews may represent pertinent job groups. Livernash has shown how job content comparisons are stronger within narrow clusters, somewhat weaker among broader clusters or functional

---

[23]A cluster is a group of jobs that are linked together by technology, administrative organization (promotion, transfer sequences), or social custom so that they have common wage-making characteristics. John T. Dunlop, in George W. Taylor and Frank C. Pierson (eds.), *New Concepts in Wage Determination* (New York: McGraw-Hill Book Company, 1957), p. 129.

groups, and weakest among broad clusters.[24] It may be that different compensable factors are required for even narrow job clusters. Present-day job evaluation practice, however, usually deals with broad job clusters or functional groups.

Employees on jobs within a cluster are likely to make job comparisons. The relationships are influenced by custom and tradition as well as the promotion and transfer sequences of the organization.

Such a classification of jobs into clusters may, in most organizations, be justified by experience. Experience justifies the prediction that the wages of jobs in different job clusters will not always move together and in equal amounts. Because there are differences in timing and amplitude of movement of values for different types of services, job cluster differentiation has an economic justification. Jobs in the same cluster thus appear to have their own set of compensable factors.

A decision is, therefore, necessary. In view of the variation in degree of relationships among jobs and job groups, is there one set of compensable factors that will permit realistic job comparisons or must different factors be found for at least broad job clusters? The usual job evaluation practice, at least in large organizations, is to employ separate compensable factors and separate job evaluation plans for each broad functional group.

In this way, it may be decided that the "clerical cluster" is being paid for academic content of jobs, length of preparatory training period, variety of problems encountered and dealt with on the employee's responsibility, seriousness of possible errors, responsibility for handling confidential information, and so on. In the executive cluster, the compensable factor selected may be the level of basic types of responsibilities delegated. Thus, for one cluster, there may be only one factor selected, whereas for another cluster several may be needed.

If different compensable factors are found to be applicable to different clusters, there is justification for carrying through the entire evaluation of jobs in one cluster at a time—which is what happens in most organizations. Factory jobs, for example, may be evaluated first, followed by clerical jobs, and so on.

METHODS OF DETERMINING FACTORS

Apparently very little study has been devoted to the process of determining compensable factors. Although most observers and students of job evaluation agree that successful plans are tailormade to the requirements of an individual organization, no guides are available to

[24]E. Robert Livernash, in Taylor and Pierson, *New Concepts,* pp. 148–153.

the parties for selecting factors on which the plan is to be based. Of course, lists of factors employed by others are available (see Figure 10), but beyond this aid the parties are on their own.

Perhaps the major reason for this lack of study of the process of determining compensable factors is the wide use of ready-made plans designed by employer associations and modifications of such plans by consultants. It may be that most organizations make such modifications of existing plans as seem appropriate or devise their plan by adapting parts of a number of existing plans.

Information is available, of course, on how the most used ready-made plans were designed. For example, the NMTA-NEMA plan (discussed in Chapter 7) was designed by a group of twenty-five experienced men who knew the fifty key jobs involved intimately. These men were asked to review the descriptions of the key jobs and to list all the job characteristics, requirements, conditions, and so on, which, in their opinion, should be considered in determining the values of the jobs. The group came up with a list of 90 job attributes or characteristics. This list of 90 compensable factors was first reduced to 15 and later to 11 by eliminating (1) factors common to all jobs in equal amount and thus not useful in determining relative value, (2) factors that applied to people rather than to jobs, and (3) factors that overlapped so greatly that one measured the other.[25] Benge and his associates, through a similar process, arrived at five factors for the factor comparison method. The United States Department of Labor, as a result of years of analyzing jobs in all types of establishments and considerable research, has determined that worker functions involved with data, people, and things, and worker traits required by jobs, are factors applicable to all jobs.

One study of job evaluation plans suggests that the factors may be reduced to job importance and job difficulty, which represent, respectively, simulated demand and supply factors as substitutes for hidden real demand and supply factors.[26] Unfortunately, this viewpoint implies that the employment exchange is solely an economic transaction, a view rejected in this book. Behrend[27] has shown that a major problem of incentive plans is that they imply that effort is the only job-related contribution recognized by the organization. But employees are aware, whether organizations are or not, that organizations require job-related

[25]Verne Fisher, "What's Right with Job Evaluation," *Industrial Management* (April, 1961), pp. 21–27.

[26]Edward Harry Bowman, *Executive Job Evaluation in the Insurance Industry,* Ph.D. dissertation (Ohio State University, 1954, L.C. Card No. MC 59-6621).

[27]Hilde Behrend, "The Effort Bargain," *Industrial and Labor Relations Review* (July, 1957), pp. 503–515.

Skill

Education
Education or Mental Development
Education or Trade Knowledge
Schooling
Experience
Previous Experience
Experience and Training
Training Time
Time Required to Become 80% Efficient
Training Required
Time Required to Learn Trade
Time Required to Adapt Skill
Job Knowledge
Knowledge of Machinery and Dexterity
    with Tools
Knowledge of Materials and Processes
Knowledge
Mentality

Accuracy
Ingenuity
Initiative and Ingenuity
Judgment and Initiative
Mental Capability
Intelligence
Resourcefulness
Versatility
Job Skill
Manual Dexterity
Dexterity
Degree of Skill and Accuracy
Manual Accuracy and Quickness
Physical Skill
Details
Aptitude Required
Difficulty of Operation
Ability to do Detailed Work
Social Skill

Effort

Mental Effort
Mental Application
Mental or Visual Demand
Concentration
Visual Application
Physical Effort
Physical Application
Physical Demand

Physical or Mental Fatigue
Muscular or Nerve Strain
Fatigue Due to Eye Strain
Fatigue
Honesty of Effort
Monotony of Work
Monotony and Comfort

Responsibility (for)

Safety of Others
Material or Product
Equipment or Process
Machinery and Equipment
Material and Equipment
Work of Others
Supervision of Others
Supervision Exercised
Cost of Errors
Effect on Other Operations
Necessary Accuracy in Checking, Counting
    and Weighing

Spoilage of Materials
Protection of Materials
Equipment
Product
Physical Property
Plant and Services
Cooperation and Personality
Dependability
Adjustability
Coordination
Details to Master
Quality

Working Conditions

Unavoidable Hazards
Hazards Involved
Exposure to Health Hazard
Exposure to Accident Hazard
Occupational Hazard Disease
Danger–Accident from Machinery or
    Equipment
Danger–from Lifting

Surroundings
Dirtiness of Working Conditions
Environment
Job Conditions
Difficulty in Locating Work Elsewhere
Attendance
Disagreeableness

FIGURE 10

Factors Selected for Factory Point–Rating Systems

Skill

Mental Requirement
Mentality
Mental Application
Creative Ability
Judgment
Analytical Ability
Initiative
Resourcefulness
Versatility
Skill Requirements
Complexity of Duties
Personal Qualifications Needed for the
  Job
Personal Requirements
Ability to Make Decisions
Managerial Techniques
Character of Supervision
  Given
Difficulty of Work

Education
Preparation for the Job
Essential Education and
  Knowledge
Basic Knowledge and
  Experience
Experience, Knowledge and Training
  Necessary
Previous Experience
Training Time
Experience and Training
Capacity for Getting Along with
  Others
Capacity for Self Expression
Social Skill
Ability to do Detailed Work
Ability to do Routine Work
Manual or Motor Skill
Office Machine Operation
Manual Dexterity

Effort

Physical Requirement
Physical Application
Physical Effort
Physical Demand
Physical or Mental
  Fatigue

Manual Effort
Pressure of Work
Mental Effort
Volume of Work
Attention Demand

Responsibility (for)

Executive Responsibility
Personnel
Supervision of Others
Work of Others
Monetary Responsibility
Commitments, Property, Money or
  Records
Company Cash
Dependability and
  Accuracy
Accuracy
Details
Quality
Effect of Errors

Material
Equipment
Records
Confidential Data
Methods
Determining Company Policy
Market
Contact with Others
Contact with Public, Customers, and
  Personnel
Goodwill and Public Relations
Cooperation and Personality

Working Conditions

Job Conditions
Tangible Surroundings
Intangible Conditions
Working Conditions

Personal Hazard
Monotony
Attention to Details
Out-of-Town Travel

FIGURE 10 (Cont.)

Factors Selected for Clerical Point-Rating Systems

Source: Jay L. Otis and Richard H. Leukart, *Job Evaluation* (Englewood Cliffs, N. J.: Prentice-Hall, Inc., 1948), pp. 90-91. Reprinted by permission.

contributions that are difficult to reduce to strictly economic terms. To provide a basis for a job evaluation plan acceptable to the employer, employees, and the union, the factors must somehow represent their respective judgments on equity as measured by contribution.

Keeping all these considerations in mind, a number of methods by which an individual organization may determine applicable compensable factors suggest themselves. The most obvious is for the parties to distill compensable factors from job descriptions. A committee could be asked to list compensable factors suggested by job descriptions and to edit the list to arrive at those most useful. Perhaps a list of factors such as Figure 10 could be studied by members as possibilities before they turned to job descriptions.

This method suggests that if the parties decide that responsibility, skill, effort, and willingness to work under certain working conditions are acceptable compensable factors, any of a large number of ready-made job evaluation plans would be acceptable to them. If, however, they decide that the jobs imply compensable factors not found in ready-made plans, a custom-built plan is required.

Research by the author and a colleague suggests the use of a questionnaire to determine the importance of various contributions to employee groups. Such a questionnaire has been developed and tested,[28] but agreement also would be required on separating job-related from performance and personal contributions. An experimental instrument shows promise of measuring the relative weights that employee groups believe should be attached to various contributions.

Still another approach to determining compensable factors is to solicit the opinions of union leaders. Joint union-management job evaluation is, after all, a process of communicating the job-related contributions that members are making and that organizations require.

An interesting development concerning compensable factors is the use of the things, data, and people functional hierarchies of jobs in a supplement to the *Dictionary of Occupational Titles.*[29] Using the proportionate involvement of the job with data, people, and things and level of involvement, it was found possible to represent the entire range of functions in jobs throughout the occupational spectrum. It is significant that these factors are those that the theory of social stratification

[28]D. W. Belcher and T. J. Atchison, "Equity Theory and Compensation Policy," *Personnel Administration* (July–August, 1970), pp. 22–33; T. J. Atchison and D. W. Belcher, "Equity, Rewards and Compensation Administration," *Personnel Administration* (March–April, 1971), pp. 32–36.

[29]U.S. Department of Labor, *Selected Characteristics of Occupations (Physical Demands, Working Conditions, Training),* 1966—A Supplement to the *Dictionary of Occupational Titles,* 3rd ed. (Washington, D.C.: United States Government Printing Office, 1966). See also U.S. Department of Labor, *Handbook for Analyzing Jobs.*

suggests determine the functional importance of occupations. In addition, the relationship between the things, data, people hierarchies, and the proportion of prescribed and discretionary tasks pointed out by Jaques has been noted.[30] Jaques[31] states that all jobs contain prescribed and discretionary tasks and that the proportion of discretionary tasks increases in higher-level jobs. Jaques' suggested single compensable factor (time-span of discretion) may thus encompass discretion with respect to things, data, and people. Although, as was mentioned in Chapter 3, Jaques' approach has not attained wide usage, other plans employing a single factor similar to time-span of discretion have been developed and used.[32]

[30]Sidney A. Fine, *The 1965 Third Edition of the Dictionary of Occupational Titles —Content, Contrasts, and Critique* (Kalamazoo, Michigan: The Upjohn Institute for Employment Research, December, 1968).

[31]Elliott Jaques, *Equitable Payment* (New York: John Wiley and Sons, Inc., 1961).

[32]S. J. Goldenberg, "Significant Difference: A Method of Job Evaluation," *Canadian Personnel and Industrial Relations Journal* (May, 1968), pp. 19–23 (judgment used); A. W. Charles, "Installing Single-Factor Job Evaluation," *Compensation Review* (First Quarter, 1971), pp. 9–21 (problem-solving).

6

Job Evaluation–
Nonquantitative Methods

DEVELOPING OR CHOOSING A SYSTEM

After compensable factors have been chosen, the next step in job evaluation is to develop or select a system that will make it possible to evaluate jobs in accordance with the amount and level of the factors present in jobs. In this step, the organization may adopt a ready-made system in use in another organization, modify an existing system, or develop a new one.

Actually there are only a limited number of methods of comparing jobs. These methods are incorporated into the basic job evaluation methods; that is, ranking, classification, factor-comparison, and point methods. Any job evaluation system adopted by an organization will make use of a basic method of comparing jobs.

Whether to use a ready-made system or a custom-built system, however, depends mainly on whether a ready-made system can be found that is based on compensable factors identical to those selected by the organization. If such a ready-made system can be found, it is advantageous to use it. There are advantages to be gained by using a system operating successfully in another organization if such a system fits the needs of the organization under study. Among these advantages are ease of comparing wage data and standardization of job titles. Equally important, adopting a ready-made plan saves the time and effort of developing a plan.

If, however, the compensable factors selected are not contained in a ready-made system, a system is developed. This may involve modifying a ready-made system or developing a completely new system. Modification is applicable where only a few of the compensable factors in the organization differ from those in the ready-made system. If many differences are apparent, a custom-built system is called for.

In any case, the job evaluation system finally applied to the organization should be based on the compensable factors determined to be applicable to its jobs.[1] Any apparent advantage to be gained from the use of a ready-made system is lost if factors inherent in the system do not apply to the organization.

The first decision probably should involve the method to be used in comparing jobs. The ranking and classification methods are relatively simple in that no attempt is made to obtain quantitative measures of job value. For this reason, they are often referred to as nonquantitative methods. The factor comparison and point methods of job comparison are more complex. They may be referred to as quantitative methods because of the quantitative job values developed through the use of the methods. As a basis for the decision on the method of job comparison to be employed and the job evaluation system to be utilized, it will be useful to examine the basic methods and some modifications of these methods.

According to a number of surveys, the ranking and classification methods (the nonquantitative methods) are used much less often than quantitative methods. Surveys in the United States tend to reveal that the nonquantitative methods are found in 10 per cent or less of responding organizations.[2] A large British survey found that of 2,065 job evaluation plans, 20 per cent were ranking plans and 28 per cent were grading plans, with a tendency for both types to be less used in larger organizations.[3]

Interpreting such surveys is somewhat difficult, however. There may be a trend toward the use of less complex plans stemming from (1) research results that show that less complex systems yield results almost identical with complicated systems, and (2) growing awareness that employee understanding and acceptance is more easily obtained with less complex plans. Also, the surveys may grossly underrate the prevalence of grade description or classification plans in that the great majority of federal, state, county, and municipal jobs are classified by this

---

[1]J. S. Gray, "Custom Made Systems of Job Evaluation," *Journal of Applied Psychology* (December, 1950), pp. 378–380.

[2]R. C. Smyth, "Job Evaluation Plans," *Factory Management and Maintenance* (February, 1951), pp. 118–121; "Job Evaluation: A Survey of Company Practice," *Management Review* (April, 1957), pp. 42–44; E. Lanham, *Job Evaluation* (New York: McGraw-Hill Book Co., 1955), p. 47; John A. Patton, "Job Evaluation in Practice: Some Survey Findings," *AMA Research Report Number 54* (New York: American Management Association, 1961), pp. 73–77; K. O. Mann, "Characteristics of Job Evaluation Programs," *Personnel Administration* (September–October, 1965), pp. 45–47.

[3]National Board for Prices and Incomes, "Job Evaluation," *Report No. 83 (Supplement)* (London: Her Majesty's Stationery Office, September, 1968), p. 8.

method.[4] Such plans are not recorded in surveys of nongovernment organizations.

THE JOB-RANKING METHOD

As the title implies, the ranking method ranks the jobs in the organization from highest to lowest. It is the simplest of the job evaluation methods and the easiest to explain. Another advantage is that the ranking method takes less time to accomplish than other methods.

Its disadvantages are attributable more to the way the method is used than to the method itself, although straight ranking can handle only a limited number of jobs. For example, the ranking method has often been employed without first securing job facts. The lack of job facts has made it essential to find individuals in the organization who know all or many of the jobs well. The difficulty of finding such people is cited as a disadvantage of the ranking method, although the availability of job facts makes this disadvantage a less serious one.

Similarly, rankers are asked to keep the "whole job" in mind and are given instructions merely to rank the jobs. This results in different bases of comparison among raters and conscious or unconscious influence by such factors as present pay rate, competence of job incumbents, and prestige values of jobs. This difficulty can be overcome by selecting one or more compensable factors and informing raters to rank jobs on the basis of those factors. Such instructions give the rater not only a basis for job comparison, but also a method of eliminating outside influences.

If the ranking method is set up in accordance with the job evaluation process, it may be expected to yield the advantages cited and to minimize the disadvantages.

STEPS IN THE RANKING METHOD

1. Obtain Job Information.   As specified by the job evaluation process, the first step is job analysis. Job descriptions for each job are prepared. Sometimes job specifications also are prepared. Because those using a ranking method will probably limit compensable factors to one or perhaps two, however, it is difficult to write job specifications in these terms. What may be more desirable, if specifications are desired, would be to use general job requirements such as those included in the USES job analysis report.

[4]The term "classification studies" is the governmental synonym for job evaluation.

2. Select Raters and Jobs to Be Rated. Most organizations have too many jobs to permit raters to know all the jobs well. Since this is adjudged to be desirable, the usual procedure is to rank jobs by department. In fact, for this reason the ranking method is sometimes called the *departmental order-of-importance* method. It is less difficult to find raters who know the jobs in a single department.

Another reason for a breakdown by department is that it is difficult to rank different clusters of jobs together. Thus, for example, it is very difficult to compare directly shop jobs and clerical jobs. However, if one compensable factor is selected for all jobs, comparison in terms of this factor is possible.

Raters who will attempt to make unbiased judgments are selected. They are trained in rating procedure, although less training is perhaps required for ranking than for other types or rating.

3. Select Compensable Factor(s). This step determines the basis on which job comparison is to be made. One factor, such as job difficulty, may be used, or more than one factor may be used. Also, a procedure is laid down for the consistent application of the factor(s). Finally, the definition of the factor(s) is carefully explained to the raters so that rankings will be based on the factor(s) selected. If job specifications are to be written in terms of the compensable factor(s) selected, they are written at this point.

4. Rank Jobs. Either of two methods may be used for obtaining job ranks—the card-sorting method or the paired-comparison method. In the first method, raters are furnished with cards (one for each job) on which job titles and job descriptions are written. Actually, although less convenient, actual job descriptions or even job specifications might be used. Then the raters are asked to rank the jobs from highest to lowest.

Although ranking may be accomplished in this manner if a limited number of jobs are involved, it becomes difficult to make distinctions if many jobs must be ranked. Another method may be advantageous in such circumstances. It might be called the "best of the best and poorest of the poorest" method of ranking and involves separating jobs into piles. First, jobs are divided into two piles. Then each of these piles is divided, and so on, until sufficient breakdown is achieved.

The paired-comparison method is perhaps capable of yielding the most accurate and reliable rankings. In this method, the rater compares each job with every other job on which ratings are required. Either of two techniques may be used to facilitate this comparison. In the first, the rater is provided with slips of paper on which two jobs appear and is asked to indicate which of the two he ranks higher. Sufficient slips are provided so that each job is compared to every other job at least once and, preferably, twice. To guard against unconscious bias, the order in which jobs appear on the slips is randomized, and an effort is made to see that a particular job appears last as often as it does first.

A second technique is to provide the rater with a table such as is illustrated in Figure 11, and ask him to check the higher of two jobs indicated by the cells of the table. The number of times a job is checked establishes its rank. This second technique is more convenient for the rater to use.

	Cost Clerk	File Clerk	Addresso-graph Opr.	Ledger Clerk	Junior Typist	Order Clerk	Mes-senger	Total
Cost Clerk								
File Clerk								
Addresso-graph Opr.								
Ledger Clerk								
Junior Typist								
Order Clerk								
Messenger								

FIGURE 11

Paired-Comparison Table

5. Combine Ratings.   It is advisable to have several raters rank the jobs independently. When this step has been completed, averaging the ranks to arrive at a composite rating is sufficiently accurate.

As mentioned, discussions of the ranking method speak of ranking the job as a whole. This presumably means that only one compensable factor (such as difficulty or importance) is employed. If more than one compensable factor is employed, the jobs are ranked on each factor and the factors bear equal weight, averaging the ranks to achieve a composite job rank seems still properly called the ranking method. If, however, the factors are assigned different weights, the plan is similar to the factor-comparison plan discussed in the next chapter.

Also, the ranking method is usually assumed to be primarily applicable to small organizations in which all the jobs can be placed into one ranking. In larger organizations, jobs are ranked by department and the departmental rankings are dovetailed by the committee.

Computers are making it possible to achieve the advantages of the ranking method without the limitation of numbers. The paired-comparison method can handle any number of raters, jobs, and factors when the computer compiles the results. One consultant assembles a committee of workers and management and has each member rank the jobs on overall importance using paired comparisons. After each rater has ranked the jobs three times, the results are fed into a computer that produces a rank-order list of jobs.[5] If desired, a more complex method is produced by having the raters rank the jobs on overall importance and a set of factors. These results are fed into the computer along with market rates to produce factors' weightings and a range of scores for each factor. This approach achieves both employee involvement and employee understanding because of simplicity.

THE JOB-CLASSIFICATION METHOD

The classification or grade description method of job evaluation involves defining a number of classes or grades of jobs and fitting jobs into the classes provided. Figuratively, the method may be described as a series of carefully labeled shelves in a bookcase. The primary task is to describe each of the classes so that no difficulty is experienced in fitting each job into its proper niche. Jobs are then classified by comparing each job to the descriptions provided.

This method of comparing jobs has the major advantage that most organizations, and employees as well, tend to classify jobs. With this fact as a beginning point, it may be relatively easy to secure agreement about the classification of most jobs. The classification method also promotes thinking about job classes among both executives and employees. If jobs are thought of as belonging in a certain grade, all the problems of compensation administration become easier to solve. In fact, many organizations, after completing job evaluation by another method, clas-

[5]"Computer-Assisted Job Evaluation," *The Executive* (New Zealand, March 1, 1970), pp. 15–16.

sify jobs into grades to aid in wage administration. This point deserves emphasis. When jobs have been placed in grades or classes subsequent to job evaluation by any method or even by informal decision or agreement, it is not unusual to find these grades the major focus of actual compensation administration. When jobs change or new jobs emerge, they may be placed in the job structure by decision or negotiation. It may be necessary to employ the formal job evaluation plan only infrequently if agreement cannot be reached without it.

Perhaps the major advantage of the method is its flexibility. Although most discussions of the grade-description method suggest that it is most useful for organizations with relatively few jobs, it has been used successfully by the largest organization in the world (the U.S. government) for a long period of years. In fact, it is the primary job evaluation method at most levels of government in the U.S. In such use, it has been able to classify successfully millions of kinds and levels of jobs.

Advocates of the classification method hold that job evaluation by any method involves much judgment and that this method permits classification of all kinds and levels of jobs flexibly but with sufficient precision to achieve employee and management acceptance and organization purposes. Although the U.S. government has investigated quantitative job evaluation,[6] it has been concluded that the wide range of jobs covered required the adaptability of the classification method. It has been suggested that applying quantitative systems in government would cost much more than the additional accuracy warrants.[7] But quantitative job evaluation has been spreading in local government installations in the U.S., often at the insistence of unions.

Disadvantages of the grade description method are (1) difficulty of writing grade descriptions and (2) judgment required in applying them. Because the grading method considers the job as a whole, compensable factors are unweighted and unscored, which means that the factors have equal weight and little of one is balanced by much of another. Thus, terms that express the amount of compensable factors in jobs in the grade are depended on to distinguish one grade from another. Also, it is quite possible that a given grade could include jobs requiring high skill and other jobs that require little skill but carry heavy responsibility.

Grade-description methods customarily employ a number of compensable factors. They typically emphasize difficulty of the work but also include performance requirements. The federal classification sys-

[6]U.S. Civil Service Commission, "Classification Principles and Policies," *Personnel Management Series No. 16* (Washington, D.C.: U.S. Government Printing Office, June, 1963), pp. 10–11.

[7]C. F. Lutz, "Quantitative Job Evaluation in Local Government in the United States," *International Labour Review* (June, 1969), pp. 607–619.

tem, for example, employs the following compensable factors: (1) difficulty and variety of work, (2) supervision received and exercised, (3) judgment exercised, (4) originality required, (5) nature and purpose of interpersonal work relationships, (6) responsibility, (7) experience, (8) knowledge required.

Terms used to distinguish differing amounts of compensable factors of necessity require judgment in the application of grade descriptions. For example, making distinctions among simple, routine, varied, and complex work and among limited, shared, and independent judgment, although quite possible, is not automatic. Also, because the classification method deals with the whole job, there may be a tendency in writing grade descriptions to employ some compensable factors only at certain levels rather than to use all compensable factors throughout. Grade descriptions of higher grades tend to be longer than those of lower grades and much more complex.

Given the long experience of governments with classification plans and the ready availability of these plans to any organization that might wish to use the grade descriptions and grading standards, it is somewhat suprising that private industry in the U.S. has made so little use of the grade-description method. It is even more surprising when it is remembered that using these plans would be free, whereas other ready-made plans usually require paying the fees of a consultant.

STEPS IN THE CLASSIFICATION METHOD

1. Obtain Job Information. The classification method, like the ranking method, if it is to function properly, begins with job analysis. Job descriptions are written for each job. Job specifications written in terms of compensable factors may be prepared.

2. Separate Jobs by Type. The next step in the grade-description method is to classify jobs by kind. Well-defined classes are used, such as shop jobs, clerical jobs, sales jobs, and so on. Even if only one compensable factor is to be used in classifying all jobs by level, it is wise to grade each kind of job individually.

3. Select Compensable Factors. At this stage a decision must be made on the factor(s) to be used in grading jobs. One factor such as job complexity may be selected for all kinds of jobs, or several factors may be used.

4. Develop Grade Descriptions. The next step involves writing grade descriptions that describe each class in terms of amount or level of compensable factor(s) in jobs. This may be accomplished by writing one statement applicable to a given class or by writing a series of grading rules that, when used, enable raters to classify all jobs of a given kind.

Part of this step is determining the number of classes or grades. The number of classes into which types of jobs are to be grouped will depend on (1) tradition, (2) the range of skills, (3) the wage or salary range of the jobs in the group, and (4) the organization's promotion policy. If a union is involved and a joint union-management job evaluation is being conducted, the number of grades is normally a matter of joint decision. In general, seven to fourteen classes will meet the needs of most types of jobs. Also, it is possible for different types of jobs to make use of different numbers of classes. Thus, shop jobs may have eight grades whereas clerical jobs have fourteen. In small organizations the number of classes may be smaller.

A committee is usually assigned the task of writing the grade descriptions or grading rules. In this task use is made of job information applying to the jobs to be evaluated. Usually, the grade descriptions of the two extreme grades are written first, then the others. If grading rules are used, these rules specify the amount or level of the compensable factor(s) that places a job in a particular class.

Actually, grade descriptions may be written either before or after classification of jobs. In small companies jobs may be classified and the job information applicable to jobs in a grade may be used in writing grade descriptions. This is essentially what is done when jobs are first evaluated by other job evaluation systems and then placed in grades for administrative convenience. Usual practice in the grade-description method calls for writing descriptions first. Grade descriptions may include typical jobs that fall into the class.

5. Classify Jobs. The committee charged with writing grade descriptions is often also assigned the task of classifying jobs. Job classification involves comparing job information with grade descriptions or grading rules. Each job is placed in its appropriate niche by checking its job description or job specification against the grade descriptions or grading rules.

Sometimes the process of classifying jobs is combined with the process of writing grade descriptions. Thus, descriptions of the two extreme grades are written first and jobs are classified into these grades. Then the remaining jobs have two extreme classes. These two grade descriptions are then written and the jobs are classified. The process continues until all jobs are classified.

SUMMARY

The job-ranking and job-classification methods of job evaluation comprise the nonquantitative methods. These two methods of job comparison place the job into a hierarchy (a job structure) without any attempt to attach numerical values to jobs. In this they differ from the quantitative methods (factor comparison and point), which result in scores or values as well as a job structure.

The nonquantitative methods may be successfully utilized in all types of organizations and jobs. Careful use of such plans can achieve a workable job structure with a minimum of time and effort.

7

Job Evaluation–
Quantitative Methods

Nonquantitative methods of job evaluation were described in the preceding chapter. This chapter deals with the quantitative methods. The latter differ primarily from the former in that they provide numerical values for jobs in addition to a job structure. In the quantitative methods of job comparison, separate judgments are made on each factor, a numerical value is attached to each factor, and these values are summed to obtain a job value.

Proponents of the quantitative methods believe that making several separate judgments with respect to each job and attaching numerical values to these judgments make the job evaluation more precise. They believe that such methods make possible a more thorough analysis of job value and a finer classification within job structures.

The two major job evaluation methods using numerical values in deriving a job structure are the factor-comparison method and the point method. The former may be thought of as a refinement of the ranking method because jobs are compared directly in both. Similarly, the point method is similar to the classification method in that jobs are compared indirectly through a written scale.

Most existing job evaluation plans are quantitative. Surveys indicate that point plans represent from 50 per cent to 85 per cent of job evaluation plans in the U.S. and that factor-comparison plans account for about 10 per cent.[1] Many job evaluation plans are combinations of

[1]John A. Patton, "Job Evaluation in Practice: Some Survey Findings," *AMA Management Report Number 54* (New York: American Management Association, 1961), pp. 73–77; K. O. Mann, "Characteristics of Job Evaluation Programs," *Personnel Administration* (September–October, 1965), pp. 45–47; Prentice-Hall, Inc., *Personnel Management —Policies and Practices* (November 1, 1966), 15, 103.

point and factor comparison. The large British survey cited previously found that about 50 per cent of plans were point plans and about 5 per cent factor-comparison plans. Industrywide and national job evaluation are almost always quantitative plans.

FACTOR-COMPARISON METHOD

The factor-comparison method of job evaluation compares jobs by making judgments concerning which jobs contain more of certain compensable factors than others. Jobs are compared to one another, one factor at a time. Original judgments, pertaining to key jobs, permit construction of a job comparison scale to which other jobs may be compared. The compensable factors used in the method are usually (1) mental requirements, (2) physical requirements, (3) skill requirements, (4) responsibility, and (5) working conditions, or combinations of these factors. It is apparent that the authors of the method[2] consider these to be "universal factors" found in all jobs. Thus, one job comparison scale applicable to all jobs in the organization would be possible. This practice is often followed in installations of the factor-comparison method. A separate job comparison scale, however, can be developed for each job cluster.

As previously mentioned, the factor-comparison method is a refinement of the ranking method in that jobs are compared on a number of factors and the results are combined and assigned a numerical value. Thus, ranking methods employing more than one compensable factor and different weights for the factors are essentially factor-comparison plans. Also, the practice of assigning factor weights statistically by computer from factor rankings and market rates employs the factor-comparison concept. So also does the use of job titles as examples of factor levels in other types of job evaluation plans. The point is that although the basic factor-comparison plan is used less often than point plans, concepts from the factor-comparison plan have found wide application.

ADVANTAGES

A major advantage of the factor-comparison method is the requirement that a custom-built installation be made in each organization. Thus, whenever the method is used, a job comparison scale is

---

[2]Eugene J. Benge, Samuel L. H. Burk, and Edward N. Hay, *Manual of Job Evaluation* (New York: Harper and Brothers, 1941).

constructed in terms of the jobs that exist in the organization. This practice of tailormaking a job evaluation system may make the results a better fit to the organization. Previous discussion of the job evaluation process stressed the desirability of such an approach. The flexibility permitted by the custom-built nature of installations has been cited as an additional advantage of the method.

Another advantage of this method is the availability of careful instructions covering installation steps.[3] In fact, the originators believe that the method is sufficiently clear to permit comparable results whether used by management, representatives of employees, or an outside consultant.

The type of job comparison utilized by the factor-comparison method may be cited as another advantage. Jobs are compared to other jobs to determine a relative value. Since relative job values are the results sought, this method of comparison is logical. Actually, this advantage has encouraged job comparison in other methods of job evaluation. For example, it has been mentioned that grade descriptions used in job classification methods often mention titles of jobs representative of that grade. Similarly, some point systems include job titles in defining degrees of factors.

Limiting factors to five or less is another advantage of the factor-comparison method. A limited number of factors tends to reduce the possibility of overlapping, with consequent overweighting of factors.

Still another advantage is the ease with which the resulting job comparison scale can be used. It is not difficult to train employees and union representatives in the use of the scale. Also, once employees have become familiar with a job comparison scale covering one type of job, evaluating other types of jobs may be simplified.

The use of a monetary unit in many systems employing the factor-comparison method is considered by some to be an advantage in that use of a job comparison scale often permits pricing the job as soon as job level is established. It is questionable, however, whether this advantage is sufficient to offset the disadvantage of possible bias being introduced by use of such units.

DISADVANTAGES

Perhaps the major disadvantage of the method is the use of "universal" factors. Discussion of the job evaluation process emphasized the

[3]Benge, Burk, and Hay, *op. cit.*; also Eugene J. Benge, *Job Evaluation and Merit Rating* (Deep River, Conn.: National Foremen's Institute, Inc., 1941).

importance of determining compensable factors applicable to the organization and the job clusters under study. Use of the same factors for all organizations and for all jobs in an organization runs counter to this approach.

Another disadvantage concerns the use made of key jobs by the factor-comparison method. A major criterion of key jobs in the factor-comparison method is the essential correctness of the pay rate. Since these key jobs are the basis of the job comparison scale, the usefulness of the scale depends on anchor points represented by these jobs. But jobs change, sometimes slowly and imperceptibly. To the extent that one or more key jobs change over time either without detection or without correction of the scale, users of the job comparison scale are basing decisions on what might be described figuratively as a badly warped ruler.

If monetary values of jobs are used in developing the job comparison scale, another disadvantage arises. Those charged with making the numerous judgments involved may be biased by such information and may unconsciously assign higher levels of the factors to a highly paid job even if such assignment is not justified. It should be noted that not all applications of the factor-comparison method use existing wage rates as a basis for judgment. If used, however, bias is probably encouraged.

Similarly, in using a job comparison scale after it has been completed, the fact that dollar-and-cent units are used may influence the evaluation of other than key jobs. Those using the scale are constantly reminded of the absolute values of jobs while they are attempting to determine the relative value of jobs. For purposes of reducing bias, it is helpful to clearly separate these two processes.

A serious disadvantage of the factor-comparison system is its complexity. The numerous and complicated steps involved in building the job comparison scale make it difficult to explain. If there is a question of confidence on the part of employees or their representatives, this complexity can make acceptance of the resulting wage structure difficult.

THE BASIC METHOD

Since the inception of the factor-comparison method of job evaluation, several variations in the basic method have appeared.[4] Some of the variations were devised to remove some of the disadvantages just

[4]See Edward N. Hay, "Four Methods of Establishing Factor Scales in Factor Comparison Job Evaluation," *The AMA Handbook of Wage and Salary Administration* (New York: American Management Association, 1950), pp. 56–65.

discussed. All such modifications, however, are based on the original method. For that reason, steps in the original method are outlined in detail before discussion of variations.

1. Analyze Jobs; Write Job Descriptions and Job Specifications. As in other job evaluation methods, the factor-comparison method begins with securing job information. Jobs are analyzed by job analysts, and job descriptions are written covering duties of each job. Although this is usual practice, a variation sometimes employed is to analyze only key jobs at this point, securing information on the remaining jobs after completing the job comparison scale.

Job specifications are written in terms of the five factors usually used with the factor-comparison method. Those writing job specifications are provided with a set of factor definitions such as those in Figure 12. Job specifications are recorded on a form similar to Figure 13.

Mental Requirements

When we speak of mental requirements, we have in mind those activities of a job which call upon the use of the intellect; also those personal traits required by the job such as judgment, patience, ability to work with others, etc. The individual that has these job requirements brings them to the job and does not have to acquire them later.

In addition, most jobs call for a certain amount of education. A job may call for the ability to read and write and do simple addition. On a job specification, this is indicated by a certain number of years of education. It does not mean that an individual must have attended school for that length of time, as he may have taught himself without the actual formal education.

Another sub-division of the mental requirement is work knowledge. If you were to hire a person to do messenger work throughout the city, you would want someone who knew the streets and how to go between specific points. This is an example of what we mean by work knowledge. It is basic information that a person must have relative to job requirements before he would be considered for the job.

Skill Requirements

Skill is the experience factor and is developed by actually doing the job. A person might learn what all the duties of a job are, but merely knowing the duties does not mean that he can do them speedily and accurately until he has had the necessary experience.

One type of skill is manual skill. This is the ability to develop muscular coordination by repetitive use of the hands, feet, arms, etc., as required on a job. A person must develop skill in such simple things as lifting, shoveling; as well as in more complex operations such as using a typewriter. They all take practice to do them properly, and practice simply means that muscles are trained to do that type of work.

Generally manual skills are learned fairly rapidly—some take a few hours and others a few weeks to gain the necessary speed and accuracy to do the work properly.

Another type of skill is what is termed sensory. Certain jobs require that certain senses such as sight, hearing, taste, touch, and smell be developed above the average to do the job properly. As an example, an auto mechanic learns to diagnose motor trouble by the sound of the running motor. A crane operator, through training his sense of sight, knows how to

FIGURE 12

Factor Definitions Used Under the Factor Comparison System

swing out the boom to proper position in order to place or pick up material without any lost time. This type of skill is generally more difficult to learn than a manual skill.

The third type of skill may be called mental skill. It is the type of skill which is used in making decisions based on past experience. It differs from mental requirements, which, as pointed out, are those mental abilities which a person brings to the job with him.

Mental skill can be seen in the decisions a supervisor makes in a given situation in order to get a certain piece of work out on time. From experience he knows how long it will normally take to do a job, given a certain number of workers, and he assigns them with this in mind. He has learned how to do these things by experience on the job; hence we term his ability "mental skill." It is very complex and is a higher type of skill than the other two.

Sub-divisions of the skill factor include necessary prior experience and time to learn and to become proficient.

Physical Factors

This factor refers to the demands of a job upon the human body. We will try to determine the exertion of bodily power, either in single actions or in a continued series of activities directed toward doing the job. We will consider whether the job demands standing, walking, sitting, lifting, bending, carrying, etc., and endeavor to break down total work time into the percentage spent on each type of physical effort.

The matter of comparing physical effort exerted on different jobs should not offer any great difficulty, and we will leave to committee discussions any clarifications of this factor. We might point out here that we are not trying to measure physical effort scientifically, but are endeavoring to arrange jobs in their relative positions with regard to this factor.

Responsibilities

There are certain responsibilities in every job for which the worker is accountable and must answer for nonperformance or wrong performance of his duties. Responsibility is evaluated in terms of the cost of failure to perform the duties properly, assuming the man is properly trained. Obviously, it is also assumed that he is not crazy or angry, or a saboteur who would willfully destroy.

Job specifications will endeavor to set out responsibilities in each job. We will specify whether the job calls for responsibility for equipment and whether it is for maintenance, operation of such equipment, or other factors relative to these. Also, we will consider responsibilities for tools and materials—for purchases, sales, sorting, storing, etc. Another division of responsibility is record-keeping, and others are supervision of men, directing and instructing others, money, methods and public contact.

Working Conditions

Under this factor, consideration is given to those influences which tend to make the job pleasant or disagreeable. It includes such items as place of work, whether it is indoors or outdoors, whether the job conditions are dirty, crowded, damp, hot, cold or otherwise unpleasant.

Under working conditions also are considered the hazards of a job, and type of accidents that may be inherent in the job.

FIGURE 12 (Cont.)

Source: Used by permission of Benge Associates, Management Engineers.

---

2. *Select Key Jobs.* With job information in hand, fifteen to twenty-five key jobs are selected by the job evaluation committee. Key jobs are benchmarks in the range of jobs under study and are thus selected so as to make them acceptable reference points. The task of selecting key jobs is an important one, for the entire method is built on them. In the original method, key jobs are assumed to carry correct rates of pay. In methods to be discussed later, this is not a requirement.

Job descriptions and job specifications are helpful in selecting key jobs. Committee discussion of this information should make possible selection of the requisite number of key jobs.

3. Rank Key Jobs by Factors.   Next, committee members are asked to rank the key jobs on each of the five factors, using job information as a basis for judgment. They are asked to make this ranking several different times to solidify their judgments. Then a meeting is held and some method found of obtaining composite ranks representing the judgment of the committee. Averaging may be employed if agreement among members is close. If not, discussion may be continued until a

Job Title Job Duties:	Dept.		Date No. Employed	
Mental	*Skill*	*Physical*	*Responsibility*	*Working Conditions*
___ years general education	Kind ___	Kind of physical effort:	Equipment	Work place
Special ed.:			Materials	Type of work
Kind of work knowledge:	Desirable prior experience:	___ % Standing ___ % Walking ___ % Sitting	Methods	Surroundings
Math used:	Time and proficiency:	Strength Fatigue	Records	Conditions
What records prepared?	Co. jobs which train for this:	Sex M___ F___		
Personal traits required:	This job leads to:	Eyesight requirements:	Supervisory	Hazards
	Other skill factors:	Other physical factors:	Other	

Prepared by_____ Approved by_____

FIGURE 13

Job Specification

group decision is reached. Committee rankings on key jobs by factors are exemplified by Table 1. Note that in the table the jobs are called "tentative" key jobs. They remain tentative until several judgments are made, after which they are either eliminated or become "true" key jobs.

TABLE 1

Average Ranks of 16 Tentative Key Jobs as Assigned by Committee

Job	AVERAGE RANK				
	Mental Require- ments	Physical Require- ments	Skill Require- ments	Responsi- bility	Working Con- ditions
Gager	2	13	2	3	15
Pattern Maker	1	12	1	1	16
Common Laborer	16	1	16	16	1
Power Shear Opr.	11	11	9	5	4
Plater	10	6	6	12	9
Riveter	12	3	12	14	8
Blacksmith	13	2	8	13	7
Punch Press Opr.	14	4	13	15	5
Automatic Screw Machine Opr.	4	8	3	2	13
Casting Inspector	3	7	4	4	10
Millwright	9	10	5	6	11
Tool Crib Attendant	7	16	14	10	14
Arc Welder	8	9	7	9	3
Electric Truck Operator	6	15	11	8	12
Crane Operator	5	14	10	7	6
Watchman	15	5	15	11	2

4. Distribute Wage Rates by Factors. The next step is for committee members to divide up the present wage being paid on each key job among the five factors, in accordance with their judgments about the importance of the factors to the job. For example, if the present wage for the job of common laborer is $3.26, this might be divided as follows:

Mental requirements . . . . $ .36
Physical requirements 1.20
Skill requirements 42
Responsibility 28
Working conditions 1.00
$3.26

This distribution is made for all key jobs. In making these judgments, the rankings illustrated in Table 1 may be used as guides. When each member of the committee has made the distribution of money several times independently, the committee meets and agrees on the amount of money to be assigned to each factor for each key job (see Table 2). This committee action, like that referred to in the preceding step, may result from averaging or discussion and eventual agreement.

TABLE 2

Average Distribution of Present Wages

| Job | Average Cents Per Hour Assigned | | | | | |
	Mental	Physical	Skill	Responsi-bility	Working Con-ditions	Present Rate
Gager	1.44	.76	2.04	1.02	.90	6.16
Pattern Maker	1.80	.78	2.26	1.20	.46	6.50
Common Laborer	.36	1.20	.42	.28	1.00	3.26
Power Shear Opr.	.82	.84	1.02	.96	.84	4.48
Plater	.88	1.02	1.18	.60	.66	4.34
Riveter	.78	1.12	.82	.52	.66	3.90
Blacksmith	.66	1.18	1.36	.54	.96	4.70
Punch Press Opr.	.60	1.08	.60	.46	.76	3.50
Automatic Screw Mach. Opr.	1.24	.96	1.96	1.14	.48	5.78
Casting Inspector	1.26	1.00	1.24	1.00	.58	5.08
Millwright	.96	.90	1.80	.94	.54	5.14
Tool Crib Attendant	1.06	.52	.58	.70	.48	3.34
Arc Welder	1.00	.94	1.06	.72	.88	4.60
Electric Truck Opr.	1.14	.64	.88	.76	.52	3.94
Crane Operator	1.20	.72	1.00	.90	.72	4.54
Watchman	.40	1.06	.46	.64	.90	3.46

5. Compare Vertical and Horizontal Judgments. The next step involves cross-checking the judgments already made. Figuratively, the two judgments may be thought of as judgments from two different directions; that is, the original rankings may be thought of as vertical comparisons and the money distributions as horizontal comparisons. If a key job is assigned the same position in both comparisons, the judgments appear to check each other. Also, it may be adjudged that if in the case of a given job the two judgments do not coincide, that job is not a true key job. To make this comparison, the money distributions may also be ranked and the two ranks compared (see Table 3).

TABLE 3

Difficulty Rank vs. Money Rank

Jobs	Mental		Physical		Skill		Responsibility		Working Conditions	
	D	M	D	M	D	M	D	M	D	M
Gager*	2	2	13	13	2	2	3	3	15	4
Pattern Maker†	1	1	12	12	1	1	1	1	16	16
Common Laborer†	16	16	1	1	16	16	16	16	1	1
Power Shear Opr.†	11	11	11	11	9	9	5	5	4	6
Plater†	10	10	6	6	6	7	12	12	9	10
Riveter†	12	12	3	3	12	12	14	14	8	9
Blacksmith*	13	13	2	2	8	5	13	13	7	2
Punch Press Opr.†	14	14	4	4	13	13	15	15	5	7
Automatic Screw Machine Opr.†	4	4	8	8	3	3	2	2	13	14
Casting Inspector*	3	3	7	7	4	6	4	4	10	11
Millwright‡	9	9	10	10	5	4	6	6	11	12
Tool Crib Attendant†	7	7	16	16	14	14	10	10	14	15
Arc Welder*	8	8	9	9	7	8	9	9	3	5
Electrical Truck Operator†	6	6	15	15	11	11	8	8	12	13
Crane Operator†	5	5	14	14	10	10	7	7	6	8
Watchman†	15	15	5	5	15	15	11	11	2	3§

*These are *not* true key jobs.
†These may be accepted as key jobs.
‡ Note that the job has a higher rank in money on the skill factor and a lower rank in money on the working conditions factor. This means that the job has been given too much for skill and too little for working conditions. In this case the committee may want to make an adjustment.
§Note that when a tie in money rank occurs, the difficulty ranking decides which ranks first.

Examination of Table 3 shows that four jobs are sufficiently out of line to make it necessary to eliminate them as key jobs. The others are close enough so that they may be retained. As suggested in note ‡ of the table, however, before the job comparison scale is constructed certain adjustments in the money distribution may be made. Comparison of vertical and horizontal rankings may suggest that on certain jobs the ranks can be adjusted by moving a small amount of money from one factor to another.

6. *Construct the Job Comparison Scale.* The next step is setting up the job comparison scale. The basis for this scale is the corrected money distribution allocated to true key jobs in the preceding step (see Table 4). In some installations, however, these values are multiplied by

TABLE 4

Job Comparison Scale

			Factors		
Cents	Mental	Physical	Skill	Responsi-bility	Working Conditions
2.30					
2.29					
2.28					
2.27					
2.26			Pattern Maker		
2.25					
2.24					
2.23					
2.22					
2.21					
2.20					
2.19					
2.18					
2.17					
2.16					
2.15					
2.14					
2.13					
2.12					
2.11					
2.10					
2.09					
2.08					
2.07					
2.06					
2.05					
2.04					
2.03					
2.02					
2.01					
2.00					
1.99					
1.98					
1.97					
1.96			Auto. Screw Mach. Opr.		
1.95					
1.94					
1.93					
1.92					
1.91					
1.90					
1.89					
1.88					
1.87					
1.86					

TABLE 4 (Cont.)

Job Comparison Scale

Factors

Cents	Mental	Physical	Skill	Responsi-bility	Working Conditions
1.85					
1.84					
1.83					
1.82					
1.81					
1.80	Pattern Maker		Millwright		
1.79					
1.78					
1.77					
1.76					
1.75					
1.74					
1.73					
1.72					
1.71					
1.70					
1.69					
1.68					
1.67					
1.65					
1.64					
1.63					
1.62					
1.61					
1.60					
1.59					
1.58					
1.57					
1.56					
1.55					
1.54					
1.53					
1.52					
1.51					
1.50					
1.49					
1.48					
1.47					
1.46					
1.45					
1.44					
1.43					
1.42					
1.41					
1.40					

TABLE 4 (Cont.)

Job Comparison Scale

			Factors		
Cents	Mental	Physical	Skill	Responsi- bility	Working Conditions
1.39					
1.38					
1.37					
1.36					
1.35					
1.34					
1.33					
1.32					
1.31					
1.30					
1.29					
1.28					
1.27					
1.26					
1.25					
1.24	Auto Screw Mach. Opr.				
1.23					
1.22					
1.21					
1.20	Crane Opr.	Com. Laborer		Pattern Maker	
1.19					
1.18			Plater		
1.17					
1.16					
1.15					
1.14	Elec. Tr. Opr.			Auto. Screw Mach. Opr.	
1.13					
1.12		Riveter			
1.11					
1.10					
1.09					
1.08		Punch Pr. Opr.			
1.07					
1.06	Tool Crib At.	Watchman			
1.05					
1.04					
1.03					
1.02		Plater	Power Sh. Opr.		
1.01					
1.00			Crane Opr.		Com. Laborer
.99					
.98					
.97					

TABLE 4 (Cont.)

Job Comparison Scale

			Factors		
Cents	Mental	Physical	Skill	Responsi-bility	Working Conditions
.96	Millwright	Auto. Screw Mach. Opr.		Power Sh. Opr.	
.95					
.94				Millwright	
.93					
.92					
.91					
.90		Millwright		Crane Opr.	Watchman
.89					
.88	Plater		Elec. Tr. Opr.		
.87					
.86					
.85					
.84		Power Sh. Opr.			Power Sh. Opr.
.83					
.82	Power Sh. Opr.		Riveter		
.81					
.80					
.79					
.78	Riveter	Pattern Maker			
.77					
.76				Elec. Tr. Opr.	Punch Pr. Opr.
.75					
.74					
.73					
.72		Crane Opr.			Crane Opr.
.71					
.70				Tool Crib At.	
.69					
.68					
.67					
.66					Riveter Plater
.65					
.64		Elec. Tr. Opr.		Watchman	
.63					
.62					
.61					
.60	Punch Pr. Opr.		Punch Pr. Opr.	Plater	
.59					
.58			Tool Crib At.		
.57					
.56					

TABLE 4 (Cont.)
Job Comparison Scale

			Factors		
Cents	Mental	Physical	Skill	Responsi-bility	Working Conditions
.55					
.54					Millwright
.53					
.52		Tool Crib At.		Riveter	Elec. Tr. Opr.
.51					
.50					
.49					
.48					Tool Crib At. Auto Screw Mach. Opr.
.47					
.46			Watchman	Punch Pr. Opr.	Pattern Maker
.45					
.44					
.43					
.42			Com. Laborer		
.41					
.40	Watchman				
.39					
.38					
.37					
.36	Com. Laborer				
.35					
.34					
.33					
.32					
.31					
.30					
.29					
.28				Com. Laborer	

a constant, a computation that results in point values. Since the job comparison scale is the instrument used in evaluating jobs other than key jobs, the use of point values instead of money removes one source of possible bias.

7. Use the Job Comparison Scale. The job comparison scale is an instrument for use in evaluating the organization's jobs. The committee may begin by selecting twenty-five to fifty supplementary key jobs and slotting them into the scale. This process serves somewhat to check the original scale. It also serves to fill in some of the gaps in the scale.

Supplementary key jobs are selected by the committee. The major criterion is the substantial correctness of the wage rate. Committee members individually rate these jobs using job specifications and the job comparison scale as guides. These jobs are fitted into the job comparison scale and serve to provide additional benchmarks for use by the committee. Any errors that appear in the scale are corrected at this point.

The remaining jobs are evaluated in the same manner. Each job is compared to the job comparison scale one factor at a time by first reading carefully the job information on the job and then comparing it with job information on jobs in the scale. Individual ratings are discussed in committee until agreement is reached and the job is slotted into the job comparison scale. In a completed job evaluation, all the organization's jobs will be in appropriate positions on this scale. As new or changed jobs appear they are evaluated in the same way.

MODIFICATIONS

One of the disadvantages of the factor comparison method was attributed to the use of dollar-and-cents units in developing job comparison scales. As suggested, one solution is to convert money units to points. Also, it occasionally occurs that key jobs with essentially correct wage rates do not exist. The per cent method of deriving job comparison scales was developed as an answer to both of these problems.

This method employs vertical and horizontal job comparisons as in the basic factor comparison method. In fact, the first three steps are identical in the two methods. At this point in the per cent method, percentage points are assigned by the committee to the vertical rankings. The money distribution in the basic method becomes a horizontal ranking of the importance of factors in the job, which is also translated into percentages. The remaining steps involve computations designed to provide a vertical and horizontal percentage value for each factor in each job by expressing each as a proportion of a common base.[5] The task of the job evaluation committee then becomes one of deciding whether one of these values or an average is the proper one. The resulting job comparison scale is in percentage points rather than money. The job comparison scale may employ the percentage values arrived at by the committee or adjusted values from a table of "equal appearing intervals" of 15 per cent. Non-key jobs are rated on the job comparison scale in exactly the same manner as in the basic method.

Another adaptation of the basic factor-comparison method employs what is called a job profile (a distribution in percentage terms of the importance of factors in a job). In the profile method, jobs are ranked on one factor, equal appearing intervals between ranks are established on this factor, and these values are derived for other factors by employing the profile percentages. Committee action develops the job comparison scale by comparing jobs factor by factor. The guide-chart profile method, designed for management positions by Edward N. Hay and Associates,[6] employs profiles for weighting factors, whereas actual evaluation of jobs employs two-dimensional point rating scales. Thus the plan uses a combination of factor comparison and point methods.

This tendency to develop combination plans making use of factor-comparison ideas is perhaps best illustrated by the well-known steel plan. The steel plan may be called a combination plan because (1) the scales were developed following the factor-comparison approach, but (2) once developed, a job evaluation manual was written that describes factors and degrees in words as well as in terms of benchmark jobs (see Figure 14). The steps followed in building the scales were those of the basic factor-comparison method with two exceptions: compensable factors were selected and defined by the parties instead of employing the universal factors; weights for factors and degrees were developed statistically by correlating job rankings by factor and the existing wage rates of key jobs instead of by committee judgment.[7] (See Figure 15 for factor and degree weights.)

After the factor and degree weights were obtained, factors and degrees were described in narrative form in a job evaluation manual. The manual was used to evaluate non-key jobs just as it is in a point system.

[5]Two different computation methods have been devised. See William D. Turner, "The Per Cent Method of Job Evaluation," *Personnel* (May, 1948), pp. 476–492; Edward N. Hay, "Creating Factor Comparison Key Scales by the Per Cent Method," *Journal of Applied Psychology* (October, 1948), pp. 456–464.
    [6]For details, see *Personnel* (September, 1951), pp. 162–170; (July, 1954), pp. 72–80; (January–February, 1958), pp. 63–72.
    [7]Paul M. Edwards, "Statistical Methods in Job Evaluation," *Advanced Management* (December, 1948), pp. 158–163.

THE POINT METHOD

The point method of job evaluation involves breaking down the job into several compensable factors, giving each job a numerical score on each of these factors and summing these scores to obtain the value of the job. It is similar to the classification or grade-description method in that a scale is set up against which jobs are measured. The difference between the two methods is that, whereas one scale is developed for the classification method, a scale for each compensable factor is developed in the point method and typically the scales are weighted differently.

In the point method a carefully worded rating scale is constructed for each compensable factor. This rating scale includes a definition of the compensable factor, several divisions (called degrees) of each factor carefully outlined, and a point score for each such degree.

These rating scales may be thought of as a set of rulers to be used to measure jobs. If the rulers measure components known to be present in the jobs and if they are carefully constructed, they become sufficiently accurate to measure jobs at the time of installation and to measure new and changed jobs.

This figurative language, however, perhaps suggests a degree of accuracy that is impossible in job evaluation. The so-called rulers must be constructed of words and the so-called measurements are still judgments—which is another way of saying that the method is no more accurate than the rating scales developed and used.

ADVANTAGES

Probably the major advantage of the point rating method is the stability of the rating scales. Once the scales are developed, they may be used for a considerable period. Jobs may change without changing the scales. Only a change in what the organization is paying for requires building a new yardstick. This creates another advantage; that is, point plans increase in accuracy and consistency with use.

The point method makes use of the types of rating scales that are usually regarded as most reliable and valid. Graphic rating scales and check lists were devised to reduce rating error and the influence of bias on ratings. Agreement among raters is close even when ratings of employees, supervisors, and personnel executives are compared.

Because the point rating method permits development of a scale for each compensable factor adjudged to apply in the organization, acceptance of results by the parties is likely. When compensable factors are chosen, those that the parties decide are important can be used.

Code	Hazards Likelihood and Nature of Injury	Bench Mark Jobs	Numerical Classifi- cation
A	Accident hazard low and usual injuries consist of minor cuts, bruises, and burns. Operate machines, machine tools, material handling equipment, or control movement of material when only occasionally exposed to moving machinery. Perform repetitive manual tasks, such as feeding or piling product or material.	Hot Bed Opr.—Bil. Mill Speed Opr.—H.S. Craneman—H.S. Blower—Bess. Mill Janitor Coupling Tap. Opr.	Base
B	Accident hazard moderate and probable injuries consist of severe cuts, bruises or fractures such as encountered when performing routine crane hooking, operating tractors and trucks, regularly adjusting moving machinery or product. Exposed to falls such as may occur when walking or climbing over bins, stock buggies, and low scaffolds. Occasionally exposed to hot objects that may cause moderate burns. Exposed to flying objects such as chips and scale. Handle or work near caustic, inflammable, or volatile liquids or gases. (Closed vessels or pipes.)	Tractor Opr.—Ram Tandem Mill Roller Nail Machine Opr. Stocker—O.H. Bricklayer "A" Scarfer—Cond. Bottom Maker—S.P. Chipper—Cond. Saturator Opr.—B.P. Dryerman—B.P. Laborer Pickler Loader—Batch	.4
C	Exposed to burns for molten metal splashes. Regularly manipulate hot product with tongs or hooks.	Charging Mach. Opr. —O.H. Strander—Bar Mill Hi Mill Plugger—Pipe Seamless	.8

FIGURE 14

Degree Definitions

Handle or control caustic inflammable or volatile liquids. (Open vessels or handling containers.)

Agitator Opr.—B.P.
Pipefitter "A"
Motor Inspector—B.M.

	Hazards		*Numerical Classification*
Code	*Likelihood and Nature of Injury*	*Bench Mark Jobs*	
	Exposed to falls such as might occur when working on high scaffolds, structures and roofs.	Stock Unloader—B.F. Millwright—B.M.	
	Occasionally exposed to high voltage electricity.		
	Exposed to severe injury from crane hooking where difficult rigging or lifting devices are involved.		
	Perform heavy maintenance work involving climbing and rigging to repair, set up, or tear down equipment and mills.		
	Climb on moving rolling stock.		
D	Exposed to severe burns from handling, transporting or controlling the flow of molten metal.	Keeper—Blast Furnace 2nd Helper—O.H.	1.2
E	Frequent exposure to a hazard where failure to exercise extreme care and judgment might cause an accident which would result in total disability or a fatality.	High Tension Lineman	2.0

FIGURE 14 (Cont.)

Source: Agreements between Carnegie-Illinois Steel Corporation and the United Steelworkers of America (CIO) (October 23, 1945; April 15, 1946; May 8, 1946; January 13, 1947 as amended; and January 27, 1947), pp. 50, 51.

Factor	A	B	C	D	Degrees E	F	G	H	J
1. Pre-employment training	Base	.3	1.0						
2. Employment training and experience	Base	.4	.8	1.2	1.6	2.0	2.4	3.2	4.0
3. Mental skill	Base	1.0	1.6	2.2	2.8	3.5			
4. Manual skill	Base	.5	1.0	1.5	2.0				
5. Responsibility for materials	Base	.3–2.3	.5–3.7	.8–8.5	1.2–10.0				
6. Responsibility for tools and equipment	Base	.2–.5	.4–1.0	.7–2.0	1.0–3.0	1.5–4.0			
7. Responsibility for operations	Base	.5	1.0	2.0	3.0	4.0	5.0	6.5	
8. Responsibility for safety of others	Base	.4	.8	1.2	2.0				
9. Mental effort	Base	.5	1.0	1.5	2.5				
10. Physical effort	Base	.3	.8	1.5	2.5				
11. Surroundings	Base	.4	.8	1.6	3.0				
12. Hazards	Base	.4	.8	1.2	2.0				

FIGURE 15

Steel Plan—Degree and Factor Weights

Source: Agreements between Carnegie-Illinois Steel Corporation and the United Steel-workers of America (CIO) (October 23, 1945; April 15, 1946; May 8, 1946; January 13, 1947 as amended; and January 27, 1947).

Job classes are easily set up in a point plan. The point values make for simple classification either in terms of arbitrary point ranges or on the basis of agreement. Point values also aid in job pricing. When each job or class of jobs is assigned a point value, consistent assignment of monetary values is possible.

As rating scales are developed, every effort is made to provide the rater with aids in reaching decisions. Factors and degrees are carefully defined and examples are provided. Judgment is not eliminated, of course, but careful steps are taken to reduce errors to a minimum.

DISADVANTAGES

The point rating method is difficult to develop, a fact that probably represents its major disadvantage. Compensable factors must be carefully and clearly defined, degrees of factors must be blocked out in terms carrying the same meaning for all raters, weights must be allocated to factors in accordance with their importance, and point values must be assigned to degrees.

The difficulties involved in developing a point plan undoubtedly account for the heavy usage of ready-made plans. In large part, point plans are used more than other types of plans because of the availability of a number of ready-made plans. If each organization had to develop its own point plan, it is quite likely that the method would be much less popular. As mentioned previously, the applicability of a ready-made plan is determined by the fit of the plan to the organization in terms of compensable factors and weights. Even modifying a ready-made plan involves technical difficulties.

The method also takes time to install. Even after scales are developed, each job is compared to the scale by at least two or three raters. Considerable clerical detail is involved in recording and collating the ratings.

Nor are the details of the method easy to explain. Terms such as degrees, point values, and weights are not easily interpreted to employees. They are concepts unfamiliar to most laymen, and unless careful instruction is provided in simple language, opposition may be aroused.

STEPS

The point rating method is the most commonly used method of job evaluation, and countless variations are in use. Fortunately, however, because the steps involved are somewhat standardized, one explanation of the steps in the point method will suffice. Some variations will be discussed as modifications later in this chapter.

1. Determine Type(s) of Jobs to Be Evaluated. Although it is possible to develop one point rating plan for all jobs in the organization, this is not usual practice. Compensable factors often are quite different for different clusters of jobs within the organization. And even if one compensable factor or set of compensable factors applies to all jobs, objective wording of rating scales may require a separate point plan for each cluster of jobs. Thus the decision may be to evaluate shop jobs, or clerical jobs, or executive jobs; and a plan is developed for the job cluster selected. The point method will be developed for only one group at a time. Consequently, the first step in the point method is to select the type of jobs to be evaluated.

2. Collect Job Information. The next step involves job analysis. Detailed information is collected on each job to be evaluated and is recorded in a job analysis schedule. A job description is written for each job.

3. Select Compensable Factors. When job information is available, compensable factors are selected that are applicable to the jobs under study. Selecting compensable factors was discussed in Chapter 5.

There the position was taken that compensable factors in job evaluation plans are the job-related contributions recognized in the employment exchange. If this view is accepted, the compensable factors selected determine the acceptability of the job evaluation plan by the parties and the workability of the plan. Thus the factors selected are those applicable to the organization and to the jobs under study.

The number of factors chosen also depends on the organization. At least the most important factors are included, and these should be decided by the parties. When the compensable factors have been selected, job information may be reported on job specifications in terms of these factors. Such specifications are useful tools in comparing jobs to rating scales.

Education

This attribute refers to the academic or technical training which is considered prerequisite for learning the job. Such training may be acquired through formal schooling or its equivalent and provides a basis or background necessary for the development of adequate job skill and knowledge.

Knowledge

This refers to what a person should know, beyond the knowledge given by the prerequisite schooling, in order to perform the job satisfactorily. This knowledge is generally gained through actual job experience or on-the-job training. It is broken down into three aspects: Knowledge of (1) procedures and methods; (2) organization; and (3) company practices and policies.

Mental Requirements

This refers to the general mental requirements of the job as expressed in resourcefulness in dealing with unfamiliar problems, interpretation of data, initiation of new ideas, creative or developmental work, etc.

Accuracy

This refers to the necessity for performing work accurately and thoroughly and to the loss which may result from failure to be accurate. Errors include those of judgment as well as those of a mechanical nature, but do not include those of a voluntary nature.

Effort

This refers to the mental and physical expenditures required in the performance of a job. Physical environment and the continuity or monotony of the work, as well as other conditions leading to nervous and/or physical strain, are to be considered.

Source: A. T. Kearney and Company, Chicago.

FIGURE 16

Factor Definitions

4. Define Compensable Factors.   When compensable factors have been chosen that are specific to the organization and to the jobs under study, it is not difficult to define the factors. Such definition is, however, an important step, for this formal statement of the significance or meaning of the factor is used extensively in later steps in the evaluation. Those charged with rating jobs will be constantly checking back against this definition as evaluation proceeds. Unless the statement is sufficiently clear to carry the same connotation to all readers, rating errors may result. Consequently, the language employed to convey factor meaning is important.

The more specific the factors chosen, the more precise the definitions may be. General factors are broader and must be defined in more general terms. Some examples of factor definitions are shown in Figure 16.

5. Define Factor Degrees.   Factors in point plans are broken up into divisions or degrees so that raters may judge the amount or level of a factor existing in jobs. For example, the working conditions (surroundings) factor may be composed of the following degrees:

Degree	Definition
A	Inside machine shop or average factory type of building. Slightly dirty, noisy, and not uniformly heated.
B	Heat in summer due to proximity to furnace of hot materials. Inside and outside conditions, but not required to remain out in in extreme weather. Outside weather conditions, but protected part of time by roofs, pulpits, or cabs. Continually dirty or greasy work, or exposure to wetness and some fumes and smoke.
C	All weather conditions where weather is severe. Exposed to considerable wetness, acids, fumes, dust, or glare necessitating the wearing of protective clothing or devices. Extreme conditions of dirt where man becomes covered with obnoxious dirt such as tar, paint, etc. Extreme heat for intervals but not for extended periods. Exposed to intense noise for extended periods.
D	Exposed to extreme heat of intense degree and for considerable time.
E	Exposed to extreme heat approaching the point of endurance where relief from surroundings at regular intervals is a necessity.

Source: Agreements between Carnegie-Illinois Steel Corporation and the United Steelworkers of America (CIO), (October 23, 1945; April 15, 1946; May 8, 1946; January 13, 1947 as amended; and January 27, 1947), pp. 48, 49.

Preparation for the Job.

　　1– 2　　No experience, high school education, average intelligence.

　　3– 4　　Requires some special training such as typing, stenography, negotiable instruments, loans, law, etc.

　　5– 8　　Experience in several jobs leading to this one.

　　9–10　　Requires fair knowledge of some particular field such as accounting, investments, loans, law, etc.

　11–12　　Requires a thorough knowledge of at least one field and also some knowledge of related fields.

　13–14　　Requires knowledge covering several fields sufficiently to discuss them intelligently. Requires wide experience.

In connection with above, consider special skills required:

Accounting	Investments	Secretarial
Correspondence	Languages	Shorthand
Filing	Law	Special Accounting
Income Tax	Negotiable Instruments	Typing

Contact with the Public, Customers, and Personnel.

　　1– 2　　Jobs rarely coming into contact with others.

　　3– 4　　Contact generally with others in the same group.

　　5– 6　　Jobs having some contact outside the group. (Do not include contacts of a delivery nature.)

　　7– 8　　Jobs coming into contact with the public and employees regularly on routine matters.

　　9–10　　Jobs for which personality and the ability to get along with people are primary qualifications.

　11–12　　Jobs having major contacts with either customers, public, or personnel.

Degree of Executive Responsibility.

　　　0　　None.

　　1– 2　　Oversees work for a group doing routine work under direction of a supervisor. Not responsible for methods. (Responsible only for proper completion of assigned work.)

　　3– 4　　Supervisor of ordinary work group under supervision of a manager. (Doing routine work; not responsible for methods.)

　　　　　　　　　　　　　　　– or –

　　　　　　Manager of a small independent department doing routine work.

　　　　　　　　　　　　　　　– or –

　　　　　　Assistant to the head of a large division.

　　5– 6　　Supervisor of a large division in a large department doing routine work. Somewhat responsible for methods. Responsible to a manager and an officer.

　　　　　　　　　　　　　　　– or –

　　　　　　Supervisor of a group doing individual work under a manager or an officer.

　　　　　　　　　　　　　　　– or –

　　　　　　First assistant to the head of a large division.

　　7– 8　　Manager of a large department doing routine work. Responsible for methods to Comptroller and responsible for all workers.

　　9–10　　Manager of a large division doing routine work. (Responsible for methods and workers.)

　　　　　　　　　　　　　　　– or –

　　　　　　Manager of a department doing individual work. (Responsible for methods and workers.)

FIGURE 17

Degree Definitions—Clerical Jobs

Source: William R. Spriegel and Elizabeth Lanham, *Job Evaluation in Banks* (Austin, Texas: Bureau of Business Research, University of Texas, August, 1951), pp. 129-131.

The process of determining degrees may be compared figuratively to determining inch marks on a rule. It is first necessary to decide the number of such divisions, then to ensure that they are either equally spaced or represent known distances, and finally to see that they are carefully defined. The number of degrees, like the factors themselves, depends on the organization and the jobs under study. If, for example, working conditions are apparently identical for most jobs, and those jobs with working conditions that differ from the general rule have, among themselves, similar surroundings, then two degrees of this factor are sufficient. If, on the other hand, seven or even more categories are clearly discernible, that number of degrees is specified.

The major problem in determining degrees is to make each degree equidistant from the two adjacent degrees. This problem is solved in part by selecting the number of degrees actually found to exist and in part by careful definition of degrees. Degree determination and definition are guided by decision rules such as the following: (1) limit degrees to the number necessary to distinguish among jobs; (2) limit degrees to those including at least one job, and applicability of the degree to the job should be apparent; (3) use terminology in degree definitions that employees understand; (4) use standard job titles as part of degree definitions.

Determining and defining degrees is a crucial step in the point method. These are the "inch marks on the ruler," and unless they are clearly marked and meaningful, resulting scales can produce unreliable and inaccurate ratings. Figure 17 illustrates some degree definitions as used in clerical and executive jobs.

In order to attain maximum flexibility in the use of factors, some plans employ what might be called two-dimensional degrees. For example, one plan in developing degrees of the factor "knowledge of job procedures and methods" uses what amounts to nine degrees by defining three degrees of complexity and three degrees of versatility and permitting raters to use the nine possible combinations (see Figure 18).

6. Determine Relative Values of Factors. Only rarely are compensable factors assigned equal weight in determining job value. It is usually determined that some factors are more important than others. In fact, the relative importance of factors becomes apparent when compensable factors are chosen.

Factor weights may be assigned statistically or by committee judgment. In the statistical method, wage or salary rates of key jobs are correlated with various weights assigned to the factors until the best fit is found. Multiple linear correlation results in a regression equation that points to factors requiring more or less weight. Gilmour provides an

Complexity	*Versatility Required*		
	Col. A *0-1* *Limited variety of tasks required.*	*Col. B* *2-4* *Variety of tasks required.*	*Col. C* *5-* *Wide variety of tasks required; new tasks added frequently.*
Row 1 0-1 Routine tasks involving very simple procedures.			
Row 2 2-4 Semi-routine tasks which follow established or standardized procedures.			
Row 3 5- Non-routine tasks which follow only generally . established procedures or methods.			

FIGURE 18

Example of Two-Dimension Degrees

Source: A. T. Kearney and Company, Chicago

excellent illustration of this approach.[8] As mentioned previously, the steel plan carries weights derived statistically. Ferguson, Sargent, and Reinfold suggest that linear programming and matrix techniques of mathematical analysis be used to set factor weights.[9]

In most existing plans relative factor weights were developed by committee judgment. The reasoning involved is that the only useful criterion is acceptance by the parties, and this acceptance can best be attained by committee decisions. The procedure is to (1) have committee members carefully study factor and degree definitions, (2) have each member rank the factors in order of importance and have the total committee agree on a ranking, (3) have each member distribute 100 per cent among the factors individually, and once more have the committee reach agreement. The result is a set of factor weights representing

[8]Robert W. Gilmour, *Industrial Wage and Salary Control* (New York: John Wiley and Sons, Inc., 1956), Chapter 4.

[9]R. O. Ferguson, L. F. Sargent, and N. V. Reinfold, "Pay Plans for Management," *Factory Management and Maintenance* (March, 1954), pp. 142–144.

committee judgment. Factor weights of a commonly used ready-made plan were developed by a committee.

But the weights specified by the committee and the weights attained in actual use of the scales may differ. Such differences are usually attributable to lack of use of some degrees because they are so defined as to be rarely used in the actual evaluation of jobs. Although it is possible to correct statistically for differences in the application of scales before committee weights are applied, a better solution is to eliminate unused degrees. Key jobs may be evaluated to determine that all degrees are used and, if not, unused degrees can be eliminated.

7. *Assign Point Values to Factors and Degrees.* When the relative value of factors has been determined, the next step is to assign points to the factors and to the degrees. These are the values that will be used in determining the total point values of jobs.

The total points assigned to a factor have been determined in percentage terms in the preceding step. Here, all that is required is a decision on the total number of points to be used in the plan. If, for example, 500 points are to be used, the value of each factor is 5 times the percentage value. This procedure also determines the point value of the highest degree of each factor. Thus, if a given factor (say, working conditions) is assigned 20 per cent of the weight, and 500 points are to be used, the total number of points allocable to working conditions is 100, and the highest degree of the factor would also carry 100 points.

Total points for each factor are assigned to degrees usually by either arithmetic progression or geometric progression. In the former, increases are in equal amounts from the lowest to the highest degree —*i.e.,* 20, 40, 60, 80, 100. In the latter, increases are in equal percentage steps—*i.e.,* 5, 10, 20, 40, 80, 160. Actually, if the plan has been developed for a specific job cluster rather than for the entire organization, it matters little which method is followed; few point plans apply to all the jobs in the organization. If desired, the effect of arithmetic or geometric progression may be tested by evaluating key jobs and noting the effect produced.

Using either progression assumes that degrees have been defined with sufficient precision to permit the assumption that they represent equal steps along a scale. If it is believed that this is not the case, the committee must decide how the total points allocated to a factor should be divided up among the degrees. Most plans, however, assume that each degree of a factor represents a step equivalent to other degrees.

It was pointed out in step 5 that factors may employ differing numbers of degrees. Thus, one factor may have three degrees and another eight. If this is the case, the simplest procedure (using arithmetic progression) to follow in assigning point values to degrees is: (1) set the value of the highest degree (as explained above) by multiplying the percentage allocated to the factor by total possible points; (2) set the minimum degree at the actual percentage figure (thus, if a given factor were allocated 30 per cent of the points and the total possible points were set at 500, the highest degree of the factor would be 150 and the lowest degree, 30); (3) subtract the two figures; (4) divide the result by the number of steps from the lowest degree to the highest (the number of degrees minus 1); (5) add this figure successively to the lowest degree. Therefore, if the factor in the example has seven degrees, points would be assigned as follows: 30, 50, 70, 90, 110, 130, 150; if five degrees: 30, 60, 90, 120, 150. If geometric progression is desired, the use of logarithms provides degree values.

Where factor weights and the resulting point values for factors and degrees have been determined by committee rather than statistically, a number of key jobs are usually evaluated to determine if the plan achieves the desired relationships among jobs. At this point adjustments in point values may be called for to ensure that the plan will be acceptable to all the parties.

8. *Write Up the Job Evaluation Manual.* A final step in preparing for job evaluation by the point method is to consolidate the factor and degree definitions and point values into a job evaluation manual. This step places in convenient form the yardsticks to be used by raters in evaluating jobs. An example of such a manual is provided in Figure 19.

9. *Rate the Jobs.* When the manual is complete, job rating can begin. Raters, usually in committee, use the scales to evaluate jobs. The jobs may be taken in any order. Key jobs, as was seen, have been rated previously, but final ratings are made at this point. In fact, key jobs may be used in steps 3 through 7 and employed as part of the degree definitions.

As jobs are rated, a record of the rating of each factor is recorded on a substantiating data sheet (see Figure 20). This becomes a permanent record of the points assigned to each factor and the reasons for assigning the particular degree of the factor to the job. Substantiating data come from job descriptions and job specifications.

EXAMPLES OF POINT PLANS

The popularity of point plans is largely attributable to the wide adoption of plans developed by employer associations and consultants. These organizations have prepared job evaluation manuals that have been used or adapted by thousands of organizations. For example, the American Association of Industrial Management-National Metal Trades Association has a job-rating plan for shop production and maintenance service jobs and another plan for office, technical, and supervisory jobs. The Life Office Management Association has a plan for life insurance companies.

The most widely used plan is that of the National Electrical Manufacturers Association and the National Metal Trades Association for factory jobs. It has been sold to members of these associations and to other organizations. It has also been adapted in various ways by consultants and user organizations. Table 5 illustrates some similarities among typical plans for blue-collar jobs. Notice the similarities in factors and weights, with the exception of the steel plan, which places extraordinary weight on responsibility. Ready-made plans and modifications of such plans for office jobs are also somewhat similar, as shown in Table 6.

Examination of these tables suggests that although the factors employed in ready-made plans are quite similar, different weightings of factors in separate plans may serve to accommodate the needs of organizations and their members. Although the model of the employment exchange implies that each organization should develop its own plan based on agreed on job-related contributions and some studies establish the superiority of custom-made job evaluation plans,[10] it appears that ready-made plans with and without modification are sufficiently flexible to accommodate the needs of the parties. It is significant that success of job evaluation does not appear to depend on the type of plan used. One survey of U.S. companies found that 93 per cent of those using a ready-made plan rated it successful.[11] The British survey cited previously found that 90 per cent of plans installed with the aid of consultants were rated as successful as compared to 89 per cent of plans wherein consultants were not used. Many, perhaps most, consultants have their own job evaluation plans.

CHECKLISTS

A somewhat different type of point plan is the checklist. Previously discussed plans are based on the graphic rating scale developed

[10]J. S. Gray, "Custom Made Systems of Job Evaluation," *Journal of Applied Psychology* (December, 1950), pp. 378–380; J. Stanley Gray and Marvin C. Jones, "Ready-Made versus Custom-Made Job Evaluation," *Journal of Applied Psychology* (February, 1951), pp. 11–14.
[11]"Job Evaluation Comes of Age," *Personnel* (November–December, 1960), pp. 4–5.

Element	TECHNICAL AND OFFICE JOBS Total Points (Weight)	Per Cent
Mental Demands	200	48.2%
Training and Experience	84	20.2%
Effect of Error	48	11.6%
Personal Contacts	45	10.8%
Job Conditions	38	9.2%

MENTAL DEMANDS

Mental Demands is the mental capacity required of an individual to perform a given job efficiently. Factors considered are judgment, analytical ability, initiative and originality. The training and experience acquired by an individual is not considered.

Degree	Factor	Point Value
1	(a) Independent judgment in making decisions, from many diversified alternatives, that are subject to general review in final stages only. (b) Analysis and solution of complex problems affecting production, sales, or company policy. (c) The establishment of procedures in a field in which pioneer work has been negligible and with no reference of detail to higher supervision.	200
2	(a) Independent judgment in making decisions from various alternatives, with general guidance only from higher supervision. (b) Analysis and solution of nonroutine problems involving evaluation of a wide variety of data. (c) The establishment of procedures in conformance with administrative policies and general instructions from supervision.	175
3	(a) Independent judgment in making decisions involving nonroutine problems under general supervision. (b) Analysis and evaluation of a variety of data pertaining to nonroutine problems for solution in conjunction with others. (c) The carrying out of nonroutine procedures, under constantly changing conditions, in conformance with general instructions from supervision.	150
4	(a) Independent judgment in planning sequence of operations and making minor decisions in a complex technical or professional field. (b) Research and analysis of data pertaining to problems of a generally routine nature. (c) The carrying out of nonroutine procedures in conformance with instructions from supervision.	125

FIGURE 19

Job Evaluation Manual

5	(a) Independent judgment in making minor decisions where alternatives are limited and standard policies have been established.	100
	(b) Analysis of standardized data for information of, or use by, others.	
	(c) Performance of semiroutine operations with guidance by supervision, but where detailed instructions are lacking.	
6	(a) Independent judgment is negligible; however, minor decisions sometimes must be made. Work is checked by others.	75
	(b) Analysis of noncomplicated data by established routine.	
	(c) Performance of semiroutine operations from detailed instructions.	
7	(a) Independent judgment is negligible but must be able to receive and transmit simple information obtained from written and verbal sources.	50
	(b) Analysis of data is negligible but must be accurate in recording information for use by others.	
	(c) Performance of routine, standardized operations under direct supervision.	
8	(a) Independent judgment is not involved.	25
	(b) Analysis not required.	
	(c) Performance of simple, repetitive tasks under close supervision.	

TRAINING AND EXPERIENCE

Training and Experience is the length of time required for an individual of average mental capacity to acquire the training and knowledge needed to perform a given job efficiently.

Degree	Factor	Point Value
1	7 years or more	84
2	5 years but less than 7 years	77
3	4 years but less than 5 years	70
4	3 years but less than 4 years	63
5	2½ years but less than 3 years	56
6	2 years but less than 2½ years	49
7	1½ years but less than 2 years	42
8	1 year but less than 1½ years	35
9	8 to 11 months	28
10	5 to 7 months	21
11	2 to 4 months	14
12	Less than 2 months	7

FIGURE 19 (Cont.)

EFFECT OF ERROR

Effect of Error is the extent to which an employee's decisions may affect the company from a cost standpoint. The loss may involve loss of own or others, time and/or loss of company funds. (Loss is considered on the basis of an average top figure for a single occurrence, not an extreme maximum.)

Degree	Factor	Point Value
1	Probable error in basic information developed independently and upon which important management decisions are based could cause substantial loss of company funds, serious delays in schedule, or loss of customers' accounts. Work is not generally subject to check.	48
2	Probable error not easily detected and may adversely affect outside relationships. Work is subject to general review only and requires considerable accuracy and responsibility.	40
3	Probable error may create a serious loss of production, waste material, or damage to equipment, but loss is usually confined within the company. Most of work is not subject to verification or check.	32
4	Probable error may result from decisions based on recommendations, but error is usually confined to a single department or phase of company activities. Most of work is subject to verification or check.	24
5	Probable error would normally result in loss of own and others' time to correct error. Practically all work is subject to verification or check.	16
6	Probable error would normally result in loss of own time to correct error. Practically all work is subject to verification or check.	8

PERSONAL CONTACTS

Personal Contacts is the nature, purpose, and level of company and public contacts required of an individual to perform a given job efficiently. Factors considered are ability to orally express ideas, maintain poise, and exercise tact and persuasiveness.

Degree	Factor	Point Value
1	Contacts are with company supervision, supervision of other companies, customers or other persons in all types of positions requiring the ability of the employee to influence and to establish and maintain company good will.	45

FIGURE 19 (Cont.)

2	Contacts with persons of substantially higher rank within the company and concerning matters requring explanation, discussion, and obtaining approvals. Contacts with persons outside the company, involving carrying out of company policy and programs, the improper handling of which will affect operating results.	35
3	Contacts with persons in other departments within the company and concerning matters of a general nature. Contacts with persons outside the company but where the primary responsibility rests with supervision.	25
4	Contacts are normally with persons within the company and outside contacts are infrequent. Contacts usually concern routine reporting and exchange or giving of information requiring little or no interpretation or discussion.	17
5	Contacts generally with immediate associates and own supervision	9

JOB CONDITIONS

Job Conditions are the environmental working conditions and unavoidable hazards involved in the performance of the job. These conditions are beyond the employees' control.

Degree	Factor	Point Value
1	Continuous exposure to one or more disagreeable factors such as fatiguing physical exertion, burns, sprains, noise, glare, weather, ventilation, and so forth.	38
2	Frequent daily exposure to one or more disagreeable factors such as fatiguing physical exertion, burns, sprains, noise, glare, weather, ventilation, and so forth.	30
3	Somewhat disagreeable conditions due to occasional exposure to noises, open drafty places, possibility of damage to clothing, and occasional exposure to minor accident hazards.	22
4	Good working conditions, but infrequently exposed to extremes in temperatures, loud noises, disagreeable odors, and so forth. Practically no exposure to any accident hazard.	14
5	Usual office working conditions.	6

FIGURE 19 (Cont.)

for employee evaluation, but checklists employ the principles involved in the forced choice system of employee evaluation. It may help to view checklists as a randomized list of degree definitions.

Early work on a job evaluation checklist was done by Bellows and Estep,[12] who attempted to utilize the United States Employment Service Occupational Characteristics Check List for job evaluation purposes. They found a correlation of 0.74 between the results of a job evaluation plan and OCCL Scores. The Life Office Management Association[13] has developed a list of 149 clerical operations for which relative values have been determined.

[12]Roger M. Bellows and M. Frances Estep, "Job Evaluation Simplified: The Utility of the Occupational Characteristics Check List," *Journal of Applied Psychology* (August, 1948), pp. 354–359.
[13]L. W. Ferguson, *Clerical Salary Administration* (New York: Life Office Management Association, 1948).

SUBSTANTIATING DATA SHEET – OFFICE JOBS		
Job Title _____ Code No. _____		
	Degree	*Points*
Education		
Job Knowledge		
Supervision Exercised		
Trust Imposed		
Errors		
Nature of Work		
Contacts With Others		
Physical-Mental Strain		
Date Rated _____ Date Re-rated _____ Total Points _____		

FIGURE 20

TABLE 5

Factors and Weights-Point Plans-Hourly Jobs

Factors	NEMA-NMTA	Appliance Mfgr.	Steel Plan	Aircraft Mfgr.	Electric Utility
Skill					
Education	14		2.4		8
Experience	22			23.8	
Initiative	14				
Training			9.3	23.8	21
Knowledge		32			
Manual Dexterity			4.7		10
Judgment		10			
Mental Skill			8.1		
Mentality				12.0	13
Total	50	42	24.5	59.6	52
Effort					
Physical	10	15	5.8	7.0	10
Mental and/ or Visual	5	5	5.8	6.0	5
Total	15	20	11.6	13.0	15
Responsibility					
General			15.1		
Equipment or Processes	5	5	9.3	12.0	5
Material or Product	5	5	23.3		5
Safety of Others	5	5	4.7		5
Work of Others	5	5			3
Total	20	20	52.4	12.0	18
Job Conditions					
Working Conditions	10	10	6.8	7.7	10
Unavoidable Hazards	5	8	·4.7	7.7	5
Total	15	18	11.5	15.4	15
Grand Total	100	100	100.0	100.0	100

TABLE 6

Factors and Weights-Point Plans-Salaried Jobs

Factors	NEMA	Employers Assn.	Consultant	Trade Assn.	Appliance Mfgr.
Education	17.5	10.6	15.0	12.3	
Experience	29.0	16.0	9.0	19.0	10.1
Training			9.0		10.1
Complexity	14.5	10.6		12.3	
Mental Skill			27.0	3.3	48.2
Responsibility for:					
Function		10.6	22.0		
Procedures		6.3			
Confidential Data		4.2		3.3	
Assets		8.0			
Errors				11.0	11.6
Monetary Responsibility	8.8				
Contacts	8.8	8.0	7.0	11.0	10.8
Working Conditions	3.8	3.7	5.0	3.3	9.2
Hazards		7.0			
Type of Supervision	8.8	7.5	3.0	11.0	
Extent of Supervision	8.8	7.5	3.0	13.5	
Total	100.0	100.0	100.0	100.0	100.0

Additional work has been done on this approach by Lawshe and his associates.[14] Building on the work of the Life Office Management Association, a checklist of 139 items has been developed and tested for clerical jobs. A portion of the checklist is reproduced in Figure 21. The checklist may be used both for describing and evaluating jobs. As a job description, it is filled out separately by the employee and his supervisor and a discussion between them straightens out any discrepancies.

Each item in the checklist has an operational weight determined statistically from studies of operations involved in clerical jobs. These weights are used as point values in determining the relative value of jobs. Miles' study showed that the five most important items found in the job should carry most of the weight. Thus, in calculating point

[14]M. C. Miles, "Validity of a Check List for Evaluating Office Jobs," *Journal of Applied Psychology* (April, 1952), pp. 97–102.

_____ 1. Makes simple calculations such as addition or subtraction with or without using a machine[†] .... ( )

_____ 2. Performs ordinary calculations requiring more than one step, such as multiplication or division, without using a machine or requiring the use of more than one set or group of keys on a calculating machine[†] .... ( )

_____ 3. Performs numerous types of computations including relatively complicated calculations involving roots, powers, formulae, or specific sequences of action with or without using a machine[†] .... ( )

_____ 4. Balances specific items, entries, or amounts periodically with or without using a machine[†] .... ( )

_____ 5. Keeps a running balance of specific items, entries, or amounts, with or without using a machine[†] .... ( )

_____ 6. Copies desired data from one form or record into the proper place on another form or record by longhand .... ( )

_____ 7. Copies desired data from one form or record into the proper place on another form or record using typewriter or some type of office machine[‡] .... ( )

_____ 8. Makes simple or routine entries in record books or on special or standard forms by longhand or using a typewriter .... ( )

_____ 9. Makes simple or routine entries in record books or on special or standard forms using some type of office machines[‡] .... ( )

_____ 10. Records on special forms or records all items of particular type(s) or classification(s) by longhand .... ( )

_____ 11. Records on special forms or records all items of particular type(s) or classification(s) using a typewriter or some type of office machine[‡] .... ( )

_____ 12. Makes out various routine forms such as checks, receipts, invoices, form letter addresses, or other items, according to standard operating procedures by longhand .... ( )

_____ 13. Makes out various routine forms such as checks, receipts, invoices, form letter addresses, or other items, according to standard operating procedures using a typewriter or some type of office machine[‡] .... ( )

_____ 14. Prepares routine lists of specific items, numerical and/or verbal, according to designated system by longhand .... ( )

_____ 15. Prepares routine lists of specific items, numerical and/or verbal, according to designated system using a typewriter or some type of office machine[‡]( )

_____ 16. Composes routine correspondence or memoranda, following standard operating procedures .... ( )

_____ 17. Composes correspondence requiring specific knowledge of methods, procedures, policies, or other information... ( )

_____ 18. Prepares routine reports, based on information at hand, following standard operating procedures.. ( )

_____ 9. Selects and/or gathers specific data, information, or desired items, according to standard operating procedures, or upon request .... ( )

_____ 20. Consults or studies specific books, manuals, catalogs, or other sources in order to obtain desired information .... ( )

_____ 21. Searches indexes, manuals, files, records, or other sources for desired or missing information on specific subjects... ( )

_____ 22. Prepares reports requiring the investigation of various sources of information, and systematic organization and presentation .... ( )

_____ 23. Prepares analyses or summaries of programs, reports, specific operational items, or other data .... ( )

_____ 24. Compiles lists of numerical, verbal, or other descriptive data .... ( )

_____ 25. Compiles numerical or statistical data for tables, charts, rate schedules, or other uses with or without using a machine.. ( )

FIGURE 21

Example of Checklist Items

_____26. Prepares or compiles financial, statistical, or numerical statements and/or accompanying descriptive reports .... (   )

_____27. Draws up contracts, specifications, or other forms requiring specific knowledge of methods, procedures, policies, or other information .... (   )

_____28. Makes out routine schedules of work, production, appointments, arrivals, departures, or other matters .... (   )

_____29. Determines need for and/or makes routine orders for necessary supplies, materials, or other items... (   )

_____30. Makes assignments of facilities, vehicles, equipment, or similar items to provide for efficient and optimal use... (   )

FIGURE 21 (Cont.)

Source: C. H. Lawshe, *The Job Description Check-List of Office Operations* (Lafayette, Indiana: Occupational Research Center, Purdue University, April 1952), pp. 2, 3. Reprinted by permission.
†Machines that may be used in items No. 1, 2, 3, 4, 5 include machines such as: adding machine, billing machine, rotary-driven calculating machine; high-keyboard type of book-keeping machine, posting machine, cash register, key-driven calculating machine, typewriter-accounting type of bookkeeping machine.
‡Machines that may be used in items No. 7, 9, 11, 13, and 15 include such machines as: high-keyboard type of bookkeeping machine, typewriter-accounting type of bookkeeping machine, billing machine, posting machine, fanfold machine, check-writing machine, cash register

values, the average value of these items is quadrupled before the average value of the rest of the items is added to obtain a total point value for the job.

The checklist method of job evaluation is an adaptation of the forced choice method of employee rating. This rating method was developed to improve the reliability of ratings and to reduce the effect of rater bias. It is essentially a series of carefully worded statements whose weights have been developed statistically and are unknown to the rater. The rater uses the checklist by checking the statements that apply. The checklist is then turned in for scoring.

If continued research shows the checklist to be a useful instrument for evaluating clerical jobs, there is no reason why it cannot be applied to other types of jobs as well. Several of the experimental approaches to job analysis discussed in Chapter 5 develop task lists that could be used in this way.

OTHER JOB EVALUATION METHODS

The four basic methods of job evaluation represent majority practice in organizations. Although a number of combinations of the basic methods exist, such as combinations of factor-comparison and point plans, combinations of grading and point plans, and combinations of ranking, factor-comparison, and point plans, discussing them would achieve no further purpose. The methods examined in this section are sufficiently different from the basic methods to demand separate treatment.

Jaques' method of distinguishing jobs in terms of "time-span of discretion," mentioned in Chapter 3, may be considered to be a method of job evaluation. Job level, in Jaques' view, is determined by time-span of discretion (the longest period of time an employee is permitted to exercise discretion without review of his actions by his supervisor). Employees are held to be intuitively aware of the level of their work and fair pay for it. This approach focuses on definitions of job-related contributions held by employees and their managers, and a number of job-related contributions are apparently grouped under this global factor.

Application of the time-span approach has been limited. One problem has been that even with Jaques' detailed instructions,[15] measuring time-spans has proved difficult and whether they can, in fact, be measured is still controversial. Atchison[16] found that time-span and the results of the job classification method of job evaluation correlated very highly for engineers and scientists. Research carried out in the Netherlands found a high correlation between the results of analytical job evaluation and time-spans for nonmanual employees, but a lower correlation for manual employees.[17] Richardson[18] reports measuring both time-span and "felt-fair pay" in a large manufacturing organization and finding a high correlation between them. Another study, however, found that time-span is not highly correlated with either individual ability or job level.[19]

Another problem with the time-span approach has been with limiting job comparisons to the one factor. Especially manual workers, but probably other employees as well, appear to believe that several factors are required to explain differences among jobs. In other words, they believe that they are making a number of job-related contributions and they want these contributions recognized. As a consequence, some job

[15]Elliott Jaques, *Time-Span Handbook* (London: Heinemann, 1964).

[16]Thomas Atchison and Wendell French, "Pay Systems for Scientists and Engineers," *Industrial Relations* (October, 1967), pp. 44–56.

[17]National Board for Prices and Incomes, "Job Evaluation," *Report No. 83* (London: Her Majesty's Stationery Office, September, 1968), p. 7.

[18]Roy Richardson, "An Empirical Study of Fair Pay Perceptions and the Time Span of Discretion," unpublished doctoral dissertation (University of Minnesota, December, 1969).

[19]Paul S. Goodman, "An Empirical Examination of Elliott Jaques' Concept of Time-Span," *Human Relations* (May, 1967), pp. 155–170.

evaluation plans incorporate time-span as one of the compensable factors.[20] If, however, time-span of discretion is defined as the decision-making aspect of jobs, at least two job evaluation plans have appeared that are based on such a single factor.[21]

At the opposite extreme from Jaques' focus on the individual as the source of the definition of equity is a method that relies on the market. Called the guideline method of job evaluation, its major criterion of relative job value is that provided by the market place. In this method a large number of key jobs are selected. It is not uncommon for 50 per cent of an organization's jobs to be selected. These jobs are employed as survey jobs—the market rate for these jobs is determined. The market rates are compared to a schedule of pay grades constructed on the basis of intervals of five per cent. This schedule includes a minimum rate, a midpoint, and a maximum rate for each grade. The range varies from 30 per cent in the lower grades to 60 per cent in the higher grades.

The job evaluation process consists of matching market rates to the closest midpoint in the schedule of pay grades. At this point, adjustments of one or two grades may be made to accommodate internal job relationships. When the key jobs have been placed into grades, the remaining jobs are positioned by ranking them against key jobs. All jobs within the organization are evaluated at one time and the final job ordering includes all the organization's jobs.

The method was developed by Smyth and Murphy Associates, Inc., and has reportedly been tested in a number of organizations.[22] Primary advantages claimed for the guideline method are the speed and ease with which it may be installed and the resulting integrated pay structure.

Economic theory and organization practice both suggest that large organizations encompassing a number of job clusters can accommodate both the market and internal relationships best by administering separate pay structures for the separate job clusters. Apparently, however, the guideline method is sufficiently flexible to reconcile disparate job clusters. Champoux compared the simulated results of the

[20]Herbert D. Rossman, "Job Evaluation Study—1960," *Personnel Journal* (January, 1961), pp. 314–318.

[21]S. J. Goldenberg, "Significant Difference: A Method of Job Evaluation," *Canadian Personnel and Industrial Relations Journal* (May, 1968), pp. 19–23; A. W. Charles, "Installing Single-Factor Job Evaluation," *Compensation Review* (First Quarter, 1971), pp. 9–21.

[22]Anthony M. Pasquale, "A New Dimension to Job Evaluation," *AMA Management Bulletin No. 128* (New York: American Management Association, 1969); Richard C. Smyth, "Job Evaluation Failures," talk before the American Compensation Association (1965).

guideline method to the actual pay structure of a government agency over a ten year period and found that, although separate job clusters varied differentially from guideline results, the overall fit produced correlation coefficients of 0.95 and above for each year.[23] These results, however, are somewhat attenuated by the fact that the government agency studied administered one integrated pay structure and made extensive and continuing use of salary surveys.

But although the guideline method can apparently deal adequately with economic forces, it seems to represent a poor fit with the model of the employment exchange used in this book. No attempt is made to specify the job-related contributions provided by employees and required by organizations, unless it is assumed that the job level determined by the method is sufficient specification. Furthermore, the method treats the employment exchange as a purely economic exchange, which the model implies is dysfunctional to the organization. Although job-related contributions have an economic base, the organization requires contributions that are difficult to reduce to strictly economic terms.

Still another approach to job evaluation is the employment of cluster analysis to determine job relationships. From cluster analysis, job relationships emerge that can be used to classify jobs. Compensable factors are specified by the job clusters that result or from those that serve to create job relationships.

In an early, exploratory study, Thorndike[24] used a distance measure and an elementary clustering technique to sort twelve Air Force jobs into three job clusters. Each job was measured on nineteen dimensions and the position that each job occupied in the space determined by its measurement on these dimensions was computed. A distance measure representing the geometric distance between pairs of jobs was also obtained. A small distance value indicates job similarity and a large distance measure, job dissimilarity. The clustering technique identified groups of jobs that had highly similar distance measures, thus demonstrating the feasibility of the technique for classifying jobs. In another exploratory study, Orr[25] successfully applied this clustering technique to three samples of jobs measured in aptitude dimensions.

A number of others have employed different forms of cluster

[23]Joseph Edward Champoux, "A Test of the Guide Line Method of Job Evaluation," unpublished master's thesis (San Diego State, 1971).

[24]Robert L. Thorndike, "Who Belongs in the Family?" *Psychometrika* (December, 1953), pp. 267–276.

[25]David B. Orr, "A New Method for Clustering Jobs," *Journal of Applied Psychology* (February, 1960), pp. 44–59.

analysis to checklists of job activities, listings of managerial job elements, individual perceptions of job similarity, and interpersonal relations in jobs.[26] One of the most interesting applications of cluster analysis to the classification of jobs is the Systematic Approach to Multidimensional Occupational Analysis mentioned in Chapter 5. In this study 350 positions were classified according to technical, organizational, and communicational dimensions by cluster analysis.

Continued development of clustering techniques may have strong implications for job evaluation as a method of creating job structures based on agreed-on contributions. One possibility is to present employees with a questionnaire designed to elicit perceived importance of contributions, having employees rank jobs in terms of these same contributions, and finally employing cluster analysis via computer to group and classify jobs on the basis of these multidimensions.

Two other experimental approaches to job evaluation may deserve mention. Patten has applied the Guttman technique of scale analysis (a method of determining if the scale is measuring only one variable) to managerial positions.[27] Triandis has applied the semantic differential technique (a method of measuring meaning) to determine how managers and workers perceive jobs and found that both employ job complexity as the major determinant.[28]

RESEARCH ON JOB EVALUATION

Studies of job evaluation have been conducted primarily by psychologists. Lawshe and his associates at Purdue made a series of early studies of ready-made point plans and some factor-comparison plans and found that they all gave heavy weight to skill and that in all installations two or three factors carried most of the weight, although the factors varied by organization.[29] These findings led to the development and successful testing of some abbreviated scales and to the finding that

[26]Marvin D. Dunnette and Wayne K. Kirchner, "A Checklist for Differentiating Different Kinds of Sales Jobs," *Personnel Psychology* (Autumn, 1959), pp. 421–429; John K. Hemphill, "Job Descriptions for Executives," *Harvard Business Review* (September–October, 1959), pp. 63–68; M. Reeb, "How People See Jobs: A Multidimensional Analysis," *Journal of Industrial Psychology* (December, 1963), pp. 113–117; Kenneth R. Brown, "Job Analysis by Multidimensional Scaling," *Journal of Applied Psychology* (December, 1967), pp. 469–475.

[27]Thomas H. Patten, Jr., "Evaluating Managerial Positions by Evalograms," *Personnel Administration* (November–December, 1966), pp. 17–26.

[28]Harry C. Triandis, "Comparative Factorial Analysis of Job Semantic Structures of Managers and Workers," *Journal of Applied Psychology* (October, 1960), pp. 297–302.

[29]Published in the *Journal of Applied Psychology* from 1944–1949.

different methods of job evaluation yield highly similar results. Reliability of job ratings was found to be improved by reducing overlap among factors, good job descriptions, and rater training.

Recent psychological research has been concerned with the problems of job-rating scale construction and job-rater behavior. As in the case of job analysis, much of this research has been conducted by military psychologists.

One series of studies tested the reliability of different scale formats and found that higher reliabilities resulted when scale levels were defined and that benchmark tasks increased reliability over numerical designations. In one study of nine variations of a rating scale using the same group of raters, jobs, and factors, it was found that ratings were affected significantly by rating scale format.[30] One study appears to establish that use of job descriptions results in more reliable ratings than the use of job specifications alone.[31]

Other studies have been concerned with rater behavior and its antecedents. One study found that the perceptual sensitivity of raters varies with the trait rated.[32] Another developed a technique to predict whether prospective raters will rate higher or lower than group average.[33] A study of the extent to which bias is removed from job evaluation by using an outside evaluator without knowledge of the job confirms the difficulty of separating man and job.[34] Rater familiarity with jobs affects some factors and not others, may not affect or raise or lower job ratings, and is not simply ego involvement. In one study, two-thirds of job ratings were unaffected by rater familiarity.[35] Employees performing the same job in different parts of the organization and with differing amounts of experience may rate the same task state-

[30]Joseph M. Madden, "A Comparison of Three Methods of Rating Scale Construction," *Journal of Industrial Psychology* (June, 1964), pp. 43–50; David L. Peters and Ernest J. McCormick, "Comparative Reliability of Numerically Anchored Versus Job-task Anchored Rating Scales," *Journal of Applied Psychology* (February, 1966), pp. 92–96; Joseph M. Madden and R. D. Bourdon, "Effects of Variations in Rating Scale Format on Judgment," *Journal of Applied Psychology* (June, 1964), pp. 147–151.

[31]Joseph M. Madden and Joyce M. Giorgia, "Identification of Job Requirement Factors by Use of Simulated Jobs," *Personnel Psychology* (Autumn, 1965), pp. 321–331.

[32]James N. Mosel, Sidney A. Fine, and Jewell Boling, "The Scalability of Estimated Worker Requirements," *Journal of Applied Psychology* (June, 1960), pp. 156–160.

[33]Llewellyn Wiley and William S. Jenkins, "Methods for Measuring Bias in Raters Who Estimate Job Qualifications," *Journal of Industrial Psychology* (March, 1963), pp. 16–22.

[34]E. P. Prien and S. D. Saleh, "A Study of Bias in Job Analysis," *Journal of Industrial Psychology* (December, 1963), pp. 113–117.

[35]Joseph M. Madden, "The Effect of Varying the Degree of Rater Familiarity in Job Evaluation," *Personnel Administration* (November, 1962), pp. 42–46; Joseph M. Madden, "A Further Note on the Familiarity Effect in Job Evaluation," *Personnel Administration* (November–December, 1963), pp. 36–42.

ments differently.[36] But a method developed to measure rater consistency and interrater agreement found rater consistency very high, and the method does measure interrater agreement and source and extent of disagreement.[37] Finally, supervisors and workers have been found to agree on the difficulty of tasks.[38]

SUMMARY

This chapter has examined quantitative job evaluation methods as sources of job-related contributions. In addition, some job evaluation approaches that differ substantially from the basic methods were appraised. Finally, some research results on job evaluation techniques were reviewed.

[36]Francis D. Harding and David A. Naurath, "Effects of Job Experience and Organization on the Rating of Tasks," *Engineering and Industrial Psychology* (Summer, 1960), pp. 63–68.

[37]Joseph M. Madden, "Policy-Capturing Model for Analyzing Individual and Group Judgment in Job Evaluation," *Journal of Industrial Psychology* (June, 1964), pp. 36–42.

[38]J. T. Hazel, J. M. Madden, and R. E. Christal, "Agreement Between Worker-Supervisor Descriptions of the Worker's Job," *Journal of Industrial Psychology* (September, 1964), pp. 71–79.

8

Performance Contributions

The second measure of contributions to the employment exchange recognized by the organization (the first is job-related contributions) is performance on the job. Organizations implicitly recognize performance contributions through rate ranges and incentive plans.

As will be detailed in Part III, both rate ranges and incentive plans are prevalent organization practices throughout the world. Rate ranges are usual for office and technical and professional employees and are not unusual for production workers. Incentive plans, although practice varies by industry and country, apply to many production and sales workers and some clerical workers. Managers and some professional employees often work under both a rate range and an incentive plan.

Both practices assume that (1) differential performance is required by the organization, (2) individuals assigned to the same job differ in performance, (3) differential performance should be rewarded separately from job assignment, and (4) performance differences can be measured. Because these assumptions are important in understanding performance contributions to the employment exchange, each deserves some discussion.

The assumption that differential performance is required by the organization was discussed in Chapter 3. There it was seen that although all organizations probably require differential performance on some jobs, very few organizations require it on all jobs. On some jobs, differential performance cannot occur. Some types of work—jobs on an assembly line in an automobile plant, for example—offer little scope for variation in performance. Each employee is asked to perform in a specific way at a fairly definite speed. In some other situations, processes are structured exactly for technical reasons. On a number of factory jobs, the learning time is relatively short and all employees are expected to work in about the same way at about the same pace. On some office jobs, performance routines are so specified that little variation in individual output is possible. Many organizations are so structured that extra performance on some jobs would disrupt the work flows in others. Other jobs, of course, not only permit but require differential performance. Many sales jobs, professional jobs, and managerial jobs are examples.

The assumption that individuals assigned to the same job differ in performance if technical conditions permit is a valid one. Some men produce two or three times as much as others, and the best man sometimes produces five or six times as much as the worst man.[1] One careful investigation found a variation of over 100 per cent on routine work and concluded that a larger range of variation is to be expected on less routine work.[2] But the point is that not all jobs permit this variation and that not all organizations want it, whether they realize it or not.

The assumption that differential performance should be rewarded separately from job assignment would seem to require that (1) organizations and employees both know what kind of performance is required, and (2) can distinguish performance contributions from job-related and personal contributions. If better performance consists of additional or higher-quality output, no problem of definition exists. But what is improved performance when additional output comes at the expense of willingness to accept technological change, willingness to save time, concern for quality, optimum utilization of materials and equipment, cooperation with other employees and organization units, and/or flexibility in meeting changed demands? Incentive plans imply that improved performance means increased effort,[3] and it may be that some of the difficulties of operating incentive plans are attributable to employee resentment of being evaluated on the basis of a single contribution (effort) and to employee recognition that other contributions required by the organization are unrewarded. Rate ranges typically leave the specification of performance contributions to the performance appraisal process, which may include factors difficult to relate to performance (such as personal traits). Also, movement through ranges often turns out to be based on seniority, even if called performance or merit.

[1] Marion W. Richardson, "Forced-Choice Performance Records," *Personnel* (November, 1949), p. 207.

[2] H. M. Douty, "Some Aspects of Wage Statistics and Wage Theory," Industrial Relations Research Association, *Proceedings of the Eleventh Meeting* (Chicago, December 28–29, 1958), p. 201.

[3] Hilde Behrend, "The Effort Bargain," *Industrial and Labor Relations Review* (July, 1957), pp. 503–515.

Thus it would seem that neither oganizations nor employees have an unambiguous definition of performance contributions. In the case of incentive plans, is effort both a job-related contribution (as a factor in job evaluation plans) and a performance contribution? In the case of rate ranges, the required performance contributions would seem to be implied by the factors used in performance appraisal and by the criteria used to move employees through ranges.

The assumption that performance differences can be measured is met differently in the two methods. Incentive plans assume that performance can be measured. Rate ranges, however, assume that performance can only be evaluated or appraised. In part, this difference is attributable to the difference in how performance is defined.

PERFORMANCE MEASUREMENT

Incentive plans pay employees for results by comparing actual results to expected results. Hence, such plans require determination of expected results (called production standards) and methods of measuring actual results. Production standards are normally a responsibility of industrial engineers and are developed by the process of work study. Work study involves a detailed definition of the work layout, equipment, materials, process, machine feeds and speeds, working conditions, product quality, and all other details affecting output. The development of such a definition requires a detailed study of work procedures and of every operation of employees. Work study makes use of two techniques, which are employed in sequence: (1) methods study, and (2) work measurement. Methods study is employed to improve methods of production. Work measurement provides a base (standard) for assessing human effectiveness. Although work study is similar to job analysis, it is much more detailed and precise.

Work measurement requires that the work involved be susceptible to standardization of methods. Such standardization is accomplished through methods study, which develops methods information, determines a proper method, and provides means whereby the proper method is made known and used.

When the method of doing a particular job has been standardized, it becomes feasible to measure the work content of the job. Most work measurement methods do not attempt to measure the work content directly, only the time required to perform work units. The methods employed by industrial engineers are time study and its derivatives; *i.e.,* standard data or predetermined elemental times, and ratios. Time study determines the time taken to perform a given task by timing the elements, adjusting the time for the pace of the operator (called "leveling" or "rating"), and adding allowances for fatigue, minor delays, and personal needs. The rating or leveling feature of time study is a source of controversy and often unions insist that at best time study is an aid to bargaining.

Standard data or predetermined elemental times consists of the results of detailed time studies of elemental motions compiled and stored for future use. Use of these data consists of determining the elements of a task, obtaining the times from the compilation of standard data, and summing these times to obtain total time. An advantage of using standard data is the consistency provided by the method, and many organizations are using such systems. A number of systems of synthetic elemental times have been published.

Activity ratio studies consist of recording a series of observations of activities. Observations are made on a sampling basis and ratios between the different types of activity involved in the work cycle are calculated. Using this procedure, the distribution of activities over a day or week can be determined within specified limits of accuracy.

Production standards consist of standard times obtained by any of these methods, plus allowances. Quality levels are, of course, carefully considered in the analysis prior to setting production standards and often are specified in the standard itself.

Measuring performance consists of comparing actual results to production standards. Units are specified during the standard setting process, and the method and frequency of recording the completed units are part of the incentive plan procedure.

This brief explanation of the process of measuring performance under an incentive plan serves to point out (1) the specific and limited definition of performance contributions under these plans, (2) the complexity of the process of measurement, (3) the subjectivity remaining in spite of these attempts to obtain objectivity, and (4) the importance of production standards in the performance measurement process. Although the explanation applies primarily to production jobs, the measurement process is similar in all types of incentive plans—for clerical workers, for salesmen, for managers. Performance measurement requires determining the performance contribution to be measured, the units of measurement, standardizing the conditions of work, and a standard against which actual performance is to be compared.

PERFORMANCE APPRAISAL

In most organizations employee performance is not measured but rather is evaluated or appraised. Performance appraisal is a formal method of evaluating employees, which assumes that employee performance can be observed and assessed even when it cannot be objectively measured. Examining performance appraisal systems should yield evidence of the performance contributions valued by organizations and the manner in which these contributions enter the employment exchange.

Although every organization appraises employees whether it wants to or not or realizes it or not, not all organizations have formal employee appraisal programs. Various surveys, however, have established that a large majority of organizations have formal employee evaluation plans, although the proportion of plans covering white-collar employees is higher than those covering blue-collar employees.[4] The lesser incidence of evaluation plans involving blue-collar workers reflects the use of job rate pay plans, rate ranges where movement is based entirely on seniority, and incentive plans. It may also reflect management's reluctance to bargain on merit rating plans if the union insists, as required by a ruling of the National Labor Relations Board.[5]

Employee appraisal plans in organizations are used for a variety of purposes. Whisler and Harper[6] point out that performance appraisals are employed by organizations to answer four recurring questions: What should the individual's reward be? Where does the individual best fit in the organization? How can the individual be helped to perform better? How well are organization programs working? Although each of these questions calls for information on employee performance, its weight in the answer varies, as does the way in which the information is used. Thus it is quite possible that use of performance appraisal for determining individual salaries could conflict with its use for improving performance. Discussing ratings with subordinates, for example, appears unnecessary in pay determination, but improving performance seems impossible without this step. One answer, of course, is the development of a different appraisal method for each use. But beyond the expense involved is the matter of signals to employees. Employees are quite likely to follow perceived payoffs.

Organizations, therefore, are unlikely to use different appraisal plans for different purposes. But they often use different appraisal plans for different employee groups. For example, there may be separate evaluation plans for the following groups: shop employees, clerical em-

---

[4]William R. Spriegel, "Company Practice in Appraisal of Managerial Performance," *Personnel* (May–June, 1962), pp. 77–83; Richard V. Miller, "Merit Rating in Industry: A Survey of Current Practices and Problems," *ILR Research* (Fall, 1959), p. 12; National Industrial Conference Board, *Studies in Personnel Policy No. 194* (1964).

[5]Harold W. Davey, *Contemporary Collective Bargaining*, 2nd ed. (Englewood Cliffs, N.J.: Prentice-Hall, Inc., 1959), p. 263.

[6]Thomas L. Whisler and Shirley F. Harper, *Performance Appraisal* (New York: Holt, Rinehart, and Winston, 1962), p. 427.

ployees, supervisors and professional employees, sales employees, managers.

Pay and promotion decisions represent major uses of performance appraisal plans. A NICB survey[7] found 69 per cent of organizations using ratings for pay decisions and 73 per cent for promotion decisions. Thus, performance appraisals seem to be logical sources of performance contributions recognized by organizations.

PERFORMANCE STANDARDS

It was mentioned in the preceding section that performance measurement requires performance standards. Actually, so does evaluating performance. It is extremely difficult to determine the level of performance of a given employee without knowing what adequate performance consists of—the performance standard for the job.

The job description forms the basis for performance standards by specifying the tasks and their purposes. The next step is to determine how well each of these tasks is to be performed to represent acceptable performance. This may be accomplished through superior-subordinate conferences, statistical analysis of past records, or work measurement (as described under performance measurement). Obviously, the more objective the performance standards, the easier is the rating task.

Sufficient experience with the development of performance standards has been accumulated to show that such standards can be developed at various levels of precision for most jobs. A spokesman for the American Management Association has insisted that performance "standards can be established for any job in terms of quantity, quality, cost and time, even though the meeting of standards may sometimes be a matter of judgment rather than exact measurements."[8] Standards may be quantitative (numerical), qualitative (expressed in words), or verifiable (with reference to records for documentation).

But although appraising performance logically requires standards of performance, the fact of the matter is that probably most performance appraisal plans operate without them. In fact, as will be seen, perhaps the chief feature of one type of performance appraisal (often called appraisal by objectives) is that the development of performance standards is an integral part of the method.

PERFORMANCE APPRAISAL METHODS

Although there are many variations of performance appraisal methods, there are only two basic methods of appraising employees: (1)

[7]National Industrial Conference Board, *Studies in Personnel Policy No. 144* (1964), p. 17.

[8]*Research Study 42* (New York: American Management Association, 1960).

compare them to a standard, and (2) compare them to one another. To the extent that the standard is well developed, the first approach becomes applicable and consistent appraisals throughout the organization may be made. But to the extent that standards are weak or unavailable, comparing employees to one another yields more reliable results, if employees can be compared.

Rating Scales.   Rating scales involve comparing employees to a "standard." They ask the rater to appraise the "degree" of a factor that best describes the employee. The various degrees of the separate factors are usually assigned point values to obtain a total score for each employee when rating is completed.

Rating scales may be figuratively described as "rulers" against which employees are compared. One ruler is developed for each factor to be rated. Then each scale is divided into "inch-marks" or degrees. The factors and degrees are defined to permit the rater to choose the degree that in his judgment best describes the employee.

Quality of Work—Accuracy

How would you rate this individual with respect to the quality of the work he turns out, the neatness and accuracy evident in the job he does?

Careless worker. Tends to repeat some types of errors.	Work is sometimes unsatisfactory because of errors or untidiness.	Usually turns out acceptable work. Not many errors.	Checks and observes his work. Quality can be relied upon.	Work is of highest quality. Errors extremely rare, if any. Little wasted effort.

Comments: _____

FIGURE 22

Example of a Graphic Rating Scale

In form, rating scales typically provide a line for each factor, with the various degrees arrayed along the line in either increasing or decreasing order. (See Figure 22.) In the graphic rating scale, the line is thought of as a continuum, and the rater may place a check anywhere along the line. In the multiple-step rating scale, one or more boxes are provided in each degree for the rater's check mark. Typically, the extreme degrees have only one box and the intermediate degrees, two or more. Thus the multiple-step scale is not a continuous scale—it provides definite marks that the rater must choose from. In actual practice, the degrees in a graphic rating scale come to be regarded as steps and are used in that manner.

Rating scales are the most commonly used merit rating method and, as a consequence, have the advantage of familiarity. Another advantage is the information available for a discussion of the rating with the ratee. To the extent that those who use the scale attach the same meaning to the degree and factor definitions, the concept of a "standard" against which employees are compared is an advantage.

If, however, raters do not agree on the meanings of degrees and factors, the "standard" is illusory and becomes a disadvantage. Another disadvantage is a tendency often observed to use the same scale on jobs only roughly similar in nature. Insofar as the jobs involve different performance factors, different scales seem to be required. A third disadvantage appears when a total score is obtained after rating. This assumes that good performance on one factor can offset poor performance on another, and this may not be true. To the degree that there is overlapping between factors, one aspect may be inadvertently overweighted.

Rating scales for employee rating are similar to the rating scales used in the point method of job evaluation. In the discussion of point systems it was pointed out that actual weighting of the scales may be quite different from the weights specified when the system is developed. Thus weights should be applied after ratings have been completed and checked statistically. This point also applies to rating scales used for appraising personnel.

Although many rating methods have been developed since the appearance of rating scales, research evidence indicates that graphic rating scales are actually just as valid as the more complex methods.[9] For these results to emerge, however, research evidence shows that the following conditions must be met: (1) unambiguous descriptions of characteristics and degrees must be used, (2) evaluations are not given to those appraised, and (3) raters, especially overly considerate ones, must be trained in the desirability of a wide range of scores.[10]

Forced Choice Method. The forced choice approach, or preference checklist, involves presenting the rater with a number of sets of statements, phrases, or words describing job performance. The rater is required to choose from each set the items most descriptive and least descriptive of the individual. In a set of four items, two appear favorable and two unfavorable. Only one of the favorable items adds to the total score; only one of the negative-appearing items detracts from it. The value of the items is determined by statistical analysis of items based on

[9]A. C. Bayroff, H. R. Haggerty, and E. A. Rundquist, "Validity of Ratings as Related to Rating Techniques and Conditions," *Personnel Psychology* (Spring, 1954), pp. 93–113.

[10]John B. Miner, "Management Appraisal: A Capsule Review and Current References," *Business Horizons* (October, 1968), pp. 83–96. This excellent review of the research on performance appraisal is used extensively in the following sections.

the performance of successful and unsuccessful employees. The score values are not available to the rater. He is forced to check items that in his opinion are characteristic of the individual without knowing whether his ratings are placing a high or low value on the individual's performance. This secrecy feature is intended to reduce the influence of bias and to result in more effective ratings.

The forced choice approach was developed by the armed services. Since the man rated had ready access to his efficiency reports, scores tended to pile up at the high end of rating scales. The forced choice approach was developed to overcome this tendency.

The method appears to have two advantages. First, reducing rater bias should produce better ratings. Second, the rater is asked to report observations, not to evaluate what he has observed. In other types of rating, the rater is often asked to form a judgment based on his observations. In the forced choice, or preference checklist, however, he is only asked to report his observations. The evaluation is performed by the statistical method used to derive the item score.

The primary disadvantage of the method also flows from the secrecy feature. Raters resist a procedure that makes it difficult, if not impossible, for them to determine how they had actually rated a man. Also, under these conditions raters find ways to determine item scores. In use, therefore, leniency was not entirely overcome. The armed forces have abandoned the approach.

The forced choice approach would also seem to be of limited value as evidence of performance contributions. If neither the rater nor the ratee knows the performance contributions valued and devalued by the organization, the performance portion of the employment exchange is unspecified.

Another disadvantage of the forced choice approach is high cost. To be most useful, the items should be developed for specific jobs, and developing them and deriving score values require technical expertise and is time consuming.

The forced choice method of rating employees is the basis for the checklist method of job evaluation. As mentioned previously, checklists have been developed to both analyze and evaluate clerical jobs.

The Critical Incident Method.   The critical incident method involves determining those behaviors that are crucial to success and failure on given jobs. When these incidents occur they are noted, along with the date of occurrence, on the employee's performance record. This method also was developed by the armed services to overcome the problem of rater leniency.

The primary advantage of the critical incident approach and the accompanying performance record is the information available and the encouragement given the supervisor to observe and record performance continually. Also, a list of critical incidents would seem to represent the performance contributions required.

The primary disadvantage of the method is its complexity and cost. It is time consuming to develop critical incidents for jobs. Also, although the method provides raw material for ratings, a rating procedure is essential to complete the rating process. The approach has been discontinued by the armed forces because it did not solve the leniency problem in spite of its complexity and cost.

Employee Comparison Systems. The employee comparison (ranking) systems compare the *relative* performance of the employees in a group, as contrasted to rating scales, which compare employees to a "standard." In many cases in which these systems are used, relative overall performance is rated rather than performance on each of several factors. The techniques are equally applicable, however, to the use of several factors.

The paired-comparison method was discussed as a technique of ranking jobs in the ranking method of job evaluation. Here, each employee on a given job is "paired" with every other employee on the job. The rater then determines which of the two employees in each pair is better in terms of overall performance or in terms of each of the factors selected.

The rank-order method is a simple, direct method of appraising relative performance of employees on a given job. The rater simply ranks the employees on the job, using as a basis for judgment either overall performance or separate performance factors. A convenient device to facilitate ranking is to provide raters with a pack of cards, one for each employee. The rater then simply numbers them in sequence.

Another device to facilitate ranking (called alternation ranking) involves providing the rater with a form with two numbered columns labeled "most" and "least." Working from a list of employees to be rated, he places the person he adjudges to exhibit the most of a quality at the top of the "most" column and the one with the least at the bottom of the "least" column. After crossing these names from the list of employees, he continues until all employees have been ranked.

In both the paired-comparison and the rank-order system it is possible to obtain a total score by averaging the ranks given an employee by several raters.

In the forced distribution system the rater is required to distribute the employees among a limited number of categories (usually five) in such a way that a specified percentage of employees is assigned to each category. Typically, the distribution is as follows: (1) lowest 10 per cent, (2) next 20 per cent, (3) middle 40 per cent, (4) next 20 per cent, (5) highest 10 per cent. Employees may be rated once on overall performance or several times, once for each of several factors. A simple facilitating procedure is to type each employee's name on a separate card, provide the raters with the pack of cards, and ask them to distribute the cards into piles in the percentages specified.

Advocates of employee comparison systems cite as their major advantage greater accuracy of employee appraisal as compared to systems using an absolute standard. They point, for example, to psychological experiments to support the viewpoint that judgments of performance based on such a relative comparison are usually more adequate than those based on a defined standard. The relative simplicity of rating employees by comparing them with one another also is an advantage. Because of this simplicity, rater training may be less intensive when employee comparison systems are used. Of the employee comparison systems, probably the simplest and yet most reliable judgments can be obtained from the paired-comparison method.

A disadvantage of the employee comparisons systems is the lack of substantiating information attached to the ratings. Normally only a rating is available, with no further information explaining why that rating was given. At most the rater is provided with the factors on which employees are to be ranked and employees are not. Thus employee comparison methods do not provide information on performance contributions.

The forced distribution method is the only one of the employee comparison methods that employs any form of performance standard. In this method the standard is the average of group performance. But the required percentages may not apply in small groups and raters tend to resist using them.

A disadvantage shared by all employee comparison methods is the problem of employee comparability. Whatever group of employees is to be ranked, it must first be determined that their jobs are sufficiently comparable so that the employees can be ranked on the same factor or factors. Then raters must have sufficient information about each individual in the group to permit ranking. Finally, numbers present problems. Ranking any group greater than twenty presents grave difficulties. But ranking smaller groups and combining the rankings raises issues of whether rank one (or the highest 10 per cent) in one group represents the same performance as equivalent positions in other groups.

In spite of these disadvantages, a number of organizations use ranking methods to appraise the performance of certain employee groups. Engineers, for example, are ranked on performance in some organizations.

Appraisal by Objectives.　Appraisal by objectives or results compares employee performance to expected results. In the usual procedure, a rater and ratee agree on key anticipated objectives for the ratee, set up a plan or timetable for achieving them, and at a later time compare actual and planned accomplishments and revise goals for the next period.[11] Because the method was devised to improve employee performance rather than to make pay or promotion decisions, the comparison between actual and planned results is often done informally. But a number of organizations use rating scales to record degree of success in meeting each goal. Others rank employees on relative success in meeting goals.

The major advantage of the method is the specification of performance contributions. The goals become the standards of performance and both rater and ratee are aware of the definition of performance in the employment exchange. In fact, the effective feature of the method for improving performance has been found to be the specification of goals.[12] This finding agrees with Locke's research,[13] which shows that people who set specific goals perform at much higher levels than those who are told to "do their best."

A disadvantage of the appraisal by objectives approach is the possibility that the goals selected are those on which performance is easily measured rather than those that are important for accomplishing organization goals. But this possibility is inherent in all performance standards. Thinking of performance standards as specifying the performance contributions required by the organization and provided by the employee should serve to focus on objectives rather than activities.

RATING FACTORS

If the previous analysis is correct, the factor or factors employed in employee evaluation should represent performance contributions. The term "performance appraisal" implies this and the information required to answer the four questions representing rating purposes confirms it. This means that a factor called overall performance might be used or such factors as quantity of work, quality of work, achievement, errors, productivity, and workmanship. Separate rating plans for different employee groups permit the use of factors defining performance for specific groups.

[11]Edgar F. Huse, "Performance Appraisal—A New Look," *Personnel Administration* (March–April, 1967), pp. 3–5ff.

[12]Herbert H. Meyer, Emanuel Kay, and John R. P. French, Jr., "Split Roles in Performance Appraisal," *Harvard Business Review* (January–February, 1965), pp. 123–129.

[13]E. A. Locke, "The Relationship of Intentions to Level of Performance," *Journal of Applied Psychology* (February, 1966), pp. 60–66.

Research on performance appraisal shows that the closer the factors are to actual behavior and results, the more raters will agree in their evaluations.[14] Also, factors should be those that can be clearly described so that all raters will have the same kind of behavior in mind.[15] An approach that has proved successful both in selecting appropriate factors and in overcoming resistance to appraisal systems is to have those who will use the plan participate fully in its construction.[16]

If the model of the employment exchange used in this book is correct, selecting factors for use in performance appraisal would involve agreement between the organization and employees on the performance contributions required by the organization. Appraisal by objectives tends in this direction. But it should be possible for the parties to agree on the performance contributions required for each job cluster.

Examination of the employee evaluation plans of many organizations shows a strong tendency to include as factors a variety of personal traits that have little, if anything, to do with effective performance and that cannot adequately be judged solely from work behavior. Such qualities as personality, attitude, ability, ambition, and character are not unusual. Even if it were possible to evaluate employees on such factors, they yield no signals to employees about performance requirements of the organization. Furthermore, many of these traits could not be changed by the individual.

Many organizations that do emphasize performance factors also ask raters to appraise potential. This practice may be questioned. Not only may such ratings be redundant in that performance is the best measure of potential, but also research results suggest that ratings of potential are quite often invalid.[17]

RATERS

Appraisals may be made by superiors, peers, subordinates, or the individual to be rated. Almost all appraisals in organizations are made by the immediate superior. Although it appears logical in many in-

---

[14]J. P. Campbell, M. D. Dunnette, E. E. Lawler, and K. E. Weick, *Managerial Behavior, Performance, and Effectiveness* (New York: McGraw-Hill Book Company, 1970), p. 125.

[15]R. S. Barrett, *Performance Rating* (Chicago: Science Research Associates, 1966).

[16]*Ibid.;* P. C. Smith and L. M. Kendall, "Retranslation of Expectations: An Approach to the Construction of Unambiguous Anchors for Rating Scales," *Journal of Applied Psychology* (April, 1963), pp. 149–155.

[17]L. L. Ferguson, "Better Management of Managers' Careers," *Harvard Business Review* (March–April, 1966), pp. 139–152; J. B. Miner, "Bridging the Gulf in Organizational Performance," *Harvard Business Review* (July–August, 1968), pp. 102–110.

stances that fellow employees would have superior information on employee performance, little use has been made of peer ratings, perhaps on the grounds that supervisors have better information on organization performance requirements.

The research evidence on the relative merits of the different raters is mixed. One study indicates that although two levels of supervision agree quite well, superiors and co-workers do not, with the latter giving the higher ratings.[18] Other studies have found the same discrepancy between superior and self-ratings.[19] It appears that self-interest can influence peer, subordinate, and self-ratings to the point where their use as a sole source of appraisals could be disadvantageous to the organization.

On the other hand, combined superior and self-ratings in the appraisal by objective approach have been shown to be effective in many organizations, as discussed previously. It also appears that peer ratings by middle-and upper-level managers are quite free of bias and therefore are useful.[20]

A combination of superior, peer, and self-ratings has been recently suggested by Lawler.[21] Not only should knowledge that ratings by superiors are being obtained reduce any bias in peer and self-ratings, but also the three different observational perspectives should improve the combined rating. If the three views of employee performance agree, decisions based on them should not only be accepted, but also should enhance achievement of organization goals. If they do not agree, the results may suggest different views of performance contributions that ought to be examined. Such combined appraisals may very well be the approach to appraisals of the future.[22]

IMPROVING RATINGS

The research evidence that the average of ratings made by several individuals is superior to that made by one person[23] tends to support

[18]D. Springer, "Rating of Candidates for Promotion by Co-workers and Supervisors," *Journal of Applied Psychology* (October, 1953), pp. 347–351.

[19]E. P. Prien and R. E. Liske, "Assessments of Higher Level Personnel: III. Rating Criteria: A Comparative Analysis of Supervisor Ratings and Incumbent Self-Ratings of Job Performance," *Personnel Psychology* (Summer, 1962), pp. 187–194; J. W. Parker, E. K. Taylor, R. S. Barrett, and L. Martens, "Rating Scale Content: III. Relationships Between Supervisory and Self-Ratings," *Personnel Psychology* (Spring, 1959), pp. 49–63.

[20]H. E. Roadman, "An Industrial Use of Peer Ratings," *Journal of Applied Psychology* (August, 1964), pp. 211–214.

[21]Lawler, in *Journal of Applied Psychology* (October, 1967), pp. 369–381.

[22]Miner, in *Business Horizons* (October, 1968), pp. 83–96.

[23]Bayroff, Haggerty, and Rundquist, in *Personnel Psychology* (Spring, 1954), pp. 93–113.

the combined approach just discussed. Although average ratings from any one source obviously are less biased than any single biased rating, it has often proved difficult to find more than one superior with sufficient knowledge of an employee's work behavior to enable him to appraise it. An obvious advantage of peer and subordinate appraisals is that they have good opportunities to observe behavior.

If adequate knowledge of employee performance permits, appraisals made by managers at several hierarchial levels improve ratings. Such managers may make their appraisals independently, or with knowledge of the appraisal made by lower-level managers. But the evidence shows that making changes in the appraisals made by lower-level managers does nothing to improve ratings.[24]

Ratings tend to be improved by relatively frequent appraisals in that research indicates that ratings are affected by recent events.[25] Perhaps every six months is the longest period that should elapse between appraisals unless raters keep notes during a longer rating period.

The research evidence indicates that the most powerful device for improving appraisals is rater training. Training has been shown to increase agreement among raters, reduce bias, increase rating accuracy, prevent inflation of ratings, and spread out the rating distribution.[26] Such training should provide opportunities for discussion of the plan and the appraisal process. When raters are involved in the development of the appraisal method, those involved have achieved a good deal of training. But training is needed in the importance of careful appraisals, the desirability of a wide range of rating scores, the influence of recent events, and how to minimize common rating errors such as central tendency, halo effect, and leniency.

Central tendency, or ratings that show little spread, is particularly amenable to rater training. When raters are cautioned to make ratings conform to the actual dispersion of individual performance, rating results are improved. Halo effect, the tendency to carry the influence of one factor throughout the rating, is also reduced by making raters aware of the tendency. Leniency can be reduced by ensuring that raters agree on the meaning of the factors used, but it has been found that particular stress must be placed on getting overly considerate managers to curb their leniency.[27]

[24]Miner, in *Business Horizons* (October, 1968), pp. 83–96.

[25]Campbell *et al.*, *Managerial Behavior, Performance, and Effectiveness*.

[26]Lee Stockford and H. W. Bissell, "Factors Involved in Establishing a Merit Rating Scale," *Personnel* (September, 1949), pp. 94–115; R. Bitner, "Developing an Industrial Merit Rating Procedure," *Personnel Psychology* (Winter, 1948), pp. 403–432; J. Levine and J. Butler, "Lecture vs. Group Discussion in Changing Behavior," *Journal of Applied Psychology* (February, 1952), pp. 29–33.

[27]M. S. Klores, "Rater Bias in Forced-Distribution Performance Ratings," *Personnel Psychology* (Winter, 1966), pp. 411–421.

In view of the consistently favorable evidence of the effect of training on appraisal programs, it is surprising to find its use by organizations limited. Lack of adequate training has been cited as the major problem of most appraisal programs.[28]

PERFORMANCE APPRAISAL PROBLEMS

In many organizations performance appraisal is a controversial matter. Some managers resist its use, often because they believe strongly in basing decisions on seniority.[29] Other managers doubt that effective performance appraisals can be made in organizations and state that a common tendency is for managers to decide on salary first and then adjust performance ratings to fit it. The evidence shows that it is the less effective managers who are most opposed to performance appraisal.[30]

Much of the controversy may be traced to the use of the same performance appraisal for the four purposes mentioned previously. The research evidence suggests that separate performance appraisals be made for the different purposes and that only those ratings designed for the purpose of aiding in employee development and in improving performance be discussed with those evaluated.[31] Following these suggestions plus involving managers in developing the system reduce resistance to appraisals. Forbidding feedback to ratees on ratings for pay adjustment purposes and training raters in the importance of appraising performance conscientiously serve to reduce the problem of biased ratings. An especially attractive suggestion is to inform managers that appraisals represent decisions of the immediate superior but the organization reserves the right to compare appraisals and other decisions made by the manager regarding the employee for consistency over time.[32] Of course, with such a policy the rater must be given the authority to make distinctions among people that he can defend and must not be required to make distinctions that he cannot defend.

As mentioned at the beginning of the discussion of performance appraisal, such plans exist to provide answers to four recurring ques-

[28]F. M. Lopez, *Evaluating Employee Performance* (Chicago: Public Personnel Association, 1968).

[29]J. B. Miner, *Personnel and Industrial Relations—A Managerial Approach* (New York: The MacMillan Company, 1969).

[30]L. W. Gruenfeld and P. Weissenberg, "Supervisory Characteristics and Attitudes Toward Performance Appraisals," *Personnel Psychology* (Summer, 1966), pp. 143–151.

[31]Meyer, Kay, and French, in *Harvard Business Review* (January–February, 1965), pp. 123–129.

[32]Whisler and Harper, *Performance Appraisal*, p. 436.

tions in organizations. The question—How much should the individual's pay be?—may be answered by an appraisal of his performance. But, as the discussion of membership and performance motivation in Chapter 3 suggests, not all jobs nor even all organizations require performance motivation. When, however, organizations do require performance motivation, the main ingredient is the credibility of the relationship between performance and rewards. Unless individuals accept the validity of performance appraisals and unless they know what kinds of performance the organization requires and accepts, obtaining performance motivation is impossible.

SUMMARY

This chapter has examined performance measurement and performance appraisal for evidence of the performance contributions to the employment exchange. This examination suggests that organizations have assumed that both they and employees are aware of the kinds of performance required and that the primary issue is measurement. As a result, performance measurement seems to imply that what the organization wants is more effort. Performance appraisal, on the other hand, implies that the organization wants more performance but has not thought through what performance it wants nor how to measure it. An unpublished study by the author and a colleague found that managers cannot classify items in a list of possible contributions taken from job evaluation and performance appraisals into job-related, performance, and personal factor classes with a reliability greater than pure randomness. Because performance motivation depends not only on the credibility of performance measures and appraisals but also on employee's knowing what kinds of performance the organization wants and can accept, it seems important for organizations to more carefully specify performance contributions. Appraisal by objectives and further development of performance standards are steps in this direction.

9

Personal Contributions

Compensation, at least in theory, represents rewards for contributions. Thus, according to the tenets of compensation administration, organizations pay first for job-related contributions and second (at least on some jobs) for performance contributions. Personal contributions (defined as personal traits not required by the job) are not rewarded because doing so would represent paying for contributions not required by the organization.

Equity theory, on the other hand, holds that there are a large number of potential contributions that may be recognized and considered relevant to the employment exchange and that if a contribution is perceived as relevant by one of the parties to the exchange, it goes into the determination of equity. Thus it seems important to examine potential contributions to determine which of them are recognized and rewarded by organizations and which of them, if perceived as relevant by employees and not recognized by the organization, can cause feelings of inequity.

Job-related and performance contributions have been discussed. To the extent that these contributions are clearly understood by employees to be involved in the employment exchange, they represent no difficulties. But to the extent that they are not understood, they too may lead to feelings of unfairness.

It is quite well established that employees expect to be paid in accordance with the level of difficulty and importance of their jobs and, often, for extra performance on the job. Organizations strongly influence the beliefs of their members, especially when they reinforce beliefs widely held in an industrial society. But for organizations to influence employee beliefs, the signals must be clear. Employees must learn what contributions the organization needs and can accept and those the organization does not need and cannot accept. In both the chapters on job-related and performance contributions, it was seen that organizations have not been careful about their signals with respect to contributions.

Also, although few organizations today employ personal rates (paying the person for what he is rather than what he does), it is not clear that this accords with the wishes of all employee groups. At least certain employee groups (craftsmen, professionals, at least some managers) appear to believe that they should be paid for individual attributes rather than for their job assignments and that organizations need these contributions whether they realize it or not, and should reward them. Organization practices that yield ambiguous signals with respect to the contributions it requires and accepts may serve to reinforce these beliefs.

This chapter examines a number of potential contributions and organization practice with respect to them. Although the chapter is entitled "personal contributions," what to include is not clear. Organizations give ambiguous signals about what contributions they need and can accept. As will be seen, some of these contributions are rewarded even though the organization denies it. Others are actively sought during the selection process but are only rewarded if required by the job assignment. Still others are interpreted by the organization as job-related contributions, but by individuals as personal contributions that should be rewarded by the organization whether used by the organization or not. Finally, the typical ambiguity with which most organizations define performance contributions means that some of them are perceived by employees to be needed by the organization but are not so perceived by the organization.

AGE AND SENIORITY

Few organizations officially recognize age or seniority as contributions. Although governmental organizations often have pay ranges wherein movement is automatic, business organizations typically officially deny such an approach by calling them merit ranges unless bargained into union contracts. In actuality, however, most pay ranges in business organizations involve movement based on seniority.[1] A study of the relationship between size of pay increases and seniority would

[1]Sumner H. Slichter, James J. Healy, and E. Robert Livernash, *The Impact of Collective Bargaining On Management* (Washington, D.C.: The Brookings Institution, 1960), pp. 604–606.

show high correlations in most organizations, and higher-level jobs tend to be filled by high-seniority people. A careful study of wage dispersion within occupations in an urban labor market found seniority to be the single most powerful explanatory variable, but that age up to a maximum was also positively associated with wage rates.[2]

The belief that seniority is a contribution that should be rewarded is not limited to lower-level employees. Many managers as well have a strong belief in the seniority principle.[3] A survey of management salaries and a number of explanatory variables found the correlation between age and salary to be 0.39 (N = 300) and between experience and salary to be 0.62.[4]

Perhaps the strongest evidence that at least certain employee groups and organizations perceive age and seniority as contributions that should be recognized in the employment exchange is the use of the maturity curve in salary determination for engineers and scientists. Maturity curves are graphs that plot salaries (on the vertical axis) against age or years of experience.

Actually, maturity curves might be more properly called progression curves and involve two somewhat different approaches. In the career curve approach, professional employees are assumed, after they finish their education, to develop at some standard rate as a result of experience. Years since degree and performance are the contributions recognized, and a chart (see Figure 23) relating salary and years for several levels of performance is used for salary determination.

The individual contribution approach is similar, but instead of separate curves for each performance level, a small number of performance groups are recognized. Figure 24, for example, recognizes three performance or ability groups. Placing an individual with a certain number of years of experience into one of these three groups recognizes age and performance as contributions and establishes an applicable salary range.[5] Although maturity curves may be said to recognize performance, they also recognize age and seniority as contributions. An additional unit of age and seniority represents additional contributions to the organization regardless of the performance level.

Elliott Jaques reports that his empirical work in a large number of organizations establishes that individual capacity grows and declines

[2]Albert Rees and George P. Schultz, *Workers and Wages in an Urban Labor Market* (Chicago: University of Chicago Press, 1970).

[3]J. B. Miner, *Personnel and Industrial Relations—A Managerial Approach* (New York: The Macmillan Company, 1969).

[4]Kenneth E. Foster, "Accounting for Management Pay Differentials," *Industrial Relations* (October, 1969), pp. 80–87.

[5]Robert E. Sibson, *Wages and Salaries,* rev. ed. (New York: American Management Association, 1967), pp. 181–185.

with age.[6] Thus he offers a family of earnings progression curves to be used in salary adjustments. Apparently, age and seniority are becoming increasingly recognized as contributions of managerial-level employees. Increasingly, the literature on managerial compensation refers to the career-path concept and salary growth charts.[7]

The idea of a "market for careers"[8] suggests that increasingly at least management and professional people will perceive themselves as associated with a field. Although they may be employed by a single employer for a long period of time, they perceive their development

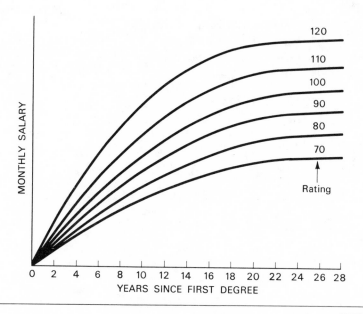

FIGURE 23

Career Curves

Source: Figures 23 and 24 from Robert E. Sibson, *Wages and Salaries: A Handbook for Line Managers* (New York: American Management Association, 1960), p. 170. Reprinted by permission.

[6]Elliott Jaques, *Equitable Payment* (New York: John Wiley and Sons, Inc., 1961).
[7]"The Career-Path Concept for Managers Overseas," *Compensation Review* (Second Quarter, 1971), pp. 50–52; Robert A. Smith, "Achieving Flexibility in Compensation Administration," *Compensation Review* (Fourth Quarter, 1970), pp. 6–14.
[8]Peter Drucker, "The New Markets and the New Capitalism," *The Public Interest* (Fall, 1970), pp. 44–79.

in their field as a contribution that should be recognized by the employer. The similarity between the idea of a career for "knowledge workers" and the craftsman (who is affiliated with his field rather than an employer and expects the standard rate for whatever level of work the employer assigns him) should not be ignored. Professionals have long expected that their growing capacities be recognized regardless of the complexity or simplicity of the client's problem. A full professor assumes that he is making greater contributions than an associate or assistant professor, although their jobs are identical.

All of this suggests that individuals believe and many organizations agree that increased age (up to a certain point) and increased experience (measured by seniority) represent additional contributions that should be recognized and, if possible, used by organizations. But, according to this viewpoint, it is up to the organization to use or permit the use of these contributions. This approach (often called the man approach as opposed to the job approach), stresses that as the individual increases his competence the contributions he brings to the organization have increased whether the organization utilizes them or not. This view of the employment exchange is quite different from viewing it as a purely economic transaction involving the purchase and sale of units of labor.

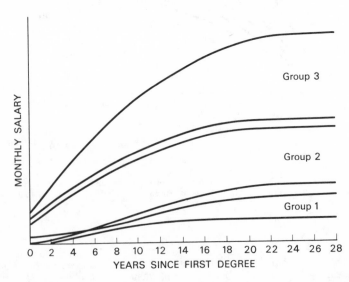

FIGURE 24

Individual Approach

SEX AND RACE

Sex and race are not to be considered in the employment exchange as a matter of social policy, and no legitimate organization counts them as (negative) contributions in determining rewards. Not only is such recognition prohibited by law, it is morally reprehensible. The tenets of compensation administration specify that jobs and performance on jobs are colorblind and sexless.

But the evidence is otherwise. The Rees and Shultz study cited previously found wages in identical occupations lower for women than for men and, in general, lower for nonwhites and workers with Spanish surnames than for whites. This finding implies either that enough organizations with personal rate systems exist and involve discrimination to influence the statistics or that organizations with merit ranges correlate race and sex with performance.

In fairness, it should be recognized that most discrimination is not due to compensation administration but to selection. Women and nonwhites with qualifications identical to those of white males are placed in lower-level jobs. Even today women college graduates receive starting salaries about 17 per cent lower than men with identical degrees.

Although job evaluation is concerned with jobs and not incumbents, in many organizations practice distinguishes men's jobs and women's jobs and, at least in the past, lower-level jobs were reserved for minorities. Although such practice is disappearing, where it exists it implies that sex and race are negative contributions.

PERSONAL APPEARANCE

The appearance and other physical attributes of employees are not considered to be contributions to the employment exchange according to the doctrine of compensation administration. Job evaluation does not consider job incumbents, and performance is presumably uninfluenced by appearance and physical attributes.

But as everyone knows, organizations do consider appearance in selecting employees at least for certain jobs. Receptionists are attractive more often than not. No one is surprised to discover that an unattractive secretary is more than normally efficient.

Physical attributes are probably counted as contributions even though organizations deny it. Taller male college graduates command higher starting salaries than shorter ones. Although solid information is unavailable, it seems possible that performance appraisals are influenced by physical attractiveness.

Very interestingly, people believe that appearance should be counted as a contribution to the employment exchange. In a number of unpublished studies the author and a colleague found that most respondents in all demographic and occupational categories considered personal appearance to be a legitimate contribution to the employment exchange, but not an important one.

LIFE STYLE

The tenets of compensation administration specify that an individual's life style is neither a positive nor negative contribution to the employment exchange. Only if an individual's personal life incapacitates him for any job or adversely affects his performance on his job do such considerations enter, and then only indirectly.

Undoubtedly, most organizations today do assiduously avoid interference in or consideration of an employee's personal life in organization decisions. But managers make organization decisions and their opinions of subordinates' life style may affect them. In another unpublished study made by the author and a colleague, a sample of 40 managers with salary determination authority considered such personal factors as divorce and irresponsible appearing recreation activities as important negative contributions and church and other positively valued affiliations as important positive contributions. In fact, these managers considered personal factors to be more important contributions than performance.

ADAPTABILITY, COMMITMENT, COOPERATION, CREATIVITY, INITIATIVE, JUDGMENT, AND RELIABILITY

These factors represent contributions required by organizations. Organizations need behavior indicating adaptability or flexibility in the face of changed conditions, commitment to the job and the organization, cooperation with other people and organization units, creativity in approaching problems, willingness to take action without urging, reasoned approaches to organization problems, and dependability. Although the requirements for these contributions vary somewhat by job, organizations need these behaviors and employees realize it. In fact, it has been suggested that a primary basis for resentment of wage incentive plans is that employees recognize that organizations need these contributions but pay only for effort.[9]

[9]John Corina, *Forms of Wage and Salary Payment for High Productivity* (Paris: Organisation for Economic Co-operation and Development, 1967).

A number of organizations include these contributions in performance appraisals. Unfortunately, however, most organizations assume that these factors are personality traits rather than behaviors that may be exhibited in varying amounts on jobs. Personality traits are particularly difficult to rate because they are viewed so nebulously that agreement on whether people possess them is almost impossible.[10] Furthermore, managers resist rating personality traits on the grounds that such traits are very difficult or impossible to change.

But behaviors representing kinds of performance the organization requires can be appraised. Definitions of the kinds of behavior the organization needs can be developed for separate job clusters together with standards of performance specifying evidence of effective behaviors. Appraisal by objectives would seem to be one approach to broadening definitions of performance to those behaviors the organization needs and employees know the organization needs.

SELF-IMPROVEMENT EFFORTS

Although organizations reward employees who improve their skills and abilities by promotion, compensation administration doctrine does not recognize self-improvement efforts as contributions unless these efforts serve to improve performance on the present job. Although this approach appears logical following the job approach, the man approach and the careers concept (discussed under age and seniority) imply that as the individual acquires greater competence the contributions he brings to the organization have increased whether the organization utilizes them or not. Individuals of all demographic and occupational categories believe that self-improvement efforts represent contributions of at least some importance to the employment exchange.

ACCEPTANCE OF RESPONSIBILITY, EFFORT EXPENDED, EDUCATION, INTELLIGENCE, JOB KNOWLEDGE, AND EXPERIENCE

These contributions are considered by organizations to be job-related and they form the basis of job evaluation plans. In job evaluation, as discussed previously, jobs are adjudged to acquire difficulty or importance based on the amounts of these contributions required of the job incumbent. If the job incumbent must carry a great deal of responsi-

[10]John B. Miner, "Management Appraisal: A Capsule Review and Current References," *Business Horizons* (October, 1968), pp. 83–96.

bility of various kinds; expend large quantities of mental and/or physical effort; possess a high level of education, intelligence, and job knowledge; and have a great deal of experience, the job is placed high in the hierarchy.

Although initiates to the cult of job evaluation understand very clearly the distinction between man and job, this distinction may not be clear to the uninitiated. To initiates, these contributions are a short-cut for appraising the level of job content.

But to the uninitiated, they are personal contributions. After all, it is people who carry responsibility, expend effort, and acquire education and experience, not jobs. If these individuals consider these contributions to be personal rather than job-related contributions, they may logically believe that individuals who bring more of these contributions to the organization are making greater contributions regardless of work assignment.

CONCLUSIONS REGARDING CONTRIBUTIONS TO THE EMPLOYMENT EXCHANGE

Our analysis of contributions to the employment exchange suggests that compensation administration is strongly influenced by a strictly economic view of employment. It views contributions as labor services purchased by the organization. Only those services actually used are to be paid for. Following this reasoning, compensation administration views itself as measuring contributions (labor services) first by job assignment and second by performance on that job assignment.

Individuals learn the broad outlines of contributions expected in work in the general socialization process and the specific contributions expected by the organization after they join it through organization socialization. The process of organization socialization is powerful. Individuals learn very quickly to make the contributions that organizations require in order to obtain the rewards that they seek from the employment exchange.

But, perhaps because organizations view employment solely as an economic transaction, they have assumed that employees clearly understand what contributions the organization requires although organization practices provide ambiguous signals. Organizations quite obviously reward for personal contributions even though they say they do not. Organizations obviously require performance contributions not recognized in the reward system. Organizations profess to pay for jobs by evaluating what appear to be personal contributions.

It would seem that better understanding of the actual employment exchange calls first for recognition that the employment exchange is broader than an economic transaction and then thinking through for each employee group what contributions the organization requires and can accept. In the case of some employee groups, the required contributions will be bargained. Members of other groups will be informed of expected contributions at the time they are hired. But all employees should know the contributions expected and accepted from their employee group.

Some, perhaps most, employee groups will be paid for job assignment. Job evaluation seems to be acceptable procedure for defining job-related contributions and can achieve understanding of the distinction between job-related and personal contributions by careful explanation. As we have seen, the most powerful explanatory device is full participation.

Some groups will be paid solely for job-related contributions. In these cases, it is particularly important that those contributions recognized are those that are actually made in the employment exchange. Unrecognized contributions may be a particularly potent source of feelings of inequity.

Some groups will be paid for job-related contributions plus seniority—a personal contribution in the terminology used here. In such cases, it seems particularly important that employees understand the distinction between job-related and personal contributions.

Some groups will be paid for job-related contributions plus performance contributions. The number of these groups would be expected to be smaller than under present arrangements, as organizations realize the stringent requirements of performance motivation. Where groups are paid for performance contributions, much more attention than presently given is called for in defining the performance contributions that the organization requires and can accept from each group. From some of these groups (management, for example) the organization may want and may be able to accept total commitment. But fewer organizations will want to limit performance contributions of any group to greater effort.

Although it will be difficult for organizations to accept (at least economic ones), some employee groups may insist on being paid for personal contributions rather than job-related and performance contributions. Such employee groups will insist on being paid for their education, experience, and competence in their field without regard to job assignment. For some of these groups, the organization may be able to design the job around the man (some managers, for example), thereby translating personal contributions into job-related contributions. In these cases, performance contributions may be defined and recognized. In other groups, personal contributions will remain the basis of the employment exchange. In these groups, it may be possible to separate performance contributions from personal contributions and separately reward performance contributions. But the difficulty of defining performance contributions in strictly organizational terms may mean that such separate recognition of performance is often largely ceremonial, representing extra rewards for growing personal contributions. Fortunately for organizations, most employees who demand to be paid for personal contributions may have a high need for achievement, and thus organizations can focus on permitting performance rather than on meeting the requirements of performance motivation.

Designing quite different employment exchanges for different employee groups is not easy. But it often represents making official what already occurs while reducing the feelings of inequity with attendant low productivity, absenteeism, and turnover.

Rewards

Rewards for work include all those things that the employee receives as a consequence of the employment exchange. In systems terms, they represent inputs to employees from the organization in exchange for outputs from employees in the form of contributions. To the organization, rewards represent outputs to employees in exchange for inputs from employees in the form of employee contributions. To both, outputs must exceed inputs if the systems are to survive and achieve their goals. Employees, in other words, must perceive their rewards as greater than their contributions and organizations must perceive rewards provided employees as less than employee contributions.

Defining rewards in this way suggests that rewards are of various kinds and that organizations may be supplying a greater variety of rewards than they are typically aware of. Organizations are, of course, aware that they are providing economic rewards and that these economic rewards are limited by organization resources. They may or may not be aware that they are providing many other kinds of rewards, only some of which are limited by organization resources.

The variety of rewards from the employment exchange is almost endless. There are several ways of classifying them. For example, rewards may be classified as economic and noneconomic or as extrinsic (provided by the organization) and intrinsic (provided by the individual to himself). Both classification systems provide useful information—the former because it emphasizes what to most of us are the primary rewards from work, the latter because it emphasizes that many rewards from work are provided by the individual and may be cost-free to the organization.

The classification used here attempts to capture the advantages of both classification systems. It also recognizes that, although organizations are not always aware of it, organization rewards divide into three types based on purpose. Job rewards are those attached to a particular job. Performance rewards are allocated on the basis of differential performance. Membership rewards are those an individual receives simply because he is a member of the organization. [1]

Thus, Part III first examines economic rewards associated with jobs, performance, and membership, and second, noneconomic rewards in terms of these same three purposes. As will be seen, some of the more important intrinsic rewards are noneconomic performance rewards.

[1]William Foote Whyte, *Organization Behavior* (Homewood, Illinois: Richard D. Irwin, Inc., 1969), pp. 74–75.

10

Economic Job Rewards—
Wage Level

The primary reward for work in the view of employees and organizations is the wage or salary. This figure determines the employee's standard of living. It, at the same time, determines a substantial portion of the organization's costs. Although it is the individual who receives the paycheck, wages are attached to the job to which he is assigned. Thus wages are job rewards. Wages are prices to the employer and income to the employee—both economic variables. Thus wages are economic job rewards.

Wages are administered prices in that they are results of decisions of the parties to the employment exchange. Although market forces influence the wage set, other forces are operating to influence the decision. Decisions imply alternatives and in wage decisions a wide range of alternatives usually exists.

Economic forces set upper and lower limits, but in the usual case a wide range of alternatives exists between them. In fact, if no alternatives exist (one wage rate exists in the market), experience shows that this result is not due to market forces but to their attenuation—usually by a strong labor union.

The range of alternatives set by economic forces involves the survival of the organization. Below some minimum wage, the organization is unable to recruit and retain employees. Above some maximum wage, the economic resources of the organization are exceeded. Obviously, these limits are influenced by the time period under consideration. For a short time, organizations might attract employees at zero or negative wages and, at the other extreme, pay out in wages all the resources the organization possesses or can command. But for any significant period of time, wages cannot go below some positive value and still attract and retain employees or above some point and still permit an organization to allocate its resources to all essential uses. The longer the period under consideration, the smaller the range between the upper and lower limits. The time period helps explain differences in union and management perspectives in collective bargaining, with the union emphasizing short-term possibilities and management, longer-term considerations.

Within this range there is room for judgment and bargaining. For example, the employer usually controls hiring specifications and can raise or lower them to attract employees at a given wage. Or he can train his own employees and promote from within and thus compete in the labor market only at starting rates. Or he can search for employees who are less interested in wages than in other rewards less costly to the organization. He can change his approach depending on general business conditions, labor turnover, or need to expand employment. Actually, the employer may not know the maximum wage he can pay until, having been forced to pay above what he honestly believed to be the maximum, he is able to survive by increasing efficiency and cutting costs. Furthermore, his competitive position may be either improving or declining, with the result that he has difficulty estimating a feasible wage for even a short period ahead.

That upper and lower limits exist does not mean that they are clearly defined in the mind of the employer. The organization may be unconcerned with its precise position in this range unless it is close to one of the limits and in danger of being pushed beyond it. The employer may also search harder for information indicating the limits if he is confronted by union demands than he would if no unions were involved.

The minimum and maximum of the range of wages are influenced by different sets of forces.[1] The minimum is influenced by conditions in the local labor market; the maximum, by conditions in the market for the organization's product or service. Accordingly, the minimum is influenced by such forces as (1) going rates in the community, (2) amount of unemployment in the area, (3) expansion or contraction of employment by labor market competitors, (4) the organization's plans regarding level of employment, and (5) its customary wage position in the area. The maximum is influenced by such considerations as (1) the elasticity of demand for the product, (2) whether product demand is rising or falling, (3) the proportion of labor costs to total costs, (4) whether product prices are set competitively or administered, and (5) the relative efficiency of the organization.

[1]Lloyd G. Reynolds, *Labor Economics and Labor Relations,* 5th ed. (Englewood Cliffs, N.J.: Prentice-Hall, Inc., 1970), pp. 616–619.

The different forces determining the minimum and maximum may mean that the range between them is wide or that they almost coincide. An organization adhering to industry wage rates may be so far above area wage rates that the minimum is meaningless. But an organization in a low-paying industry located in a high-wage area may find that its maximum and minimum almost coincide.

Although the organization in a high-wage industry located in a low-wage area has a wide range of economic alternatives, its actual alternatives may be restricted. Other organizations in the industry may exert upward pressure by holding that paying less than industry rates involves unfair competition. Organizations in the area may exert downward pressure to avoid upsetting the labor market. The strength of these pressures varies greatly by industry. In large-scale, prominent, competitively insulated industries, organizations are likely to follow industry rates. In small-scale, less visible, highly competitive industries, the organization is more likely to be influenced by area wage rates.

The existence of a range between maximum and minimum wages also permits union pressures to operate. Union pressures may force organizations closer to their wage maximums, especially if the organization is part of high-wage industry in a low-wage community. Unions attempt to equalize wage rates of organizations competing in the same product market. Union pressure may even raise an organization's wage maximum by forcing it to pay more than it honestly believed possible. In such cases reduction in profit level prompts management action to reduce costs and increase efficiency, thereby increasing the organization's wage maximum. Such union pressures are subject to miscalculation, however, in that an organization forced beyond an unalterable wage maximum may not survive.

Both the minimum and maximum of the range of wage rates may be changed by economic conditions as well as by employer and union actions. An increase in the demand for the organization's product or service permits an increase in the employer's maximum, as does any improvement in the efficiency with which labor is utilized. In inflationary periods, wage increases may be passed on to consumers as price increases with no loss of sales. In recessions, both the maximum and minimum may be lowered as demand for product or service falls and as potential employees become available at lower wages.

Organizations of different kinds, of course, have quite different economic limits on wages. Business organizations vary by industry in demand elasticity and labor cost to total cost ratios and thus have widely varying wage possibilities. Public organizations compete in the same labor markets but differ greatly in sources of revenue, labor cost ratios, and demand elasticity. Some, such as public educational organizations, are limited by tax revenues, which may be more affected by political than economic realities. Others, such as public hospitals, have an inelastic demand fostered by government and high labor cost ratios. But all employing organizations are subject to some range of possible wage rates.

Perhaps enough has been said to establish that (1) for every organization there are upper and lower limits on wages determined by economic forces, (2) these limits can be estimated but not known precisely except at the cost of organization survival, (3) the limits change over time and are affected as well by economic conditions and actions by unions and management.

WAGE LEVELS AND WAGE STRUCTURES

Before proceeding to examine the decision process by which wages are determined within this range of possibilities, it is useful to distinguish wage levels and wage structures. Wage levels are averages. Thus it is possible to speak of the wage level of the economy, an industry, or an organization. In fact, the previous analysis (see pages 229–232) could have used the term wage level in referring to the wages of an organization or an industry.

Wage structures are wage relationships. Thus it is possible to speak of the wage structure of the economy, an industry, or an organization in which the relationships among wages within that entity are highlighted. It is also possible, of course, to speak of the interindustry wage structure and the intraindustry wage structure.

An organization may be thought of as having a single wage structure made up of the wages (or salaries) of all the jobs within it. It is often more useful, however, to think of an organization as made up of a number of wage structures—one for each job cluster. The wages in each of these structures can be averaged, of course, resulting in a wage level.

The previous discussion of economic limits to wage determination is oversimplified by implying that organizations face one set of limits. In practice, even small organizations include a number of separate job clusters and quite different economic limits apply to each. For example, the economic limits applicable to production jobs are quite different from those applicable to sales jobs, or to professional or administrative jobs.

The following discussion of wage level decisions assumes that the wage level applicable to a particular job cluster is under consideration but it is equally applicable if the organization thinks of itself as one large cluster of jobs. The section on wage structure (pricing job structures) likewise assumes particular job clusters. Obviously, wage levels and wage structures are related. (The average of the wages of any group of jobs is the wage level of those jobs, whereas a compilation of the separate job rates is the wage structure.)

In many organizations and union-management negotiations wage decisions are approached as a change in wage level. An absolute or percentage change in wage level is decided on and applied to all jobs. In these organizations, wage structures are considered a separate problem to be approached separately. In other organizations, rates for jobs are bargained and the decision becomes at once a change in wage level and wage structure.

WAGE LEVEL DECISIONS

The forces that influence wage level decisions were discussed extensively in chapters 2 and 3. In Chapter 2 we saw that wage levels are influenced by the productivity of the economy, unions, conditions in the product market, conditions in labor markets, profits, unemployment rates, and wage levels of certain heavy industries. Unemployment and profits show the highest correlations with wages. Labor cost per unit and willingness of organizations to pass on cost increases as price increases also influence wage levels. The effect of unions on wage levels is still controversial. Size of organization is a major influence on wage levels. Competitive industries have lower wage levels in all industrial countries.

In Chapter 3 we saw that wage levels are influenced by employee definitions of equity, social pressures, custom, and reference groups. The distinctive features of separate sociological labor markets produce a strain toward separate wage levels for each. The status value of pay exerts upward pressure on wage levels.

EMPLOYER STRATEGY

Employer strategy in wage level decisions involves choosing some position within the range of alternatives, a rationale for this position, and a plan for achieving it. For example, the organization may decide to be a wage leader on the grounds that such a policy permits the organization to select the cream from all labor markets and the plan to achieve leadership involves paying more than any labor market competitor. At the other extreme, economic realities may force the employer to pay as little as it can to keep its jobs manned, to dilute job requirements where feasible, and to adjust wage levels only in the face of high turnover and absenteeism.

Most organizations, however, choose a position midway between these extremes—say, 5, 10, or 15 per cent above (or below) the labor market average. The position chosen is typically meant to apply in all labor markets, but economic realities may force a different position for some groups. The rationale for the position chosen is highly dependent on whether the organization is a business organization or some other type of employing organization, and within business by industry and, often, size. The rationale also may be prestige or custom. Other explanations are paying community or industry wage levels represents equity, recruitment problems and costs, labor turnover costs, employee satisfaction, product market competition, profit prospects, and labor relations problems.

Plans for actuating the strategy chosen typically involve collecting information on labor markets, economic conditions, union settlements, and organization prospects and problems, and using this information to maintain the organization's desired position. Many organizations emphasize community wage levels alone or in conjunction with industry wage levels but also monitor employee satisfaction levels, company prestige, labor supply, and union pressures.[2] Others emphasize product market competition, union pressures, labor supply considerations, or profit prospects depending on industry, size, and other considerations.[3] Noneconomic organizations may place more emphasis on labor market information than do economic organizations, and economic organizations not severely constricted by economic realities may place more emphasis on organization status and prestige than do noneconomic organizations.

Most organizations, regardless of type, recognize that their wage level strategy, although meant to be organizationwide, may be adhered to more closely for some employee groups than for others. For some groups, organization strategy is much influenced by unions; for others, by labor supply considerations; for still others, by organization goals. Perhaps the ultimate standard of wage level strategy is employee acceptance.

Organization strategy, however, is strongly influenced by the belief that equity is defined by what the organization decides it can pay.

    [2]Richard A. Lester, *Company Wage Policies* (Princeton, N.J.: Princeton University Press, 1948).
    [3]George P. Shultz, *Pressures on Wage Decisions* (New York: John Wiley & Sons, Inc., 1951); Charles A. Myers and George P. Shultz, *The Dynamics of a Labor Market* (Englewood Cliffs, N.J.: Prentice-Hall, Inc., 1951); George P. Shultz, Irwin Herrnstadt, and Elbridge S. Puckett, "Wage Determination in a Non-Union Labor Market," Industrial Relations Research Association, *Proceedings of the Tenth Annual Meeting* (New York City, September 5–7, 1957), pp. 194–206; L. G. Reynolds, *The Structure of Labor Markets* (New York: Harper & Brothers, 1951).

As emphasized in Chapter 3, however, equity in the employment exchange is defined by employee perceptions of rewards and contributions. Although these perceptions may be influenced by the position of the organization, membership motivation depends on employee definition of equity.

UNION STRATEGY

Union strategy in wage level decisions has frequently been simply stated as "more." But this is a serious oversimplification that ignores both differences among unions and the evidence of union concern with the consequences of wage level decisions.

Defining unions as political organizations operating in an economic environment[4] is still useful in discussing union wage strategy. Political factors—union rivalries, membership sentiments, relative strength of intraunion factions, strong needs for union leaders to deliver results if they wish to remain in power, gains made by other unions, the needs of the union as an organization—are all elements in union strategy. Equity considerations are also present in the insistence on preservation of customary relationships with other unions.

But economic factors—state of the labor market, movements in the cost of living, demand for the employer's product, product market competition, and nonunion competition—also influence union wage strategy.[5] Which of these forces bears the greatest weight is still a matter of controversy.

Unions facing unfavorable economic conditions are concerned with employment effects. Unions unhampered by economic strictures emphasize political considerations. Thus the major determinants of union wage strategy vary in importance over time and among different product and labor markets. Particularly important are conditions in particular industries and organizations.

A balanced statement of union wage strategy determinants stresses economic pre-conditions within which political pressures operate.[6] In good times, when employment and profits are high, political factors predominate. Union wage policy under such conditions is determined by the gains of other unions in similar circumstances and custom-

---

[4]Arthur M. Ross, *Trade Union Wage Policy* (Berkeley: University of California Press, 1948).

[5]John T. Dunlop, *Wage Determination Under Trade Unions* (New York: Augustus M. Kelley, Inc., 1950).

[6]M. W. Reder, "The Theory of Union Wage Policy," *Review of Economics and Statistics* (February, 1952), pp. 34–45. See also, Daniel J. B. Mitchell, "Union Wage Policies: The Ross-Dunlop Debate Reopened," *Industrial Relations* (February, 1972), pp. 46–61.

ary relationships. Economic restraints are at a minimum because most employers can pass on wage increases as price increases. Unemployment, for example, resulting from the unwillingness of an employer to meet union demands is no deterrent because union members will have no difficulty finding other jobs.

Under such conditions, wage patterns tend to develop and are followed. But a pattern to persist must be compatible with the economic survival of organizations. It cannot persist if adherence to the pattern means lost jobs and lost production. The ability of an organization to meet a pattern depends on several conditions. The ratio of labor cost to total cost cannot be too high. The extent of nonunion competition must be limited. Perhaps most important is the ability of the organization to pass on wage increases to consumers in the form of price increases, without losing business.

Thus even in good times, the very different relationships between product and labor markets in poorly organized, highly competitive industries and those of highly organized industries with less price competition become important to union strategy. In the former, wage costs are a strategic competitive cost, price increases reduce product demand, and wage levels of nonunion organizations set limits in unionized organizations unless the latter are courting suicide. In the latter industries, however, economic restraints are attenuated.

There are identifiable patterns within narrowly defined industries, and a looser pattern force in more broadly defined industries and within the jurisdiction of certain unions. But there is a great deal of variation in pattern-following within an industry, and the strength of the pattern varies over time. Beyond the pattern forces in particular industries, beyond the jurisdiction of a particular union, and away from national product markets, patterns among industries are less clear.[7]

During a downturn in general business conditions, union wage policies are more satisfactorily explained by economic factors than by political factors. If a union faces unemployment in the firms with which it bargains, this fact usually influences wage policy. The extent to which unemployment affects union wage policy, however, depends on several factors, both economic and political. If the industry is not completely organized, nonunion competition will force the union to adjust wage policy in the face of unemployment. Similarly, the feasibility of permitting one employer to maintain a lower wage level than another employer will have an effect. If this practice is feasible, the union may

[7]E. Robert Livernash, "Wages and Benefits," in Woodrow L. Ginsburg, E. Robert Livernash, Herbert S. Parnes, and George Strauss (eds.), *A Review of Industrial Relations Research* (Madison, Wisconsin: Industrial Relations Research Association, 1970), p. 110.

permit a firm with substantial unemployment a lower wage level. The extent to which this course is followed, however, will depend on whether the union believes that a lower wage level will increase employment for its members. Also, an attempt may first be made to lower labor costs in various ways without tampering with the wage policy. To the extent that this course is possible, other employers will not become aware of the discrimination.

But political considerations also enter here. The extent to which the union adjusts wage policy to unemployment will depend on the extent to which the union leader is convinced that taking employment considerations into account will be to union advantage. This will depend on (1) whether or not unemployed workers are still union members, (2) the number of unemployed union members, and (3) the attitude of the majority.

If unemployment in general is low, if union members express unwillingness to work at wages below union scales, and/or if wage discrimination among employers is adjudged by the union leader to be impolitic, union wage policy will be maintained and the firm may be forced out of business. This seldom occurs, however, if unemployment is general.

Union wage policy is strongly influenced by the nature of competition in the product market of firms with which it deals. In highly competitive industries, economic forces hold sway. Unions that organize many firms competing strongly in the same product market usually pursue a standard wage policy within a given product market. The purpose of this policy is to "take labor out of competition." In this situation, unions can seldom make concessions in wages to individual firms in economic difficulties. To do so would give these firms a competitive advantage that would threaten the jobs of union members working for other employers. However, such unions might help firms in economic difficulty to lower labor costs in ways not obvious to other employers. Or they might attempt to reduce competitive pressures in the industry by (1) suppressing price competition among employers; (2) inducing governments to pass minimum wage laws, public contract laws, fair trade laws, and protective tariffs, thus reducing competition; (3) inducing governments to provide a market for products and jobs (through government contract allocation); and (4) financing advertising campaigns.

Where unions bargain with diverse employers who do not compete in the same product market, patterns are not stressed at the expense of local conditions, especially in the case of small firms. In such instances, if a union fears that a pattern increase would hurt employment in a given firm, the pattern is broken. Because a below-pattern increase would not create a competitive threat to employment in other firms bargaining with the national union, it is accepted.

Even during periods of inflation, where such insulation from competition exists, prosperous firms are expected to follow the pattern, but in firms in which employment might be adversely affected, substantial deviations from union wage policy are approved. Of course, even here, an attempt is often made to reduce labor costs in the firm rather than the wage level, because labor costs are much less apparent to other firms.

Although these considerations are all important, one or a few take precedence in a specific situation. If business conditions in the economy are good, union organization needs prevail and the other factors are restraining influences only. If business conditions are poor, the needs of union organizations are pushed into the background. In good times and bad, product market competition, nonunion competition, and special conditions applicable to an industry or a particular firm impose limits on an otherwise applicable policy.

Union wage strategy appears to be more pragmatic than employer wage strategy and less concerned with rationale. This, too, fits with the definition of a union as a political organization operating in an economic environment.

But unions, as mentioned previously, do surround wage policy with ethical connotations. Equity is to be achieved by meeting union demands. Union wage policy is based on information regarding other wage settlements, economic conditions, and forward prospects for the industry and the organization. In this it is like employer wage policy. Also, like employer wage strategy, equity is defined by what the union believes the employer should pay.

In both employer and union definitions of equity the standard is external to the individual. In contrast, equity in the employment exchange is defined by employee perceptions of rewards and contributions. Although the requirement for member ratification of union contracts appears to bring the external and internal definitions of equity together, employee perceptions are influenced by but not controlled by union wage policy. In fact, it is quite possible that union wage strategy may contribute to inflationary pressures in the economy without improving employee perceptions of equity.

WAGE LEVEL DETERMINATION

The process of wage level determination involves the use of certain comparison standards to arrive at wage level decisions. Although these comparison standards are examined in some detail in Part IV, their use in wage level determination is discussed here. The comparison standards analyzed in Part IV are (1) laws and other social pressures on compensation, (2) wage and salary surveys, and (3) wage criteria. Because the following sections emphasize the manner in which comparison standards are used in wage level determination rather than descriptions of the standards, for obvious reasons, laws and other social pressures are not discussed here. If laws and regulations direct the parties to take certain actions or follow certain procedures, they do so.

The range of wage level alternatives and employer and union strategies discussed earlier in this chapter suggest that comparison standards may be used to guide wage level decisions or to rationalize decisions that have been made. As will be seen, using them as precise yardsticks would yield almost as many different wage levels as there are standards.

Use of Wage and Salary Surveys. Although almost all organizations use surveys, there are no hard data on how they are used. The reason for this lack is undoubtedly the range of actual usage of such surveys by different organizations and differential usage by some organizations for separate employee groups. For example, many government organizations adjust wage levels to accord with statistical measures of survey results by placing these values at predetermined positions in pay ranges. In the guideline method of job evaluation, computation of average rates of jobs from surveys serves to place the job into the labor grade closest to this figure.

But most organizations use wage survey data solely as guides for contemplating possible changes in wage level. Although they may employ a variety of statistical analyses to increase comparability of survey data from one survey period to another, they treat the results only as guides. Judgment in the application of such guides is often regarded as a skill of an effective compensation administrator.[8]

Also, survey usage varies by job cluster. In recent years, professional employees have often been in short supply and many organizations gear wage levels of engineers and scientists quite closely to surveys. Also, in some labor markets, a shortage of clerical employees has necessitated close attention to wage levels of these employees. Surveys of management salaries, however, are typically used only as rough guides.

The use of wage survey results in collective bargaining negotiation is perhaps typical of survey usage. If management presents wage survey

<hr>

[8]Kenneth E. Foster, "The Plus Side of Wage Surveys," *Personnel* (January–February, 1963), pp. 35–43.

results and the union presents tabulations of contract rates, neither will likely be given much weight. If management designs and conducts a survey with union assistance, there is likely to be more reliance on the results. But even in this case, the weight to be given to data typifying the area and that representing the industry is likely to be a source of controversy.

The following anecdote, supplied by a colleague,[9] perhaps illustrates a not atypical use of wage survey data in collective bargaining. In this situation, the industry is primarily located in two major areas, the firm has installations in both areas, and a national union represents workers in both. Wage survey data were available for both areas and for the industry. In one location, area rates were above industry rates by 12.5 per cent. In the other, area rates were below industry rates by 20 per cent. In the former, the company negotiator argued for industry rates and the union negotiator for area rates. In the latter location, the union negotiator demanded industry rates and the company negotiator, area rates. Neither negotiator showed evidence of schizophrenia in either situation and both believed that they were making legitimate use of wage survey data.

Although this example represents the use of both area and industry data, the same usage is conceivable with either alone. Wage survey data are usually presented in a manner that would permit calculation of several statistical measures representing the entire sample of responding organizations or selected parts of the sample. Although documentation is unavailable, a situation is conceivable in which the two parties stoutly defended their interpretation of the data. A careful study of a large labor market found that "keeping up with the area" meant quite different things to different employers.[10]

This section has emphasized the use of wage surveys in wage level determination. Wage surveys, it should be pointed out, however, have other uses in compensation administration. One, as will be seen in the next chapter, is to validate wage structure decisions. Another is to permit comparison of pay increase rates and practices among organizations and trends toward and away from various types of pay plans.

But the major use of wage and salary surveys appears to be as a guide to wage level decisions. In this connection, regardless of the actual use made of survey results, one consequence of making and/or using wage surveys is to assure employees that the organization is keeping up with the labor market.

Use of Wage Criteria.   If possible, there is even less in the way of documentation of the use of wage criteria than of wage survey data.

[9]Henry L. Sisk, personal correspondence, September 3, 1970.
[10]Reynolds, *Structure of Labor Markets*, p. 157.

Logic and experience suggest that they are used (1) to point out the consequences of decisions, (2) as bases for negotiation, and (3) as supplements to judgment. As has already been pointed out, wage criteria may be used by organizations and unions to rationalize positions taken as well as to arrive at these positions. Also, strictly applying the various criteria would in many situations result in conflicting decisions. For example, if the cost of living is up 10 per cent and ability to pay is down 10 per cent, comparable wages in the area justify a 5 per cent increase, and comparable wages in the industry call for a 5 per cent decrease, what change in wage level is justified?

The *comparable wage*[11] criterion has already been discussed as wage survey data. All that is necessary here is to place it in perspective with other wage criteria. Comparable wages is, without doubt, the most widely used wage criterion, perhaps because of its apparent fairness. Such usage was greatly expanded by the Federal Pay Comparability Act of 1970 wherein the pay of all federal employees is determined by salary surveys conducted by the Bureau of Labor Statistics. To most people, wages paid by other employers for similar work represents a fair wage. Employers find it reasonable because it implies that competitors are paying the same wages.

Furthermore, comparable wages have a certain measurability. Although, as will be seen in a later chapter, obtaining market rates is not simple and the going wage is an abstraction, wages are prices and measuring them contains a good deal of economic wisdom.

Comparable wages greatly simplify the task of the negotiators, because once the appropriate comparisons have been agreed on, difficulties are minimized. A wage level can be set that is satisfactory as income and also as costs in that unit labor costs can be widely different among organizations with identical wage rates.

In a tight labor market, comparable wages is likely to be the primary criterion of wage level determination because paying going wages may be necessary to obtain and keep a work force. Organizations are forced to maintain traditional relationships in order to keep a labor force. The result is that comparable wages are a force for generalizing changes in wage levels.

When strong competition in the product market appears, however, the emphasis is likely to change from emphasis on income to emphasis on costs. Under such circumstances, less emphasis is placed on the comparable wage criterion, and other criteria emphasizing wages

[11]The phrase "going wages" in industry and "prevailing wages" in the public service are comparable terms, but the distinction between them is important. Business organizations distinguish between "going wages" (wages paid in the labor market) and "prevailing wages" (set by the Secretary of Labor and based on union rates). Government organizations do not make this distinction and use the term "prevailing wages."

as cost will become the focus of attention. In other words, comparable wages are followed as long as other criteria are not more compelling.

The *cost of living* criterion has been widely applied in recent years because of pronounced increases in living costs. If the cost of living is rising, there is great pressure from workers and their unions to adjust wages to offset reductions in real wages.

In recognition of the influence of cost of living changes, escalator clauses have been written into many labor contracts. Organizations desiring contracts longer than one year find that such contracts must either include escalator clauses tying wages to changes in the cost of living or deferred increases anticipating increases in living costs. Although the popularity of escalator clauses varies greatly over time, inflation greatly increases their popularity.

The cost of living criterion, like the comparable wages criterion, emphasizes wages as income. Tying wages to the cost of living helps ensure keeping up with changes in the labor market. It is quite possible that increasing levels of sophistication means that employees' estimates of their worth are adjusted upward during inflationary periods so that organizations failing to keep up will encounter trouble in getting and keeping a labor force.

The apparent simplicity of the cost of living criterion is appealing as well as its apparent fairness. But, as will be seen later, measuring the cost of living is not simple and use of these measures for wage level adjustments raises a number of issues, not the least of which are the inflationary effects of the use of the cost of living criterion.

The cost of living criterion, in inflationary periods, reinforces the comparable wage criterion. Wage levels are increased to compensate for increases in the cost of living and wage comparisons generalize these changes. As long as influences in the labor market are stronger than influences in the product market, the tendency to use the cost of living criterion may persist. But if employers are faced with strong competition in the product market and a choice must be made between maintaining the employees' real wages and maintaining jobs, cost rather than income considerations become paramount. Under these circumstances, the cost of living criterion loses much of its force.

The *living wage* criterion is similar conceptually to the cost of living criterion in that both are concerned with standards of living. But the living wage is an ideal concept, whereas cost of living measures changes. The living wage criterion is seldom used in wage level determination, although unions may present minimum budgets as ethical arguments in wage negotiations. As will be seen later, the primary use of the living wage criterion is to guide social policy—*i.e.,* minimum budgets may justify changes in minimum wage laws.

The *ability to pay* criterion emphasises the effects of wage levels on costs to organizations rather than as income to employees. It is widely used in wage level determination in part because it represents the process by which an employer must approach wage levels, in part because it represents the final decision rule for wage level changes justified on other grounds, and in part because profit levels are related to wage levels.

Any organization faced with a prospective change in wage levels must compare the projected wage bill with projected resources. Noneconomic organizations have budgetary constraints. Economic organizations estimate whether the increase in wage costs will increase labor cost per unit and, if so, if these increased costs can be passed on to consumers without loss in sales. In all organizations, the comparison of costs and resources determines its ability to pay.

Also, organizations may find that wage level increases justified on other grounds—say, comparable wages or cost of living—simply cannot meet the test of ability to pay. Unions as well as employing organizations have shown sensitivity to organizations' ability to pay. Unions are aware that large wage increases when a significant proportion of an industry is nonunion can cost jobs. Even in inflationary periods, business organizations must be sure that their labor costs are not out of line with those of competitors.

In a sense, the ability to pay criterion to the employer might better be called inability to pay. But unions use it positively by pointing to high profit levels as evidence of an organization's ability to pay. Numerous instances could be cited of large increases won in negotiations by unions emphasizing the high profits of the organization or industry.

But ability to pay is used only at the extremes. As long as an organization believes it can meet the projected wage level, it may consider ability to pay no business of the union. Unless unions see profits as abnormally high, they are likely to consider ability to pay as irrelevant.

More important, measuring ability to pay is difficult at best and highly controversial. Obtaining agreement on whether or not profits are a proper measure and the proper measure of profits is probably impossible. Nor does the measurement problem disappear in noneconomic organizations. Furthermore, neither employing organizations nor unions would advocate strict application of ability to pay.

The *productivity* criterion is not widely used in wage level determination in specific organizations at present. But there are some reasons for expecting that it may find wider use in the future. At present, specific use of the productivity criterion is largely limited to the automotive industry. In these organizations an annual improvement factor provides annual increases geared to changes in productivity in the economy. Beginning in 1948, General Motors and the United Auto Workers bargained long-term agreements incorporating this feature, along with a cost of living escalator clause. Although the annual improvement factor specifically relates the annual increase to economy-wide productivity advances, it may also be interpreted as the price of a period of labor peace—long-term contracts. The spread of long-term labor contracts with deferred increases but no tie to productivity suggests this interpretation. There is no question that employees want improvements in their pay, and requests to share in advancing productivity is one way to get them. As shown in Chapter 2, productivity is the main force behind increases in the level of real wages in all countries.

Actually, the productivity criterion may be an attempt to apply measurement to ability to pay. Improved physical productivity is a measure of increased ability to pay.

As will be seen in a later chapter, however, measuring productivity is not simple. Productivity may be measured at several levels and these different measures have quite different wage level implications. Furthermore, productivity advances attributable to different sources cannot be identified. More important, productivity sets limits to wage advances that, if exceeded, contribute to further inflation.

But the use of the productivity criterion may increase in the future. In Great Britain, productivity bargaining is being used to correct high cost situations by bargaining on higher contributions to the employment exchange.[12] Low productivity advances in recent years in the U.S. and wage increases greatly exceeding productivity increases may be expected to focus attention on similar approaches in this country. In fact, productivity bargaining has been suggested as a way of increasing productivity in higher education.[13]

The *labor supplies* criterion is usually latent to other criteria that emphasize wages as income to employees (comparable wages and cost of living). But for certain employee groups and in certain labor markets, the labor supplies criterion becomes the major one.

There is no question but that a major test of the adequacy of a wage level is whether it serves to obtain and hold a labor force. A number of studies have revealed the labor supply problems of low-wage industries and the tendency of organizations to meet these problems by "paying the market" where possible and lowering hiring standards

---

[12]Allan Flanders, *Collective Bargaining: Prescription for Change* (London: Faber and Faber, Ltd., 1967).

[13]Joseph W. Garbarino, "Precarious Professions: New Patterns of Representation," *Industrial Relations* (February, 1971), pp. 1–20.

where this was impossible.[14] These results show that the labor supplies criterion becomes primary for some organizations.

But even for economically robust organizations, certain employee groups in short supply may require use of the labor supplies criterion in wage level decisions. Engineers, scientists, and computer programmers have been obvious examples of such groups. Managers may be another. Also, in a number of local labor markets, clerical workers represent shortage occupations. The point is that shortage occupations may require separate attention to the labor supplies criterion in wage level decision.

The *purchasing power* criterion is sometimes employed by unions in wage negotiations as an argument that expanded purchasing power in the hands of consumers is a requirement of a prosperous and expanding economy. Employing organizations reject the purchasing power criterion on the grounds that wage level decisions in single organizations or even industries are unrelated to their product demand and that no single bargain in this country appreciably affects the total economic situation. Although, as will be seen later, a more sophisticated counterargument would show that purchasing power represents a gross oversimplification of economic reality, the use of the purchasing power criterion is sufficiently limited to preclude its use here.

Wage level determination for a specific organization is a decision-making process. The decision is reached unilaterally in the case of a nonunion employer, at the bargaining table in the case of the union employer. In either case, a number of factors influence the decision reached, the most important of which have been discussed in this chapter.

Comparative wage rates probably bears the greatest influence, for this factor plays two roles. It is a standard of comparison and a method of dispersing wage movements. Cost of living and ability to pay enter the decision as pressures for movement. They operate as initiators of wage movements. In upward movements, cost of living furnishes the thrust. Inability to pay operates as a ceiling and, in downward movements, a pressure. Productivity, an independent factor in some decisions, operates in most cases through ability to pay. The final decision must meet the test of ability to attract and hold an adequate labor force and provide it with motivation.

Minimum budgets and the concept of the living wage are too

[14]Shultz, Herrnstadt, and Puckett, in IRRA, *Proceedings of the Tenth Annual Meeting*, pp. 194–206; Irwin L. Herrnstadt, "The Reaction of Local Unions to Economic Adversity," *Journal of Political Economy* (October, 1954), pp. 425–439; R. A. Lester, *Adjustments to Labor Shortages* (Princeton, N.J.: Princeton University Press, 1955).

indefinite to be very useful as standards. Purchasing power is too broad a consideration to be applicable to a particular wage level decision.

Key bargains may have a substantial impact on wage levels in both unionized and nonunion organizations. The key negotiations may employ all or most of the wage criteria. Once the key bargain is reached, the process of wage comparison holds the spotlight and transmits both product market and labor market pressures. Ross' centrifugal and centripetal forces provide an excellent explanation of the manner in which the three most pertinent criteria (comparable wages, ability to pay, and cost of living) apply. Wage comparisons exert a centripetal force, pulling separate wage level decisions together. Ability to pay operates as a centrifugal force since no two employers have exactly the same wage-paying capacity. Comparisons run in limited orbits and are strongest when the economic position of most employers is moving in the same direction (when the cost of living is moving rapidly). Ability to pay supersedes comparisons if ability to pay is more compelling. It may be possible to accommodate both wage comparisons and ability to pay by increasing the wage level but taking actions to prevent a rise in unit labor costs.[15]

WAGE LEVEL ISSUES

To most organizations, the problem of wage level appears in terms of changes in the wage level—the question of how large an "across-the-board" change in wage rates is to be made. Such changes are called "general" increases or decreases. When the decision has been made that such a change is desirable, some additional issues must be faced.

PERCENTAGE VERSUS FLAT INCREASES

One question, for example, is whether the general increase or decrease should be made a flat amount to all recipients or should be a percentage change. Whether or not an employer favors a flat or a percentage change depends on a number of considerations. If faced with problems of (1) recruiting skilled workers, (2) maintaining differentials in a finely divided wage structure, or (3) satisfying employee demands for equal or greater differentials, he is likely to favor a percentage change. In this way an employee earning $2.00 an hour might receive a 20-cent increase, and a worker earning $4.00 an hour

[15]Arthur M. Ross, "The External Wage Structure," in George W. Taylor and Frank C. Pierson (eds.), *New Concepts in Wage Determination* (New York: McGraw-Hill Book Company, Inc., 1957), pp. 190–192.

would receive a 40-cent increase. A flat increase would give both employees the same increase. Employers faced with problems of (1) recruiting beginning employees, (2) reducing a wage increase to the minimum in terms of cost, or (3) satisfying the largest number of employees may favor an increase of a flat amount.

Unions, especially of the industrial type, tend to favor flat increases for political reasons. In these unions the majority of workers are in lower-pay categories and represent a politically potent group. Also, if changes in wage levels are based on changes in living costs, it is possible to argue that higher-paid workers pay less proportionately for necessities and are thus no more affected by changes in the cost of living than lower-paid workers. In this form, the argument becomes another political reason for union insistence on flat increases.

In any case, many increases in wage levels in unionized organizations have been of the cents-per-hour variety rather than percentage changes. The result is a reduction in percentage skill differentials. If the process continues over a period of time, political pressures for restoring of traditional differentials begin to build up as skilled workers become more vociferous in their demands. The result is often a demand for a flat cents-per-hour increase, with additional amounts for skilled workers in various classifications. Another solution sometimes adopted is alternating absolute and percentage changes in wage levels.

Nonunion employers with formal compensation administration programs may prefer percentage changes in wage levels in order to maintain percentage skill differentials among jobs. Over any significant period of time, reduction of differentials between unskilled and skilled labor may have an adverse effect on the supply of skilled labor. A function of skill differentials is presumably to compensate for the time, trouble, and expense incident to acquiring additional skills.

The unemployed in recent years have included high proportions of unskilled workers. High unemployment of such workers often occurs in labor markets with serious shortages of skilled workers. It may be that relative skill differentials must be increased to induce acquisition of needed skills.

TANDEM WAGE ADJUSTMENTS

Another question concerns relationships among segments of the organization. In many organizations, solution to the problem of wage and salary levels is complicated by the fact that only a portion of employees is unionized. Thus, collective bargaining sets the level for organized employees and the employer makes decisions unilaterally for other groups. Although such decisions are based on considerations such as those laid down in this chapter, usual practice appears to be to make tandem adjustments—that is, to give such increases (or decreases) to unorganized groups in order to prevent inequities from occurring. Here the employer may adhere strictly to percentage rather than flat adjustments. For example, a flat rate adjustment to shop workers may be translated into percentage terms and applied to other groups.

Actually, the principle on which tandem adjustments are based is applicable more generally. Whenever wage level adjustments are made that apply to specific groups within the organization, customary relationships are considered in making wage level decisions applicable to other groups.

11

Economic Job Rewards– Wage Structures

Wage and salary rates within an organization are paid for jobs. Wage level decisions are concerned with general changes applying to all jobs in the organization or to all jobs in a cluster or family. Wage or salary structures are concerned with the rates for specific jobs and the relationships among these rates. Obviously, wage levels and wage structures are related, but because wage structure decisions involve determination of pay rates for specific jobs, they involve considerations not present in wage level decisions.

WAGE STRUCTURE CONSIDERATIONS

Jobs are developed by organizations to get their work done. Labor services acquire specific economic meaning only in relation to the particular jobs to which these services are attached. Thus the typical situation is that the organization designs jobs and selects employees to fill them. The jobs designed by the organization are the primary source of contributions required and thus the rewards for the job. In this way, organizations are determining the organization division of labor and the kinds of services they need, and both are calculated for organization purposes. These are the jobs the organization fills from a heretofore unstructured market for labor services.[1]

---

[1] George H. Hildebrand, "External Influence and the Determination of the Internal Wage Structure," in J. L. Meij (ed.), *Internal Wage Structure* (Amsterdam: North-Holland Publishing Company, 1963), pp. 260–299, is probably the best single source of internal wage structure considerations. This section owes much to it.

Other organizations are doing the same thing. But they differ in technology, management, competitive economics, and collective bargaining. As a consequence, the jobs that they design are quite unlikely to be identical to those of other organizations. Furthermore these decisions are not made once and for all but are subject to continuous revision as market conditions, technology, and institutional influences change. The result is that the division of labor in society is an abstraction that provides people who are imperfect fits for any organization's jobs, ranging from quite close fits to almost none. Thank God for the flexibility of people.

But people and institutions also have a hand in structuring labor markets. Craft unions, for example, determine the kinds of work their members do and expect employing organizations to adjust to this decision. The market for clerical workers is structured by the institutions that train them, with the result that clerical jobs are often quite similar in different organizations. Professional employees and managers insist on having something to say about the design of their jobs and part of the result comes from the influence of the institutions that train them. At the other extreme are semiskilled factory employees. Organizations employing semiskilled factory employees are subject to little influence on job design by either employees or unions, except in job redesign decisions. Unions of semiskilled factory workers typically insist, however, on participating in decisions with respect to job redesign. This participation is guided by customary relationships among and within employee groups. Custom also operates in nonunion situations to resist change in job design.

One of the major influences on job and wage structures is the technology of the field in which the organization is located and changes in technology. But technology seldom provides rigid boundaries. It typically provides choices within which management, unions, and competitive pressures can operate in designing jobs and job relationships.

The labor market influences the wage structure through labor supply. But often only a few of the organization's jobs are market-oriented and the labor supply for most jobs is provided from within the organization. For example, in manufacturing, often hiring-in jobs, standard maintenance jobs, and clerical work are the only market-oriented jobs. Clerical work includes several labor-market-sensitive jobs and the wage structure of clerical jobs must accord with market forces to ensure an adequate labor supply. Craft work, on the other hand, is controlled by craft unions rather than the labor market unless craft workers are in short supply. In fact, any group in short supply includes market-sensitive jobs but given relatively adequate labor supplies only those groups wherein the labor market is structured by unions or otherwise well organized are labor-market oriented.

The product market affects wage structures through cost-oriented jobs. Such jobs exist where profit margins are sensitive to changes in unit labor cost. If the ratio of unit labor cost to price is critical, the jobs involved become cost-oriented jobs and organizations will strongly resist changes in their wage rates, especially changes not made by other organizations. Organizations that compete in the same product market, those whose prices are interrelated, or those experiencing or anticipating increased competition or decreased demand may regard any increase in unit labor costs as a threat, especially when labor cost is a significant proportion of total costs.

Unions affect wage structure, but the differential effects of craft and industrial unionism and the type of bargaining relationship are considerable. Craft unions tend to determine craft rates for all organizations employing members of the craft as well as the design of craft jobs. The limit of craft rates is the cost-price resistance of employers. Industrial unions, on the other hand, are more concerned with employing organizations than craft unions, but less concerned with product markets because they often bargain with organizations in many product markets. Thus industrial unions may attempt to impose a common wage structure on organizations with which they deal that clashes with product market realities.

Within organizations, industrial unions are concerned with equalities and differentials among particular groups of jobs. They often serve to reinforce custom and tradition in job and wage structures and to resist change that might decrease employee security. If the industrial union deals with organizations in a common product market, it may attempt to impose a common job and wage structure by comparing rates of a number of reasonably comparable jobs. But even in such cases, the influence of industrial unions on wage structure is slight compared to that of craft unions.

Unions also affect wage structures by resisting lower wage rates for jobs downgraded by technological change and by demanding that increased productivity on jobs arising from any source result in wage increases. Typically this means that wages of changed jobs are not cut but often increased when the change results in increased productivity. Such job rates distort rational job and wage structures and a cumulative series of them can so impair the organization's cost-profit position that management is forced to fight for a revised, rational wage structure.

· The union's strategy with respect to general increases can also affect wage structures. As mentioned in the previous chapter, flat cents-per-hour or dollars-per-month increases maintain absolute differentials but compress the structure in relative terms, whereas flat percentage increases maintain relative differentials and increase absolute differentials. Industrial unions especially may follow a policy of cents-per-hour increases because most of their members are in lower-paid groups. But unions cannot maintain this strategy in the face of opposition from higher-paid groups. In fact, worker preferences and resulting labor supply shortages force restoration of relative differentials in both union and nonunion situations.

But probably the strongest influence of unions on wage structures operates through the quality of the union-management relationship. As mentioned previously, some unions take an active part in job evaluation and their interest in a rational wage structure results in reduced grievances over wage inequities. Other unions, primarily of the craft variety, seek to preserve customary relationships and job security, resist changes in job content and structure, and are uninterested in the employer's problems of maintaining economic efficiency. Still other unions seem totally uninterested in job and wage structures of the organization and insist on (1) no wage cuts when job content changes, (2) wage increases for all increases in job productivity, (3) strong resistance to job content and other changes calculated to increase productivity, and (4) encouragement of wage inequity grievances. In such cases, job and wage structures become chaotic and correcting the irrationalities may require long and bitter strikes often prolonged by union internal political struggles resulting from the wage inequities.

Organization decisions with respect to job and wage structures represent a balancing of these forces—technology and management decisions regarding its use, aided or impeded by unionism and competitive forces in the labor and product markets. But the strength of these forces varies by organization type and within organizations by job clusters. Organizations made up largely of members of craft unions have union-oriented wage structures in which the wage structure is almost completely determined by the union. Organizations in construction, printing and publishing, the railroads, longshoring and maritime, and entertainment are examples of union-oriented wage structures.

Organizations consisting largely of members coming from a well-organized and competitive labor market but with no union have what might be called market-oriented wage structures. Organizations of this type have only limited choices because jobs are easily identified and are quite uniform throughout the market. Banks, insurance companies, department stores, and restaurants are organizations with primarily market-oriented wage structures.

Organizations with many specialized jobs, dealing in labor markets too disorganized to provide adequate grading and pricing, and in which no unions function, have primarily internally determined wage structures. Such wage structures may be influenced by product markets, but only if labor cost is high relative to total cost. Internally determined wage structures are management decisions and may range from highly rational structures flowing from job evaluation to a system of personal rates. Organizations in small towns, isolated locations, or nonunion communities provide examples, as do unique organizations in larger communities, and government employment.

Most large unionized organizations have what might be called union-and-product-oriented wage structures. In these organizations wage structures represent management decisions shaped and restrained by technology, unions, and cost-price relationships and the product market. Technology provides some uniformity in job structures in organizations engaged in common lines of production. Unions, through their insistence on traditional relationships, establish some key jobs and job clusters and provide an upward thrust to the entire structure. Cost-price relationships and the product market compel the organization to resist the upward push and to make changes in jobs and job relationships to keep cost-price relationships in line. Low ratios of labor cost to total cost and inelastic product demand, however, reduce competitive pressures on organizations. Organizations in many branches of manufacturing, in mining, and some service industries are examples of organizations with union-and-product-oriented wage structures.

Organizations with internally determined and union-and-product-market-determined wage structures leave large portions of wage structure decisions to management. Wage structure determination in these organizations follows closely the key job, job cluster, wage contour formulation offered by Dunlop and explained in Chapter 2. Key jobs acquire their status from labor markets, product markets, and comparisons with other organizations, often fostered by unions. Job clusters come from technologies and employee skill groupings. Wage contours originate with customary comparisons with other organizations, often fostered by unions. Custom strongly influences all three.

But although organizations can be classified as having wage structures that are primarily union-oriented, market-oriented, internally oriented, or union-and-product-market-oriented, organizations of any considerable size have job clusters that fall more comfortably into one or more of the other categories. Organizations employing craftsmen, unless they are members of an industrial union, are usually forced to develop a wage structure for this job cluster that bears the stamp of a union-oriented wage structure. All organizations employ clerical workers and the wage structure of the clerical job cluster is largely market-oriented. Professional employees (engineers and scientists) have salary structures that combine market orientation and internal determination regardless of the major activity of the organization. Managerial salary structures are primarily internally determined except in very tight labor markets without regard to organization type. The result is that the typical organization develops and administers at least four or five of the following separate wage structures: shop, clerical, draftsmen and technicians, administrators, engineers and scientists, sales, supervision, and executives. Although, obviously, there will be relationships among these separate wage structures, the strength of these relationships varies by organization and over time.

The above discussion of wage structure considerations shows that wage structures keyed solely to the labor market are likely to be few in number, to result from very tight labor markets, and to be characteristic of organizations well-insulated from product-market competition, unions, and technological change. Most organizations must consider labor cost ratios, product-market competition, and union demands as well as labor markets in determining wage structures. Furthermore, many labor markets are abstractions that do not provide a close fit for any organization's jobs or wage-paying ability because dissimilar organizations structure them and, within limits, control them and decide their place within them.[2]

PRICING THE JOB STRUCTURE

Wage structures result from pricing job structures. Job structures result from application of formal or informal job evaluation (see chapters 6 and 7). The pricing of job structures is subject to the influences discussed in the preceding section plus some technical ones.

For example, the manner in which job relationships were determined may influence job pricing. If a formal job evaluation plan was employed, the type of plan has an effect. The extent of union involvement in the formal job evaluation program may also influence job pricing. If informal job evaluation was used to determine the job structure, the pricing process may be influenced by whether the informally derived job structure makes use of pay grades or separate jobs. Both unions and management tend to favor simplification of pay structures, however, and this agreement reduces the variation in pricing procedures.

Present wage and salary rates of the organization are often the data used in the pricing process. The tendency of job evaluation, both formal and informal, to sharpen the distinction between payment for

[2]See Charles T. Stewart, Jr., "Wage Structure in an Expanding Labor Market: The Electronics Industry in San Jose," *Industrial and Labor Relations Review* (October, 1967), pp. 73–91; D. Robinson, "The Myths of the Local Labour Market," *Personnel* (Great Britain, December, 1967), pp. 36–39.

the job and the wage level of an organization and between payment for the job and payment to individual employees on the job,[3] permits the job pricing process to deal with present rates, even under union conditions.

Often, however, the job structure is priced out by making use of market rates. This means the employment of wage surveys. Wage survey results are often employed as an important, but not the only, consideration in pricing job structures. Some reasons for this are that surveys usually secure data on a limited number of key jobs that vary in importance and cost significance from one organization to another. Also, evaluated rates may easily be above market rates for certain jobs. Hence, market rates are only one consideration in job pricing. As will be seen later, however, if market rates are higher than evaluated rates, market rates are often followed.

Often just as influential on job pricing as market rates are the cost consequences of jobs. In most organizations there is a fairly well-defined group of jobs that represents an important segment of the total labor costs of the company.[4] Although some organizations are more restricted by labor cost considerations than others, it is important to note that prices assigned this group of jobs may greatly affect an organization's competitive position. In pricing the job structure, rates assigned these jobs largely determine the wage level of the firm, and wage structure relationships are built around this cost center.

PRICING PROCEDURES

So far in this section, job structure has been employed so as to imply a single job structure. Actually, of course, there may be one job structure for the entire organization or several job structures, one for each broad job cluster. The difference may result from whether formal or informal job evaluation is employed, as well as the type of system if a formal job evaluation plan is used. It was seen that the ranking, classification, and factor-comparison methods can, if desired, derive one job structure for the organization. Even these methods, however, are often applied to distinct job clusters. The point method is customarily built for a single job cluster.

Pay grade job classification and individual job rates might be called informal job evaluation. In the first method, a number of pay grades are established and decisions are reached on which jobs belong

[3]Sumner H. Slichter, James J. Healy, and E. Robert Livernash, *The Impact of Collective Bargaining on Management* (Washington, D.C.: The Brookings Institution, 1960), p. 593.

[4]E. Robert Livernash, in George W. Taylor and Frank C. Pierson (eds.), *New Concepts in Wage Determination* (New York: McGraw-Hill Book Company, Inc., 1957), p. 158.

in which pay grade. The method is similar to formal classification job evaluation except that no rules or descriptions are established to guide decisions. In unionized companies, such as in the meat packing industry, the existence of pay grade classification usually denotes opposition to formal job evaluation. In such cases pay grades are established for the bargaining unit.

Individual job rates have elements of job classification and informal evaluation. Such structures frequently establish identical wage rates for comparable jobs. An informal classification may consist of broad occupational titles that include a variety of more narrowly defined jobs. In fact, the term "job classification" employed in many organizations in place of the term "job" may imply that more than one job is included in the category. Examples of individual job rates are the crafts, the oil industry, and the automobile industry. Like the pay grade structure, the individual job rate structure applies to the bargaining unit.

RESPONSIBILITY FOR JOB STRUCTURE PRICING

If the job structure is determined through formal job evaluation, pricing responsibility depends heavily on whether the organization has a union and the degree of union participation in the job evaluation program. If job evaluation is a joint union-management venture, the union is obviously represented on the committee that prices the job structure. If job evaluation is conducted on a unilateral basis by the employer, the union in collective bargaining may accept the job structure developed, may accept it in part, or may ignore it. In each of these cases, the pricing process is the result of collective bargaining at least on key jobs and possibly on all jobs. To some managements, the process of pricing a job-evaluated job structure by collective bargaining is disturbing because the resulting wage structure may perpetuate or produce inequities that the job evaluation plan was designed to eliminate. To others, collective bargaining is seen as introducing needed flexibility into the system. Some managements insist that they need a logically developed job structure to prepare for bargaining. In nonunion organizations, pricing the job structure derived from formal job evaluation is the responsibility of the committee or individuals charged with the program.

Informal job evaluation is priced through collective bargaining in unionized organizations and by management in nonunion organizations. In fact, pay grade pricing is usual practice in both formal and informal arrangements.

ESTABLISHING JOB CLASSES OR GRADES

If job structures of individual jobs are developed, as in ranking, point, and factor-comparison methods, it is possible to assign dollar values to each job. As pointed out previously, however, a trend toward simplified wage and salary structures is encouraged by both managements and unions. One of the results is a tendency to group similar jobs into grades for pay purposes. In this way, in large organizations at least, much time and effort are saved. For example, dealing with, say, ten pay grades rather than hundreds of job rates represents a convenience to both unions and management. Even small changes in duties where job rates are used may require changes in pay rates.

Unfortunately, perhaps, the original term applied to these job groupings was "labor grades." Today the terms "job grades," "job levels," "pay levels," and "pay grades" are becoming common. The term "pay grade" will be employed here. A pay grade is defined as a grouping of jobs of approximately equal difficulty or importance as determined by job evaluation. If a point job evaluation plan is employed, a pay grade consists of jobs falling within a range of points; if a factor-comparison plan is used, a range of evaluated rates; if a ranking plan is used, a number of ranks. In the classification method of job evaluation, pay grades are established by the plan.

There appears to be no optimum number of pay grades for a particular job structure. In practice, pay grades vary from as few as four to as many as sixty. If there are few grades, the number of jobs in each grade will be relatively large, and the increments from one grade to another will be relatively large. If, on the other hand, there are many pay grades, the number of jobs in each grade will be relatively small, and the increments between grades also will be relatively small.

A number of considerations determine the optimum number of pay grades for a given job structure. An obvious one is organization size. Another is whether the job structure was determined for a broad job cluster or a narrow one. If, for example, all factory jobs are included, the number of pay grades may be larger than if a separate structure was developed for assembly or maintenance jobs. Another consideration is company pay increase and promotion policy. The two extremes are (1) identical rates for all incumbents on a particular job along with rapid promotion and (2) wide rate ranges so that a number of pay increases are possible for the incumbent on a job together with limited promotional opportunity. In the former case, a larger number of pay grades is called for and in the latter, fewer pay grades. A given organization may take a position at either extreme or between them. Still another consideration is the slope of the wage structure measured by the pay differential between the highest and lowest paid job in the structure. The steeper the slope, the more grades are possible while still maintaining meaningful pay distinctions between grades and the incentive to progress to a higher grade.

Although organization practice varies greatly, there is a tendency to reduce the number of pay grades. Ten to sixteen grades for a given job structure appears to be common practice. Ten grades for nonsupervisory factory jobs is typical as is thirteen for clerical job structures.[5] Broader job structures, of course, contain more grades. For example, salary plans that encompass clerical, professional, and administrative employees have an average of sixteen grades. Pay steps between grades are commonly 5 to 7 per cent for hourly and clerical jobs and 8 to 10 per cent for professional and administrative jobs.

Standard practice is to establish grades of equal width or point spread. Increasing spreads could also be justified. Employers and unions agree that if pay grades are to be employed there must be cut-off points. Random widths, however, are difficult to defend.

At one time, pay grades were numbered from the top down, with the highest level jobs in grade 1. Under present practice, placing jobs at the lowest level in grade 1, pay grades can be added as higher-level jobs are designed.

The actual establishment of pay grades is a decision-making process designed to (1) place jobs of the same general value in the same pay grade, (2) ensure that jobs of significantly different value are in different pay grades, (3) provide a smooth progression, and (4) ensure that the grades fit the organization and the labor market. Examination of job evaluation results may yield natural cut-off points.

To determine the proper number of pay grades, it is often useful to plot the jobs on a chart. When this has been done, it may be found that a certain point spread (say, 50 points) will work quite satisfactorily. Sometimes, however, certain groups of jobs dictate that judgment be used in allocating jobs to pay grades. To obtain a workable system, careful attention should be paid to these job groups. For example, in Figure 25, an unworkable system would result if the grouping in the center of the chart were divided into two pay grades.

Before final determination of pay grades, it may be wise to determine not only how many jobs, but also how many employees are affected by the number of grades and the division chosen. Figure 25, for example, plots only jobs and wage rates. Each plotted point includes

[5]Richard M. Story, "Trends in Wage Administration," *Business Studies* (Denton, Texas: North Texas State University, Fall, 1967), p. 114; U.S. Department of Labor, "Salary Structure Characteristics in Large Firms," *Bulletin No. 1417* (1963).

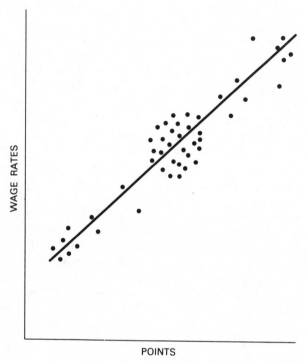

POINTS

FIGURE 25

Scatter Diagram for Selecting Pay Grades

one or more employees. Thus, before final determination of pay grades, it is wise either to plot each employee on such a chart or to note on a similar chart the number of employees represented by each plotted point. Since large numbers of employees may be affected by small changes in pay grades, great care and fairness must be used in final determination of pay grades. Grievances can be avoided by seeing that pay grades with large numbers of employees are not affected adversely.

Because jobs in a pay grade are treated as identical for pay purposes, it is extremely important that grade boundaries be accepted. For this reason, practice often calls for placing jobs very close to the maximum cut-off point into the next higher grade.

PRICING

As mentioned previously, the pricing process may work with individual jobs or with pay grades. In fact, if the organization is to employ rate ranges with differential pay rates for individuals on the same job, time may be saved by making decisions on the wage line, pay grade boundaries, and rate range limits at the same time. This is especially the case if pricing makes use of both present rates and wage survey results, because wage survey results always represent a sizable range.

Because this chapter is concerned with job rewards, however, discussion of rate range decisions is deferred until a later chapter. Also, because most organizations employ pay grades, the pricing process as discussed here employs them.

Usual practice employs present wage rates in the pricing process with adjustments made to make the final results accord with the market. (This is not true, of course, of the guideline method of job evaluation, which places jobs into pay grades closest to their market value.)

If present rates are used, the present rates of jobs in each pay grade may be averaged or the midpoint found and the results plotted on a chart. Figure 26 is an example of such a chart. To create a smooth progression between pay grades, a "wage line" is fitted to the plotted points. The line may be straight or curved and may be fitted by a number of different methods. When plotting job structures of single job clusters, a straight line is usually employed. The most frequently employed of the possible lines are the low-high line, the freehand line, and the least squares line.

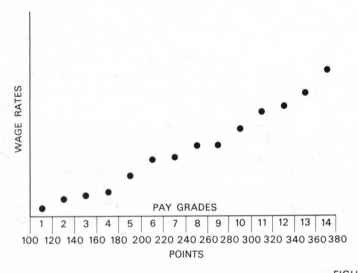

FIGURE 26

Graph of Pay Grades and Present Rates

The low-high line is a straight line connecting the highest and the lowest of the plotted points (often called anchor points). The rates of intervening grades are made to fall on the line. The low-high line appears especially useful in bargaining the wage structure because of its flexibility. Either end of the line may be raised separately or the entire line may be raised when a final bargain is reached. Figure 27 is an example of the low-high line.

Another possibility is the freehand line. After the points have been plotted on the chart, the trend of the data can often be easily visualized. If such conditions exist, it is possible to draw a freehand line that best describes the plotted points. In drawing such a line, it is useful to follow the principle that vertical deviations from the line are minimized as the line follows the obvious slope of the data. Although the line may be either straight or curved, its advantages are greatest when a straight line fits. The obvious advantages of using a freehand line are that it is easy to plot and simple to explain. It is often found that a least squares line produces such a small margin of additional accuracy that its computation is not worth the time involved nor the difficulty of explanation. Figure 28 is an example of a freehand line.

The least squares line determines mathematically the line that follows the principles specified for the freehand line. If a least squares line is desired, it may be fitted by calculating the equation for the line and plotting the line obtained from the solution.

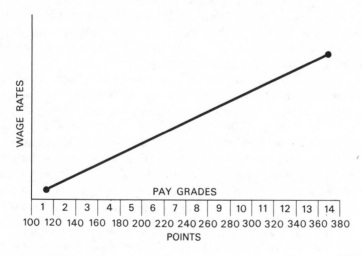

FIGURE 27

Low-High Line

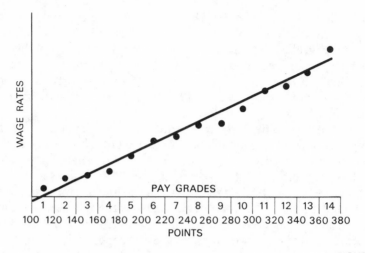

FIGURE 28

Freehand Line

Experience suggests that the additional accuracy of the least squares line is seldom sufficient to offset the added difficulty of explaining the method involved to the statistically unsophisticated. It may be useful to test wage lines developed by simpler methods against a least squares line.[6] Professionals or other statistically sophisticated groups, however, may prefer a wage line calculated by least squares.

In most cases, the low-high (anchor point) line or a freehand line achieves all the accuracy inherent in job evaluation results. Furthermore, both permit adjustment to achieve agreement of committee members or union and management.

As pointed out above, wage survey results in usual practice are used as an input in adjusting the wage line derived from present rates. It is possible, of course, to use wage survey results instead of present rates in determining the wage line. In both cases it is well to recognize that because jobs vary greatly in significance to organizations, even if they are identical (and this is unlikely), a range of rates is inevitable. Thus it is useful to employ a chart such as Figure 29, in which survey results have been presented in terms of the pay grades of the organization using quartiles. Such data when compared to present rates enable

[6]Any standard statistics textbook provides instructions for computing a least squares line. The equation for a straight line is: $Y = a + bX$ (where a is the point where the line crosses the Y axis and b is the slope of the line). Normal equations for computing a and b are $\Sigma Y = Na + b\Sigma X; \Sigma XY = a\Sigma X + b\Sigma X^2$. N = number of grades (or jobs). ΣX = sum of the points or other values for pay grades. ΣY = sum of the average rates for pay grades. ΣXY = sum of the product of point values and wage rates for each pay grade. ΣX^2 = sum of the squared point values for each pay grade. The normal equations are solved simultaneously.

the parties involved to make decisions on the wage structure. The medians (midpoints) or averages of survey results may, of course, be used in place of present wage rates determining the wage line. But the inevitability of a range of rates (minimum 50 per cent) raises questions about the usefulness of any single figure.[7] Recognition of this fact may account for the practice of establishing rate ranges at the same time as standard rates for pay grades when wage survey results are used to price job structures. The starting rate of a pay grade must be sufficient to attract employees to those jobs, and wage survey results provide evidence of what that rate must be.

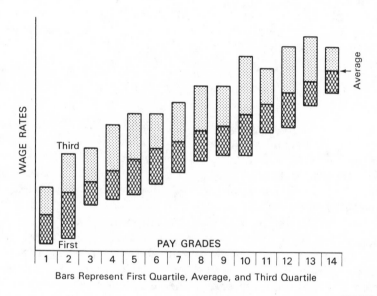

Bars Represent First Quartile, Average, and Third Quartile

FIGURE 29

Wage Survey Results

PRICING JOBS

When pay grades are priced, rates for jobs are those attached to the pay grade in which the job is classified. A system of code numbers to identify jobs with their proper pay grade is a helpful device in control and record keeping.

Some organizations prefer to work with a job structure composed of individual jobs rather than pay grades, in some cases because of the

---

[7]Although one author reports that survey findings are accurate within 5 per cent for clerical positions and 10 per cent for top level positions when the best survey techniques are utilized. Robert E. Sibson, *Wages and Salaries,* rev. ed. (New York: American Management Association, 1967), p. 69.

difficulty of convincing department heads that cut-off points are necessary and that efforts to move borderline jobs into higher pay grades destroy the usefulness of the system. In other cases, it is due to the small size of the organization, in which event pay grades may result in little savings. In still others, the union or unions involved may prefer job rate structures.

If a job structure of individual jobs is to be priced, the procedures are largely the same as those covered. The essential difference is that adjustments are made to accommodate the different job evaluation plans. If a point plan is involved, points and rates for separate jobs may be plotted on scatter diagrams. If a factor-comparison plan is used, evaluated rates instead of points are plotted and a choice may be made between plotting only key jobs or all jobs in the pricing process. In a ranking plan, jobs are recorded by rank and job rate adjustments are made to correspond with the ranking.

MARKET RATES VERSUS EVALUATED RATES

The first section of this chapter examined in some detail the influences on wage structures. One of these influences was the labor market, or more correctly, the numerous labor markets in which the typical organization deals. Because of the possibilities of conflict between market rates and rates that accord with job evaluation, it may be useful to highlight them here.

Job evaluation is an attempt to substitute rationality for a variety of nonrational influences on wages and salaries by appraising jobs in terms of their contribution to the organization. The process presumably produces a hierarchy of jobs that accords with both organization requirements and employee values, including customary relationships. This internally developed job structure is logically, at least, somewhat different from that of any other organization.

Market rates, on the other hand, represent an agglomeration of prices paid by organizations of every size and type. Some jobs are never filled from the labor market, but rather by employees trained by the organization. Some organizations are almost completely insulated from most labor markets, except for jobs they cannot provide training for. Even if jobs in different organizations are identical, the chance of their occupying the same position in the job hierarchy is small. Even highly skilled jobs may vary in importance to the various employing organizations.

Thus no job evaluated wage structure is immune to conflict with market rates. The only way that an organization could avoid such conflict would be to pay at or above the market on every job. But the severity of the conflict varies considerably from one organization to another. Low-wage organizations may experience conflict on many jobs. Likewise, organizations employing largely semiskilled workers and promoting from within have less conflict than organizations employing large numbers of highly skilled workers who must be hired for these jobs. If there is unemployment in the local labor market, less conflict between market rates and evaluated rates occurs even in low-wage organizations. Geographically isolated organizations or those with large numbers of unique jobs experience less conflict.

The fact that the position and meaning of the same job rate varies from organization to organization makes the solution of the conflict easier. If the job is a hiring-in job, the organization may have no choice but to pay the market rate. If not, the importance of the conflict depends on the position of the job within a job cluster. If it is a job more strongly related to associated jobs than to the market, the market rate is much less important. If jobs that are keyed to the market are at or above market rates, internal relationships are likely to prevail.

Some job clusters are market-oriented, usually because the organization cannot provide the training needed or because the union discourages intraorganization comparisons. Other job clusters are essentially insulated from the market, except for hiring-in jobs. But tight labor markets tend to make any job cluster in which the organization does not provide its own labor supply by promotion or transfer from within market-oriented. Although changes in market rates vary in amount and even direction for separate job clusters, in periods of generally tight labor markets there is some similarity among the movements.

The basic solution to conflict between market rates and evaluated rates is to develop a number of wage structures. In this way, a job cluster that must be tied closely to the labor market can be so tied without seriously disturbing other wage and salary structures. A less preferable solution is to exempt certain jobs or job clusters from job evaluation. This solution is difficult to defend and endangers internal relationships. A third solution is the guideline method of job evaluation that, in effect, determines internal relationships by market relationships.

Wage structure decisions as outlined in this chapter attempt to balance internal and external considerations (market rates). Most organizations achieve this by developing a number of separate wage structures and by emphasizing flexibility in pricing job structures. Low-wage employers in competitive industries, especially those operating in tight labor markets, may have to abandon interest in internal relationships and concentrate on keeping jobs manned by paying market rates. In fact, they may have to lower their hiring standards as well.

Solution to conflicts between market rates and evaluated rates may be made easier or more difficult by unionism. If the job evaluation plan is a joint one or if the union is interested in consistent internal relationships, solution is facilitated. Craft unionism, rival unionism, and lack of interest in internal relationships make solution more difficult.

OCCUPATIONAL DIFFERENTIALS

Job evaluation is ostensibly a device for maintaining occupational differentials.[8] Whether or not this result has been achieved is not known. One study found that job evaluation plans often provide for an increase in the skill differential and suggests that occupational narrowing has been less where the proportion of skilled workers is high.[9] The job evaluation plan in the basic steel industry has maintained occupational differentials. One of the announced purposes of the Dutch national job evaluation plan was to preserve occupational differentials.[10]

Most economists contend that there has been a long-term tendency for occupational differentials to decline, although it has been pointed out that the facts are not unambiguous.[11] It is generally agreed that in the short run, occupational differentials change little during normal periods, but contract sharply during periods of very high employment.

To the extent that job evaluation serves to maintain relative occupational differentials, it gives employees an incentive for accepting or undergoing training to enhance their skills and in the long run contributes to the supply of skilled people. Although wage differentials are certainly not the sole motive for acquiring additional skills, a latent function of job evaluation may be to preserve occupational differentials, especially during periods when employees, unions, and organizations have little reason for maintaining them.

WAGE STRUCTURE ADMINISTRATION PROBLEMS

Decisions concerning internal wage structure must not only contend with the numerous considerations discussed in this chapter, but

[8]Harry Ober, "Occupational Wage Differentials in Industry," in W. S. Woytinsky and Associates, *Employment and Wages in the United States* (New York: Twentieth Century Fund, 1953), p. 474.

[9]Slichter *et al., Impact of Collective Bargaining,* p. 622.

[10]H. M. Douty, "The Impact of Trade Unionism on Internal Wage Structures," in Meij, *Internal Wage Structure,* p. 238.

[11]Melvin Reder, "Wage Differentials: Theory and Measurement," in Universities-National Bureau Committee for Economic Research, *Aspects of Labor Economics* (Princeton N.J., 1962), pp. 257–318.

also with continuous change in employees, jobs, and organizations. Jobs change by the addition or subtraction of duties according to the needs of the organization. Jobs also change as a result of changes in technology, with consequent changes in method and equipment. New jobs are added and old ones disappear. Employees also change, through leaving the organization and being replaced by others, and through transfer and promotion to different jobs. Employees must be classified as assigned to certain jobs for which they are to be paid. Organizations also change in response to these internal changes and in response to changes in the external environment—product markets, labor markets, and the union or unions representing employees.

Responding to these changes involves wage structure maintenance. This section examines a number of wage structure problems and methods of dealing with them.

JOB CHANGES—JOB DESCRIPTIONS

Job changes call for changes in job descriptions and job evaluations to ensure that the changed job carries the appropriate pay rate. New jobs call for job analysis and job evaluation to determine the appropriate rate.

Both represent additional effort for busy supervisors and managers, even if the analysis and evaluation are done by others. As such, there may be a tendency for managers to neglect these chores under the general press of work.

Unfortunately, however, consistent wage structures require that these changes be made and made promptly. In addition, under union conditions failure to make them can foreclose the organization's right to make changes in job descriptions. In a number of cases, management has lost a considerable portion of its right to make job changes by failing to make prompt changes in job descriptions.[12] By custom and practice, employees may acquire the right to do certain work and to refuse to do work not called for in job descriptions. Major union-management problems have been caused by laxity in wage administration, so that established custom limits management's rights to make changes.

Much of the problem can be attributed to failure to educate managers on pay administration. Unless managers realize the importance of keeping pay structure changes in tune with job changes, any program of pay structure maintenance is likely to degenerate into detective work.

[12]Slichter *et al., Impact of Collective Bargaining,* p. 582.

EMPLOYEE CHANGES—EMPLOYEE CLASSIFICATION

When employees change jobs and when new employees are assigned to jobs, employee classification determines the job description that applies to the work the employee is doing and the appropriate pay rate. A pay rate cannot be assigned an employee until he has been classified as performing a certain job.

Proper employee classification of new employees and changing classifications when employees change jobs are essential to maintaining consistent pay structures. But, like job changes, they represent additional work for busy managers. Again, unless managers understand that employee misclassification destroys pay relationships and creates vested interests that are difficult to change, they are likely to neglect reporting employee changes and to inappropriately classify employees. The extent of the problem is illustrated by an organization that conducted an employee audit bimonthly and still found misclassification in 2 to 4 per cent of the classifications.

TECHNOLOGICAL CHANGE

Technological change affects wage structures by making changes in jobs. As mentioned previously, when jobs change, their place in the structure may change.

The issue of whether or not automation brings a net upgrading or downgrading of jobs has created a lively controversy in the literature. Although most predictions have been that automation will bring a general upgrading, the evidence from actual cases has been mixed.[13] Evi-

---

[13]Peter F. Drucker, "Integration of People and Planning," *Harvard Business Review* (November–December, 1955), p. 38; George B. Baldwin and George P. Shultz, "Automation: A New Dimension to Old Problems," Industrial Relations Research Association, *Proceedings of the Seventh Annual Meeting* (Detroit, December 28–30, 1954), pp. 114–128; James R. Bright, "Does Automation Raise Skill Requirements?" *Harvard Business Review* (July–August, 1958), pp. 85–98; Herman J. Rothberg, "Labor Adjustments for Changes in Technology in an Oil Refinery," *Monthly Labor Review* (September, 1957), pp. 1083–1087; Jack Stieber, "Automation and the White-Collar Worker," *Personnel* (November–December, 1957), pp. 8–17; H. F. Craig, "Administering Technological Change in a Large Insurance Office—A Case Study," *IRRA Proceedings* (1954), pp. 129–139; Charles R. Walker, "Life in the Automatic Factory," *Harvard Business Review* (January–February, 1958), pp. 111–119; William A. Faunce, "Automation and the Automobile Worker," *Social Problems* (Summer, 1958), pp. 68–78; Arthur N. Turner, "A Researcher Views Human Adjustment to Automation," *Advanced Management* (May, 1956), p. 23; Martin Richmond, "Automation—Tool of Cost Reduction," *Manufacturing Series No. 222* (New York: American Management Association, 1956), pp. 48–58; Robert L. Aronson, "Automation—Challenge to Collective Bargaining," in Harold W. Davey, Howard S. Kaltenborn, and Stanley R. Ruttenberg (eds.), *New Dimensions in Collective Bargaining* (New York: Harper & Brothers, 1959), p. 63.

dence of upgrading and downgrading has been reported as well as increased tension and better working conditions. Skills, at least sometimes, are of a different kind rather than more or less.

Experience shows that adjustments in job and wage structures have been less troublesome than expected. Skill levels on affected jobs have not been significantly raised or lowered.[14] The steel plan, with its 50 per cent weight on responsibility, has accommodated automated jobs without apparent difficulty.[15] Others report that present job evaluation plans are adequate to adjust to the changes.[16]

It appears to have been established, however, that automation reduces the number of separate job classifications.[17] Broader job classifications take account of the interdependence of automated jobs and the tendency to move men from job to job.[18]

Broader job classifications mean broader job descriptions and less frequent changes in employee classification. Thus if the broad job descriptions represent reality, problems of maintaining wage structures may be reduced.

In practice, few jobs are actually downgraded.[19] This may mean that job changes resulting from technological change do not reduce job-related contributions. It may also mean that automation creates new rather than changed jobs. A third possibility is that some jobs do require less contributions but organizations do not choose to evaluate them downward. But there is no evidence that downgrading is more frequent in nonunion than in unionized organizations.

Technological and other changes over a period of time may require basic revision of the job evaluation plan—in factors, weights, or both. If the model of the employment exchange used in this book is correct in its implication that many employees want to make more contributions than organizations have chosen to recognize, these desires plus technological change may require it. The NBPI study of job evaluation suggests a careful audit of job evaluation plans and pay structures at least every three years.

[14]Robert L. Aronson, "Jobs, Wages and Changing Technology," *Bulletin 55* (School of Industrial and Labor Relations, Cornell University, Ithaca, New York, 1965).

[15]G. L. McManus, "Steel Pay Rates Meet Challenge of Growing Automation," *Iron Age* (March 13, 1958), pp. 61–63.

[16]Faunce, in *Social Problems* (Summer, 1958), p. 75; Herman J. Rothberg, "Adjustment to Automation in a Large Bakery," *Monthly Labor Review* (September, 1951), pp. 1037–1040.

[17]Jon M. Shepard, "Functional Specialization and Work Attitudes," *Industrial Relations* (February, 1969), pp. 185–194.

[18]Julius Bezler, "Effects of Automation on Some Areas of Compensation," *Personnel Journal* (April, 1969), pp. 282–285.

[19]Slichter *et al., Impact of Collective Bargaining,* p. 585.

ENVIRONMENTAL CHANGES

Product markets, labor markets, and union-management relationships also change and require adjustment of job and pay structures. Product market changes may change the cost incidence of jobs and force organizations to husband their economic resources. Labor market changes may produce shortages of certain employee groups and compress pay structures. Changes in unions, in the internal political situation of unions, in collective bargaining agreements, and in union-management relationships may foster or inhibit union interest in internal wage structures and may make wage structure administration easy or difficult. Unions can aid or hinder organizations in making the adjustments in wage structures that environmental changes require.

In the United States in recent years, union contracts and the practice of nonunion organizations with regard to white-collar employees have resulted in yearly changes in the pay rates of jobs in response to environmental changes. Union contracts often call for deferred increases on a yearly schedule. Organization practice with respect to clerical, administrative, and professional employees makes yearly adjustments.[20]

MAINTENANCE PROCEDURES

Problems of wage structure administration emphasize the importance of job evaluation maintenance. Maintenance, at a minimum, consists of (1) keeping job descriptions and job ratings up to date, and (2) seeing that employees are actually performing the jobs outlined in the job descriptions. A central agency may be assigned to (1) analyze new or changed jobs, (2) see that job changes are reported, (3) see that old descriptions and evaluations are still adequate, (4) see that identical jobs have identical job titles, and (5) receive and process appeals and grievances with respect to job ratings.

Supervisors are normally responsible for advising this department of any changes in job content that they are planning to make or have made. They are likewise responsible for seeing that employees are assigned to tasks and duties included in the job descriptions. To facilitate carrying out these responsibilities, supervisors may be required to review at regular intervals with each employee the job description of his job and, if the job description is not adequate, to request a new analysis and evaluation. A form for such requests is shown in Figure 30.

[20]U.S. Department of Labor, *Bulletin No. 1417.*

```
┌─────────────────────────────────────────────────────────────────┐
│              REQUEST FOR JOB EVALUATION OR RESTUDY                │
│                                                                   │
│                                      Department _____       │
│                                        Yes    No                  │
│  Job Title: _____ New Job:  ──    ──            │
│                                                                   │
│  Present Job Code No. _____                                │
│  1. Has job content changed since last evaluation? Yes ___ No ___ │
│  2. Describe change _____  │
│     _____   │
│     _____   │
│     _____   │
│     _____   │
│  3. A. When did change occur? _____   │
│     B. Or, did change occur over an extended period of time? Yes ___ No ___ │
│  4. Has this work been performed in another department? Yes ___ No ___ │
│     If so, in what department? _____  │
│  5. Remarks: _____   │
│     _____   │
│     _____   │
│                                                                   │
│                                                                   │
│                                Foreman: _____           │
│                                Date: _____              │
│                                                                   │
│                                Superintendent                     │
│                                                                   │
│  Original to Wage Administration                                  │
│  1 copy for Superintendent                                        │
│  1 copy for Works Manager                                         │
│  1 copy for Foreman's follow up                                   │
└─────────────────────────────────────────────────────────────────┘
```

FIGURE 30

Source: **Allis-Chalmers Manufacturing Company, Milwaukee, Wisconsin. Reprinted by permission.**

Some organizations require that approval for job changes be obtained before such change is made. It is doubtful that this practice can be justified in a dynamic organization. If job changes are reported and consequent re-evaluations are made promptly, such rigidity would not seem to be called for. If, however, supervisors are guilty of shifting duties in order to manipulate pay rates, some method must be found to discourage the practice.

In addition to supervisory requests for job restudy, other methods may be used to maintain the system. The central wage department may be set up to audit jobs by department on a continuing basis. Thus, each department's jobs would be subject to audit at regular intervals. Interim checks might be made, however, by checking departmental job lists at regular intervals against a list of standard job titles.

Another device is to limit the life of job descriptions. Thus, a job description would be valid only for a certain definite period, after which time the job must be restudied.

A further check on the adequacy of job information and the correctness of job values is the grievance or appeal procedure. Employees should be encouraged to appeal whenever they believe their job description or job rating is incorrect. If the organization is unionized, the regular grievance procedure may be used. If the organization is nonunion, an appeal procedure may be devised. In either case, a request for restudy of the job is made early in the procedure. After the wage department has made a re-evaluation of the job, if the matter is still not settled, it is sent up the line until agreement is reached.

Standard job titles are an essential part of job evaluation maintenance. Such standard titles should apply to all jobs that entail identical duties and responsibilities wherever found in the organization. A central department polices the use of these job titles to see that they are used only where they apply.

12

Economic Performance Rewards—Rate Ranges

Organizations act as if they believe that they use pay to reward superior performance. Almost all organizations have wage or salary ranges for a considerable proportion of their employees and they typically insist that movement through these ranges is based on merit. Most organizations have incentive plans that apply to many employee groups. Pay ranges apply to many production employees and to almost all clerical, professional, and managerial employees. Incentive plans apply to many production employees, a large proportion of salesmen and managers, and a smaller proportion of clerical workers and professional employees. Most employee groups are paid under either ranges or incentive plans. Managers, however, typically are paid under both arrangements.

But in spite of the prevalence of merit ranges and incentive plans, the fact is that very few employees are actually paid for performance. As pointed out in chapters 3 and 8, not only are the requirements for using pay to reward performance difficult to meet, but also organizations have not been diligent in meeting them.

Few organizations have been careful in specifying what performance contributions the organization requires and can accept, with the result that few employees know what performance contributions are rewarded. If organizations have specified what performances are required (as in the case of incentive plans), they usually exclude performance contributions that employees know that the organization requires but for which employees are not rewarded. Nor have organizations been careful to distinguish employee performance from changes over which the employee has no control.

Furthermore, organizations for both good and bad reasons have not convinced employees that measurements of employee performance are reliable and valid. Even more important, organizations have not convinced employees that rewards depend on performance, often because they don't and often because pay secrecy hides from superior performers the fact that they receive more rewards.

Studies show that pay is not closely related to performance in many organizations that claim to have merit ranges.[1] Typically, pay is much more closely related to job level and seniority than to performance. Low, zero, and even negative relationships between pay and supervisory ratings of performance occur even among managers, where the relationship would be expected to be high. In union situations it has been found that typically over 80 per cent of employees are at the top of the range even where management strongly endorsed the merit philosophy and that unions often prefer a merit range to an automatic range because movement is faster under the merit range.

Studies of incentive plans also show numerous instances wherein performance is poorly or negatively related to pay.[2] In these instances, both organizations and employees recognize that the incentive plan is malfunctioning, although they may disagree about the reasons for it. But in the case of ranges, a persistent mythology appears to have convinced organizations that calling pay increases merit increases makes them performance rewards even if they are not. Employees accept the increases but not the myth that they are based on performance.

It has been shown that, given some positive indicators, employees are willing to believe that pay is based on performance.[3] But in the absence of these indicators, employees refuse to accept the relationship.

[1]E. E. Lawler and L. W. Porter, "Predicting Managers' Pay and Their Satisfaction with Their Pay," *Personnel Psychology* (Winter, 1966), pp. 363–373; B. Svetlik, E. Prien, and G. Barrett, "Relationships between Job Difficulty, Employee's Attitude Toward His Job, and Supervisory Ratings of the Employee's Effectiveness," *Journal of Applied Psychology* (October, 1964), pp. 320–324; M. Haire, E. E. Ghiselli, and M. E. Gordon, "A Psychological Study of Pay," *Journal of Applied Psychology Monograph* (August, 1967), pp. 1–24; M. H. Brenner and H. C. Lockwood, "Salary as a Predictor of Salary: A 20-Year Study," *Journal of Applied Psychology* (August, 1965), pp. 295–298; Sumner H. Slichter, James J. Healy, and E. Robert Livernash, *The Impact of Collective Bargaining on Management* (Washington, D.C.: The Brookings Institution, 1960), pp. 602–606.

[2]Slichter *et al., Impact of Collective Bargaining,* Chapter 17; Robert H. Roy, "Do Wage Incentives Reduce Costs?" *Industrial and Labor Relations Review* (January, 1952), pp. 195–208; Donald Roy, "Quota Restriction & Goldbricking in a Machine Shop," *American Journal of Sociology* (March, 1952), pp. 427–442; Donald Roy, "Work Satisfaction and Social Reward in Quota Achievement: An Analysis of Piecework Incentive," *American Sociological Review* (October, 1953), pp. 507–514; Donald Roy, "Efficiency and 'the fix': Informal Intergroup Relations in a Piecework Machine Shop," *American Journal of Sociology* (November, 1954), pp. 255–266.

[3]Edward E. Lawler, III, *Pay and Organizational Effectiveness: A Psychological View* (New York: McGraw-Hill Book Company, Inc., 1971), p. 159.

As discussed in Chapter 3, organizations have not perceived the distinction between membership motivation and motivation to perform, nor the fact that although the former is essential to organizations, the latter may not be because (1) it may not be needed, (2) it can be secured in other ways, or (3) it is too costly for the organization to obtain. As long as organizations fail to make this distinction, there is a strong tendency to expend organization resources in a futile attempt to obtain motivation.

In fairness, it should be recognized that there appears to be a cultural expectation on the part of employees of yearly pay increases. If this is true, it is understandable for organizations to attempt to get as much as possible in return for the expenditure of organization resources. But until organizations realize that additional pay not tied to performance can achieve membership motivation but not motivation to perform, programs to provide performance rewards are largely myths.

In the following discussions of ranges and incentive plans, it will be seen that in many cases, wage and salary increases actually represent membership rewards rather than performance rewards. An effort will be made, however, to point up the conditions under which each can be performance rewards.

RATE RANGES

Rate ranges probably apply to most employees in this country. The most comprehensive survey reported, covering 10 million employees in 40 urban labor markets, found that in 32 of them a majority of office workers worked under formal rate ranges and a majority of production workers in 11 of the markets.[4] A summary of area wage surveys made by the Bureau of Labor Statistics in 1968–69 reported that the majority of office workers in almost all areas worked under rate ranges, as did the majority of plant workers in many areas. Single-rate programs were very seldom used for office workers and represented majority practice for plant workers in only a very few areas.[5] But single-rate plans appear to be growing for plant workers in manufacturing, wholesale trade, and services.[6] Basic steel and the automobile industry are examples of single-rate systems for production workers, and individ-

---

[4]Otto Hollberg, "Wage Formalization in Major Labor Markets, 1951–1952," *Monthly Labor Review* (January, 1953), pp. 22–26.

[5]U.S. Department of Labor, "Area Wage Surveys, Selected Metropolitan Areas, 1968–69," *Bulletin No. 1625–90* (1970), pp. 68–69.

[6]John Howell Cox, "Time and Incentive Pay Practices in Urban Areas," *Monthly Labor Review* (December, 1971), pp. 53–56.

ual job rates are the rule in the crafts. But government workers almost universally work under rate ranges.

Organizations justify rate ranges on the grounds of individual differences in employee proficiency. Workers assigned to the same job often differ greatly in productivity. Differences in individual productivity between the best and worst employee of up to five or six times have been documented.[7] One study found variations of over 100 per cent on routine work and concluded that a greater range of variation is to be expected on more complex work.[8]

Managers typically believe that rate ranges provide an incentive for employees to improve performance. As pointed out in Chapter 3, however, the existence of a range is only one of a number of requirements for performance motivation. Some unions have accepted rate ranges as a method of securing higher maximum rates than a single rate system would provide.

Individual differences in employee productivity exist only if jobs permit them. Not all jobs permit significant variation in individual productivity. Some types of work—jobs on an assembly line, for example —offer little scope for variation in performance. Each employee is expected to perform in a specific way at a fairly definite speed. In some other situations, processes are structured precisely for technical reasons and the resulting jobs leave no scope for individual variation in performance. On a number of jobs in a wide variety of organizations, the learning time is very short and in a matter of hours or a few days all employees are expected to work in about the same way at about the same pace.

In such situations, the rationale of individual differences in productivity is absent, and a single-rate system, in which a single rate is set for each job or pay grade, may be employed. Any employee assigned to a given job receives the rate for the job. Such a system is simple to administer and it can operate without difficulty (1) if little variation in output is possible, and (2) if it is acceptable to the parties concerned. Unions often favor the single-rate principle because it eliminates judgment-based differentials in individual pay. Obviously, if single rates exist, performance rewards are not being employed.

In single-rate systems, either job rates or grade rates may be used. If the job rate is used, a wage line such as that shown in Figure 31 provides the job rates. If the grade rate is used, rates for pay grades appear as in Figure 32.

[7]Marion W. Richardson, "Forced-Choice Performance Records," *Personnel* (November, 1949), p. 207.

[8]H. M. Douty, "Some Aspects of Wage Statistics and Wage Theory," IRRA, *Proceedings of the Eleventh Meeting* (Chicago, December 28–29, 1958), p. 201.

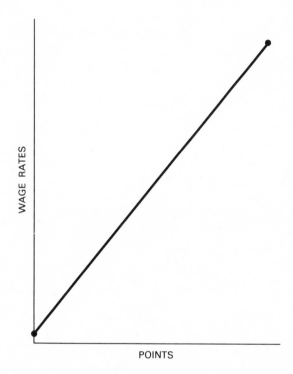

FIGURE 31

Single Job Rates

If different levels of job performance are possible, however, performance differences are a logical justification for rate ranges. If two employees of widely different efficiency are assigned to the same job and receive the same pay rate, it is quite likely that the more efficient worker will feel that he is being treated unfairly. In such instances, the lack of performance rewards may encourage the higher performer to seek an employment exchange that will match his rewards more closely with his contributions.

But observation of situations in which rate ranges are employed shows that organizations use ranges where they appear difficult to justify in terms of individual differences in performance and that rate ranges if so justified are seldom as wide as performance differences. Both phenomena suggest that the rationale behind rate ranges is more complex than a simple reflection of performance differences and deserves examination.

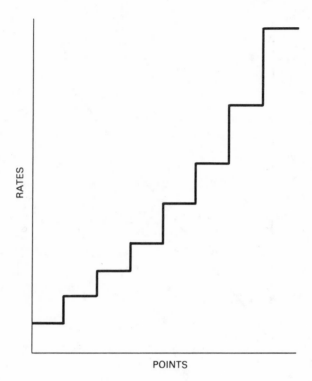

FIGURE 32

Rates for Pay Grades

RATE RANGE RATIONALE

One study reported the rationale of rate ranges in most large organizations was the need to provide for performance differences, but in some cases the rationale was industry practice.[9] The second explanation suggests that the labor market dictates the use of ranges.

A careful analysis of the purposes of rate ranges confirms this implication and shows that ranges serve a number of purposes, whether or not organizations are aware of this.[10] For example, if there is a significant range of quality variation in individuals seeking a given kind

[9]U.S. Department of Labor, "Salary Structure Characteristics in Large Firms," *Bulletin No. 1417* (1963).

[10]Walter Fogel, "Wage Administration and Job Rate Ranges," *California Management Review* (Spring, 1965), pp. 77–84.

of job, rate ranges permit organizations to vary pay rates with employee quality. But quality differences are difficult to assess and job experience is usually assumed to measure it. Experienced employees are usually difficult to attract away from other organizations because membership rewards are often tied to length of service. Thus, in these labor markets, rate ranges may be essential but are usually wider than necessary to retain experienced employees. Notice also that rate ranges based on worker quality do not provide performance rewards—they merely ensure that rewards are sufficient to attract the quality of employee required.

Rate ranges may, as suggested above, be justified by performance differences. But the relationship between pay and performance can only be assured if movement through ranges is based on merit. If movement is based on length of service, the relationship between pay and performance may be destroyed. It also follows from this rationale that if there is no variation in employee performance, there will be no ranges. Finally, only ranges based on merit entail performance rewards.

A third rationale for rate ranges is employee expectations. If employees expect wage increases irrespective of improved performance, rate ranges may provide an alternative to a general increase. To the extent that not all employees get increases or that varying increases are given, such increases may be less costly to the organization than a general increase. But such rate ranges do not provide performance rewards.

Still another rationale for rate ranges is collective bargaining. In contract negotiation the employer may agree to rate ranges or an expansion of rate ranges because they involve less cost then a general increase. The union may demand ranges with movement based on length of service to reward members with high seniority. It hardly needs to be said that such ranges do not provide performance rewards.

A study of a large number of collective bargaining relationships suggests that the concept of a rate range has changed.[11] The original concept of a rate range was that the average qualified employee should receive the rate for the job, presumably the rate that would be assigned under a flat rate system—the job rate or pay grade rate. According to this concept two types of ranges are possible. In one, new employees are brought in at a starting rate and in a relatively short period they are advanced to the top of the range, often through a series of steps. In such plans the standard rate (job rate or pay grade rate) is the maximum of the range. Such ranges, which may be job rates or rates for pay grades, are portrayed in figures 33 and 34. Movement is automatic, based on

[11]Slichter *et al., Impact of Collective Bargaining*, p. 604.

length of service. Actually this is very similar to a flat system since all employees are expected to reach the maximum rate. If jobs are such that after a period of time all workers have reached a uniform standard of performance and further improvement is unlikely or impossible, this type of range appears justified. All employees become average after a period of time. Above-average performance is impossible.

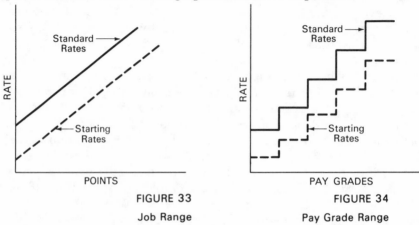

FIGURE 33	FIGURE 34
Job Range	Pay Grade Range

In the other type, standard rates are placed at the midpoint of the range. Average employees are expected to attain the standard rate after they become proficient on the job. Below-average employees are expected to remain below the midpoint and only superior employees are expected to receive rates in the upper half of the range. Such ranges are depicted in figures 35 and 36. The purpose of such ranges is to provide an incentive for above-average performance.

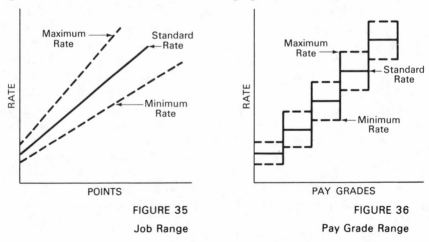

FIGURE 35	FIGURE 36
Job Range	Pay Grade Range

   Both types of ranges are applicable to an organization or even to a single broad job cluster. Figure 37 shows a pay schedule in which grades 1 through 5 employ the first type of range and the balance of the grades, the second. The assumption is that only average performance is possible on the first five grades but superior performance becomes possible on higher-level jobs.

   It appears that the original concept of the range has been undergoing gradual change. The study found evidence that this expectation of the "average" employee's being paid at the middle of the range has been gradually changed so that the maximum is now the expected rate. Since all employees expect to reach the maximum of the range, this rate calls for merely satisfactory rather than superior performance. Only a few companies retained the original viewpoint of average rates for average performance.

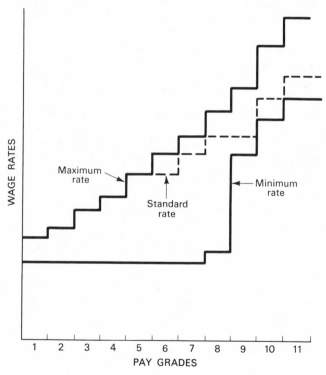

FIGURE 37

Example of Rate Ranges with Varying Spreads

This discussion of the rationale of rate ranges raises some real questions concerning the propriety of calling pay increases within rate ranges performance rewards. Only one of four purposes of ranges entailed performance rewards and then only under certain conditions. Furthermore, the changed concept of a rate range seems to greatly restrict its use for this purpose. Clearly, the requirements of performance motivation outlined in Chapter 3 do not fit closely with rate range rationale.

ESTABLISHING RATE RANGES

The width of rate ranges employed in practice reflects the range rationale emphasized by organizations. For example, the within-grade spread for hourly jobs typically varies from 10 to 25 per cent, from 25 to 35 per cent for office jobs, and from 30 to 100 per cent for management positions. The progression presumably follows the opportunity for differential performance on jobs so that limited ranges are employed where only small differences in performance are possible and wider ranges, where large performance differences are possible.

The variation in range widths employed by different organizations for each employee group suggests that other considerations are operating. For example, the concept of "average employee receives job rate" would entail a broader range than the "satisfactory employee receives maximum rate" concept. If ranges are employed to account for employee quality differences, actually discernible differences would be a consideration. Practices of other organizations in the industry or area may provide some indication of discernible quality differences in the labor market as well as employee and union preferences.

Organization promotion policy and practice may affect the width of ranges in that job families in which promotion is rapid may be accommodated with narrower ranges than job families in which promotions come more slowly. Organization practice with respect to the number of separate pay schedules affects the width of ranges. For example, separate pay schedules for clerical employees have an average spread of 30 per cent in large organizations; combined professional and administrative schedules, 37 to 47 per cent; and combined clerical, professional, and administrative schedules, 35 to 45 per cent.[12] Range width is also affected by the size of a pay increase required in order to be noticeable.

Establishing range maximums is particularly difficult. There is some logical maximum for every job such that regardless of how well an individual performs, the result is worth no more to the organization.

[12]U.S. Department of Labor, *Bulletin No. 1417.*

When this point is reached, the ideal solution is to promote the individual if he has the abilities required in higher-level jobs. Unfortunately, promotions are not always available immediately and promotable people should be informed that they are temporarily at the top of their range and that pay increases on the present jobs will be limited to general increases. There are, of course, people worthy of the top pay of the job but not promotable. These individuals should know that further increases will be limited to general increases in pay and benefits.

Perhaps because of the difficulty of establishing range maximums, about one-fifth of large organizations report that they have provisions for pay increases beyond the maximum for professional and administrative employees. A somewhat smaller proportion of organizations have such provisions for clerical employees.[13]

Ranges may be established arbitrarily or empirically. If determined arbitrarily, a decision is made on the percentage or dollar spread and lines are drawn in around the wage line. If pay grades are employed, a minimum and maximum rate for each pay grade are established. If, for example, it is decided that the range shall be 10 per cent above and 10 per cent below the wage line, lines are drawn at these levels. Grade range minimums and maximums are determined by drawing lines parallel to the base of the chart at the height where the lines cross the midpoint of the grade. (See Figure 38.) The spread of the range may be either a constant dollar amount or a percentage. Percentage spreads are more often used. Some pay schedules increase the percentage spread on higher-pay grades.

The empirical method of determining ranges employs past practice of the organization and often wage survey data. Past practice on pay rates is examined on the theory that this represents what the organization was trying to do. Wage survey data report the range of rates paid by other organizations. One way to depict past practice of the organization is to plot average pay for the lowest- and highest-paid job in each pay grade as well as the average of all jobs in the grade on a chart and to fit lines to these points to create ranges for each grade. Another is to plot pay rates of all present employees on a scatter diagram and fit lines to the minimums and maximums in each pay grade. Wage survey data are then used to adjust the ranges developed.

The empirical method should suggest the possibility of determining pay grades and rate ranges at the same time. In actual practice, as suggested previously, this is often done.

Examination of Figure 38 may serve to illustrate how the number of pay grades and the slope of the wage line affect another consideration

[13]*Ibid.*

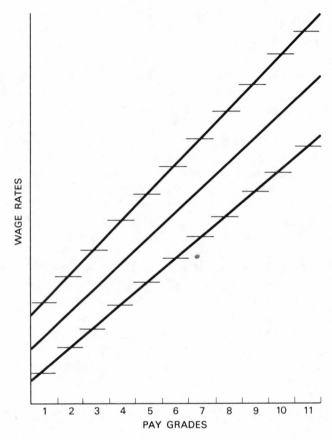

FIGURE 38

Setting Rate Ranges for Pay Grades

in establishing ranges; *i.e.,* overlap. Overlap occurs when rate ranges are established so that individuals in a lower-pay grade may be paid more than individuals in higher grades. It is apparent that overlap can only be prevented if the wage line slopes steeply, there are few pay grades, and the ranges are narrow.

Theoretically, overlap produces employee dissatisfaction if individuals in lower-pay grades receive a higher rate than some individuals in higher grades. In practice, however, little difficulty has been encountered and typical pay schedules involve overlap of three or four pay grades.

The common use of rate ranges with this amount of overlap may be additional evidence that the concept of a range has shifted away

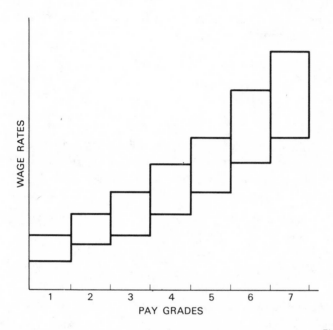

FIGURE 39

Example of Overlap Between Adjacent Pay Grades with No Overlap Between
Alternate Pay Grades

from that of performance reward to that of membership reward. If individuals promoted to jobs in the next higher grade always receive pay rates above the midpoint of the new range (because promoted people, of course, receive at least their former rate), it is difficult to believe that only superior performers are in the upper half of the range. To preserve incentive values of both ranges and promotions, a pay schedule such as that shown in Figure 39 would seem to be required.

CLASSIFYING EMPLOYEES

The process of employee classification—deciding for each employee which job description identifies the work he is doing—was discussed in Chapter 11. The problems discussed there, although present under a single rate system, become even more serious when ranges are employed. Rate ranges with any degree of overlap perhaps not only make misclassification harder to detect from records, but also may cause supervisors to underrate its importance. Actually, ranges make proper employee classification more important.

Preferable practice may be to have each supervisor, with the help of a job analyst who is familiar with the job information, classify the employees reporting to him. Calling each supervisor into the compensation administration department to perform the task probably assures that the task will be accomplished in the shortest possible time.

As each employee is classified, an employee classification record is prepared that includes (1) name, (2) employee identification number, (3) department, (4) job title, (5) job number, (6) present wage rate, (7) job value (points), and (8) pay grade. To maintain this record, it is necessary that all employee and job changes be reported. Thus all accessions, separations, transfers, and promotions necessitate changes in the employee classification record, as do new jobs or changes in existing jobs.

CORRECTING OUT-OF-LINE RATES

When wage and salary ranges have been determined and employees have been classified, it is usually discovered that some employees are being overpaid and some underpaid according to the rate ranges set up.

There also will be overpaid and underpaid employees under a flat rate system. Such rates require policy decisions. The policies below apply to both flat rate and range systems. They typically protect employee interests but vary widely by organization.

UNDERPAID EMPLOYEES

Little question exists regarding appropriate action on underpaid employees. Underpaid employees, if they are to be retained, should have their wages raised to the minimum of the rate range, either immediately or in one or two steps. If the employee is adequately performing the job in which he is classified, the difference between his rate and the minimum of the range is an account payable of the employer.

It is possible, of course, that the employee is not worth the minimum of the range. There are several possibilities here. First, if the labor market is so tight that such marginal employees must be retained, a lower classification may be assigned to the job. Similar reasoning would apply to handicapped or superannuated employees unable to perform the regular job. A second and preferable alternative is either to transfer the employee to a job he can perform or to release him from the organization. Another possibility exists if new employees have not learned the job—a learning classification at a lower rate.

Usually there will be few underpaid employees, and a policy of bringing their rates into line immediately serves to protect the integrity of the pay schedule. If many employees are underpaid, a careful review is required not only because of cost considerations, but also because of the possibility of creating inequities between newly raised employees and those already at the minimum of the range. Also, a phasing-in period may be appropriate.

OVERPAID EMPLOYEES

Overpaid employees present more of a problem, but a problem so common that special terminology has been developed to handle it.[14] The rates involved have been variously called red circle, ringed, flagged or personal rates, red allowances, adders, over rates, and personal out-of-line differentials. Various solutions are possible. A National Industrial Conference Board study found much variation in practice.[15] The two extremes are (1) do nothing and (2) bring the rate into line at once. Both policies cause morale problems, and the first encourages whipsawing.

The most common solutions are the following: (1) freeze the rate until general increases bring it into line; (2) transfer or promote the employee to a job that will carry his rate; (3) freeze the rate for six months, during which time every effort is made to transfer or promote the employee, but at the end of six months bring the rate into line; (4) withhold a part of each general increase until the rate is in line with the proviso that if the employee refuses a transfer to a job that will carry his rate, his rate is adjusted immediately; (5) red circle the job rather than the employee for a limited period; (6) eliminate the differential after one year; (7) eliminate the differential according to a time period that varies with the seniority of the employee. These solutions are presented in order of frequency in practice.

A number of less common arrangements exist. One, the adder, is a payment to the employee in quarterly installments of the difference between his rate and the job rate or range maximum. The employee is

---

[14]In fact, a special terminology seems to be developing for the various kinds of out-of-line rates. Sibson refers to red-circle situations (overpaid employees), gold-circle situations (overpaid employees who are exempted from the pay schedule), green-circle situations (under-paid employees), and silver-circle situations (very long service employees overpaid for this reason but not for performance). Robert E. Sibson, *Wages and Salaries,* rev. ed. (New York: American Management Association, 1967), pp. 129–131.

[15]George W. Torrence, "Correcting Out-of-Line Rates of Pay," *Management Record* (September, 1960), pp. 10–13.

given 100 per cent of the differential the first year and the amount is reduced by 25 per cent each year until it is eliminated. In another variety of the adder, the difference is reduced at once to the increment between pay grades. In both arrangements the amount of the adder is reduced by general increases. The advantage of the adder involves a separation from regular earnings, calling the attention of both employer and employee to its exceptional character.

Another arrangement is the lump-sum settlement. The employee, for example, may be paid the difference times 2,000 hours and his rate brought in line immediately or paid the difference times 1,040 hours and a like amount six months later if he is still on the same job.

Still another arrangement is to arrange with the union to leave red circle rates out of bargaining until they are back in line. This is essentially the same as withholding generals.

Any solution adopted involves questions of equity. Overpayment is obviously not the fault of the employee and any reduction in rate is very likely to appear unfair to him. On the other hand, the question of inequities involving all employees is the concern here. A plan accepted by the parties to correct inequities logically must be permitted to correct inequities discovered. The various practices above attempt to achieve justice both for individual employees and for the entire employee group. Failure to correct red circle rates means that (1) pay range maximums are meaningless, (2) the employee involved is being paid more than is justified for outstanding performance and more than others doing outstanding work, and (3) organization resources are going to red circle employees at the expense of other employees who are paid less for equal or better performance.

MOVING EMPLOYEES THROUGH RATE RANGES

Rate ranges make possible different pay rates for individuals on the same job. To operate such ranges, some method is called for that differentiates between employees. Such a method specifies the position of each employee between the starting rate and the maximum of the range.

STEP RATES

To facilitate use of ranges, a very few nongovernment organizations, but most government organizations, divide the entire range into a series of steps. Three or more steps are usually provided within the range. The size of the steps will vary, of course, with the size of the range, and the number of steps will depend on the period of time required to achieve proficiency in the job.

Step rates facilitate the process of granting increases. A given increase may consist of one or, at the most, two steps, and the amount is specified by the step rates. This removes the necessity of making a decision on the size of the increase.

Most organizations object to the inflexibility of such an arrangement, preferring to determine in each instance what the amount of the increase will be. They feel that some of the incentive value of the range is lost if the amount of an increase is specified.

Whether or not step rates are employed will depend somewhat on the method of progression through the rate ranges. Automatic progression requires the use of steps. Merit progression may or may not make use of step rates.

METHODS OF PROGRESSION

Methods of progression through rate ranges are (1) automatic progression, (2) merit progression, and (3) a combination of (1) and (2). A given organization may confine its use of one of the methods to certain types of jobs, or it may use all three methods on one type of job. Some organizations, for example, use all three methods of progression on shop jobs in the following manner: (1) pay grades 1–5 employ automatic progression throughout the range, (2) pay grades 6–9 use automatic progression to the midpoint of the range and merit thereafter, (3) pay grades 10 and above employ merit progression exclusively.

Automatic Progression. Automatic progression (sometimes referred to as scheduled increases) refers to wage increases based automatically on length of service. Thus, in the automobile industry a common rule is a small increase at the end of the first month and another one at the end of three months. One firm in heavy industry has a starting rate, a three-months' rate, a six-months' rate, and a rate granted automatically at the end of one year's service for all shop jobs. Another firm has two automatic increases at three-month intervals for pay grade 1, three such increases for pay grade 2, four for pay grade 4, and five for pay grade 5. A not uncommon arrangement is a specified automatic increase every sixteen weeks until the maximum rate is reached. This arrangement often applies to both factory jobs and office jobs on hourly rates and may include as many as one-half of the pay grades in a job cluster. In all these cases, the last automatic increase is the end of the progression because it is anticipated that the worker will be fully proficient at the end of that period. Many such progression systems are installed at the insistence of a union that is not convinced that a merit system will be handled fairly.

A fully automatic progression plan is actually a variation of the single-rate system or flat rate system. If all employees may expect to reach the maximum of the range on completing a given period of service, the assumption is that the maximum is the rate for the job.

In some automatic progression plans, the scheduled increase is granted only if the employee's proficiency has progressed to the degree expected. If the employee is adjudged not deserving of the increase, under some plans it may be withheld, especially if such a plan is applied to clerical workers. Often, however, an employee not granted the increase is transferred to another job for another chance or released from the organization. This type of automatic progression includes an element of merit and necessitates a method of determing whether or not the employee deserves the scheduled increase.

Some element of merit may be permitted also in fully automatic plans, although in a limited way. Under some such plans an employee may be granted a scheduled increase before it is due. For example, an employee may be adjudged to have progressed sufficiently after one month to receive the three-months' rate, or after three months to receive the six-months' rate. Thus, merit may be used to speed up the progression. It may not be used, however, to slow down progression.

Merit considerations in automatic progression plans, however, should not be overemphasized. The major element in automatic progression plans is the automatic movement through the range by all employees. Common union policy has been to accept rate ranges if this meant a higher rate than a single rate would provide and to achieve automatic movement through ranges.[16]

Organizations make much more use of automatic progression than is commonly assumed. A report of the results of area wage surveys[17] conducted in 1968–69 by the Bureau of Labor Statistics shows that automatic progression is used more often than merit progression for plant workers in 39 of 45 geographic areas across the country in all industries. In six of the areas automatic progression was also more prevalent than merit progression for office workers, but a combination of automatic and merit progression was prevailing practice in fifteen areas.

Combinations of Automatic and Merit Progression. It was pointed out at the beginning of the discussion of methods of progression that combinations of automatic progression and merit increases have been employed. Some such combinations have already been men-

---

[16]Slichter *et al., Impact of Collective Bargaining,* p. 602.
[17]U.S. Department of Labor, *Bulletin No. 1625–90.*

tioned. In one, fully automatic progression was employed for lower-pay grades and merit increases for higher-pay grades. In another, automatic increases were granted only to those that were adjudged to deserve them.

Probably most usual of the combinations, however, is fully automatic progression to the midpoint of the range, with merit controlling from that point on. Under the original concept of rate ranges, this plan is based on the reasoning that all employees may be expected to reach average proficiency in the time required under automatic progression to reach the midpoint of the range, but not all employees can be expected to reach above-average proficiency calling for rates in the upper portion of the range. To the extent that all employees do achieve average efficiency by the time they have reached the midpoint of the range, the plan may be justified from a labor cost standpoint. To the extent that they do not, labor costs rise.

It is, of course, possible to employ combination progressions along with the changed concept of a range (all employees eventually reach the top of the range regardless of proficiency). Under this arrangement all employees would get an increase based on length of service and some would get more because of their performance. It is impossible to determine from published reports whether combination progressions represent automatic progression to the midpoint and merit thereafter or combinations of length of service and merit at all points within ranges. Some indication of practice in large firms (1000 or more employees) is provided by a BLS survey covering clerical, professional, and administrative employees wherein 60 per cent of the schedules regarded the midpoint of the range as representative of the market value of the job.[18] It is quite likely that pay schedules of plant workers more often regard the top of the range as the job rate and that schedules applicable only to managers and professionals include a higher percentage than that reported.

Automatic progression plans are simple to administer since they are purely mechanical. Introducing the element of merit complicates administration, but at least preserves some possibility of securing performance motivation from pay. It is well known that individual differences in performance do not disappear after employees have a certain period of service with an organization. Nor are employees with long service with the organization always more proficient than those with less service.

Merit Progression.   Merit progression is presumably based on the theory that wage or salary increases should be earned through increased proficiency or quality of performance and that such increases

---

[18]U.S. Department of Labor, *Bulletin No. 1417.*

should be viewed by employees as incentives toward further improvement. As the analysis of rate range rationale showed, however, the theory is a quite imperfect explanation of most so-called merit ranges.

Under the original range concept, a rate range consisting of a minimum rate, a midpoint or standard rate, and a maximum rate is particularly applicable to a system of merit progression. In such a system employees of less than average proficiency receive rates below the midpoint, average employees are paid the standard rate for the job, and only employees exhibiting superior performance are paid rates above the midpoint. Thus employee incentive is provided and labor costs are kept in line.

Theoretically, under such a system an employee could be paid any rate in the range that was in accord with his level of proficiency at a particular time. Thus, in theory, if an employee's performance dropped below standard, his wages would be reduced, just as his wage or salary rate would be increased if his performance was above standard.

Actually, however, wage increases may be granted for increased proficiency and wage increases may be withheld if performance is below standard, but wage or salary rates are seldom reduced when employee proficiency drops. A few organizations have programs whereby performance pay increases are not included in the wage or salary but involve a separate bonus based on performance in the preceding period and thus may vary from zero upward.[19] But organizations that employ pay ranges do not reduce pay when performance declines.

There is some question about how much merit progression exists in practice. One large study found that the concept of the range had changed, and that, in practice, often over 80 per cent of employees were at the maximum of the range, even in cases in which management stressed the merit philosophy. Very few companies held to the original concept of the range and enforced it by insisting on superior performance for rates above the midpoint.

Unions have exerted pressure for the fastest possible movement through ranges when they have accepted rate ranges. In one instance, the union turned down a management proposal for an automatic progression plan because the existing merit progression plan provided faster progression to the maximum.[20] Engineering unions endorse the merit principle, but investigation of actual progression shows that in most instances poorer engineers move to the maximum as fast as efficient ones.

[19]This practice has often been advocated. See Timothy W. Costello and Sheldon S. Zalkind, "Merit Raise or Merit Bonus: A Psychological Approach," *Personnel Administration* (November–December, 1962), pp. 10–17; Burt K. Scanlon, "Is Money Still the Motivator?" *The Personnel Administrator* (July–August, 1970), pp. 8–12.

[20]Slichter *et al., Impact of Collective Bargaining,* pp. 604–605.

Unions, under a merit progression plan, often follow the practice of presenting a grievance whenever any member does not receive the maximum merit increase permitted under the plan. Apparently management has been unwilling to defend merit decisions against grievances. The evidence suggests that, except for probationary and learning period pay decisions, very little of the original merit concept remains.[21]

Not only unions are involved, however. Labor shortages have played a part. If starting rates were too low to attract candidates, new employees were brought in at higher positions in the range. Then older employees were given increases to partially maintain the customary relationships between new and older employees. Often these increases raised marginal employees above the midpoint. These increases, called merit.increases, were actually general increases.

Using merit increases to grant general increases is in large part responsible for the breakdown in the merit principle. Part of the problem is failure to understand the distinction. Managers at all levels, but especially at lower levels, may perceive all pay increases as identical and fail to distinguish between increases granted because of changed economic conditions and increases granted for improved performance. This may be attributable to the generally held opinion that money itself is a motivator rather than more money as evidence of accomplishment.

Equally important is management concern that nonunion employees who get general increases after the union negotiates an increase for its members will believe that the union got them their pay increase. This concern has caused many companies to discontinue general increases and grant increases to nonunion employees on an "individual basis," informing the employee that part of the increase is an economic adjustment and part is for merit.[22] To the extent that economic adjustments are kept separate from merit increases and to the extent that merit increases are limited to those whose performance warrants it, the merit principle may be preserved. If rate ranges are moved upward by the amount of economic adjustments and marginal and satisfactory employees are limited to these economic adjustments, merit increases to above-average employees may be expected to hold incentive values. To the extent that economic and merit increases are combined, the merit principle appears to be lost.

The fact that an average of 50 to 60 per cent of salaried employees (sometimes as high as 95 per cent), even in large organizations, get annual pay increases implies that merit progression is a misnomer. Although there is an understandable trend away from merit progression on hourly jobs, it appears that organizations feel that calling pay

[21] *Ibid.*, p. 606.
[22] George W. Torrence, "Individual vs. General Salary Increases," *Management Record* (May, 1961), pp. 18–20.

increases merit increases convinces salaried employees that they represent performance rewards.

DETERMINING INDIVIDUAL PAY RATES

In most organizations pay rates of individuals within rate ranges reflect a number of considerations, of which performance is only one. Typical considerations are (1) the individual's performance appraisal, (2) his pay history, (3) his position in the range, (4) his experience, (5) time since last pay increase, (6) the amount of his last increase, (7) various pay relationships within the department, (8) pay relationships with other departments, (9) labor market considerations, and (10) state of the organization's financial resources. The balance of these often conflicting considerations determines whether an individual gets a pay increase and its amount. Although all of these inputs appear essential, calling the result a merit increase would seem to invite disbelief.

A few organizations have retained merit increase programs by converting performance appraisal scores directly into pay rates with no adjustment for other considerations.[23] Although some of the reported cases involve large organizations, it may be that small organizations are more able to maintain such programs.

But most organizations appear to believe that the facts of organization life dictate that performance be only one element in individual pay determination. A study of the members of the *Fortune* 500 list reports that although 93 per cent claim to subscribe to the merit-reward philosophy, the majority do not relate pay to performance.[24] One study of a large organization shows that "the careers that people make for themselves in large-scale organizations attenuate the role of pure performance in pay."[25] A corporate compensation director argues that merit is extremely difficult to define when economic forces are forcing substantial yearly increases and that merit increases become visible to recipients through careful maintenance of pay relationships within an organization.[26]

[23]Avery S. Raube, "A Point System Merit Rating Plan," *Management Record* (January, 1948), pp. 21–22; "A Merit Rating Plan Your Employees Will Really Buy," *Factory Management and Maintenance* (May, 1955), pp. 118–120; Slichter *et al., Impact of Collective Bargaining,* p. 605.

[24]William A. Evans, "Pay for Performance: Fact or Fable," *Personnel Journal* (September, 1970), pp. 726–731.

[25]Thomas H. Patten, Jr., "Merit Increases and the Facts of Organizational Life," *Management of Personnel Quarterly* (Summer, 1968), pp. 30–38.

[26]Kenneth E. Foster, "What is a Merit Increase?" *Personnel* (November–December, 1961), pp. 18–24.

An apparently troublesome problem of pay relationships in organizations in inflationary periods occurs when new employees are hired at rates close to those of present employees with some years of service with the organization. This so-called *compression* problem is assumed to consist of feelings of inequity on the part of present employees. Presumably these employees are disgruntled because their inputs of years of service become undervalued.

Although suggestions for solving compression have appeared in the literature,[27] organization recognition of the phenomenon seems a curious contradiction in compensation administration. Organizations profess to pay for jobs and performance on jobs and very few organizations profess to recognize length of service in individual pay. Thus if the new employee is qualified for the job and performs satisfactorily, theoretically only superior performers should feel an inequity if employees accept the employers' definition of the employment exchange. If, however, employees perceive that what the organization calls a merit increase is based on length of service, they may be expected to see this input as underrewarded when new employees receive pay rates close to their own. Existence of the phenomenon of compression seems to be additional evidence that ranges do not represent performance rewards.

In determining individual pay rates, most organizations of at least moderate size apparently are convinced that consistency of relationships and employee treatment are at least as important as performance. Consequently, there is a tendency for pay increase decisions to be centralized in a compensation department in which the numerous and often conflicting considerations can be balanced. Although supervisors have the best information on employee performance, they do not have the other information needed nor the perspective to balance these considerations from an organization viewpoint.

A common organization response to the need for organization-wide perspective in balancing pay increase constraints and the need for managerial input on employee performance is *pay planning*. These formal programs are designed to ensure that the information inputs required and the influence of various organization members are brought together with performance data possessed by the employee's supervisor when individual pay decisions are made. A common program is to (1) provide the manager with the required information, (2) provide the manager with counseling by staff specialists to interpret these data, (3) and ask him to pre-plan the amount and time of pay increases for all his employees for a year in advance.

[27]Robert M. McCaffery, "Equity vs. Compression in Production Planning," *Compensation Review* (Fourth Quarter, 1970), pp. 15–22.

A part of these programs is commonly called *pay increase budgeting* whereby department managers complete worksheets provided by the compensation department that include for each employee (1) pay grade, (2) minimum, midpoint, and maximum points in the applicable range, (3) present pay rate, (4) date and amount of last increase, and (5) proposed increase and date. When each department manager has completed his pay adjustment forecast, departmental comparisons are made before pay increase budgets are approved.

Advantages claimed for this approach include (1) intraorganizational consistency because decisions are based on information from all departments at the same time, (2) intradepartmental consistency because all employees are considered for pay adjustment at the same time, (3) the possibility of predicting the cost impact of pay increases in advance, (4) the benefit of making pay decisions affecting all employees at one point in time separate from the time of employee appraisal, and (5) delegation of individual pay decisions to supervisors.

Such approaches to individual pay determination may illustrate the realities of organization life in a bureaucracy. Administration, including compensation administration, deals with realities rather than with what conditions ought to be. But under such approaches it should not be assumed that rate ranges provide performance rewards. It would be useful to recognize that such pay increases where granted are membership rewards—rewards for continued participation in the organization. It may well be that organizations have discovered that getting and keeping employees is the primary problem and that securing performance motivation from pay is either too difficult or impossible. If that is the case, it would seem wise to stop calling these pay adjustments merit increases and concentrate on achieving membership motivation. Expending organization resources on the assumption that these expenditures will achieve performance motivation under conditions wherein this result is clearly impossible is waste.

OPERATING RANGES AS PERFORMANCE REWARDS

Although it is admittedly not easy to accomplish, individual pay decisions under ranges can be made to provide performance rewards. The performance motivation model in Chapter 3 shows that for pay to motivate performance the following conditions must exist: (1) employees must believe that good performance will lead to higher pay, (2) employees must want higher pay, (3) negative consequences of high performance must be minimized, and (4) other desired rewards are also related to good performance.

The first condition is the most basic and apparently the most difficult to obtain. Obviously, it requires that pay actually be tied to performance. But it also requires that employees (1) know what good performance consists of, (2) accept the performance measures as valid and inclusive, (3) see that the better performers actually get higher pay.

The best way to insure that pay is tied to performance and that the relationship can be seen by employees is to divide pay into three parts, as suggested by Lawler.[28] One part, pay for the job, would be the same for everyone assigned to the job. A second part would be different for employees of different length of service and perhaps for other personal contributions. The third part would be pay for performance during the preceding period, which could be zero or low for poor performers and high for superior performers. This third portion of pay, because it was based solely on performance, would vary over time with an individual's performance from zero to a high figure.

But visibility even under such an arrangement would seem to depend on employees' knowing the amount of others' performance rewards. It has been found that secrecy results in managers overestimating the pay of peers and underestimating the pay of superiors and in high performers underestimating the differences between their pay raises and those of others.[29] Thus the results of secrecy seem to be that the visibility of an actual performance-reward relationship is destroyed.

Many organizations inform employees of the minimum, midpoint, and maximum of their respective ranges.[30] But few organizations make the pay of individuals public and many go to great lengths to preserve secrecy. However, a report of an organization that emphasizes performance increases implies that fellow employees are aware of the high pay increases of high performers.[31]

The required size of performance rewards is somewhat controversial. Gellerman argues that if pay is to motivate performance, very large amounts are needed—enough to create the prospect of becoming wealthy.[32] Lawler believes that it requires that the organization be willing to give high performers large raises. Some organizations in the *Wall Street Journal* report cited above were giving superior performers 20 per cent increases.

---

[28]Lawler, *Pay and Organizational Effectiveness,* p. 167; see also Costello and Zalkind, in *Personnel Administration* (November–December, 1962), pp. 10–17; and Scanlon, in *The Personnel Administrator* (July–August, 1970), pp. 8–12.

[29]Lawler, *Pay and Organizational Effectiveness,* pp. 174–175.

[30]Two out of three offices and five out of six plants, according to a Prentice-Hall survey in 1966.

[31]John F. Lawrence, "Some Firms Abandon Uniform Pay Increases, Reward Big Producers," *Wall Street Journal* (New York, April 23, 1968), p. 1.

[32]Saul W. Gellerman, *Management by Motivation* (New York: American Management Association, 1968).

But it is quite possible for performance rewards to be so high that they violate the employee's sense of a fair reward or lower his interest in money. Thus it is important for the organization to determine for its employees what a fair raise is considered to be.

This may also be the place to emphasize that to secure performance motivation through pay employees must want more pay based on their performance. As pointed out in Chapter 3, people differ in the importance they attach to money. A number of studies have found that managers and salesmen want their pay to be based on performance.[33] Workers are not so favorable toward merit pay, but it is quite possible that they may have been objecting to plans they were familiar with. But it seems clear that a performance pay plan is unlikely to be successful if employees do not want to be paid for performance. Thus it seems essential that an organization determine whether or not the employees for whom a performance pay plan is being considered want to be paid for performance.

Because people differ in the importance they ascribe to money and in their willingness to be paid for performance, organizations should want to know what kinds of employees they have. It may be possible, however, to select employees who will respond to performance pay.

Managers may also differ about whether they wish their subordinates to be paid for performance. The evidence suggests that managers in the United States do and that good managers are more likely to than poor managers. But managers in Europe are less likely to prefer performance pay plans for their subordinates.[34]

Although performance measurements and appraisals are very much involved in performance pay, they were discussed at length in Chapter 8. It only seems necessary to emphasize here that unless such measurements and appraisals are accepted as valid and as including all important performance contributions, employees are unlikely to accept the performance-reward tie as credible. In complex organizations, in which much of the work is interdependent, the difficulty of measuring the performance contributions of individuals may raise special problems. But, as suggested in Chapter 8, appraisal by objective may, because of mutual superior-subordinate influence, achieve the necessary credibility.

This section attempted to show how individual pay decisions within rate ranges may become performance rewards. As repeatedly stressed, not all organizations need performance rewards and the need

[33]Lawler, *Pay and Organizational Effectiveness*, pp. 159–160.
[34]*Ibid.*, p. 162.

varies among employee groups. Also, organizations requiring performance rewards may or may not be able to meet the conditions required to base pay within rate ranges on performance. For those organizations or jobs wherein the requirements cannot be met, there is nothing to be gained by maintaining the myth that ranges represent performance rewards but a large potential waste of organization resources.

13

Economic Performance Rewards—Incentive Plans

Organizations utilizing incentive plans believe that they are offering performance rewards and providing performance motivation. As will be seen in this chapter, although incentive plans appear to accord with the performance motivation model, in practice, they may or may not. Incentive plans may yield substantial increases in productivity and lowered costs to organizations together with increased earnings to employees. But they may also lead to increased employee earnings with no increase in performance, together with increased costs and numerous employee relations problems.[1]

Incentive plans are controversial. Opponents range from those who oppose the idea of performance rewards on the grounds that performance is a function of the organization of work and management practices rather than employee effort, to those who oppose incentive plans on the grounds that they don't work and cause more problems than they solve. The decline, perhaps the disappearance, of incentive plans is often predicted.[2]

Proponents of incentive plans often believe that a "fair day's work" is not normally attainable in the absence of an incentive plan because time workers produce only about 50 to 60 per cent of the output attained by incentive workers.[3] Although they admit that some

[1]Sumner H. Slichter, James J. Healy, and E. Robert Livernash, *The Impact of Collective Bargaining on Management* (Washington, D.C.: The Brookings Institution, 1960), p. 502.
[2]AFL-CIO, "Decline of Wage Incentives," *Collective Bargaining Report* (November, 1960); R. Marriott, *Incentive Payment Systems,* 3rd ed. (London: Staples Press, 1968), p. 259.
[3]H. K. von Kaas, *Making Wage Incentives Work* (New York: American Management Association, 1971), p. 11.

300

incentive plans malfunction, they insist that this is usually due to poor installation and maintenance rather than the concept of incentive.

The belief that incentive plans motivate performance appears to be widely held by employers.[4] It has, in fact, been argued that if both employers and employees accept the belief, it becomes a self-fulfilling prophecy.[5]

INCENTIVE PLAN PREVALENCE

The controversy has had little effect on the utilization of incentive plans over the years. A comparison of recent surveys in the United States with similar surveys seven years earlier, however, suggests that there may be a trend away from incentive plans in the U.S.[6] In other countries incentive plans often apply to a majority of employees and in some countries their use is expanding.[7]

U.S. Bureau of Labor Statistics' surveys in the 1968–70 period show that about 20 per cent of plant workers in manufacturing work under incentive plans, but other industries reveal much smaller proportions. Very few office workers work under incentive plans.[8] Although incentive plans are more prevalent in manufacturing than in non-manufacturing, there is a great deal of variation by industry and area. For example, in the textile, clothing, cigar, and steel industries, the proportion of covered employees is over 60 per cent, whereas in the aircraft, bakery, beverage, chemical, and lumber industries the proportion is less than 10 per cent. Area variation is just as great. In some cities in the Northeast and North Central areas, from 35 to 40 per cent of plant workers work under incentive plans; in the South some cities range from 20 to 25 per cent; on the West Coast the percentage is less than ten.[9] Even within these areas there is wide variation. Forty per cent of plant workers in Waterloo, Iowa, work under incentive plans, but only 4 per cent do so in Detroit. Even within an industry the variation by area is substantial.

One analysis of incentive plan coverage suggests that they tend to be used if labor costs are large and the market is cost-competitive, if

[4]Hilde Behrend, "Financial Incentives as the Expression of a System of Beliefs," *British Journal of Sociology* (June, 1959), p. 257.

[5]John Corina, *Forms of Wage and Salary Payment for High Productivity* (Paris: Organisation for Economic Co-operation and Development, 1970), pp. 63–64.

[6]John Howell Cox, "Time and Incentive Pay Practices in Urban Areas," *Monthly Labor Review* (December, 1971), pp. 53–56.

[7]Corina, *Forms of Wage and Salary Payment,* p. 35.

[8]Cox, in *Monthly Labor Review* (December, 1971), pp. 53–56.

[9]U.S. Department of Labor, "Area Wage Surveys, Selected Metropolitan Areas, 1968–69," *Bulletin No. 1625–90* (1970).

technology is not advanced, and if production bottlenecks are likely to occur.[10] But the variation in industry and/or area coverage suggests that tradition and ideology as well as economics and technology are variables that determine the use of incentive plans.

Some incentive plans have been abandoned.[11] But new installations and expanded coverage of existing plans represent an offsetting tendency. The expansion of incentive coverage in the basic steel industry has undoubtedly been a factor, as has expanded coverage in other industries. The noticeable tendency toward broader coverage of employees in the plant in which incentive plans are found and the extension of work measurement systems to virtually all kinds of work suggest that incentive plans may expand outside of manfacturing. But the limited application of incentive plans to office workers argues against it.[12]

The apparent decline of incentive plan utilization in the United States is in sharp contrast to other countries. In Europe, incentive coverage appears to be growing, with many countries having over 50 per cent of employees covered. In Great Britain, coverage may have stabilized, but it is growing in many other countries. A recent report placed coverage at 80 per cent in Portugal, 65 per cent in Sweden, 60 per cent in Holland and Belgium, 50 per cent in France, and 40 per cent in Germany.[13] The highest proportion of worker coverage is probably still in the U.S.S.R., where some form of incentive plan applies to all workers.

As in the U.S., incentive coverage in Europe varies greatly by industry. For example, in Belgium 68 per cent of workers in paper processing are paid time rates, whereas 97 per cent of steel workers are under an incentive plan.

In spite of the apparent expansion of incentive plans in Europe, incentive plans may be as controversial there as in the U.S. A 1967 survey in Great Britain found 40 per cent of employers extremely dissatisfied with incentive plans.[14] Even the U.S.S.R. has revised incentive plans by establishing ceilings on the growth of bonuses and premi-

---

[10]Robert B. McKersie, Carroll F. Miller, Jr., and William E. Quarterman, "Some Indicators of Incentive Plan Prevalence," *Monthly Labor Review* (March, 1964), pp. 271–276.

[11]Robert B. McKersie, *Incentives and Daywork: A Comparative Analysis of Wage Payment Systems,* DBA dissertation (Harvard Graduate School of Business Administration, 1959); Lawrence F. Mihlon, "Wage Incentives vs. Measured Daywork," *Factory* (February, 1962), p. 64.

[12]In none of the metropolitan areas surveyed by the Department of Labor in 1968 and 1969 did office worker incentive coverage reach 0.5 per cent. *Bulletin 1625-90* (1970).

[13]Corina, *Forms of Wage and Salary Payment,* pp. 34–42.

[14]*Ibid.,* p. 40.

ums.[15] But in Germany, Austria, and Switzerland, employer sentiment at least is strongly favorable to incentive plans. In other countries, although questions may be raised regarding some of the consequences of incentive plans, employing organizations intend to keep them.[16] The conclusion reached in an excellent review of the literature of incentive plans that wage incentives will be around for a long time seems justified.[17]

This review of the prevalence of incentive plans has not differentiated plans by type but included all arrangements whereby payment to employees is based at least in part on employee output. Thus individual, group, and plantwide plans are included as well as various arrangements for computing premiums and bonuses. The term "incentive plan" as used in the U.S. includes a wide variety of plans. In Europe, the term "piecework" tends to be used for individual plans and "plant bonuses" for broader plans, although usage varies between countries. As a consequence, statistics for different countries are difficult to compare and a stable or increasing proportion of incentive coverage may include a changing proportion of different types of plans; *i.e.,* more plantwide and less individual plans, for example.

In the United States, most incentive plans are either piecework or standard hour plans. Outside of what might be called the piece-rate industries (the needle trades), piece rates are being displaced by standard hour plans.[18] Most plans provide for individual incentives, but small group plans and plantwide incentives are being increasingly used.

INCENTIVE PLAN RESULTS

Most reports of experience with incentive plans suggest that wage incentives result in greater output per man-hour, lower unit costs, and higher employee earnings. Typically, these reports come from company experience with incentive plans with no attempt to determine the source of change nor to compare results of incentive workers with a control group. When incentive plans are installed, many changes are made in conditions of work and if no effort is made to determine the effects of each, observed changes may be due to something other than the incentive plan. It is quite possible, for example, that the results

---

[15]M. Kabaj, "Evolution of Incentive Systems in U.S.S.R. Industry," *International Labour Review* (July, 1966), pp. 22–38.

[16]Emile Boursier, in Corina, *Forms of Wage and Salary Payment,* p. 146.

[17]Garth L. Mangum, "Are Wage Incentives Becoming Obsolete?" *Industrial Relations* (October, 1962), pp. 73–96.

[18]Slichter *et al., Impact of Collective Bargaining,* p. 495.

obtained are attributable to changed management practices employed as a prerequisite to installation of an incentive plan.

Such reports often cite employee earnings increases of 10 to 70 per cent and cost decreases of 25 to 65 per cent under incentive plans. A survey of the results of 2500 incentive plans reported an average productivity increase of 63.5 per cent, an average rise in employee earnings of 20.6 per cent, and an average savings in unit labor costs of 25.9 per cent.[19]

Although these surveys imply that observed results are attributable to the incentive plan, no attempt is made to determine whether the source of improvement was better management, increased employee effort, or other changes accompanying the installation. Some evidence that not all the improvement results from the incentive plan is available from the experience of a five-plant company, two of which had incentive plans and three, measured daywork (production standards but no wage incentive). In this company, the most and least efficient plants, separated by a wide margin, are the two incentive plants.[20] Some other evidence is available from a study that compared productivity, costs, worker effort, and earnings in a number of companies with similar jobs but different payment plans and concluded that productivity was due more to methods analysis and time-studied standards than to incentive plans.[21]

It thus appears that although reports of company experience show that incentive plans are associated with increased output, lower unit costs, and higher employee earnings, a sizable proportion of these gains may be attributable to other changes accompanying incentive plans, especially improved management practice. Methods improvements, performance standards, performance measurements, and other prerequisites to successful incentive plans may contribute as much or more than the incentive plan.[22]

Fortunately, there are some studies that attempted to determine the effects of the incentive plan alone. Before-and-after studies involving only a change from fixed pay to an incentive plan have found quite substantial productivity increases.[23] Carefully designed laboratory studies employing control groups also found that offering financial in-

[19]"Wage Incentives and Productivity," *Personnel* (May–June, 1955), pp. 4–5; see also M. S. Viteles, *Motivation and Morale in Industry* (New York: W. W. Norton & Company, Inc., 1953).

[20]Slichter *et al., Impact of Collective Bargaining,* p. 49.

[21]Robert E. Lane, "A Comparison of Controlled Day Work and Incentive Systems," unpublished master's thesis (University of Wisconsin, 1956).

[22]von Kaas, *Making Wage Incentives Work,* p. 4, says 50 per cent but offers no data.

[23]F. J. Roethlisberger and W. J. Dickson, *Management and the Worker* (Cambridge, Mass.: Harvard University Press, 1939); S. Wyatt, "Incentives in Repetitive Work: A Practical Experiment in a Factory," *Industrial Health Research Board Report No. 69* (London: H. M. Stationery Office, 1937), pp. 43–46.

centives increases productivity and that subjects working on a piece-rate system produce about 20 per cent more than subjects on an hourly rate.[24] Lawler, after a careful review of the evidence on incentive plans, concluded that even the most conservative studies seem to suggest that individual incentive plans can increase productivity by 10 to 20 per cent.[25]

Most of the reports and studies have been concerned with incentive plans applied to individual employees. Reports of experience with incentive plans applied to small groups and organization subunits tend to show productivity increases equivalent to those claimed for individual plans.[26] Suggestions have been frequently made that under conditions of modern technology, cooperation and coordination rather than individual effort determine productivity and that group rather than individual incentives are called for.[27] A careful review of a number of studies covering a variety of situations in which individuals were rewarded differently showed that if the work was interdependent, productivity showed no increase—only if individuals did not depend on others did productivity increase in response to differential rewards.[28] Only a very few studies of the effects of group plans have been made. A study conducted in two British factories found that productivity decreased as group size increased and that workers on individual incentives were higher producers than workers on group incentives.[29] Another study found that production under group incentives was higher than under a fixed hourly rate but lower production characterized larger groups because employees saw less relationship between their pay and their performance.[30] A group sales plan was found to encourage cooperation.[31]

Plantwide incentive plans report substantial increases in produc-

[24]J. W. Atkinson and W. R. Reitman, "Performance as a Function of Motive Strength and Expectancy of Goal Attainment," *Journal of Abnormal and Social Psychology* (November, 1956), pp. 361–366; E. A. Locke and J. F. Bryan, *Goals and Intentions as Determinants of Performance Level, Task Choice and Attitudes* (Washington, D.C.: American Institute for Research, 1967); E. E. Lawler, "Equity Theory as a Predictor of Productivity and Work Quality," *Psychological Bulletin* (December, 1968), pp. 596–610.

[25]Edward E. Lawler, III, *Pay and Organizational Effectiveness: A Psychological View* (New York: McGraw-Hill Book Company, 1971), p. 124.

[26]Paul Broadstone, "Group Incentive in a Job Shop," *Factory Management and Maintenance* (September, 1951), pp. 132–133; Harold B. Maynard, "Changing Philosophies of Wage Incentives," *Mechanical Engineering* (March, 1952), pp. 277ff.

[27]B. M. Bass, *Organizational Psychology* (Boston: Allyn and Bacon, Inc., 1965).

[28]L. Keith Miller and Robert L. Homblin, "Interdependence, Differential Rewarding, and Productivity," *American Sociological Review* (October, 1963), pp. 768–778.

[29]R. Marriott, "Size of Working Group and Output," *Occupational Psychology* (January, 1949), pp. 47–57.

[30]H. Campbell, "Group Incentives," *Occupational Psychology* (January, 1952), pp. 15–21.

[31]N. Babchuk and W. J. Goode, "Work Incentives in a Self-Determined Group," *American Sociological Review* (October, 1951), pp. 679–687.

tivity and cooperation among employees.[32] But the effectiveness of these plans is very hard to document because (1) installing such plans involves a number of other changes, and (2) control groups are almost impossible to obtain. The evidence suggests that these plans improve cooperation among employees, improve productivity over a fixed pay plan, and can tie other rewards to improved performance but attenuate even beyond small group plans the connection between performance and pay.

INCENTIVE PLAN PROBLEMS

Although there is a great deal of evidence that incentive plans can improve employee performance, there is also much evidence that they have dysfunctional consequences. There is a tremendous amount of evidence, for example, that incentive plans, especially individual ones, result in restriction of output. Such studies show that restriction of output under incentives is widespread and results in productivity much below worker capability.[33]

The reasons for restriction of output have been shown to be worker beliefs that additional productivity will lead to a rate cut or to their working themselves out of a job.[34] These beliefs presumably result in group pressures to restrict output, with the result that both social and economic reasons for restriction exist.

It has also been shown that the competition created by individual incentive plans can cause serious problems if the work calls for cooperative effort.[35] People can be expected to exhibit behavior that is rewarded, and cooperative behavior is not rewarded or recognized under an individual incentive plan. In fact, it has been suggested that incentive plans cause employee resentment because such plans reward only effort, although employees know that many other contributions are

[32]E. S. Puckett, "Productivity Achievements—A Measure of Success," in F. G. Lesieur (ed.), *The Scanlon Plan* (Cambridge, Mass.: M.I.T. Press, 1958), pp. 109–117; Gilbert K. Krulee, "Company-Wide Incentive Systems," *The Journal of Business* (January, 1955), pp. 37–47.

[33]O. Collins, M. Dalton, and D. Roy, "Restriction of Output and Social Cleavage in Industry," *Applied Anthropology* (Summer, 1946), pp. 1–14; M. Dalton, "The Industrial 'Rate-Buster': A Characterization," *Applied Anthropology* (Winter, 1948), pp. 5–18; D. Roy, "Quota Restriction and Gold Bricking in a Machine Shop," *American Journal of Sociology* (March, 1952), pp. 427–442; W. F. Whyte (ed.), *Money and Motivation* (New York: Harper & Brothers, 1955).

[34]D. J. Hickson, "Motives of Workpeople Who Restrict Their Output," *Occupational Psychology* (July, 1961), pp. 110–121; Viteles, *Motivation and Morale in Industry.*

[35]E. E. Ghiselli and C. W. Brown, *Personnel and Industrial Psychology*, 2nd ed. (New York: McGraw-Hill Book Company, 1955); Babchuk and Goode, in *American Sociological Review* (October, 1951), pp. 679–687.

required by the organization.[36] Worker beliefs concerning incentive plans may well be a problem in that the model of performance motivation presented in Chapter 3 clearly shows that unless employees believe that increased performance will result in an increase in desired rewards, they will not perform. Although it is difficult to determine their prevalence, a number of negative worker beliefs with respect to incentive plans have been reported.[37] For example, it has been suggested that workers often believe that (1) incentive plans result in the speedup; (2) rates will be cut if increased earnings are made under the plan; (3) incentive plans encourage competition among workers and the discharge of slow workers; (4) incentive plans result in unemployment through "working yourself out of a job"; (5) incentive plans break down crafts by reducing skill requirements through methods study; (6) workers do not get their share of increased productivity; (7) incentive plans are too complex; (8) standards are set unfairly; (9) industrial engineers are out to rob workers; (10) earnings fluctuations make it difficult to budget household expenditures; (11) incentive plans are used to avoid a deserved pay increase; (12) incentive plans increase strain on the worker and may impair his health; (13) incentive plans increase the frequency of methods changes; (14) incentive plans ask workers to do more than a "fair day's work"; (15) incentive plans imply a lack of trust in workers by management. If such beliefs exist, it is obvious that incentive plans cannot provide performance motivation. Unless they can be changed, they would seem to provide difficult problems for the installation and operation of incentive plans.

It would be incorrect, however, to assume that a majority of employees and union leaders are averse to incentive plans. Employees are often strongly favorable to incentive plans and union attitudes are diverse. Some unions object to wage incentive plans on principle, some believe that incentive plans have been used in their industry so long that they would be difficult to eliminate, and some actively advocate incentive plans.[38]

An apparently serious problem of incentive plans is the existence of "demoralized" plans. In such plans there are (1) sizable inequities in earnings and effort, (2) large and growing incentive yield accompanied by low and declining effort levels, and (3) high proportions of payments

---

[36]Hilde Behrend, "The Effort Bargain," *Industrial and Labor Relations Review* (July, 1957), pp. 503–515.

[37]Solomon Barkin, "Labor's Attitude Toward Wage Incentive Plans," *Industrial and Labor Relations Review* (July, 1948), pp. 553–572; Russell A. Hedden, "Labor's Attitude Toward Wage Incentives," *The Conference Board Management Record* (August, 1946), pp. 265–267.

[38]William Gomberg, "Union Attitudes on the Application of Industrial Engineering Techniques to Collective Bargaining," *Personnel* (May, 1948), pp. 443–454.

of average earnings and other guarantees for nonincentive work by incentive employees. Such distorted plans typically involve poor union-management relationships, a high rate of grievances, and frequent wildcat strikes and slowdowns. Typically, a demoralized incentive plan denotes a continuing struggle for looser rates and higher earnings until low output, high costs, and poor labor relations threaten organization survival. One study found a surprising number of demoralized incentive plans.[39]

No data exist on the degree to which incentive plans do become demoralized, but from published reports it is apparent that it is not an isolated phenomenon. One survey of incentive plans in 316 companies concluded that 78 per cent of the plans had failed or developed serious problems.[40] As the studies cited earlier in this section show, demoralization is not inevitable. But, particularly with changing technology, methods, and materials, it can be avoided only by careful, vigilant administration. Management is probably chiefly responsible for demoralization because of failure to maintain the plan under the inevitable informal employee pressures and grievances stoutly defended by the union.

An incentive problem implied above is the high administrative costs of such plans. Although there is no question that determining standards, measuring output, and maintaining the plan are more costly than administering a pay for time-worked plan, studies are not available that accurately show the costs of installing and operating an incentive plan. Studies cited earlier concerning cost reductions under incentives suggest that productivity increases can and often do offset the additional costs.

Still another problem of incentive plans is the tendency for internal wage and salary relationships to be distorted such that lower-skilled incentive workers may earn more than high-skilled workers not under the plan.[41] Interestingly, this problem as well as intergroup conflict has been credited with the move toward expanding incentive coverage within plants and entire organizations.[42] It may be responsible for the very high coverage of steel workers, even on machine-paced jobs.

[39]Slichter *et al., The Impact of Collective Bargaining,* p. 497; see also Herbert R. Northrup, "The Other Side of Incentives," *Personnel* (January–February, 1959), pp. 32–41.

[40]Bruce Payne, "The How and Why of Incentives," *Dun's Review and Modern Industry* (January, 1954), p. 60.

[41]Leonard R. Sayles, "The Impact of Incentives on Inter-Group Work Relations— A Management and Union Problem," *Personnel* (May, 1957), pp. 483–490; William Foote Whyte, "Economic Incentives and Human Relations," *Harvard Business Review* (March–April, 1957), pp. 73–80.

[42]Mangum, in *Industrial Relations* (October, 1962), pp. 73–96.

Several of these problems, especially the last one and the need for cooperation between workers on interdependent jobs, have encouraged the adoption of group and plantwide incentive plans. Although the studies made to date have not proved that these broader plans do avoid these problems, there is evidence that they can encourage cooperation and offer suggestions (not proof) that output restriction is less likely. The numerous changes that accompany the installation of a companywide plan make determining the source of results especially difficult. At any rate, there is no reliable evidence comparing the relative effectiveness of individual, group, and companywide plans.

PAY FOR TIME vs. PAY FOR OUTPUT

Up to this point, the discussion has implied that an organization desiring to provide economic performance rewards in exchange for increased performance has a choice of whether to use ranges or some form of an incentive plan. In principle, this is true. In practice, however, the decision often becomes whether to pay for time or for results.

Our model of the employment exchange specifies that what is involved is contributions and the units in which the organization recognizes them. Payment on the basis of time, in practice, subsumes a large number of unspecified contributions. Payment for output appears to require that contributions produce measurable results before they are recognized as contributions. In practice, however, payment for results often turns out to be payment for one contribution—effort—while ignoring other contributions required by the organization.

The apparent payment for results under incentive plans, however, suggests that the work itself largely determines whether or not an incentive plan is applicable. Thus, it would appear that time wages are more applicable if (1) units of output are difficult to distinguish and measure, (2) employees are unable to control quantity of output, (3) there is not a clear relationship between effort and output, (4) delays in the work are frequent and beyond employee control, (5) quality considerations are especially important, (6) good supervision exists and supervisors know what a "fair day's work" consists of, (7) precise advance knowledge of unit labor costs is not required by competitive conditions.

Similarly, output wages appear preferable if (1) units of output can be measured; (2) there is a clear relationship between employee effort and quantity of output; (3) the job is standardized, the work flow is regular, and delays are few or consistent; (4) quality is less important than quantity or, if quality is important, it is easily measured; and (5) competitive conditions make it imperative that unit labor costs be definitely known and fixed in advance of production.[43]

Actually, even these criteria are not so clearcut as they appear. Management, with the aid of industrial engineers, has been able to extend greatly the area of measurable work. As will be seen later, indirect work of all kinds, including office and sales work, has yielded to measurement. Even management jobs have been measured to yield quantitative standards of performance. Also, adaptations of incentive plans have been developed to permit their application in cases in which the relation between effort and output is not so clear as the above rule implies. In some cases this has been done with group plans; in others, by assessing the importance of certain types of indirect work to the production work.

Other important criteria are (1) community attitudes, (2) employee attitudes, and (3) labor relations climate. The statistics on prevalence of incentive plans suggest that communities differ greatly in worker efficiency and labor relations climate. It is often observed that smaller and more rural communities have a better industrial climate than large industrial communities. Employee attitudes are more receptive to incentive plans in some organizations than others. The labor relations climate may be such as to make any incentive plan an additional source of conflict or to provide a channel for further cooperation.

Technological considerations may, of course, enter into the decision. As the proportion of machine time increases, incentive possibilities are reduced. As the production flow becomes more regulated by conveyor or process, the need for incentive is reduced. But under these conditions, incentives can be applied with greater reliability. Incentive plans are more likely to be successful in industries with a stable technology than in those undergoing continual technological change.[44]

Many predictions have been made about the effects of automation on incentives. One is that incentives will disappear because work can no longer be measured.[45] Another is that automation will spawn more incentive plans based on quality of output, material and machine utilization, and maintenance time and cost.[46] Most predictions are for

[43]See Sumner H. Slichter, *Union Policies and Industrial Management* (Washington, D.C.: The Brookings Institution, 1941), pp. 288–291.

[44]Slichter *et al., The Impact of Collective Bargaining,* p. 519.

[45]William A. Faunce, "Automation and the Automobile Worker," *Social Problems* (Summer, 1958), p. 69; Charles R. Walker, "Life in the Automatic Factory," *Harvard Business Review* (January–February, 1958), p. 116.

[46]Mathew J. Murphy, "Automation and Other Technological Advances," *Manufacturing Series Number 205* (New York: American Management Association, 1953); "Management Problems in the Factory of the Future," *Management Review* (August, 1952), pp. 481–483.

group or plantwide incentive plans.[47] A study by the Bureau of Labor Statistics of an automated rubber plant found no change required in man-paced tasks, but on machine-paced jobs the incentive was based on the work required of the operator plus seeing that the machine achieved capacity operation.[48] The individual incentive plan required minimum adaptations to automation.

It appears that as machines take over substantial portions of the job, incentive plans, where applied, will be broader in coverage. This results from lowered worker resistance to incentives, less requirement for heavy physical effort, and the difficulty of maintaining clear distinctions between incentive and nonincentive jobs.[49] Incentives are becoming all or nothing decisions.

It thus appears that, in practice, the decision on whether or not an incentive plan is applicable is the result of a system of beliefs. If the parties to the decision believe that an incentive plan is appropriate, a way will usually be found to install one. If a result is not discernible, a process may be. If measurement is impossible, appraisal may not be. If an individual plan is not feasible, a group or plantwide plan may be. Often, in fact, the distinction between an incentive plan and a range is more apparent than real.

Actually, of course, the decision is based in part on the characteristics of the plans themselves. The following section is an examination of the workings, advantages and disadvantages, and conditions of applicability of specific plans.

TYPES OF INCENTIVE PLANS

Incentive plans imply that employees receive additional pay for additional contributions measured by results. Whether these results are measured for each individual or for small or larger groups and whether results are measured directly or by some indirect means are the major variables in types of plans. But these two variables have yielded such a great variety of plans that it would be impossible to discuss them all. This section examines most of the types of plans in use.

[47]Jack Rogers, *Automation* (Berkeley: Institute of Industrial Relations, University of California, 1958), p. 83; George P. Shultz and Arnold R. Weber, "Technological Change and Industrial Relations," Chapter 6 in Herbert G. Heneman, Jr., and others (eds.), *Employment Relations Research* (New York: Harper & Brothers, 1960), pp. 190–221.
[48]Joseph W. Childs and Ralph H. Bergmann, "Wage-Rate Determination in an Automated Rubber Plant," *Monthly Labor Review* (June, 1958), pp. 610–611.
[49]Slichter *et al., The Impact of Collective Bargaining,* pp. 514–515.

INDIVIDUAL PLANS

Most incentive plans are based on the performance of individuals. Many of the following plans, but not all of them, can also be applied to groups.

Measured Daywork. Under measured daywork, formal production standards are developed and employee performance is judged relative to these standards. As originally developed and in some current usage, measured daywork involves periodic revision of hourly rates corresponding to employee performance relative to production standards. Under this arrangement, individual employee performance is appraised at least quarterly, and the employee's hourly rate is adjusted upward or downward in accordance with this appraisal.

This plan is similar to the rate range discussed in Chapter 12. One difference is that standards employed in measured daywork are usually more formal than those employed with ranges, and employee review is more frequent. Time study and its derivatives are typically used in setting standards under measured daywork. Another difference, and perhaps an even more important one, is the fact that the hourly rate under measured daywork may be revised either up or down.

Some advantages attributed to this plan are that (1) workers can easily understand it; (2) effective supervision is encouraged because of the existence of standards and the relatively frequent appraisals; (3) time standards may be less controversial and more easily changed without worker resistance; (4) worker cooperation in methods changes may be more easily obtained if such cooperation is reflected in their ratings; (5) better performers are paid more than average and poor performers; and (6) time standards facilitate interdepartmental comparisons and thus cost control and organization planning.

Disadvantages of the plan may be that (1) the limited incentive may result in a gradual decline in effort; (2) high performers may be discouraged by the failure of the plan to sufficiently reflect differences in performance; (3) worker acceptance of methods changes and changes in standards may be inversely correlated with the strength of the connection between performance and pay; and (4) management may have less motivation to maintain correct standards.

Measured daywork with the incentive feature may be applicable if there are numerous unstandardized conditions in the work and if much of the task is process or machine controlled. It provides some incentive but not a strong incentive. Strong supervision seems to be a definite requirement. This plan has been used successfully by General Motors with the approval of the UAW and has been employed in clerical incentive installations. Also, some managerial incentive plans are of this type.

But measured daywork may also be used without the incentive feature, in which case employees are paid hourly rates in association with some type of control of worker efficiency by means of production standards. But hourly rates are not adjusted in accordance with employees' average performance against standard over a period of time. It might better be called, and is often called, a "fair day's work program."

In some cases organizations with unsatisfactory incentive plans have adopted this plan. In others, companies have installed the plan in place of an incentive plan in a new plant. No knowledge is readily available on the number of such plans in existence. Although experience with worker efficiency under such plans has not been uniform, easier adjustment of workers to technological change, gains in product quality, and improvement in labor relations are frequently reported.

The obvious difference between nonincentive measured daywork and incentive plans is the absence of the money motivation. Management retains the responsibility for employee efficiency. Work standards are required as is a higher supervisor-to-worker ratio.

The supervisor's job under such plans is quite different from his job under incentive plans. Under incentive plans he may be so busy with decisions involving the plan that he loses interest in the level of employee efficiency above the required minimum. More important, he may have a vested interest in preserving the status quo, because new methods, layout, or work flow are highly likely to create new problems for him. Hence, his interest in searching for work improvement may be limited.

Under nonincentive measured daywork, direct responsibility for employee effort rests with the supervisor. He is likely, however, to have more time to devote to the task and be motivated to solve employee efficiency problems through work improvement.

Production standards in these plans may be either "ultimate" or "attainable."[50] Ultimate standards make no allowance for nonstandard conditions and represent a set goal. Attainable standards include allowances for nonstandard conditions. Incentive plans employ attainable standards. Most nonincentive-measured daywork systems make use of ultimate standards. Good performance under ultimate standards involves as well as reasonable employee effort removal of nonstandard conditions.

In administering measured daywork, in addition to the choice of ultimate or attainable standards, decisions must be made on whether or not to advise employees of the standards and on whether or not to make reference to standards in disciplining employees. Two arrangements

[50] *Ibid.,* p. 540.

are common: (1) attainable standards made known to employees with direct reference to standards in discipline for low production, (2) ultimate standards not publicized and indirect discipline.

The first arrangement appears to preserve incentive values of the plan, but it may make both production standards and employee efficiency discipline cases matters of dispute between union and management. The second approach appears to limit the plan to cost and other management purposes, but standards are not subjects of union-management dispute because discipline is not based on standards. Actually, the very fact that supervisors know production standards has resulted in great improvements in employee efficiency.

Although little incentive to exceed standard exists under measured daywork plans without the incentive feature, and although such plans vary greatly in effectiveness, a number of advantages may accrue from them. Methods changes are easier to make under such plans than under incentive plans, for example. Much less conflict appears to arise over production standards, and management freedom in establishing standards is seldom challenged. Good labor relations may be easier to attain under such plans than under incentive plans. Management attention to employee efficiency is maintained.

Midway between measured daywork with hourly rates adjusted for employee performance and measured daywork without incentive is measured daywork with two hourly rates—a lower rate for those employees who fail to make standard and a higher one (usually by 20 per cent) for those who meet or exceed standard. Called the multiple-time plan, it provides a strong incentive to reach standard, thus correlating with supervisory effort. But no incentive is provided above standard and this feature may be resented by good performers. Also, the sharp focus on production standards may generate resistance to technological change and numerous standards grievances.

Piecework. This is the most common type of incentive plan. Piecework is sufficiently familiar to all of us as to require almost no explanation. Straight piecework pays a man so much for each item produced. If Jim Green gets 15¢ a piece for stamping out lid covers, he knows that if he turns out 100 covers a day he makes $15, and if he can turn out 1000, he will make $150. Straight commission plans for salesmen are piecework plans in that earnings are based directly on the number or dollar value of items sold. Piecework pays a man for what he does and leaves him free to choose his own speed.

Piece rates are set for specific jobs. A time standard is set, usually through time study. By applying the time standard against the base rate, a rate per piece is determined. Thus, if Jim Green in the above example holds the job of punch press operator, the rate for which is

$3.00 per hour and the time standard for stamping out lid covers is determined to be 20 lid covers per hour, the piece rate is 15¢ per piece.

Piecework to most of us implies straight piecework, a strict proportionality between results and rewards regardless of the level of output. Frequently, this strict proportionality is modified in practice by guaranteeing the employee's time rate if he fails to make standard. Under guaranteed piece rate, Jim would be paid his hourly rate for any hour he failed to stamp out 20 lid covers. For any hour in which he turned out 20 or more, he would be paid by the piece. Generally, this time rate or guaranteed base rate is set for each job by job evaluation.

Direct labor costs are constant for all levels of output where no guarantee is used. If base rates are guaranteed, direct labor costs are constant for all levels above standard. Total unit costs, however, may be expected to decrease for levels of production above standard because fixed costs decline when spread over increased output.

The chief advantages of·piecework are its simplicity in calculation, incentive value, and understandability. It appears just in principle and it facilitates cost accounting, because labor costs are constant for all outputs under straight piecework and for outputs above standard under guaranteed piecework.

Its primary disadvantage is its unsavory reputation among many employees. Another disadvantage results from the fact that standards are expressed in monetary terms. This means that all changes in wage rates call for changing piece rates. More important psychologically, it means that the standard and the rate are inseparable. Thus changes in standards tend to be resisted even if fully justified and agreed on because changing standards means changing piece rates.

Also, because rate and standard are inseparable, equity demands that every employee producing a given piece receive the same rate. It is thus impossible under piecework to incorporate other contributions into the incentive plan. It is also impossible to differentiate between employees on the basis of seniority or experience if either were deemed desirable.

Some of the early piecework plans were less concerned with equity. The Taylor Differential Piecework plan consisted of two piece rates—one for employees who did not make standard and a much higher one for those who exceeded standard. The Merrick Differential Piecework plan had three piece rates—a low piece rate, an intermediate piece rate, and a high piece rate, depending on whether workers were producing at zero to 85 per cent of standard, 85 to 100 per cent, or above 100 per cent. The Gantt Task and Bonus plan guaranteed the base rate to those who produced below standard but offered a high piece rate to those who produced above standard. These plans may be called selective because they were devised to encourage high performers and to discourage low performers.

Plans that pay different workers different piece rates for producing the same piece are not unlikely to be perceived as unfair by employees. Perhaps these early selective plans are in part responsible for the widespread distaste for piecework.

Piecework is the most common type of incentive plan in this country primarily because of what might be called piecework industries, largely the needle trades. These industries are characterized by many small employers engaging in strong product market competition. The stability that exists in the industry may be largely attributable to unionism. Time study is used but piece rates are bargained. Bargaining piece rates is actually bargaining unit labor cost, apparently a necessity because of product market competition. In spite of the disadvantages of piecework, long tradition and union-management agreement serve to make such plans work well in these industries. Plants vary widely in efficiency, but demoralized incentive plans in the sense of runaway standards with high pay for low effort do not exist in these industries. Relatively stable technology is largely responsible.

Before concluding our discussion of piecework, it is useful to delineate their essential characteristics. The chief characteristic is that all gains or losses in the output of a worker go to him, unlike time wages, wherein all gains and losses in output accrue to the employer. It also contrasts with sharing plans (to be discussed later) in which gains and losses are shared between the employer and the employee.

Another characteristic of such plans is the proportional relationship between output and earnings at all levels of production. Thus additional output is equally profitable to the employee regardless of previous output. This contrasts with selective plans in which additional output may be more or less profitable to the employee depending on the level of his production.

A third characteristic of plans of this type is the high standards on which they are based. Such plans make use of "high task" or 100 per cent efficiency, which is defined as an amount of production derived through motion and time study that a normal operative can accomplish day after day without physical or mental impairment. "High task" may be contrasted with "low task," which is obtained from past production records and is assumed to be at the 62½ per cent level of efficiency. Sharing plans are often based on low task.

Successful piecework plans require accuracy in measuring both standards and individual output. Inaccuracy in these measurements gives rise to wage inequities and may result in failure of the plan due to employee dissatisfaction.

These characteristics of piecework plans are important because they appear to hold out some elements of equity to both employee and employer. It seems fair to the employee, for example, to reward him for all of his output above standard and to maintain a proportionate relationship between output and earnings at all levels of output. Furthermore, such a plan is easily understood. Likewise, it seems fair to the employer that additional rewards be based on performance above a reasonable standard.

But as we saw, piecework has a number of serious disadvantages that flow from the inseparability of standard and rate. It seems logical that an incentive plan could be devised that provided the desirable characteristics of piecework without its drawbacks.

The Standard Hour Plan. Such a plan, sometimes called the "standard time plan," "time piecework," "hour-for-hour plan," "the 100 per cent bonus plan," but more usually called "the standard hour plan," is essentially the same as piecework. The only major difference is that under the standard hour plan the standards are expressed in time per unit of output rather than money. Outside of the piece-rate industries, it is the most-used incentive plan.

The standard hour plan and the straight piecework plan both reward employees in direct proportion to their output. However, in the case of the standard hour plan, instead of a price per piece, a "standard time" is allowed to complete a particular job, and the employee is paid for the standard time at his time rate if he completes the job in standard time or less. Thus, if an employee completes in eight hours a job for which the standard time is ten hours, his earnings for the job are ten times his time rate. If he takes more than standard time to do the job, he will be paid at his time rate for the time actually spent on the job. Actually, of course, most standards are in minutes. Earnings can be calculated either in terms of time saved or as a percentage of efficiency. In the first arrangement, the worker is paid at his base rate for time taken and time saved. In the second, standard time divided by actual time yields an efficiency percentage. Multiplying the efficiency percentage by base rate yields earnings for the job.

Advantages of the standard hour plan are the same as those under piecework, with the additional advantage of standards being stated in time units. It is much easier to administer in group installations and to compare the relative performance of departments and individuals. All disadvantages of straight piecework are met by this plan.

The standard hour plan is sometimes referred to as a straight line plan because earnings are in direct proportion to output. As mentioned previously, this feature promotes employee acceptance because of its apparent fairness and because it is easy to understand. The same feature makes payroll computations simple and facilitates efficiency comparisons between departments and plants.

But standard hour plans assume that the work and all the conditions surrounding it have been standardized so that time standards at high task are accurate. Under these conditions production above standard can be assumed to result solely from worker input. If, however, conditions or operations have not been well standardized or if fluctuations in methods or materials exist, the result is often a wide fluctuation in incentive earnings with consequent problems of employee grievances over apparent inequities. If frequent changes in conditions and methods are characteristic of the organization, these problems are made worse. Thus the standard hour plan would seem to work best if the work is well standardized, repetitive, and not subject to frequent change. It has been suggested that because of their simplicity and apparent fairness, standard hour plans have been used in situations not well suited to them.[51]

Figure 40 depicts the manner in which earnings and direct labor costs vary under straight piecework and under the standard hour system. Two curves of earnings are shown, which represent what are probably the upper and lower limits of present practice. Both employ high task as standard.

Curve 1 illustrates a plan in which 135 per cent of base rate is paid at 135 per cent efficiency. Curve 2 illustrates a plan in which 135 per cent of base earnings is paid at 100 per cent efficiency. Either plan may exist with or without the guarantee. Standard hour plans, however, almost always guarantee the time rate. Most standard hour plans assume that the average incentive operator will earn 125 per cent of his hourly rate.

Sharing Plans. Under sharing plans the worker does not receive 100 per cent of his additional output but shares the increased output with the employer. One result of this flatter earnings curve is that superior performers do not receive earnings as high as they would under piecework and the standard hour plan and below-average operators receive some incentive earnings at lower levels of performance.

Such plans tend to be applied if the work has not been standardized and if there is considerable variation in materials and processes. In such cases it is difficult to set standards accurately because of varying conditions, and often considerable averaging has been employed. The original reason for sharing plans was the inability to set reliable standards, chiefly because standard-setting techniques were undeveloped

---

[51]von Kaas, *Making Wage Incentives Work,* p. 15.

and many standards were derived from past production records. But they are applied today if standardization is limited and fluctuations in materials and methods are inherent in the work.

The major advantage of sharing plans is the reduced fluctuation in employee earnings that would exist under a standard hour plan under nonstandard conditions and frequent variations in materials and processes. Another advantage is ease of transition to incentives in that incentive earnings under sharing plans begin at lower output levels. Still another is that earnings are less affected by methods changes. Thus sharing plans require less attention to maintenance of standards and worker grievances with respect to changed earnings. The principal disadvantages of sharing plans are (1) the reduced incentive, especially for high performers; (2) possible objections by workers to sharing their increased productivity with management; and (3) the more complex

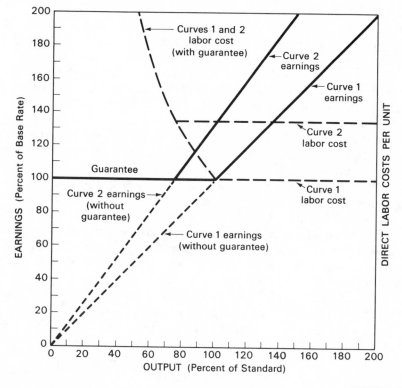

FIGURE 40

Earnings and Direct Labor Costs for Straight Piecework and Standard Hour Plans earnings curves that complicate payroll calculations and make employee understanding of the plan difficult.

The Halsey Plan—Under the Halsey plan, a standard time is allowed for completing a piece of work or a job. If the work takes this amount of time or more than this amount of time, the employee is paid a wage equal to his time rate for the time actually spent on the job. Thus the worker is guaranteed a minimum wage for output below standard. If, however, the job is completed in less than standard time, the worker is paid his time rate for the actual time taken and receives, in addition, a bonus at his time rate for the time saved. In practice, the bonus is calculated to give the employee from 30 to 70 per cent of the time saved, but the usual percentage is 50. The other 50 per cent is the employer's share. For example, if a worker's hourly rate is $3.00 and the standard time for a job is five hours, completing the job in four hours calls for payment of $12.00 ($3.00 X 4) and, assuming 50-50 sharing, a bonus of $1.50 ($3.00 X ½ hour). Thus he would receive $13.50 for four hours worked.

Standard times under the Halsey plan were originally set from past production records. Today such standards are set by time study or its derivatives, but nonstandard conditions and changes in materials and methods reduce their precision because the variables are averaged. This means that such standards are below those that would be set under ideal conditions. Standards under the Halsey plan are usually set at low task (62½ per cent of time-studied standards) and incentive earnings begin at that point. Fast-changing job shop work, maintenance work, or multiple-duty office work are all situations wherein recurring changes may reduce the precision of standards.

The rationale for the sharing arrangement in the Halsey plan is that standards are imprecise and that incentive earnings above the base rate begin at low task. It would, of course, be possible to meet the latter situation with a standard hour plan employing a pay curve such as Curve 2, Figure 40. But varying conditions and imprecise standards would result in widely fluctuating employee earnings and high costs to the organization.

Figure 41 illustrates the manner in which employee earnings and direct labor costs vary with output under the Halsey 50-50 system.

The Rowan Plan—Under the Rowan plan, like the Halsey plan, a standard time is allowed for completion of a job, and a bonus is paid for any time saved. The bonus in the Rowan plan, however, takes the form of a percentage of the employee's time rate. The bonus percentage is equal to the proportion of time saved to standard time. Thus, if an employee's hourly rate is $3.00 and he completes in four hours a job for which the standard time is five hours, the bonus percentage is 20 per cent, since the time saved (one hour) is 20 per cent of the standard time (five hours). The worker is paid for the time he took to do the job (four hours) at his hourly rate ($3.00) plus 20 per cent. He will thus be paid $3.60 per hour, and his total pay for this job will be $14.40. The employee is guaranteed his time rate if he fails to reach standard.

The Rowan plan, like the Halsey plan, was devised when standards were set not by time study but, usually, from past production records. Under the plan, wages increase with output but at a decreasing rate, and, regardless of output, it is impossible for an employee to make more than twice his hourly rate. There is thus no incentive for the employer to cut the rate.

A major disadvantage of the plan is its complexity. It is not simple to explain to employees, and calculations of earnings are time consum-

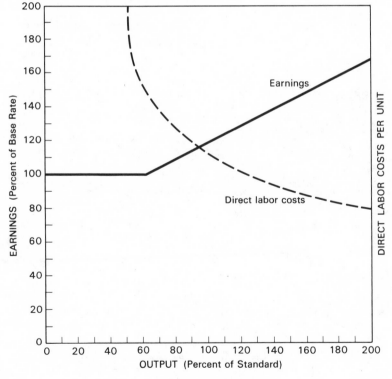

FIGURE 41

Earnings and Direct Labor Costs Under the Halsey (50-50) System

ing. Second, the sharing arrangement is not likely to be favored by employees. Third, budget and cost considerations are made difficult by the varying labor costs under the plan.

The Rowan plan may be applied if there are variable working conditions and operations and if the parties insist that only one plan be used. It may also be useful in the case of learners who need encouragement within the narrow limits of their capacity.

If high-task standards are available, but still a plan is desired that will protect the company against excessive labor costs from occasional loose standards, a modified Rowan plan may be employed. Here bonus is deferred until 100 per cent efficiency. Daywork wages are guaranteed for all levels of efficiency below 100 per cent. A strong incentive to reach and maintain a high standard of performance is provided.

Figure 42 illustrates the operation of the Rowan plan at both low-task and high-task standards on earnings and direct labor costs.

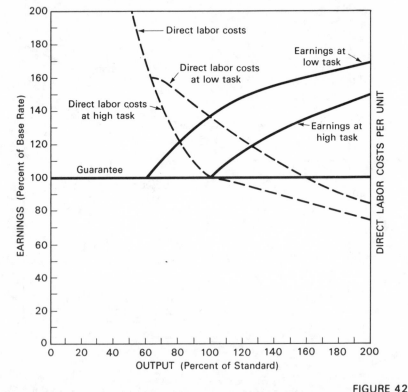

FIGURE 42

Earnings and Direct Labor Costs Under the Rowan Plan

The Bedaux Plan—The Bedaux plan is basically a Halsey sharing plan that gives 75 per cent of the time saved to the employee and the remaining 25 per cent to foremen, servicemen, and other indirect personnel, presumably for their support of his work. In the Bedaux plan, the standard time for a job is determined by time and motion study. Allowed time is stated in "points" or "B's." A B is the amount of work plus a suitable proportion of rest that is found to be normal for one minute. Sixty B's are standard performance per hour. A standard number of points is specified for completion of each job. An employee receives, in addition to his hourly rate, a bonus equal to 75 per cent of the number of points earned in excess of 60 per hour multiplied by 1/60 of the hourly rate. Thus, if standard for a job is five hours, actual time is four hours, and the hourly rate of the employee $3.00, bonus computation is made as follows: (1) 300 points (5 × 60) were earned in four hours, which means that the employee earned 60(300–240) extra points; (2) bonus therefore equals 75 per cent of (60 × $3.00) divided by 60, which is $2.25. If an employee does not reach standard, he is paid at his time rate.

Today, where the Bedaux plan is employed, often the sharing feature does not exist; that is, employees are paid a bonus of 100 per cent of all production above standard. Where this is the case, the plan is equivalent to the standard hour plan.

Standard in the Bedaux plan is usually set so that when employees reach 100 per cent of production they are paid 120 per cent of base earnings. This might be called intermediate task.

Actually the Bedaux plan is more than an incentive system. The units permit production and cost control. Similarly, they enable forward planning of production and costs. Comparisons between the relative efficiency of individuals, supervisors, departments, and so on, are made possible. The plan was originally devised to provide for a situation in which workers were shifted often from one job to another.

Figure 43 illustrates variations in earnings and direct labor cost for both the 75 per cent and the 100 per cent plans.

GROUP INCENTIVE PLANS

Just as some situational factors (frequent change, for example) determine the applicability of some individual incentive plans and preclude others, other situational factors may suggest that an incentive plan to be appropriate must be applied to groups rather than individuals. As organizations become more complex, a growing number of jobs become interdependent with other jobs in either of two senses. Some jobs are embedded in a sequence of operations so that performance on

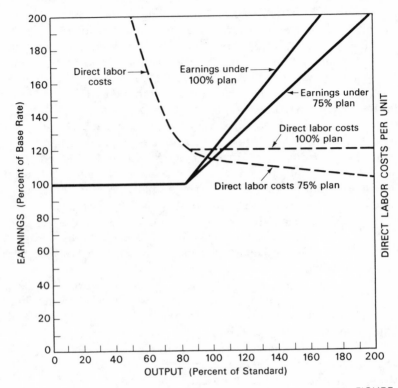

FIGURE 43

Earnings and Direct Labor Costs Under the Bedaux Plan

jobs that precede them and follow them affect performance on them. Other jobs require joint efforts to achieve results. In both cases, job interdependence makes measurement of individual performance difficult and perhaps impossible. Interdependence also requires cooperation among individuals and organizational units, and individual incentive plans do not measure or reward such behavior. Organizations in which there is a large number of interdependent jobs may be forced to reward the cooperation that they require. One way of doing so may entail an incentive plan keyed to groups.

The increasing number of incentive plans applied to small groups and plantwide incentive plans[52] may be evidence that organizations are recognizing that changing technology often creates interdependent jobs. But it may also be evidence that organizations have become disen-

[52]Slichter *et al., The Impact of Collective Bargaining,* p. 496.

chanted with demoralized individual incentive plans with higher costs and lower effort levels than exist in nonincentive organizations. If, as has been suggested, incentive plans represent a system of beliefs, some organizations could be expected to turn to group or plantwide incentive plans in such situations.

There is no question but that the increased proportion of work not directly connected with producing goods and services, the increasing variety of jobs, and the increasing proportion of work done by machines tend to make individual plans difficult to maintain. Changing technology often means that productivity is less a matter of individual effort than of teamwork and coordination. This suggests incentive plans that encourage teamwork rather than individual effort.

Also, the lack of knowledge of whether results of individual incentive plans are mainly attributable to improved methods and other changes or to the incentive plan appears to be an argument for group incentive plans. If productivity gains are in large part attributable to these other changes rather than to greater employee effort, an argument that employee effort is greater under individual plans loses much of its force. If it turns out that changes in technology and methods encounter less resistance under group plans, this is a strong argument in their favor. If, furthermore, it turns out that group norms and thus restriction of output are less likely to develop under group plans, this is a strong argument in their favor. Certainly the ubiquitous observation that rate of production is socially determined suggests a plan that encourages the group to set a higher level of production and employ group discipline against loafers.[53]

It has been suggested earlier in this chapter that employees under an individual incentive plan may resent being rewarded only for additional effort if it is obvious to them that other contributions are needed for organization effectiveness. If, for example, cooperation with other individuals or organization units, flexibility in the face of obstacles, acceptance of frequent changes in the work, and other such contributions are needed, an individual incentive plan is not only unlikely to obtain these inputs because they are not rewarded but may cause resentment by employees who perceive organizational need for these inputs.

Group incentive plans represent one way to reward cooperation and other contributions because they are based on group performance. In fact, rewarding group performance implies that a number of additional contributions are being recognized and rewarded by the organization. Thus group incentive plans may serve to convince employees

---

[53]Krulee, in *Journal of Business* (January, 1955), pp. 37–47.

that they are being rewarded for all the important contributions by measuring results at an organization level higher than the individual. Measuring the productivity of the group in either dollar or physical units may accomplish this. But it is also possible that it may not. Whatever measure is developed should encompass the behaviors the organization requires and inform employees that they are being evaluated on the basis of these inputs. Otherwise they will not be motivated to supply them.

The measure should also be an objective one in order to convince employees that it does measure group performance. As suggested, it is often possible to obtain an objective standard by measuring the performance of larger groups. It is conceivable that a group incentive plan can be based on some subjective measure but only if employees believe that it measures performance and encompasses the required behaviors. If, however, employees question the validity of the subjective measure, any incentive in the plan is lost.

A final requirement is that employees be able to affect the measure by their performance. If the performance measure is unrelated to an individual's efforts, it cannot motivate performance. It is for this reason that profit sharing plans are not included in the group and plantwide incentive plans described below. The individual is not in a position to influence the profits of the organization and for this reason there is little reason to believe that a profit standard can motivate performance.

Group incentive plans are of two quite different types. Most common are group adaptations of individual plans whereby the plan is applied to a group of employees or to a subunit of the organization. Less common but growing in use is the plantwide or organizationwide incentive plan.

Small-Group Incentives.   Most incentive plans applied to small groups or organization subunits are group adaptations of individual incentive plans. Many of the individual incentive plans described previously can be easily adapted to groups. The standard hour plan, for example, and any of the sharing plans, can be so adapted. In group installations, base rates are paid up to group standard output and, above this, group efficiency applied to the earnings curve determines the premium for the individuals in the group. Group efficiency of, say, 125 per cent under a standard hour plan would earn each member of the group 1.25 times base rate for each hour worked.

In such installations, group size, group stability, and the nature of the work are important variables. Plans applied to larger groups result in productivity increases lower than those of smaller groups and individual plans because it is more difficult for employees in larger groups to see the relationship between their performance and their earnings.[54] Reasonable stability in the work group appears to be a requirement.[55]

Perhaps most important is the degree of worker interdependence created by the nature of the work. If cooperation is required by the work, group plans may encourage teamwork in groups as large as 35 to 40. Although little research has been conducted on group incentive plans, it has been shown that they can encourage cooperation.[56] It is also possible that group plans can reduce some of the undesirable effects of individual plans, such as restriction of output, but this has not been shown to be the case.

The advantages of group over individual incentive plans include the greater ease of determining group standards and measuring group output than individual standards and individual output. On jobs other than direct production, setting individual standards can entail long and careful study, and setting group standards may save time and effort. In situations wherein individual performance is very difficult to separate from group performance, group incentives seem advantageous. Group plans may also ease the load of supervisors in administering the incentive plan. It is also conceivable that disciplinary action against slackers and training new group members may be taken over by the group in group incentive plans.

The chief disadvantage of plans of this type is the possibility of intergroup friction.[57] Although cooperation among members of the group may increase, there is nothing in such plans to encourage cooperation among groups themselves. Groups may restrict output, resist revision of standards, and attempt to gain rewards at the expense of other groups. Group pressure can be more formidable than individual pressure and beyond union control. Another disadvantage is the weakened incentive for the high producer. He is less likely to stay and maintain his high pace under group incentives because his rewards are no different from those of lower producers in the group.

Small-group and departmental incentive plans are expanding as a result of technological change and employee and union pressures.[58] As machine-paced operations increase, worker and union resistance to

[54]Campbell, in *Occupational Psychology* (January, 1952), pp. 15–21.

[55]Leslie Buck, "The Influence of Group Size and Stability Upon the Effectiveness of an Incentive Plan," *Occupational Psychology* (October, 1957), pp. 270–280.

[56]Babchuk and Goode, in *American Sociological Review* (October, 1951), pp. 679–687.

[57]William B. Wolf, *Wage Incentives as a Managerial Tool* (New York: Columbia University Press, 1957), p. 120.

[58]Mangum, in *Industrial Relations* (October, 1962), pp. 73–96.

incentives decrease, and there has been an extension of incentive coverage to machine-paced operations and to workers who have little or no direct effect on production.[59] Unfavorable earnings comparisons between incentive and nonincentive workers have been one of the reasons for extending incentive coverage. If, as has been suggested, these plans pay incentive rates for the same production available at time rates with effective supervision,[60] it would be improper to consider them as performance rewards.

Plantwide and Companywide Incentives. A number of forces serve to foster a growing interest in incentive plans covering the entire plant or company. One is the need for cooperation among employees. If employees must cooperate both within and between departments, a plantwide plan may encourage it. Another is technological change, which makes separate measurement of individual and even departmental performance difficult. Still another is demoralization of individual incentive plans and the difficulties of maintaining such plans.

As a result, a substantial number of companywide or plantwide incentive plans have been tried. The number of such plans in operation is unknown. One study reports that about 7 per cent of United States firms have plantwide bonus plans, but the definition employed includes profit sharing.[61] The common feature of these plans is that they offer everyone in the organization a bonus or some form of extra payment based on a measure of organization performance. Typically, the bonus is a percentage of the base rate of the employee, so employees receiving the same wage or salary rate would get an equal bonus. Plans differ in the manner in which organization effectiveness is measured.

Most well-known of plantwide incentive plans are the Scanlon Plan and the Rucker Share-of-Production Plan. The Kaiser Plan, although similar to the Rucker Plan, is an example of an individual company plan that differs in details from the basic plans but follows the same principles.

Plantwide incentives in the definition used here employ measures of organization effectiveness within the control of organization members. This definition excludes profit sharing on the grounds that profits are a measure of organization performance only partially within the control of the organization and largely beyond the control of most organization members. For this reason, profit sharing is assumed to be a membership reward rather than a performance reward and discussion of it is deferred until the next chapter.

[59]As of November, 1970, 91 per cent of employees represented by United Steelworkers were covered by incentive plans, according to the union. "Incentive Pay," *Monthly Labor Review* (January, 1971), p. 68.

[60]Mangum, in *Industrial Relations* (October, 1962), pp. 73–96.

[61]Corina, *Forms of Wage and Salary Payment,* p. 73.

The Scanlon Plan—The Scanlon Plan is as much an employee-management or union-management cooperation plan as an incentive system. It features employee participation as a philosophy of industrial relations. Employees, supervisors, and management have an opportunity to criticize one another's suggestions for improving efficiency. The plan has two essential features: (1) a direct incentive to employees to improve efficiency, and (2) a system of departmental committees and a plant screening committee to evaluate employee and management cost-savings suggestions.

The Scanlon Plan was developed by Joseph Scanlon in 1937 to help reduce costs in a steel mill in which he was a union representative. As a result of the success of the plan, Scanlon was moved to national headquarters of the steelworkers' union and helped install a number of the plans. He later moved to the Massachusetts Institute of Technology, where encouragement and study of the plan continues. A 1956 study reported sixty Scanlon plans in operation.[62] Although Scanlon considered a union essential to stimulate employee participation, the plan has been installed in nonunion as well as union plants.

The philosophy of the plan is that efficiency depends on effective companywide cooperation. The purpose of the incentive is to produce teamwork. The bonus is based on savings in labor cost. A ratio of payroll to sales value of production (monthly sales plus or minus inventory adjustment) is computed from past records. Each month (sometimes bimonthly) actual payroll is compared to this ratio. Any savings between actual and expected payroll goes into a bonus fund, 75 per cent of which goes to employees and 25 per cent to the company. In practice, 25 per cent of the bonus fund for a given month is held in reserve for possible deficits and the account is closed at the end of the year.

An example may aid in understanding the plan. Assume that the normal ratio of payroll to sales value of production is 40 per cent. On sales of $1 million, normal payroll is $400,000. If through increases in efficiency this volume was produced for a payroll of $350,000, a $50,000 bonus results, of which three-quarters, or $37,500, goes to the employees. The employee's share is determined by converting the bonus fund to percentage of payroll and applying this percentage to the employee's pay for the month.

There is no incentive under the Scanlon Plan for one part of the work force to try to gain at the expense of others. Usually, all employees are included in the plan.

Case studies of Scanlon plans in operation show the following results: (1) employee willingness to provide large numbers of useful,

[62]W. B. Wolf, "The Scanlon Plan—Device to Increase Profits and Productivity," *Pacific Northwest Business* (June, 1956), pp. 18–27.

cost-saving ideas; (2) employee willingness to accept technological change and to make new equipment and methods work; (3) a better work pace and a work climate hostile to loafing; (4) greater interest in quality, (5) greater willingness of workers to help one another and share knowledge of shortcuts; (6) more flexible administration of seniority clauses in promotion, transfer, and recall to aid efficiency; (7) less overtime; (8) employee insistence on efficient management; (9) greater awareness on the part of employees of company sales problems and problems of meeting competition; (10) more realistic contract negotiations; and (11) fewer grievances. Productivity increases of 60 per cent have been reported as well as employee earnings increases of over 50 per cent.[63]

Not all Scanlon Plan installations have been successful, however.[64] Much depends on the willingness of employees and management to make it work. Most of the installations have been in plants of 1,000 employees or less. The employee may lose some of his feeling of responsibility for costs in larger plants.

Calculating the ratio and adjusting it to changed conditions causes some problems. Original calculation involves questions of breadth of coverage and finding a normal period. Changes in wages, product mix, market conditions, and proportions of direct to indirect workers call for changes in the ratio and agreement on the new ratio.

Not completely solved is the changed position of management under Scanlon plans. The more successful the plan, the more employees concern themselves with company problems. They may be critical of management, especially supervisors. Supervisors may fear a loss of their authority.

The effect of recessions on such plans is uncertain. In some cases suggestions stop but efficiency stays constant. In others, suggestions for improving efficiency increase. Loss of bonus does not seem to harm the plan.

A problem concerning former incentive earnings may occur if Scanlon plans replace individual or group incentive plans. Such plans

---

[63]Russell W. Davenport, "Enterprise for Everyman," *Fortune* (January, 1950), pp. 55ff.; Whyte, *Money and Motivation,* Chapter 14; Joseph N. Scanlon, "Profit Sharing under Collective Bargaining: Three Case Studies," *Industrial and Labor Relations Review* (October, 1948), pp. 58–74; Fred Lesieur, "Local Union Experience with a Cooperation Plan," IRRA, *Proceedings of the Fourth Annual Meeting* (Boston, December 28–29, 1951), pp. 174–181; Robert C. Tait, "Some Experiences with a Union-Management Cooperation Plan," *ibid.,* pp. 167–173; Lesieur, *The Scanlon Plan;* Fred G. Lesieur and Elbridge S. Puckett, "The Scanlon Plan has Proved Itself," *Harvard Business Review* (September–October, 1969), pp. 109–118.

[64]Thomas Q. Gilson and Myron J. Lefcowitz, "A Plant-Wide Productivity Bonus in a Small Factory," *Industrial and Labor Relations Review* (January, 1957), pp. 284–296.

are usually discontinued if Scanlon plans are installed, and returning to base rates means a drastic cut in earnings for some employees. A common solution is to pay average earnings as "red circle rates" until bypassed increases bring earnings back into line. Some unions have refused to red circle any rates, insisting that the plan be installed with reasonable rates for each job.

Departmental committees under the Scanlon Plan are usually composed of two people—an elected employee representative and a management representative. The screening committee consists of departmental committee members and others who pass on suggestions beyond the authority of the departmental committees. Both management and employee suggestions are submitted, criticized, and adopted. Many more suggestions are both submitted and adopted than under conventional suggestion plans.

Although case studies have reported substantial increases in productivity under Scanlon plans, so many changes are made in organizations when the plan is installed that it is impossible to comment about the effects of the plan. There seems to be no doubt, however, that companywide incentive plans can increase cooperation, but they break even further than small groups plans the connection between individual performance and pay.

The case studies suggest that Scanlon plans are most successful in small organizations with stable product lines and cost-price ratios, competent supervision, good labor relations, strong top management interest in and participation in the plan, and management willingness to take criticism from employees and to discuss company problems. Small organizations permit effective communications that may enhance employee perception of the relationship between their performance and organization effectiveness. Stability of product-line and costs reduce the frequency of change in the standard and the bargaining over the standard. Good supervision, healthy labor relations, and top management support of the plan may increase employee trust and ensure acceptance of the performance-reward relationship.

Rucker Share-of-Production Plan—The Rucker Plan is similar to the Scanlon Plan in philosophy but is based on much more sophisticated analysis. A historical relationship is established between total earnings (including indirect compensation) of hourly rated employees and production value created by the company. If major changes in products or production processes occur, the plan is re-engineered. Because of the careful analysis that goes into the original ratio, however, adjustments occur less often than with a Scanlon plan.

An economic engineering audit of several years of past operation is conducted, including a detailed study of approximately two years, broken down by monthly operating results. Production value or value added by the company is sales value of output less cost of raw materials purchased and related costs such as supplies and power. A standard productivity ratio is calculated that expresses the amount of production value required for each $1.00 in wages paid, including benefits. The productivity ratio also determines production shares; that is, the share of production attributable to labor and the share due the company. The analysis is conducted for each plant.

Assume that the company put $.55 worth of materials, supplies, and power into production to obtain a product worth $1.00. Value added or production value is thus $.45 for each $1.00 of sales value. Assume also that analysis shows that 40 per cent of production value is attributable to labor. The productivity ratio becomes 2.5, and for a payroll (plus benefits) of $100,000, standard production value is $250,-000. If actual production value for the month is $300,000, a gain of $50,000 is available for bonus and is distributed 40 per cent to labor and 60 per cent to the company. Labor's bonus share for the month is $20,000. Actually, 25 per cent of the gain in any month is placed in a reserve account to offset poor months. The reserve account is distributed at the end of the year. The $20,000 bonus fund is distributed *pro rata* to individuals on the basis of their regular pay (including overtime and shift differential) for the month.

The plan is most often applied to production workers, but it may be developed to cover all the employees in the company. Analysis determines standard shares of production value for each group or team. A common arrangement is to determine the shares of the employee team (all hourly rated employees) and the company. The Rucker Plan provides an integrated incentive to reduce costs of producing the same production value or to produce a greater production value for the same costs. All savings go to the groups covered on the basis of their share of production value.

Employee committees are used to obtain and appraise suggestions for improvements in production and costs. Typical "share-of-production" committees consist of worker representatives from each major department plus a lesser number of shop supervisors. Usually there are two chairmen—a top executive, and the union president. If there is no union, an employee representative replaces the union leader. Committee members may serve terms of one year, or shorter periods may be specified to encourage new thinking.

Apparently these committees achieve results quite similar to those produced by Scanlon plans. One study reports that committee members in successful Rucker plans are just as aggressive and critical of poor management as in Scanlon-Plan companies.[65] It appears that the results and problems in Rucker plans are very similar to those existing in Scanlon plans.

One difference may be that Rucker plans have been successfully added to existing individual incentive plans. Another is that the standard under the Rucker Plan is based on a careful study of accounting records and not considered bargainable, whereas the standard in the Scanlon Plan, although starting from past records, is typically negotiated. Thus, in the Rucker Plan, negotiated wage increases that cannot be matched with either increased productivity or compensating price increases affect the performance ratio, whereas in the Scanlon Plan they would call for renegotiation of the standard. Still another is that the Rucker Plan offers an incentive for savings not only in labor but in other costs, whereas the Scanlon Plan is limited to savings in labor costs. This difference suggests that the Rucker Plan may be advantageous if material costs are high and if employee attention to quality can reduce costs. With this exception, the conditions of applicability of the Scanlon and Rucker plans appear identical.

No estimate is available of the number of Rucker plans in operation, but there may be as many as there are Scanlon plans. Although at one time there was union objection to the plan, none is apparent today.

The Kaiser Plan—A notable exception to small-company application of plantwide incentive plans is the Kaiser Steel Long Range Sharing Plan. It is similar to the Rucker Plan in providing an incentive for saving in material and supply costs as well as labor costs and in being based on a careful study of company costs. It is also somewhat similar to the Scanlon Plan in that many of the plan's details were established by negotiation between Kaiser Steel and the United Steelworkers. It is similar to both in the use of committees to encourage cost savings suggestions.

Actually, the plan is much more complex than either of the other two. For example, it has sixteen objectives, including the prominent one of protecting employees against unemployment resulting from technological change. Among its objectives is the elimination of individual incentives.

The percentage of cost savings that goes to employees was determined by analysis of company records and is not bargainable. Bonus is distributed monthly to covered employees.

[65]Frances Torbert, "Making Incentives Work," *Harvard Business Review* (September–October, 1959), pp. 81–92.

The plan has received wide publicity, especially the average $.50 per hour bonus that employees received during the first year. Since that time bonus payments have dropped and several revisions of the plan have been made to maintain employee and union acceptance.[66]

It appears that at least some of the objectives have been realized. The company reports improved cooperation and fewer grievances, but restrictive practices have not disappeared. Productivity has increased as evidenced by employee bonuses but the reduction in these bonuses suggests that the productivity increases are falling off over time.

When the plan was installed, approximately 1500 separate standards were developed from historical records to supplement the bonus percentage in showing employees the relationship between their performance and their rewards.[67] These standards and the communication accompanying installation of the plan may have served to show employees the relationship between their performance and their bonus in spite of the large size of the organization. The drop in productivity gains since the first year may attest to the difficulty of maintaining the belief in the relationship, especially in large organizations.

Other Cost Savings Sharing Plans—Other plans similar to the Scanlon and Rucker plans have been worked out by individual companies, often with the aid of unions. Reports of such plans are often too limited to determine whether only the mechanical features are similar or the philosophy as well.

One plan, known to include both, may antedate both the Scanlon and Rucker plans. This is the plan of the Nunn-Bush Shoe Company. An analysis of wages to sales from 1926 through 1934 showed that the relationship was very close to 20 per cent. This figure was chosen as a basis for a sharing program and a guarantee of fifty-two paychecks a year.

Although there is no union, employee relations are excellent and employees share in many company decisions. In 1948, after learning of the Rucker Plan, the workers voted to change to 36 per cent of value added rather than 20 per cent of sales as the standard. Solicitation of employees' ideas on production problems and unusually good employee relations make the plan a success.

[66]Harold Steiglitz, "The Kaiser Steel Union Sharing Plan," *Studies in Personnel Policy No. 187* (New York: National Industrial Conference Board, 1963); *The Long Range Sharing Plan* (Fontana, California: Kaiser Steel and United Steelworkers of America, May, 1965); Robert A. Bedalis, "The Kaiser Sharing Plan's First Year," *The Conference Board Record* (July, 1964), pp. 37–42; Robert A. Bedalis, "The Kaiser Sharing Plan's Second Year," *The Conference Board Record* (July, 1965), pp. 37–39.

[67]Ralph L. Vaugh, "Kaiser Steel's Long Range Sharing Plan," an address at San Diego State (April 20, 1966).

Much of the plan's success, however, must be attributable to the personality and employee relations philosophy of H. L. Nunn. An interesting question involves the extent to which the success of these employee participation or employee-management cooperative incentive plans is due to the ability of the author of the plan to imbue others with his philosophy.

INCENTIVE PLAN ADMINISTRATION

The various types of incentive plans and the variation in effectiveness of incentive plans in operation suggest that there are conditions under which a particular plan is applicable and conditions that make for the success or failure of an incentive plan. Knowledge concerning these conditions is a product of the experiences of individual organizations or consultants rather than careful research. This section reports what appear from experience to be the conditions for successful incentive plan operation.

TECHNICAL CONDITIONS

It is obvious that whether or not an incentive plan is applicable, and the most applicable type of incentive plan, should be based on the kind of work being performed.[68] A plan suited to highly repetitive, standardized, short-cycle manual operations is unlikely to fit less structured work. Highly variable unstandardized work may make incentives unworkable.

Standardized repetitive operations permit incentives, but the rate of change in operations, methods, and materials may determine the type most applicable. Infrequent change permits precise measurement and such conditions may suggest an individual standard hour plan providing maximum incentive with few major problems of plan maintenance. More frequent changes reduce the precision of measurement and under these conditions sharing plans reduce earnings fluctuations and problems of plan maintenance. Under such conditions a plantwide plan would be workable, perhaps at some cost in incentive value.

If operations, methods, and materials have been only partially standardized, a standard hour plan is difficult to administer. In such cases a sharing plan would reduce earnings fluctuations and make it easier to develop standards. Here also a plantwide incentive would be workable.

[68]von Kaas, *Making Wage Incentives Work.*

On unstandardized operations, such as job shops, operations and methods are usually determined by the worker. In these situations operating an individual incentive plan is difficult. Measured day work with or without the incentive feature based on performance compared to past records (estimates) may be workable, a sharing plan less so. If the labor content of most of work is reasonably uniform, a plantwide plan would be possible.

If the work pace is controlled mechanically or by the process, the operators' tasks primarily involve supplying material, removing finished outputs, and monitoring the machine. As mentioned previously, in such operations, because the work often requires less worker effort and output is not a function of worker effort, there is less reason for an incentive plan but much less worker or union objection to one. Thus numerous organizations have adopted machine-utilization plans in these cases, called "incentives not to slow down" by one author.[69] Another possibility is a multifactor plan based on standards for material usage, product yield, scrap, and machine utilization. Also workable in this instance is a plantwide incentive plan.

If the work cannot be measured directly by the usual work measurement techniques (as in repair work, experimentation, model-making, watchmen), an indirect measure such as is involved in plantwide incentives may be workable. Often, however, such work is simply not amenable to an incentive plan.

Most organizations have jobs that fall into all of these categories. Thus, an organization desiring to place all or most employees on incentives may find that a plantwide incentive plan is the most feasible alternative. Some organizations may find that their work is such that a heavy commitment in industrial engineering capability will permit broad coverage of a standard hour or sharing plan. But in most organizations the work is sufficiently varied to require either a number of different plans, each geared to a limited segment of the organization, or an organizationwide plan.

Seldom mentioned in reports of experience with incentive plans but pointed out increasingly by others[70] is that the work often demands that workers cooperate with one another and with other organization units rather than compete. Such requirements, which are becoming the norm in complex organizations, argue against individual incentive plans and in favor of group and organizationwide incentive plans. Obtaining cooperation between interdependent workers and organization units is difficult under the best conditions and logically impossible when the reward system encourages competition.

[69]Mangum, in *Industrial Relations* (October, 1962), pp. 73–96.
[70]Corina, *Forms of Wage and Salary Payment;* Lawler, *Pay and Organizational Effectiveness.*

ENVIRONMENTAL CONDITIONS

The information concerning incentive plan prevalence suggests that in certain industries and certain communities incentive plans are the norm. In such industries and communities, employee and management attitudes may require an incentive plan and a favorable employee attitude may contribute to its effectiveness through the mechanism of a self-fulfilling prophesy. Unions in these circumstances can be expected to foster a labor relations climate amenable to incentives. In traditionally nonincentive industries and communities, however, attitudes may present a roadblock to the use of wage incentives even if all other conditions are favorable.

ORGANIZATIONAL CONDITIONS

Size of the organization may affect the success of incentive plans. A large organization can typically make the commitment to work measurement and industrial engineering that individual incentive plans require, whereas many small organizations cannot. Plantwide incentive plans apparently require fairly small organizations in order to be successful. Thus, large organizations would seem to be limited to individual or small-group incentive plans or to none at all, and small organizations with limited industrial engineering commitment or capability would seem to be limited to plantwide plans.

Also involved, of course, is the proportion of total costs represented by labor costs. If labor costs are a high proportion of total costs, organizations can afford the attention to work measurement that individual incentive plans require. But if labor costs are a small proportion of total costs and thus incentive plans appear unnecessary, employees and unions may demand an incentive plan as a method of increasing employee earnings.

Management attitudes are very much a condition of incentive plan success. Unless management is committed to maintaining the relationship between performance and pay and backs this commitment with expenditures and effort for standardization, work measurement, and incentive plan maintenance, an individual incentive plan can fail or become obsolete very quickly. Management attitudes will depend in part on the nature of competition in the industry and on business conditions. Unless management is sufficiently concerned about productivity and costs to maintain the effort to make any kind of an incentive plan work, but especially an individual one, the organization may be better off without an incentive plan.

Union-management relationships also determine the kind of incentive plan that is feasible, or even if an incentive plan can work at all. A hostile relationship argues against any kind of an incentive plan, because the union may be motivated to use it as an additional arena of controversy. A formal, arms-length relationship suggests limiting incentive coverage to situations wherein sufficient objectivity can be achieved to preclude disagreement. If, however, the relationship is characterized by mutual respect and trust, incentive plans dictated by technical conditions may be employed—*i.e.,* a plantwide incentive plan or a sharing plan based on imperfect measurement may be employed if the work requires it.

ADMINISTRATIVE CONDITIONS

Careful attention to incentive policies and procedures in advance of installation is a condition for the successful operation of incentive plans. Wide participation in the development of these policies and procedures, including union-management negotiation, is a part of this condition. A careful statement of policy goes far toward preventing situations in which rewards are offered for results not desired by either the organization or employees. Participation in policy-making helps ensure both the commitment of resources and energy required by management and the favorable attitudes of employees and the union on which the success of the incentive plan depends.

Incentive plans require a heavy commitment of resources to industrial engineering. Unless the industrial engineering function has the capability to carry out the standardization and measurement work as well as plan maintenance, incentive plans quickly become obsolete.

Management must also expect pressure to expand incentive coverage to nonincentive workers in order to bring their earnings up to the level of earnings of incentive workers. Ensuring that such expansion is economically justified may require especially competent industrial engineering people and additional time and effort. But failure to commit these resources may dilute the effectiveness of the basic plan.

Incentive plans require good supervision. This requirement may mean selecting more capable supervisors. But it certainly means training supervisors to understand the workings of wage incentives and, equally important, showing supervisors that wage incentives are an important means of obtaining the quality, cost, and output objectives that are their responsibility and the basis of their rewards. Unless supervision acquires the necessary skills and a strong interest in making the plan work, the incentive plan will quickly deteriorate.

Employees and union representatives must accept the incentive plan as fair if it is to work. In nonunion organizations, obtaining this belief may require a giant, continuing communications effort. In unionized organizations, union help in explaining the plan may ease this task. Emphasizing the prospects for steady employment and allaying other fears of employees is necessary to obtain belief in the fairness of the plan.

Keeping the incentive plan simple and understandable to employees is essential. All procedures should be as simple as possible. Complicated earnings formulas should be avoided. Employee trust requires that employees understand how the plan works and affects their pay.

Standards must be accepted by employees and guaranteed against change except under agreed-on conditions. Employee fear of rate cutting is the force behind restriction of output and employee distrust of incentive plans. Accepted standards require capable industrial engineering staffs and supervisors who are not only technically competent but competent in securing employee approval of standards and the standard-setting process. Successful incentive plans emphasize measurement rather than negotiation in setting standards.[71] Obviously, acceptance of measurements requires confidence in management's fairness and good labor relations.

Union time study stewards work with industrial engineers in many organizations in setting standards. The procedure seems to work well if the time study steward is well trained and accepted by both parties as an independent expert. Standards disputes are typically settled between the time study steward and the industrial engineer on the basis of the results of a joint study and solutions acceptable to employees, the union, and the company.

Developing acceptable original standards is not so difficult as obtaining employee and union acceptance of circumstances dictating changes in standards. Because of employees' fear of rate cutting and union insistence on protecting employees' interests, any change in standards is likely to be resisted no matter how justified. But changes in materials, methods, and equipment require changes in standards if the incentive plan is not to become uneconomical for the organization.

The logical solution is to change standards if a significant change has occurred in the work since the original standard was developed. Also, if the change is attributable to a change in method developed by a worker, he should be well paid for his innovation. Contract clauses requiring some percentage of change in materials, methods, or equipment before the standard can be changed, which have been included in numerous labor contracts, represent workers' fears of rate cutting and worker desire to benefit in earnings from change. But such clauses

[71]Slichter *et al., The Impact of Collective Bargaining,* p. 520.

prohibit adjusting standards to creeping changes and it is the cumulative effect of such changes that most often make an incentive plan obsolete. The fact that in successful incentive operations such clauses are often bargained into contracts and then ignored in practice suggests that the only practical solution to keeping standards up to date is to convince employees and unions that standards will be changed only when changed circumstances in the work require it.

Failure to meet or exceed standards should be carefully investigated, and the reasons found and corrected. The failure may be due to poor standardization of materials and equipment, in which case employees have the right to request a revision of the standard. Or it may be due to inadequate training or failure to follow the prescribed methods. Neither of these cases calls for a revision of the standard but for better supervision and training. The provision for paying the worker "average earnings" if he fails to reach standard rather than finding and correcting the reason for the failure weakens incentive plans.

Workers should be encouraged to use the grievance procedure if they question any part of the operation of the incentive plan. Such grievances help management uncover "trouble spots" in the system and permit their prompt correction. These grievances should be handled promptly because they represent an opportunity to obtain favorable employee reaction to the program.

A base rate should be established for each job on incentive and this rate should be guaranteed regardless of the production of the worker. The relationship among base rates should be determined by job evaluation. The base rate for the job should be unaffected by whether the worker is or is not on incentive. A successful incentive plan is not a scheme to avoid a justifiable increase in base rate. Conversely, an incentive plan should not be used to increase pay without a corresponding increase in performance.

Pay relationships become more important, if possible, under an incentive plan. If earnings of low-skilled employees on incentive exceed those of high-skilled employees not on incentive, the latter's resentment may destroy confidence in the plan and lead them to pressure for additional earnings whether or not they have earned them. Monitoring pay relationships continually involves an additional commitment of resources under individual and small-group incentive plans.

Employees favor plans that provide earnings in direct proportion to the increase in output above standard, and unions encourage them in this. As mentioned previously, technical conditions often prescribe less than direct proportionality between performance and earnings. In such cases management must recognize that they have an additional hurdle to clear in convincing employees of the fairness of the performance-reward relationship.

In any case, extra earnings under the plan must be sufficient to provide incentive for extra effort. With reasonable effort, most workers should be able to attain some incentive earnings. The average worker at incentive pace is usually expected to earn a 25 to 30 per cent bonus. Individual workers are expected to vary around the normal bonus rate.

Because of individual differences, there is theoretically no ceiling on earnings, and establishing one is the equivalent of cutting rates and reducing the plan's incentive value for high producers. Some organizations, however, have placed a ceiling on earnings, sometimes with union approval, to reduce pressures on standards.[72]

Undoubtedly, the administrative condition most supported by experience is adequate maintenance of the incentive plan and all of its supporting procedures. More incentive plans fail because of inadequate maintenance than for any other reason. Many organizations with successful incentive plans audit all phases of incentive operation at regular intervals of one year or less. Standards are audited by analyzing an operation selected at random, almost as if an original standard were being developed—*i.e.*, materials, methods, operator proficiency, and equipment are checked and compared to the existing standard. The timekeeping and reporting systems are also audited, as are earnings relationships among individuals and groups, by statistical analysis of earnings distributions.

An advantage of the periodic audit is the assurance that high earnings are not used as a signal to revise standards but that every standard is periodically audited and revised up or down as prevailing circumstances dictate. Union officials, recognizing the desirability of a consistent rate structure and the elimination of inequities, find the approach logical. Employees are less likely to resent changes wrought by an agreed-on system than by an individual making decisions that affect them.

INCENTIVE PLAN APPLICATIONS

There is a tendency to think of incentive plans as applicable primarily to direct production jobs, with merit ranges the appropriate performance rewards for other employees. This tendency applies pri-

[72] *Ibid.,* p. 516.

marily to individual and small-group incentives rather than plantwide or organizationwide incentives in that the name of the latter does imply coverage of all employees.

The fact is, however, that individual and small-group incentive plans have been and are being applied to almost all varieties of work. In the opinion of many industrial engineers, the applicability of incentive plans is virtually limitless. All that is required in this viewpoint is that the savings to the organization resulting from the incentive plan exceed the cost of measuring and operating the plan. There is scarcely any type of employment activity that someone in this country has not successfully measured, and applied to it a reasonably successful incentive plan.

The premise on which this reasoning is based may be simply stated. All tasks, jobs, or functions must have a purpose if their existence is justified. Better performance of this purpose is worth money to the organization. Devising a yardstick to measure this improved performance will therefore permit rewarding the individual or group who achieves it.

This conception of the application of incentive plans has led to such applications as maintenance and repair work, materials handling, inspection, stockroom work, janitorial work, warehousing, shipping, office work, transportation, hospital work, and even construction work.[73] Incentive plans are widely applied to sales work of all kinds. Supervisory, professional, and middle-management jobs are paid at least partially on an incentive basis in a minority of employing organizations. Top management jobs are almost universally paid partially on the basis of an incentive plan.

The general approach in all these applications has been (1) identifying measurable work as yardsticks of performance,[74] (2) setting standards on the basis of these yardsticks, (3) measuring performance against these standards, and (4) providing extra pay for performance above standard. It has been found in all of these applications that certain aspects of work results can be measured. Obviously, the more similar the work is to factory production jobs, the more conventional work measurement approaches apply. As large offices, for example, become white-collar factories, they become amenable to traditional

[73]See Barry D. Whelchel, "Informal Bargaining in Construction," *Industrial Relations* (February, 1971), pp. 105–109.

[74]For an excellent discussion of this process, see Executive Office of the President, Bureau of the Budget, *Techniques for the Development of a Work Measurement System* (Washington, D.C.: Government Printing Office, March 1950); "Now Those Unmeasurable Jobs are Measurable," *Factory Management and Maintenance* (February, 1959).

work measurement.[75] Although clerical incentive plans do not seem to be numerous, they are in use both in the U.S. and in Europe.

Most applications of incentive plans, regardless of the type of work involved, employ the traditional work measurement techniques—time study and standard data, with either times developed within the organization or a system of basic elemental times developed by a consulting organization. Some consultants have developed standard times for special kinds of operations. For example, the originators of Methods Time Measurement have time standards for maintenance operations. Industrial engineers are increasingly using day-long time studies, work sampling, and various statistical and operations research techniques to measure work in situations wherein the traditional techniques are less applicable. The computer is increasingly being used as an aid in work measurement.[76]

The widely varied applications of incentive plans attest to the fact that with diligent effort and ingenuity it is possible to find and measure aspects of work. But it may be useful to remember that the kind of behavior measured is the kind of behavior that people exhibit.[77] Thus, organizations must be certain that the incentive plan is based on measures of output that the organization requires rather than on those that can be measured. If what is measured is only peripherally related to organization goals and if what is not measured remains unmeasured and neglected by employees, the incentive plan impedes attainment of organization goals. Worse, attainment of what is measurable may work against the attainment of unmeasurable goals.[78]

Incentive plans may be perceived as pay for the outputs of the employee rather than for inputs of the employee, as in other payment methods. Thus, incentive plans may assume that one or a very few measures of employee output represents the performance contributions that the organization requires from employees and that it is possi-

[75]Harold W. Nance, "Four Myths of Office Work Measurement," *Personnel* (November–December, 1965), pp. 8–16; "Measuring How Office Workers Work," *Business Week* (November 14, 1970); Borje Strender, "Methods of Raising the Efficiency of White-Collar Work," in *International Conference on Automation, Full Employment, and a Balanced Economy* (The American Foundation on Automation and Employment, Inc., 1967), pp. 1–5.

[76]Kenneth K. Kopp, "A Computer Based Janitorial Standards Program for Colleges and Universities," in Paul S. Greenlaw and Robert D. Smith (eds.), *Personnel Management: A Management Science Approach* (Scranton, Pa.: International Textbook Co., 1970), pp. 392–410; von Kaas, *Making Wage Incentives Work,* p. 168, reports that Management Sciences, Inc., Appleton, Wisconsin, has two systems for developing standards via computer—one for repetitive and another for nonrepetitive operations.

[77]Lawler, *Pay and Organizational Effectiveness,* p. 168.

[78]See V. F. Ridgway, "Dysfunctional Consequences of Performance Measurements," *Administrative Science Quarterly* (September, 1956), pp. 240–247.

ble to measure these outputs. The emphasis has been placed on the latter assumption—the measurement aspect. Unfortunately, however, less attention has been given to whether or not what has been measured represents the performance contributions organizations want from employees. It may be that incentive plans serve to tell the employee that the organization considers the employment exchange as a purely economic transaction wherein goods or services produced are exchanged for pay. Undoubtedly, some employees prefer this kind of an employment exchange. But if employees do receive this signal, it should surprise no one if they seek to limit their contributions to those apparently sought, to get the highest price, and to resent the organization for failing to recognize and reward other performance contributions it obviously needs.

DO INCENTIVE PLANS FIT THE PERFORMANCE MOTIVATION MODEL?

As the chapter title suggests, organizations believe that incentive plans motivate performance. The research evidence shows that this belief has foundation—incentive plans can increase performance above that attainable at a fixed pay rate. But incentive plans do not always result in increased performance, as evidenced by demoralized incentive plans, and numerous studies have shown that incentive plans can also result in restriction of output and cause employee relations problems. Also, it has been shown that the different kinds of incentive plans produce different results. Thus it seems useful to examine incentive plans in terms of the performance motivation model outlined in Chapter 3.

The model specifies that for an incentive plan to motivate performance (1) employees must believe that good performance will lead to more pay, (2) employees must want more pay, (3) employees must not believe that good performance will lead to negative consequences, (4) employees must see that other desired rewards besides pay result from good performance, (5) employees must believe that their efforts do lead to improved performance. Although the model specifies that the relationship among these variables is multiplicative (anything multiplied by a 0 yields a 0), the first variable is clearly most important.

Incentive plans do foster the belief that good performance leads to more pay. Individual plans create a stronger belief than group and plantwide plans in that in group plans, results only imperfectly reflect individual performance. Plans based on objective standards and measurements create a stronger belief in the performance-pay relationship than plans based on less objective standards. In the latter, the belief is based in part on the employee's confidence that the measurements do reflect his performance.

But as discussed earlier, people do attach different values to pay. If employees do want more pay and nothing about the plan serves to reduce its importance to them, this part of the model is met. If, however, an incentive plan is applied to employees who don't want more pay or who don't want their pay based on their performance, it is not.

The belief that negative consequences will result from good performance is quite possible under incentive plans. In individual plans, especially, it has been shown that employees can believe that rates will be cut if they produce too much and that social rejection by peers, working yourself out of a job, or even getting fired if you fail to meet standard can be anticipated consequences. It is quite possible in individual plans that the perceived negative consequences could offset the perceived positive consequences. Small-group plans may generate conflicts among competing groups that are perceived as negative consequences. Plantwide or organizationwide plans, however, are less likely to produce negative consequences, although resentment of employees who no longer get overtime has been reported under Scanlon plans, and the employees who refuse to go off individual incentives may arouse resentment toward the Kaiser Plan.

The belief that other desired rewards result from good performance is more likely to appear in group and organizationwide plans than in individual ones. Especially in plantwide plans, good performance is likely to result in social acceptance, esteem, respect, and feelings of achievement. If a person feels that he benefits from another's good performance, he is quite likely to encourage him to perform well. It has been suggested that the real strength of the Scanlon Plan is that it can tie other rewards to good performance and reduce the negative consequences.[79]

Employee beliefs that their contributions to the organization result in the performance measured by the organization may be the weakest link in incentive plans. If employees feel that the performance measured is affected by so many things beyond their control that what they do has little effect, this belief must be weak. If employees feel that the performance measure does not reflect a number of contributions that they make and that they feel the organization needs, the belief is weak.

This point was made in the last section but it seems important enough to repeat here. If the incentive plan is based on such a limited

[79]Lawler, *Pay and Organizational Effectiveness,* p. 132.

conception of employee contributions that employees believe that it neither reflects the contributions they make nor those that the organization really requires, not only will the incentive plan not work, it may weaken membership motivation because of resentment.

DO INCENTIVE PLANS AFFECT MEMBERSHIP MOTIVATION?

If incentive plans work by creating or confirming beliefs, they can also affect the beliefs (perceptions) that form the basis of membership motivation. If the incentive plan provides signals to an employee that more of the rewards that he wants are available in this employment exchange in return for the contributions he wants to make, his commitment to the exchange is likely to increase. If, however, the signals carry the message that additional money is the only reward available for increased performance and he doesn't want more money, that other rewards that he values will be reduced by good performance, that only those contributions that result in the measured performance result in more rewards and he does not want to provide more of those contributions, or that the contributions he wishes to increase are not going to result in higher rewards, his commitment to the employment exchange may be significantly depressed. In fact, he may seek an employment exchange that meshes more closely with his reward-contribution desires.

This is an example of the dilemmas faced by organizations in compensation administration. Attempts to improve performance motivation may weaken membership motivation. Fortunately, it is usually possible to treat different employee groups differently in matters of pay.

14

Economic Membership Rewards

A large proportion of the economic rewards that organizations provide employees are not designed to compensate for the specific job to which the employee is assigned or for his performance, but for his membership in the organization. The rationale for this statement is that the economic rewards discussed in this chapter are attached to neither the job nor performance but to affiliation with the organization.

The emergence of rewards for membership attests to the differences between the employment exchange and the usual economic exchange. Such rewards indicate that organizations are aware that in the employment exchange they are not purchasing labor services alone but sufficient organization attachment on the part of employees to enable the organization to accomplish its purposes. Thus, membership rewards are evidence that organizations have a broader view of the employment exchange than they generally profess in matters of compensation determination.

If this view is correct, membership rewards in organizations would be expected to vary with the breadth of the organization's view of the employment exchange. Organizations that view the employment exchange as a purely economic transaction would be expected to have few membership rewards and to view employment of most members as temporary. On the other hand, organizations holding a broader view of the employment exchange would be expected to have many membership rewards to attempt to secure a long-term commitment from most members. These latter organizations recognize that keeping the organization together is a prerequisite to organization effectiveness.

But employees have not been passive in this broadened view of the employment exchange, which dictates membership rewards in addition to rewards for labor service. Those employee groups with the strongest commitment to the organization have always received membership rewards. As new employee groups are asked to or wish to extend their commitment to the organization, they demand membership rewards. As all employee groups perceive that their continued affiliation with an organization is a contribution, they demand increased rewards for membership.

Fortunately, the process that has just been described does not have to be conscious on the part of either organizations or their members in order to be valid. The membership rewards discussed in this chapter may be considered performance or even job-related rewards by some employee groups and by some organizations. It is the author's contention, however, that each of them represents rewards for membership rather than for the provision of labor services.

MATURITY CURVES

An example of a membership reward that may be conceived by employees or even organizations as a performance reward is the maturity curve, progression curve, or career curve concept discussed in Chapter 9. Although maturity curves do include performance appraisals, the major explanatory variable is assumed to be years of experience since obtaining the degree. Thus membership in the field or organization is the basis of the reward. An additional unit of age and seniority is assumed to represent additional contributions regardless of the performance level.

Actually, maturity curves represent a measurement of membership in the field rather than the organization. Although he may be employed by a single employer for a long period of time, the employee perceives his development in his field as a contribution that should be recognized by the employer whether he has been with one or several employers during the period. Membership in this case may be said to accrue to the field, but because the employer of the professional gets the professional's total commitment, the employer is expected to pay for this membership. It is up to the organization to use the contributions that membership implies.

PROFIT SHARING

Another membership reward, perceived as a performance reward by some organizations, is profit sharing. As mentioned in the preceding chapter, profit sharing plans are often considered to be organization-wide incentive plans. Joseph Scanlon called his plan a profit sharing plan. The Council of Profit Sharing Industries includes cost-savings sharing plans as profit sharing, although they pay off whether or not the organization makes a profit.

Increasing production has been cited as one of the goals of profit sharing, and reported results include increased efficiency and lower costs.[1] Many early reports of profit sharing results attributed large increases in production to the plan.[2] More recent reports find profit sharing companies more successful financially than nonprofit sharing companies but are more careful in attributing the findings to profit sharing.[3]

PROFIT SHARING PREVALENCE

Profit sharing arrangements have a long history both in this country and abroad. Some evidence of the recent growth of profit sharing in the United States is the estimate that the number of profit sharing companies has doubled every five years since 1951, to some 125,000 plans in 1967.[4] Some portion of this growth can be attributed to the favorable tax treatment given employees under deferred plans, but such rapid growth suggests that organizations believe profit sharing produces some positive results for the organization.

DEFINITION AND PURPOSE

According to the Council of Profit Sharing Industries, profit sharing is "any procedure under which an employer pays or makes available to regular employees subject to reasonable eligibility rules, in addition to prevailing rates of pay, special or deferred sums based on the profits of the business."[5] Although the word "incentive" does not appear in this definition, it is stated or implied in most compilations of objectives of profit sharing. For example, the following objectives were compiled from a survey of 298 profit sharing companies: (1) to instill a sense of

---

[1]"Sharing Profits with Employees," *Studies in Personnel Policy No. 162* (New York: National Industrial Conference Board, 1957).

[2]Dwight B. Baird, "Profit-Sharing Doubles Production," *Mill & Factory* (May, 1953), pp. 133–136; James F. Lincoln, *Incentive Management* (Cleveland: Lincoln Electric Company, 1957).

[3]Bert L. Metzger and Jerome A. Colletti, *Does Profit Sharing Pay?* (Evanston, Illinois: Profit Sharing Research Foundation, 1971).

[4]William J. Howell, "A New Look at Profit Sharing, Pensions, Productivity Plans," *Business Management* (December, 1967), p. 27.

[5]Council of Profit Sharing Industries, *The Constitution and Bylaws of the COPSI* (Chicago, October 17, 1962), p. 1.

partnership, (2) to serve as a group incentive, (3) to provide employee security, (4) to be fair, (5) to provide benefits beyond basic wages without incurring fixed commitments, (6) to attract desirable employees and reduce turnover, (7) to encourage employee thrift. These objectives are in the order of frequency in which they appeared in the survey.[6]

Profit sharing organizations hope that a sense of partnership between employees and management will emerge and that employees will come to appreciate some of the problems confronting the organization and the interdependence of all organization members. As such, they see profit sharing as a form of worker education.

The incentive effect is assumed to flow from this sense of partnership, such that employees will see that their cooperation, flexibility, and acceptance of change are required for organization effectiveness. Employee security is presumed to flow from enhanced organization effectiveness.

The objective of providing benefits beyond basic wages without fixed commitments by the organization expresses the concept of flexible compensation such that employee earnings respond to changes in economic conditions through sharing in the profits. Employees, it is hoped, may be more reasonable in their wage demands in prosperous periods if they recognize the relation between wages and profits and know that they will receive a share of profits realized.

The objectives of attracting and holding desirable employees and of showing the employer's attempts to be fair are perhaps the most realistic ones. As an attempt to increase employee rewards as the organization can afford such increases and as an attempt to improve the perceived fairness of the employment exchange, profit sharing may increase the attractiveness of the organization to many employee groups.

The objective of encouraging employee thrift, however, would seem to be reasonable only in profit sharing plans that accept employee contributions. Plans limited to disbursing company profits do not appear to encourage employee thrift.

TYPES OF PLANS

Profit sharing plans are typically differentiated on the basis of when profit shares are distributed. Cash or current distribution plans pay out profit shares at regular intervals as earned. Deferred plans put the profits to be distributed in the hands of a trustee and distribution

[6]P. A. Knowlton, *Profit Sharing Patterns* (Evanston, Illinois: Profit Sharing Research Foundation, 1954), p. 55.

is delayed until some event occurs. Combination plans do both by distributing part of the profit share as earned and deferring distribution of the balance.

Cash Plans. Cash or current distribution plans provide for distribution of profit shares at regular intervals. It is hoped that distribution, at monthly or quarterly intervals will provide incentive effects by paying out the profit shares shortly after they are earned. Some cash plans, however, distribute profits annually or semiannually. Current distribution plans make up an estimated 40 per cent of profit sharing plans.[7] An estimated 75,000 to 85,000 cash plans existed in the United States in 1971.

Cash plans are usually found in small organizations. In small organizations it may be possible to show employees the relationship between their efforts and their profit share if the payment interval is short. But there is also the possibility that employees will associate these payments with regular wages and believe that they are part of their earnings to which they are regularly entitled. The percentage of profits distributed under various cash plans varies from a low of 8 to 10 per cent to a high of 50 to 75 per cent, depending on whether or not part of total profits has been reserved for specific company needs. The median distribution found in one study was 15 per cent in plans without such reservations and 17.5 per cent in plans with them.[8]

Current distribution plans are quite likely to encounter employee reaction to nonprofit periods whether or not the plan achieves the incentive objective. If employees perceive their profit share as part of their regular pay, they will logically resent the paycut. If employees believe that their previous profit shares have reflected their efforts, no rewards in return for the same efforts may seriously shake their faith in the plan.

Perhaps the most famous of the current distribution profit sharing plans is that of the Lincoln Electric Company of Cleveland, Ohio. The well-known Lincoln Incentive System consists of a number of plans of which the year-end bonus based on profits is only one. Most employees are on piecework with a guarantee. In addition, profits above 6 per cent are distributed each year among employees in accordance with their merit rating. Over the years since 1934 the year-end bonus has not been less than 20 per cent of annual wages and often has been well over 100 per cent.

Wage-dividend plans that fix the percentage of profits distributed to employees according to the amount of dividends paid to stockholders

[7]Metzger and Colletti, *Does Profit Sharing Pay?* p. viii.
[8]B. L. Metzger, *Profit Sharing in Perspective,* 2nd ed. (Evanston, Illinois: Profit Sharing Research Foundation, 1966), p. 62.

are cash-distribution plans. The assumed advantage of wage-dividend plans is that they emphasize the identity of interests between employees and stockholders. Because such plans divide profits between employees and stockholders according to a fixed formula and because employees are declared a wage dividend whenever stockholders are declared a dividend, employee-stockholder identity is assumed to result from the plan.

Deferred Plans.   In deferred plans a part of the profits is normally put in the hands of a trustee who keeps individual employee accounts. Contributions from employees into their fund may be made in about half of deferred plans. The amount in each employee's account is held in trust to be released only under definitely stated circumstances such as (1) retirement, (2) permanent total disability, (3) death, (4) layoffs, (5) severance, (6) other contingencies.

The trust agreement includes a predetermined formula for determining the profits to be shared and a predetermined formula for distributing the funds to employees. These formulas are required for Treasury approval, a necessary prerequisite if the company is to be permitted to deduct payments as made for tax purposes, and the employee is to be permitted to defer such income until received. With this approval, company contributions must be limited to a stated proportion of total payroll.

The tax advantages to employees under deferred plans, together with compound interest on their fund, may make such plans especially attractive to employees. But whether or not they do so depends in part on the vesting provisions of the plan. Vesting (full nonforfeitable right of the employee to the fund) is complete in the case of employee contributions and usually complete in the case of employer contributions when the employee retires, dies, or becomes permanently disabled. If, however, the employee leaves the organization prior to these events, vesting provisions vary from immediate full vesting to full vesting after twenty-one years. Fortunately for employees, vesting provisions are becoming more liberal and employees are permitted to draw on their fund for a wider variety of contingencies. The median percentage of company profits distributed under deferred plans was found in one study to be just under 14 per cent when no prior reservations on profit had been made, to one-third after prior reservations.[9]

Deferred profit sharing plans are expanding much more rapidly than cash plans. As of the end of 1970, over 101,000 deferred plans were reported in existence.[10] This expansion may be attributed to (1) em-

[9]Metzger, *Profit Sharing in Perspective*, p. 62.
[10]Metzger and Colletti, *Does Profit Sharing Pay?* p. viii.

ployee desire for greater security, (2) employer attempts to provide additional employee security without fixed commitments, (3) less employee resentment to nonprofit years under deferred plans, and (4) the tax advantages to employees.[11] Deferred plans are more prevalent than cash plans in larger firms.

The famous Sears, Roebuck and Company plan is a deferred-distribution plan. Under this plan company and employee contributions combine to provide very satisfactory retirement benefits. One of the features of the plan has been the limitation of employee contributions to effectively equalize the participation of lower- and higher-salaried employees. It seems quite apparent that this plan has been successful in attracting and holding employees.

Deferred plans emphasize membership rather than performance objectives. This seems wise in view of the deferred nature of the rewards. The question of whether any kind of profit sharing plan can motivate performance is discussed later in this section.

Combination Plans. Combination plans, as the name implies, are combinations of cash and deferred plans. One plan may place part of the profit share in trust and pay the balance in cash. Or two separate plans—one cash and one deferred—may cover the same employees. Combination plans are more likely to be found in organizations of 50 to 100 employees rather than in larger organizations, where deferred plans dominate, or very small organizations (under 20 employees), where cash plans are the rule.[12]

RESULTS OF PROFIT SHARING

The rapid growth in profit sharing in the United States suggests that the results are positive for both organizations and employees. Unfortunately, however, the heterogeneous objectives of profit sharing, the broad coverage of most plans, and the numerous changes in organizations that profit sharing implies make measurement of results difficult. As with other types of pay plans, individual company reports are often glowing. Numerous surveys have reported the opinions of organization members on the operation of the plan.

A 1957 National Industrial Conference Board survey[13] reported that approximately 55 per cent of companies reported important benefits from the plan, while 6 per cent failed to find any benefit. Over one-third of the companies with cash plans and one-quarter of those

---

[11]Gustave Simons, "Economic and Legal Aspects of Profit-Sharing Plans," *Industrial and Labor Relations Review* (October, 1948), pp. 76–89.

[12]Metzger, *Profit Sharing in Perspective,* p. 31.

[13]NICB, *Studies in Personnel Policy No. 162.*

with deferred plans were not wholly satisfied with profit sharing, usually because employee efficiency had not been stimulated.

A survey of 108 profit sharing companies by the Profit Sharing Research Foundation in 1963[14] reported positive organization ratings on a number of profit sharing objectives. Combining very effective and moderately effective ratings, the range was from 93 to 24 per cent on nine objectives. Fifty-four per cent of organizations with cash plans and 30 per cent of organizations with deferred plans rated them as very effective in attracting and holding desirable employees. However, 50 per cent of organizations with deferred plans reported a doubtful or no effect on productive efficiency, and 45 per cent, little effect on cost savings. Cash plans also were not rated clearly positive on incentive effects.

Unions have been ambivalent toward profit sharing. Profit sharing organizations with unions are somewhat less likely to cover union members than to cover them. Few labor agreements include profit sharing provisions. An exception is the American Motors-UAW agreement. About 35 per cent of the membership of the Council of Profit Sharing Industries is unionized.[15]

There is some evidence that employee attitudes toward the organization and the employment exchange improve with profit sharing. Employees are more likely to believe that they receive their share of company growth and that they are recognized for their contributions to company growth. They are much more likely to approve of the way management is doing its job. They are more likely to approve cost-cutting suggestions. They are more likely to have a feeling of partnership with management. But they do not believe that an individual can link his own work to profit results or that profit sharing eliminates free-loaders.[16]

PROFIT SHARING PLAN PROVISIONS

Profit sharing plans vary widely in administrative provisions concerning organization contributions, employee allocation, eligibility requirements, payout provisions, and other administrative details. Two-thirds of plans define the contributions of the organization by formula, and in the balance the contribution amount is determined by the board of directors. Most formulas specify a straight percentage of before-tax profit after prior reservations for stockholders and reserves.

[14]Reported in Metzger, *Profit Sharing in Perspective*, p. 120.
[15]*Ibid.*, p. 137.
[16]Robert D. Best, "Profit Sharing and Motivation for Productivity," in *A Symposium of Profit Sharing and Productivity Motivation* (Madison, Wisconsin: Center for Productivity Motivation, University of Wisconsin, February 23–24, 1961).

Allocation to employees or employee accounts is usually based on employee compensation but may be influenced by length of service, employee contributions, employee performance, or responsibility. In most plans all full-time employees are eligible after a short or no waiting period, but a substantial minority of plans exclude union employees or are limited to specific employee groups. Payout provisions are usually determined by plan designation (cash, deferred, or combination), but deferred and combination plans are increasingly incorporating vesting provisions and payout under a wide variety of circumstances.

Current distribution plans involve fewer administrative problems than do deferred plans. Deferred plans require approval by the Internal Revenue Service, a trustee, and typically an administrative committee. In all types of plans there is apparently a continuing problem of maintaining the visibility and credibility of the plan to employees. The two most common solutions adopted are (1) broad employee participation in installing and administering the plan, and (2) constant communication efforts. Because profit sharing is technical and deferred plans involve legal matters, most profit sharing organizations advise careful study of existing plans and perhaps professional help prior to installation.

PROFIT SHARING AND THE MOTIVATION MODELS

Our discussion of profit sharing suggests that such plans do not closely fit the performance motivation model. Profits are influenced by so many variables that it is very difficult for an individual to feel that his contributions influence organizationwide results. Thus it is difficult for an individual to believe that his profit share is related to his performance. In small organizations with cash plans and continuous communication efforts, it may be possible for an organization to maintain employee belief in the performance-reward relationship, but such beliefs are vulnerable to any occurrence that reduces profits while the employee maintains his performance level. Larger organizations with cash plans are less likely to be able to foster these beliefs initially and they may be even more vulnerable to changing circumstances. Deferred plans involve the additional hurdle that payment of the reward is not immediate but often delayed for years. In such plans employee belief in the performance-reward relationship may be impossible, even in small organizations.

On the other hand, profit sharing may closely fit the membership motivation model even in large organizations, at least for certain groups of employees. The promise to provide additional economic rewards when profits of the organization permit it and the implied acceptance of all employee contributions that will advance the profit goal serve to increase both the numerator and the denominator of the membership motivation model. In this way employees may enlarge their commitment to the organization.

This enhanced membership motivation appears to be the real strength of profit sharing. The profit sharing objective of instilling a sense of partnership is met to the extent that employees want to continue their membership and to make additional contributions that enhanced membership implies. Improved performance may result not because employees see a performance-reward relationship, but because they want to broaden and deepen the employment exchange by increasing their contributions in return for more intrinsic and perhaps extrinsic rewards.

COMPENSATION SECURITY PLANS

Perhaps the most clearcut economic membership reward is a compensation security plan in which the organization signals its desire for continued employee membership in the organization by providing a guarantee of employment or income. Such plans are not numerous but they deserve some discussion both because they represent an example of a pure economic membership reward and because they illustrate the issue encountered later in indirect compensation of whether or not they represent a reward or a social responsibility of employing organizations.

In symbolizing continued employee membership, compensation security plans are similar to another symbol—salaried status. Because salaries employ a time unit of a week, a month, or a year, they imply continued membership, whereas the hourly wage implies a short-term employment relationship. The symbolic nature of a salary is reinforced by the knowledge that salaried workers as well as hourly workers are laid off under adverse economic conditions. But the status superiority of a salary over a wage is well established, as are the larger lifetime earnings of those paid a salary rather than wages. Thus a salary implies not only continued membership but higher status and increased rewards.

A limited number of organizations have placed all employees on salary. For example, the Gillette Safety Razor Company and International Business Machines Corporation have paid all employees on a salary basis for some time. Other organizations pay at least part of blue-collar employees by salary.[17] Unions such as the United Auto

---

[17]Paul G. Kaponya, "Salaries for *All* Workers," *Harvard Business Review* (May–June, 1962), pp. 49–57; David A. Weeks, "Salaries for Blue Collar Workers," *The Conference Board Record* (November, 1965), p. 15.

Workers, the United Rubber Workers, and the Steelworkers have made demands in negotiations that their members be placed on salary.

Salaried status for all employees seems to represent another dilemma in compensation administration. Salaried status should increase membership motivation of former wage earners at no increase in payroll. But in many organizations, salaried employees acquire additional benefits and privileges and, more important, when former wage earners acquire salaried status and the additional benefits, the former salaried employees will surely demand pay increases to compensate for their loss in relative status.

More organizations have provided some form of compensation security plan than salaried status for all employees, but the number is still quite limited. One study reported that less than 3 per cent of responding firms guaranteed wages or employment for a definite period.[18] Another but quite different form of compensation security plan, supplemental unemployment benefits (SUB), has been written into a limited number of labor agreements primarily in the auto, steel, container, and rubber industries.

The difference between the two approaches to compensation security is a fundamental one. Guaranteed wages or employment emphasize employment security wherein the employer underwrites the cost of a specified period of employment. Supplementary unemployment benefits, on the other hand, emphasize income security wherein the employer in effect contributes a limited amount to an insurance fund that indemnifies the employee against the loss of income from unemployment.

Only a limited number of guaranteed wage or employment plans have appeared, although the first ones were installed in the 1880s.[19] A few plans guaranteeing employment or wages to all employees on a yearly basis—the George A. Hormel Company, the Nunn-Bush Shoe Company, and the Procter & Gamble Company, for example—have been in effect for many years. But most such plans limit the guarantee to a portion of the year and/or a portion of employees or limit the organization's liability in numerous ways.

One reason why guaranteed wage and employment plans have seen such limited application is that few economic organizations have been able to underwrite the contingent liability that such plans imply. Even with the numerous limitations customarily specified in the plan, the employer is liable for the period guaranteed for the employees covered. Actual costs are difficult to forecast in advance. They may be

---

[18]"Personnel Practices in Factory and Office: Manufacturing," *Studies in Personnel Policy, No. 194* (New York: National Industrial Conference Board, 1964), p. 113.

[19]Murray J. Latimer, *Guaranteed Wages: Report to the President of the Advisory Board* (Washington, D.C.: Government Printing Office, 1947).

zero if all covered employees are kept at work or equal to the full wages of all covered employees if work is not available. Careful analysis of past experience permits forecasting but does not remove the contingent liability.

Such plans imply continuous effort on the part of the organization to stabilize employment because employment instability increases the cost of the guarantee. The possibilities of employment stabilization vary widely by industry and apparently by organization size. The three long-term plans mentioned are all in consumers goods industries and involve small or moderate-size companies. Limited coverage may provide stable employment for covered employees at the cost of other employees whose jobs become less secure.

Another reason for limited application of wage or employment guarantee plans is that almost every decision of the organization in some way affects the guarantee. This means that unions and employees have strong reasons for concerning themselves with production schedules, technological improvements, and even plant location, as well as all decisions affecting work and employees. Contract clauses with respect to overtime, hours, shifts, seniority, layoff, recall, notice to report, and transfer and reassignment all affect the guarantee. Flexibility in work assignment tends to reduce the employer's cost of the guarantee but may dilute previous gains for employees acquired by the union.

Thus, although wage or employment guarantees continue to appear often at the insistence of strong unions, employers tend to resist them because of the contingent liabilities they imply, uncertainties about employment stabilization possibilities, and their encouragement of employee and union concern with any management decision that might affect the guarantee. In turn, many unions (especially craft unions) oppose them because maintaining the guarantee may require dilution of already acquired gains and because they are skeptical of the organization's ability to make good on a guarantee in many industries. Only about 500,000 employees were covered by such plans in 1965.

Income security plans represent an attempt to meet the disadvantages of wage and employment guarantees and still provide a measure of income security to employees. First, they limit the liability of the employer to an amount specified in advance. Second, most of them employ insurance principles and build on the existing public program of unemployment compensation. Third, they are designed to augment employee security without diluting previously acquired union gains or seriously affecting management decisions in areas not directly affected by the plan. Unfortunately, perhaps, for our society, these plans do little to encourage employing organizations to stabilize employment.

The most well-known of these plans is the supplementary unemployment benefits (SUB) plan incorporated into the automobile labor agreements in 1955. Since that time these plans have been extended to a number of other industries, primarily in durable goods manufacturing but also in a few nondurable goods manufacturing and a very limited number of nonmanufacturing industries.[20] Although these plans have expanded greatly since their inception, they cover less than 3 million employees.

The original SUB plan specified a maximum company contribution of $.05 per hour worked into a trust fund until the fund reached a maximum funding position. The purpose of the maximum funding position was to encourage company efforts toward employment stabilization because maintaining the fund at maximum halted company contributions. Employee eligibility for SUB was tied to eligibility for unemployment compensation, but one year's seniority was also required. Benefits were a percentage of after-tax straight time earnings less unemployment compensation and any other earnings, but high seniority employees were protected by relating benefits to both the status of the fund and the seniority of the employee. The plan was designed to yield 60 per cent of earnings for twenty-six weeks, including UC payments.

Since the original plan was installed in 1955 benefits have been improved in each contract. The $.05 per hour payment into the fund was sufficient to sustain both increased weekly benefits and longer duration. In addition, the fund has provided severance pay and short-week payments. At present, benefits of 95 per cent of take-home pay for fifty-two weeks are provided senior employees, and payments into the fund have been increased.

SUB plans in other industries differ in details but are quite similar in concept. They, too, have increased benefits and extended the duration of benefits since their inception with only small increases in costs.

Not all income security plans have been integrated with unemployment compensation. A plan originating in the flat glass industry in 1955 provided for a company contribution of $.05 per hour to an individual trust account for each individual employee. The account maximum was set at $600 and any excess over this amount was to be used to increase vacation pay. The benefits are not related to unemployment compensation. Instead, they represent a fund for each employee to draw on at his discretion if he is laid off for one pay period or out of work because of illness or injury for two periods. The money in the employee's account is to be paid to him at termination or to his estate at his death. Although there are only a few individual trust account plans, other income security plans are not tied to unemployment compensa-

---

[20]United States Department of Labor, "Supplemental Unemployment Benefit Plans and Wage-Employment Guarantees," *Bulletin No. 1425-3* (Washington, D.C.: Government Printing Office, June, 1965), p. 4.

tion and provide income security if absence from work results not only from unemployment but from disability or even legal proceedings.

Income security plans have been successful in providing employees a large measure of income security when unemployed and, in some arrangements, when absent from work for other reasons. Perhaps most interesting, this security has been provided at a low cost to employing organizations in cyclical industries.[21] Cyclical industries are those in which guaranteed wages and employment seemed least feasible because they presented employing organizations with extremely high contingent liabilities.

In addition, income security plans have in many cases provided severance pay and short-week benefits because financing through trust funds permitted it.[22] Short-week benefits are essentially a guaranteed weekly wage—at least the equivalent of a weekly salary.

These benefits to employees have been found not to affect employer layoff and hiring decisions.[23] But they probably hamper rather than induce employer efforts to stabilize employment. Also, it is not inconceivable that a paid layoff at almost full take-home pay may be regarded as more attractive than work. An unintended consequence has appeared in the proposal that senior employees with full SUB protection be laid off to allow short-service employees to continue to work. Senior employees are quite likely to favor this "inverse seniority" as a method of enabling them to benefit from the plan. Employers are less likely to favor the idea because short-service employees may be both less skilled and less effective.

Thus, although compensation security plans in theory represent an example of a pure economic membership reward, they are in practice a vivid illustration of the issues raised by indirect compensation or employee benefits. Employing organizations think of them as means of getting and keeping employees. Employees, on the other hand, may think of them as safeguards against insecurity provided by the employer as part of his social responsibility because society has not seen fit to do so through adequate public plans. The fact that this arrangement means that some employees have more protection than others and some have none may not affect either view.

---

[21]Joseph M. Becker, *Guaranteed Income for the Unemployed* (Baltimore: The Johns Hopkins Press, 1968).

[22]Emerson H. Beier, "Financing Supplementary Unemployment Benefit Plans," *Monthly Labor Review* (November, 1969), pp. 31–35.

[23]Beverly K. Schaffer, "Experience with Supplementary Unemployment Benefits: A Case Study of the Atlantic Steel Company," *Industrial and Labor Relations Review* (October, 1968), pp. 85–94.

INDIRECT COMPENSATION

The hodgepodge of economic rewards lumped under the terms "fringe benefits," "wage supplements," "nonwage benefits," "social wages," "supplementary employee remuneration," "supplementary compensation," and "indirect payment practices" all represent rewards for membership in the organization rather than rewards for the job or for performance. It seems clear that indirect compensation represents payment or benefits to the employee not for his work but for his acceptance of the role of employee.

Unfortunately, neither party to the employment exchange has clearly established the boundaries of these rewards. There is lack of agreement on what is or is not to be included, the purposes to be served, responsibility for programs, the costs and values of the various elements, the units in which the costs and values are to be measured, and the criteria that decisions are to meet. As a result, decisions with respect to indirect compensation are more complex than those concerned with wages and salaries.

Part of the complexity may be traced to the view of the employment exchange held by most employing organizations. Because the employment exchange has been viewed by employing organizations as a strictly economic transaction, organizations perceive themselves as paying solely for productive services. Thus it appears incongruous and perhaps somewhat embarrassing to organizations to pay for employee needs in order to obtain continued employee membership in addition to paying for productive service. As a result, the organization is quite likely to consider indirect compensation as full substitutes for direct economic rewards geared to the same purposes.

But at least as much of the complexity may be traced to the view of employees and unions that employing organizations are charged with a responsibility to provide for certain employee needs as a condition of the employee's membership in the organization. Thus these benefits may not be seen as rewards from the employment exchange but as basic conditions of work required of responsible employers.

DEFINITIONS

There is no generally accepted definition of what is included in what this book calls "indirect compensation."[24] Because two organiza-

---

[24] Nor in the terms applied to the category. The most-used term is still fringe benefits, but supplementary compensation or supplementary payment practices may be gaining in usage.

tions (U.S. Chamber of Commerce and the Bureau of Labor Statistics) have been conducting surveys of benefit costs for about twenty years, it could be argued that indirect compensation is what these organizations include in their surveys.[25] Unfortunately, however, they don't agree. Although both include social insurance, private welfare plans, and paid leaves, BLS includes premium pay whereas the C. of C. does not. The C. of C., however, includes paid company time off the job and certain employee services but BLS does not.

Other classifications of existing benefits have been offered. Sargent,[26] for example, employed the following categories: (1) pay for time not worked; (2) monetary awards and prizes for special activities and performance; (3) bonuses, contributions, and profit sharing; (4) payments to provide employee security; and (5) practices and services that benefit employees. Fisher and Chapman[27] employed the following classification: (1) premiums for time worked, (2) pay for time not worked, (3) employee benefits, and (4) employee activities. The National Industrial Conference Board has employed a similar set of categories: (1) extra payments for time worked, (2) payments for time not worked, (3) payments for employee security, and (4) payments for employee services.[28] In addition to the different items included in these classifications, controversy over the inclusion of elements has appeared among employing organizations and between organizations and unions. Some employers, for example, would not include legally required benefits or benefits expected to yield an immediate benefit to the company.[29] Some unions would exclude most employee services, premium pay, and paid leave time.[30]

An interesting analysis of employer and union purposes in installing benefits and services led Allen[31] to conclude that penalty payments, paid leave, and protections from economic hazards were not compensation at all but obligations of employers for the social welfare of employees assumed by employers as a condition of the employment exchange. A basic premise of the analysis is that unions turned to private employers to provide these benefits when it became apparent that

[25]Harland Fox, "Comparing the Costs of Fringe Benefits," *Conference Board Record* (May, 1967), pp. 29–35.

[26]Charles W. Sargent, *"Fringe Benefits": Do We Know Enough About Them?* (Hanover, New Hampshire: The Amos Tuck School of Business Administration, Dartmouth College, December, 1963).

[27]Austin M. Fisher and John F. Chapman, "Big Costs of Little Fringes," *Harvard Business Review* (September–October, 1954), pp. 35–44.

[28]"Computing the Cost of Fringe Benefits," *Studies in Personnel Policy No. 128* (New York: National Industrial Conference Board, 1952).

[29]"What's a Fringe?" *Dun's Review and Modern Industry* (August, 1960), p. 56.

[30]Nelson M. Bortz, "The Measurement of Fringe Benefit Expenditures," *Personnel* (July, 1956), pp. 87–94.

[31]Donna Allen, *Fringe Benefits: Wages or Social Obligation?* (Ithaca, New York: Cornell University Press, 1964).

they could not be obtained through social legislation. In the process of wresting these "working conditions" from employers, according to the analysis, unions sometimes referred to the benefits as wages, sometimes as substitutes for wages; but their purpose was to achieve them as "rights."

This is a minority viewpoint. In most views, including that of most economists and BLS, the benefit package constitutes an important portion of total compensation.[32] The elements of compensation have been shown to be interchangeable to some extent. Since 1964, BLS has defined total compensation as all payments to workers subject to income tax withholding and all payments made by the employer to government agencies, insurance companies, or trustees for insurance and welfare. Employee compensation by this definition does not include employee services, largely on the grounds that their costs are not readily identifiable.

Notice that this definition of total compensation does not differentiate parts of compensation by purpose. Attempts to define fringe benefits by purpose typically emphasize that they are payments unrelated to the job or performance.

The viewpoint of this book is that indirect compensation is a part of total compensation but represents payments to employees not for job and performance contributions but for membership in the organization. It takes no position on whether a particular employer expenditure that goes to employees is or is not a part of indirect compensation. But, following the membership motivation model, any reward to enter the employment exchange must be perceived by the employee. Thus, if any item of indirect compensation is not recognized as relevant to the exchange, it is not seen as a reward. Figure 44 is a list of possible inclusions.

GROWTH OF INDIRECT COMPENSATION

Indirect compensation, however defined, has grown rapidly over the years and the growth shows no signs of abating. One study found that benefits have expanded after allowing for inflation at almost triple the growth rate of wages and salaries and predicted that they would reach 50 per cent of payroll by 1985.[33] The BLS and the Chamber of Commerce studies show that benefit costs have been growing by at least double the rate of wages.[34]

[32]Alvin Bauman, "Measuring Employee Compensation in U.S. Industry," *Monthly Labor Review* (October, 1970), pp. 17–24.
[33]T. J. Gordon and R. E. LeBleu, "Employee Benefits, 1970–1985," *Harvard Business Review* (January–February, 1970), pp. 93–107.
[34]See the continuing series of surveys by the U.S. Chamber of Commerce; William Davis and Lily Mary David, "Pattern of Wage and Benefit Changes in Manufacturing," *Monthly Labor Review* (February, 1968), pp. 40–48.

1. *Extra payments for time worked:*
   Holiday premiums
   Overtime premiums

   Shift premiums
   Weekend premiums

2. *Nonproduction awards and bonuses:*
   Anniversary awards
   Attendance bonus
   Christmas bonus
   Quality bonus
   Safety awards

   Service bonus
   Suggestion awards
   Waste-elimination bonus
   Year-end bonus

3. *Payments for time not worked:*
   Call-back pay
   Call-in pay
   Clean-up time
   Clothes-changing time
   Dental care time
   Down time
   Family allowances
   Holidays paid for but not
     worked
   Jury duty time
   Lay-off pay
   Medical time
   Military induction bonus
   Military service allowance
   National Guard duty
   Paid death-in-family leave

   Paid lunch periods
   Paid sick leave
   Portal-to-portal pay
   Religious holidays
   Reporting pay
   Reserve military duty
   Rest periods
   Room and board allowances
   Severance pay
   Supper money
   Time spent on contract
     negotiation
   Time spent on grievances
   Vacation pay
   Voting time
   Witness time

4. *Payments for employee security:*
   Contributions toward:
     accident insurance
     disability insurance
     hospitalization insurance
     life insurance
     medical insurance
     surgical insurance

   Contributions to State disability
     insurance
   OASI contributions
   Contributions to unemployment
     compensation
   Supplements to unemployment
     compensation

   Contributions to workmen's
     compensation
   Supplements to workmen's
     compensation
   Contributions to employee thrift
     plan
   Contributions to employee stock
     purchase plans
   Credit union
   Employee loan association
   Health and welfare funds
   Home financing
   Mutual benefit association
   Payment of optical expenses
   Pensions
   Savings Bond administration

5. *Payments for employee services:*
   Annual reports to employees

   Income tax service

Beauty parlors
Cafeteria
Canteen service
Charm courses
Company athletic
  teams
Company housing
Company orchestra
Company stores
Cooking schools
Dietetic advice
Educational assistance
Employee counselling
Employee discounts on
  purchases
Employee parties
Employee pleasure trips
Employee publications
Financial advice
Flowers for ill and deceased
  employees and families
Free laundry
Free meals
Functions for retired
  employees
Health education
Hospital facilities

Information racks
Legal aid
Lunch period entertainment
Medical examinations
  (voluntary)
Music at work
Nursery
Paid club memberships
Paid subscriptions to magazines
Parking space operation
Purchasing service
Reading room facilities
Recreational facilities
Rest room facilities
Safety clothes at company
  expense
Safety programs
Scholarships
Shower and locker rooms
Transportation
Vacation facilities
Visiting nurse
Vitamins and salt tablets
Wedding gifts
Work clothes at company
  expense

FIGURE 44

Selected Fringe Items

A number of factors have been operating to bring about this fundamental change in the nature of compensation. One is the changing nature of our economy as a result of continued industrialization. Increases in productivity have permitted choices in the way the worker's share is distributed. Part of the productivity increase, for example, has been taken in increased leisure in the form of vacations and holidays as well as shorter hours.

Growing industrialization and changes in modes of living have brought new risks to the employee and have increased old ones at the same time that increased productivity has permitted programs to provide security against these risks. Economic security in a society in which most individuals are employees depends on finding and keeping a job. Any threat to continuing employment becomes a risk to the employee and his family and creates demands for methods of insuring against such risks. With the increase in demands, arrangements have appeared to permit the employee to take part of his compensation as protection from insecurity.

Another factor has been the growing social determination of the way in which compensation is distributed.[35] Collective decisions involving government, labor, and management are made in compensation determination along with the manner in which it is to be allocated. The influence of governments in the allocation of compensation was first felt in social legislation. The earliest legislation called for employer contributions for workmen's compensation. Later, the social security program called for employer contributions to unemployment compensation and contributions of both employers and employees to old age, survivors, and disability insurance. More recently, state legislation has provided for employer and employee contributions to ensure against nonwork accidents and illnesses.

An equally important role of government has been income tax legislation. High corporate income tax rates have encouraged the expansion of indirect compensation programs. Because much of the employer's cost of such programs is deductible for income tax purposes as business expense, companies have had an incentive to install indirect compensation plans. As long as benefit costs are deductible for tax purposes, it makes no monetary difference to the employer whether compensation is direct or indirect.

But it may make a tremendous difference to employees. Given a demand for protection from insecurity, much more protection can be purchased with pre-tax dollars than with after-tax dollars paid to employees. Also, the purchase of protection on an individual basis not only costs more but usually provides less benefits than those purchased on a group basis.

Wage stabilization during World War II gave a strong impetus to growth of indirect compensation by permitting improvements in benefits while discouraging wage and salary increases on the grounds that the latter would contribute to inflationary pressures whereas the former would not. The broadened definition of "wages" by the National Labor Relations Board and the courts to include pensions and health and welfare plans encouraged union drives to include benefit programs in labor agreements.

Union demands have served to increase indirect compensation as a proportion of total pay. The growth in unionism since the mid-1930s was largely accomplished by organizing the mass-production industries.

---

[35]Michael T. Wermel, "The Changing Nature of Compensation," in Robert D. Gray (ed.), *Frontiers in Industrial Relations* (Pasadena: California Institute of Technology, 1959), pp. 621–637.

Workers in these industries were much more prone to the risks of industrial life than were craft workers, and union leaders of industrial unions demanded protection from insecurity for their members.

Union leaders of large industrial unions have fostered member interest in programs providing protection from insecurity. Sometimes a benefit has been demanded to establish a principle of employer responsibility for certain risks facing workers. Often indirect compensation has been increased when wage increases did not appear feasible. Allen's analysis, cited previously, suggests that union strategy with respect to benefits has been constant (the achievement of certain protections from insecurity as "rights"), but that union tactics varied in order to achieve the greatest gains. Ross has suggested that unions have sought to expand indirect compensation for a number of reasons, including (1) desire for increased status, (2) demand for security of income, (3) a method of shortening working hours, (4) a method of enabling the union to gain strength with members, and (5) the rise of the doctrine of the plant as a community.[36]

Most of these reasons imply a strong interest in benefits on the part of workers. It appears that employee interest in benefits has been growing over the years. An early study by Reynolds found benefit programs quite unimportant to workers.[37] Lester, however, found evidence that workers' preference for compensation in the form of benefits has been increasing during the past two decades and that they place a high value on benefits entirely apart from tax and price (group purchase) advantages.[38] Although employee preferences for benefits vary with their personal situation, some employee groups report that they would prefer an increase in benefits to an increase in wages.[39] Employee preferences appear to be based on perceived needs rather than benefit costs.[40]

The fact that over half of indirect compensation represents protection from insecurity[41] suggests that both employees and employers are aware that life in an industrial society requires these protections. Although indirect compensation has expanded greatly through collec-

---

[36]Arthur M. Ross, "Fringe Benefits Today and Tomorrow," *Labor Law Journal* (August, 1956), pp. 467–482.

[37]Lloyd G. Reynolds, *The Structure of Labor Markets* (New York: Harper & Brothers, 1951), p. 94.

[38]Richard A. Lester, "Benefits as a Preferred Form of Compensation," *Southern Economic Journal* (April, 1967), pp. 488–495.

[39]Ludwig A. Wagner and Theodore Bakerman, "Wage Earners' Opinions of Insurance Fringe Benefits," *The Journal of Insurance* (June, 1960), pp. 17–28.

[40]Stanley M. Nealey, "Pay and Benefit Preference," *Industrial Relations* (October, 1963), pp. 17–28; Mark R. Greene, *The Role of Benefit Structures in Manufacturing Industry* (Eugene, Oregon: The University of Oregon, 1964).

[41]Bauman, in *Monthly Labor Review* (October, 1970), pp. 17–24.

tive bargaining, many of the benefits were provided by employers prior to their inclusion in labor agreements apparently in the recognition that maintaining a labor force requires an investment quite apart from paying for productive service. Employer beliefs that indirect compensation aids the organization in getting and keeping employees suggest that these benefits represent expenditures to protect present investment in employees and to ease problems of recruitment.

COSTS OF INDIRECT COMPENSATION

The growth of indirect compensation as a proportion of pay has focused attention on the cost of benefit programs. From the viewpoint of the employer, at least, changing the form of compensation does not reduce its impact on costs.

A number of studies have called attention to the increasing cost of indirect compensation. Although the results of these studies vary because of variations in the benefits included, there is agreement that indirect compensation costs organizations from 20 to 30 per cent of payroll.

As mentioned previously, the U.S. Chamber of Commerce has been making benefit cost surveys since 1947. One part of this survey presents the percentage of payroll representing benefit costs for an identical group of companies. This percentage was 16.1 in 1947, 24.2 in 1957, and 29.9 in 1967. Although this figure for identical companies has advanced faster than the average of all companies in the survey, the latter figure was 27.9 per cent for 1969 as compared to 26 per cent in 1967.[42] There were substantial variations between companies and industries. In wholesaling and retailing, benefits represented 21.7 per cent of payroll, whereas banks and other financial institutions averaged 33.9 per cent. The petroleum, food, chemical, and public utility industries all paid out at least 30 per cent of payroll in indirect compensation. There is also substantial variation by region (higher in the North and in metropolitan areas) and by organization size (higher in large firms).

Periodic surveys have been made by the Bureau of Labor Statistics. The 1968 figures show that supplementary compensation, using BLS definitions, represents 20.5 per cent of total compensation.[43] BLS studies show that benefits provided to union workers are greater than those provided nonunion workers, manufacturing industries provide higher benefits than nonmanufacturing, and white-collar employees

---

[42]"Compensation Currents," *Compensation Review* (First Quarter, 1971), pp. 2–3.
[43]Bauman, in *Monthly Labor Review* (October, 1970), pp. 17–24.

receive a slightly larger proportion of their compensation in the form of benefits.

Unions take credit for the larger benefits paid to union than to nonunion employees.[44] But one study found that variations in benefit expenditures are explained largely by variations in employee earnings levels and that the apparent causal relationship between benefit expenditures and union status is spurious in that it merely reflects that unionism's strength is in high-wage sectors of the economy.[45]

Broad surveys can only detect trends. Differences in (1) definitions of items to be included, (2) payroll accounting practices, (3) scheduled working hours, (4) pay rates, (5) composition of the work force, and (6) company employee relations philosophy make comparison difficult. Variations in accounting practices present the most serious problem. The Bureau of Labor Statistics studies found accounting procedures in a large proportion of firms unable to provide the breakdowns to supply meaningful data. The U.S. Chamber of Commerce studies provide reporting firms with a schedule for reporting comparable data. In the biennial surveys since 1947 they have sampled identical firms. In this way the surveys not only provide reliable trends in costs of the benefits covered but may contribute to common accounting procedures for indirect compensation expenditures.

INDIRECT COMPENSATION DECISIONS

Decisions with respect to indirect compensation are made more complex because of confusion of purpose, lack of agreement on which benefits do and do not represent compensation, and the rapid growth of benefits and benefit costs. Perhaps the major point of agreement between the parties is that the nature of compensation is changing.[46]

To the employer, decisions on indirect compensation represent a large and growing proportion of compensation expenditures—so defined because they represent a large part of his contributions to the employment exchange. To the union, these benefits are social obligations of responsible employers, gains to hold out to present and potential members, and strategic considerations in bargaining. To the employee, they represent protections from insecurity and rewards associated with membership in the organization.

[44]Rudolph Oswald and J. Douglas Smyth, "Fringe Benefits—on the Move," *American Federationist* (June, 1970), pp. 18–23.

[45]Robert Rice, "Skill, Earnings and the Growth of Wage Supplements," *Papers and Proceedings of the American Economic Association* (May, 1966), pp. 583–593.

[46]Arnold Strasser, "The Changing Structure of Compensation," *Monthly Labor Review* (September, 1966), pp. 953–958.

Superficially, indirect compensation decisions are similar to wage-level decisions. In both, the basic issue to the employer is one of labor costs. The employer's decision in both cases involves expenditures resulting from the employment exchange, and from a cost viewpoint he is indifferent whether the money goes for direct or indirect compensation. The tendency to combine wages and benefits into a "package" at the bargaining table suggests that direct and indirect compensation decisions are made on similar grounds.

Actually, however, decisions on indirect compensation involve a number of considerations not present in wage decisions. Unions sometimes do and sometimes do not consider benefits to be pay equivalents. Employees differentially value various benefits, depending primarily on their personal situation but also on the effectiveness of unions or employers in convincing employees of their value. Employing organizations differ greatly in work force composition and thus on employee needs and desires for various protections from insecurity and other rewards for membership in the organization. Furthermore, employers must recognize that although expenditures on indirect compensation can motivate membership, they do not represent rewards for the job or for performance. Finally, indirect compensation decisions hold a number of implications for the parties to the employment exchange, for the economy, and for society that are not present in decisions involving direct compensation. The remaining portions of this section examine the considerations involved in indirect compensation decisions.

LEGISLATION

Social legislation requiring employing organizations to make contributions to programs protecting employees from certain insecurities nicely illustrates the issues we have been discussing. Such legislation requires that the employer make expenditures for the health and safety of his employees and for various forms of insurance to indemnify employee loss of income from illness and injury, unemployment, and old age. These expenditures are required whether or not the employer wants to make them and whether or not employees desire the resulting benefits.

It might thus be argued that these expenditures do not represent compensation resulting from the employment exchange but are merely a convenient method whereby society insures that its members are protected from certain insecurities. But to the employer they represent expenditures that arise from the employment exchange, are for the benefit of employees, and substitute for direct compensation that could be provided employees in the absence of social legislation.

If the model of the employment exchange is correct in specifying that a reward must be recognized as such by the employee, it is quite possible that employer expenditures for social insurance are not considered to be rewards by employees. But the employer probably has no choice but to consider them as a part of his contribution to the employment exchange and to hope that he can convince employees of their relevance.

Such legally required benefits cost the average employer almost 6 per cent of payroll, according to the U.S. Chamber of Commerce and the Bureau of Labor Statistics. These payments represent direct employer outlays required by legislation and do not include expenses involved in providing safe and healthful working conditions and in administering programs.

INDIRECT COMPENSATION SURVEYS

Another consideration in indirect compensation decisions is industry and area practice regarding benefits. One of the organization considerations in the decision to install a new benefit or broaden an existing one is the extent to which these benefits are offered by other employers in the labor market.

Surveys of prevailing practice in indirect compensation are conducted for the same reasons as are wage and salary surveys—to obtain information on compensation offered by labor market competitors. Community wage surveys conducted by the Bureau of Labor Statistics include a number of supplementary benefit practices. Employer association wage and salary surveys customarily include indirect compensation programs. Individual organizations may seek such data along with wage and salary information or in separate surveys. The usual survey seeks prevailing practice—descriptions of each program and its coverage. Tabulations consist of the number of responding organizations having each specific type of program and often variations in programs for different employee groups.

Such surveys of prevailing practice show employer concern with the membership rewards of labor market competitors. They also accord with union interest in prevailing practice. But the information obtained is quite different from that obtained in wage and salary surveys. Wage surveys are surveys of wage costs, whereas an identical benefit may represent widely different costs in different organizations because of varying work forces and methods of financing benefits.

Ideally, an organization faced with indirect compensation decisions would know both the benefits offered by labor market competitors and other organizations' benefit plan expenditures. But benefit plan expenditures are not readily available in most organizations because accounting practices vary and because costing out individual benefits is difficult. Actually, although it seems important for organizations to know their total benefit costs,[47] and it would seem useful to know labor market competitors' total indirect compensation expenditures, cost information on individual benefits is less meaningful to other organizations because of differences in work force composition and other differences among organizations.

As the following section emphasizes, much more useful than either prevailing practice or benefit cost surveys would be surveys of benefit preferences of employee groups within the organization. The model points out that to be a reward, a benefit must be recognized and considered relevant by the employee. Only if an employee wants additional indirect compensation will it be considered by him as a reward.

Benefits provided by other employers may or may not be considered important by an organization's employees. If they are, it is the cost of the benefit to this organization rather than other organizations that enters the indirect compensation decision. This suggests that prevailing practices from surveys of other organizations should be costed out in this organization and this information used, along with employee preferences, in making indirect compensation decisions.

This section reinforces the complexity of indirect compensation decisions. Organizations are charged with ensuring that all expenditures redound to the benefit of the organization. As indirect compensation becomes a larger proportion of total compensation, organizations can be expected to be more careful in indirect compensation decisions. In wage decisions, comparison with other organizations may be an important consideration in order to permit the organization to be competitive in the labor market. In indirect compensation decisions, however, although benefit practices of other organizations are one consideration, they are much less important than employee preferences. Unless employees want a particular benefit, they are quite unlikely to consider it a reward, and expenditures by the organization for this benefit do not enter the employment exchange and cannot achieve a benefit for the organization.

ORGANIZATION BENEFIT PLAN ANALYSIS

Surveys of prevailing benefit practices may have the dysfunctional consequences of encouraging particular benefit programs not because they are needed or wanted by employees but because they exist in

---

[47]See Michael T. Wermel and Geraldine M. Beideman, *How to Determine the Total Cost of Your Employee Benefit Programs: A Guide for a Company Survey* (Pasadena: Industrial Relations Section, California Institute of Technology, 1960).

other organizations. The present benefit structure in this country suggests that indirect compensation decisions have been motivated by competition among organizations based on a vague feeling that more benefits help an organization get and keep a work force rather than on careful analysis of employee needs and preferences.

Organization analysis of indirect compensation practices would seem to require an examination of present programs and the needs and preferences of employees. Our designation of indirect compensation as membership rewards is an aid in this analysis in that it specifies organization purpose in these programs as obtaining and retaining employees. But organizations employ many different employee groups with different needs and preferences.

The most important question in the analysis concerns the needs and preferences of employees. Employee needs depend on the composition of the organization's work force—age, sex, family status, labor market commitment, and length of company service, for example. An organization whose employees are primarily composed of young unmarried women, likely to leave the labor force upon marriage, with organization length of service unlikely to exceed three years, requires quite different benefits than an organization composed of married men likely to stay with the organization until retirement. The needs for protection against loss of income from various causes are much greater in the latter organization. Benefit programs designed for such an organization would involve wasted resources if applied to the former.

Employees may be expected to vary in needs and preferences for benefits not only according to their personal situation (age, marital status, family responsibilities) but by the employee groups to which they belong and their commitment to the organization. Thus, white-collar employees may want different benefits from blue-collar employees, professionals may want benefits that signify their status, and managers may want benefits that reflect a long-term commitment to the organization. It is for these reasons that surveys of employee preferences have been suggested.

Present and proposed benefits should be compared against employee needs. Unmet needs of employees may call for additional benefits. But overlapping benefits that provide more protection than is needed are a waste of resources. Fortunately, the rapidly increasing costs of indirect compensation are focusing the attention of organizations on the need for analysis of existing benefit programs and more careful thought to the existing benefit structure when a new one is proposed.[48] There is some evidence that decisions are no longer made on the basis

---

[48]Arthur J. Deric (ed.), *The Total Approach to Employee Benefits* (New York: American Management Association, 1967).

of a benefit-by-benefit comparison with other companies but on a comparison of present and proposed benefits with employee and organization needs. Such an approach permits correcting past mistakes through the elimination of waste and overlapping while filling gaps.

A part of the analysis is also concerned with the relationship between direct and indirect compensation both in terms of organization costs and employee needs. Not only do increases in wages and salaries increase the costs of indirect compensation (overtime, vacations, and holiday pay are the most obvious examples), but they serve to increase employee needs for protection against loss of income.

Analysis of benefit costs and the protection afforded employees often involves some technical expertise. For example, the protection provided and administrative costs may vary widely with different methods of financing benefits. A knowledge of insurance principles may be required. Less technical but equally important may be analysis of the potential costs of not providing a particular benefit. It may be that an informal practice meets employee needs, but at a higher cost than a benefit program designed for the purpose.

Costs not only vary between organizations because of work force composition, as discussed previously, but because of such organization and industry characteristics as ratio of labor cost to total cost, variability of demand, technical considerations requiring round-the-clock operations, profitability, and so on. Companies with high profits tend to have high indirect compensation and so do larger organizations, unionized organizations, and organizations in low labor-cost industries. Benefit expenditures also vary by size of community and section of the country.

Such analyses as outlined in this section suggest that benefit programs be planned rather than put together in the patchwork fashion many programs evidence. They serve to prepare the organization for bargaining on benefits and to redesign indirect compensation programs in terms of employee and organization objectives. Employee preference surveys based on the benefits and costs derived from such an analysis can permit choices that ensure that indirect compensation consists of desired rewards.

COLLECTIVE BARGAINING ON INDIRECT COMPENSATION

Most indirect compensation decisions are made at the bargaining table. If it is assumed that union demands are mirrors of employee desires and that organizations have analyzed the needs of their employees and the organization, the results of the bargaining should be advantageous to employers as well as employees and their union. The employees should be receiving the benefits that they want and unions are motivated to convince employees of the value of the benefits.

Unfortunately, however, unions have goals beyond representing the desires of employees in specific employing organizations. They may, for example, strive for a benefit attractive to the majority of the members, whether or not it is needed or desired in a particular organization. Because of the political nature of unionism, union leaders have learned that they must always achieve gains or something that can be made to appear as a gain to the majority of their constituents. Benefits can often be made to appear to be larger gains than an equivalent pay increase and have often been won from employers unable to increase wages. Such experiences may suggest to union leaders that benefit programs involve small cost to employers but represent gains to employees when properly merchandized.

Furthermore, if Donna Allen is correct in concluding that benefits are not perceived by unions as compensation but as social responsibilities of employers obtained at the bargaining table because they could not be obtained through social legislation, then unions have no reason for considering the needs and desires of particular employees and organizations. By this reasoning, benefits become prerequisite to the employment exchange rather than rewards from it, and unions may seek to attain them by calling them wages or nonwages or following any strategy that achieves the goal. In so doing, unions would be representing not just their members but all employees.

But if benefits are part of compensation as organizations assume because they involve expenditures by the organization and go to employees and if, furthermore, neither unions nor employers have sought out the needs and desires of these employees and this organization, collective bargaining may result in benefit programs dysfunctional to both their members and to organizations. In such cases, a large part of employees' compensation goes for benefits they neither need nor want and organizations are placed at a competitive disadvantage. Fortunately, there is mounting evidence that both unions and management are recognizing the need for careful analysis as indirect compensation becomes a larger proportion of total compensation.

THE CAFETERIA APPROACH

An approach to indirect compensation decisions often suggested[49] is that rather than having the organization or unions and management make benefit decisions, the employee be permitted to make the decision. Called the cafeteria approach, the employee is assigned a certain

[49]Nealey, in *Industrial Relations* (October, 1963), pp. 17–28; E. E. Lawler, "The Mythology of Management Compensation," *California Management Review* (Fall, 1966), pp. 11–22; J. R. Schuster, "Another Look at Compensation Preferences," *Industrial Management Review* (Spring, 1969), pp. 1–18.

amount of compensation that he can divide between benefits and cash.

The cafeteria approach is based on research evidence that there are large individual differences among people in the value they attach to various benefits. As discussed previously, people may or may not want a particular benefit based on their personal situation, and to some extent, on the employee group to which they belong. This method should also ensure that people recognize benefits as rewards because they get only those that they choose.

It would appear that the cafeteria approach would be favorably viewed by employees. One study[50] found that more than three-quarters of the employees of a large aerospace firm would change the components of their pay package if they were free to do so. Drucker[51] has suggested that shaping benefits to the wants of specific major groups of employees is one solution to the waste of large amounts of benefit expenditures in this country.

But the cafeteria approach has not been widely applied. One reason undoubtedly is that it would complicate payroll accounting. With computerized accounting, this problem should be minor. At least one computer software firm, System Development Corporation, has developed a computer program that permits employees to choose among a number of options.[52] Another is that cafeteria plans would be applicable only to nonunion employees because unions would resist such plans. Although this may be true, it has not been tested inasmuch as both management and unions seem to be in agreement on the notion that for purposes of indirect compensation the work force is homogeneous. There seems to be no good reason why a limited number of pay-benefit packages that seem to fit different employee groups could not be developed by surveying employee opinions regarding equal-costing benefits. It is also possible that a choice of two or three of these packages could be bargained into labor agreements. One author suggests the development of a limited number of packages through research that follow what he calls the "stages of man" approach so that each package would fit a man's situation for a five-year period.[53]

Perhaps another reason for the hesitance in adopting the cafeteria approach is the belief that employees should have some protection from insecurity whether they choose it or not. Although this issue could be met by placing these basic items in each of the packages, it would

[50]Schuster, in *Industrial Management Review* (Spring, 1969), pp. 1–18.

[51]Peter F. Drucker, "What We Can Learn from Japanese Management," *Harvard Business Review* (March–April, 1971), pp. 110–122.

[52]Jay R. Schuster, Lewis D. Hart, and Barbara Clark, "Epic: New Cafeteria Compensation Plan," *Datamation* (February 1, 1971), pp. 28–30.

[53]J. Taylor, "A New Approach to Compensation Management," *Compensation Review* (First Quarter, 1969), pp. 22–30.

be done at the risk of some employees not valuing these rewards that they were forced to accept.

Another problem is that the cost of insurance programs is typically geared to proportion of employee coverage. Developing packages from surveys of employee opinion should advise organizations in advance of the number of employees who would be expected to choose each option. Higher costs of lower coverage should be offset by the advantage of employees recognizing chosen benefits as rewards.

There is also some danger that in combining job rewards (pay) and membership rewards (benefits) and permitting employee choices among items, some employees may choose so many benefits that their pay distorts the job status alignment. This possibility is remote for employee groups who think of their compensation as a package of disparate items, and there is some evidence that this is true even of blue-collar employees. Also, the packages from which the employee is permitted to choose could be designed to eliminate this possibility.

The major advantage of the cafeteria approach, it bears repeating, is to ensure that employees are fully aware of the economic rewards that they receive from the employment exchange. As will be observed later in this chapter, employees are not aware of organization benefit expenditures in spite of major efforts to communicate this information to them. The cafeteria approach brings clearly to the attention of the employee how much the organization is spending to compensate him, and it assures that money is spent only on benefits the employees want.

OTHER CONSIDERATIONS IN INDIRECT COMPENSATION DECISIONS

On several occasions in this chapter the additional complexities of indirect compensation decisions beyond those encountered in wage decisions have been mentioned. This section briefly examines some of the issues that face employing organizations, unions, our economy, and society because of the method we have chosen to solve the problems of employee insecurity in this country.

Americans have chosen very largely to solve the problems of insecurity arising from an industrial society by private means. Thus, employees of large, unionized organizations in metropolitan areas are well protected from insecurity and receive appreciable chunks of leisure both on and off the job. These benefits vary by industry and area as well as by organization size and unionization. Some employees of small, nonunion organizations have only the limited protection of social legislation, and some have none at all. This range between the "haves" and the "have nots" grows wider with the growth of benefits that shows no signs of abating.

It is hard to believe that this disparity can continue to exist without strong pressures being created for public programs to redress the balance. If public programs are developed, it makes a tremendous difference whether benefits continue to be rewards from the employment exchange as they are viewed in this country at present or as prerequisites to the employment exchange or working conditions. Donna Allen has suggested that unions, perhaps inadvertently, have forced on employers a set of social responsibilities that are prerequisites of the employment exchange. If she is correct, organizations would be wise to consider the consequences of removing up to 30 per cent of economic rewards from the employment exchange. Also, unions would be wise to consider the consequences to employment of a system wherein a prospective employer must expend a sum equal to 30 per cent of each employee's yearly earnings as a prerequisite to employment.

The significance of indirect compensation in employee motivation is no longer in question. Benefits can motivate membership but not performance,—at least not in the way they are administered now. Because most benefits go to all employees equally or are tied to seniority rather than performance, they cannot motivate performance. Organizations may be wise to keep it that way. Not only would these arrangements be difficult to change, there may be an advantage to separating membership rewards from rewards for other purposes. There is some danger of organizations' discouraging employees who would be more productive elsewhere from leaving, but such problems can probably be handled in other ways more easily than by trying to tie benefits to performance.

But organizations must be aware that to motivate membership, employees must recognize these benefits and consider them relevant before they become rewards. If employees are not aware of these benefits or do not consider them to be relevant, they do not influence membership motivation. The primary attractiveness of the cafeteria approach is its promise of making employees aware that benefits are rewards.

Indirect compensation decisions greatly increase the responsibilities of employing organizations. Because benefit programs are membership rewards, they imply the existence of a long-term rather than short-term employment relationship. The moral commitments involved reduce labor-cost flexibility of organizations because additional commitments are made with the addition of each benefit and as each new employee achieves permanent status.

The fact that the value of programs to employees is not perfectly correlated with costs to the organization increases the organization's responsibility. Although benefits tend to have greater values than costs because of tax considerations and group purchase, it would seem that with the acquisition of each benefit the employer accepts new responsibilities for seeing that employee values equal or exceed organization costs.

But carrying out these responsibilities also becomes more difficult. Many of the programs require administration by specialists whose concern is often with technical details of specific programs rather than with ensuring that employee value is maximized. This technical myopia, enhanced by the fact that benefits are usually installed at different times, tends to hide problems of consistency among programs and of overlap in benefits.

Indirect compensation decisions also increase the responsibilities of unions. With each additional benefit, union responsibilities for ensuring value to members would seem to increase along with the difficulties of carrying out this responsibility. Union technical experts can be just as myopic as those of employing organizations. Also, although the political nature of unionism may explain obtaining benefits that some members may not need or already have in another form, it does not remove the moral issue. Furthermore, the tendency for unions to demand benefits obtained by other unions has resulted in benefits crossing industry lines, perhaps destroying economically justified differentials. More serious for unions in partially organized industries, the larger benefit programs in unionized firms appear to have intensified union-nonunion competition to the disadvantage of the union. The tendency of small firms to have less costly benefit programs may have increased intraindustry differentials as interindustry differentials are decreased. Multiple employer plans and direct-service health plans may have the effect of creating union paternalism to replace the employer paternalism of earlier years.

The point is that union demands for indirect compensation have unintended consequences for members, employing organizations, and unions themselves. These consequences increase unions' responsibilities and deserve more attention than they have received.

Indirect compensation decisions of employers and unions may have unintended consequences for our economy. Our method of providing benefits by private means may have reduced our ability to compete in foreign markets. Although other industrialized economies appear to have equal or higher benefits, the cost incidence is quite different. Although it can be argued that benefits are a social cost, paid for in their entirety by workers, whether these benefits are provided through the employer, unions, governments, or each worker's personal resources, the effects on an employer's labor costs are quite different in the various cases. In this country, benefits are provided through employment and most costs appear in labor costs of employers. In many other countries, benefits are largely provided by employee contributions and general tax revenues and thus do not appear in employer labor costs. Also, in other countries there appears to be more attention to gearing benefits to actual needs of employees and employee groups rather than providing them to all employees regardless of need, as in this country. Both our method of financing benefits and our lack of concern with need and overlapping benefits may serve to decrease the competitiveness of our economy.

Indirect compensation decisions may have contributed to the problem of maintaining price stability in this country. When total compensation gains exceed productivity gains in the economy, inflationary consequences are the likely results. To the extent that indirect compensation costs are not fully added to wage costs in computing total compensation, total compensation gains may exceed productivity gains inadvertently. Our method of financing benefits may tend to hide some indirect compensation costs and ignore the fact that some items of indirect compensation (overtime, for example) increase in proportion, and some more than in proportion to wages.

Whether or not indirect compensation decisions have reduced total employment in this country is still a controversial matter. To the extent that benefit commitments made in hiring a new employee encourage employers to work the present force overtime, total employment is reduced. Although the 30 per cent of payroll represented by present benefit expenditures obviously does not approach the 50 per cent overtime premium, adding hiring, training, and turnover costs may tip the balance.[54] For example, in very tight labor markets employers may assume that additional costs of employing marginal workers when added to benefit expenditures are greater than paying overtime premiums to present employees. Union demands for double time for overtime have been based on the premise that benefit costs encourage overtime rather than expansion in employment.[55]

The effect of present benefit arrangements on labor mobility is also unsettled. Although logic and some studies suggest that benefits are

---

[54]Joseph W. Garbarino, "Fringe Benefits and Overtime as Barriers to Expanding Employment," *Industrial and Labor Relations Review* (April, 1964), pp. 426–442; Ronald G. Ehrenberg, "The Impact of Overtime Premium on Employment and Hours in U.S. Industry," *Western Economic Journal* (June, 1971), pp. 199–207.

[55]"Labor Urges Double-Time for Overtime Assignments," *IUD Bulletin* (March, 1964), p. 10.

among the factors that serve to tie individuals to organizations,[56] it has not even been shown conclusively that pension plans do so.[57] Part of the difficulty lies in designing studies that uncover the effect of one or a few factors among many, but it appears that people who are tied to an organization by benefits would be tied without them by other items in the employment exchange.[58]

The issue of whether protections from insecurity provided through employment have weakened community efforts to stimulate citizen participation in programs designed to provide group protection would seem to deserve more attention than it has received. Also, although industrial societies do increase insecurity, must the protections involve either employer or union paternalism? To what extent (if any) should an individual bear the responsibility for protecting himself from insecurity?

ADMINISTERING INDIRECT COMPENSATION

The complexities involved in indirect compensation decisions suggest that administrative problems exist. The technical details of insurance and retirement plans, for example, require specialists. The various types of benefits suggest the need for someone to coordinate them. But confusion of purpose has made coordination difficult.

When indirect compensation is recognized as consisting of various membership rewards, however, administration is simplified. These benefits are part of compensation to be coordinated with other portions of compensation by the compensation administrator.

The model points out that to be rewards, indirect compensation, just as wages, salaries, and other forms of compensation, must be recognized and considered relevant by the employee. No question exists any longer whether employees value benefits.[59] But it is quite well established that they are often not aware of the amount of compensation that benefits involve,[60] even after extensive efforts to inform them.

[56]Hugh Folk, "Private Pension Plans and Manpower Policy," U.S. Department of Labor, *Bulletin 1359* (1963).

[57]Herbert S. Parnes, "Labor Force and Labor Markets," in Woodrow L. Ginsburg *et al.* (eds.), *A Review of Industrial Relations Research* (Madison, Wisconsin: Industrial Relations Research Association, 1970), p. 51.

[58]Arthur M. Ross, "Do We Have a New Industrial Feudalism?" *American Economic Review* (December, 1958), pp. 903–920.

[59]Lester, in *Southern Economic Journal* (April, 1967), pp. 488–495.

[60]Arthur A. Sloane and Edward W. Hodges, "What Workers Don't Know about Employee Benefits," *Personnel* (November–December, 1968), pp. 27–34.

The cafeteria approach suggests itself as the superior method of informing employees of the costs and values of benefits. In this method, because employees chose the benefits that they receive, they know exactly what they are getting. Gearing benefits to employee groups based on group needs and desires (determined by employee surveys) would seem to be an acceptable alternative to the cafeteria approach. Because employee groups are thus assured that they are receiving benefits tailored to their needs and desires, they will at least logically value these rewards more highly than if the benefits were designed for everyone.

But because indirect compensation involves deferred rewards, organizations have discovered that a continuing communications program is required to ensure that employees are aware of the rewards that they are receiving. Perhaps the most effective of the communications media is the individual benefit statement prepared by computer and given to the employee each year.[61] All forms of communication media are employed, however—booklets, pamphlets, pay envelope stuffers, company newspaper articles, films, and meetings.

Effective communication of benefits appears to depend on getting across (1) the total value of benefits to the employee at a given point in time, (2) the value of individual benefits, (3) the incremental value to the employee of the organization's providing the benefit over direct employee purchase, and (4) the cumulative value of all benefits.[62] Explaining the details of specific plans and benefit policy seems both less necessary and less effective. Benefit plan communications are effective if they achieve employee perception of the value of these rewards, not if information on plan details has been learned by employees.[63]

[61]"New System Fills in the Blanks on Benefits," *Business Week* (March 1, 1969), p. 94.

[62]Stanley Hauser, "Designing the Employee Benefit Message and Getting It Across," *Pension and Welfare News* (March, 1968), pp. 20–21.

[63]Thomas H. Patten, Jr., *Communicating the Salary Administration Package* (Stamford, Connecticut: Motivation, Inc., 1969), p. 26.

15

Nonfinancial Rewards

Compensation as defined in this book includes nonfinancial as well as economic rewards. The vast number and variety of nonfinancial rewards that may be provided to employees through the employment exchange are the subject matter of this chapter. Many of these rewards issue from the organization, others from supervisors, others from fellow employees, and still others from the employee himself.

Organizations have available and often provide many nonfinancial rewards that they do not seem to be aware of or at least do not utilize to obtain either membership motivation or performance motivation. Also, organizations often act as if they are unaware of or choose to ignore the nonfinancial rewards provided by supervisors, work groups, or the employee himself. In fact, the nonfinancial rewards that organizations are conscious of providing employees are often administered in a manner that precludes getting either type of motivation from them.

Employees are probably more conscious than employing organizations of the many nonfinancial rewards that may become available through the employment exchange. But employees differ widely in the rewards they want and how much value they place on each. Some of these employee differences are related to occupations. Others are related to demographic characteristics of employees.

These differences in the values placed on nonfinancial rewards by different employee groups, although not well-researched, appear to be very great. It is quite possible that some employee groups are willing to substitute nonfinancial rewards for economic rewards. If this is true, employing organizations may be wasting economic resources by failing to give sufficient attention to nonfinancial rewards.

Both of the models presented in Chapter 3 specified that to be a reward an outcome from the employment exchange must be recognized and considered relevant by the employee. They also show that the more a reward is valued by the employee, the more weight it carries in motivating both membership and performance. Thus it is important that organizations be aware of the range of nonfinancial rewards that may be provided employees, the values employee groups place on these rewards, and methods by which these rewards may be administered to motivate membership and performance.

Organizations, of course, differ in the nonfinancial rewards that they have available or are able to influence. Also, organizations may be expected to vary even more on this dimension in the future. But it is doubtful if any organization can any longer afford to ignore the existence or the consequences of nonfinancial rewards.

The purpose of this chapter is to emphasize the tremendous variety of available nonfinancial rewards, to suggest how different employee groups may differentially value some of the categories of nonfinancial rewards, and to show how organizations can improve their administration. As with economic rewards, nonfinancial rewards are classified into job, performance, and membership reward categories. An additional dimension exists in the case of nonfinancial rewards, however, in that the sources of these rewards are not only the organization but also supervisors, work groups, and the individual himself. Also, the value placed on the different nonfinancial rewards probably varies much more widely among employee groups than the value placed on economic rewards.

VARIETY OF NONFINANCIAL REWARDS

The variety of nonfinancial rewards from work is almost endless. Even a casual attempt by most of us to delineate the rewarding outcomes of any particular employment exchange would yield quite a number. Likewise, attempts to study even simple employment exchanges experimentally in laboratories lead to the conviction that a large number of nonfinancial rewards are operating that have not been specified or controlled.

But although it is apparent to all of us that this myriad of nonfinancial rewards are present in most, if not all, employment exchanges, few attempts have been made to ferret them out systematically. Organizations and unions, because their major focus has been on the economic basis of the employment exchange, have had little reason to do so. Economists have also understandably focused on economic rewards.

Psychologists have distinguished a sizable number of nonfinancial rewards in studies of job satisfaction. Such studies have made use of from five to seventy-one separate factors.[1] An excellent study of job satisfaction research resulting in a standardized instrument to measure job satisfaction has reduced sources of job satisfaction to five types: characteristics of the work, pay, promotions, supervision, and co-workers.[2] The factors employed by Herzberg,[3] however, are probably more representative of the number of rewards that job satisfaction research distinguishes. These factors are recognition; achievement; possibility of growth; advancement; salary; interpersonal relations with superiors, subordinates, and peers; technical competence of supervision; responsibility; company policy and administration; working conditions; the work itself; personal life; status; and job security.

Sociologists also have pointed out a number of nonfinancial rewards from work. Dubin,[4] for example, has distinguished power pay (a job of greater importance, exclusive jurisdiction over a job), authority pay (promotion, more authority), status pay (giving the individual higher status), and privilege pay (giving the individual opportunities for informal relationships with people of higher authority). But he believes that employing organizations have somewhat over 100 distinguishable possible rewards from work, many of which organizations do not appear aware of. Recent work by Dubin and his students has resulted in a classification of 124 sources of attachment to work.[5]

Recent work on motivation and organization theory has greatly extended the list of nonfinancial rewards from the employment exchange. Table 7 presents what may be a representative compilation of nonfinancial rewards from work derived from a broad sampling of published behavioral science research. No pretence is made that is complete. All the rewards in the table are positive. It is, of course, possible to point to negative rewards or punishments such as boredom, danger,

[1]Edward E. Lawler, III, *Pay and Organizational Effectiveness: A Psychological View* (New York: McGraw-Hill Book Company, 1971), p. 42.

[2]Patricia Cain Smith, Lorne M. Kendall, and Charles L. Hulin, *The Measurement of Satisfaction in Work and Retirement* (Chicago: Rand McNally & Company, 1969).

[3]Frederick Herzberg and others, *The Motivation to Work,* 2nd ed. (New York: John Wiley & Sons, Inc., 1959).

[4]Robert Dubin, *Working Union-Management Relations* and *The World of Work* (Englewood Cliffs, N.J.: Prentice-Hall, Inc., 1958).

[5]R. Dubin, "Attachment to Work" (unpublished paper, 1968); Robert A. Hedley, "Freedom and Constraint: A Study of British Factory Workers," (unpublished doctoral dissertation, University of Oregon, June, 1971); Thomas C. Taveggia, "Voluntarism, Satisfaction, and Attachments to Work" (unpublished doctoral dissertation, University of Oregon, 1971).

TABLE 7

Nonfinancial Rewards

I. Associated with the job

Reward	Source			
	Organization	*Supervisor*	*Group*	*Individual*
The work flow system	X			
Optimum information flows	X			
The number of operations	X			
Complexity of the work	X			X
Skill requirements	X			
Attention required by the work	X			X
Predictability	X			
Knowing in advance what the tasks are	X			X
Job status and prestige	X		X	
Job importance and level	X		X	
Opportunity to think of other things while working	X			X
Interruptions in the work	X	X	X	
Having enough time for personal needs	X			
Safety of the job	X			
Cleanliness of the work	X			
Pleasant working conditions	X			
The quality of tools and equipment	X			
Making a quality product	X			X
Value of product or service	X			X
Importance of product or service	X	X	X	X
Usefulness of the product				X
Clear authority symbols	X	X		
Well-defined rules	X			
Knowing how my work fits in	X	X		
Opportunity to teach new people	X	X		
Compatibility of interactions required by the job with preferred interaction pattern	X			X
Dominance over other people	X			X
Authority over other people	X			X
Power	X	X		
Opportunity to compete with others	X			
Low-pressure supervision	X	X		
Democratic supervision	X	X		
Competent supervision	X	X		
Representation by supervision	X	X		
General supervision		X		
Nonpunitive supervision		X		
Fair supervision		X		

TABLE 7

Nonfinancial Rewards (Cont.)

	Source			
	Organization	*Supervisor*	*Group*	*Individual*
Consideration by supervision		x		
Opportunity to develop friendships			x	
Acceptance by other people			x	
Emotional significance of the task				x
The job as a "cause"				x
Job familiarity				x
Enjoyment of the activity				x
Enjoyment of energy expenditure				x
Amount of physical work				x
Keeping busy				x
Feeling of contributing				x
Feeling of having a purpose in life				x
Feeling of completion				x
How the work pulls me along				x
Flexibility required by the work	x			x
Freedom of movement while working		x		x
Pride in work results				x
Seeing the results of my work				x
Knowing exactly how my equipment works		x		x
How fast the time goes				x
Compatibility of work requirements with other roles				x
Compatibility of work requirements with self-image				x
II. Associated with performance				
Opportunity for promotion (advancement)	x			
Status	x		x	
Recognition (appreciation) (praise)	x	x	x	
Power	x	x	x	
Influence on decisions	x	x	x	
Participation in problem-solving	x	x		
Setting performance goals	x	x		
Variety	x		x	x
Responsibility	x			x
Autonomy	x			x
Freedom	x	x		x
Independence	x	x		x

TABLE 7

Nonfinancial Rewards (Cont.)

	Source			
	Organization	*Supervisor*	*Group*	*Individual*
Using one's highest skills and abilities	x	x		x
Developing one's highest skills and abilities	x	x		x
Personal growth	x	x		x
Feeling of accomplishment				x
Achievement				x
Ego-involvement				x
Self-fulfillment				x
Commitment				x
Challenge				x
Interest				x
Self-respect (esteem)			x	x
Self-control				x
Identification with organization goals				x
III. Associated with organization membership				
Prestige of organization (community approval of occupation)	x			x
Size of organization	x			
Visibility of the organization	x			
Age of the organization	x			
Profits of the company	x			x
Importance of the organization	x			x
Flexibility of the organization	x			
Company policy and administration (Proper procedures)	x			
Decentralization	x			
Delegation	x			
Authority system (clarity of authority symbols)	x			
Work flow system	x			
Communication systems (optimum information flows)	x			
Conflict resolution methods	x			
Management competence	x	x		
Company rules (well-defined rules)	x			
Justice determination systems (evaluation by fair standards) (fair evaluation) (equity of rewards)	x			x

TABLE 7

Nonfinancial Rewards (Cont.)

	Source			
	Organization	*Supervisor*	*Group*	*Individual*
Uniform administration of system rewards	x			
Feeling of security	x			x
Pleasant working conditions (cleanliness, convenience, safety)	x			
Predictability	x			
Work schedules (hours, shift work)	x			
Treatment of employees	x	x		
Adequacy of training	x	x		
Opportunity for self-improvement	x			
Legitimized decisions (consensual validation of decisions)	x		x	
Participative management (consultative management)	x	x		
Power equalization	x	x	x	
Interaction patterns (amount, duration, source)	x			
Power (power pay)	x			
Influence	x	x	x	
Authority (authority pay)	x			
Status pay	x		x	
Confidence organization has in the individual	x			x
Level in organization	x			
Privilege pay	x			
Knowing important people	x		x	
Opportunity to use knowledge and abilities	x			x
Opportunity for promotion	x			
Recognition of seniority	x		x	
Compatibility of work requirements with other roles	x			x
Supervision (quality of, consideration of, general, low-pressure, democratic, non-punitive, competent, representation of)		x		
Interpersonal relationships with supervisor		x		
Size of work group	x		x	
Power of the work group (influence)			x	
Support from the work group			x	
Group affiliation (identification with group)			x	

TABLE 7

Nonfinancial Rewards (Cont.)

| | *Source* | | | |
	Organization	*Supervisor*	*Group*	*Individual*
Group spirit, pride, solidarity, cohesiveness			x	
Group control of how work is done			x	
Participation in group decisions			x	x
Contributing to group perform-ance			x	x
Sharing in rewards for group accomplishments			x	x
Working with fellow workers as a team			x	
How well group members work together			x	
How much co-workers depend on me			x	
Ethnic makeup of the work group			x	
Mutual likes and dislikes			x	
Acceptance by the work group (co-workers)			x	
Knowledge of one's standing in the work group			x	
Influence in the work group			x	
Status congruence			x	x
Agreement of group norms and organization objectives	x		x	
Association with others (inter-personal relationships, social satisfactions, feeling of be-longing, participation in the social system)			x	
Opportunity for friendships at work (talking to others at work)			x	
Opportunity to meet new people			x	
Seeing fellow workers off the job			x	
Helping others do their job			x	
Liking the organization				x
Union rules and procedures			x	
Shop steward's competence, influence, philosophy			x	
The kind of people who belong to the union			x	

TABLE 7

Nonfinancial Rewards (Cont.)

	Source			
	Organization	*Supervisor*	*Group*	*Individual*
Social activities of the union			x	
How well the union is run			x	
Size, importance, power of the union			x	x
Number of unions in the organization			x	
Interpersonal relations with subordinates			x	
Organization goals have personal value (identification with organization goals, subsystem goals, or professional goals)				x
Relevance of organization goals				x
Compatibility of organization membership with self-image				x
Self-esteem				x
Feeling of having a purpose in life				x
Familiarity with the organization				x
Opportunity to live the kind of life one wants				x
Commuting distance and time				x
Transportation facilities				x
Liking the union				x

(Items in parentheses are assumed to be equivalent to the foregoing item.)

or discomfort, which may be outcomes of the employment exchange. The author prefers, however, to retain the positive connotation of rewards and to think of willingness to accept adverse conditions as a contribution.

The reader will notice that not all the nonfinancial rewards catalogued are clearly distinguished from financial rewards nor from other nonfinancial rewards. A promotion, for example, is clearly both a financial and a nonfinancial reward. Likewise, praise is a form of recognition, but it may imply increased status and enhanced social relationships at work and may result in greater work commitment by the individual.

Because such ambiguities suggest that nonfinancial rewards deserve a great deal more research and analysis, this chapter is limited to emphasizing (1) the vast number and variety of these rewards available for use in the employment exchange, (2) some differences among employee groups in their evaluation of these rewards, and (3) some indications of how organizations can utilize these rewards. To attempt a complete analysis of this form of compensation, however, would require another book.

NONFINANCIAL JOB REWARDS

Table 7 suggests the variety of nonfinancial job rewards that employees may recognize and consider relevant. Many of them are provided by the organization as a result of job design. For example, the work flow system; information flows; the number of operations; the complexity of the work; the skill and attention requirements; and the status, importance, or level of the job may be rewards for many employee groups. Other employee groups may value the predictability of the work, the opportunity to think of other things while working, interruptions in the work, and/or having enough time for personal needs. To some employee groups, the safety features of the job, the cleanliness of the work, and pleasant working conditions are rewards. Some employee groups place value on the quality of the tools and equipment and the quality, value, importance, or usefulness of the product or service of the organization. Clear authority symbols and well-defined rules are rewards to some employee groups. To most people, knowing how their work fits into the total task is an important reward. Some employees place a high value on the opportunity to teach new people. Some place importance on the compatibility of interactions required by the job and their preferred interaction pattern. Some employee groups consider the opportunity to dominate others, to hold authority, and to exercise power over people and situations as important rewards from the job. Some welcome the opportunity to compete with other individuals and groups.

The source of most of the above nonfinancial job rewards is the organization. In some cases, the organization is the sole source of the reward. In others, the supervisor, the work group, and/or the employee himself also provide the reward.

Although little is actually known about which occupational or demographic employee groups place high values on these organization-provided nonfinancial rewards, the reader has probably developed some hypotheses. Some of them may be important to all employee groups. Some of them would appear important to work-committed groups, others to the less committed. Some rewards would appear most important to employee groups strongly affiliated with the organization. Some are obviously reserved for employees at higher levels of the organization.

If particular employee groups place a substantial value on one or more types of nonfinancial job rewards, the organization should know what they are so that the jobs and the organization may be designed to provide them. Many of these rewards appear to be cost-free to the organization. Certainly, designing nonfinancial rewards in terms of the desires of employee groups makes more sense than ignoring the existence of these rewards.

A number of nonfinancial job rewards are provided by the supervisor. Although the influence of the climate of the organization on supervisory practice is well-known, as are the different procedures used in selecting and training supervisors, these rewards are seen by employees to be provided or withheld by the supervisor. Thus, general supervision; low-pressure supervision; democratic supervision; and considerate, fair, nonpunitive supervision may be differentially valued by different employee groups. Likewise, competent supervision and competent representation by supervision may be more important to some employee groups than to others.

Only two nonfinancial job rewards appear to be provided by the work group, *i.e.,* opportunity to develop friendships and acceptance by other people. The relevance of these rewards would not seem to differ greatly among employee groups.

A very large number of nonfinancial job rewards are provided by the employee himself. The importance of these intrinsic rewards would be expected to vary greatly among employee groups. To some employee groups, the emotional significance of the task is an important reward. The job may be seen as a "cause" or a "calling." To other employees, the familiarity of the job is rewarding. Some, perhaps the same employee groups, enjoy the work activity, the energy expenditure, the amount of physical effort involved. To some employees, merely keeping busy is a reward. The feeling of contributing or having a purpose in life is a self-administered nonfinancial job reward to some employee groups. Some groups value the feeling of completion provided by the work. A similar reward is the feeling that the work pulls the individual along. Some employee groups consider the flexibility required by the work a nonfinancial job reward. Other groups value the freedom of movement permitted by their work. Perhaps many kinds of employees place value on seeing the results of their work. Some experience pride in the work results. Some employee groups consider knowing exactly how their tools and equipment operate to be a reward. Some employees appreciate the speed with which time passes at work. It seems certain that the compatibility of the work requirement with other (nonwork) roles is a reward to some employee groups. A more limited set of employee groups value the compatibility of work requirements with their self-image.

Perhaps the most significant feature of nonfinancial job rewards, besides their variety, is that numerous rewards are available to all types of occupational and demographic groups. Not only are rewards available to groups at higher levels of the organization, but also to those in lower-level jobs. There are rewards for those whose work is their life as well as for those whose work is not their central life interest. There are rewards for those affiliated with their field, for those affiliated with the employing organization, and for those whose affiliation to either the field or the organization must be regarded as marginal. Some of the rewards are likely to be valued by all employees. Although it would be possible to hypothesize which rewards are likely to be valued by which group, organization and work force differences could easily refute them. For example, an organization's technology may demand a work force of work-committed people with either managerial or professional ideologies at all organization levels. Conversely, the organization may require only a very limited number of work-committed or highly affiliated members, with most employees' main interests being outside the organization or the work. These two extremes suggest quite different rewards and imply that organizations should design their nonfinancial job rewards for their own work forces.

The sources of nonfinancial job rewards appear, not surprisingly, to be primarily the organization and the employee himself. The supervisor as a source may be underrepresented because the supervisor may influence many of the rewards provided by the organization. The work group does not appear to be a major source of nonfinancial job rewards. The appearance of numerous intrinsic rewards for the job accords with the findings of Herzberg.[6]

NONFINANCIAL PERFORMANCE REWARDS

Although less in number than job rewards, there are many nonfinancial rewards associated with performance. The most well-known, of course, is opportunity for promotion or advancement. But there is little evidence that organizations are careful to associate promotions with performance, even at the managerial level.[7] This is unfortunate because promotions represent an opportunity for the organization to

---

[6]Frederick Herzberg, *Work and the Nature of Man* (Cleveland: The World Publishing Company, 1966).

[7]John P. Campbell, Marvin D. Dunnette, Edward E. Lawler, III, and Karl E. Weick, Jr., *Managerial Behavior, Performance, and Effectiveness* (New York: McGraw-Hill Book Company, 1970), p. 61.

show employees that good performance results in both financial and nonfinancial rewards.

Status is a powerful nonfinancial reward because it is highly valued by all employee groups. Unfortunately, however, although it is potentially a performance reward, organizations typically attach status to organization level rather than to performance.[8] Thus if promotions are not based on performance, both promotions and status are devalued by the organization and also by its members.

Potentially, status may be tied to good performance on all types of work and thus could be offered by the organization to all employee groups. But status may also be conferred by work groups, conceivably on different scales than those used by the organization. If status is provided by the organization and the work group on the basis of performance, it is a powerful incentive. If, however, the work group employs different measuring scales, a reward provided by the organization may be denigrated by the group. If neither the organization nor the work group ties status to performance, status is obviously not a performance reward. Thus, the value of status as a performance reward varies among employee groups.

Recognition may be provided by the organization, the supervisor, or the work group. Like status, the value of recognition is probably widely shared by employee groups. But although recognition is a potential performance reward, it may or may not be, depending on whether recognition is tied to performance and whether the organization, the supervisor, and the work group provide it for the same behavior.

Power and influence may be highly valued performance rewards for most employee groups. These nonfinancial rewards may be provided by the organization, the supervisor, and the work group. Tannenbaum has shown that influence in organizations is not in limited supply but may be increased for all employee groups without decreasing it for any.[9] Thus if influence is tied to performance, it can be a reward for most employee groups.

Participation in problem-solving is likely to be highly valued by some employee groups, but not others. Fortunately, the possibility of tying participation to performance is probably greatest for employee groups that consider participation relevant. Unfortunately, however, organizations do not tie participation to performance, but rather treat it as a membership reward—offering or not offering it to all members.

The opportunity to set performance goals appears similar to participation in relevance to employee groups and in effects. Some em-

[8] *Ibid.,* p. 61.
[9] Arnold S. Tannenbaum, *Social Psychology of the Work Organization* (Belmont, California: Wadsworth Publishing Company, Inc., 1966).

ployee groups welcome the opportunity to set performance goals and react favorably to its use as a performance reward, whereas other groups do not consider it relevant and might resent it. Organizations, however, tend to offer this reward indiscriminately to all groups and do not appear to recognize that it may be a reward to some groups but not to others.

Variety is a nonfinancial reward that may be offered by the organization and may be provided by the individual himself. Not all employee groups or individuals within the groups place a high value on variety. If it is highly valued, organizations can tie increased variety to good performance, but there is little evidence that they do so. Fortunately, as the sociologists have shown,[10] employee groups and individuals who want variety provide it, but not as a performance reward.

Responsibility, autonomy, freedom, and independence are nonfinancial performance rewards provided by the individual himself if the organization offers the opportunity to do so. Some employee groups place high value on these rewards and tend to make the tie to performance wherever the organization permits them to do so. Organizations often provide these rewards to these groups without being aware that they are performance rewards and withhold them from other groups for whom these rewards have high relevance and for whom they would be performance rewards. Less often, organizations attempt to offer these rewards to groups that do not value them and for whom they cannot be performance rewards.

Using one's highest skills and abilities is similar to the preceding rewards in that they are provided by the individual himself if the organization provides the opportunity to do so. The individual also makes the tie between the reward and performance. Employee groups undoubtedly differ greatly in the importance placed on this reward. Remembering the imperfect tie between promotions and performance in most organizations, it can only be hoped that organizations offer the opportunity to use the highest skills and abilities to those who wish to do so and that this opportunity is provided on the basis of performance.

The developmental rewards—developing one's highest skills and abilities and personal growth—are also provided by the individual if the organization and supervisors provide the opportunities. Although not all employee groups place a high value on these rewards, it is probably true that organizations provide the most opportunities to those groups that consider these rewards important. It is probably also true that these same groups tie these rewards to performance. But organizations have

[10]Donald F. Roy, "Banana Time—Job Satisfaction and Informal Interaction," *Human Organization* (Winter, 1959–1960), pp. 158–168.

been less careful in tying these rewards to performance. In many organizations, the developmental rewards are membership rather than performance rewards.

As Herzberg, and what might be called the job design and job enrichment movement, point out, a large number of performance rewards are provided entirely by the individual himself. These intrinsic rewards—feelings of accomplishment, achievement, ego-involvement, self-fulfillment, commitment, challenge, and interest, for example—are nonfinancial rewards that the individual provides himself in accordance with his performance. The organization provides neither the rewards nor the tie to performance. It provides only the arena in which occur the activities that permit these rewards.

Although it is difficult to overestimate the advantage that intrinsic rewards give to organizations, the major question is the employee groups that provide themselves with these rewards. Advocates of job enrichment appear to believe that all employee groups place a high value on these rewards.[11] Others have found considerable differences among employee groups in the value placed on these rewards.[12] The most reasonable possibility appears to be that some work-committed groups consider these rewards to be highly relevant. At the other extreme there are undoubtedly groups to whom work is chiefly instrumental in achieving other goals. It is theoretically possible, but not very likely, for an organization to select only members who value these rewards highly.

Other intrinsic performance rewards are feelings of self-control and identification with organization goals. Both of these may be considered highly relevant by some employee groups, but not by others. Organizations are probably fortunate that this is the case.

A final nonfinancial performance reward suggested in Table 7 is self-respect or feeling of esteem. This reward is provided by both the individual himself and the work group and would seem to be highly relevant to most employee groups. But for many employee groups it is quite possible that the tie between the reward and performance is quite tenuous and organizations might be hard-pressed to provide it.

Perhaps the most significant feature of nonfinancial performance rewards is that they consist primarily of intrinsic rewards that sometimes depend on the organization's providing an opportunity for the individual to reward himself, but often are quite independent of the organization. Another significant feature of these rewards is that they

[11]M. Scott Myers, "Every Employee a Manager," *California Management Review* (Spring, 1968), pp. 9–20.

[12]Charles L. Hulin and Milton R. Blood, "Job Enlargement, Individual Differences, and Worker Responses," *Psychological Bulletin* (January, 1968), pp. 41–55.

are probably extremely important to some employee groups but not to others. Finally, nonfinancial performance rewards provided by the organization and supervisors are frequently not closely tied to performance and may in fact be perceived by employees as membership rather than as performance rewards.

NONFINANCIAL MEMBERSHIP REWARDS

By far the largest number of nonfinancial rewards are associated with membership in the organization rather than with the job or performance. As in the case of economic rewards, most of the rewards are designed to maintain the organization—to get and keep members. This conclusion may be a source of surprise to managers, but if the analysis on which Table 7 was built is sound, it is hard to dispute. It is probably also true that organizations are not aware that many of these nonfinancial membership rewards are present in the employment exchange.

Many of the rewards arise from characteristics of the organization. For example, organization size, prestige, visibility, importance, and level of profits may be rewards to many employee groups. Even the age of the organization may be a reward.

Other organization-provided rewards are associated with the way the organization is run. Instances of these rewards are the flexibility of the organization, organization policies and procedures, the extent of decentralization employed, the extent of delegation of authority, the clarity of authority symbols, the work flow system, the communications system, and conflict resolution methods. Although the relevance of these rewards may vary among employee groups, they may also be important to all members. Management competence, another reward in this category, may be highly valued by all employee groups.

A large number of rewards involve the organization's relations with employees. Well-defined rules, for example, are a valued reward to some employee groups. Pleasant working conditions are important to most employee groups.

An important reward to all employees in some organizations and to certain employee groups in others is a feeling of security. A number of unpublished studies conducted by the author and a colleague to determine the importance employees assign to various rewards suggest that some organizations have members at all levels who value security highly, that other organizations have members some of whom consider security important whereas other groups do not, and that some organizations are made up of members who attach a low importance to security. But it appears hazardous to predict from either occupational or demographic characteristics which employee group will highly value security.

A nonfinancial reward that appears to be of increasing importance to all employee groups in most organizations is the justice determination system. It appears that today's labor force expects evaluation by fair standards, fairness in the evaluation process, equity in the reward process, and uniform administration of membership rewards. In fact, it has been suggested that organizations may in the near future have to offer an explicit justice determination process, including final determination by an independent, impartial person, to attract members.[13]

Some employee groups place a high value on the predictability of life in the organization. Others may consider the work schedule as an important reward—scheduled working hours and the presence or absence of shift work, for example. Most employee groups place a high value on the general treatment accorded employees by the organization and the supervisor.

The adequacy of training programs and the opportunity for self-improvement are rewards valued differentially by employee groups in most organizations. Many managers, for example, consider the quality of the management development program as part of their rewards. Organizations have discovered that providing employees with more training than the job requires may be valued by employees as evidence of the employer's interest in a long-term employment exchange.

Some employee groups place a high value on consensual validation of decisions, participative or consultative management, and what is often called power equalization in the organization. As pointed out previously, however, it appears to be a mistake to assume that all employee groups consider these rewards important.

The customary interaction patterns required or permitted by the work of the organization may be highly valued by employees. It has been shown that the compatibility of interactions required (in amount, duration, and source) and the pattern preferred by the individual is rewarding to many people.[14]

It is often assumed that power, influence, and status are rewards that must be reserved by the organization to particular employee groups. But as Tannenbaum's work (cited previously) has shown, influence may be dispensed much more broadly with advantages to organizations. Likewise, Dubin, as previously mentioned, has shown that

[13]Phillip Selznick, *Law, Society, and Industrial Justice* (New York: Russell Sage Foundation, 1969).

[14]William Foote Whyte, *Organizational Behavior* (Homewood, Illinois: Richard D. Irwin, Inc., and The Dorsey Press, 1969); Eliot D. Chapple and Leonard R. Sayles, *The Measure of Management* (New York: The Macmillan Company, 1961).

what he calls power pay, authority pay, status pay, and privilege pay may be valued rewards to all employees. Observation of any organization suggests that organization level is a reward highly valued by employees. Knowing important people is a relevant reward to many employees. The confidence that the organization displays in the individual is highly valued by many people in most employee groups.

The opportunity to use one's knowledge and skills is a highly valued reward to some employee groups. In fact, observation suggests that this reward may quite often be a good substitute for economic rewards. Most of us know someone who apparently chose an employing organization on the basis of this reward rather than money.

The opportunity for promotion was discussed previously as a potential performance reward. Evidence concerning the manner in which most organizations administer promotion programs, however, suggests that the typical organization holds out the opportunity for promotion as a reward to all employee groups in return for continued membership. Given the desire of most people for increased status, organizations in which the major problem is membership motivation rather than performance motivation may be following the wiser course.

Recognition of seniority or length of service is a major reward for some employee groups in most organizations and for all employee groups in some organizations. Although industrial unions are often criticized for their emphasis on seniority, it is difficult to believe that the emphasis would prevail without positive employee evaluation. And certainly unions cannot be blamed for the use of seniority in nonunion organizations, nor in management circles. Gardner's suggestion[15] that the evaluative criteria of merit and equality continually compete in our society may better explain how seniority may be a valued reward to some members of all employee groups.

The compatibility of work requirements with other roles may be an important reward to some employee groups. Certainly, to employee groups to which work does not represent a central life interest, it is a valued reward. But if the characterizations of the new labor force and of typical life styles involving an almost complete separation of work, family, political, religious, and recreational institutions are correct, this reward will certainly become more important to most people, with the possible exception of professionals.

The primary source of the nonfinancial membership rewards discussed up to this point is the employing organization. Some of them are also provided by the supervisor and by the work group. A few of them are also intrinsic rewards in the sense that both the organization and the individual must provide them before they become rewards.

[15]John W. Gardner, *Excellence* (New York: Harper & Row, 1961).

As mentioned in the preceding section, the supervisor is probably underrepresented as a source of these rewards. Many of these organization-provided rewards may not become visible unless the supervisor is perceived as making them available. There are also a number of nonfinancial membership rewards that are provided solely by the supervisor. For example, general supervision, quality of supervision, the consideration shown by supervision, low-pressure supervision, democratic supervision, nonpunitive supervision, competent supervision, and representation by supervision may be highly valued rewards to particular employee groups. Likewise, interpersonal relations with the supervisor may be an important reward to some employee groups but not to others.

For most employee groups, the work group may be as likely a source of nonfinancial membership rewards as the organization. For these employee groups, the size of the work group; the power and influence of the work group; identification with the work group; group spirit, pride, solidarity, cohesiveness; group control of how work is done; participation in group decisions; contributing to group performances; sharing in rewards for group accomplishment; working with fellow workers as a team; how well group members work together; how much co-workers depend on the individual; the ethnic makeup of the work group; and mutual likes and dislikes held by the work group may be highly valued rewards. Although employees may well place different values on these rewards, it would seem to be folly to suggest that some employees do not consider these group-provided rewards important, given the proclivity of work groups to form as a result of interactions required by the work.[16] It seems significant that March and Simon suggest that work groups strongly influence not only the rewards that individuals perceive, but also which rewards they value and how much they value them.[17]

Additional possible nonfinancial membership rewards from the work group are acceptance by the work group, knowledge of one's standing in the work group, and influence in the work group. Status congruence may be conferred by or fought for and obtained by the group. For some employee groups, agreement between group norms and organization objectives is an important reward.

A number of interpersonal rewards may be provided by members of the work group—association with others, feeling of belonging, oppor-

[16]Leonard R. Sayles, *Behavior of Industrial Work Groups* (New York: John Wiley & Sons, Inc., 1958); George Strauss and Leonard R. Sayles, *Personnel,* 2nd ed. (Englewood Cliffs, N.J.: Prentice-Hall, Inc., 1967); Joe Kelly, *Organizational Behaviour* (Homewood, Illinois: Richard D. Irwin, Inc., and The Dorsey Press, 1969).

[17]James G. March and Herbert A. Simon, *Organizations* (New York: John Wiley & Sons, Inc., 1958), Chapter 3.

tunity for friendships at work, opportunity to meet new people, the opportunity to help others, seeing fellow workers off the job, are examples. Although the importance of these rewards undoubtedly varies among individuals, it would seem silly to hypothesize that they are unimportant to any employee group. Supervisors may place great value on interpersonal relationships with subordinates.

A number of nonfinancial membership rewards are provided by the union. Although it is obvious that unions and work groups are no more identical than work groups and employing organizations, for present purposes perhaps not too much understanding will be lost by assuming that rewards provided by the union are provided by a large group of employees. Some of the union-provided rewards are union rules and procedures; the competence, influence, and philosophy of shop stewards; the kind of people who belong to the union; social activities of the union; how well the union is run; the size, importance, and power of the union; and the number of unions in the organization. Although these rewards are available only to members of the bargaining unit, they may vary greatly in importance to members of this group. It should not be assumed, however, that these rewards are valued by and available only to blue-collar workers. In some organizations professional employees are organized and in Great Britain, lower levels of management.[18]

Finally, there are a number of nonfinancial membership rewards provided by the employee himself. For example, liking the company; identifying with organization goals, subsystem goals, or professional goals; perceived relevance of organization goals; compatibility of organization membership with self-image; and self-esteem may be relevant rewards for many employee groups. Others, such as feeling of having a purpose in life, familiarity with the organization, opportunity to live the kind of life one wants, commuting distance and time, transportation facilities, and liking the union may be valued rewards to some employee groups but not to others.

Nonfinancial membership rewards are apparently sufficiently numerous and varied to provide a positive balance to the employment exchange for all occupational and demographic groups. Some of them appear relevant to all employees. Others seem obviously designed for particular employee groups. Most of the membership rewards are provided by the organization, but a very substantial number are provided by work groups and the union. In the list are even a limited number of intrinsic rewards for membership.

[18]Kelly, *Organizational Behaviour;* see also Alfred T. DeMaria, Dale Tarnowieski, and Richard Gurman, *Manager Unions?* (New York: American Management Association, 1972) for suggestions that manager unions may be forthcoming in the U.S.

ADMINISTERING NONFINANCIAL REWARDS

Both the membership motivation and the performance motivation models presented in Chapter 3 emphasized that to be a reward an outcome from the employment exchange must be recognized and considered relevant by the employee. Thus the first obvious requirement in administering nonfinancial rewards is that organizations be aware of the nonfinancial rewards provided in the employment exchange and of the importance placed on the different rewards by different employee groups. The performance motivation model also indicated that in order for a reward to incite a particular kind of behavior, the employee must believe that the behavior will lead to the kind of rewards he desires. Consequently, a second requirement in administering nonfinancial rewards is that organizations concern themselves with the behavior-reward connections and attempt to tie the rewards the different employee groups value to the kinds of behavior the organization needs. As was pointed out in the preceding section, some nonfinancial rewards are potential rewards for the job, others for membership (getting and keeping employees), and still others for performance. An additional complication is that only part of these rewards is provided by the organization. The balance is provided by the supervisor, the work group, and the individual himself.

Nonfinancial rewards for the job and for membership have been typically ignored rather than administered by organizations. Most organizations appear unaware of them or, if aware, ignore them. Perhaps because they conceive of the employment exchange as solely an economic transaction, they are not aware of nonfinancial rewards. Even if aware of nonfinancial job and membership rewards, organizations may assume that job incumbency and organization membership behaviors are minimal contributions purchased by economic rewards and relatively unaffected by nonfinancial rewards. Thus they may see the nonfinancial job and membership rewards as behaviorally neutral even though they may recognize that the organization, the supervisors, work groups, and employees themselves may provide employees with nonfinancial rewards.

But the facts of the matter are quite different. The different employee groups want quite different nonfinancial rewards in return for job incumbency and organization membership, and ignoring nonfinancial rewards or attempting to treat all employee groups alike may mean that some groups are provided rewards they don't consider relevant whereas other groups are so underrewarded that only marginal people join or remain in the organization. Because nonfinancial rewards can partially substitute for economic rewards,[19] the organization may be wasting resources while attracting and keeping only marginal members in some employee groups. This implies that organizations must pay as much attention to nonfinancial job and membership rewards as to economic rewards in order to attract and keep the kinds of members it wants in all employee groups.

Organizations are much more likely to be aware of the potential nonfinancial performance rewards but no more likely to administer them effectively. The major administrative deficiency is the failure to tie these rewards to performance. As pointed out previously, promotion —one of the most powerful nonfinancial (as well as financial) rewards —is not unambiguously related to performance in organizations. Other organization-provided performance rewards such as status, recognition, and responsibility are often likely to be based on organization membership or job incumbency rather than performance.

Fortunately for organizations, most of the nonfinancial performance rewards are intrinsic (provided by the individual himself), and if employees value these rewards and if the jobs are designed to permit them, employees reward themselves for performance. But because it is doubtful that all employee groups consider these rewards important, administration is still essential. Also, although employees who value these rewards want to believe that these rewards are tied to effective performance, the organization could conceivably destroy this belief by designing the jobs of those who do not value these rewards and the jobs of ineffective performers to permit them to receive the same rewards as effective performers. Presumably strong evidence that intrinsic rewards go to all employees could destroy the performance-reward connection.

Thus, it appears that all nonfinancial rewards require much more attention from employing organizations than they have received. Just as in the case of economic rewards, particular nonfinancial rewards must be offered to those employee groups that consider them important and they must be tied to the kinds of behavior the organization requires.

ORGANIZATION REWARD ANALYSIS

A first step in administering nonfinancial rewards is for the organization to think through the nonfinancial rewards it can and wishes to make available to each employee group. Some organizations may wish to continue the employment exchange as a purely economic transac-

[19]Lawler, *Pay and Organizational Effectiveness,* p. 216.

tion. Other organizations, because of their traditions or technology, may find that the nonfinancial rewards they can offer are severely limited. Some organizations may decide that their technology and work force demand that numerous nonfinancial rewards be made available to all employee groups. Most organizations will presumably decide to offer different nonfinancial rewards to different employee groups.

The nonfinancial rewards made available by organizations will consist of the three categories discussed above—job, performance, and membership. If our analysis of economic rewards applies to nonfinancial rewards as well, many organizations will decide to offer job and membership rewards to most employee groups and to reserve performance rewards to high-level, organizationally-committed employee groups. Some organizations may decide to offer nonfinancial rewards of all three types to all employee groups.

SURVEYS OF EMPLOYEE PREFERENCES

A second step in administering nonfinancial rewards is to survey employee desires for particular nonfinancial rewards. Porter and Lawler suggest such an approach for managers and offer a survey instrument that they have found useful in research.[20] Their approach is to ask respondents three questions concerning each possible reward: How much is there now? How much should there be? How important is this to me? A seven-step scale is provided for each response.

The author and a colleague have applied the approach to separate employee groups in the same organizations and to distinct occupational and demographic groups in dissimilar organizations.[21] Without exception, the results have shown that employee groups assign quite different importance to the rewards. Our research has shown that combining the first two questions into a discrepancy question (plus and minus) and using the importance question yields similar results and facilitates analysis.

For research purposes the number of reward items has been limited to twenty or less. But there appears to be no reason why an organization conducting a survey of its employees could not use a much larger number. As mentioned previously, Dubin was successful in obtaining employee responses to over 100 items.

---

[20]Lyman W. Porter and Edward E. Lawler, III, *Managerial Attitudes and Performance* (Homewood, Illinois: Richard D. Irwin, Inc., 1968), pp. 174 and 190–192.

[21]See D. W. Belcher and T. J. Atchison, "Equity Theory and Compensation Policy," *Personnel Administration* (July–August, 1970), pp. 22–33; T. J. Atchison and D. W. Belcher, "Equity, Rewards & Compensation Administration," *Personnel Administration* (March–April, 1971), pp. 32–36; and a number of unpublished studies.

EMPLOYEE SELECTION

Reward preference surveys not only show the rewards that employee groups value, but also permit a comparison between the rewards employees want and those that the organization can and will make available. Discrepancies may be met by changes in organization reward systems to meet the preferences of employee groups or by selecting employees who value the rewards the organization wants to make available. Lawler[22] has suggested that organizations that wish to use a merit pay system select people who place a high value on pay. There seems to be no good reason why an organization cannot select people who place a high value on the rewards the organization wants to offer, perhaps by using a variation of the employee preference survey instrument in selection.

Undoubtedly, however, the organization, when making a reward preference survey, will discover that a good deal of self-selection has occurred in the organization so that the employees who stay are those who value the rewards that the organization makes available. Employees of organizations known to offer a great deal of security, for example, turn out in our research to place a high value on security.

As the organization reward analysis section suggested, however, most organizations probably want to offer different rewards to different employee groups. It is doubtful if any organization really wants security-oriented employees in management. Self-selection would seem to yield organization effectiveness only if the organization had planned the reward system of the separate employee groups. Certainly, offering the same nonfinancial rewards to all employees or ignoring them can yield appropriate self-selection only by chance.

JOB DESIGN

Job design or redesign is the most frequently suggested approach to administering nonfinancial rewards in organizations. Broadly speaking, this approach involves designing jobs to provide the incumbent with rewards other than economic.

Actually, what might be called the job design movement has been evolving for a number of years and deals with varying kinds of nonfinancial rewards. Davis, who appears to hold the broadest view of job design, pointed out in an early article that organizations typically design jobs guided by narrow economic criteria and custom, with the result that people find them boring and stultifying; jobs, he stated, should be designed to meet a much broader set of organizational, technical, and

---

[22]Lawler, *Pay and Organizational Effectiveness,* pp. 177 and 67–70.

personal criteria to achieve both organization objectives and individual motivation.[23] Davis argues that designing jobs by following the logic of the industrial engineer has resulted in jobs that are not only uninteresting and demotivating for people, but also, on balance, costly for the organization. Analysis of case studies involving job design and redesign following this broad view suggests that the nonfinancial rewards made available to employees include some from all three categories (job, performance, and membership) and are provided by the organization, supervisors, work groups, and the employee himself.[24] Davis' approach in specifying individual as well as organizational and technical criteria in the design of jobs implies that different employee groups require different job designs. In fact, his recent work suggests that jobs be restructured in terms of (1) getting untutored, unskilled individuals into productive work; (2) the needs and desires of organization members; and (3) making jobs a stage in an integrated career.[25] The concept of redesigning jobs in terms of the needs and desires of available manpower has been implemented by the Manpower Administration, U.S. Department of Labor.[26]

Proponents of job enlargement and job enrichment appear to have a somewhat more limited perspective of job design in that they imply that the nonfinancial rewards that become available through the design of jobs are intrinsic rewards for performance. Herzberg, for example, insists that job enrichment, because it provides rewards of achievement, growth, and recognition, is the only route to performance motivation.[27] Myers also implies that job enrichment provides intrinsic performance rewards for all employee groups.[28] It has also been suggested that job enrichment is a requirement for meeting the changing values of youth.[29]

In fact, job design may have come to be largely synonomous with job enlargement and job enrichment and call for designing jobs to permit the individual to reward himself for good performance. To ac-

[23]Louis E. Davis, "Toward a Theory of Job Design," *The Journal of Industrial Engineering* (September–October, 1957), pp. 305–309.

[24]Louis E. Davis, "The Design of Jobs," *Industrial Relations* (October, 1966), pp. 21–45.

[25]Louis E. Davis, "Restructuring Jobs for Social Goals," *Manpower* (February, 1970), pp. 3–6; Louis E. Davis, "Job Satisfaction Research: The Post-Industrial View," *Industrial Relations* (May, 1971), pp. 176–193.

[26]See *A Handbook for Job Restructuring* (Washington, D.C.: U.S. Government Printing Office, 1970).

[27]Frederick Herzberg, "One More Time: How do you Motivate Employees?" *Harvard Business Review* (January–February, 1968), pp. 53–62.

[28]M. Scott Myers, "Every Employee a Manager," *California Management Review* (Spring, 1968), pp. 9–20.

[29]Gloria Cowen, "The Changing Values of Youth," *Personnel Administration* (November–December, 1971), pp. 21–27.

complish this result it is suggested that jobs be designed so that (1) the individual receives meaningful feedback on his performance, (2) the job is perceived by the individual as requiring him to use abilities that he values, and (3) the individual feels that he has a high degree of self-control over setting his own work goals and defining the paths to these goals.[30] Operationally this may require changing jobs in the horizontal dimension (the number and variety of operations), the vertical dimension (planning, decision-making), or both.

As Lawler points out, however, individuals differ in whether or not they place a high value on these rewards and in whether they believe they should reward themselves for quality or quantity of performance. If members of some work groups do not place a high value on these intrinsic rewards, they cannot result in improved performance. If the performance for which employees reward themselves is improved quality rather than increased quantity but the organization requires the latter, job design does not provide performance rewards. Lawler's review of ten job enlargement studies showed that all resulted in higher quality work but only four out of ten led to higher productivity.

The National Industrial Conference Board defines job design quite similarly but includes rewards provided by the group in the nonfinancial rewards available from enlarged or enriched jobs by assigning much planning and decision-making to the work group.[31] The assumption here also is that the work group highly values these intrinsic rewards. It may also be worth pointing out that in our analysis of nonfinancial rewards, rewards provided by the group were likely to be associated with membership rather than with performance.

The concept of job design employed by Davis accords with that of the Tavistock Institute of Great Britain and employed in Europe. A group of case studies in Norway show that planning and decision-making by the work group is an integral part of the approach, as are group reward systems. In addition, individual workers are paid extra for each additional skill they acquire regardless of the job they are performing at the moment. Although the successful situations do report increases in productivity, an apparent ubiquitous result of successful experiments is reduced turnover and absenteeism.[32] Job enrichment programs in the Bell system in this country also appear to result in reduced turnover.[33] These results suggest that the rewards from job redesign involv-

[30]Edward E. Lawler, III, "Job Design and Employee Motivation," *Personnel Psychology* (Winter, 1969), pp. 426–435.
[31]Harold M. F. Rush, *Job Design for Motivation* (New York: The Conference Board, Inc., 1971).
[32]Eileen Mackenzie, "Job Design in an Industrial Democracy," *International Management* (August, 1971).
[33]Harry Holloway, "Job Enrichment and the Bell System," *The Personnel Administrator* (July–August, 1971), pp. 28–30.

ing employees at lower levels of the organization can be membership and job rewards for the employees involved even if they are not performance rewards.

But the research evidence shows that job enlargement procedures increase attendance and sometimes productivity only if applied to certain work groups. White-collar employees, supervisory workers, and rural or small-town blue-collar workers may react positively to job enlargement. Positive reactions appear much less predictable for urban blue-collar workers.[34] Those who are tempted to experiment with job enrichment and job enlargement as a panacea for performance motivation for all types of employees need to be reminded that the research evidence shows that *some* people doing *some* lines of work respond to the opportunity to participate in determining how this work is done with higher productivity. But even these people do not respond to nonfinancial rewards alone.[35]

In fact, there is some evidence that the combination of financial and nonfinancial performance rewards that are characteristic of the employment exchange represent another dilemma of compensation administration. Deci, as reported by Vroom,[36] has conducted some experiments in which students were first provided with only intrinsic rewards for a task; second, were paid on a wage incentive plan; and third, returned to the intrinsic-rewards-only condition with the result that pay increased performance when offered but decreased performance when it was withdrawn. Although these results are difficult to interpret, they may mean that economic performance rewards can reduce the performance motivation value of nonfinancial rewards.

Job Design and the Motivation Models. The models presented in Chapter 3 should help us attain some perspective on how organizations can use job design to achieve membership and performance motivation. The membership motivation model shows that any reward that the employee recognizes and considers relevant enters the employment exchange and that the combination of these rewards when compared to contributions produces a positive balance that results in the membership decision. Any nonfinancial reward made available by job design can increase membership motivation if the employee values it and if it serves to increase the total of his perceived rewards. Thus designing jobs so that employee groups get more of the nonfinancial

---

[34]Hulin and Blood, in *Psychological Bulletin* (January, 1968), pp. 41–55.

[35]See Martin Patchen, "Participation in Decision-Making and Motivation," *Personnel Administration* (November, 1964), pp. 24–31; George Strauss and Eliezier Rosenstein, "Workers Participation: A Critical View," *Industrial Relations* (February, 1970), pp. 197–214.

[36]Victor H. Vroom, "The Effects of Extrinsic Rewards on Intrinsic Motivation," a paper presented at the Western Psychological Association (San Francisco, April 24, 1971, mimeographed).

rewards they want, other things being equal, should reduce absentee-ism and turnover. But designing jobs to provide nonfinancial rewards that employees do not value should have no effect or might even reduce the balance.

The performance motivation model shows that job design must not only provide rewards that employees value, but that employees must believe that (1) increased effort will result in improved perfor-mance, and (2) improved performance will result in more of these rewards. Moreover, these relationships are multiplicative so that if the value attached to the reward or either of the beliefs is zero, perform-ance motivation will be zero. Thus if any employee group does not value the nonfinancial rewards that the design of the job makes attain-able, or does not believe that increased effort will improve performance or that improved performance will mean obtaining the reward, job design cannot motivate performance in that group. In some employee groups, positive values on all three variables are quite likely, but in others are almost impossible to obtain.

Administering the Design of Jobs.   Both motivation models show that administering job design requires that the organization (1) think through what nonfinancial rewards it wishes to and can make available to employee groups, (2) determine what rewards each employee group values, and (3) build a reward system for each employee group that matches (1) and (2) and is designed to motivate membership in some employee groups and both membership and performance motivation in others. Although organizations and their work forces are extremely diverse, it may be useful to suggest some of the possibilities.

Small organizations in advanced technology may find that they can design jobs for all levels of employees that provide nonfinancial performance rewards. Assuming that all employees value these rewards and that the organization can create the appropriate effort-perform-ance and performance-reward beliefs, the organization may find that it can create a single reward system that motivates both membership and performance. But small organizations in more prosaic technologies will probably have to design one reward system for management made up largely of performance rewards, and another for nonmanagerial employees consisting entirely of job and membership rewards. Manage-rial employees are likely to hold the positive beliefs that performance motivation requires unless the organization is at pains to destroy them. But nonmanagerial employees may place no importance at all on the performance rewards but highly value some of the job and membership rewards.

Larger organizations, probably regardless of technology, will need a number of quite different reward systems. The managerial reward system will consist primarily of performance rewards. The reward system for professionals will be similar but may be different for those from whom organization commitment is expected and for those who are committed to their professional field. The reward system for other white-collar groups may consist of performance, job, and membership rewards. For sales groups, performance rewards may be emphasized. But for clerical groups, although organizations may be able to design jobs to provide performance rewards and these employees may want them, beliefs in the effort-performance and performance-reward relationships may be just too difficult to maintain. If so, the reward system of clerical employees will consist of job and membership rewards. The reward system for production employees will in these organizations presumably be confined to job and membership rewards. In fact, they may often consist mainly of membership rewards provided by the work group or, when provided by the organization, consist of those signifying the compatibility of work and other roles. The point is that the design of jobs to make nonfinancial rewards available to employees involves designing a significant part of the reward system and, as such, must be designed in terms of both organization objectives and the desires of different employee groups.

As part of the reward system—in fact, a very significant portion for some employee groups—it is important that job design be coordinated with other rewards. For this reason, the compensation administrator must be involved in job design as well as in determining economic rewards. Coordination is essential to ensure that the financial and nonfinancial rewards combine positively for each employee group in order to motivate membership. Coordination is even more important, however, in connection with performance motivation in that it is not what the organization says but what it does that creates the performance-reward belief. Here, at least, action speaks louder than words.

In suggesting the possibilities of reward systems for organizations, the broad categories of job, performance, and membership rewards were used rather than the specific and widely varying nonfinancial rewards within each category. It should be understood, however, that in designing jobs to provide nonfinancial rewards, the elements are the specific rewards. For example, both logic and a good deal of research suggest that the compatibility of interactions required by the job and the preferred interaction pattern of individuals is an important nonfinancial job reward.[37] Jobs designed to provide this compatibility and to contain this reward offer an additional reward, whereas those that do not have presumably lowered the total rewards of the employee.

[37]Whyte, *Organizational Behavior.*

ADMINISTERING OTHER NONFINANCIAL REWARDS

Not all the nonfinancial rewards are specified through job design. Others are specified through the policies and procedures of the organization. Although the requirements for securing membership and performance motivation are exactly the same as those specified in the discussion of job design, some of these rewards appear to call for some attention.

Promotion, for example, can be a powerful performance reward for most, if not all, employee groups. But to be a performance reward, employees must believe that good performance is the route to it. As mentioned previously, organizations have not been very successful in fostering this belief, even among managers, usually because their actions speak louder than their words. Organizations would be wise to think through the employee groups for which they wish to make promotion a performance reward and for those for whom they wish it to be a membership reward and administer promotions accordingly. Telling employees that promotion is a reward for performance but actually tying promotions to length of service or some other nonperformance variable not only destroys the performance-reward belief for promotions but probably makes the belief difficult to inculcate for other rewards.

Status symbols are another potentially powerful performance reward, but few organizations use them in this way. In most organizations status symbols are tied to organization level rather than performance. Thus, if promotion is not administered as a performance reward, status symbols are not a performance reward either.

Numerous opportunities are available to organizations to tie several other nonfinancial rewards to performance, at least for certain groups. For example, the opportunity for the individual to schedule his own hours of work or to accrue time off to be spent in personal development or community activities would be a powerful performance reward for certain groups.[38] Likewise, the opportunity to work in other segments of the organization or even other organizations for a time might be made rewards for performance for certain employee groups.

But it is equally important for organizations to devote attention to job and membership rewards. The analysis that produced the classification of nonfinancial rewards employed in this chapter shows that rewards from supervisors, work groups, and the individual himself can become available for job incumbency and membership in the organization. This suggests that organization policies and procedures be admin-

---

[38]See Margaret A. Howell, "Time Off as a Reward for Productivity," *Personnel Administration* (November–December, 1971), pp. 48–51.

istered to make these rewards visible to those employee groups to which they are relevant. Efforts to upgrade the quality of supervision can become job rewards for supervisors and membership rewards for subordinates.[39] Work groups are such an important source of membership rewards that organizations might give serious thought to giving certain groups at least a voice in selecting new members. More attention should also be given to designing physical working conditions for groups to which working conditions are important rewards. Organizations that can offer a large measure of security and have attracted many employees who value it would be wise to make it a visible reward for employee groups that consider it important and obviously remove it for groups that do not.

REINFORCEMENT SCHEDULES

Designing reward systems to secure the kind of behavior the organization wants suggests the applicability of operant conditioning.[40] The basic process in operant conditioning is obtaining the desired behavior by selectively reinforcing already existing behavior in such a manner as to insure the desired response. The process, called shaping, involves initially rewarding almost any behavior and, by progressive steps, requiring closer approximations of the desired behavior to obtain the reward. Organizations usually employ just the opposite approach in administering rewards, in that most rewards are provided for almost any behavior or withheld completely.

Operant conditioning suggests that organizations administer reward systems so as to help people learn the desired behaviors and to maintain them by scheduling the rewards. Possible reward schedules are (1) continuous reinforcement (reward every correct response); (2) fixed-ratio (reinforce every nth response); (3) fixed-interval (reinforce after a specific period of time); (4) variable-ratio (vary the ratio of reinforcement around an average); and (5) variable-interval (vary the time interval of reinforcement around some average time period). A graphic example of the effectiveness of the variable schedules is easily observable at the slot machines in Las Vegas.

Organizations have made very little use of operant conditioning in designing reward systems. But a few have. One organization reduced tardiness and absenteeism by making all employees with perfect attendance for a month eligible for a drawing that yielded one prize for every twenty-five employees and also held a drawing for a larger prize

[39]J. A. Belasco and H. Trice, "Unanticipated Returns of Training," *Training and Development Journal* (July, 1969), pp. 12–17.
[40]B. F. Skinner, *Science and Human Behavior* (New York: Free Press, 1967).

for which all employees with six months of perfect, punctual attendance were eligible.[41] Fixed-interval attendance rewards have been employed as well[42] but there appears to be no reason why still other schedules could not be used for nonfinancial rewards.

Emery Air Freight Corporation is reported to be successfully using operant conditioning by improving feedback of operating results to employees and by using praise and recognition to improve performance. Reports of interest by other organizations in operant conditioning and reinforcement schedules suggest that reward systems of the future will be designed to achieve the behavior desired rather than be copied from other organizations.[43]

[41]Walter Nord, "Improving Attendance Through Rewards," *Personnel Administration* (November–December, 1970), pp. 37–41.

[42]E. E. Lawler and J. R. Hackman, "Impact of Employee Participation in the Development of Pay Incentive Plans: A Field Experiment," *Journal of Applied Psychology* (December, 1969), pp. 467–471.

[43]"New Tool: 'Reinforcement' for Good Work," *Business Week* (December 18, 1971), pp. 76–77.

The Comparison Process

Completion or continuation of the employment exchange logically requires not only rewards and contributions but a comparison
process whereby both parties (employers and employees) evaluate the
projected rewards and contributions and the balance between them.
The comparison process involves a decision on the rewards and contributions to be compared, a comparison standard, and presumably some
decision rules with respect to the appropriate balance between rewards
and contributions. Like the process of determining the relevant and
important contributions and rewards, the comparison process is perceptual in that each party makes the comparisons he deems appropriate
and his decision determines whether he will make or continue the
employment exchange.

The chapters in Part IV focus on the comparison process. Chapter
16 contrasts the comparisons made by organizations with those made
by employees and offers some suggestions on how they may be brought
closer together. Chapters 17, 18, and 19 examine typical comparison
standards used by organizations (compensation policy; wage, salary, and
benefit surveys; and wage criteria) and outline what research and theory suggest would bring the resulting comparisons closer to those made
by employees.

The basic assumption of Part IV is that the employment exchange
can more closely approach the desires of both parties if what is being
compared and comparison standards are similar. Although recognizing
that the employment exchange works because each party places different values on what is being exchanged, it assumes that differences in

415

what is compared and differing comparison standards if they result in an employment exchange produce one that is unstable and fraught with conflict.

16

Comparison Standards

In determining whether or not the employment exchange is to be made or continued, both employers and employees make use of some comparison standards to evaluate rewards and contributions and the balance between them. Both parties presumably engage in a comparison process that involves a decision on what to compare, the use of some comparison standards, and some decision rules to determine whether or not the employment exchange is to be made or continued.

Just as in the case of determining the relevance and importance of rewards and contributions, appropriate comparisons are perceptual —they exist in the eyes of the beholder. Thus it is not only possible but quite likely that the employer and the employee will differentially perceive the rewards and contributions to be compared and which comparison standards are appropriate.

Although some evidence exists of what organizations compare and somewhat less about how they do so, much less is known about the comparison practices of individuals. What little is known about the comparison process of individuals suggests that they compare a broader range of rewards and contributions than organizations and employ quite different comparison standards. But it must be emphasized that the comparisons made by both parties must be largely inferred from observed behavior and from theory that needs additional testing.

This chapter examines the comparison process of organizations and of employees. Although organizations would seem to differ in what and how they compare, organization compensation practices suggest that what organizations compare and how they do so are largely similar.

But although the limited evidence suggests an underlying similarity in comparisons made by employees, there are vast differences among employee groups that carry important implications for organization compensation practices. Thus an attempt is made in this chapter to differentiate employee groups in terms of the comparison standards they employ. Finally, some suggestions are offered of what organizations may be able to do to better integrate employee comparisons with organization comparisons. Unless organization and employee comparisons are made on similar grounds, securing both membership motivation and performance motivation may be difficult.

ORGANIZATION COMPARISONS

What organizations compare and how they compare is evidenced by organization compensation practices and studies by labor economists of wage determination. This evidence shows that organizations use other organizations and internal relationships among jobs as comparison standards. Other organizations in the industry or area are the primary standard,[1] but the results of these comparisons are interpreted in terms of organization policy. Conditions in product and labor markets are also employed as standards as well as more general economic criteria (cost of living, ability to pay, productivity, minimum budgets).[2] These comparison standards employed by organizations are external to the organization and the data compared are economic. The organizations employed as comparison standards are chosen by the organization making the comparison, but interpretations of the results of the comparisons may be influenced by organization policy, economic conditions, and union pressures.

Furthermore, organization comparisons are of rewards and are limited primarily to economic rewards. Wage and salary surveys are made or used by most organizations[3] and benefit surveys are made by many. The fact that benefit surveys are more often of prevailing practice than of benefit costs suggests that benefits are not entirely economic rewards, but organizations consider benefits to be economic rewards—wages or salaries in a different form.

Wage and salary surveys may imply a comparison of contributions in that data are usually collected by occupation. But typical wage survey

[1]Arthur M. Ross, "The External Wage Structure," in George W. Taylor and Frank C. Pierson (eds.), *New Concepts in Wage Determination* (New York: McGraw-Hill Book Company, 1957), pp. 173–205.

[2]Paul Bullock, *Standards of Wage Determination* (Los Angeles: University of California, Institute of Industrial Relations, 1960).

[3]Orval R. Grigsby and William C. Burns, "Salary Surveys—The Deluge," *Personnel Journal* (June, 1962), pp. 274–280.

practice[4] and the manner in which the data are used suggest that occupational wages are collected to make economic rewards comparable and that contributions are either assumed to be unimportant in comparisons or noncomparable.

If this interpretation of wage and salary survey practice is accurate, organizations make comparisons of economic rewards with other organizations. Noneconomic rewards are apparently not considered to be an essential part of the employment exchange. Likewise, contributions are compared only to the extent that occupations imply contributions. It seems that organizations do not look closely at what they get in return for the rewards.[5]

These generalizations need to be tempered by the recognition that some wage and salary surveys take elaborate steps to ensure job comparability and that organizations in similar technologies make informal comparisons as part of the process of job and organization design. But compensation practice focuses on external comparisons of economic rewards while largely ignoring other rewards and all contributions.

Interestingly, compensation practices with respect to professional employees have fostered organization comparisons of contributions as well as rewards. Salary surveys of professionals present salary rates by age (or years since degree) and performance level rather than jobs.[6] These maturity curves force organization attention to contributions not ordinarily considered. In fact, an interesting study of the compensation of engineering-scientific managers found that contributions relating to both the position and the position-holder were required to predict pay level.[7]

Organizations also make internal comparisons. But these comparisons emphasize contributions rather than rewards. Job evaluation, for example, compares the responsibility, skill, effort, and willingness to accept certain working conditions required by jobs. Performance evaluation compares the performance of job incumbents.

Thus, organizations typically use other organizations as comparison standards and largely limit comparisons to pay and benefit practices. Little attention is paid to contributions except when making internal comparisons. In both external and internal comparisons, the rewards and contributions considered show that organizations conceive

[4]N. Arnold Tolles and Robert L. Raimon, *Sources of Wage Information: Employer Associations* (Ithaca: Cornell University Press, 1952).

[5]Edward E. Lawler, III, *Pay and Organizational Effectiveness: A Psychological View* (New York: McGraw-Hill Book Company, 1971), pp. 11–12.

[6]George W. Torrence, "Maturity Curves and Salary Administration," *Management Record* (January, 1962), pp. 14–17.

[7]Kenneth E. Foster, "Accounting for Management Pay Differentials," *Industrial Relations* (October, 1969), pp. 80–87.

of the employment exchange as an economic transaction. But, curiously, the rewards and contributions are not compared as they are in other economic transactions.

INDIVIDUAL COMPARISONS

The evidence available on the comparison standards of individuals and what they compare stands in sharp contrast to comparison practices of organizations. It shows, for example, that individuals often compare with standards within themselves or with other individuals and that they compare all the rewards and contributions that they consider relevant against one another in appraising the employment exchange.

INDIVIDUAL COMPARISON STANDARDS

The work of Elliott Jaques suggests that the employee uses a comparison standard within himself.[8] Vroom agrees that an individual employs his self-concept as a comparison standard.[9] Weick states that an individual uses an internal standard if objective reality is not available as a standard.[10]

Festinger's theory of social comparison processes holds that if objective means are not available for comparison, people compare with other people, that objective standards are preferred, and that subjective evaluations are based on perceived similarity of comparison persons.[11] But Festinger also points out that even if it is possible to test an opinion against objective reality, the test frequently is not made. An important issue in application of the theory is the definition of objective reality by the individual. Presumably, if he accepts the information available to him, it represents reality. If, however, he does not receive information or does not accept what he receives, it does not represent objective reality and he compares himself with other people.

Whether the individual accepts wage survey data presented to him by the organization as objective reality is an empirical question. The fact that such data are typically collected and interpreted by the organization without any input on his part, and the fact that information on other rewards and on contributions is not readily available, may

[8]Elliott Jaques, *Equitable Payment* (New York: John Wiley & Sons, Inc., 1961).

[9]Victor H. Vroom, *Work and Motivation* (New York: John Wiley & Sons, Inc., 1964).

[10]K. E. Weick, "The Concept of Equity in the Perception of Pay," *Administrative Science Quarterly* (December, 1966), pp. 414–439.

[11]L. Festinger, "A Theory of Social Comparison Processes," *Human Relations* (May, 1954), pp. 117–140.

mean that use of comparison persons is more likely than use of objective reality.

Equity theory as formulated by Adams[12] and much of the research on equity theory[13] employ another individual or group as the comparison standard used by individuals. Pritchard, however, argues that an internal standard is more likely to be used in the employment situation.[14]

To sociologists, comparison standards represent an application of reference group theory that is concerned with "those processes of evaluation and self-appraisal in which the individual takes the values or standards of other individuals and groups as a comparative frame of reference."[15] Reference group theory states that reference groups and reference individuals are selected by the individual on the basis of perceived similarity to himself or to his situation. Groups selected may be those in which the individual holds membership or which he hopes to join. Although it is possible for an individual to employ multiple reference groups, this possibility is reduced by the tendency to compare himself with individuals of similar status with whom he is or has been in actual social relations and with those whose situation he has some knowledge of.[16]

A number of other suggestions regarding the determinants and consequences of reference groups flow from the theory. Individuals and groups who are subordinate to the same authority are likely to use one another as reference groups. But perceived group membership is also important in that membership in a large group or class promotes comparisons with others in the large group, whereas membership in a smaller group promotes face-to-face comparisons. Organizations, unions, and governments may influence the choice of reference groups by focusing the attention of individuals on common reference groups, but only if these new reference groups are accepted as legitimate and consistent with previously existing norms of equity. If such influence results in conflicting frames of reference, dissatisfaction is a likely consequence. Perceived legitimacy of comparisons strongly influences the

[12]J. S. Adams, "Inequity in Social Exchange," in L. Berkowitz (ed.), *Advances in Experimental Social Psychology,* Vol. 2 (New York: Academic Press, Inc., 1965), pp. 267–299.

[13]See E. E. Lawler, III, "Equity Theory as a Predictor of Productivity and Work Quality," *Psychological Bulletin* (December, 1968), pp. 596–610, for an excellent review.

[14]R. D. Pritchard, "Equity Theory: A Review and Critique," *Organization Behavior and Human Performance* (May, 1969), pp. 176–211.

[15]Robert K. Merton and Alice Kitt Rossi, "Contributions to the Theory of Reference Group Behavior," in Herbert H. Hyman and Eleanor Singer (eds.), *Readings in Reference Group Theory and Research* (New York: Free Press, 1968), pp. 28–68.

[16]Hyman and Singer, *Readings in Reference Group Theory,* pp. 3–21.

choice of reference groups. In stable, tradition-bound societies, individuals are likely to make intragroup rather than intergroup comparisons. In highly mobile, "open" societies, on the other hand, less clearly defined reference groups are generated, and perhaps more discontent. If relationships have been defined as morally right, situational changes that result in the use of new reference groups may or may not result in what are regarded as legitimate comparisons. Efforts to manipulate the reference groups employed by individuals may or may not be successful and, if successful, the consequences of change may not coincide with intentions. Organizations, unions, and governments, for example, may fail in attempts to broaden reference groups. If they are successful in changing them, they are likely to be unsuccessful in ending comparisons with new groups. Members of certain occupations, industries, and communities may have such intense reference group orientations that any efforts to change them would prove to be futile.[17]

Groups with which the individual frequently interacts, in which he considers himself a member, and in which others consider him to be a member are the most likely reference groups. But if individuals are strongly oriented toward achieving membership in another group, anticipatory socialization focuses his comparisons on the group to which he wishes to belong. For most people, the focus of attention is on their current role, with only a very small proportion of it tied to future roles and even less to past roles.[18] Although all of us fulfill a number of roles, the tendency of these roles to be separated physically, temporally, and functionally in modern society[19] probably means that comparisons pertinent to the work situation are becoming relatively uninfluenced by comparisons within family, religious, political, or other social roles.

Although many elements of reference group theory require much more empirical test, some studies of comparisons have been made. British manual workers, for example, have been found to choose comparisons close to their situation and to very rarely compare themselves to nonmanual workers.[20] Frenchmen have been found to compare themselves to members of the same occupation, to family members, and to members of their own social circle.[21] A study of over 500 manual

[17]Seymour Martin Lipset and Martin Trow, "Reference Group Theory and Trade Union Wage Policy," in Mirra Komarovsky (ed.), *Common Frontiers of the Social Sciences* (Glencoe, Illinois: Free Press, 1957), pp. 391–411.

[18]Robert K. Merton, *Social Theory and Social Structure* (New York: Free Press, 1968), Chapter 11.

[19]Robert Dubin, "Work and Non-work: Institutional Perspectives," in Marvin D. Dunnette (ed.), *Work and Leisure in the Year 2001* (Belmont, California: Wadsworth Publishing Company, Inc., in press).

[20]W. G. Runcimon, "Reference Groups and Inequalities of Class," in Hyman and Singer, *Readings in Reference Group Theory*, pp. 207–221.

[21]Eric Stern and Suzanne Keller, "Spontaneous Group References in France," *ibid.*, pp. 199–206.

workers in Michigan found that comparisons were made among those on the same occupational level and of similar social origin and that work associates and male family members were comparison persons. Only those individuals who had accepted the middle-class ideology of opportunity shifted their comparisons to persons above themselves.[22] Canadian oil refinery workers have been found to be able to identify persons with whom they compare their wages. Although the study asked individuals to make a comparison with someone whose wages were different from their own, comparison persons were chosen with attributes similar to those of the comparer. If the comparison person's attributes were superior to those of the comparer, a wage differential in the comparison person's favor was acceptable, and vice versa. Although both consonant and dissonant comparisons were made, the latter were found to be unlikely unless reality brought such comparisons to an individual's attention.[23]

American managers at different organization levels in both private and public organizations have been found to have different comparison standards. Lower-level managers compare with their peers within the organization. Higher-level, more educated, and higher paid managers tend to compare with managers in other organizations.[24] But Lawler and Porter's[25] determination that managers on the same organization level have similar pay expectations may also be interpreted to agree with Jaques[26] and Vroom;[27] *i.e.*, that individuals use their own self-concept as a standard. An interesting study found that the comparison standard chosen is influenced by the result of the comparison so that when inequity appears inevitable to the comparer he prefers remote comparisons.[28]

Some unpublished data obtained from a pilot study by the author and a colleague indicate that different occupational groups vary widely in their comparison standards. Although the results must be regarded as tentative because they are based on small samples, they represent the comparison standards reported by individuals in different occupational groups employed by several different organizations. Interest-

[22]William H. Form and James A. Geschwender, "Social Reference Basis of Job Satisfaction: The Case of Manual Workers," *ibid.*, pp. 185–198.

[23]Martin Patchen, *The Choice of Wage Comparisons* (Englewood Cliffs, N.J.: Prentice-Hall, Inc., 1961).

[24]I. R. Andrews and Mildred M. Henry, "Management Attitudes Toward Pay," *Industrial Relations* (October, 1963), pp. 29–39; Mary Jo Hamilton, "A Study of Public Management Attitudes Toward Pay," unpublished master's thesis (San Diego State, 1966).

[25]Edward E. Lawler, III, and Lyman W. Porter, "Perceptions Regarding Management Compensation," *Industrial Relations* (October, 1963), pp. 41–49.

[26]Jaques, *Equitable Payment.*

[27]Vroom, *Work and Motivation.*

[28]K. E. Weick and B. Nesset, "Preferences Among Forms of Equity," *Organization Behavior and Human Performance* (November, 1968), pp. 400–416.

ingly, unskilled workers were the only group that used objective reality (the labor market for their services) alone as the comparison standard. Skilled workers (craftsmen) compared with fellow union members and with information provided by the union. Female clerical workers compared with others similar to themselves in the same employing organization and preferably in the same organization unit. Nurses compared primarily with others in their field, but as a result of collective bargaining activities of their professional association also compared themselves with other members of their employing organizations. Public school teachers typically compared themselves with an idealized self-concept and others in their field, but a sizable proportion of them made dissonant comparisons with people of similar educational attainment in other organizations. Engineers and scientists compared themselves with others in their profession. Managers, however, had a strong tendency to compare their present situation with a previous one.

A more carefully designed study[29] of social workers showed that at least among professionals, comparison standards are strongly influenced by the cosmopolitan vs. local orientation of the individual.[30] Cosmopolitans (those whose orientation is with the profession rather than the organization) employed other members of the profession and information provided by the union as comparison standards. Locals (those whose orientation is toward the employing organization), on the other hand, compared with others within the organization.

WHAT INDIVIDUALS COMPARE

Although organization practice and economic theory imply that individuals limit comparisons to economic rewards and ignore noneconomic rewards and contributions, this does not seem to be the case. It is true that individuals' comparisons are hampered by lack of information at the time they enter an employing organization but the evidence that individuals today highly value benefits,[31] make relative comparisons (implying comparison of contributions), and are aware of the effects of changes in the cost of living suggests that even at this time actual comparisons are broader than assumed. Once within an employing organization, comparisons include the full range of rewards and contributions.

[29]T. J. Atchison, D. W. Belcher, and J. Hunt, "Measuring the Employment Exchange," (unpublished manuscript).

[30]Alvin W. Gouldner, "Cosmopolitans and Locals: Toward an Analysis of Latent Social Roles," *Administrative Science Quarterly* (December, 1957), pp. 444–480.

[31]Richard A. Lester, "Benefits as a Preferred Form of Compensation," *Southern Economic Journal* (April, 1967), pp. 488–495.

Patchen's study of Canadian oil refinery workers, although limited to wage comparisons, showed that individuals made them by comparing not only wages but the contributions of the comparer and the comparison person.[32] Equity theory[33] and the studies made to test it[34] have shown that the individual compares rewards and contributions by making use of a long list of both. Studies in ongoing organizations have found that individuals consider about twenty separate rewards and an equivalent number of contributions as relevant and important to the employment exchange.[35] The high importance assigned by individuals to most of these rewards and contributions makes it difficult to believe that individual comparisons are made on rewards alone or on a limited number of rewards and contributions. One of the fascinating abilities of human beings is that of making complex comparisons of only subjectively comparable entities with only limited information available.

Thus both theory and research evidence show that individuals compare both rewards and contributions and a wide variety of each. Economic rewards and contributions are only a part of the considerations. Furthermore, unlike organizations, individuals may first make comparisons with their own self-concept, then with others with whom they come into direct contact, and finally with the labor market. The difference between individual and organization comparisons implies that the employment exchange will be differentially viewed except by individuals strongly attuned to the external labor market.

DIFFERENCES AMONG EMPLOYEE GROUPS

Although the direct evidence is fragmentary and comes from a wide variety of sources, it seems useful to attempt to distinguish employee groups in terms of the comparisons they are likely to make. Although the following distinctions must be regarded as tentative, they are based on reference group theory and research, equity theory and studies, sociological analyses of labor markets,[36] and some experience in and studies of organizations.[37]

---

[32]Patchen, *Choice of Wage Comparisons.*
[33]Adams, in Berkowitz, *Advances in Experimental Social Psychology,* pp. 267–299.
[34]See reviews by Lawler and Pritchard.
[35]D. W. Belcher and T. J. Atchison, "Equity Theory and Compensation Policy," *Personnel Administration* (July–August, 1970), pp. 22–33; T. J. Atchison and D. W. Belcher, "Equity, Rewards, and Compensation Administration," *Personnel Administration* (March–April, 1971), pp. 32–36.
[36]Theodore Caplow, *The Sociology of Work* (New York: McGraw-Hill Book Company, 1954), Chapter 7.
[37]I am indebted to my colleague, Professor Thomas J. Atchison, for some of the conclusions reached in this section.

Unskilled workers appear to make comparisons that come closest to the economic model of the employment exchange. In making the decision to accept an offer of employment, they compare the pay offered with the value they place on their time; *i.e.,* the comparison standard is objective reality. As soon as they enter an organization and become embedded in a group, however, they broaden the factors compared and the peer group is their comparison standard.

Semiskilled workers probably compare a broader range of rewards and contributions than is commonly assumed and use peers as their comparison standard. If semiskilled workers are members of a union, peer group comparisons are supplemented by union-directed comparisons. But the influence of union-directed comparisons is hampered by (1) possible conflicts with strongly held views of appropriate relationships, (2) the danger of convincing members to make new comparisons before these comparisons are accepted by management, and (3) the difficulty of changing standards that have become internalized by members.

Craftsmen are likely to make comparisons with others in their field rather than within the employing organization. Skilled workers in large organizations probably make broader comparisons and compare with peers as well as members of their field in other organizations but are probably less influenced by union directed comparisons than semiskilled workers unless represented by a craft union.

Female clerical workers, although recruited from a well-organized labor market and thus inclined to make some use of objective reality as a comparison standard, are even more likely to compare with organization peers than with any other group, especially on working conditions. The result is that market data show a broader range of economic rewards than most other groups.

Salesmen probably have more difficulty with comparisons than any other employee group. Because they cannot become too committed to the organization and still be effective, organization commitment may be ruled out as both a contribution and a reward. Because the salesman gets most of his information from outside the organization (other salesmen and customers) and economic information is easy to transmit, his comparisons are based primarily on economic rewards and contributions rather than on other rewards and other contributions. The result is that salesmen are likely to make poor decisions with respect to the employment exchange.

Foremen or first-line supervisors tend to be of two types in making comparisons. The college-educated foreman is likely to make use of anticipatory socialization—to compare himself to individuals in higher management. The comparisons are likely to be broad ones, including many different kinds of rewards and contributions, and to be consonant to the comparer. The noncollege foreman, on the other hand, compares with his subordinates both because his pay is tied to that of his subordinates and because further promotion is highly unlikely. Comparison with peers may also be made but is less probable because it is likely to result in dissonance if some of the foremen are college men.

Professionals and mobile middle managers are like craftsmen in making comparisons with others in their field rather than with peers within the organization. But both professionals and mobile middle managers experience conflict between the pull of the profession and the pull of the organization. Those who emphasize comparisons outside the organization (the cosmopolitans) are likely to fluctuate between dissonant comparisons produced by comparisons outside the organization but limited in the rewards and contributions considered and consonant comparisons produced by anticipatory socialization involving a much wider range of rewards and contributions. Those who emphasize comparisons within the organization (locals) are likely to make consonant comparisons based on anticipatory socialization.

Neither the cosmopolitan-local nor the mobile-nonmobile dichotomies, however, serves to explain the tendency of at least some managers to compare their present situation with a previous one. It may be that the reality of uneven upward progress in organizations means that anticipatory socialization results in such dissonance that looking backward at the progress made to date is more comfortable.[38]

Some middle managers and professionals, because of their jobs, are more likely to have more contacts outside the organization. Thus "relations" people are more likely to be found on the cosmopolitan-mobile end of the continuum than are production managers. (It is also probable that research and development people are more likely to be cosmopolitan-mobile because like salesmen too much commitment to the organization can mean lessened effectiveness.)

Top management, like unskilled employees, are likely to make primarily economic comparisons but for different reasons. Top managers are more privy to economic information with respect to the organization; and because they are placed where their decisions affect organization success, they are likely to compare their economic contributions and their economic rewards and demand a "piece of the action." They are also in a position in which anticipatory socialization no longer provides comparison standards. Finding comparison persons or groups outside the organization is complicated by differences among industries and between economic and noneconomic organizations.

[38]Professor Atchison calls this "mid-career crisis."

WHAT ORGANIZATIONS CAN DO

By recognizing that individuals compare all the rewards and contributions that they recognize and consider relevant and that different employee groups make different comparisons and use different comparison standards, organizations can take one or both of two approaches to improving employee evaluation of the fairness of their employment exchange. Organizations can, for example, find out what rewards and contributions each employee group considers relevant and what reference groups or individuals each group compares with and provide information to facilitate these comparisons. Or they may be able to change comparisons of some employee groups in ways that benefit the organization.

Determining what employee groups compare and their comparison standards is probably the simpler part of the first approach. The major problem is that of providing information that becomes accepted by employees and used in comparisons. Because the entire employment exchange is perceptual, the information provided employees must be of sufficient quantity and quality. But more important, it must be believed.

If employee groups emphasize economic rewards and make comparisons outside the organization, the wage and benefit surveys must be conducted in such a way that employees will accept the results. This may mean participation by employee groups in designing the surveys; *i.e.,* determining what jobs are to be surveyed and what organizations are to be included.[39] Such an approach not only serves to provide information of the type the employee groups use, but also employee participation in survey design should assure acceptance of the results.

If employee groups emphasize economic rewards but compare with their peers within the organization, a number of steps seem necessary to improve comparisons. One suggested frequently is the elimination of pay secrecy in organizations.[40] If employees compare with peers, pay secrecy means that comparisons are made on the basis of inaccurate information and often lead to overestimates of the pay of peers. An unpublished study by the author and a colleague found much less perceived inequity among government employees where pay rates are known than in private organizations in which pay secrecy is the norm.

But because individuals compare not only rewards but rewards with contributions, it is important that employees have information with respect to contributions. Here the primary step would be em-

[39]Lawler, *Pay and Organizational Effectiveness,* p. 197.
[40]*Ibid.,* p. 255.

ployee participation in job evaluation so that employees accept the difference in contributions represented by different jobs. Employee acceptance is, as stated previously, the primary criterion of the effectiveness of job evaluation. Employee participation should result in greater employee acceptance. Also, there is some evidence that job holders are less prone to overpay jobs than are managers.[41]

Individuals, however, compare other contributions than those encompassed by job evaluation. Here the primary requirement is that organizations be straightforward in specifying the other contributions that are accepted and rewarded. If performance, for example, is to be rewarded, employees must know how performance is defined and be shown that better performance does in fact result in higher rewards. Accomplishing the latter may require the elimination of pay secrecy.

Other contributions require equal attention by organizations. If the organization does in fact require other contributions (such as cooperation or versatility) that are not recognized in the reward system, the reward system should be changed to recognize them.

If, however, employees believe that certain contributions should be rewarded but the organization does not, the organization would seem to have no alternative but to attempt to show employees why these contributions cannot be accepted. In most cases the latter can probably be accomplished by a careful explanation of the reward system of the organization, emphasizing what contributions are rewarded. Because organizations have done so little thinking and communicating with employees about the employee contributions the organization wants and can accept, employees not unreasonably make inferences about appropriate contributions. Organization specification of acceptable contributions may serve to show some employees that they have selected the wrong organization. But hopefully, specification of contributions will enable organizations to keep good performers and lose marginal ones.

If employee groups emphasize noneconomic rewards regardless of whether comparison standards are within the organization or without, the organization is in an excellent strategic position. Because many of the rewards these groups want are intrinsic rewards that the individual rewards himself if given the opportunity to do so and are balanced by additional contributions, the organization is in a position to gain at no cost. In fact, some evidence exists that people who receive larger noneconomic rewards are more satisfied with their pay.[42]

[41]E. E. Lawler and J. R. Hackman, "The Impact of Employee Participation in the Development of Pay Incentive Plans: A Field Experiment," *Journal of Applied Psychology* (December, 1969), pp. 467–471.

[42]D. D. Penner, *A Study of the Causes and Consequences of Salary Satisfaction* (Crotonville, N.Y.: General Electric Behavioral Research Service, mimeographed, 1966).

As was pointed out in Chapter 15, however, there is a large variety of noneconomic rewards that organizations can use to increase the reward package of separate employee groups. Providing these rewards often requires only that the organization know what rewards employee groups desire and is willing to design jobs and organization relationships to permit these groups to receive these rewards.

But it is important that total reward packages be designed for specific groups. To help these groups in making comparisons, it seems even more important to inform these groups that the organization desires to develop a long-term employment exchange and wishes to offer the rewards desired and to accept the contributions (including commitment) that these employee groups wish to make. It perhaps does not need to be said that in this communication process action speaks louder than words.

Such efforts by organizations should be especially fruitful in the case of professionals and mobile middle managers who are continually balancing the pull from outside and the pull of the organization. But they should also help with groups that are prone to make comparisons primarily on economic grounds (salesmen). In both situations, the organization can offer what is perceived to be a broader and deeper employment exchange than may be obtained elsewhere.

The other approach by the organization is to attempt to change the comparison standards of employee groups by emphasizing comparisons that the organization considers more appropriate. Although this approach is within the power of organizations, it is fraught with dangers and requires careful analysis in advance. Organizations may promote the adoption of new comparison standards by presenting information on the situations of other groups. But organizations may discover, as have unions, that if the previously employed standards were adjudged to be morally right, they cannot be changed. More important, an attempt to change comparison standards must be carefully considered for long-term effects. If the change is successful, any attempt to change back to the former frame of reference is doomed to failure.

17

Compensation Policy

Organization compensation policy was cited in the previous chapter as a comparison standard employed by organizations in making compensation decisions. These organization intentions, generalized decisions, or ground rules are typically employed to determine the response of the organization to information that might affect the employment exchange. As such, organization compensation policy (whether consciously determined or not) represents the ultimate comparison standard of organizations.

Organization compensation policies are not determined in a vacuum, however. Public policy, union policy, and the culture all constrain organization policy. But organization response to constraints existing in its environment may be passive or active; *i.e.,* organizations may passively accept constraints as limits upon organization freedom to act or they may regard them as guides to positive actions that the organization may initiate.

This chapter examines public, union, and organization policy on compensation. Public policy may be treated as a set of constraints on organization policy. Union policy may be considered as another type of constraint with respect to employer policy concerning union members or as another comparison standard. Organization policy is treated as a comparison standard shaped by the organization as the result of a passive or active response to the environment. As such, organization compensation policy may react to constraints as an opportunity to better integrate organization and employee comparisons with a view to improving the employment exchange.

PUBLIC POLICY

Public policy on compensation is expressed in federal and state legislation and in regulations imposed by executive branches of these governments. It represents our society's major intentions with respect to compensation. Because these stated social goals express only a portion of our broader social and economic purposes, they are not always clear or consistent with one another. At the risk of oversimplification, public policy may be represented as stating that compensation must not be too low nor (at times) too high, but that within these limits compensation decisions should be left to the parties at interest. Also, in the interests of fairness, certain groups have been protected and all groups must be paid when such payment is due.

FAIR LABOR STANDARDS ACT

National policy setting a floor under wages is stated in the Fair Labor Standards Act of 1938 and in subsequent amendments. The national minimum for workers in interstate commerce has been increased whenever the floor falls to about 50 per cent of average hourly earnings.[1] Coverage of the act has also been expanded.

Increases in the legal minimum wage and in the coverage of the act imply a social concern for increasing standards of living. Another feature of the act specifying that certain employees must be paid premium rates (time and one-half) for overtime beyond forty hours per week implies that public policy is concerned not only with compensation rates but also with earnings. It may also imply the desirability of adequate leisure for employees.

To the employer, the distinction in the law between *exempt* and *non-exempt* employees is of major importance. In fact, the distinction has become so crucial to compensation administration that some employers administratively separate the function for the two groups. The exempt employee is not covered by the provisions of the act; the nonexempt employee is. Executive, administrative, and professional employees are exempt from the minimum wage, overtime, and record-keeping provisions of the law if their work, responsibilities, and pay meet specific criteria. Other employees are covered. Exempt employees, of course, receive compensation well above the floor provided for nonexempt employees. See Table 8 for definitions of exempt employees. Placing employees on salary does not make them exempt from the act unless the specific requirements are met.

[1]Thomas Gavett, "Youth, Employment and Minimum Wages: An Overview," *IRRA Proceedings* (Detroit, December 28–29, 1970), pp. 106–116.

TABLE 8

Definitions of Executive, Administrative, and Professional Employees

I. *Definition of an executive employee.* The term "employee employed in a bona fide executive . . . capacity" in section 13 (a) (1) of the act shall mean any employee:

(a) Whose primary duty consists of the management of the enterprise in which he is employed or of a customarily recognized department or subdivision thereof; and

(b) Who customarily and regularly directs the work of two or more other employees therein; and

(c) Who has the authority to hire or fire other employees or whose suggestions and recommendations as to the hiring or firing and as to the advancement and promotion or any other change of status of other employees will be given particular weight; and

(d) Who customarily and regularly exercises discretionary powers; and

(e) Who does not devote more than 20 per cent of his hours worked in the workweek to activities which are not directly and closely related to the performance of the work described in paragraphs (a) through (d) of this section: *Provided,* That this paragraph shall not apply in the case of an employee who is in sole charge of an independent establishment or a physically separated branch establishment, or who owns at least a 20-per cent interest in the enterprise in which he is employed; and

(f) Who is compensated for his services on a salary basis at a rate of not less than $125 per week (or $115 per week if employed in Puerto Rico or the Virgin Islands) exclusive of board, lodging, or other facilities:

Provided, That an employee who is compensated on a salary basis at a rate of not less than $200 per week (exclusive of board, lodging, or other facilities), and whose primary duty consists of the management of the enterprise in which he is employed or of a customarily recognized department or subdivision thereof, and includes the customary and regular direction of the work of two or more other employees therein, shall be deemed to meet all of the requirements of this section.

II. *Definition of an administrative employee.* The term "employee employed in a bona fide . . . administrative . . . capacity" in section 13 (a) (1) of the act shall mean any employee:

(a) Whose primary duty consists of the performance of office or nonmanual field work directly related to management policies or general business operations of his employer or his employer's customers; and

(b) Who customarily and regularly exercises discretion and independent judgment; and

(c) (1) Who regularly and directly assists a proprietor, or an employee employed in a bona fide executive or administrative capacity (as such terms are defined in this subpart); or

(2) Who performs under only general supervision work along specialized or technical lines requiring special training, experience, or knowledge; or

(3) Who executes under only general supervision special assignments and tasks; and

(d) Who does not devote more than 20 per cent of his hours worked in the workweek to activities which are not directly and closely related to the performance of the work described in paragraphs (a) through (c) of this section; and

(e) Who is compensated for his services on a salary or fee basis at a rate of not less than $125 per week (or $100 per week if employed in Puerto Rico or the Virgin Islands) exclusive of board, lodging, or other facilities:

Provided, That an employee who is compensated on a salary or fee basis at a rate of not less than $200 per week (exclusive of board, lodging, or other facilities), and whose primary duty consists of the performance of office or nonmanual field work directly related to management policies or general business operations of his employer or his employer's customers, which includes work requiring the exercise of discretion and independent judgment, shall be deemed to meet all of the requirements of this section.

III. *Definition of a professional employee.* The term "employee employed in a bona fide . . . professional . . . capacity" in section 13 (a) (1) of the act shall mean any employee:

(a) Whose primary duty consists of the performance of work—

TABLE 8 (Cont.)

(1) Requiring knowledge of an advanced type in a field of science or learning customarily acquired by a prolonged course of specialized intellectual instruction and study, as distinguished from a general academic education and from an apprenticeship, and from training in the performance of routine mental, manual, or physical processes; or

(2) Original and creative in character in a recognized field of artistic endeavor (as opposed to work which can be produced by a person endowed with general manual or intellectual ability and training), and the result of which depends primarily on the invention, imagination, or talent of the employee; and

(b) Whose work requires the consistent exercise of discretion and judgment in its performance; and

(c) Whose work is predominantly intellectual and varied in character (as opposed to routine mental, manual, mechanical, or physical work) and is of such a character that the output produced or the result accomplished cannot be standardized in relation to a given period of time; and

(d) Who does not devote more than 20 per cent of his hours worked in the workweek to activities which are not an essential part of and necessarily incident to the work described in paragraphs (a) through (c) of this section; and

(e) Who is compensated for his services on a salary or fee basis at a rate of not less than $140 per week (or $125 per week if employed in Puerto Rico or the Virgin Islands) exclusive of board, lodging, or other facilities:

Provided, That this paragraph shall not apply in the case of an employee who is the holder of a valid license or certificate permitting the practice of law or medicine or any of their branches and who is actually engaged in the practice thereof;

Provided, That an employee who is compensated on a salary or fee basis at a rate of not less than $200 per week (exclusive of board, lodging, or other facilities), and whose primary duty consists of the performance of work either requiring knowledge of an advanced type in a field of science or learning, which includes work requiring the consistent exercise of discretion and judgment, or requiring invention, imagination, or talent in a recognized field of artistic endeavor, shall be deemed to meet all of the requirements of this section.

Source: *WH Publication* 1363 (Washington, D.C.: U.S. Department of Labor, May, 1972).

A large part of the importance employers place on the provisions of the Fair Labor Standards Act is due to the heavy penalties involved in violating its provisions. Wage and hour investigators from the U.S. Department of Labor are charged with enforcing the act and collecting back wages from employers who violate the minimum wage and overtime provisions.

Although coverage of the act has been expanded greatly in recent years (over 80 per cent since 1966), some employees are not covered by the act. Many of these receive rates below the federal minimum wage.

STATE MINIMUM WAGE LAWS

Employees not covered by federal minimum wage legislation are often covered by state laws. Minimum wage laws were in force in forty states in 1971.[2] Although in the past most state laws limited coverage to women and children, many of them now apply to men as well. State laws are also expanding in coverage and raising minimums to meet or exceed the federal minimum. Some state laws provide for automatic adjustment when changes are made in the federal minimum.

PREVAILING WAGE LAWS

Both federal and state governments have laws requiring employers contracting with the government to pay "prevailing" rates. The Davis-Bacon Act requires the Secretary of Labor to determine the prevailing rates on federal construction contracts. The Walsh-Healey Act has the same requirement for all public contracts with the federal government in excess of $10,000. In both instances, the Secretary of Labor must determine the prevailing rates for the industry in the locality. The rate determined by the Secretary of Labor becomes the minimum under the contract. The Walsh-Healey Act also requires that time and one-half be paid for all work in excess of eight hours in one day or forty hours in one week on these contracts. All states have prevailing wage laws covering public contracts, but the type and size of contracts covered vary.

EFFECTS

The effects of minimum wage laws have long been a matter of controversy. High teenage unemployment in recent years has served to further fuel the debate. Economic theory and a number of studies point out that minimum wages reduce employment, especially of marginal employees.[3] Studies by the Bureau of Labor Statistics, on the other hand, find that actual employment effects are substantial in only a few low-paying industries and areas[4] and offset only partially the wage increases granted low-paid employees. Some significant indirect effects

[2]Sylvia Weissbrodt, "Changes in State Labor Laws in 1971," *Monthly Labor Review* (January, 1972), pp. 29–39.
[3]George J. Stigler, "The Economics of Minimum Wage Legislation," *American Economic Review* (June, 1946), pp. 358–365; Arthur F. Burns, *The Management of Prosperity* (New York: Columbia University Press, 1966); Yale Brozen and Milton Friedman, *The Minimum Wage Rate* (Washington: The Free Society Association, 1966); Lloyd Reynolds and Peter Gregory, *Wages, Productivity and Industrialization in Puerto Rico* (Homewood, Illinois: Richard D. Irwin, Inc., 1965); John M. Peterson and Charles T. Stewart, Jr., *Employment Effects of Minimum Wage Rates* (Washington: American Enterprise Institute, August, 1969).
[4]L. Earl Lewis, "Minimum Wage: Fertilizer Industry," *Monthly Labor Review* (January, 1951), pp. 33–37; Harry S. Kantor, "Economic Effects of the Minimum Wage," *Monthly Labor Review* (March, 1955), pp. 307–311; Norman J. Samuels, "Effects of the

of increasing wages of workers not covered have been noted. These and other studies suggest that minimum wage laws do reduce employment but not nearly enough to offset the increased wage rates.[5] But the reduction in employment appears not only to have been small but also to result from improved labor utilization. For example, some employers have responded to increases in the minimum wage by discharging some employees, screening applicants more carefully, increasing production standards, reducing overtime, increasing mechanization, changing layouts, changing product lines, increasing production, and increasing prices.[6]

The controversy over the employment effects of minimum wage laws has focused recently on the issue of the relationship between the minimum wage and high teenage unemployment. A number of studies conclude that minimum wages have an adverse effect on the employment of teenagers. Other studies find no evidence of such an effect.[7] A BLS study, although accepting the conclusion that a significant relationship between the minimum wage and youth unemployment exists, finds that other variables not included in most studies cast doubt on the importance of minimum wages as an explanatory variable.[8] For example, the rapid growth in teenage population, the decrease in teenage agricultural employment, the heavy demand by teenagers for part-time jobs while still in school, and the uncertainties in the minds of employers caused by the military draft have all served to raise the unemployment of teenagers. An attitude survey of employers found that approximately 65 per cent did not believe the minimum wage was important in the decision to employ teenagers. A regression analysis of unemployment data from 1954 through 1968 (through seven changes

$1 Minimum Wage in Three Seasonal Industries," *Monthly Labor Review* (September, 1957), pp. 1087–1091; Norman J. Samuels, "Effects of the $1 Minimum Wage in Five Industries," *Monthly Labor Review* (May, 1958), pp. 492–501; Louis E. Badenhoop, "Effect of the $1 Minimum Wage in Seven Areas," *Monthly Labor Review* (July, 1958), pp. 737–743; "Effects of the Minimum Wage on Employment and Business," *Monthly Labor Review* (May, 1965), pp. 541–543; Jack I. Karlin, "Economic Effects of the 1966 Changes in the FLSA," *Monthly Labor Review* (June, 1967), pp. 21–25.

[5]N. Arnold Tolles, "The Purpose and Results of the U.S. Minimum Wage," *Monthly Labor Review* (March, 1960), pp. 238–242; Isador Lubin and Charles A. Pearce, "New York's Minimum Wage Law: The First Twenty Years," *Industrial and Labor Relations Review* (January, 1958), pp. 203–219.

[6]Paul A. Brinker, "The $1 Minimum Wage Impact in 15 Oklahoma Industries," *Monthly Labor Review* (September, 1957), pp. 1092–1095.

[7]For a review of these studies see J. M. Kreps, "Youth Employment and Minimum Wages: Some Further Questions," *Nebraska Journal of Economics and Business* (Winter, 1971), pp. 14–21.

[8]"Youth Unemployment and Minimum Wages," *BLS Bulletin 1657* (Washington, D.C.: Government Printing Office, 1970).

in the FLSA) found that teenagers are less affected by minimum wage changes than adults.[9] This unsettled controversy may result in a lower minimum wage for teenagers in future revisions of the FLSA. Whether a lower minimum wage for teenagers will result in employers' preferring teenagers over adults is another unsettled question.

The effects of prevailing wage laws have been less carefully studied. One study found that the Walsh-Healey Act served to increase wage levels both by the prevailing wages set and by the "target effect" for labor unions.[10] This effect operates by providing a standard against which unions may compare firms not covered by the act and through restoring customary relationships after covered firms have changed wage levels to comply with prevailing rates. A presidential proclamation (No. 4031) in 1971 suspending the Davis-Bacon Act temporarily for the purpose of lessening the inflationary impact of wage settlements in construction implies that the act raises wage levels.

Obviously, the target effect operates with minimum wage laws as well as prevailing wage laws. If customary relationships are disturbed by raising the floor, forces are set in motion to restore them whether among organizations or within them.

SOCIAL LEGISLATION

Just as minimum and prevailing wage laws place a floor under wage rates and earnings, so social legislation may be interpreted as placing a floor under benefits provided employees. Thus the Social Security Act's provisions for security against old age, disability, and unemployment represent public policy on minimum benefits. State workmen's compensation laws and state disability laws are similar. Such social legislation not only states the kinds of protection from insecurity public policy deems appropriate, but it requires that employees be provided basic benefits in these areas. If unions and employees consider these benefits as basic minimums to be supplemented by improved benefits, improvements in social legislation also provide a target effect.

WAGE CONTROLS

Although public policy has long placed floors under wages and benefits, it has usually avoided ceilings. But at times of strong inflationary pressures it has attempted to control the pace at which wages and

[9]Peter S. Barth, "The Minimum Wage and Teenage Unemployment," *IRRA Proceedings* (New York City, December 29–30, 1969), pp. 296–310.
[10]Herbert R. Northrup, "Wage Floors by Walsh-Healey," *The Conference Board Business Record* (June, 1950), pp. 220–221.

salaries advance. During World War II and Korea, for example, wage controls were instituted in an effort to hold back upward pressures on wage levels. In both instances a tripartite board with representatives of employers, labor, and the public was assigned the task of administering controls. Both boards limited increases in compensation to those that could be justified on the basis of equity. *Intraplant inequities,* evidenced by different rates paid by an employer for the same work or rates that failed to reflect differences in jobs, were recognized as situations demanding correction. Thus, job evaluation was encouraged as a means of correction. *Interplant inequities,* evidenced by rates lower than those paid for the same jobs by other employers in the same industry or localities, were recognized as a more pervasive source of unfairness. To permit correction of interplant inequities, wage surveys were conducted by the Bureau of Labor Statistics. Wage adjustments for changes in the cost of living were also permitted under World War II wage controls. Wage controls during Korea also permitted adjustments in situations that could be justified by productivity, ability to pay, substandard wages, or inequity resulting from the particular date at which controls were installed.

World War II wage controls are usually adjudged to have been successful undoubtedly because the superordinate motive of patriotism maintained reasonable unity among the three parties. Korean wage controls, on the other hand, were much less successful, because wages but not prices were controlled and employers, labor, and public members did not agree on the need for controls.

The wage-price guidelines of the early 1960s represented the first peacetime attempt in the United States to control the advance of wages and prices by direct means. In this relatively mild attempt at controls, the President's Council of Economic Advisers stated that wages should not be permitted to advance faster than economywide increases in productivity and that prices should be kept stable. To account for industry differences, industries in which productivity changes exceeded the national average were to limit wage increases to the national growth rate of productivity and to cut prices. Industries experiencing productivity growth rates at the national average were to grant the same wage increases but keep their prices stable. Only industries whose productivity growth rates were below the national average were to be permitted to increase prices, but their wages, too, were to be advanced only as fast as economywide increases in productivity. No administrative machinery was erected to police the guidelines but the President publicly criticized violations of them—thus the term "jawboning."

Whether the guidelines were successful in slowing the pace of wage and price advances has been highly controversial. Obviously, wage changes resulting from large union-management agreements and price changes involving entire industries, and thus most visible, were the focus of presidential attention. Less visible changes were largely unchallenged. Guideline proponents applaud their educational value and believe that by influencing the actions of large, visible industries and unions, the pace of wage and price advance was slowed. Opponents of the guidelines believe that at best they were ineffective and at worst they encouraged misallocation of resources by controlling only visible industries and unions and by providing a target effect often unjustified by economic reality. Although there is a vast volume of economic literature covering the controversy, the reader can find most of the issues discussed in one volume.[11]

Much more stringent wage and price controls were installed in the United States in 1971. Beginning with a ninety-day freeze on all wages and prices, administration of price changes was later assigned to a price control board consisting of public members and administration of wage changes to a wage control board consisting of employer, labor, and public members. Later, administration of both price and wage changes was assigned to an all public member cost of living council.

The control program has gone through a number of changes alternately involving tightening and loosening of restraints by stating relatively precise or loosely defined wage and price goals as guidelines and by treating exceptions rigidly or flexibly. In all of them, attempts have been made to impose restraint with minimal distortion of the economy and without establishing elaborate administrative machinery. The approach was to require advance approval or notice of wage and price decisions by the largest economic units, periodic reports of such decisions by smaller units, and exemption from controls of small organizations and some industries and sectors of the economy. Controllers were granted authority to delay or rescind increases. The Internal Revenue Service was enlisted to help police the controls.

Whether wage and price controls have been successful is a matter of some controversy. The original wage freeze was both a political and economic success—the public approved and wages and prices remained largely unchanged for ninety days. But once the freeze was lifted problems began to appear. Labor objected to tampering with union-management agreements and to tight controls over wages without effective price controls and with no controls on profits and dividends, but approved of flexibility in administering wage guidelines. Employers objected to price controls tied to profit margins but ap-

[11]George P. Shultz and Robert Z. Aliber (eds.), *Guidelines, Informal Controls and The Market Place* (Chicago: University of Chicago Press, 1966).

proved of tight wage controls and price controls permitting pass-through of cost increases.

It appears that controls over a significant period of time face a dilemma of whether political or economic effectiveness can be achieved. Consensus can often be obtained with ineffective controls. But effective controls have difficulty retaining consensus.

These problems with wage and price controls have appeared throughout the industrial world.[12] Called incomes policies, they are designed to improve the tradeoff between wage and price stability and unemployment (the Phillips Curve) by political means. European countries have been experimenting with incomes policies for twenty-five years. Although they have not been notably successful, incomes policies do improve the tradeoff on a short-term basis. As a result, Europeans continue to use them. Apparently, a workable incomes policy requires a fair degree of cooperation from unions and some degree of compulsion. Since wage costs are the primary target of incomes policies, labor believes that it is being asked to sacrifice more than other segments of society. Thus, a good consensus that includes labor is essential.[13]

Most incomes policies have been stop-go; *i.e.,* a freeze, severe restraints, moderation, and finally abandonment until the next crisis. Unfortunately, such stop-go policies appear to have political payoffs and for this reason may continue to be used.[14]

A long-term incomes policy probably requires some real income gains to workers rather than just money gains, perhaps through some redistribution of income to low-paid workers. Such a manpower policy rather than a wage restraint policy has been the basis of a long-term incomes policy in Sweden, where unions are strong and engage in national bargaining with a national employers' association. Other European unions have expressed interest in a real incomes policy implying cost-of-living compensation.[15]

The decentralized nature of collective bargaining in the United States probably makes such a long-term incomes policy unattainable. An alternative approach suggests restructuring the economy to promote competition in the labor and other markets by reducing the privi-

[12]D. C. Smith, *Incomes and Wage-Price Policies* (Kingston, Ontario: Industrial Relations Centre, Queen's University, 1967).

[13]Lloyd Ulman and Robert J. Flanagan, *Wage Restraint: A Study of Incomes Policies in Western Europe* (Berkeley: University of California Press, 1971).

[14]*Ibid.;* see also "Incomes Policies: What Europe Learned," *Business Week* (November 13, 1971), pp. 142–146.

[15]Andrew Martin, "Organized Labor and the Shaping of Economic Policy in Western Europe," *IRRA Proceedings* (New Orleans, December 27–28, 1971), pp. 176–185; Lloyd Ulman, "Inflation Policies and Collective Bargaining," *Monthly Labor Review* (August, 1971), pp. 48–52.

leges and immunities that have been granted unions and by measures to increase labor mobility and reduce structural unemployment.[16] But restraining unions implies that unions are responsible for inflation, which careful economic analysis has failed to show.[17] Also, free collective bargaining is a national goal that holds some parity with price stability. It is true that collectively bargained wage increases in a decentralized economy probably make for larger increases than individual bargaining. Also, structural reform of labor and product markets would reduce wage pressures and can be obtained under our system at a price of some labor peace. Unless the U.S. is willing to employ both an incomes policy and a structural reform policy, incomes policy is likely to be of the stop-go variety.

Wage Controls and Reference Groups. One of the unsolved problems of wage controls is the tendency of government boards to impose their comparison standards on those already in operation. If these arbitrarily imposed standards conflict with those used by workers, the result may not be the equity desired by controllers but increased inequity on the part of all groups affected by the decision. A further question involves the permanence of the effect of these administrative decisions on reference groups. Although the imposition of uniform standards by wage control authorities may seem necessary and rational, in a decentralized system of wage determination the consequence may be greatly increased inequity.[18]

LAWS AFFECTING COLLECTIVE BARGAINING

Public policy on compensation, although setting wage floors and sometimes ceilings, obviously intends that most compensation decisions be made by the parties to the employment exchange. Our federal and state laws that specify the rules of the game in collective bargaining imply concern with the method by which decisions are reached rather than with the decisions themselves. These laws and the regulations of administrative agencies specify collective bargaining as the method of determining compensation (as well as other issues surrounding work) if employees prefer it. They also offer guidelines for the collective bargaining process when it is used. But with very minor exceptions (union

[16]Gottfried Habeler, "Incomes Policy and Inflation: Some Further Reflections," *IRRA Proceedings* (1971), pp. 132–142.

[17]Edmund S. Phelps, "Money-Wage Dynamics and Labor-Market Equilibrium," *The Journal of Political Economy* (July–August, 1968), pp. 678–711.

[18]Seymour Lipset and Martin Trow, "Reference Group Theory and Trade Union Wage Policy," in Mirra Komarovsky (ed.), *Common Frontiers of the Social Sciences* (Glencoe, Illinois.: Free Press, 1957), pp. 391–411

security clauses and nondiscrimination) they leave the decisions to the parties. If employers and employees prefer to strike individual bargains on compensation, public policy offers no guides on method and almost none on the decisions reached.

EQUAL PAY LAWS

The most obvious exception to the "hands-off" public policy on compensation decisions (outside of floors and ceilings) is embodied in equal pay laws. These laws are designed to prevent discrimination in compensation based on sex. Until the passage of the federal Equal Pay Act of 1963, public policy on equal pay was confined to states. Forty-one states had laws requiring equal pay for women in 1971.[19]

The federal act prohibits employers from discriminating on the basis of sex by paying wages less than they pay to employees of the opposite sex for equal work on jobs that require equal skill, effort, and responsibility, and that are performed under similar working conditions.[20] Because the Equal Pay Act is an amendment to the Fair Labor Standards Act, it is policed by the Wage and Hour Division of the Department of Labor. "Inconsequential differences" among jobs do not justify unequal pay. To justify pay differentials on the same job, an employer must show that there are bona fide differences in either seniority, merit, incentive, or factors other than sex.[21]

Actually, equal pay legislation is only a portion of public policy prohibiting employment discrimination. Title VII of the Civil Rights Act of 1964 prohibits discrimination in compensation related to race, color, religion, sex, or national origin. The Age Discrimination in Employment Act of 1967 prohibits arbitrary discrimination in compensation against persons from 40 to 65 years of age. A number of state laws and local ordinances similarly prohibit discrimination in compensation. Some of them prohibit discrimination against the handicapped.[22] Because these laws apply to employment practices in general rather than to compensation in specific, enforcement is typically accomplished through conciliation with employers. But public policy clearly intends to eliminate discrimination in compensation not clearly based on job, performance, or required personal inputs.

[19]Morag MacLeod Sinichak, "Equal Pay in the United States," *International Labour Review* (June, 1971), pp. 541–557.

[20]"Equal Pay for Equal Work Under the Fair Labor Standards Act," U.S. Department of Labor, *Interpractices Bulletin,* Title 29, Part 800 (1967).

[21]"Equal Pay Issues," *Compensation Review* (Fourth Quarter, 1971), pp. 6–8.

[22]Weissbrodt, in *Monthly Labor Review* (January, 1972), pp. 29–39.

ASSURANCE OF PAYMENT

A final type of public policy on compensation is the requirement that workers be paid wages due them. State legislation typically specifies that wages be paid at regular intervals (one week or two) and that they be paid in cash or its equivalent. Payment in scrip (private currency) is usually prohibited, as is paying employees in barrooms. These laws also specify immediate payment if an employee is discharged. Laws pertaining to garnishment and wage assignment regulate debt collections from employees and typically restrict the amount of wages subject to garnishment and prohibit employee discharge or suspension because of such actions. Bankruptcy and lien laws give employees prior claims over the assets of the employer. Many states have agencies that assist employees in collecting wages due them.

The federal anti-kickback statute—the Copeland Act of 1934—makes illegal any requirement that employees return a part of their earnings to employers or others for the privilege of working. The act applies to all federal projects and contracts and applies strict penalties to anyone who tries to collect kickbacks. Several states have similar laws designed to ensure that employees receive the agreed-on rates.

UNION COMPENSATION POLICY

Union compensation policy emerges from studies of unions and collective bargaining and the effects of unions on wage levels and wage structures. Discussion of union compensation policy is complicated by differences among unions, although recent studies suggest that union policy in general and apparent policy differences can be explained by a limited number of variables.

Union wage policy has frequently been simply stated as "more." This is a serious oversimplification. Although union wage policy presumably calls for increasing the wages and other rewards of its members, the evidence suggests that few unions pursue this goal without regard to consequences.

Union compensation policy appears to be in reasonable agreement with public policy. Union support for increases in minimum wages is well known. Also, unions agree with public policy that compensation decisions should be largely left to the parties. But unions are understandably reluctant to go along with the idea of ceilings on compensation, although experience has shown that they have cooperated with the incomes policies of several countries for varying periods of time. Also, union policy on nondiscriminatory compensation has varied widely among unions.

Although it is well known that union policy is formulated by union leaders subject to consultation and veto by members, knowledge concerning the relative weight of the various pressures that shape the policy is imperfect. A reasonably complete compilation of these pressures would include (1) membership sentiment; (2) internal political pressures operating on union leaders; (3) wage programs and accomplishments of other unions; (4) business conditions facing the firm, the industry, and the economy; (5) unemployment in the local labor market; (6) product market competition; (7) industry wage comparisons; and (8) nonunion competition.

What has been called the Ross-Dunlop controversy over the determinants of union wage policy serves to group these pressures into political and economic categories. Ross'[23] study of union wage policy concludes that a union is a political organization operating in an economic environment. He found union wage policy to be determined largely by political factors—union rivalries, relative strength of intraunion factions, strong needs for union leaders to deliver results if they wish to remain in power, comparisons with gains made by other unions, and the needs of the union. Ross found little evidence that union wage policy was influenced by economic pressures; *i.e.,* the potential effects on employment of wage policies were not seriously considered. Ross' concept of "coercive comparisons," used to explain the comparison process of unions, is a close fit with reference group theory.

Dunlop's[24] study found union wage policy primarily determined by economic considerations—state of the labor market, movements of the cost of living, demand for the employer's product, and product market competition. Unions, Dunlop found, were sensitive to economic conditions that produce employment effects.

These two positions are useful in understanding union wage policy. Both are correct. Unions do respond to membership sentiments and to intraunion and interunion rivalries and make "coercive comparisons" with other unions. One study found that in nineteen major bargaining relations covering eleven different industries the increases granted over a twelve-year period were so similar as to be unexplainable on solely economic grounds.[25] These "wage patterns" do develop and are followed.

[23]Arthur M. Ross, *Trade Union Wage Policy* (Berkely: University of California Press, 1948).
[24]John T. Dunlop, *Wage Determination under Trade Unions* (New York: Augustus M. Kelley, Inc., 1950).
[25]John E. Maher, "The Wage Pattern in the United States, 1946–1957," *Industrial and Labor Relations Review* (October, 1961), pp. 3–20.

But union settlements often deviate from these key bargains for economic reasons. The classic demonstration of this deviation is a study of steel contracts from 1946 through 1950.[26] Even among the settlements made by the powerful steelworkers' union in a boom period there were several types of deviation from the pattern. For a pattern to persist it must be compatible with the economic survival of the firm. The ability of a firm to meet a pattern depends on several conditions. The labor cost to total costs ratio is one. Another is the extent of nonunion competition in the industry. If a union firm follows the pattern and a nonunion firm does not, the union firm may lose business quickly. Even more important is the ability of the firm to pass on wage increases as price increases without losing sales.

It appears to be primarily economic pressures on the product market rather than the labor market that constrain union wage policy. The combination of a highly competitive product market and the existence of nonunion competition is especially likely to restrict union wage gains. But unions are not completely helpless in the face of adverse product markets. Unions, by (1) suppressing price competition among firms, (2) inducing governments to pass minimum wage laws, public contract laws, fair trade laws, and protective tariffs, can reduce competition among firms, (3) inducing governments to provide a market for products and thus jobs (through government contract allocation), and (4) financing advertising campaigns, are sometimes able to limit the operation of economic forces and to increase the ability of firms to survive and adhere to the pattern.

Unions, by organizing a complete product market (especially if the entry of nonunion organizations is difficult),[27] can manipulate market conditions to their advantage. Because wage changes are the same for all producers, the union can limit the effects of competition among producers of a particular product.

But the possibilities of union manipulation of market forces should not be exaggerated. The union must adjust itself to product market conditions that it can affect only to a limited extent. Its power to gain wage increases is limited by its own recognition of the impact of wage changes on employment, particularly in terms of economic adversity in its industry.

This ability of unions to recognize the effect of wage changes on employment has been called the key to the Ross-Dunlop controversy; *i.e.,* Ross unions cannot perceive the tradeoff whereas Dunlop unions

[26]George Seltzer, "Pattern Bargaining and the United Steel Workers," *Journal of Political Economy* (August, 1951), pp. 319–331.
[27]Harold M. Levinson, *Determining Forces in Collective Wage Bargaining* (New York: John Wiley & Sons, Inc., 1966).

can.[28] Unions emphasizing political pressures, however, can perceive employer resistance and, in extreme situations, unemployment of its members.

Perhaps the more real issue is union reaction to unemployment of its members. If the industry is not completely organized, nonunion competition may force the union to adjust wage policy in the face of unemployment. Similarly, the feasibility of permitting an employer to maintain a lower wage level may have an effect. If this practice is feasible, the union may permit a firm that has been laying off workers a lower wage level. But this would depend on whether the union believes that a lower wage level will increase employment for its members. Or an attempt may be made to lower the employer's labor cost without tampering with the wage policy if this course is feasible without other employers becoming aware of it.

The extent of these economic reactions will in turn depend on such political considerations as whether or not unemployed workers are still union members, the number of unemployed union members, and the attitude of the majority. An alternative approach available to politically oriented unions is to bargain for devices that protect the union from employment decreases (work rules, limits on subcontracting).

Thus, both political and economic forces shape union wage policy and it seems impossible to predict which will be emphasized at a particular time or place. Coercive comparisons do result in wage decisions different from those that would obtain from economic forces alone, but economic forces just as clearly impose limits on political pressures. When a union adjusts its demands to a firm's adverse competitive position, it usually adopts over time a new comparison standard, perhaps another firm in similar economic circumstances. The parties to every bargaining relationship do refer to some pattern, but this does not mean that political forces have overridden market forces. It also appears true that political influences are more emphasized during good times than bad, in protected product markets more than in competitive product markets, and in highly unionized rather than in only partially unionized industries. But both political and economic influences are present in every bargaining relationship at all times.[29]

If one were forced to decide whether political or economic forces are more influential in determining union wage policy, it would be easy

[28]Daniel J. B. Mitchell, "Union Wage Policies: The Ross-Dunlop Debate Reopened," *Industrial Relations* (February, 1972), pp. 46–61.

[29]See M. W. Reder, "The Theory of Union Wage Policy," *Review of Economics and Statistics* (February, 1952), pp. 34–45; Albert Rees, "Union Wage Policies," in IRRA, *Interpreting the Labor Movement* (Madison, Wisconsin: IRRA, 1952), pp. 130–148.

to side with Reynolds.[30] In his view, the most important pressures are (1) rank-and-file sentiments, (2) interunion and intraunion rivalries for members and prestige (and thus coercive comparisons), and (3) the constraints imposed by the economic environment. The political nature of unionism does suggest that union wage policy is strongly influenced by member acceptance. Members' demands are discussed in union meetings before negotiation begins, and the terms agreed on must usually be submitted to a membership vote before final ratification. As is well known, in recent years union members have frequently rejected the terms recommended by their officers. Reports of the reactions of the "new-life-style" worker[31] indicate that unions must remain and perhaps grow even more sensitive to membership acceptance.

UNION WAGE POLICY AND REFERENCE GROUPS

In spite of the sensitivity of unions to member acceptance, there is a strong tendency of unions to emphasize comparisons external to the organization. Comparisons are typically made within the industry rather than the community. If members accept these comparison standards, few difficulties are likely to appear. But if members compare with others on similar jobs within the organization or with other employees with similar personal attributes, trouble is likely.

The evidence suggests that unions have been successful in adjusting to membership demands for attention to internal inequities between jobs and individuals and in balancing the parts of the compensation package. But union egalitarian philosophy is likely to emphasize external standards of comparison unless other pressures are overriding. There are sufficient examples of unsuccessful union attempts to change members' comparison standards, however, to suggest that unions need to give more attention to determining the reference groups that members actually use. Although unions have been able to influence members' choice of reference groups, they may be increasingly unable to do so.

Unions have also assumed (along with employers) that individuals compare only rewards rather than rewards and contributions. In the past, the level of employees organized and largely inadvertent attention to contributions in labor agreements have provided a rough-and-

[30]Lloyd G. Reynolds, *Labor Economics and Labor Relations,* 5th ed. (Englewood Cliffs, N.J.: Prentice-Hall, Inc., 1970), pp. 614–615.

[31]Edward E. Lawler, III, "Compensating the New-Life-Style Worker," *Personnel* (May–June, 1971), pp. 19–25; see also "The World of the Blue Collar Worker," *Dissent* (Winter, 1972), entire issue, but especially Part 1.

ready form of equity. But as new groups are organized and members become more sensitive to contributions made but not recognized within organizations, unions may be forced to give more explicit attention to members' comparisons.[32]

EMPLOYER COMPENSATION POLICY

Employer compensation policy is of necessity more operational than public or union policy. Because it is within organizations that most compensation decisions are made, organizations must have policies covering at least the following areas: (1) position in labor markets (average or below or above), (2) organization level of compensation decisions, (3) basis of compensation changes (merit or seniority), (4) communication regarding compensation (secrecy or openness), and (5) form of compensation.

Employer compensation policy is determined within constraints imposed by public policy, and often union policy as well. Further constraints are imposed by the culture; economic conditions; other organizations; and the size, structure, technology, and climate of the organization. But in large part, the policy and resulting compensation programs flow from whether the organization takes an active or passive approach in dealing with these constraints. An organization may actively set out to improve the employment exchange and thus organization functioning or it can passively accept constraints as rules to be followed.

Public policy sets floors and sometimes ceilings but these limits apply only to financial rewards and do not constrain either contributions or decisions pertaining to the vast majority of employment exchanges that are left to the parties to decide. Union policy is somewhat flexible, places tighter limits on rewards than on contributions, and, in any case, seldom applies to more than a part of the organization. The culture determines the broad outlines of acceptable employment exchanges but organization climate can mold them within these broad outlines.

Economic conditions do place severe limits on organizations but these limits vary among organizations and over time. Furthermore they limit financial rather than total rewards, are less limiting on the contributions organizations can accept or require, and thus may have differential effects on separate employee groups. There are maximum and

[32]John Corina, *Forms of Wage and Salary Payment for High Productivity* (Versailles: OECD, 1967), pp. 87, 118.

minimum limits on an organization's wage levels set by its position in product and labor markets—a minimum below which it could not go and hold enough employees to meet organization objectives, and a maximum above which it cannot go for budgetary reasons. But these limits are not clearly defined unless the organization feels it is close to either limit and in danger of being pushed beyond it. Furthermore these limits depend on the time period under consideration. The organization can exceed either limit for short periods, but for the longer periods the range between them is narrower.

The maximum and minimum wage levels are determined by different kinds of forces and there is no necessary connection between them. The maximum is set by conditions in the product market and the organization's ability to operate within them in terms of costs and prices. The minimum is determined by conditions in the labor market that result in part from supply and demand for labor, but at least as much from customary relationships, union pressures, and pressures from other organizations.

Other organizations affect employer wage decisions in two directions. Other organizations in the community may exert downward pressure to keep from "upsetting the market." Other organizations in the industry may exert upward pressures to forestall "unfair competition" in wages. Thus an organization in a high-wage industry in a low-wage community must somehow balance these two opposing forces.

Although some organizations are seriously restricted in compensation policy by one or more of these external constraints, the typical organization has a good deal of leeway. But many organizations are constrained by their size, structure, technology, and organization climate,[33] often without realizing it, and thus do nothing to deal with these constraints. Typical compensation programs with minor exceptions are so similar as to suggest that compensation policy is determined without regard to these variables.

Organization size can serve to free or restrict organization compensation policy. Although small size may restrict wage and salary levels because of limited economic resources, in every other organization compensation policy area the smaller organization is at a distinct advantage. Compensation decisions may be made at the lowest levels. Pay increases may be closely tied to performance and employees can see and thus believe that pay is tied to performance. Communication regarding pay may be completely open. Employment exchanges may be carefully designed for each individual so that he receives the kinds

[33]Edward E. Lawler, III, *Pay and Organizational Effectiveness: A Psychological View* (New York: McGraw-Hill Book Company, 1971), Chapter 16.

of rewards he wants and fully understands the contributions that the organization can accept.

Large organizations, on the other hand, may have more economic slack, but are more restricted except for policy with regard to pay level. Large organizations as well as small ones can carefully specify rewards and contributions at the time employees are hired. But seeing that the bargain is kept is more difficult in large organizations. Also, permitting lower-level managers in large organizations to make pay decisions probably ensures inconsistency. Communication programs are also probably somewhat vulnerable to differences in organization units. There is also an understandable reluctance in large organizations to accept the administrative inconvenience of different reward packages for different individuals throughout the organization.

But the most serious constraint on compensation policy in large organizations is the difficulty of maintaining the belief that pay changes are based on performance. Because action speaks louder than words and inconsistent actions are almost ensured by large size, it is probably impossible for large organizations to obtain performance motivation throughout the organization.

Decentralization helps because it enables units of the organization to utilize the advantages of small size. However, different compensation policies, and thus programs for the different employee groups, is a strategy available to organizations regardless of size and organization structure. That compensation policies must be confined to securing membership motivation from one employee group does not mean that compensation policy for other employee groups is similarly restricted. But it does mean that employment exchanges must be carefully designed and maintained for each employee group.

The technology of the organization has a strong influence on appropriate compensation policy. Organizations engaged in process production (as opposed to mass production and unit production)[34] usually have lower labor cost to total cost ratios and thus more freedom in decisions on wage levels, but employees are much more interdependent and individual performance is much more difficult to measure. Thus, compensation policy in process industries, although it may specify a high position in labor markets, is limited in designing pay to motivate performance unless contributions are carefully specified at the time of hiring or the payoff involves group performance. Organizations in process industries, however, are often small in terms of number of em-

[34]J. Woodward, *Industrial Organization: Theory and Practice* (London: Oxford University Press, 1965).

ployees, thus permitting the policy advantages of small organizations.

Technology, however, has more dimensions than type of production process. Classifying organizations as routine or nonroutine in two senses (probability of the appearance of new problems, programmed or nonprogrammed solutions to problems) results in differentiating four types of organizations[35] that would seem to require quite different compensation policies. The four types of organizations have quite different types of employees as typical rank-and-file members. Routine organizations (routine in both senses) are likely to be primarily composed of production people and the organization is likely to be centralized. Craft organizations (few new problems, search for solutions) are likely to be composed of employees who demand a strong voice in how the work is done and who resist performance-based pay plans. Engineering-type organizations (unfamiliar problems, programmed solutions) are likely to be largely manned by professionals who combine the viewpoints of their professions and those of the organization. Nonroutine organizations (nonroutine in both senses) are composed of individuals who may possess highly technical training but whose work and hopefully their attitudes make all of them managers of the organization. The compensation policies of these four types of organizations may be expected to vary greatly. The first two would be expected to emphasize membership motivation except for a limited number of employee groups. Although the first type may attempt a performance-based pay plan for rank-and-file employees, it will probably not work. The second (craft type) would probably be unwise to try. The third and fourth types would be expected to motivate both performance and membership, but a performance-based pay plan would encounter many more difficulties in the third type.

Organization climate may be a more important determinant of compensation policy, however, than any other organization variable. Because motivating performance by compensation depends on beliefs that are fostered by organization actions rather than words, authoritarian organizations are limited to making pay decisions that are objectively based. Unless employees in such organizations can actually see pay-performance relationships, they are unlikely to believe they exist. In organizations in which members receive more information and have more influence on decisions, they are more likely to trust management and to believe that a performance-reward relationship exists even if the

---

[35]Charles Perrow, *Organizational Analysis: A Sociological View* (Belmont, California: Wadsworth Publishing Company, Inc., 1970).

evidence is not unequivocal. In such organizations, compensation policy is subject to far fewer constraints, and the employment exchange may be fashioned to achieve the goals of both the organization and members.

This last point suggests that compensation policy may be employed to change the organization.[36] Because pay is one of the strongest signals in organizations, the organization may use it to broadcast a change in management style. A more open compensation communications policy and more discussion of the contributions the organization needs and can accept can be such a start. Even more important is showing the relationship between performance and reward by actually delivering. Involving employees in pay decisions is another clear signal. But, to repeat, it is action not words that produces changes.

Although some organizations respond positively to these constraints and give a good deal of attention to compensation policies and resulting programs, the evidence suggests that most organizations assume that the employment exchange is a simple economic transaction that requires little thought. Most employer compensation policy calls for comparing economic rewards with what other organizations are paying for similar work. Contribution is assumed to be measured by the job to which the employee is assigned and by his performance on that job. Thus, job comparison and employee comparison are also called for by compensation policy. But noneconomic rewards and contributions not specifically required by the job tend to be ignored in compensation policy, and desired performance is typically not well defined.

Fortunately, however, most organization compensation policy assumes that the ultimate test of equity is employee acceptance. This assumption is probably responsible for making compensation work as well as it does. At worst, it probably assures that the organization's jobs are filled with some quality level of employees. At best, it encourages communicating policies that inform employees of the organization's aims in compensation. It probably also serves to legitimize informal managerial practices regarding noneconomic rewards and contributions not recognized by formal policy.

INTEGRATING EMPLOYER COMPENSATION POLICY AND EMPLOYEE COMPARISONS

The contrasts between the comparisons made by organizations as shown by employer compensation policy and the comparisons made by individuals suggest some ways by which they may be integrated. Orga-

---

[36]Lawler, *Pay and Organizational Effectiveness*, pp. 281–284.

nizations compare economic rewards with other organizations and assume that contributions are entirely economic and measured by jobs. Thus, organizations assume that the employment exchange is a strictly economic transaction. Individuals, on the other hand, compare with objective evidence, their self-concept, other individuals, and reference groups. Furthermore, they compare both rewards and contributions and a wide variety of each that go much beyond the economic. Unlike organizations, individuals appear to make comparisons first with their own self-concept, then with others with whom they come into direct contact, and finally with the external labor market. Some individuals are attuned to the external labor market, but the others are making comparisons quite different from those made by organizations.

This difference suggests that the organization needs to know the comparison criteria employed by the different employee groups within the organization—the comparison standards, the factors compared, and the decision rules used. Group differences may follow occupational lines but they may also be influenced by demographic variables. Although it seems quite well established that rewards and contributions are compared, which rewards and which contributions are compared may be expected to vary with employee groups.

Periodic surveys have been suggested to determine the value that employees place on possible rewards and contributions.[37] Employee groups in a number of employing organizations have been shown to be able to report the relative importance they place on particular rewards and the importance they attach to particular contributions. They are also able to report the discrepancy between (1) the amount of a reward received and the amount they desire, and (2) the amount of a contribution recognized by the organization and the amount by which they wish it to be recognized. Comparison standards used and probable reactions to perceived inequity have also been supplied by these groups.[38]

Organizations making surveys of employees to determine the comparison standards and the important rewards and contributions of particular employee groups can use these results to obtain and provide the kinds of information each employee group needs to make its comparisons. Groups that make economic comparisons can be provided with economic information with respect to their reference group. Although noneconomic information is harder to handle, the fact that most

[37]Lyman W. Porter and Edward E. Lawler, III, *Managerial Attitudes and Performance* (Homewood, Illinois: Richard D. Irwin, Inc., 1968), Chapter 9.

[38]D. W. Belcher and T. J. Atchison, "Equity Theory and Compensation Policy," *Personnel Administration* (July–August, 1970), pp. 22–33; T. J. Atchison and D. W. Belcher, "Equity, Rewards, and Compensation Administration," *Personnel Administration* (March–April, 1971), pp. 32–36.

comparisons are likely to be within the organization and knowledge of the pertinent comparison standard should make it easier to accomplish.

Organizations also measuring perceived discrepancy with respect to rewards and contributions can use this information along with importance measures to appraise the present employment exchange of particular employee groups. Logically, rewards and contributions considered highly important by employees should carry low discrepancy scores if the employment exchange is to be perceived as equitable by employees. Even if the organization cannot make all the changes in the employment exchange that such analysis suggests,[39] knowing the sources of inequity perceived by employees is useful to organizations.

One course always available to organizations attempting to integrate employee and organization comparisons is the provision of information to employees. It seems likely that comparisons are made on the basis of available information, with emphasis on the quantifiable. If so, the concentration on pay and benefits as the primary rewards and time and effort as the primary contributions by some employee groups is understandable. It is quite possible that the emphasis given by organizations to economic variables in the employment exchange has served to make wage demands legitimate solutions to inequity arising from any source.

When comparisons are made on the basis of available information, increasing the amount and quality of information should serve to broaden comparisons to the advantage of both employees and organizations. An unpublished study by the author and a colleague suggests that government employees for whom economic matters are published experience less inequity. Lawler's[40] findings on the undesirable effects of pay secrecy suggest that organizations could enhance employees' perception of equity by giving them more information. But there seems to be no good reason why increased communication by the organization should be limited to economic rewards. Greatly increased communication to employee groups about all parts of their particular employment exchange should help integrate employee and organization compari-

---

[39] An example is a public organization of professionals in which it was found by such an analysis that rewards were designed for local-oriented employees and the contributions for the cosmopolitan-oriented. Although designing such an employment exchange was undoubtedly inadvertent, any change would probably result in greater inequity for either employee group. T. J. Atchison, D. W. Belcher, and J. W. Hunt, "Measuring the Employment Exchange" (unpublished manuscript).

[40] E. E. Lawler, "Managers' Perception of Subordinates' Pay and of Their Superiors' Pay," *Personnel Psychology* (Winter, 1965), pp. 413–422.

sons. Although there are undoubtedly limits to the extent to which organizations can influence employees' comparisons, it is quite possible that additional economic information, although somewhat useful, will be less influential than additional information of a noneconomic nature. But organizations can teach employees to value the rewards offered by the organization and that the contributions required by the organization are legitimate.[41]

Different employee groups, of course, make different kinds of comparisons. But not much is known about which particular rewards relate to which particular contributions for various groups. Responsibility may be both a contribution and a reward for professionals and managers. Production and clerical employees may directly relate pay and benefits to time worked and effort expended. Until more is known, presumably the best course for organizations is to provide more information on the rewards and contributions each employee group considers highly important.

Employee groups appear to fall on a continuum in terms of the inclusiveness of the employment exchange. Thus to some employee groups, discussing their employment exchange is the equivalent of discussing their lives. At the other extreme, the employment exchange is limited to a very few rewards and contributions.

Employee groups also differ in whether or not they wish to expand the employment exchange. Some groups want to continue the employment exchange with the same balance of a limited number of rewards and contributions as when they were hired. Some groups, however, want to expand the employment exchange and do so by providing more contributions in return for additional intrinsic rewards that they provide themselves. If members of these latter groups see the reward-contribution balances as positive, they expand their views of legitimate organization demands.[42] If the balance is perceived as positive by both the individual and the organization, both want to make the employment exchange more inclusive. The individual wants to contribute more than his time and energy if the employment exchange includes many valued rewards. The organization tends to increase its contributions to members who provide the most positive balance. Attempts by the organization to obtain more contributions from members of these groups will be welcomed and result in commitment to organization goals. But such attempts by the organization with groups that prefer to

---

[41]Sherman Krupp, *Patterns in Organization Analysis* (New York: Holt, Rinehart and Winston, Inc., 1961), p. 97.

[42]C. I. Barnard, *The Functions of the Executive* (Cambridge, Massachusetts: Harvard University Press, 1938).

maintain the original exchange may be interpreted by these groups as an opportunity to haggle continuously over the terms of the agreement.[43]

Probably the most fruitful course for organizations in integrating employee and organization comparisons is to broaden their view of the employment exchange. The employment exchange is becoming more inclusive for all employee groups and both individuals and organizations are demanding more from it. Even in economic terms the expansion of benefits indicates a desire by individuals for a broader reward package. But individuals expect much more than economic rewards, and organizations have them available whether they realize it or not. Also organizations demand and can accept many more different kinds of contributions than they previously recognized.

Organizations must also be prepared to make a greater variety of employment exchanges. The employee mix of organizations is changing and the work force is becoming more diverse, including more professionals, more women, more members of minority groups. The rewards that some of these employee groups expect are quite different from those expected by other groups. Organizations must be prepared to respond with different reward packages for separate employee groups both because of organization requirements and social pressures.

The typical organization will thus be required to develop a number of different reward packages that vary both by occupational and demographic groups. Organizations may be expected to offer individuals more choices in determining their reward package. These choices will change with the individual's circumstances.

But differentiating rewards for different employee groups creates needs for coordinating them. In most organizations the responsibility for the different kinds of rewards is assigned to a number of separate organization units, and some rewards are no one's responsibility. The need for coordination suggests that one particular individual or organization unit be assigned the responsibility for developing reward packages based on the characteristics of the organization's work force. There seems to be no other way of removing the contradictory signals that uncoordinated reward systems give to individuals, nor for the organization to gain maximum value from rewards.

It is equally important that rewards be integrated with contributions. Organizations need to give more attention to the kinds of contributions they require and can accept and to the relationship between desired rewards and desired contributions for each employee group.

---

[43]Hilde Behrend, "The Effort Bargain," *Industrial and Labor Relations Review* (July, 1957), pp. 513–515.

This need suggests that job and organization design be integrated with the employment exchange. It might also prove useful to analyze labor contracts in terms of the employee contributions they imply.

For most organizations, designing employment exchanges for special employee groups probably means a considerable amount of bargaining, presumably more individual bargaining with highly educated professionals but more collective bargaining as well with employee groups not presently thought of as unions, possibly including middle managers.[44] It also implies a more careful spelling out of the employment exchange at the time of hiring.

Better integration of the employment exchange with the desires of employee groups should improve the compensation process for the organization as well as for employees. Organizations have limited resources and determining the optimum allocation of these resources to achieve organization goals is a crucial decision. Thus the organization must determine the contributions it needs from each employee group and how it can best distribute its available rewards to attain them. This suggests that organizations should be willing to accept minimum performance and commitment from some employee groups while insisting on high performance and commitment from others. Some work can be highly programmed, requiring only that the individual maintain his membership at the minimum level of performance. For these employee groups performance is built into the organization structure and the technology and rewards are primarily economic and are defined explicitly.

If, however, the organization requires that considerable discretion be exercised by the individual, more commitment is needed and this requires that the individual see a connection between his performance above the minimum level and additional rewards. Although these employment exchanges can probably never be completely specified, they can be expanded through further understanding of contributions relevant to both individual and organization and the availability of intrinsic rewards. These relationships are likely to be of longer duration and to imply future contributions by the individual and additional rewards for efforts to develop them.

[44]See Alfred T. DeMaria *et al., Manager Unions?* (New York: American Management Association, 1972).

18

Wage and Salary Surveys

The primary comparison standard of most organizations is the market value of employee services. Organizations seek to maintain a position with respect to the labor market—above the market rate in the case of wage leaders, at or near the market rate in the case of other employing organizations.

This emphasis on "comparable wages" or "going wages"[1] implies that organizations view the employment exchange as an economic transaction in which labor services are purchased. But it also represents a form of equity. Paying what other organizations pay does imply fairness in compensation.

Whether paying the market rate represents an economic or a sociological approach to wage determination is an interesting question. It does involve determining market value of employee services. But it also implies the force of custom, in which organizations pay what they do because other organizations do so, while the other organizations follow the same practice.

At any rate, for the vast majority of employers, discovering "comparable wages" in the area and/or industry provides a first approximation in wage and salary determination.[2] The particular rates employed may apply to organizations operating in the local labor market, to organizations in the same industry in the local labor market, to organizations in the industry without regard to location, or to some combination of these. Although organizations differ in their degree of orientation to

[1]Often referred to as "prevailing wages" by public organizations.
[2]Richard A. Lester, *Company Wage Policies* (Princeton, N.J.: Princeton University Press, 1948).

industry and area, no organization can ignore the local labor market in which it operates. Comparable wage and salary information is usually obtained by using some form of wage survey.

WAGE SURVEYS

Although there are records of wage surveys made as early as 1891,[3] they were relatively infrequent until World War II. When the National War Labor Board developed the concept of "interplant inequities" and enlisted the aid of the Bureau of Labor Statistics in determining comparable wages, they apparently began what could be called the wage survey movement. At any rate, since that time employers have emphasized wage surveys.

A survey of manufacturing companies employing approximately 2 million workers in the late 1940s found that ninety out of ninety-five companies made use of wage surveys and fifty-two of them not only made use of surveys compiled by others but also made surveys of their own.[4] A 1950s study reported that comparative wage information was collected from 62,000 employers employing 10 million workers by employer associations.[5] Presently, wage and salary surveys are conducted by individual organizations, employer associations, professional societies, and consulting organizations, as well as the Bureau of Labor Statistics. Union research departments frequently compile wage information from labor agreements for use by their negotiators.

It is not unusual for a large employing organization to make surveys at regular intervals, usually once or twice a year in each labor market, more frequent special surveys when necessary, and to participate in and thus receive copies of numerous surveys conducted by others. In fact, participation in wage and salary surveys has become such a burden to some organizations that they have been forced to limit it. One organization reported requests to participate in nearly 100 surveys each year.[6] Compensation administrators report that such an experience is not unusual.

Such a volume of data collection suggests that an enormous need exists, but it may also suggest a reliance on quantity rather than quality

---

[3]The Bureau of Labor Statistics' first study of occupational wage statistics was made in 1891. See United States Department of Labor, "BLS Handbook of Methods for Surveys and Studies," *Bulletin No. 1458* (Washington, D.C.: Government Printing Office, October, 1966).

[4]Lester, *Company Wage Policies,* pp. 10–11.

[5]N. Arnold Tolles and Robert L. Raimon, *Sources of Wage Information: Employer Associations* (Ithaca, New York: The New York State School of Industrial and Labor Relations, Cornell University, 1952), p. 335.

[6]Orval R. Grigsby and William C. Burns, "Salary Surveys—The Deluge," *Personnel Journal* (June, 1962), pp. 274–280.

of information. Because it seems fair to employers and employees to have wages related to those paid for comparable work in the labor market or the industry of which the organization is a part,[7] organizations are motivated to seek such information. Also, although excellent occupational information is collected and published by the Bureau of Labor Statistics, not all occupations are covered.[8] Furthermore, organizations under our system of wage determination largely design their own jobs and decide which jobs they need information on, which labor market competitors they wish to compare with, and what kinds of information are needed. The result is that organizations conduct or participate in wage and salary surveys designed to obtain information on the specific jobs that they wish to compare from particular organizations in particular labor markets. Not all surveys are designed to secure data with respect to particular jobs, nor to obtain the same sort of compensation information. But all of them are assumed to provide organizations with information useful in making compensation decisions.

It is difficult to predict whether private wage and salary surveys will continue to proliferate or will become less frequent in the future. The tendency of some organizations to adopt benchmark job evaluation, which requires organizations to obtain labor market information on as many jobs as possible, argues for continued proliferation.[9] On the other hand, the time-consuming nature of wage survey participation and the expanding use of BLS surveys argue against it. For example, more than 50,000 copies of the BLS Professional, Administrative, Technical, and Clerical Salary survey are sold each year,[10] and public employers are increasingly using these surveys in salary administration.[11]

Another factor that should make for fewer, more careful surveys is expanding knowledge of the complexity of wage information and of the difficulty of making appropriate wage comparisons. One of the fall-outs from surveys of occupational wage rates by the BLS is the development of wage survey techniques that permit the collection of reliable information.[12] For example, such requirements as proper sample selection and size, good job descriptions, personal visit determina-

[7]H. M. Douty, *Wages: An Introduction* (Los Angeles: University of California, Institute of Industrial Relations, 1951), p. 30.

[8]H. M. Douty, "Survey Methods and Wage Comparisons," *Labor Law Journal* (April, 1964), pp. 222–230.

[9]Matthew J. Murphy, "Keeping Pace with the Labor Market under Inflationary Conditions," *Compensation Review* (Second Quarter, 1969), pp. 8–13.

[10]Douty, in *Labor Law Journal* (April, 1964), pp. 222–230.

[11]Thomas W. Gavett, "Comparability Wage Programs," *Monthly Labor Review* (September, 1971), pp. 38–42.

[12]See USDL, *Bulletin No. 1458* (October, 1966), pp. 114–125 and 145–157.

tion of job comparability and individual pay rates, and careful specification of the information sought serve to show that many wage surveys that purport to provide occupational wage data are at best unreliable and at worst, worthless. Hopefully, users of wage survey data and participants will insist on knowing the characteristics of the survey in advance and act on that knowledge. Sophisticated participants and users are aware that although nonoccupational wage information may be usefully collected by mail, reliable occupational data obtained in this way are unlikely. They are also aware that because the usefulness of an occupational wage depends very basically on the skill and care with which the job matching process is conducted, job title inquiries are meaningless except among individuals who have previously established job comparability.

Of course, the reliability of the information that the organization requires depends on the use to be made of it. If interest is confined to general wage and salary movements in the market, high reliability may not be essential. If, however, the information is to be used to determine a change in wage level or a change in the internal wage structure, high reliability may be required. With these provisos in mind, an organization requiring wage survey data has available several choices: (1) a government survey may be used, (2) union wage data may be available, (3) surveys by trade or employer associations may be available, (4) surveys by consulting or professional organizations may be available by subscription, (5) an informal group of employers may form and make a survey, (6) an organization may make its own survey. Although these choices are probably arrayed in terms of costs to the organization, the reliability of the information may vary greatly. Government surveys are highly reliable but may not provide all the required information.

The reliability of the others is largely a matter of the way the surveys are conducted. For this reason, an organization requiring wage data must be in a position to evaluate the procedures used in wage and salary surveys.

GOVERNMENT OCCUPATIONAL WAGE AND SALARY SURVEYS

Government occupational wage surveys have contributed greatly to wage survey techniques. As an aid to understanding the procedures necessary to produce reliable occupational wage and salary data, the BLS surveys are discussed in some detail with particular reference to methods used.[13] In subsequent examination of private wage surveys,

[13]USDL, *Bulletin No. 1458* (October, 1966).

procedures will be compared to those used in BLS surveys as aids in judging survey reliability.

The Bureau of Labor Statistics presently has three programs that provide compensation data by occupation: industry wage surveys; community wage surveys; and the national survey of professional, administrative, technical, and clerical pay. Industry wage surveys provide data for selected occupations in fifty manufacturing and twenty nonmanufacturing industries nationally on a three- and five-year cycle that varies by industry. These surveys provide data on straight-time first-shift rates for individual workers in selected occupations; weekly work schedules; shift operations and differentials; paid holiday and vacation practices; and health, insurance, and pension benefits. Although industry surveys provide data by occupation that should be highly useful to employing organizations, their relatively long-term cycle and national coverage somewhat attenuate their usefulness.

Community wage surveys, however, come much closer to organization requirements. They are made annually in eighty-six local labor markets. They cover selected clerical and manual jobs common to a variety of manufacturing and nonmanufacturing industries. In addition to earnings data, these surveys provide information on weekly work schedules; paid holiday and vacation practices; and health, insurance, and pension benefits. Shift operations and differentials are provided for plant workers. Minimum entrance rates for inexperienced office workers are furnished. Data are classified by industry division as well as occupation and presented in frequency distributions showing the number of individuals in each wage rate class. Unfortunately, however, the occupations covered in community wage surveys are limited to white-collar, skilled maintenance, and other indirect manual jobs that are common to a variety of industries. They do not include processing jobs that are specific to particular industries. Although some of these occupations are included in industry surveys, the time delay in the latter undoubtedly serves to explain the need for many nongovernment surveys.

The national survey of professional, administrative, technical, and clerical pay provides salary distributions and means, medians, and inter-quartile ranges for seventy-seven occupations annually. Definitions of these occupations provide for classification of employees by work levels (for example, there are eight work levels for engineers). Although reflecting duties and responsibilities in industry, the definitions were designed to be translated into specific pay grades of federal civil service employees. In addition to salary data, weekly hours and salary systems are presented as well as industry salary differences. As mentioned previously, the PAT survey appears to be widely used by employing organizations, but its use may be limited by its national coverage. Although it is true that many of the occupations covered have a national rather than a local labor market and that clerical jobs that are primarily locally-oriented are summarized from community surveys, some occupations (such as job analysts, engineering technicians, and draftsmen) are usually filled from local labor markets.

All three of these occupational surveys are designed and conducted in such a manner as to insure the reliability and usefulness of the data. The wage rate, for example, is a highly specific measure—the rate of pay for individual workers excluding premium pay for overtime and for weekend, holiday, and shift work. The pay of incentive workers is made equivalent by dividing straight-time earnings by corresponding hours worked. Production bonuses, commissions, and cost-of-living bonuses are counted as earnings but nonproduction payments (for safety, attendance, etc.) are not. Nor are tips or allowances for meals, room, or uniforms included. The pay rate thus represents cash straight-time wages before deductions.

Benefits included (paid holidays; paid vacations; and health, insurance, and pension plans) are limited to those that are applicable to all nonsupervisory workers. Informal plans and those that are paid for entirely by employees are excluded.

Occupational classifications are defined in advance of the surveys. Although the job descriptions are designed to permit comparisons between organizations and areas and are thus somewhat brief, they provide sufficient detail to identify the essential elements of skill, difficulty, and responsibility. Only full-time regular workers are included in the survey; this means that working supervisors, apprentices, learners, trainees, and handicapped, probationary, part-time, and temporary workers are excluded.

The surveys are planned in consultation with management, labor, and government representatives. The needs of major users are a major consideration in the design and conduct of the surveys.

A minimum size of organization included in the survey is set at a point at which exclusion would have negligible effects for most occupations. Occupations are selected to represent a reasonably complete range of rates for the employment categories involved. They thus hopefully provide sufficient benchmark data to permit interpolating rates for other jobs.

Data are collected by personal visit by trained people who perform the job-matching task within organizations and secure the wage and salary rates for individuals from the organization's records. Community wage surveys involve personal visits every second year. In the intervening year the organization receives a transcript of the preceding year's job matching and wage rates. The work of surveyors is checked with special attention to the accuracy of job matching.

The sample of organizations included in the surveys is carefully selected to be representative of the area and industry. The size of the sample in a particular survey depends on the size of the universe, the diversity of occupations and their distribution, the dispersion of earnings among organizations, the size distribution of establishments, and the degree of accuracy required. The greater the dispersion of data, the larger the sample required for a given level of accuracy. Information from organizations is weighted to reproduce the universe that was sampled. The sample is designed so that the chances are nine out of ten that the published average does not differ by more than 5 per cent from the average that would be obtained if all organizations in the universe had been surveyed. This 5 per cent sampling error applies to the smallest breakdown published. Thus, broader classifications have less sampling error.

PRIVATE OCCUPATIONAL WAGE SURVEYS

Although apparently widely used by organizations to appraise their position in labor markets, BLS surveys provide only a small fraction of occupational wage and salary data. As mentioned previously, unions, employer and trade associations, consulting and professional organizations, and employing organizations (both public and private) conduct wage and salary surveys. These surveys are of widely varying quality. Obviously, however, appraisal of quality depends on the purpose the survey is designed to serve.

If the purpose consists of obtaining a sufficiently precise picture of the labor market pertinent to a particular employee group to permit the organization to determine wage level and/or wage structure, wage survey quality may be indispensable. In such cases it seems necessary for the organization conducting the survey to follow procedures similar to those used in BLS surveys. If, however, the purpose consists of keeping abreast of gross changes in labor markets and results are considered as only a minor influence on wage decisions, much less precision is necessary. Hence, determining the purpose of the survey is a major step in designing a survey or appraising one made by others. In fact, definition of purpose is a major step in channeling judgments on the area to be covered, the organizations and jobs to be included, and the types of information required.

Determining the area to be covered by the survey is essentially a matter of finding the boundaries of the labor market. Organizations designing their own surveys can determine the boundaries of applicable labor markets, but surveys designed by others may or may not coincide with these boundaries. A local labor market may be defined in terms of the home addresses of present employees or in terms of travel time to work. For some organizations, the pertinent labor market consists of other organizations in the industry within the geographic area. For others, it is the industry regardless of location. In the case of some occupations, the labor market is not restricted by either area or industry, but is national or even international. The area surveyed is an important variable to organizations appraising the usefulness of surveys made by others. Surveys covering broader areas than that encompassing an organization's labor market may be of marginal usefulness. But in the case of organizations hewing to industry rates, a survey covering members of the industry may be of some use even if poorly designed.

The organizations to be included in the survey are in part determined by the area covered. Although BLS surveys include all the organizations (above a certain size calculated so as to not affect results) in the area or industry by carefully selecting a sample that represents the total, few private surveys do so. Most private surveys select participant organizations without a census of the organizations in the universe and with little regard for sampling principles. Often, the primary criterion for inclusion in the survey is willingness to participate. Organizations conducting their own surveys can, of course, select for participation the organizations that they consider to be their labor market competitors. Participant organizations can be selected by area, industry, size, or some combination of these variables. If all organizations selected provide information, no sample is involved—the entire universe has been surveyed. But if some organizations decline to participate or if participants are selected from the universe, a sampling problem emerges that may well attenuate the value of the data. When it is remembered that the greater the variability of the data, the larger the sample needed for representativeness, surveys limited to small numbers of organizations unless they comprise the universe can seriously affect the results of the survey. For this reason, organizations attempting to appraise surveys conducted by others should be alert to the possibility of a biased sample.

The jobs included in the survey are especially important in determining the value of the survey to an organization. Obviously, a survey that includes only one or two jobs existing in the organization is of little use. Most private surveys include from twenty to thirty key jobs defined as those (1) representing the complete range of jobs surveyed; (2) numerically important; (3) traditionally employed as benchmarks; (4) well known; (5) relatively stable in job content; (6) representing good reference points in job structures concerning level of difficulty and responsibility; (7) susceptible to clear, concise description. Organizations conducting their own surveys, of course, can select key jobs that meet these criteria within the organization. But the "keyness" of jobs varies widely by organization. Although this variation would be expected to be less in surveys confined to one industry, it is unusual to find two organizations that organize tasks in the same way. Surveys designed and conducted by other organizations may or may not include enough key jobs within a particular organization to be useful. The tendency noted in benchmark job evaluation to survey all or most of an organization's jobs,[14] although it will produce more points of reference for organizations, will do nothing to reduce the diversity in job keyness in different organizations. Hopefully, including more jobs in surveys will not force organizations making surveys to cut corners in organization coverage or in determining job comparability.

The method used to insure comparability between the jobs designated in the survey and the jobs existing in participating organizations is the key to the reliability of occupational wage and salary data. If job matching is carefully and skillfully conducted, the wage and salary data presented are meaningful. Otherwise, they are not. Good methods of determining job comparability include careful comparison by trained analysts of survey job descriptions and jobs in participating organizations and the application of a common system of job evaluation. Both require personal visits to participating organizations by trained analysts. However, organizations already using a common system of job evaluation are in a position to exchange reliable wage data. Presumably, also, two knowledgable compensation administrators are able to establish sufficient job comparability to exchange wage and salary information between themselves on a very limited number of jobs by telephone.

But determining job comparability is a difficult task at best. The different ways of organizing work even in the same industry are so numerous as to make the task of determining job comparability a formidable one. In fact, in the view of some it is impossible, at least on any job in which the incumbent is able to change the job to fit himself. Research by the BLS, however, shows that trained interviewers using good job descriptions can obtain reliable wage survey data.

Some occupational wage surveys conducted by organizations do determine job comparability through the use of personal visits by trained analysts.[15] Also, in some localities a common job evaluation system is so widely used as to permit organizations to conduct surveys without job comparability problems emerging. But most private occu-

[14]Murphy, in *Compensation Review* (Second Quarter, 1969), pp. 8–13.
[15]The Metropolitan San Diego Salary Survey, for example.

pational wage surveys are conducted by mail thereby leaving the determination of job comparability in the hands of respondents. Some of these surveys provide the respondent with classification scales to permit the respondent to slot the organization's jobs into levels corresponding to survey jobs. But given the unavoidable variation in the respondents' skill and conscientiousness and the general press of work, results of these surveys must contain data of uneven reliability.

The specifications of the data sought in private wage and salary surveys strongly influence the value of the survey to an organization. Most surveys collect information on wages and salaries and on wage policies and practices. But the terms "wage" or "salary" are subject to numerous interpretations and require careful specification if the survey is to be meaningful. Average wages or salaries for an occupation could be interpreted in many different ways depending on what is included and excluded and on the method used to compute the average.

Some private occupational wage surveys use precise specifications of wage rates, as are used in BLS surveys—the base rate (before deductions) for scheduled hours excluding overtime, shift differentials, and nonproduction bonuses, but including cost-of-living increases and production bonuses. These surveys also specify the manner in which the wage or salary rate of incentive and salaried workers is to be computed so that method of payment does not distort comparisons. These specifications recognize that workers in any occupation may be paid by the hour, week, month, or year, or by some incentive arrangement. Such surveys often request the actual rates being paid to individuals, as do BLS surveys.

But many private surveys are less precise in their definitions and many request information on hiring rates, rate ranges, earnings, wage changes, and wage policies and practices rather than rates applying to individuals. As mentioned previously, many private surveys are conducted by mail. Although wage policy and practice data and information with respect to wage changes (general increases, for example) may lend themselves to collection by mail; hiring rates, rate ranges, and earnings data probably do not if accuracy is required. There are just too many possible interpretations of these concepts, as well as variations in inclusions and exclusions within organizations, to ensure accurate data without a personal visit. Situations wherein compensation practices of organizations within a community or industry are reasonably standardized and well known by the surveying organization would be an exception.

The method used to tabulate and present results of an occupational wage survey also affects the usefulness of the results. Many private surveys tabulate and present calculated measures of wage data classified by responding organization and job. (See Figure 45). Although the ability of survey users to make comparisons with particular organizations may be justified if that organization is known to be a comparison standard used by employees, such tabulations conceal much of the data in the calculated measures. For example, there is no way to calculate the median (the middle rate) or the mode (the most frequently occurring rate) nor in many of such tabulations any way of determining how the "average" was computed. They may also focus comparisons on particular jobs rather than on the job structure. The BLS method of presentation shown in Table 9 seems much superior in that it presents a frequency distribution of the number of employees in each rate classification. This method permits users to make use of the computed average or to develop their own measures of the data.

Although interest in survey data may sometimes attach to a single job because of recruiting difficulties, most organizations are interested in how their wage structure compares with the wage structure of the community or industry. Some surveys provide charts that present average rates for survey jobs and average rates for each participating organization. (See Figure 46). In the situation depicted, the cooperating organizations all used a common job evaluation plan. A similar method is to calculate a wage line for the total survey and a wage line for each participating organization and present a chart comparing community and organization wage lines for each participant. (See Figure 47). Although the second method serves to emphasize the differences in both level and slope of community and organization wage structures, it assumes (as does Figure 46) that the calculated measures are appropriate and that each organization has all the jobs surveyed. Because neither of these assumptions may be true, a presentation such as that provided by the BLS permits organizations using the data either to use the calculated averages or compute its own measures and to plot its own wage or salary rates against survey rates for all the organization's jobs for which the survey supplies data.

Wage policy and practice (including benefits) information presents particular problems for wage surveys. As explained in Chapter 14, although it is increasingly recognized that benefits are a part of total compensation, benefit cost information is so difficult to interpret, when it is available, that surveying benefit practices that the user organization prices out using its costs seems preferable. BLS practice of limiting benefit information to those easily quantifiable seems a partial solution. Most private surveys present the prevalence of wage policies, practices, and certain benefits among the organizations surveyed.

COMPANY CODE LETTER

Job	A				B				C				D				E				F				G				H				Summary Weighted Average
	Average	Minimum	Maximum	No. of Employees	Average	Minimum	Maximum	No. of Employees	Average	Minimum	Maximum	No. of Employees	Average	Minimum	Maximum	No. of Employees	Average	Minimum	Maximum	No. of Employees	Average	Minimum	Maximum	No. of Employees	Average	Minimum	Maximum	No. of Employees	Average	Minimum	Maximum	No. of Employees	
Shop Jobs																																	
Assembler																																	
Heavy Laborer																																	
Rammer																																	
Poleman																																	
Carpenter's Helper																																	
Drill-Press Operator																																	
Pipe Fitter																																	
Summary																																	
Office Jobs																																	
Messenger																																	
Stenographer																																	
Payroll Clerk																																	
Duplicating Machine Operator																																	
Typist																																	
Summary																																	

FIGURE 45

469

TABLE 9
Professional and technical occupations: Weekly earnings

(Average straight-time weekly hours and earnings of workers in selected occupations by industry division, San Diego, Calif., November 1972)

Occupation and industry division	Number of workers	Weekly earnings[1] (standard) Mean[2]	Median[2]	Middle range[2]	Average weekly hours[1] (standard)	$100 & under 110	110–120	120–130	130–140	140–150	150–160	160–170	170–180	180–190	190–200	200–210	210–220	220–230	230–240	240–250	250–260	260–270	270–280	280–290	290–300	300 & over
Men and Women Combined																										
Computer operators Class A	48	$190.00	$186.50	$172.50–211.50	40.0	—	—	—	—	—	1	1	1	18	7	1	6	—	2	4	—	—	—	—	—	—
Computer operators, Class B	106	172.50	184.00	146.50–193.50	40.0	—	—	3	8	19	8	2	4	12	49	—	—	—	—	—	—	—	—	—	—	—
Manufacturing	78	183.50	191.50	181.00–194.50	40.0	—	—	—	—	8	4	1	3	12	49	—	—	—	—	—	—	—	—	—	—	—
Nonmanufacturing	28	142.50	144.00	126.00–154.50	39.5	—	—	3	8	11	4	1	1	—	—	—	—	—	—	—	—	—	—	—	—	—
Computer operators, Class C	53	142.00	147.50	126.00–153.00	40.0	—	—	12	3	6	8	18	2	4	—	—	—	—	—	—	—	—	—	—	—	—
Computer programers, Business, Class A	73	245.00	247.00	231.00–265.00	40.0	—	—	—	—	—	—	—	—	1	—	3	4	6	16	11	11	14	5	2	—	—
Manufacturing	61	244.50	244.00	231.00–254.50	40.0	—	—	—	—	—	—	—	—	1	—	2	4	6	16	11	11	6	4	1	—	—
Computer programers, Business, Class B	80	201.00	199.00	188.00–218.50	40.0	—	—	—	—	—	1	11	1	10	19	9	12	6	8	1	—	1	1	—	—	—
Manufacturing	61	203.00	203.50	186.00–221.00	40.0	—	—	—	—	—	—	10	1	9	9	6	11	5	7	1	—	1	1	—	—	—
Computer systems analysts, Business, Class A	75	299.00	295.00	279.50–322.00	40.0	—	—	—	—	—	—	—	—	—	—	—	—	—	2	—	—	7	11	14	12	*29
Manufacturing	47	297.50	295.00	277.50–322.00	40.0	—	—	—	—	—	—	—	—	—	—	—	—	—	2	—	—	4	11	3	9	18
Nonmanufacturing	28	301.50	292.50	282.50–324.00	40.0	—	—	—	—	—	—	—	—	—	—	—	—	—	—	—	—	3	—	11	3	11
Computer systems analysts, Business, Class B	47	246.50	236.50	222.00–268.50	39.5	—	—	—	—	—	—	—	—	—	—	1	7	10	8	3	3	5	3	3	—	2
Manufacturing	32	246.50	239.00	223.50–268.00	40.0	—	—	—	—	—	—	—	—	—	—	1	1	9	6	2	2	5	2	2	—	2
Draftsmen, Class A	315	218.50	230.00	185.00–234.50	40.0	—	—	—	—	—	—	10	33	37	5	17	13	38	124	12	8	7	11	—	—	—
Manufacturing	251	211.50	227.00	182.50–232.50	40.0	—	—	—	—	—	—	10	33	37	4	16	12	32	96	9	2	—	—	—	—	—
Draftsmen, Class B	130	185.50	190.00	168.50–201.50	40.0	—	—	—	2	—	13	21	16	12	—	26	13	12	2	—	—	—	—	—	—	—
Manufacturing	92	181.00	177.50	165.00–201.00	40.0	—	—	—	2	—	13	20	15	12	—	21	12	6	2	—	—	—	—	—	—	—
Nonmanufacturing	38	197.00	194.00	185.00–204.00	40.0	—	—	—	—	—	—	1	1	—	—	5	—	6	—	—	—	—	—	—	—	—
Draftsmen, Class C	105	145.00	146.00	125.00–165.50	40.0	1	4	33	12	14	5	25	6	2	—	3	—	—	—	—	—	—	—	—	—	—
Electronics technicians	651	188.00	185.00	169.00–203.50	40.0	—	—	—	23	12	40	104	64	95	50	165	39	31	28	—	—	—	—	—	—	—
Manufacturing	586	186.50	183.50	168.50–203.00	40.0	—	—	—	23	12	39	101	58	92	41	161	3	29	27	—	—	—	—	—	—	—
Nurses, industrial (registered)	31	191.00	201.00	191.00–203.00	40.0	—	—	—	—	—	3	3	1	1	6	17	1	—	—	—	—	—	—	—	—	—
Manufacturing	30	190.50	200.50	186.00–203.00	40.0	—	—	—	—	—	3	3	1	—	6	17	—	—	—	—	—	—	—	—	—	—

* Workers were distributed as follows: 9 at $300 to $320; 14 at $320 to $340; 3 at $340 to $360; and 3 at $360 to $380.

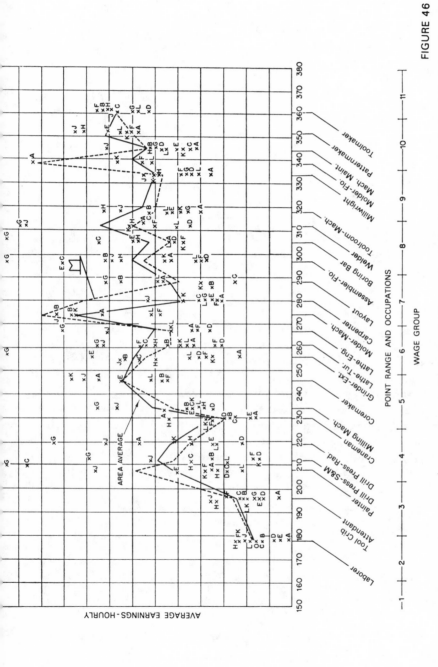

FIGURE 46

Source: "Conducting Wage Surveys," *Research and Technical Report 4* (Minneapolis: University of Minnesota, Industrial Relations Center). Reprinted by permission.

PERSPECTIVE ON OCCUPATIONAL WAGE SURVEYS

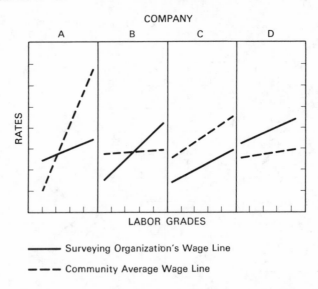

FIGURE 47

If this appraisal of private occupational wage surveys is reasonably accurate, many of the thousands of wage and salary surveys conducted each year are somewhat blunt instruments. Thus, their continued and increasing use[16] would call for some perspective.

In one view, many private surveys are so unreliable as to be almost worthless. Although the BLS has found that good job descriptions, trained interviewers, careful sampling procedures, and careful specification of concepts are essential for reliable data, a study of employer association surveys found that field men were used in less than 10 per cent, job descriptions were used in only 50 per cent, and no attention was paid to sampling.[17] One study defined survey reliability in terms of spread of results and adjudged 40 to 50 per cent spreads as normal but 75 per cent or greater spreads as evidence of unreliability.[18]   A British study[19] of 77 occupations in 40 firms, however, concluded, after

[16]A 1960 report states that some 96 per cent of employers make some use of surveys in compensation decisions. "Wages in Industry: A Survey of Company Policies," *Management Review* (June, 1960), p. 42. The available evidence leads one to believe that usage is increasing, if anything. William A. Groenkamp, "How Reliable Are Wage Surveys?" *Personnel* (January–February, 1967), pp. 32–37.

[17]Tolles and Raimon, *Sources of Wage Information.*

[18]John B. Harker, "Making Sense out of Salary Surveys," *Personnel Journal* (September, 1952), pp. 131–134.

[19]D. Robinson, "The Myths of the Local Labour Market," *Personnel* (Great Britain, December, 1967), pp. 36–39.

finding a spread of 50 per cent on 49 of the occupations and over 100 per cent on 12, that terms such as "the going rate" are meaningless. The implication of this conclusion is that occupational wage surveys are futile. But if spreads at or beyond 50 per cent are adjudged as unreliable, even BLS surveys are questionable and management compensation surveys with common spreads of 200 per cent are worthless.

In a more positive view, wage surveys are adjudged to be both indispensible and sufficiently reliable in the hands of skilled users.[20] Wage surveys, according to this view, are not micrometers but yardsticks; and although absolute job comparability is probably impossible, good job definitions and classifications yield good data. An interview study of makers and users of wage surveys concludes that improved sophistication on the part of both surveyors and users of survey data can result in improved surveys and survey usage.[21] The author is inclined to this latter view. Although there has undoubtedly been a tendency to overuse wage surveys and some tendency to misuse them because of lack of critical appraisal of survey methods, increased knowledge hopefully will result in better occupational surveys and better use of them.

NONOCCUPATIONAL WAGE AND SALARY SURVEYS

The difficulty of determining job comparability in wage and salary surveys has led to the development of survey methods not dependent on this process. One, for example, employs functions or broad occupational groups (industrial engineering, procurement) and responding organizations are asked to provide pay rate and employment data on all jobs falling within the function. Responding organizations are also asked to identify levels within the functions and to report pay rate and number of employees by levels.[22] Another[23] asks responding organizations to furnish salary and employment data from payroll records in $100 intervals for a number of categories of employees. Analysis of

[20]Kenneth E. Foster, "The Plus Side of Wage Surveys," *Personnel* (January–February, 1963), pp. 35–43.
[21]Groenkamp, in *Personnel* (January–February, 1967), pp. 32–37.
[22]Morton Adelberg, "Wage and Salary Surveys: The Occupational Approach," *Personnel* (November–December, 1960), pp. 36–44.
[23]Kenneth E. Foster, Gerald F. Wajda, and Theodore R. Lawson, "Global Plan for Salary Administration," *Harvard Business Review* (September–October, 1961), pp. 62–66.

these frequency distributions permits organizations using such data to compare their payroll expenditures for these employee categories with those of respondents. Medians, modes, and cumulative frequency distributions, for example, serve to inform organizations employing such surveys how their salary profile for each occupational group compared with those of competitors. This method was developed for use of organizations within one industry.

A third and more familiar nonoccupational approach involves the salary surveys of professional employees. These surveys, typically called maturity curves because they collect pay rates by age or years since degree, are made by a number of professional associations and private research organizations. Although such surveys typically present classifications by scholarly discipline, degree level, and supervisory status, they make no reference to job assignment.[24]

One of the most interesting developments in salary surveys is the Salary Information and Retrieval System developed by System Development Corporation and later acquired by Industrial Relations Counselors. In this system organizations provided salary and other data on professional employees to a data bank from which subscribers could conduct their own surveys by querying the computer. The data bank was originally designed to provide a wide variety of maturity curve analyses and later provided a method of job matching employing job families.[25]

USES OF WAGE AND SALARY SURVEY DATA

Although organizations appear to use wage and salary surveys as an important comparison standard, the manner in which they do so is highly variable and knowledge about the process is meager. The conclusion from an early study that employers attach different meanings to "keeping up" with the area or industry[26] apparently still stands. A small interview study found that organizations use industry and area surveys differently, usually giving great (perhaps too much) emphasis to industry surveys in wage determination but limiting area surveys that cross industry lines to determination of trends.[27] This corresponds with

[24]For an example, see *National Survey of Compensation Paid Scientists and Engineers Engaged in Research and Development,* conducted by Battelle Memorial Institute, Columbus, Ohio.

[25]See Industrial Relations Counselors Service, Inc., *Salary Information Retrieval System* (225 Santa Monica Blvd., Santa Monica, California, 90401, mimeographed, no date).

[26]L. G. Reynolds, *The Structure of Labor Markets* (New York: Harper & Brothers, 1951), p. 157.

[27]Groenkamp, in *Personnel* (January–February, 1967), pp. 32–37.

informal evidence from discussions with compensation administrators. There is an understandable tendency to rely on surveys that the organization has helped design and regularly participates in and these are often industry-oriented. There is also a tendency by compensation administrators to subject wage and salary data to detailed analysis to attempt to secure meaning from the data.[28] The discussion of private occupational wage surveys suggests that although some of them may be reliable and their data amenable to creative analysis, many are not.

In spite of the statements of advocates of guideline or benchmark job evaluation that survey data are "indicators of what going salary levels should be,"[29] most employers apparently use such data for background purposes or as guides for contemplating general wage or salary changes. Nonprofit organizations and government agencies are exceptions. Federal salary changes are directly keyed to changes shown by specific surveys, as are salary rates in many other government jurisdictions. Nonprofit organizations appear to rely more on surveys in making wage and salary changes than do profit-oriented organizations. Profit-oriented organizations appear to use survey results in different ways, depending on conditions in product and labor markets. In one period, hiring rates and rate increase policy may be problems on certain jobs and thus matters of interest. Average wage and salary rates of certain employee groups may be the emphasis in another. If there is a constant in the use of surveys, it probably is to enable organizations to inform employees that wage and salary surveys are made and used.

Our previous analysis of private surveys suggests that for many of them this lack of formula use is fortunate. In the case of less reliable surveys, use only as a guide seems proper. But even reliable surveys only tell what others pay. They don't tell why. For this reason organizations tend to use compensation policy as the ultimate comparison standard.

Although wage and salary levels in most organizations depend only partially on the results of surveys, survey results may be used for a number of other purposes. One is to compare the internal wage structure of the organization against the wage structure exhibited by the labor market. Although survey results may not dictate a change in the internal wage structure, the organization needs to know about major differences in order to determine whether internal or external forces will rule. Although it is probably a mistake to let the market determine hiring rates, they must reasonably be one element in the

[28]An example is the *constant population index*, which includes only jobs and organizations on which data are continuous, thus hopefully uncovering changes uninfluenced by the addition of new jobs and new organizations.

[29]Murphy, in *Compensation Review* (Second Quarter, 1969), pp. 8–13.

decision. Also, in decisions with respect to rates of progression and merit and length-of-service increases, practices in the community and/ or industry must represent an input. Trends toward or away from various types of incentive plans, profit-sharing plans, guaranteed wage plans, or salary for all employees plans help organizations make decisions on payment methods. The same statement may of course be made about the prevalence of certain benefits.

INTEGRATING WAGE SURVEYS AND EMPLOYEE COMPARISONS

Although organizations use wage and salary surveys as comparison standards, they represent comparison standards of the organization, not of employees. Our previous discussion of both government and private wage and salary surveys showed that neither was designed in terms of the organizations and groups that employees use for comparison purposes.

Our previous discussion of reference groups suggests that surveys of organizations and groups not used as comparison standards by employees are ignored by employees as useless, irrelevant information. Although the same discussion showed that reference groups may be changed, the process of doing so is not an easy one and, if successful, may result in unanticipated consequences.

This suggests that integrating wage surveys and employee comparisons involves employee participation in planning the survey. If employees are involved in selecting the jobs and organizations to be surveyed, they are much more likely to accept the results.[30]

Until this is done it is impossible to predict the effect on survey practice. But a reasonable prediction seems to be that less time and effort would be spent on surveys. Surveys designed with the participation of separate employee groups would be limited to jobs and organizations they compare with and would probably include fewer jobs and far fewer organizations. If so, the time and effort saved from participation in many surveys yielding what employees consider to be irrelevant information could be devoted to improving the reliability and creditability of those that are made. This approach would not stop organizations from also using other surveys of high reliability, if necessary, but it will ensure that survey information presented to employees is believed.

[30]Lawler, *Pay and Organizational Effectiveness,* pp. 197–198 and 260–261.

19

Wage Criteria

Another set of comparison standards used to determine compensation policy and to make compensation decisions are called wage criteria. Their use by organizations and unions once again implies that the employment exchange is viewed as purely an economic transaction in that wage criteria appear to represent economic variables. But although the evidence on the manner in which wage criteria are used is less than complete, what does exist suggests that in use they are behavioral and ethical standards as well as economic.

These wage criteria are used implicitly or explicitly by organizations, unions, arbitrators, and wage boards as comparison standards against which possible compensation policies and compensation decisions are appraised. Decisions about which wage criteria apply to a particular organization at a particular time, and the extent to which they apply, are seldom made explicit and no mathematical weighting technique appears to be used. But the evidence suggests that they are used to narrow the range of wage level possibilities permitting one to be chosen.

This chapter examines the major wage criteria: comparable wages, cost of living, the living wage, ability to pay, productivity, labor supplies, and purchasing power.[1] Attention is given to their usefulness

[1]For more detailed treatment of wage criteria, see Sumner H. Slichter, *Basic Criteria in Wage Negotiations* (Chicago Association of Commerce, 1947); Abraham L. Gitlow, *Wage Determination Under National Boards* (Englewood Cliffs, N.J.: Prentice-Hall, Inc., 1953); Jules Backman, *Wage Determination, An Analysis of Wage Criteria* (Princeton, N.J.: D. Van Nostrand Company, Inc., 1959); Paul Bullock, *Standards of Wage Determination* (Los Angeles: University of California, Institute of Industrial Relations, 1960).

and limitations as separate comparison standards. Although separate treatment of each of the criteria is an expository convenience and should aid understanding, it should be recognized as an abstraction from the reality of wage decisions. In practice, such complete separation is seldom possible. Wage decisions in the real world represent a rich amalgam of numerous forces only partially identifiable.

USE OF WAGE CRITERIA

Wage criteria may be used as yardsticks, plausible arguments by parties to wage decisions, or rationalizations of decisions made on other grounds. It has been suggested that they are used more to rationalize positions than to make them, on the grounds that application of the various criteria would often produce conflicting decisions.[2] For example, if the cost of living is up 10 per cent, ability to pay down 10 per cent, comparable wages in the area justify a 5 per cent increase, and comparable wages in the industry call for a 5 per cent decrease, the problem of reconciliation requires judgment that may easily be labeled after the fact as rationalization.

But wage criteria are used in making wage and salary decisions. The wages and salaries of federal employees are determined by comparable wages and salaries.[3] Public employee bargaining often involves advisory arbitration and fact-finding in wage disputes, and both procedures deal with most of the wage criteria. In fact, the growth in public employee bargaining at all levels will probably require that wage decisions be justified on the basis of comparable wages, ability to pay, productivity, labor supplies, or a combination of all of them. Although arbitration of new contract terms is a seldom-used practice in private union-management relationships in the U.S., the arbitrators make use of wage criteria.[4] The Australian system of compulsory arbitration leans heavily on such criteria as the living wage, fair wages, and ability to pay.[5]

Wage control boards make extensive use of wage criteria in determining government wage stabilization policy and in appraising wage decisions. Wartime wage controls specifically recognized cost of living,

---

[2]George W. Taylor, "Ground Rules for the Use of Statistics in Collective Bargaining," in Industrial Relations Research Association, *Proceedings of the Fifth Annual Meeting* (Chicago, December 28–29, 1952), pp. 10–20.

[3]Thomas W. Gavett, "Comparability Wage Programs," *Monthly Labor Review* (September, 1971), pp. 38–43.

[4]Irvin Bernstein, *The Arbitration of Wages* (Berkeley: University of California Press, 1954).

[5]Carl M. Stevens, "Is Compulsory Arbitration Compatible with Bargaining?" *Industrial Relations* (February, 1966), pp. 38–52.

comparable wages, and labor supplies as appropriate criteria. The guideposts of the 1960s heavily emphasized the productivity criterion. The guidelines set by the 1972 wage board incorporated cost of living and productivity criteria and by exempting low-paid employees from wage controls implied the living wage criterion.

Examination of differentials between wage levels of organizations in an area or an industry show that organizations are using wage criteria consciously or unconsciously.[6] More profitable organizations tend to pay higher wages for the same occupations than less profitable organizations, implying the effect of ability to pay. Capital-intensive organizations tend to be more profitable, implying both the ability to pay and the productivity criteria. But although small organizations are not always less profitable, small organizations tend to pay lower wages (and benefits) than large organizations,[7] implying ability to pay and perhaps both productivity and labor supply criteria. The fact that the size of establishment differential is higher in the South may imply the cost of living criterion. Service industries that tend to be labor-intensive, low-profit, and low-wage are often composed of small organizations.

Although high-profit organizations do have higher wage-paying ability, they may or may not do so. Some of them do to simplify recruitment problems, implying the labor supply criterion. Others do so because above-average profits whet the appetites of workers and their unions, again implying the ability to pay criterion.

Organizations tend to adopt a position in the wage structure of the community and to attempt to maintain this position as wage levels move up and down. This position implies the comparable wage criterion. An organization's position in the local labor market is largely a function of its profitability, implying ability to pay. But its position is also influenced by organization size and the kinds of employees who select move up and down. This position implies the comparable wage criterion. An organization's position in the local labor market is largely a attempts to change its position in the local labor market to enable it to expand employment or improve the quality of its work force.

Local labor markets also vary in wage levels, depending on industrial composition. Communities with large proportions of organizations in high-profit industries tend to be high-wage communities, implying both ability to pay and comparable wage criteria. Communities com-

---

[6]An especially lucid analysis of the interplay of forces on wage decisions of organizations is to be found in Chapter 18 of Neil W. Chamberlain and Donald E. Cullen, *The Labor Sector,* 2nd ed. (New York: McGraw-Hill Book Company, 1971). See especially pp. 391–415.

[7]Richard Lester, "Pay Differentials by Size of Establishment," *Industrial Relations* (October, 1967), pp. 57–67.

prising a high proportion of organizations in low-profit industries tend to be low-wage. Sometimes wage levels of particular communities experience short-term increases in wage levels because labor demands increase without an increase in labor supply or decreases because of an increase in labor supply without an increase in demand. In such cases, of course, the labor supply criterion is operating.

Differentials among local labor markets are limited by a tendency for workers to leave low-wage communities and for organizations to locate new plants in low-wage areas, thereby increasing labor demand. Both imply the labor supply criterion. But unions often attempt to eliminate these differentials through concessions in productivity,[8] thus implying the productivity criterion. The fact that the cost of living tends to be higher in high-wage areas implies the cost of living criterion.

Wage levels tend to increase faster in good times both because profits increase and because workers become both more demanding and more mobile. Here again the ability to pay and labor supply criteria are implied. Unions reinforce the process by insisting on gains made elsewhere (comparable wages). But even in good times less efficient organizations get by by paying lower wages to their employees and lower salaries to management and lowering their standards of employability, implying the use of both the ability to pay and labor supply criteria.

The reader will recognize in the above discussion both the use (perhaps largely unconscious) of most of the wage criteria by organizations and unions, and the operation of economic forces. Because wages and salaries represent conscious decisions and because other considerations not of an economic nature are operating, wage criteria are only a partial explanation. But they are operating in all wage decisions.

Finally, wage criteria as often used in collective bargaining do represent rationalizations. Unions will cite increases elsewhere (comparable wages), improvements in productivity, high profits, and rapid changes in cost of living as reasons for a wage increase. Employers in turn will cite other wage comparisons, inability to pay, and excess labor supply (unemployment) as reasons for lower or no wage increases. In both cases the wage criteria are chosen to justify positions taken rather than to make them.

These conscious and unconscious uses of wage criteria suggest that an appraisal of them would be useful. The reader is cautioned once more, however, that the distinctions made among the criteria in the following analysis are much less true in practice.

[8]Harold M. Levinson, "Pattern Bargaining by the United Automobile Workers," *Labor Law Journal* (September, 1958), p. 672.

COMPARABLE WAGES

Comparable wages represent, without doubt, the most widely used wage criterion. As mentioned previously, the wages and salaries of federal employees are keyed directly to comparable wages in labor markets, as are the wages of public employees in other jurisdictions. Also, unions emphasize "coercive comparisons" and private organizations consciously try to keep up with changes in labor markets. Perhaps the main reason for this widespread use is its apparent fairness. To most people, an acceptable definition of a "fair" wage is the wages paid by other employers for the same type of work. Employers find it reasonable because their competitors are paying the same wages. Another reason is its apparent simplicity. At first glance, it appears quite simple to obtain comparable wages and to base wage levels on them.

This illusion of simplicity vanishes, however, in the attempt to give meaning to comparable wages in a particular situation. As was seen in the preceding chapter, precise techniques carefully employed are required to find comparable jobs and comparable wage rates. Comparisons may be made of wage adjustments, actual rates, starting rates, rate ranges, earnings, benefits, or wage policies and practices. The influence of regularity of employment may be important in defining comparable wages. Determining the extent to which regularity of employment should reflect itself in wage rates, however, is not an easy task. There is the problem of deciding on the criterion of "comparable" organizations. Wage comparisons may involve organizations in the area, in the industry wherever located, or even outside the industry. Unions favor industry or even wider comparisons based on (1) desires of union members for wages equal to those received by others, (2) union goals of wage uniformity, and (3) rivalry within the labor movement. Organizations may favor community or industry comparisons, depending on the industry. In some industries, patterns are set that organizations in the industry or even in other industries follow. In some communities, a wage leader emerges that is followed by others regardless of industry. The important question is determining when differences in competitive conditions in the product market are so significant as to warrant a different wage level regardless of labor market influences.

The going wage is an abstraction. Some organizations always pay on the high side of the market in order to obtain goodwill or to insure an adequate labor supply. Others pay on the low side because they have to or because by lowering hiring requirements they can keep jobs adequately manned. The result is a range of rates to which various statistical measures may be applied, yielding different standard rates.

Various interpretations may be made and different determinations of the going rate arrived at—all quite easily justified.

To rely on comparable wages as a criterion of wage levels is to concentrate on wages as income. Comparable wage rates may represent entirely different levels of labor costs in two different organizations. Thus, setting wage levels strictly on the basis of going wages may impose severe hardships on one organization and a much lower labor cost on another.

These difficulties are not insurmountable, however, as attested by the number of employers leaning heavily on this criterion of wage levels. In addition to offering a certain measurability, such a policy also contains a good deal of economic wisdom. Wages are prices. A function of prices in a competitive economy is the allocation of resources. Use of comparative wage data operates roughly to allocate resources among labor markets.

Furthermore, comparisons greatly simplify the task of the negotiators. Once the appropriate comparisons have been agreed on, difficulties are minimized. A wage level can be set within which the wage, when taken along with other economic and noneconomic rewards, becomes satisfactory as income and operates reasonably well in its allocation function. Wages as costs are likewise satisfied because unit labor costs can be widely different between two organizations with identical wage rates, and unit labor costs can be identical in two organizations with widely different wage rates. And the fact that unit labor costs fluctuate more than wage rates[9] and are, at least in some measure, capable of variation through employer action[10] permits satisfactory adjustment to some level within this range.

Finally, comparable wages appear to operate as a force for generalizing changes in wage levels, although the impetus for such changes may have come from other factors. This latter fact is, however, the greatest disadvantage of the comparable wage criterion. Although it can explain how wage levels are determined, it cannot explain why. To find out why, it is necessary to attempt to trace the wage adjustment back to its origin. Such key bargains must rely on considerations like those expressed by the other criteria. Other disadvantages are (1) the lack of a single, universally acceptable type of comparison, and (2) the possibility that customary differentials among organizations and industries may satisfy social norms but disrupt economic objectives.

[9]Lloyd G. Reynolds, "Wages in the Business Cycle," *American Economic Review* (May, 1952), p. 85.

[10]Lloyd G. Reynolds, "Toward a Short-Run Theory of Wages," *American Economic Review* (June, 1948), p. 299.

In other words, although the comparable wage criterion is a major force in setting wage levels, it is not simple in its operation. In a tight labor market, when it is likely to be the compelling factor, paying comparable wages may be necessary in order to obtain and keep a labor force. Here, competitive forces in the labor market are likely to be more compelling than those in the product market. Because tight labor markets appear in prosperous periods, not only will organizations making industry comparisons increase wages, but those making local comparisons will be forced to maintain historical relationships in order to keep a labor force. When strong competition in the product market appears, however, the emphasis is likely to change to an attempt to equalize labor costs. Under such circumstances, the comparable wage criterion may not be abandoned, but will be less influential. A position will still be taken within the range of comparable wages, but wages as cost will influence the level set more than will wages as income. That is, comparable wages are followed as long as other criteria are not more compelling.

COST OF LIVING

Cost of living as a wage criterion is emphasized by workers and their unions when the cost of living is rising rapidly. In such times, they exert pressure on employing organizations to adjust wages to offset rises in living costs. In part, these demands represent a plea for equity (to offset reductions in real wages) and, in part, they represent recognition that when the cost of living is rising rapidly the economic position of most employers is changing in the same direction. Although wage pressures resulting from changes in the cost of living fluctuate with the rapidity with which living costs rise, price rises in most years since 1940 have produced expectations among employees of at least annual pay increases.

Although increases in the cost of living are translated into wage increases through comparable wages for most employees, longer-term contracts with unions have fostered other methods of applying the cost of living criterion. One is the wage reopening clause permitting wages to be renegotiated during a long-term contract. Another is the deferred wage increase that attempts to anticipate future economic changes at the time the contract is signed. The third employs an escalator clause by which wages are adjusted during the period of the contract (usually quarterly) in accordance with changes in the cost of living. In this third method, living cost changes are measured by changes in the Consumer

Price Index—either the national index or one published for a particular city.

Escalator clauses vary in popularity from year to year, fluctuating in coverage over the past twenty years from under 2 million workers to almost 4 million. Their popularity varies directly with the rapidity of cost of living increases during the period immediately preceding the signing of the contract and anticipation of future rises. Deferred increases are a satisfactory substitute for escalator clauses from the viewpoint of workers only when projected wage increases exceed changes in the cost of living.

Longer-term contracts may be interpreted as attempts by organizations to purchase longer periods of labor peace (typically three years), thereby reducing costs of annual negotiations and attendant uncertainties. All three methods of adjusting wages during the contract period suggest that organizations accept the cost of living wage criterion as valid.

But although both employees and organizations appear to employ this criterion and changes in wage rates tend to follow changes in the cost of living in the short run,[11] the effects of using cost of living as a wage criterion require some examination. Tying wages to changes in the cost of living does contain a measure of equity for employees by assuring them that their real wages are not devalued. It also provides organizations with some assurance that employees will not reduce their contributions to the employment exchange to match the reduced value of rewards, nor leave the organization.

But the equity provided employees is limited in that adjusting wages in accordance with changes in living costs implies a constant standard of living—a treadmill. Historically, unions have opposed the principle for this reason.[12] Employee equity is also impaired by common methods that provide the same absolute cost of living adjustment for all employees. Such flat adjustments assume that everyone's cost of living is the same and has changed by the same amount.

The Consumer Price Index, widely used to measure changes in the cost of living, measures the average change in the price of a comprehensive bundle of goods and services consumed by urban manual and clerical workers and their families.[13] Like any general index it is an

[11]Clark Kerr, "The Short-Run Behavior of Physical Productivity and Average Hourly Earnings," *Reprint No. 18* (Berkeley: University of California, Institute of Industrial Relations, 1950).

[12]See Executive Council Report, *Convention Proceedings of the American Federation of Labor* (1921), pp. 68–69.

[13]"The Consumer Price Index: History and Techniques," *BLS Bulletin 1517* (Washington, D.C.: Government Printing Office, 1966).

abstraction that rarely corresponds with actual living cost changes of any given family. Differences in consumption patterns among family units due to differences in family composition, age, income, taste, and other characteristics, and the possibilities of substituting goods and services yielding roughly equivalent satisfaction for those measured by the index, mean that the CPI varies greatly in its ability to measure cost of living changes for various groups. These perhaps unavoidable technical problems of measuring changes in the cost of living mean that flat cost of living wage adjustments are probably inequitable. Moreover, they compress the wage structure so that, over a period of time, the percentage differential between unskilled and skilled jobs is considerably narrowed.[14]

Organizations may experience adverse consequences in obtaining and keeping a work force from adjusting wages to changes in living costs. A compressed wage structure resulting from flat cost of living increases may produce difficulties in recruiting and keeping higher-level employees. Even more important, changes in the cost of living do not closely parallel changes in the supply-demand situation of any specific employee group. Thus an index of cost of living is a highly fallible barometer of the current market value of any employee group. Also, particular organizations and industries may be involved in competitive situations in product markets that run counter to changes in living costs.

A final problem with the cost of living criterion applies not to particular wage decisions but to the economy as a whole. Wage increases that fully reflect increases in living costs have the effect of building higher prices permanently into the cost structure and giving a twist to the upward spiral.[15] Escalator clauses especially serve to narrow the time gap between price and wage changes in an inflationary period, but deferred wage increases that anticipate price increases have the same effect. For this reason several other countries have attempted to build in some lag between price and wage changes by (1) requiring that cost of living changes be above some minimum amount before wage changes are made, (2) only partially compensating for price changes, and (3) measuring cost of living changes over longer periods.[16] Although labor contracts in the U.S. containing either wage reopeners, deferred increases, escalators, or some combination of them are extremely prevalent, the fact that most wage and salary decisions are

[14]H. M. Douty, "The Growth, Status, and Implications of Wage Escalation," *Monthly Labor Review* (February, 1953), pp. 126–129.

[15]H. M. Douty, "Living Costs, Wages, and Wage Policy," *Monthly Labor Review* (June, 1967), pp. 1–7.

[16]Jules Backman, "Cost-of-Living Escalator Clauses—Here and Abroad," *Labor Law Journal* (September, 1959), 615–622

widely decentralized and emphasize comparable wages as a criterion may provide enough of a lag between price and wage changes to prevent runaway inflation.

These varied consequences of the use of the cost of living criterion suggest caution in its use. Although attractive to employees, unions, and employing organizations in periods of rapidly rising prices, it is deceptively simple and blindly following it could produce more problems than it corrects. When influences in the labor market are stronger than influences in the product market, there is a tendency to use it to permit the employer to adjust quickly to changes in the labor market. When, however, an employer is faced with strong competition in the product market, employees may be faced with a choice between maintaining their real wages and their jobs. The cost of living criterion is never used as a sole standard of wage adjustment. Unions tend to regard cost of living increases as a minimum equity correction. In inflationary periods, cost of living changes serve to reinforce the comparable wage criterion.

THE LIVING WAGE

A wage criterion similar conceptually to the cost of living criterion is the living wage. Both are concerned with standards of living. But whereas the cost of living concept involves measuring changes in living costs statistically, the living wage concept is concerned with determining an appropriate standard of living.

Used as a wage criterion, the living wage calls for setting wages at a level that permits employees to maintain at least a certain standard of living. Minimum budgets are available for this purpose. The Bureau of Labor Statistics, for example, publishes annual costs of budgets for three living standards—lower, moderate, and higher.[17] The budgets are keyed to a family of four persons (husband, wife, boy of 13, girl of 8). In addition, the BLS publishes an equivalence scale for estimating budget costs for families of different size, age, and type, and a moderate budget for a retired couple.

These budgets are developed from criteria selected by specialists in such areas as public assistance, social and welfare services, public housing, unemployment compensation, minimum wages, collective bargaining, college scholarships, social security, and so on. Within these criteria, specific items and quantities are determined by consumer studies made by the BLS. All three budgets assume that the social goals of

[17]U.S. Department of Labor, "Three Standards of Living," *Bulletin No. 1570-5* (Washington, D.C.: Government Printing Office, Spring, 1967).

maintaining health and social well-being, nurturing children, and participating in community activities are met. Although all the budgets meet the standards of adequacy of scientists and experts, they recognize that these standards can be implemented at various levels of cost. The moderate budget is the same as the "modest but adequate" budget originally developed by the BLS in 1946. The lower budget was developed in response to requests from state public assistance agencies. The three budgets have been priced out in thirty-nine metropolitan and four nonmetropolitan areas.

The total average cost in urban areas of the U.S. in the spring of 1967 was $5,915 for the lowest of the three budgets, $9,076 for the moderate budget, and $13,050 for the highest budget. Price increases raised the lowest budget to almost $7,000 in 1972.

Use of minimum budgets in wage determination of individual employing organizations is limited. Unions sometimes present them as evidence of employee need. Both private organizations and public agencies may examine such budgets in considering the adequacy of present wage levels. But their use as a wage criterion is limited by such considerations as the following: (1) although higher living standards are widely regarded as socially desirable, the entire national income would be insufficient to provide the working population with either the moderate or highest budget; (2) both organizations and employees perceive rewards as based on contributions and although both may recognize need as a criterion of minimum rewards, neither regard it as sufficient in determining wages above the minimum; (3) individual employers cannot afford to base wage levels on minimum budgets unless their competitors are forced to do the same.

Actually, the living wage criterion is much more appropriately used as a guide for broad social policy than as a wage criterion. Thus, minimum budgets are a focus of discussion in considering changes in minimum wage laws and in formulating exemptions from wage controls.

ABILITY TO PAY

As mentioned earlier in this chapter, ability to pay does influence the wage levels of organizations. More profitable organizations tend to pay higher wages whether their profitability is based on the product market, technical efficiency, management ability, size, or some other factor. But the correlation between ability to pay and wage levels is far from perfect. Unions and employees of high-profit organizations make demands for higher wages. Organizations, however, may have the ability but not the willingness to pay. Some of them do, of course, submit to union and employee pressures. Others voluntarily choose to pay more to simplify recruitment and to permit higher selection standards.

In a very real sense the entire process of wage determination on the part of the organization is an assessment of its ability to pay. The weight attached to other wage criteria may be determined by this estimate. A prospective wage increase may or may not increase labor costs per unit (determined by wage rates and physical productivity), depending on anticipated changes in productivity. A wage increase that would be offset by increases in productivity does not increase labor costs and meets the requirement of ability to pay. A wage increase that increases labor costs, however, requires determining whether the increase can be passed on to customers or offset by reductions in other costs. Success in either effort again meets the requirements of ability to pay.

Similarly, a union presumably attempts to estimate an organization's ability to pay before making its demands. High current profits or favorable future prospects signal ability to pay and strengthen the union's bargaining power.

The ability to pay criterion has been employed in wage negotiations that link wages directly to profits, prices, sales, or output. For example, a 1919 printing agreement tied wages to economic conditions in the industry. Motion picture operators have signed contracts basing wages on the seating capacity of theaters. Coal industry agreements have tied wages to the productivity of coal fields. "Sliding scale" agreements have geared wages to selling prices.[18]

Attempts by unions to tie wages to ability to pay have been publicized. In 1945, for example, UAW used statistical techniques to forecast General Motors' profit levels to justify wage increases.[19] An even more elaborate attempt was made by the steelworkers in 1947 to forecast the wage-cost-price-profit relationships in the U.S. Steel Company at every level of production.[20]

It is therefore apparent that the ability to pay wage criterion has some usefulness in wage determination both at the bargaining table and when used unilaterally by the employer. One study found a number of organizations that estimated ability to pay by inserting a projected

[18]Z. Clark Dickinson, *Collective Wage Determination* (New York: The Ronald Press, 1941), pp. 189–210.

[19]Walter P. Reuther, *Purchasing Power for Prosperity: The Case of the General Motors' Workers for Maintaining Take-Home Pay* (Detroit: UAW-CIO, General Motors Department, 1945), pp. 55–76.

[20]Robert R. Nathan, Oscar Gross, and G. Griffith Johnson, *Economic Factors Relating to Wage Negotiations in the Steel Industry for 1947* (Pittsburgh: United Steelworkers of America, January 10, 1947).

wage increase into the latest income statement.[21] The ability to pay criterion is in actuality a composite of the economic forces facing the company. Although it seldom determines the precise wage adjustment, it usually sets the range within which the actual wage level is set. Often it would be more appropriately referred to as inability to pay in that it serves to set a limit to increases apparently justified on other grounds.

The ability to pay standard may be used by either unions or employers. Unions use it positively by pointing to "excess" profits. Employers often use it negatively as inability to pay. Neither party is likely to urge strict application of ability to pay, however, since it could lead to very undesirable results.

It would, for example, completely disorganize wage relationships. Wage levels would bear no relationship to the going rate in the labor market. Organizations in the same industry would have vastly different wage levels. Wages would fluctuate widely along with profits. All semblance of industry wage uniformity (usually strongly desired by unions) would disappear. Low-profit firms employing high proportions of skilled labor could have lower wage levels than high-profit firms employing nothing but unskilled labor. Thus, unskilled labor could receive higher wages than highly skilled labor—an effect not at all conducive to acquisition of skill or increased productivity.

Strong limits would be placed on economic efficiency. Under a system wherein increases in profits are absorbed by wages, an efficient managment would have nothing to gain from additional effort and inefficient management would be subsidized by low wages. Nor could employees leave inefficient organizations for more efficient ones because expansion of output and employment in efficient organizations would be forestalled by paying out increased profits in wages to present employees. Thus, incentive to management to improve efficiency would be seriously impaired. Possibilities of expansion would be limited.

Strict use of the ability to pay criterion would also require specific definition of ability to pay and agreement between the parties on some controversial issues. For example, how should profits be measured? Should profits unrelated to production and sales be included? Before or after taxes? As a percentage of net worth or of sales? Over what time period? What rate of return should be standard in determining ability to pay? Should management decisions on capital structure, expenditures for product development, product mix, pricing policy, and so on, which must affect profits, be bargained?

[21]Lloyd G. Reynolds, *The Structure of Labor Markets* (New York: Harper & Brothers, 1951), Chapter 6.

Thus, although strict application of the ability to pay criterion is likely to hold little attraction for the parties, the general economic environment of the economy, the industry, and the organization is important in wage level determination. When the demand for the product of the company is strong, when labor is relatively scarce, and when prices can be increased without reduction in sales, unions are likely to point to ability to pay and management is unlikely to plead inability to pay. When economic conditions facing the economy, the industry, or, especially, the organization, are unfavorable, management estimates of inability to pay may set a low limit to upward wage adjustments.

Union reaction to situations in which a company faces financial hardships was discussed in an earlier chapter. It was seen there that the reaction is a highly pragmatic one, strongly opposed to subsidizing inefficient organizations but strongly influenced by economic considerations.

Attempts to apply the ability to pay standard to bargaining in other than general terms or in other than crisis situations not only run afoul of the problems raised previously but also of strongly held opinions. Most labor leaders consider a company's ability to pay as irrelevant except if high profits are apparent. Most employers consider it as no business of the union.

Nevertheless, ability to pay or, conversely, inability to pay, will probably continue to influence wage determination in negotiations and in unilateral employer decisions. Its effect will be felt at the extremes —in judging whether a wage adjustment apparently justifiable on other grounds can or cannot be met. Strong presumptive evidence of favorable prospects in the future causes employers to resist less stringently a prospective increase in wage levels. Similarly, strong presumptive evidence of unfavorable future prospects reduces pressure for a wage increase, especially if it is feared that such a wage adjustment might cause loss of jobs, and greatly increases employer resistance. Although in a sense the concept is an expression of the entire process of wage level determination, it is limited by problems of measurement and of ability to forecast the significant economic variables as they bear on the organization.

PRODUCTIVITY

Possibly no wage criterion has received as much publicity as productivity. The "improvement factor" provided for in automotive labor contracts since 1948 has focused the attention of both managements and unions on productivity. The wage-price guideposts of the early 1960s, in their attempt to limit wage increases to increases in economy-wide productivity, constituted in effect a national educational campaign. Wage-price control policies instituted in 1972 have emphasized increased productivity as a source of wage increases and as a means of securing price stability. Productivity bargaining, a concept imported from Western Europe whereby productivity increases are negotiated in return for increased wages, has received increasing attention in this country.[22]

The reason for this interest is not hard to find. Increases in national productivity have been the chief determinant of the trends in the national level of real wages.[23] Thus, money wage increases have come from two primary sources—increases in economywide productivity and increases in the general price level.[24] The policy implication of these relationships seems exceptionally clear—a zero inflation economy could be achieved by tying wages to national productivity changes.

But although such a policy suggests wage determination by formula, neither economists nor the parties to wage determination agree that such formula wage determination is either desirable or possible. The annual improvement factor, although continued in automotive labor contracts, has shown no signs of great expansion in other industries. Both unions and employing organizations resisted the application of the guideposts and wage-price controls to their particular situations.

Nor does productivity appear to be widely used as a wage criterion. Most wage decisions are not related in any explicit way to productivity.[25] Although productivity data may be presented by both parties in wage negotiation, the extent to which it influences wage determination may be negligible. In wage arbitration cases, the use of productivity as a criterion is negligible.[26]

Use of the productivity criterion is probably hampered by some lack of understanding of the definition and measurement of productivity, in spite of the educational effects of the Council of Economic Advisers during the period of the guideposts and national concern with productivity. What is productivity? How is it measured?

Productivity refers to a comparison between the quantity of goods or services produced and the quantity of resources employed in turning

[22]Jerome M. Rosow, "Now is the Time for Productivity Bargaining," *Harvard Business Review* (January–February, 1972), pp. 78–89.

[23]Solomon Fabricant, *A Primer on Productivity* (New York: Random House, 1969), p. 106. This small paperback is an excellent explanation of the economics of productivity written in layman's language.

[24]*Ibid.,* p. 99.

[25]Douty, in *Monthly Labor Review* (June, 1967), pp. 1–7.

[26]Bernstein, *Arbitration of Wages,* pp. 28–29.

out these goods or services.[27] It is thus the ratio between output and input. But output can be compared with various types of inputs—man-hours, the total of labor and capital inputs, or with something in between. The results of these different comparisons are different, as are their meanings, and different comparisons are appropriate to different questions.

Two main concepts and measurements of productivity are used, but for different purposes. The first, output per man-hour, or labor productivity, answers questions concerning the fruitfulness of human labor under varying circumstances of labor quality, amount of equipment, scale of output, methods of production, and so on. The second, output per unit of capital and labor, or total productivity, measures efficiency in the use of labor and capital combined. This second measure is more complex but also more limited than the first. It measures whether efficiency in the conversion of labor and capital into output is rising or falling as a result of changes in technology, size and character of economic organization, in management skills, and many other determinants.

The first measure—output per man-hour—reflects the combined effect of changes (1) in efficiency with which labor and capital are used, (2) in the amount of tangible capital employed with each man-hour of labor, and (3) in the average quality of labor. It is thus the appropriate measure to employ on wage questions because these three changes are those that economists have found best explain the long-term trend in the general level of real wages. Short-term movements in earnings, however, are less well explained by labor productivity.

It should be emphasized, however, that labor productivity, or output per man-hour, measures not just the contributions of labor alone but of all input factors. In fact, improved quality of labor is estimated to contribute about 20 per cent, increased tangible capital about 17 per cent, and greater efficiency in the use of labor and capital the balance of the average annual rate of increase in economywide labor productivity.

Output per man-hour can, of course, be measured at several levels (job, plant, industry, or economy) and its appropriateness as a wage standard is very different at the various levels. At the job level, it is possible to measure worker application and effort separately from other inputs as the basis of wage incentive plans. At the plant level, estimates of the source of productivity increases can be made the basis of plant-wide incentive plans. At the industry level, productivity improvements can neither be traced separately to the behavior of workers, managers,

[27]Fabricant, *Primer on Productivity,* p. 3.

and investors in the industry nor can the contributions of one industry to another's be separated.[28] For these reasons, plus questions concerning the reliability of industry productivity indexes and predictable adverse economic consequences, industry productivity is seldom used, although sometimes is suggested as a wage determinant. At the level of the economy, however, changes in labor productivity are measured and have been suggested as appropriate for wage determination by many but not all economists. Economywide changes in productivity are the basis of the improvement factor in automotive labor contracts.

The concept of labor productivity described here is not synonymous with value or marginal productivity discussed in economic wage theory. Value productivity may be attributable to higher prices for the same output or a larger output at the same or lower prices as well as improved productive efficiency. According to economic theory, marginal or value productivity is a major determinant of wages and sets a ceiling on wages that cannot long be exceeded without adverse effects on production and employment. In the real world, wages above marginal productivity become obvious through inability to pay, thus showing the relationship between productivity and ability to pay. Improvements in labor productivity increase value productivity but so does increased demand for the product or service. Increased labor productivity with unchanged wages reduces unit labor costs and increases marginal productivity. But wage increases greater than labor productivity increases result in increased unit labor costs and may exceed marginal productivity.

An understanding of these relationships enables an appraisal to be made of productivity as a wage criterion. An appropriate beginning point would seem to be the formula use of productivity found in the improvement factor and the guideposts of the 1960s. The improvement factor bargained originally into the 1948 General Motors contract and continued in automotive contracts since that time provides for a yearly wage increase based on estimated increases in economywide productivity. The long-term trend (since 1889) in national labor productivity has been a growth of 2.4 per cent per year.[29] Although the amount of the improvement factor has increased in each contract since the original one, the formula holds that workers should be allowed to share in the gains resulting from productivity advance in the nation.

It seems significant that the improvement factor (plus the cost of living escalator) served to persuade the union to sign long-term agreements (for two and later, three years). It may be that the annual im-

---

[28] *Ibid.*, pp. 38–39.
[29] *Ibid.*, p. 14.

provement factor is simply a bargaining device to assure yearly wage increases beyond increases based on movements in living costs. Evidence for this position is provided by the rise of contracts providing for deferred wage increases in other industries with long-term contracts.

But the wage-price guideposts of the 1960s definitely advocated that wage increases of organizations be determined by economywide advances in productivity. Although the post-war trend figure of 3.2 per cent was used rather than the long-term trend of 2.4 per cent, the formula specified annual economywide productivity increases.

This formula use of productivity had been advocated by some economists for some years.[30] The suggestion that general wage levels in specific organizations be raised in accordance with annual increases in productivity in the economy was based on the belief that such a distribution of productivity gains is preferable to reducing prices in that the latter may contribute to economic instability. The method was also believed to ensure that productivity gains are distributed rather than withheld by organizations able to administer prices.

Other economists have argued against formula use of productivity on a number of grounds. For example, it has been pointed out that although there is a long-run relationship between productivity and wages, the short-run relationship is highly variable, suggesting that other wage-determining factors are more pertinent.[31] The fear has also been expressed that distributing productivity gains in the short run may so upset the long-term trend that there will be no gains to distribute.[32]

Perhaps the strongest argument against the formula use of productivity, however, is that tying wages to productivity yields stable prices only when productivity increases are accepted as a limit to wage increases. The guideposts did pose productivity increases as the limit of wage increases and broke down when price increases made wage increases limited to productivity impractical. When the cost of living is increasing rapidly, limiting wage increases to national productivity increases is unpalatable to employees. The improvement factor avoids the problem by the accompanying escalator clause. But, as stated previously, wage increases that reflect the trend increase in productivity plus the increase in living costs have the effect of building higher prices permanently into the cost structure.[33]

[30]John C. Davis and Thomas K. Hitch, "Wages and Productivity," *Review of Economics and Statistics* (November, 1949), pp. 292–298.

[31]Clark Kerr, "The Short-Run Behavior of Physical Productivity and Average Hourly Earnings," *Review of Economics and Statistics* (November, 1949), pp. 299–309.

[32]Jules Backman and M. R. Gainsbrugh, "Productivity and Living Standards," *Industrial and Labor Relations Review* (January, 1949), pp. 163–194.

[33]Douty, in *Monthly Labor Review* (June, 1967), pp. 1–7.

The inflationary potential of productivity formulas that are not accepted as limits is enhanced by a tendency to search for a productivity measure that makes larger wage increases feasible. Industry productivity increases in some industries, for example, may be larger than those in the economy. But not only are industry productivity indexes less reliable and more variable,[34] they reflect the greater possibilities of productivity increases in some industries while hiding the contributions of other industries to this rise. In fact, even national labor productivity overstates the noninflationary wage increase possibilities by including productivity increases resulting from transfers of workers from low-productivity to high-productivity industries and other sources of increase in labor quality. It has been shown that the trend in real wages is better explained by an index of national output per weighted man-hour in which higher grades of labor are weighted more heavily than low-grade labor.[35]

This controversy suggests that productivity is not a simple formula for wage level determination. Although there is a great deal of truth in the statement that productivity is a basis for wage increases in the long run, and in the statement that increased productivity in a specified establishment tends to reduce unit labor costs, productivity as a wage criterion has a number of limitations.

Advancing wage levels in strict accordance with productivity increases in specific organizations would lead to chaotic wage relationships. Different organizations and different industries have such varying rates of change in productivity as to throw wages based solely on productivity completely out of line with other wage considerations. Soon common labor in industries with rapid technological change would be paid more than the most skilled labor in other industries.

Increasing wage levels in proportion to productivity in the industry would prevent these industries from lowering prices and expanding production and employment. Thus the growth of employment would be impeded at the very points at which labor was gaining most in productivity. The result would seriously limit the incentives that have produced advances in productivity.

Productivity statistics may not be sufficiently accurate to use in wage determination. Although the national index published by the BLS is more reliable than industry indexes, it excludes an estimate for government and may not take adequate account of improvement in quality of output.[36] A special task force assigned to develop an index of govern-

---

[34]Fabricant, *Primer on Productivity,* Chapter 3.
[35]*Ibid.,* p. 110.
[36]*Ibid.,* p. 21.

ment productivity had included only about 50 per cent of the federal government's work force in 1972.[37]

Year-to-year increases in productivity are much more variable than the long-term rate of increase. Annual increases tend to be greater when business is expanding and less when business contracts. Moreover, although it is reasonable to expect that productivity will continue to rise, predictions that depart from the long-term trend are hazardous. In fact, there are probably more reasons for predicting decreases in the rate of productivity growth than increases (lower productivity growth in the growing service sector, rising crime rates, hiring hard-core unemployed, growth in spending on ecological problems).[38] Basing wage determination on either varying annual productivity measures or a declining trend rate would present problems.

If all wages were adjusted in accordance with economywide changes in productivity, wage relationships would be frozen and other influences could not be taken into account. If employees of some industries receive wage adjustments for both productiviy and cost of living whereas others do not, the result may be uneconomic interindustry differentials.[39]

Although annual productivity increases vary directly with business cycles, some increase typically occurs even in depression years. Basing wage increases on either the annual increase or the trend rate when output and employment are declining may well result in more unemployment.

Nor does distribution of productivity gains through wage increases assure fairness in income distribution. If wage increases are limited to economywide productivity increases and the price level is stable, the relative income share going to labor remains unchanged. If, however, the price level is rising, wage adjustments corresponding with national productivity gains result in a shift in income shares toward profit. Finally, wage increases exceeding productivity increases produce either inflation or a reduction in other shares.

Because of these limitations, it would seem that the applicability of the productivity criterion to wage determination in specific organizations is limited. If employed as recognition that increases in labor productivity in the organization at constant wages lowers labor costs per unit, it operates through ability to pay. If employed in the narrower

---

[37]"The Push to Boost Government Productivity," *Business Week* (May 13, 1972), p. 160.

[38]"Lower Productivity Threatens Growth," *Business Week* (January 1, 1972), pp. 36–37.

[39]Joseph W. Garbarino, "Wage Escalation and Wage Inflation," *Reprint No. 155* (Berkeley: University of California, Institute of Industrial Relations, 1961), p. 5.

sense that a productivity increase attributed to increased performance on the part of employees calls for an equivalent increase in employee rewards (as with merit increases and incentive plans), it is also applicable. But attempts to develop formulas to distribute national productivity increases within specific organizations ignore other, perhaps more important, wage-determining factors and probably raise more issues than they solve. Although the parties to wage determination do employ productivity data in negotiations, their effect on the final results is minimal.

LABOR SUPPLIES

One consideration always present in wage determination is the ability of the employing organization to obtain and hold an adequate work force. The wage level must be sufficient to perform this function or the organization cannot operate.

Perhaps the usual way this wage criterion operates is for an organization to evaluate the present effectiveness of its recruitment program and to determine whether its present level of labor turnover is too high or too low. It is true, of course, that the wage level is only one determinant of recruitment effectiveness and labor turnover. But it is an important one and evidence of its operation may be obtained from employment and exit interview records.

If no difficulty has been experienced in either of these areas, the presumption is that the present wage level is adequate to permit securing and holding a labor force. Other questions remain to be answered, however. Is the quality of the labor force being maintained, or have employees of lower efficiency been the only ones available at the present wages? Is the quality of the present labor force adequate? Is it more than adequate? Is a change in standards of employability desirable? Can it be accomplished at the present wage and salary level?

Such questions emphasize the fact, too often overlooked, that maintenance of a labor force in a numerical sense is not sufficient. Quality considerations are perhaps more important than quantity considerations. A labor force of low quality at a given wage level may be more costly to the organization than a labor force of higher quality obtained at a higher wage level, for the latter arrangement may yield lower unit labor costs. If an employer can lower his unit labor costs by raising his wage level and his standards of employability, such a course may deserve careful consideration.

This course at least partially explains the existence of wage leaders. Organizations that lead in upward movements of wage levels and those that pay "above the market" do so in the hope of attracting a higher quality labor force. It is obvious, of course, that if all organizations did this, none would gain. But because employers differ in their understanding of the relationship between wage levels and labor costs, this course will probably continue to be available.

Wage leadership may not only permit "skimming the cream" off the present labor force, it may ensure a continuing supply of high-quality personnel from new entrants. Some companies always have a waiting list of applicants, whereas others must continually make use of an aggressive recruitment program. Labor market studies have consistently shown that most employees find jobs by applying at the gate and through information supplied by friends and relatives. Such practices work to the advantage of establishments known as high-paying organizations.

Decisions regarding wage levels based on labor supply considerations must, however, be made in the light of forward prospects of the organization and the industry. Those in declining industries may be forced to allow wage levels to correspond with reduced value productivity of employees and to plan on less efficient and lower-paid work forces in the future. An expanding organization, on the other hand, may want to upgrade the quality of its work force by paying above the market and raising its standard of employability.

The extent to which labor supply considerations affect wage levels apparently varies greatly from one employing organization to another. Organizations in high-wage industries in low-wage areas experience few labor supply problems. But those in low-wage industries may face serious labor supply problems in their local labor market. Local labor market forces are important factors in wage determination even in the unionized sector of manufacturing.[40] The tendency of organizations to create their own labor markets by hiring only for beginning jobs and promoting from within serves somewhat to insulate them from the labor market.[41] Even such organizations, however, touch the labor market at some points and the usual employing organization is forced to "pay the market" or lower its hiring standards.

The typical employing organization, of course, operates in a number of separate labor markets corresponding to the separate employee groups discussed in an earlier chapter. Some of these labor markets are local, some national or international. In some of them, labor supply is

[40]T. W. McGuire and L. A. Rapping, "The Supply of Labor and Manufacturing Wage Determination in the United States: An Empirical Examination," *International Economic Review* (June, 1970), pp. 258–268.

[41]Martin Bronfenbrenner, "Potential Monopsony in Labor Markets," *Industrial and Labor Relations Review* (July, 1956), pp. 577–588.

controlled by a union or a professional society. The extent of labor market information varies greatly among these markets so that some are highly structured and others are amenable to control by employing organizations. Thus the organization's ability to insulate itself by training and promoting from within varies with labor markets. But in almost all labor markets the organization is able to vary both wages and salaries and hiring standards.

Also, as previously mentioned, employees from these separate groups differ greatly in the extent to which they emphasize economic and noneconomic rewards and in the contributions they want to make. Thus, organizations, although limited by forces operating in labor markets, are often less limited both in wage and salary determination and in hiring standards than they think they are. Although all employee groups place some value on wages and salaries, some of them are more attracted and held by intrinsic rewards flowing from the contributions they are permitted to make.

In making use of the labor supply criterion of wage levels, then, the following questions require answers: (1) What wage level will assure that the organization may secure and hold the work force needed? (2) What wage level will assure that the organization is able to maintain the quality of personnel it desires?

PURCHASING POWER

The purchasing power criterion is sometimes employed by unions in wage negotiations. Unions in large mass-production industries often use the purchasing power argument in negotiating key bargains. Basically, the argument goes as follows: A high-productivity economy requires expanded purchasing power in the hands of consumers to match the continuous expansion in goods and services offered for sale; if this additional purchasing power is not forthcoming, production declines and unemployment results. It should be pointed out that the argument is made in economywide terms and that it is not unlike the reasoning encountered in discussing economywide changes in productivity.

Several fallacies exist in the purchasing power argument. It assumes an identity between wages and total purchasing power. Actually, wages are only a part of total income. If raising wages reduces other incomes, total income may remain unchanged. A further assumption is that wage-earners are more likely to spend their total income than others, thus increasing total expenditures. This is a generalization that may not be true. Many wage-earners are in income brackets that account for substantial savings.

Nor is there an identity between income and purchasing power. Actually, purchasing power is the quantity of *goods and services* that can be bought with the money income distributed to all individuals in the system. Thus, purchasing power depends on the relation between aggregate personal income and the price level. Personal income includes income from profit, interest, and so on, in addition to wage income. Moreover, the amount of wage income depends on employment as well as wage rates. There are, therefore, at least four determinants of purchasing power: money wage rates, employment, income other than wages, retail prices. Raising one of these factors, such as wage rates, will not necessarily increase purchasing power. There may be offsetting changes in the other factors.

Actually, a more sophisticated formulation must make assumptions regarding the behavior of not only wages, but prices, propensity to consume, savings, investment, and productivity. And although it is possible to construct models in which increases in wages would increase, decrease, or leave employment unchanged, depending on the assumptions made, none corresponds closely with the real world. Sumner Slichter once remarked that if fluctuations in the business cycle could be controlled by increasing wages, economists have been wasting an awful lot of time studying control of the business cycle over the years.

From the foregoing discussion, it becomes apparent that not only is the purchasing power theory questionable but it has little to do with the problem of wage levels in a single organization. No single organization's wage level is so extensive as to permit changes to affect directly and appreciably the purchasing power expended on its products or services. No wage bargain in this country deals with the total economic situation. Thus, purchasing power is not a wage criterion in the sense that it is useful in solving the problem of wage levels in individual organizations.

PERSPECTIVE ON WAGE CRITERIA

Wage determination for a specific organization is a decision-making process. The decision is reached unilaterally in the case of a nonunion employer, at the bargaining table in the case of the union employer. In either case, a number of factors influence the decision reached, some of the most important of which have been discussed in this chapter.

Comparative wage rates probably has the greatest influence, for this factor plays two roles. It is a standard of comparison and a method of dispersing wage movements. Cost of living and ability to pay enter the decision as pressures for movement. They operate as initiators of wage movements. In upward movements, cost of living furnishes the thrust. Inability to pay operates as a ceiling and, in downward movements, a pressure. Productivity, an independent factor in some decisions, operates in most cases through ability to pay. The final decision must meet the test of ability to attract and hold an adequate labor force.

Minimum budgets and the concept of the living wage are too indefinite as standards to be very useful. Purchasing power is too broad a consideration to be applicable to a particular wage decision.

Key bargains may have a substantial impact on wage levels in both unionized and nonunion organizations. The key negotiations may employ all or most of the wage criteria. Once the key bargain is reached, the process of wage comparison holds the spotlight and transmits both product market and labor market pressures. Ross' centrifugal and centripetal forces provide an excellent explanation of the manner in which the three most pertinent criteria (comparable wages, ability to pay, and cost of living) apply. Wage comparisons exert a centripetal force, pulling separate wage level decisions together. Ability to pay operates as a centrifugal force since no two employers have exactly the same wage-paying capacity. Comparisons run in limited orbits and are strongest when the economic position of most employers is moving in the same direction (when the cost of living is moving rapidly). Ability to pay supersedes comparisons when the former is more compelling. It may be possible to accommodate both wage comparisons and ability to pay by increasing wages but taking action to prevent a rise in unit labor costs.[42]

INTEGRATING WAGE CRITERIA AND EMPLOYEE COMPARISONS

Because organizations have considered the employment exchange to be an economic transaction, wage criteria have been used as comparison standards by organizations and unions. Their use by employees has been largely limited to the information provided by unions on the progress of wage negotiations.

Integrating wage criteria and employee comparisons would seem to require determining which of these criteria employees use in appraising the employment exchange and providing sufficient information with respect to those criteria to permit employees to make rational

[42]Arthur M. Ross, "The External Wage Structure," in George W. Taylor and Frank C. Pierson (eds.), *New Concepts in Wage Determination* (New York: McGraw-Hill Book Company, 1957), pp. 190–192.

comparisons. The last chapter discussed how the comparable wage criterion may be integrated with employee comparisons. Although it seems certain that employees do consider changes in the cost of living in appraising the employment exchange, whether or not they consider the employer's ability to pay, measures of productivity, and relative supply of labor is unknown. Determining whether or not they do so is a simple matter of asking them. Once it is determined which of the criteria employees use as comparison standards, integration of employer and employee comparisons becomes a matter of providing sufficient information to enable employees to make rational comparisons.

Because it is quite certain that employees consider changes in the cost of living, it is important that organizations explain how they measure changes in living costs and how they adjust wages and salaries to compensate for these changes. If employees consider the employer's ability to pay, it seems necessary for organizations to carefully explain organization prospects and how they affect wages and salaries. Certainly, there are sufficient well-publicized cases in which employees have tempered wage demands and even accepted wage cuts in the face of employer adversity to show the wisdom of this course. The same point can be made about productivity measures. In fact, as mentioned numerous times in this book, one of the common failings of most organizations involves not thinking through and specifying what the organization wants to receive from the employment exchange, with the result that most employees don't know what the organization means by performance or productivity. Finally, there seems to be no good reason for failing to inform employees of conditions in their respective labor markets if employees consider labor supplies. In fact, supplying such information is not much different from supplying employees with wage comparison information.

V

Compensation Problems of Special Employee Groups

Organizations typically consider the compensation problems of such employee groups as salesmen, professionals, and managers as unique and so different from those of other employee groups as to warrant separate treatment. As has been repeatedly emphasized in this book, there are great differences in the employment exchange as perceived by different employee groups. The question, however, is whether the differences in compensation practices for these separate groups accord with differences in these employee groups and their jobs or to tradition or unwarranted assumptions.

Often, unfortunately, differences in compensation treatment by organizations of separate employee groups involve differences in terminology rather than substance. Some substantive differences, however, do exist; and they appear to intuitively recognize that the employment exchange of salesmen, professionals and managers is qualitatively different from that of other employees. For example, they may represent a recognition that these employment exchanges need to be more carefully designed to motivate performance as well as membership and that organizations have a greater opportunity to do so with these groups. They may also represent a recognition that these groups not only desire broader and deeper employment exchanges but that unless they meet both individual and organization objectives they cannot do so. Unfortunately, however, there is only a limited amount of evidence that organizations take advantage of the opportunities that designing employment exchanges for these groups should provide both organizations and employees.

The next two chapters examine the compensation practices of organizations with respect to salesmen, professionals, and managers. Emphasis is given to the probable effectiveness of these practices in achieving membership and performance motivation. Chapter 20 gives attention to sales compensation and Chapter 21 to the compensation of professionals and managers. Actually, as will be seen, there is a growing similarity in the way organizations design compensation for the three groups. But there are still more differences between sales compensation and the compensation of managers and professionals than between compensation programs of the latter two groups.

20

Sales Compensation

Without doubt, the dominant difference between sales compensation and the compensation of other employees is the emphasis in the former on incentive pay. Although incentive plans for employees other than managers are declining, no such tendency is appearing in sales compensation. True, the incentive plans are changing to better reflect the nature of the sales job, but a 1970 study of 375 organizations showed that almost 80 per cent of them included one or more incentive features in sales compensation.[1]

This emphasis on incentive probably is due in large part to tradition, but it is also a reflection of the importance of the sales function, the relatively unsupervised nature of much sales work, and a prevalent belief that salesmen not only need them to exert their best efforts but want to be paid on incentive. Some evidence of the preference of salesmen for incentives is a 1958 survey of the salesmen in sixty-four machinery manufacturing companies, which found that 95 per cent of them wanted to be paid on an incentive basis.[2] This finding has been interpreted as showing that salesmen place a high importance on money.[3] However, the reported experience of one organization that unintentionally paid salesmen so much that money became relatively

---

[1]Jack R. Dauner, "Salesmen's Compensation: Have We Kept Pace?" *Akron Business and Economic Review* (Summer, 1972), pp. 33–37.

[2]*Sales Compensation Manual* (Washington, D.C.: Machinery and Allied Products Institute, 1958), pp. 219–221.

[3]Richard C. Smyth and Matthew J. Murphy, *Compensating and Motivating Salesmen* (New York: American Management Association, 1969), p. 14.

unimportant to them[4] is not only a reminder that people vary in the desire for money but evidence that this desire can change.

Actually, both the desire to work under an incentive plan and the importance accorded money may vary as widely among salesmen as it does in the general population. There are so many kinds of sales jobs that a ranking of occupations by earnings placed them in the first, second, and fourth quarters of the distribution.[5] Just as with other work, there is a growing number of sales jobs that do not lend themselves to incentive plans.[6]

All of this suggests that the employment exchange for salesmen involves the same type of analysis used throughout this book. Accordingly, it seems useful to examine the salesman's employment exchange in terms of contributions, rewards, and comparison standards. Although it may be true that organizations and people who become and remain salesmen need and want the kind of employment exchange that sales compensation practice suggests, it may also be true, as with other employee groups, that tradition is the strongest factor operating.

CONTRIBUTIONS

The employment exchange as perceived by both organizations and salesmen emphasizes performance contributions but it also includes recognized job contributions and usually a number of unrecognized personal contributions. This section examines sales compensation practice in terms of the contributions it implies.

JOB CONTRIBUTIONS

Sales work, strictly speaking, involves working with buyers to secure orders. This job contribution takes the major proportion of the salesman's time, but it seldom comprises the totality of the job contributions needed by the organization. Also, many other employees in organizations who perform activities that aid the sales effort are not called salesmen. Thus the job contributions of the employee group called "salesmen" need specification.

Many sales jobs call for such job contributions as the following: soliciting orders, servicing customers, seeking out buyers, obtaining

[4]S. W. Gellerman, *Management by Motivation* (New York: American Management Association, 1968), p. 22.

[5]Max A. Rutzick, "A Ranking of U.S. Occupations by Earnings," *Monthly Labor Review* (March, 1965), pp. 249–255.

[6]Robert E. Sibson, *Wages and Salaries: A Handbook for Line Managers,* rev. ed. (New York: American Management Association, Inc., 1967), p. 172.

information, making credit and perhaps price and product modification decisions, performing such "missionary" work as product promotion and merchandising, training customer personnel, and giving technical advice and administrative assistance. All sales jobs involve such administrative work as making reports and keeping records. Notice that many of these activities involve what are usually regarded as management responsibilities. The tremendous variety in markets, products, competition, substitution possibilities, distribution systems, product demand, nature of the sales transaction, and buyer sophistication means that sales jobs vary widely among and often within organizations.

Job descriptions are used to spell out these job contributions in most organizations. Organizations that have sales jobs with any appreciable complexity find job descriptions essential, especially if they have a number of different sales jobs. Sales job descriptions typically include not only what the salesman does but such information as number of customers, volume of sales, diversity of products sold, and areas covered.

Most organizations that have sales jobs that include any job contributions besides straight selling use some form of job evaluation. Usually sales jobs are placed within the organization job structure by using the job evaluation plan used to evaluate administrative, supervisory, and middle-management jobs. If the organization's sales jobs are highly similar, the organization may differentiate among them by the use of such criteria as number of customers, number of product lines, sales volume, and responsibility for supervision, in addition to using the formal plan. If, however, sales jobs vary in complexity, the formal job evaluation plan is used not only to distinguish between sales and other types of jobs but between sales jobs.

Thus, organizations and salesmen recognize that sales work typically includes a number of job contributions in addition to selling. They also recognize that these job contributions differ from one sales job to another. Finally, both appear to accept that organizations need and expect to reward for these contributions and salesmen expect to provide these contributions and be rewarded for them.

PERFORMANCE CONTRIBUTIONS

But sales compensation emphasizes performance contributions. As mentioned previously, 80 per cent of a sizable sample of organizations included incentive features in sales compensation plans. In addition, most organizations also use rate ranges and assign individual base salaries within them.

As pointed out in Chapter 8, both rate ranges and incentive plans assume that (1) differential performance is required by the organization, (2) individuals assigned to the same job differ in performance, (3) differential performance should be rewarded separately from job assignment, and (4) performance differences can be measured. Because sales jobs always include some direct selling and because sales volume is so important to the success of most businesses, the organization is correct in assuming that it needs more sales. It is also well known that individuals typically differ widely in sales performance. Thus, organizations are correct in assuming the correctness of the first two assumptions with regard to sales, but not necessarily with regard to other activities. Organizations may well need better performance on these other activities and individuals may differ in them, but neither may be true. But rewarding differential performance on any activity requires that both organizations and employees know what kind of performance is needed and agree on the performance standards and measurements. Although these requirements may be met with regard to sales without too much difficulty, experience with incentive plans for other employees suggests some difficulty on other activities. Performance measurement requires determining the performance contribution to be measured, the units of measurement, standardizing the conditions of work, and a standard against which actual performance is to be compared. Performance appraisal, on the other hand, assumes that employee performance can be observed and assessed even if it cannot be objectively measured. Performance measurement often encounters problems of employee acceptance because it implies that what the organization wants is more effort, whereas performance appraisal encounters problems of credibility regarding whether or not the organization knows what performance it wants or can measure it. Because performance motivation is dependent not only on the credibility of performance measures and appraisals but upon employees' knowing what kinds of performance the organization wants and can accept, organizations cannot assume that either rate ranges or sales incentive plans will provide it automatically. This last point may help to explain the frequency of change in and expressed dissatisfaction with sales compensation.[7]

PERSONAL CONTRIBUTIONS

Sales compensation, with its emphasis on incentives, implies that organizations pay for performance contributions. As already mentioned, organizations also pay for job-related contributions. But few organizations and probably few salesmen consider it appropriate for organizations to pay for personal contributions (defined as personal

[7]Dauner, in *Akron Business and Economic Review* (Summer, 1972), pp. 33–37.

attributes not required by the job) on the grounds that doing so would represent paying for contributions not required by the organization.

But, as is well known, organizations recognize personal contributions even while denying it. Sales compensation increases with age to a peak in the late and middle thirties, implying age as a recognized contribution.[8] Rate ranges for salesmen, although regarded as recognizing performance contributions, in practice reward increased knowledge, extra experience and skill, and potential.[9] These variables certainly do not represent performance and they are usually paid for whether or not required by the job. In fact, salesmen, as well as other employees, perceive their development in the field (often measured by seniority with the organization) as representing additional contributions that should be recognized and, if possible, used by organizations. Organizations, in turn, sometimes gear salaries and bonuses for salesmen to achievements as compared to expectations, specifying neither. In such "incremental compensation plans,"[10] expectations are undoubtedly derived in part from personal traits of individuals—personal appearance, physical attributes, personal life style. But, hopefully, expectations are derived from such characteristics as adaptability in the face of changed conditions, commitment to the job and the organization, cooperation with other people and organization units, creativity in approaching problems, willingness to take action without urging, reasoned approaches to organization problems, and dependability. At any rate, organizations need these personal contributions and employees realize it. But sales compensation plans probably recognize this fact less than plans designed for other employee groups.

Finally, individuals and organizations recognize that acceptance of responsibility, effort expended, education, intelligence, job knowledge, and experience are contributions needed and rewarded by organizations. Although organizations that use job evaluation consider them to be job-related contributions in that these factors are used to distinguish among jobs, individuals (presumably including salesmen) consider them to be personal contributions that should be rewarded whether required by the job or not.

This analysis of contributions in the employment exchange involving salesmen shows that although organizations emphasize performance contributions, they also recognize job-related contributions and often implicitly, personal contributions. Although the importance of sales volume to organizations understandably encourages organizations to perceive the employment exchange for salesmen as an economic

[8]Smyth and Murphy, *Compensating and Motivating Salesmen,* p. 35.
[9]Sibson, *Wages and Salaries,* p. 168.
[10]*Ibid.,* p. 183.

transaction in which orders are exchanged for money, the organization's requirements for other less easily measured contributions and the self-directed character of much sales work imply a much broader employment exchange. Fortunately for organizations, the difficulty of defining and measuring these other contributions is probably offset by the high need for achievement of most salesmen. Because of this need many organizations could profitably devote their energies to permitting salesmen to perform by making personal contributions that both organizations and individuals recognize implicitly rather than to the more difficult task of defining and measuring performance contributions. But because of strong tradition, organizations will probably continue to try to develop sales incentive plans that reward performance contributions, even though in many cases, they are largely ceremonials representing growing rewards for growing personal contributions.

ECONOMIC REWARDS

Because of the emphasis on performance contributions by organizations, the rewards offered salesmen place heavy emphasis on economic performance rewards. But organizations also provide economic job rewards and, increasingly, economic membership rewards. They also increasingly provide noneconomic job, performance, and membership rewards, but less than to other employee groups.

ECONOMIC JOB REWARDS

Almost 85 per cent of organizations in 1970 paid salaries to salesmen, 20-plus per cent salary only, and 64-plus per cent salary plus incentive payments.[11] Salaries are paid primarily for job incumbency and thus represent economic job rewards. Salesmen's salaries are determined by the factors outlined in chapters 10 and 11 but are probably more influenced by the economics of the organization than most other jobs. The industry determines the profitability of product lines, the market structure and competition, and the character of sales jobs. Because industry economics and practice dictate sales jobs that range from selling nontechnical, heavily advertised products to negotiating the design, development, and delivery of custom-made technical systems for single customers, sales compensation varies widely by industry. But not by organization size. Small organizations often pay their salesmen more than large organizations.[12]

[11]Dauner, in *Akron Business and Economic Review* (Summer, 1972), pp. 33–37.
[12]Richard C. Smyth, "Financial Incentives for Salesmen," *Harvard Business Review* (January–February, 1968), pp. 109–117.

Sales salaries are also influenced by the labor market. Surveys of sales compensation are made by trade associations, consulting organizations, and organizations themselves. The American Management Association's Executive Compensation Service provides a comprehensive sales personnel report for its members. The variation shown by these surveys for any type of sales job tends to be even greater than for surveys of other types of positions, except manager.

Salary relationships within the organization also influence sales salaries. Primary among these relationships are sales management positions and positions in sales support functions. Other important internal relationships are jobs from which salesmen might be recruited and to which they might be promoted. But, as mentioned in the contributions section, job evaluation is used by most organizations to relate sales jobs to one another and to other jobs in the organization.

The man assigned to the sales job also influences salary. In fact, sales salaries in many organizations are, like management salaries, much influenced by the personal abilities of the incumbent. As pointed out in the discussion of personal contributions, organizations recognize personal contributions even when they deny doing so.

But perhaps the strongest influence on sales salaries is the form of payment. If sales jobs are paid on straight salary, salaries are obviously higher than if sales jobs are paid on the basis of salary plus incentive because in the second arrangement base salaries are adjusted downward to account for expected incentive earnings. In fact, comparing compensation of sales jobs involves comparisons of total compensation (salary plus incentive), thereby making comparisons difficult. Salesmen on incentive tend to earn about one-third more than salesmen on straight salary.[13] Salary averages from 75 to 80 per cent of the total compensation of salesmen paid on salary plus incentive,[14] but may be much higher or lower depending on the product sold, the nature of the market and competition, and organization sales objectives. A suggested range is 65 to 90 per cent.[15]

ECONOMIC PERFORMANCE REWARDS

As stressed previously, organizations favor some form of incentive compensation for salesmen. In 1970, about 15 per cent of salesmen were paid on commission and about 64 per cent salary plus some form of incentive, according to a large survey.[16]

[13]Sibson, *Wages and Salaries,* p. 166.
[14]Smyth, in *Harvard Business Review* (January–February, 1968), pp. 109–117.
[15]Frederick E. Webster, Jr., "Rationalizing Salesmen's Compensation Plans," *Journal of Marketing* (January, 1966), p. 56.
[16]Dauner, in *Akron Business and Economic Review* (Summer, 1972), pp. 33–37.

Before discussing these incentive arrangements, it may be useful to point out that, although salary ranges are usual in sales compensation, there is less tendency to characterize salary adjustments within ranges as performance rewards than is the case for other employees. For example, a study of 2,000 sales forces in 1965 found that although 58 per cent of organizations adjusted salaries on the basis of general performance or merit, the balance did so on such bases as (1) meeting competition, (2) large volume of sales, (3) length of service, (4) living costs, and (5) selling costs.[17] A compensation consultant states that merit pay adjustments for salesmen are usually based on increased knowledge, extra experience and skill, long-range demonstrated potential, and general economic factors.[18] Unfortunately, however, he finds that in practice organizations tend to give small merit increases in years of high incentive earnings and vice versa, suggesting that neither represents a pure performance reward.

There are literally thousands of sales incentive plans geared to the organization's products, markets, and marketing objectives. There is also a rough correspondence of sales compensation plans with pay plans for production employees. Straight salary plans, for example (although obviously not incentive plans), correspond with day work for production employees and tend to be used for inside salesmen and for outside sales jobs if the product is highly technical, individualized, and sold through group efforts. Straight commission plans correspond with straight piecework in that salesmen's earnings are in direct proportion to sales. Although often used in such industries as hardware and tools and in door-to-door sales, straight commission plans appear to be disappearing because organizations find that other marketing objectives are neglected or even thwarted and many salesmen dislike taking all the risk.

Most sales compensation plans are combinations of salary and incentive payments. Sales incentive plans are variously called commission plans, bonus plans, commission and bonus plans, and point plans; but the incentive plans carrying each designation overlap considerably. Commission, for example, in plans designated as salary and commission, may reward for sales, contribution to profit, or activities or efforts.[19] A 1970 survey found that 59 per cent paid off on sales, 17 per cent on orders, 17 per cent on profit measures, and the balance on other activities.[20] Commission rates may vary for the different activities and increase, decrease, or remain unchanged for different levels of activity.

[17]Research Institute of America, *Sales Compensation Practices* (New York, 1965).
[18]Sibson, *Wages and Salaries,* p. 168.
[19]Thomas R. Wotruba, *Sales Management* (New York: Holt, Rinehart and Winston, Inc., 1971), p. 402.
[20]Dauner, in *Akron Business and Economic Review* (Summer, 1972), pp. 33–37.

Commissions tend to be paid more frequently than bonuses, a point that may encourage use of the term.

Bonus plans may also be geared to sales but typically are based on a number of organization goals such as obtaining new accounts, improving market penetration, increasing order size, reducing sales expenses, and so on. Bonuses are typically established for various time periods but common practice is to pay bonuses annually. Unfortunately, many bonus plans have either no definite measurable goals or else are based on arbitrarily selected goals.

Commission and bonus plans, of course, are based on various combinations of objectives. Commissions and bonuses may be paid at different intervals.

Point plans assign point credit or monetary values for selling various commodities and for performing specified activities.[21] If carefully developed performance standards and measurements are the basis for the points or money values, point plans can provide valid performance rewards. But they can get complicated and administratively cumbersome. A compensation consultant insists that a sales incentive plan should not include more than two or three of the organization's most important sales and marketing objectives.[22]

Most sales incentive plans reward individuals rather than groups, although group plans do exist. There is general agreement that sales incentives should pay off monthly or quarterly. There appears to be more emphasis in sales incentive plans than in production incentive plans on testing the plan on paper before installation and perhaps on trying it out in selected organization units. There may also be more emphasis on explaining the plan to those it will cover. This emphasis is certainly understandable in terms of the complexity of sales incentive plans.

Organizations believe that sales incentive plans constitute performance rewards, as attested by their widespread use. Although not all organizations pay salesmen on incentive, there appears to be a widespread belief that they should whenever possible and that the typical salesman profits by such an arrangement.[23] Also there is some evidence that such plans do motivate salesmen. For example, an often cited Dartnell Corporation study of 1500 heavy equipment salesmen indicated that although those on straight salary produced an average sales volume of $135,000 a year, those on incentive averaged $262,000 a year.[24] As mentioned in Chapter 13, if both organizations and salesmen

[21]T. H. Patten, "Trends in Pay Practices for Salesmen," *Personnel* (January–February, 1968), pp. 54–63.

[22]Smyth, in *Harvard Business Review* (January–February, 1968), pp. 109–117.

[23]Smyth and Murphy, *Compensating and Motivating Salesmen.*

[24]Patten, in *Personnel* (January–February, 1968), pp. 54–63.

believe that sales incentive plans work, the result is a self-fulfilling prophesy.

But, as in the case of production incentive plans, no convincing evidence has been produced that the positive results have been produced by the incentive plan rather than some other of the many changes that accompany installation of the incentive plan. Furthermore, not all incentive plans are successful, and the frequent changes made in sales incentive plans and expressed dissatisfaction with them (one out of five organizations)[25] suggest that appraisal of these plans in terms of the performance motivation model would be useful.

The model specifies that for an incentive plan to motivate performance (1) employees must believe that good performance will lead to more pay; (2) employees must want more pay; (3) employees must not believe that good performance will lead to negative consequences; (4) employees must see that other desired rewards besides pay result from good performance; (5) employees must believe that their efforts do lead to improved performance. The relationship among these variables is multiplicative.

Perhaps most sales incentive plans create the belief that good performance leads to more pay, especially individual plans. Also, plans keyed to sales and other activities that are based on objective standards and measurements foster a stronger belief in the pay-performance relationship than plans based on less objective standards. It may be, also, that salesmen tend to have a management orientation that promotes confidence that the measurements in any sales incentive plan do reflect their performance. But it is difficult to believe that this is always the case.

Although it is widely believed that salesmen as a group place a great deal of importance on pay, it seems somewhat dangerous to assume that any particular group of salesmen does or that this importance is a constant. If salesmen do want more pay and nothing about the plan serves to reduce its importance to them, this part of the model is met. But if, as in the example mentioned previously, the plan reduces its importance or if the salesmen don't want more pay or don't want their pay based on performance, it is not. Organizations may be safe in assuming that people self-select themselves for most sales jobs so that those that apply fit the model. But as sales jobs become more complex and technical, such an assumption may no longer hold.

The belief that negative consequences will result from good performance would seem to be quite likely in sales incentive plans. The frequent change in sales incentive plans and the frequent admonition

[25]Dauner, in *Akron Business and Economic Review* (Summer, 1972), pp. 33–37.

to organizations not to overpay their salesmen[26] would seem to create the belief that high performance will result in cuts in incentive rates. Also, the complexity of many sales incentive plans may create the belief that improvements in one kind of performance will so reduce other kinds of performance as to make good total performance impossible. Sales incentive plans may also inadvertently encourage behavior that creates conflicts between sales and other parts of the organization. Although, hopefully, sales incentive plans are designed with solid knowledge of the sales jobs and salesmen are consulted in the design and fully informed of changes, it is not impossible that plan objectives sometimes conflict. Of course, if salesmen believe that negative consequences offset the positive ones, the plan won't work.

The belief that other desired rewards besides more pay result from good performance is probably provided by most sales incentive plans. Feelings of achievement, esteem, and respect are quite likely to occur along with higher incentive earnings for most salesmen. It is worth noting, however, that if the plan encourages behavior that salesmen believe detracts from their perception of good total performance, these nonfinancial rewards are less likely.

The belief that their contributions to the organization result in the performance measured by the organization probably varies widely among sales incentive plans. If salesmen feel that the performance measured is affected by so many things beyond their control that what they do has little weight, this belief is low. If salesmen feel that the measurements are faulty, standards are incorrect, or that important contributions they make are not reflected in the plan, this belief is low. Although the heavy weight given sales volume in most sales incentive plans and the achievement orientation of most salesmen may provide enough of this belief in most sales incentive plans to make them workable, organizations with highly technical products or using plans with poorly developed standards and measurements may encounter difficulties. The dilemma encountered by most plans of (1) sufficiently limiting the factors measured to achieve creditability and to reduce administrative costs, and (2) sufficiently expanding the factors measured so that important contributions are rewarded is probably inescapable.

Although probably less true in the case of salesmen than of other employees, organizations should be aware that attempting to motivate performance may reduce membership motivation. In organizations in which a sales incentive plan is clearly inapplicable because of the technical nature of the product, requirements for joint sales efforts, or some other reason, attempts to install one may well encourage salesmen to

[26]Smyth, in *Harvard Business Review* (January–February, 1968), pp. 109–117.

seek an organization that provides the rewards they want and accepts the contributions they want to make.

ECONOMIC MEMBERSHIP REWARDS

In spite of the heavy emphasis on performance rewards in sales compensation, there is a growing recognition by organizations of the need for membership rewards to obtain salesmen and to retain them in the organization. Although earlier practice conceived of salesmen (especially commission salesmen) as independent businessmen rather than employees,[27] with the result that salesmen seldom participated in employee benefits, present practice implies that organizations consider salesmen one of their most important employee groups. Benefits provided salesmen are rapidly approaching those provided to management.[28] According to a 1965 report, less than 10 per cent of straight commission salesmen failed to receive benefits at all.[29] Salesmen paid straight salary or salary plus incentive received a larger package of benefits. Former practice also often assumed that salesmen preferred to purchase their own benefits. But apparently organizations have been intuitively aware of the need to provide membership motivation for salesmen and have provided them with the benefits provided other employees.

Not only do salesmen receive the usual benefits, but a growing proportion of them are provided with a car that they may use for personal as well as business purposes.[30] Obviously, this benefit is an indirect addition to income. Moving expenses, when included in salesmen's benefit packages, can also be such an indirect addition. Some salesmen are granted stock options. There appears to be a growing trend for organizations to attempt to reduce tax burdens of salesmen by paying earnings above a certain level on a deferred basis. In a number of organizations, part of salesmen's compensation is in the form of profit sharing.[31]

An early study found that salesmen underestimate the cost of benefits by about one-half.[32] This finding suggests that salesmen will be among the first employee groups to be offered a cafeteria plan so that

[27]Smyth and Murphy, *Compensating and Motivating Salesmen,* p. 38.

[28]Patten, in *Personnel* (January–February, 1968), pp. 54–63.

[29]Research Institute of America, *Sales Compensation Practices,* p. 7.

[30]Dauner, in *Akron Business and Economic Review* (Summer, 1972), pp. 33–37.

[31]*Ibid.*

[32]Marvin Hoffman and David J. Luck, "Salesmen's Fringe Benefits," *Marketing and Transportation Paper No. 6* (East Lansing, Michigan: Michigan State University Press, 1959), p. 8.

they can choose the benefits they want. A sales compensation plan that permitted salesmen to choose (between 10 and 35 per cent limits) the incentive portion of their pay[33] seems to be evidence of organization willingness to permit salesmen to make compensation choices.

Thus, although sales compensation appears (from the incentive elements) to suggest that the sales employment exchange is viewed by organizations as an economic transaction (effort for money), in practice organizations recognize a much broader employment exchange that fosters membership motivation. Salesmen are provided with large measures of protection from insecurity in the hopes of securing their continued affiliation with the organization. Perhaps the ultimate evidence of this recognition is the planned compensation approach[34] in which compensation is geared to progress in the salesman's career.

NONFINANCIAL REWARDS

The tentative listing of nonfinancial rewards in Table 7 includes a rather large number that seems to apply to salesmen. Although as stressed in Chapter 15, not much is known about which nonfinancial rewards are desired by which employee groups, knowledge of sales jobs and salesmen suggests that organizations neglecting to administer especially nonfinancial performance rewards for salesmen are missing an opportunity. Recognition that salesmen's compensation includes such nonfinancial rewards as advancement opportunities, recognition of merit, self-improvement through education, interesting and challenging assigments, participation in decisions, adequate facilities and a stimulating environment, responsibility, and authority has appeared in the literature.[35] But the emphasis in salesmen's compensation on economic performance rewards has probably obscured the importance of nonfinancial rewards to salesmen in most organizations. As will be seen, there is a large number of nonfinancial performance rewards that could be used to secure performance motivation. But perhaps even more important to organizations are the nonfinancial job and membership rewards. Because of their many contacts outside the organization, salesmen unaware of the nonfinancial rewards from the organization seem particularly likely to make invalid comparisons of their present employment exchange and other possible ones.

[33]Webster, in *Journal of Marketing* (January, 1966), p. 56.

[34]Sibson, *Wages and Salaries,* p. 172.

[35]Roger E. Dewhurst, John Wilding, and Waino W. Suojanen, "Managerial Goals and Individual Needs in Salesmen's Compensation Plans," *Atlanta Economic Review* (April, 1969), pp. 14–16. See also Wotruba, *Sales Management,* Chapter 13.

NONFINANCIAL JOB REWARDS

Without doubt, the most important nonfinancial job reward for salesmen is the design of the job. The complexity of most sales jobs, the autonomy they provide, the opportunity to use important skills and abilities, the opportunity to exercise power and influence over people and situations, and the opportunity to compete with others are important nonfinancial job rewards to most salesmen. Thus, organizations that devote attention to sales job design in terms of the personal criteria of salesmen as well as organizational and technical criteria are providing nonfinancial job rewards to salesmen.

Another important organization-provided nonfinancial job reward is the quality of supervision. Salesmen need and want competent supervision and competent representation by supervision, as well as considerate, fair, nonpunitive supervision.

Some nonfinancial job rewards are provided by the salesman himself. To some salesmen the job is a "calling." Perhaps most salesmen value the variety provided by their work, their sense of contributing to important organization goals, the relative freedom of movement, and the sense of pride in the results of their work.

NONFINANCIAL PERFORMANCE REWARDS

Organizations do make some use of nonfinancial performance rewards for salesmen. There is some evidence, for example, that organizations are making use of the most well-known nonfinancial performance reward—opportunity for advancement or promotion in the case of salesmen. These opportunities and their relationship to performance have been spelled out in career paths.[36] If promotions and resulting increases in status are tied to performance, they become important performance rewards.

There is also some evidence that organizations use recognition as a performance reward for salesmen through certificates, plaques, articles in house organs, and personal letters from the president of the organization.[37] Contests, although perhaps decreasingly used because of the recognition of the possibility of improving one form of performance while decreasing more important ones,[38] have been used to

---

[36]J. D. Koser, "Career Paths: A Tool for Motivating Field Salesmen," in F. E. Webster, Jr. (ed.), *New Directions in Marketing* (Chicago: American Marketing Association, 1965), pp. S151–S159; Andral E. Pearson, "Sales Power through Planned Careers," *Harvard Business Review* (January–February, 1966), pp. 105–116.

[37]"Incentives for Salesmen," *Experiences in Marketing No. 14* (New York: NICB, 1967), pp. 93–94.

[38]David R. Hampton, "Contests Have Side Effects, Too," *California Management Review* (Summer, 1970), pp. 86–94.

provide recognition as well as financial rewards. Increased influence and participation in problem-solving may be usefully tied to performance of salesmen but probably seldom are. Also, although the opportunity to set performance goals is widely granted salesmen, it is seldom tied to performance. There appears to be some tendency, however, for organizations to reward high performing salesmen with jobs of greater variety.

Most of the nonfinancial performance rewards, however, are provided by the salesman himself. Such intrinsic rewards as responsibility, autonomy, freedom, and independence are provided by the salesman when the organization provides an opportunity to do so. Using one's highest skills and abilities and developing one's skills and abilities are also provided the individual. The salesman also ties these rewards to performance unless the organization prevents him from doing so.

If the assumption that salesmen tend to be a work-committed group is correct, they may be expected to provide themselves with the intrinsic rewards of feelings of accomplishment, achievement, ego-involvement, self-fulfillment, commitment, challenge, and interest in accordance with their performance. Other intrinsic rewards that may be provided by the individual are feelings of self-control and identification with organization goals. It hardly needs to be said that although organizations do not provide these nonfinancial performance rewards, they can nullify them through poor job and organization design.

NONFINANCIAL MEMBERSHIP REWARDS

But most of the nonfinancial rewards provided salesmen, as well as other employees, are membership rewards. These rewards are typically provided employees without awareness on the part of the organization. Many of these rewards are characteristics of the organization —size, prestige, visibility, importance, profit level, even age. Others are associated with the way the organization is run, including the organization's relations with employees.

A nonfinancial membership reward that was formerly largely denied to salesmen is security. Although organizations are unlikely to want salesmen who place high importance on security, it was shown previously that most organizations now recognize a desire by salesmen for a modicum of this reward.

A system of organization justice is undoubtedly a highly valued nonfinancial membership reward desired by many salesmen. The fact that some kinds of salesmen are union members is some evidence of this desire. But organizations might well consider an explicit justice determination process for salesmen to offset the apparent attractions offered by other organizations.

Salesmen also appear to place a high value on sales training programs and other opportunities for self-improvement. Both not only provide an opportunity to increase personal effectiveness, but also signal the organization's interest in a long-term employment exchange.

The opportunity to use one's knowledge and skills is probably a highly valued reward for salesmen. In fact, casual observation suggests that at times this reward is an acceptable substitute for economic rewards.

On certain sales jobs, such as those in which team selling is involved, the work group can be a source of nonfinancial membership rewards. The quality of work associates, how well members work together, and opportunities for cultivating friendships can be important rewards. On most sales jobs the opportunity to meet new people, the opportunity to help others, and the kinds of customers called on can be nonfinancial membership. rewards.

Finally, a number of nonfinancial membership rewards may be provided by the individual salesman. If, for example, he likes the company, identifies with organization goals, and finds membership in the organization compatible with his self-image, he has rewarded himself for membership.

This discussion of nonfinancial job, performance, and membership rewards must be regarded as somewhat speculative. Although different employee groups want different rewards, which groups want which rewards is simply not known. As a result, the nonfinancial rewards assumed to represent the desires of salesmen reflect the biases of the author. Also, only those that appeared to distinguish salesmen from other employee groups were chosen for discussion. For suggestions on reward preference determination and administration, see Chapter 15.

COMPARISON STANDARDS

Salesmen, for a number of reasons, probably have more difficulty in making comparisons to evaluate their employment exchange than any other employee group. First, the emphasis of organizations on incentives focuses salesmen's attention on economic rewards. People who become and remain salesmen thus probably tend to place high importance on economic rewards and to think of the employment exchange as an economic transaction. Second, because the salesman works outside the organization he gets a great deal of information from other salesmen and customers. Also, because economic information is easy to transmit and his orientation tends to be economic, economic information tends to be emphasized. Third, because sales success requires that salesmen consider the interests of the customer as well as the interests of the organization, he cannot become as committed to the organization as other employees. Thus, organization commitment is somewhat ruled out as a nonfinancial reward and the salesman who thinks of himself as an independent businessman has another reason for focusing on economic rewards.

All of these reasons would seem to lead the salesman to make poor decisions about his employment exchange. Salesmen would be expected to have high turnover and to express dissatisfaction with their compensation.

Many of the conclusions reached in this chapter suggest means of circumventing these difficulties. Organizations, in spite of their emphasis on incentives, provide salesmen with economic job and membership rewards and a large number of nonfinancial rewards. Through these rewards organizations are signaling their salesmen that they are interested in developing a long-term employment exchange with them. What seems to be called for on the part of organizations is to inform salesmen that the organization wants both membership and performance. Organizations are probably also going to have to be more open in providing salesmen with information on how and why job, performance, and membership rewards, both economic and nonfinancial, are determined. Participation by salesmen is often encouraged in determining sales incentives. But it probably needs to be expanded in salary surveys and in benefit and in nonfinancial reward determination.

Providing more information to salesmen would be facilitated by knowing more about salesmen's reference groups. Reference group theory suggests that salesmen do compare with others with whom they interact within the organization (especially sales managers and sales support personnel), as well as with other salesmen. It also suggests that the more they consider themselves to be members of the organization, the more pertinent these comparisons become. Also, the more information they have about their own employment exchange and those of others with whom they compare within the organization, the more rational their comparisons will become. It is also quite possible that they will be more prone to compare themselves with their own self-concept.

But salesmen will continue to compare themselves with other salesmen and receive sales compensation information of various levels of reliability from customers. Hopefully, the full information provided by their employing organization will permit them to place this outside information in perspective. Although the large variation in sales compensation by industry probably assures some continued dissatisfaction, salesmen made aware of their full employment exchange can be expected to make more rational employment decisions.

21

Compensation of
Managers and Professionals

Organizations typically separate the administration of compensation for exempt and nonexempt employees. This separation, flowing from the overtime provisions of the Fair Labor Standards Act, may be due in part to an assumption by organizations that the employment exchange of exempt employees is different from that of nonexempt employees. There are also differences in compensation policies and practices within the exempt group. Executive compensation, for example, includes such highly complex programs as to require a separate expertise. Professional compensation often employs approaches and techniques that are quite different from those used with other employees. Sales compensation employs techniques largely designed by sales management and emphasizes incentives.

At first glance, these differences suggest that organizations have perceived the need for different employment exchanges for different employee groups, as advocated in this book. But the differences represent primarily differences in rewards with little or no recognition of differences in contributions. It is true that organizations have intuitively recognized that with exempt employees more emphasis must be given to the individual and that some degree of organization commitment is a hoped for contribution. But there is no evidence that organizations have given much thought to the contributions they want from these employee groups and that these employees want to make.

In fact, the differences may well reflect differences in rewards based on (1) absence of union pressures and thus increased possibilities of individual treatment, (2) reactions to labor shortages, (3) responses to changes in tax laws, and (4) imitation of the practices of other employers. There is also reason to question whether the differences in compensation practices for different exempt groups represent differences in substance or merely differences in terminology.

If organizations perceive the employment exchange of the exempt group as basically an economic transaction differing only from that of the nonexempt group in the necessity for more individual treatment, there are plausible reasons for treating the employee groups similarly. In a broad sense, all the exempt groups can be considered to be performing executive work in that they make decisions, take actions, and carry responsibilities that are especially important to organizations. If executive work is defined as consisting of (1) creating production and jobs, (2) making decisions, (3) providing leadership, (4) allocating resources, (5) reconciling claimant interests, (6) introducing innovations, (7) accumulating and using capital, and (8) taking risks,[1] the exempt group is heavily involved in it. Managers are involved in all of these functions but their degree of responsibility varies with their level in the organization hierarchy. Nonmanagerial professionals are often assigned heavy responsibility in several of the functions. In addition, nonmanagerial professionals are often assigned as staff assistants to managers. When professionals are assigned to head staff departments, they are managers. Increasing professionalism of management, in fact, suggests an overlap in the terms.

Because of the differing reward practices and terminology employed for the separate exempt groups, separate chapters to discuss the compensation of supervisors, middle management, top management, and professional employees could be justified. But combining the analyses of organization compensation practices in terms of contributions, rewards, and comparison standards of all the exempt groups has the virtue of emphasizing the need for separate employment exchanges for each. In this chapter, the exempt employee groups considered are three management levels—supervisors, middle management, and top management—and professional employees. Sales compensation was discussed in the preceding chapter. Technicians are assumed to be subprofessionals and to require employment exchanges sufficiently similar to those of professional employees as to not require separate discussion. Administrative exempt employees are assumed to be either supervisors or professionals. Some reference is made to compensation of international managers.

---

[1]Charles C. Abbott, J. D. Forbes, and Lorin A. Thompson, *The Executive Function and Its Compensation* (prepared in The University of Virginia Graduate School of Business Administration for the General Dynamics Corporation, January, 1958), p. 19.

CONTRIBUTIONS

The employment exchange of the various levels of management and of professionals is perceived by organizations to include job contributions and performance contributions but not personal contributions. Personal contributions, however, are implicitly recognized by permitting top and some middle managers and often professional employees to largely determine the boundaries of their jobs. This section examines compensation practice of the various exempt groups in terms of the contributions it implies.

JOB CONTRIBUTIONS

Organizations obviously require different job contributions from different levels of managers and still different contributions from professional employees. Business organizations tend to define management positions as those that have a significant effect on profits and limit the management group to about 1 per cent of employees. But compensation practice suggests that contributions of all the members of the exempt group are limited only by those that employees want to make.

Top Management. The job contributions of top management are assumed to represent an identity between the individual and the organization. These individuals are expected to hold such a measure of organization commitment that what they contribute determines what the organization is and does. In business organizations, top management is variously assumed to be a partner of the owners and a trustee of the interests of various organization claimants, including themselves. Action and decision areas of management have been described as strategic, administrative, and operative, with emphasis of top management on strategic and administrative decisions.[2]

Distinguishing top management from other levels of management has been a difficult problem in executive compensation. Because organizations have done very little thinking about the specific contributions they want from each employee group and still less about those the individual wants to make, they tend to assume that they want all the contributions each individual manager and professional is capable of making. As a result, there is much overlap between the treatment of different groups and only a limited amount of distinction in terms of the needs and characteristics of each group.

In most organizations, top management is defined by position in the hierarchy. One study defined top management as the highest paid

---

[2]H. I. Ansoff, "Toward a Strategic Theory of the Firm," in H. Igor Ansoff (ed.), *Business Strategy* (Baltimore: Penguin Books, 1969), pp. 11–40.

10 per cent of management, which, in turn, was defined as the highest paid 1 per cent of employees.[3]

Organizations have undoubtedly been fortunate in permitting top management almost complete freedom in designing their jobs. To the extent that these individuals do want to make unlimited contributions, organizations have in this way properly specified the contributions of this group.

Most organizations have job descriptions of management jobs. Developing these descriptions is difficult, costly, and time-consuming. A well-conceived management job description probably takes about five hours of the executive's time.[4] In fast-changing organizations, these job descriptions must be frequently rewritten and, in most organizations, probably regularly revised every two years. Organizations have also found that management job descriptions must be developed by relatively high-level employees.

Management job descriptions are typically written in terms of broad functions, areas of responsibility, scope and impact of assignments, degree of accountability, and the extent and nature of supervision and influence involved, rather than in terms of tasks and duties, as in lower-level jobs. Because of this they are often called responsibility guides rather than job descriptions. Management job descriptions involve a careful determination of what the job has been made by the incumbent, because such individuals are often permitted wide latitude in changing their jobs. Draft descriptions are reviewed and coordinated, however, to insure proper definition of responsibilities.[5]

Because of the time and effort involved in writing management job descriptions, many organizations use them as a basic management tool in assigning work, communicating responsibilities, establishing authority limits, setting performance standards, and reviewing management performance. In this way management job descriptions are used for organization planning, manpower planning, and management development, as well as compensation.

Job evaluation methods applied to management jobs reflect the differences in the character of management jobs and jobs at lower levels of the organization. Different factors are employed and frequently adaptations of the basic methods of job evaluation. In most cases, management job evaluation involves adaptations of the point and

[3]Arch Patton, *Men, Money and Motivation* (New York: McGraw-Hill Book Company, 1961), pp. 91–95.
[4]Jack Mendleson, "Improving Executive Job Descriptions," *Management of Personnel Quarterly* (Spring, 1969), pp. 26–35.
[5]Richard A. Allaway, Jr., "Developing the Basis for Executive Compensation," in Russell F. Moore (ed.), *Compensating Executive Worth* (New York: American Management Association, 1968), pp. 35–58.

factor-comparison methods. Quite a number of organizations, however, use the guideline method of job evaluation for management jobs. The ranking and classification methods have not been found very useful in distinguishing degrees of management responsibility except in very small organizations.

There has been some controversy over the propriety of using formal job evaluation for top management jobs. A well-known management consultant objects to the use of job evaluation for these jobs on the grounds that formal plans tend to ignore the difficulty of separating the man and the job and to assume that the top jobs in different functions have equal value to the organization. Instead of formal job evaluation he advocates distinguishing top management jobs in terms of actual decision-making and decision-influencing by job incumbents.[6] These objections are typically well met in the adaptations of job evaluation to management jobs.

Most job evaluation plans employed on management jobs are tailor-made to the organization. Perhaps the most widely used methods are adaptations of the basic factor-comparison method.

The *modified factor-comparison* method, for example, involves the per cent method of job evaluation discussed previously. Factors selected for the particular organization may be used or more common factors such as know-how, problem-solving, and accountability. In any case, the factor definitions are based on the organization's work and the weightings are tailor-made to the organization. A management consultant finds that fewer than four or more than six factors make the plan unworkable.[7] In some use of the modified factor-comparison method, the per cent application is supplemented by guide charts that summarize the evaluations under each factor.

Multiple evaluation is another modification of the factor-comparison method applied to management jobs. In this method all the jobs are evaluated at least twice and the results compared. For example, in one widely used plan, all jobs are evaluated three times by defining job worth separately in terms of scope and impact of the job, requirements of the job, and difficulty of performing the job. Different factors are used in each of the three evaluations. After the jobs have been evaluated by the three methods, the results are compared and any inconsistencies resolved.

Profiling is another method of multiple evaluation in which a profile of each management job is developed in terms of the importance of factors to the job. Then the profile is compared to an analysis

[6]Patton, *Men, Money and Motivation,* pp. 69–75.
[7]Robert E. Sibson, *Wages and Salaries,* rev. ed. (New York: American Management Association, 1967), p. 213.

of the relative importance of the factors. All three adaptations of the factor-comparison method owe a great deal to the work of Edward N. Hay and Associates.[8]

Although point plans have been developed to evaluate managerial jobs, many of them have been developed for specific organizations.[9] Some of these point plans incorporate factors similar to Jaques' concept of time span of discretion.[10] Some of the newer point plans incorporate a factor that adjusts for size of organization.[11]

Job evaluation methods that employ factors of some kind represent attempts by organizations to distinguish management jobs in terms of job contributions. Benchmark, marketplace, and guideline job evaluation, however, ignore job contributions and create a hierarchy of jobs based on their position in the labor market. Benchmark and marketplace methods involve the development of job relationships based on salary surveys.[12] The guideline method uses salary survey data to place jobs into a pre-established system of pay grades. These methods, although appealing because of their apparent simplicity, imply that the employment exchange of managers is a simple economic transaction of money for unspecified services. More important, their apparent simplicity is a delusion. Not only is the accuracy of surveys highly dependent on survey methods, but the difficulty of determining comparability of management jobs and the broad and varied nature of management labor markets make for unreliable market data.

Some studies of salary structures of organizations, although they do not specify job contributions, do provide some signals to incumbents of the relative value organizations place on job contributions. For example, the second highest paid man tends to receive from 65 to 75 per cent of the compensation of the chief executive, the third man, 55 to 65 per cent, and so on.[13] But not only do these percentages vary widely by industry and organization size, but the function represented by the second, third, and fourth man varies by industry.[14] A plausible explana-

---

[8]For details, see *Personnel* (September, 1951; July, 1954; January–February, 1958).

[9]Otis Lipstreau and W. J. D. Kennedy, "Pricing the Management Job," *Personnel* (January–February, 1967), pp. 63–69; A. R. Childs, "A Compensation Program for Managers of Professionals and Non-Technical Personnel," in *Conference Series No. 13* (Iowa City: Center for Labor and Management, 1969), pp. 24–32.

[10]Lipstreau and Kennedy, *op. cit.*

[11]Robert L. Sauer, "Measuring Relative Worth of Managerial Positions," *Compensation Review* (First Quarter, 1972), pp. 9–18.

[12]Graef S. Crystal, *Financial Motivation for Executives* (New York: American Management Association, 1970), pp. 57–72.

[13]"Is Your Internal Pay Scale in Balance?" *Business Management* (January, 1968), pp. 36–37.

[14]"How Management Functions Rank According to Pay," *Business Management* (January, 1968), pp. 34–35; Harland Fox, "Top Executive Compensation," *Studies in Personnel Policy, No. 204* (New York: National Industrial Conference Board, 1965).

tion of steep and flat pyramids has been offered by a management consultant in terms of organization philosophy. Organizations that always promote from within, dilute jobs to fit work incumbents, and never fire anyone have narrow spreads according to this theory, but organizations that insist on the best man for the job, have high standards of performance, and discharge incompetents have wide spreads.[15]

Thus organizations do recognize job contributions of managers. Most organizations no longer question the need for some kind of plan for determining the relative worth of management positions.[16] But the manner in which they do so often suggests that organizations are too little concerned with the job contributions they get from the employment exchange.

Middle Management.   Although job evaluation is still sometimes questioned at the top management level, there is almost universal use of job evaluation of some sort on middle-management jobs. Such jobs are less subject to change by the incumbent so that job descriptions are easier to develop and have more permanence. More important, determining realistic market values becomes even more difficult for middle management jobs because such jobs are variable among organizations and because middle-management labor markets are not structured by industry and organization size, as they are for top management. Hence, where organizations use formal job evaluation plans for middle managers, they have specified job contributions. If, however, organizations employ labor market or guideline methods, they have failed to specify job contributions required of middle managers.

Professionals.   As mentioned earlier in this chapter, from the standpoint of organizations there are some strong similarities between middle managers and professional employees. Both tend to come from national or international labor markets. Professionals are often staff assistants to managers. Some professionals become managers. Many managers believe themselves to be professionals.

But professional employees are usually nonsupervisory and include such knowledge workers as engineers, scientists, attorneys, economists, physicians, psychologists, sociologists, editors, and artists. Professional employees have a good deal to say about their work. In this they are more akin to top management than to middle management. Top managers, however, are assumed to accept the goals of the organization, whereas professionals may accept the organization only as a client for their services. "Since the work of a profession involves an essential service which no one else can perform, no one else can claim the right to tell the member of the profession how to do it or even how

---

[15]Patton, *Men, Money and Motivation,* pp. 69–75.
[16]Sauer, in *Compensation Review* (First Quarter, 1972), pp. 9–18.

it should be evaluated."[17] This statement suggests that the professional does not expect to make job or performance contributions, only personal contributions.

Actually, of course, professional employees differ in whether they consider the organization to be employer or client. Although some studies report that engineers and scientists perceive themselves as entrepreneurial professionals,[18] some careful research shows that engineers are essentially oriented toward organization objectives.[19]

Writing job descriptions has been a problem because of the growing importance of technology and tight labor markets for some types of professionals, which have led organizations to permit professionals to design their own jobs rather than defining where professionals fit in the organization. Often, the work assignment of the professional varies greatly over a short period of time. Furthermore, professionals who are reluctant to give up the status of free professionals are likely to resist job descriptions and insist that each member of the profession is a unique individual.

Many organizations, however, have developed job descriptions for professional employees. One type, called a functional job description, identifies the duties of the job and is likely to be found in organizations in which there is a steady flow of work and less variation in level of duties. Other organizations have developed what are called generic descriptions, which define in very broad terms the level of work involved. Still other organizations make no effort to describe professional jobs at all.

Organizations also differ in whether or not they employ job evaluation on professional jobs. One survey found that 85 per cent of reporting organizations used job evaluation on engineering jobs.[20] Although two members of an organization that specializes in modifications of the factor-comparison method report no problems in evaluating professional jobs,[21] job evaluation plans developed specifically for professional jobs seem to work better. The federal government successfully applies the classification method to professional jobs.

[17]Edward Gross, "When Occupations Meet: Professions in Trouble," *Hospital Administration* (Summer, 1967), p. 41.

[18]Robert D. Best, "The Scientific Mind vs. The Management Mind," *Industrial Research* (October, 1963), pp. 50–52.

[19]R. Richard Ritti, *The Engineer in the Industrial Corporation* (New York: Columbia University Press, 1971).

[20]Sang M. Lee, "Salary Administration Practices for Engineers," *Personnel Journal* (January, 1969), pp. 33–38.

[21]Charles W. G. Van Horn, "Compensating Technical and Professional Personnel," *Management Report Number 163* (New York: American Management Association, 1961), pp. 37–47; William F. Dinsmore, "The Case for Evaluating Professional Jobs," *Personnel* (November–December, 1964), pp. 54–60.

A rather large number of organizations[22] make use of maturity curves. Some highly technical organizations make no attempt to describe and evaluate professional jobs and use maturity curves instead. In this approach organizations do not specify job contributions but rather emphasize personal contributions of professionals.

Supervisors. Supervisors are usually defined as employees no more than one or two levels removed from nonsupervisory employees. About 90 per cent of supervisors are covered by job descriptions and some form of job evaluation. Most organizations have discovered that applying the management job evaluation plan to supervisory jobs works much better than extending nonsupervisory plans to include supervisors. Organizations typically also have established customary pay differentials between supervisors and subordinates, thereby emitting another signal regarding the importance of supervisory job contributions. Thus, organizations have probably specified the job contributions of supervisors more carefully than they have for the balance of the exempt groups. In part, this result is due to the common practice of selecting supervisors from within, thereby increasing the importance of internal job relationships.

PERFORMANCE CONTRIBUTIONS

Organizations assume that they want performance contributions from all exempt groups and that they have specified these performance contributions by providing salary ranges and incentive plans. But the assumptions (from Chapter 8) that (1) differential performance is required by the organization, (2) individuals assigned to the same job differ in performance, (3) differential performance should be rewarded separately from job assignment, and (4) performance differences can be measured, fit the groups quite differently.

Top Management. There is no question concerning whether or not organizations need additional performance from top management or whether incumbents differ in performance. They do. There is also no question of whether top management knows what kind of performance is needed because they decide what is needed.

But even with top management there may be questions concerning agreement on performance standards and measurements. What are appropriate standards of performance in a world of fast-changing values? Is performance to be measured over the short term, the long term, or both?

[22]55.8 per cent, according to Lee's survey.

Fortunately for business organizations, the unit of measurement is accepted by top management as an appropriate measure of their performance. Business and other organizations are also fortunate that top management tends to identify with the organization so that any improvement in organization effectiveness is accepted as measuring top management performance. But there may be some question concerning whether or not top management should be rewarded separately for performance and for job assignment. If these individuals are fully committed to the organization, won't organizations get optimum performance by assigning them to the job?

Middle Management. There is also no question concerning the need of organizations for additional performance from middle management or individual differences in performance. But there are real questions concerning agreement on performance standards and measurements. Although management by objectives undoubtedly helps, middle managers are not well informed on the performance contributions measured, the units used in measurement, and the standards of performance for their jobs. Furthermore, there are often real problems of creditability regarding whether or not the organization knows what performance it wants or can measure it.

Fortunately for organizations, middle managers want to expand their performance contributions to the organization and usually want to believe that organizations know what performance they want and can measure it. But unless organizations emit reasonably consistent signals that they want and can measure these performance contributions, even this strong faith can be destroyed.

Professionals. Although organizations are certain that professional employees, like other employees, differ in performance, they often don't know if the organization requires differential performance from professionals because they usually leave the definition of what professionals can contribute up to them. Furthermore, there may be strong disagreement between organizations and professionals over the kind of performance needed and over performance standards and measurements. To the extent that professionals are oriented to their professional field and perceive the organization as a client, it is unlikely that they consider organization performance measures relevant. In the professional ethic, nonuse of knowledge is misuse,[23] and thus professionals, not organizations, must channel and measure performance.

---

[23]Wilbert E. Moore, *The Professions: Roles and Rules* (New York: Russell Sage Foundation, 1970), p. 242.

Fortunately for organizations, at least some professional employees (engineers are one example) accept organization goals and want to make performance contributions desired by the organization. These professionals tend to have motivations similar to those of middle management. But in cases in which professionals are oriented toward their field, organizations would be wise to abandon attempts to define and measure their performance contributions and to concentrate on removing obstacles to performance as defined by professionals.

Supervisors. Although organizations require differential performance from supervisors and supervisors differ in performance, organizations have difficulty in communicating to supervisors the kind of performance wanted and in devising credible performance measures. Part of the difficulty in communicating the kind of performance the organization wants flows from the often conflicting demands of the job. Much of the difficulty in devising credible performance measurements comes from failure to get agreement from supervisors on the performance contribution to be measured, units of measurement, when conditions are sufficiently standardized to yield valid measurements, and standards of performance. Because supervisors are often promoted from nonsupervisory jobs, they may or may not want to expand their performance contributions and may not believe that organizations know what performance they want nor can measure it. Although some supervisors may share the values of middle management, it is doubtful that most of them do.

PERSONAL CONTRIBUTIONS

Although organizations are aware that exempt employees are permitted more voice in the design of their jobs than nonexempt employees, most of them would deny that once jobs are designed, personal contributions (defined as personal attributes not required by the job) are rewarded. But the facts are otherwise. Although recognition of personal contributions varies widely from one employee group to another, it exists on all exempt jobs.

Top Management. Organizations imply that top management is paid primarily for performance and secondly for the job to which they are assigned. Personal contributions are not assumed to be recognized.

A recent study[24] reported that length of service did not affect executive salary levels in any measurable degree and that age does not correlate very well with executive salary levels. But another survey

[24]Robert E. Sibson, "Executive Pay—The Long Term Is Where the Action Is," *Nation's Business* (November, 1971), pp. 29–33.

found that new chief executives usually received lower compensation than their predecessors.[25] Still another survey found that outstanding performers among executives were underpaid until they reached age 45.[26] The latter studies correspond with the observation that top management expects to be rewarded for increased knowledge and greater experience and skill and that movement through salary ranges typically reflects this expectation.

Because top management positions are usually designed by the incumbent to fit his personal attributes, the issue of whether personal contributions are required by the job is less likely to arise. Hence such contributions as intelligence, education, acceptance of responsibility, and experience are accepted by both the organization and the individual as job rather than personal contributions. The same conclusion is likely, however, to apply to personal appearance, health, physical attributes, and even personal life style, which would be considered personal contributions for any other group.

But, without doubt, the major personal contribution recognized in top executive compensation is the individual's income tax situation. This factor, labeled a contribution because it represents a cost of the employment exchange to the individual, is emphasized in executive compensation. In fact, it is undoubtedly responsible for the tremendous complexity of the field. As a result, many organizations have recently added as a benefit personal financial planning for executives.[27]

Middle Management. Personal contributions loom larger in the employment exchange involving middle management. Movement through salary ranges is often based in part on increased knowledge, experience, and skill. *Salary planning* includes such considerations as the individual's salary history and his potential.[28] Potential, which is emphasized in the case of the "fast-track" executive,[29] undoubtedly is influenced by such personal traits as personal appearance, physical attributes, and personal life style. The new manager's "personality maturity," based on age and military experience and years of education and related work experience, often influences his starting salary.[30] Sal-

[25]McKinsey & Company, "A Study of Executive Compensation in 216 Large Publicly Held West Coast Companies" (1970, mimeographed).

[26]Arch Patton, "Are We Sabotaging Executive Motivation?," *The McKinsey Quarterly* (Summer, 1970), pp. 52–67.

[27]Donald J. Petrie, "Executive Financial Planning—A New Fringe Benefit," *Personnel* (November–December, 1971), pp. 17–25.

[28]Sibson, *Wages and Salaries*, p. 219.

[29]Thomas J. Murray, "The Rise of the Fast-Track Executive," *Dun's Review* (January, 1968), pp. 34, 72–74.

[30]"New College Grads' Pay Becoming More Individualized," *The Manager's Letter* (March, 1969), p. 2.

ary growth charts that gear manager's salaries to years in position are apparently being increasingly used by organizations.[31] Concern with *compression* in management salaries has resulted in salary increases tied to length of service.[32] A careful study of management pay differentials found that years of professional experience and education account for a substantial proportion of the variance in management pay.[33]

Because middle management's influence on the design of their jobs is less than complete, the contributions that managers want to make and those the organization recognizes as job contributions may conflict. These individuals usually expect to contribute their acceptance of responsibility, effort, education, intelligence, job knowledge, and experience whether or not these attributes are required by the job.

Organizations need such personal contributions as adaptability in the face of changed conditions, commitment to the job and the organization, cooperation with other people and organization units, creativity in approaching problems, willingness to take action without urging, reasoned approaches to organization problems, and dependability from middle management, whether they realize it or not. Fortunately for organizations, most middle managers want to make these contributions whether or not the organization recognizes them. Hopefully, these are the personal attributes rather than the physical ones that organizations use to measure potential.

Professionals. Many professional employees consider the organization more a client rather than an employer and expect to make personal rather than job or performance contributions. In some measure they have influenced organizations to accept these personal contributions through the use of maturity curves that measure these personal contributions in terms of age or years of professional experience. It is true that maturity curves also account for performance but the manner in which performance is often "measured" suggests that it too may be a measure of personal contributions. Although not all organizations base professional salaries on maturity curves, one measure of the success of professionals in influencing organizations to pay for personal contributions is the use of salary growth charts for middle managers.

Professionals who consider themselves to be employees and accept the goals of the organization are probably best thought of as mid-

[31]Robert A. Smith, "Achieving Flexibility in Compensation Administration," *Compensation Review* (Fourth Quarter, 1970), pp. 6–14.

[32]Agnes Bogart, "Dealing with Wage and Salary Compression," *Compensation Review* (Fourth Quarter, 1969), pp. 6–14.

[33]Kenneth E. Foster, "Accounting for Management Pay Differentials," *Industrial Relations* (October, 1969), pp. 80–87.

dle management. Engineers, for example, expect to make personal contributions but also job and performance contributions.

Supervisors. Personal contributions probably play less part in the employment exchange of the supervisor than in any other exempt group. Because of the importance of internal salary relations in determining supervisors' pay, job contributions are emphasized. Also, because of the key role of supervisors in explaining the organization's compensation programs to nonsupervisory employees, supervisors are likely to emphasize job contributions. Performance contributions play a small part primarily because only limited authority and responsibility and much latent conflict is built into most supervisory jobs and because organizations have spent so little effort in attempting to measure supervisory performance. Hence, although movement through salary ranges for supervisors is influenced by age and seniority, other personal contributions are probably largely absent.

CONTRIBUTIONS—A SUMMARY

This analysis of contributions in the employment exchange of exempt employees shows that although organizations prefer to think that they emphasize performance contributions, they actually give more weight to job contributions and, with some groups, to personal contributions. Organization compensation practice emphasizes personal contributions for professionals, job contributions for supervisors, and job and performance contributions for top management. In the case of middle management, about equal weight seems to be given to job, performance, and personal contributions.

ECONOMIC REWARDS

Rewards for the exempt group are examined in this section in terms of economic and nonfinancial job, performance, and membership rewards. Although our analysis of contributions would lead us to expect an emphasis on rewards equivalent to that found in contributions, organization concern for performance contributions suggests that heavy emphasis on economic performance rewards is more likely.

ECONOMIC JOB REWARDS

Salaries are paid for job incumbency and thus represent economic job rewards. But they are also the basic membership reward and usually the basis on which other economic membership rewards are allocated. Also, organizations adjust salaries partly on the basis of performance, thus making salaries one form of economic performance reward. Because, however, the basic purpose of salaries is assumed to reward job incumbency, they are discussed here as economic job rewards. Almost all exempt employees are paid salaries on a weekly, monthly, or yearly basis rather than hourly wages, as is the case for most nonexempt employees.

Salary determination in organizations is strongly influenced by the fact that exempt groups come from a number of distinct labor markets. The market for top management is national or international in scope but segmented by organization size and by industry. The market for professionals is likewise national or international and is segmented by scholarly disciplines and somewhat by education level. The professional labor market overlaps somewhat with the market for middle management because professionals are often managers of staff departments. The market for middle management is also national or international but it is essentially formless because of the great variety of organizations and jobs in which middle managers are employed. There is some tendency for the market for middle management to be segmented by functional area (finance, marketing, manufacturing, and so on), which tends to make it less shapeless, but not much. What market exists for supervisors is local and varies by industry. But because most organizations select at least first-line supervisors from within the organization, it is less logical to speak of a supervisory labor market.

Top Management. For a number of reasons, the economic job rewards of top management are not confined to salary but to total compensation. One is the income tax consequences, which prompt some top executives to search for payment in forms that protect them from high income taxes. Unfortunately for our purposes, this has the effect of confounding rewards for the job and rewards for personal contributions. Another is the cold, hard fact that the compensation of the chief executive sets the ceiling on pay within the organization. A third reason, which applies to middle management as well, is that organizations that pay bonuses pay salaries 10 to 20 per cent lower than non-bonus-paying organizations. Unfortunately for our purposes, the latter practice has the effect of confounding rewards for the job and rewards for performance. But for all three reasons, salary determination for top management really means determining total compensation, although in some practice total compensation means salary and bonus rather than all forms of economic rewards.

The level of total compensation of top management is influenced by a number of considerations. The main ones, organization size and industry, largely flow from a pioneering study of salary data published in Securities and Exchange Commission reports that showed that top management compensation surveys could be useful if the data were classified by industry and company size.[34] Based on these findings, the American Management Association inaugurated its executive compensation service. These widely used surveys collect data on top management total compensation (salary and bonus), integrate them with SEC data, and classify them by organization size and industry. These surveys define size in terms of sales, except in organizations that commonly use other measures of size (notably financial and insurance firms).

There are, of course, other possible indexes of organization size besides sales. Although sales seems to be the most frequently used, other breakdowns are sometimes employed. Surveys by McKinsey and Company, for example, have classified the data by industry, sales, total assets, profits, and size of payroll. Organizations that make their own surveys appear to use a sales breakdown, although others are, of course, possible.

Studies conflict on whether sales or profits are better predictors of executive compensation. Although two careful studies show that profits are a better predictor than sales,[35] a recent survey found no evidence that highly profitable companies within an industry pay significantly more than less profitable companies.[36] A management consultant reports that in his experience highly profitable companies do pay more. Interestingly, he attributes the reduced relationship between profits and executive compensation to the heavy use by organizations of compensation surveys that gauge company size by sales volume.[37]

The same author has offered a plausible explanation of the variation in top management compensation between industries.[38] The explanation offered is based on the competitive characteristics of industries and holds that low-paying industries tend to be monopolistic, government-regulated, static, seniority-oriented, and centralized. High-paying industries were held to be dynamic, results-oriented, and decentralized.

Apparently, wide use of compensation surveys has served to reduce executive compensation differences among industries.[39] This

---

[34]Arch Patton, "How Much Should An Executive Be Paid?" in *Financial Management Series No. 97* (New York: American Management Association, 1951), pp. 16–22.

[35]Joseph W. McGuire, John S. Y. Chiu, and Alvar O. Elbing, "Executive Incomes, Sales and Profits," *American Economic Review* (September, 1962), pp. 753–761; Wilbur G. Lewellen and Blaine Huntsman, "Managerial Pay and Corporate Performance," *American Economic Review* (September, 1970), pp. 710–720.

[36]Sibson, in *Nation's Business* (November, 1971), pp. 29–33.

[37]Arch Patton, "Top Executive Pay: New Facts and Figures," *Harvard Business Review* (September–October, 1966), pp. 94–97.

[38]Patton, *Men, Money and Motivation,* pp. 46–54.

[39]Patton, in *McKinsey Quarterly* (Summer, 1970), pp. 52–67.

would hardly seem surprising if economic conditions permit low-paying organizations to raise executive compensation. The embarrassing characterization of low-paying industries could harm membership motivation. But, if the characterization is true, eliminating it could harm performance motivation.

An idea of the variation in executive compensation found in surveys is obtained by noting that graphic presentations employ log-log scales (equal percentage differences rather than equal absolute differences represent equal distances on the scales). Typically, for each doubling in size, executive compensation increases by about 20 per cent.[40] Although classifying survey information by organization size reduces the variation, it is still extreme. It is not unusual to find the spread on these jobs to be 500 to 800 percent. Given this wide variation, the wide use of surveys is somewhat surprising. But the variation does help explain some tendency for organizations to make their own surveys.

The use of compensation surveys obviously calls for subjecting these data to organization policy in making decisions. Organization policy is typically influenced by such other factors besides size and industry as functional assignment, centralization or decentralization, organization structure, location of corporate headquarters, the values of top management, and the organization's stage of growth.[41]

Compensation relationships within top management may be more important to the individuals involved than level. Because these relationships signal which responsibilities and activities are important to the organization, they deserve careful consideration. Although, as mentioned previously, various studies report relationships between the pay of the top man and that of the second, third, and fourth man and between the pay of the chief executive and the top man in each function,[42] these relationships should be determined by the needs of the organization. The wide variation in compensation differentials by industry suggests that they do vary with the relative difficulty and importance of jobs. It has been pointed out that organizations with high and low differentials accord with the level at which important decisions are made.[43] As discussed in connection with job contributions, most organizations today use some form of job evaluation as an aid in determining compensation relationships even at the top level.

[40]Arch Patton, "Deterioration in Top Executive Pay," *Harvard Business Review* (November–December, 1965), pp. 106–118.

[41]Glenn L. Engelke, "Relating the Executive Compensation Plan to Corporate Organization and Objectives," in Moore, *Compensating Executive Worth*, pp. 59–82.

[42]See, for example, the cost of management study, *Business Management* (January, 1968), pp. 28–38.

[43]Patton, *Men, Money and Motivation*, pp. 69–75.

Middle Management.   Determining salaries of middle management is a particularly difficult task for organizations. Not only are labor markets for middle managers national or international in scope, they are not structured by industry because the skills are widely transferable. Even more of a problem is the infinite variation in middle management jobs between organizations due in part to organization practice and in part to permitting incumbents some leeway in designing their jobs.

Salary surveys are frequently used—both published surveys and those conducted by employing organizations. But attaining job comparability in either type of survey is extremely difficult. Even the common practice of using both job descriptions and measures of scope (usually sales) and responsibility levels leave big questions concerning the reliability of the data. Also, the use of personal visits by trained analysts— usual practice in surveys made by individual organizations—has been unable to solve the job comparability problem. The result is that middle management surveys yield data much less reliable than surveys of compensation at higher or lower levels.

As with top management surveys, it is essential to distinguish bonus-paying and nonbonus-paying organizations because the former pay lower salaries than the latter. Hence, presentations of survey data typically show base salary and total cash compensation.

It perhaps needs to be said that private organization middle management surveys for all the above reasons are extremely costly. Although many large organizations use both private surveys and published surveys, smaller organizations may find that the former cost more than they are worth.

The somewhat questionable reliability of middle-management compensation surveys means that internal salary relationships become more important salary determinants. As noted in connection with job contributions, job evaluation is almost universal with respect to middle-management jobs. Unfortunately, although the apparently increasing use of marketplace job evaluation may solve organization problems of shortage of management talent, it relies on uncertain market data rather than planned internal relationships.

It seems extremely important that organizations study the pattern of internal salary relationships and determine that this pattern not only follows and reinforces organization objectives but emits signals about valued behaviors to managers. But some organizations, apparently believing that both surveys and job evaluation are insufficiently precise to determine middle-management compensation, are employing *salary planning.*[44] In this arrangement, salaries are keyed primarily to the

---

[44]Sibson, *Wages and Salaries,* p. 219.

individual's potential and salary history as well as to internal and external pay relationships. Salary planning involves treating middle managers as many organizations treat professional employees—rewarding personal instead of job contributions.

Professionals.   As previously stated, there is overlap in salary determination of professionals and middle management. National or international labor markets are characteristic of both groups. Some professionals are middle managers. Some professionals (notably engineers) tend to have management aspirations.

Salary determination of professional employees presents at least as many complexities to organizations as salary determination for middle management. If organizations make their own surveys, selecting appropriate organizations to include and determining job comparability may be even more difficult. Because professionals tend to be oriented to their field, organizations of all sizes and types are potential labor market competitors, regardless of location. Finding comparable professional jobs in other organizations is even more difficult than finding comparable management jobs. As a result, private salary surveys based on job comparability can involve even more effort and cost. Regional industry surveys (aircraft or electronics in southern California) may solve a good part of the job comparability problems, but at the cost of excluding other potential employers. Global salary surveys[45] that collect frequency distributions of payroll data for categories of professional employees can yield useful labor market information, but they do not provide information on what responding organizations pay for jobs.

The effort and cost involved in private surveys encourage the use of published surveys. The Bureau of Labor Statistics' PAT survey is widely used. The fact that job comparability is personally established by trained analysts and organizations included are selected on a careful sampling basis encourages its use. But the limited number of job classifications covered and the difficulty organizations encounter in comparing surveyed jobs to those in the organization limit it. The Administrative and Technical Positions Report of the American Management Association's Executive Compensation Service is also widely used. But because the survey is conducted by mail and respondents determine job comparability, the data are less reliable.

But the most widely used salary surveys for professional employees are those made by professional associations and various organizations following the same approach. These surveys ignore the jobs to which professionals are assigned and report the salaries of profession-

[45]Kenneth E. Foster, Gerald F. Wajda, and Theodore R. Lawson, "Global Plan for Salary Administration," *Harvard Business Review* (September–October, 1961), pp. 62–66.

als by age or years since attainment of degree and performance. They often provide breakdowns by discipline, industry, supervisory status, degree level, organization size, and geographic region.

One effect of these surveys is the maturity or career-curve approach to salary determination for professionals. In this approach professional salaries are based on the age and experience of individual professional employees rather than on job assignment. If this approach is used, salary is not a reward for the job but for personal contributions.

Another effect of these surveys (and, of course, labor market shortages) has been the incorporation of time as a factor in salary determination. Because the curves show that salaries increase each year along with age, organizations using them tend to follow the practice of annual salary increases for professionals. Some measure of the pervasiveness of this effect is the increasing tendency of organizations to incorporate time into salary determination of middle managers as well as professionals.[46]

The extent to which the career-curve approach is used as the sole or primary determinant of professional salaries is unknown. Large, highly technical organizations often do so as well as some large research and development divisions of organizations in less-advanced technologies. But the majority of organizations employing engineers make at least some use of maturity curves.[47] The appearance of methods for translating maturity curve information into the traditional approach[48] may suggest that most organizations pay professionals for job contributions. Such organizations may also use maturity curves for setting starting rates and to adjust salary levels. One author believes that the use of maturity curves is most prevalent in what he calls the "floating labor market" of southern California and is unlikely to spread.[49]

The overlap between salary determination of professionals and middle management has prompted some organizations to integrate the salary structures of at least these two groups. Other practice calls for a double-track or parallel ladder so that professionals could advance in salary and organization status without becoming managers. Although the similar complexities in salary determination of the two groups do argue for integration, organizations would be wise to question whether the two groups want to make and be paid for the same contributions.

[46]Smith, in *Compensation Review* (Fourth Quarter, 1970), pp. 6–14.
[47]Lee, in *Personnel Journal* (January, 1969), pp. 33–38.
[48]Ralph A. Kulberg, "Relating Maturity Curve Data to Job Level and Performance," *Personnel* (March–April, 1964), pp. 45–50.
[49]Thomas H. Patten, Jr., "Maturity-Pay Curves in a Floating Labor Market: The Case of Southern California," *The Quarterly Review of Economics and Business* (Fall, 1967), pp. 57–72.

Present limited knowledge suggests that middle managers and some professionals want to be paid for job contributions given that they have some voice in designing the job around their attributes, but that most professionals expect to be paid for personal contributions without respect to job assignment. To the extent that this picture is correct, integration would seem to make salaries for both groups more a reward for personal contributions than job contributions. Our model of the employment exchange would suggest separate treatment for the two groups.

Supervisors.   Salary determination for supervisors is influenced primarily by two considerations: pay relationships to subordinates and the labor market. The labor market is the weaker of the two influences because most supervisors are selected from within the organization. On the other hand, the market for supervisors is local and because supervisory jobs are not difficult to describe, including them in local private surveys can yield solid salary data. Use of organization policy in interpreting such data is essential because supervisory salaries are influenced by industry factors and the tendency of some national organizations to pay jobs equally regardless of location. As discussed previously, almost all supervisory jobs are evaluated, usually in the middle-management plan.

The major influence on supervisory salaries is the pay of subordinates. Although organization practice varies, a supervisor usually receives at least 15 per cent more than the straight-time earnings of his highest paid subordinate, 10 per cent more than the gross pay of the highest paid subordinate, or 25 per cent more than the average gross pay of all subordinates.[50]

ECONOMIC PERFORMANCE REWARDS

Organizations, undoubtedly because they assume the need for them is great, emphasize economic performance rewards for exempt employees. As a result, the field called "executive compensation" is a complex morass of devices assumed to provide performance motivation. Some of these devices are designed to permit individuals in high income tax brackets to retain rewards presumably flowing from their performance. Some are assumed to be short-term incentives; some, long-term. Among these devices are salary ranges, bonus plans, deferred payment plans, and various forms of stock options.

Because of the widely held assumption that these devices provide incentives to performance, it seems wise to begin the analysis of eco-

[50]Sibson, *Wages and Salaries,* p. 194.

nomic performance rewards with a review of our model of performance motivation. The model specifies that for an incentive plan to
motivate performance (1) employees must believe that good performance will lead to more pay; (2) employees must want more pay; (3)
employees must not believe that good performance will lead to negative consequences; (4) employees must see that other desired rewards
besides pay result from good performance; and (5) employees must
believe that their efforts do lead to improved performance. The relationships among these variables in the model are multiplicative, which
means at the extreme that if one of them is zero, performance motivation will be zero.

Minimal reflection suggests the immediate conclusion that the
assumed incentive devices vary widely on each of the variables and
vary widely from one employee group to another. Although all exempt
groups probably want to believe that good performance leads to more
pay, they differ widely in the fragility of this belief in the face of reality.
The importance of pay undoubtedly differs both between and within
employee groups. The belief that negative consequences may flow from
better performance probably correlates positively with the perceived
complexity of jobs in which improvements in one kind of performance
come at a cost of other kinds. Although all exempt employees may
believe that other desired rewards besides more pay result from good
performance, it would seem to vary with the kind of performance
rewarded and the organization commitment of employee groups. The
belief that contributions to the organization result in the performance
measured probably varies directly with organization level. Any employee group that feels that the performance measured is beyond its
direct control or that the measurements are faulty and based on unrealistic standards is likely to be low in this belief. More serious, if a group
does not believe that its contributions are reflected in what the organization calls "good performance," not only performance motivation
but membership motivation will be adversely affected.

The following analysis of economic performance rewards for various employee groups is based on this model. Payment devices offered
each group are examined in terms of the possibility of their providing
performance motivation for that group and under what conditions.
Because, however, of the tremendous complexity of the executive compensation field, detail with respect to the various plans is kept to a
minimum.[51]

Top Management.   Because members of top management tend
to think of themselves as synonymous with the organization, the re-

---

[51]For details see Crystal, *Financial Motivation for Executives.*

quirements of the model are more easily satisfied in their case with almost any device. With most of the devices, little question is raised about any of the variables in the model except the assumption that these employees want more pay. Although some authors believe that they do not[52] and individuals undoubtedly vary, it is probably wise to assume that top management wants a "piece of the action" as a score of their achievements, if for no other reason.

Salary ranges are universally employed for management positions. These ranges are wider than those designed for nonexempt employees, reflecting both the greater range of performance possible and the larger increases deemed necessary to be meaningful. Range width often varies from 40 per cent at the bottom of the exempt group to as much as 100 per cent at the top. Although one compensation consultant has suggested that a range of 50 to 60 per cent on top-management positions is sufficient,[53] others imply that 100 per cent or more is justifiable.[54] The existence of a bonus plan affects the width of the range in that organizations with bonus plans pay lower salaries (by 10 to 20 per cent) on the assumption that outstanding performance is rewarded with a bonus. Alternatively, salary ranges are wider in organizations without bonus plans. Salary ranges also reflect organization design and growth on the assumption that rapid promotion offsets the need for wide ranges. Overlap between salary grades at this level is not only necessary but probably desirable because of low precision in determining the salary structure.

Movement through salary ranges for executives comes from salary increases almost universally called merit increases. It is widely observed, however, that these salary increases reflect the individual's pay history, internal pay relationships, and economic conditions as often as performance. Often, outstanding performers receive the same increases as lesser performers.[55]

Because, however, top executives are more likely to hold the beliefs specified in the model, salary increases are likely to be considered by them as performance rewards whether they are or not. Hopefully, at this level, salary increases are based on performance more than on other factors, although there is much evidence that this is not the case.[56]

[52]John Kenneth Galbraith, *The New Industrial State* (Boston: Houghton Mifflin Company, 1967); Robin Barlow, "Motivation of the Affluent," in *IRRA Proceedings of the Twentieth Annual Winter Meeting* (Washington, D.C., December 28–29, 1967), pp. 236–243.

[53]Richard C. Smyth, *Financial Incentives for Management* (New York: McGraw-Hill Book Company, 1960), p. 68.

[54]Sibson, *Wages and Salaries*, p. 221; Crystal, *op. cit.*, p. 119.

[55]Crystal, *Financial Motivation for Executives*, p. 113.

[56]Patton, in *McKinsey Quarterly* (Summer, 1970), pp. 52–67.

About half of business organizations have *bonus plans,* as do an increasing proportion of nonprofit organizations. Such plans are widely assumed to motivate performance and are generally approved by the stockholders. Bonus plans, although typically geared to profits, are quite different from profit sharing because they are presumably based on individual (although sometimes group) performance rather than paid as a proportion of salary.

Bonus plans are usually based on a formula designed to reflect the participants' contributions to profits. Hence, those eligible to participate greatly affect the motivational value of the plan. If eligibility is limited to those whose judgments and decisions have a significant impact on profits, it should meet most of the requirements of the model.

Members of top management meet the eligibility requirement and thus bonus plans would seem to be an ideal incentive plan for this group. But bonus plans are almost never restricted to top management and the question is whether the expanded coverage reduces the performance motivation of the top-management group. Organizations are becoming more precise in defining eligibility, although large organizations (25,000 employees) typically extend participation to about 1 per cent of employees and smaller ones to 1 or 2 per cent.[57] Eligibility levels also vary by industry with labor-intensive, highly technical, decentralized, successful organizations having higher percentages of employees eligible.

Average bonus levels range from 80 per cent of base salary at the top to 20 per cent for the lowest-level participant.[58] Some organizations set bonus ceilings at about 130 per cent of salary but others have paid bonuses to outstanding performers of 300 per cent of salary. There may be a trend toward placing lower ceilings on bonuses. One author places the usual limit at 50 per cent of base salary.[59] Organizations doing so appear to have either decided that bonuses do not motivate performance or that other objectives are more important than manager performance.

Bonus-funding formulas represent a contract between stockholders and executives. Such formulas vary widely with the economic characteristics of organizations. Most plans prescribe a deduction from profits for the owners and then a percentage above this may be accrued into a bonus fund. Most bonus-fund formulas are related to the financial goals of the organization. This relationship seems the proper one for top management, although there are organization goals that cannot be reduced to monetary terms. Other bonus formulas are keyed to goals

[57]Crystal, *Financial Motivation for Executives,* p. 130.

[58]*Ibid.,* p. 137.

[59]James A. Engel, "What are Top Executives Paid?" *Compensation Review* (First Quarter, 1969), pp. 16–21.

for sales, productivity, research and development, personnel development, public responsibility, balance between short- and long-range goals, and so on. This type seems preferable for managers and professionals whose impact on profits is difficult to trace.

As organizations become more complex, the question of whether bonuses should be based on corporate or division performance looms larger. Apparently, most organizations base the bonus on both, deciding in advance the percentage of each type of performance that is to be reflected. But determining the allocation to divisions becomes more difficult as organizations become more complex.[60] An encouraging trend is to develop separate corporate bonus plans based on profits and bonus plans for operating managers based on specific predetermined goals for division profit, sales, cost reduction, and so on. Another is for multibusiness organizations to develop custom-built incentive plans for executives in separate fields.[61] Obviously, bonus plans based on corporate and division performance and more than one goal (necessitating weighting) can become quite complex.

Distribution of bonus funds involves first allocating the funds to organization units and then assigning payments to individuals. Some organizations pay bonuses on a group basis and award bonuses in proportion to relative salaries of members. Others base rewards solely on individual performance. Still others use a combination of individual and group awards. Presumably, individual bonuses are determined by comparing individual performance to standards of performance. In some cases, the performance of eligibles is ranked as part of bonus determination. Formerly, bonus determination was at the discretion of top management. Increasingly, guides have been developed that tie bonuses to performance as compared to pre-established goals.

As mentioned previously, executive salaries in nonbonus-paying organizations are about 10 to 20 per cent higher than in bonus-paying companies. But because bonuses average 25 to 30 per cent of salary, salary plus bonus in bonus-paying organizations tends to be about 15 per cent higher.[62]

Most bonus plans pay off in cash. Some plans pay part or all of the bonus in stock. Some organizations pay the bonus over a number of years. For example, some organizations pay each year's bonus in three to five annual installments. In the usual arrangement, the individual must remain with the organization to collect it. Some organizations

---

[60]John P. Kensey, "Allocating Incentive Funds in Divisionalized Companies," *Compensation Review* (First Quarter, 1971), pp. 45–49; John Dearden, "How to Make Incentive Plans Work," *Harvard Business Review* (July–August, 1972), pp. 117–124.

[61]Sibson, in *Nation's Business* (November, 1971), pp. 29–33.

[62]Sibson, *Wages and Salaries*, p. 225.

permit executives to defer collecting the bonus until retirement or termination.

Both of these latter arrangements emphasize membership motivation rather than performance motivation and may secure the former at the expense of the latter.

In fact, there is less than full agreement that bonus plans as presently structured do motivate performance in any case.[63] Many organizations pay bonuses to all eligible participants. Many organizations have bonuses based on profits, although profits in the industry are beyond management's control. Many organizations with bonus plans have been unable to convince executives that their performance has been fairly appraised. Many plans have too many participants, with the result that executives have good reasons to doubt that individual contribution to profits does affect rewards.

But it still seems reasonable to assume that bonus plans motivate top-management performance. To the extent that these individuals are entrepreneurial risk-takers[64] and to the extent that they perceive that their performance is reflected in organization accomplishments, the requirements of the performance motivation model are essentially met. The major problem would seem to be whether or not the inclusion of other managers in the plan dilutes its effects.

Although bonus plans can be geared to both short- and long-term objectives of the organization, the more usual method of focusing attention on long-term goals is to make arrangements for managers to become owners. Logically, this approach encourages the manager to accept the role of entrepreneur or partner to the owners.

Stock options, one of the most popular executive compensation devices, were designed in part to achieve this objective. But they were also designed in response to what we referred to earlier as a personal contribution—the high income tax bracket of the executive. Hence, through stock options it was hoped that the executive could retain a larger share of his income from the organization.[65] Because this latter purpose makes stock options membership rather than performance rewards, and because the performance motivation value of stock options has been questioned for all except perhaps the two top positions in the organization, they are discussed as membership rewards. The

[63]Arch Patton, "Why Incentive Plans Fail," *Harvard Business Review* (May–June, 1972), pp. 58–66; John Perham, "What's Wrong with Bonuses?" *Compensation Review* (Third Quarter, 1971), pp. 40–44.

[64]Frank H. Cassell, "Seniority or Enterprise: What Should Incentive Plans Reward?" *Compensation Review* (First Quarter, 1969), pp. 44–52.

[65]See Arch Patton, "Executive Compensation: Tax Gimmicks vs. Incentives," *Harvard Business Review* (November–December, 1953), pp. 113–119.

compensation an executive receives from a stock option is determined by three factors: the size of the grant, the market behavior of the stock, and the executive's investment skill. Only the first can be directly related to performance. The second can be only partially controlled, even by the two top executives. The third is totally unrelated to performance in the organization.[66] In a survey conducted by Booz, Allen, and Hamilton, 57 per cent of executives stated that the relationship between their performance and their option rewards was moderate or weak. Thus, the belief required by the model that good performance will lead to more pay is quite low.

Deferred compensation arrangements are likewise assumed to be membership rather than performance rewards because of the same belief. Although a few older top executives in very high income tax brackets may perceive enough of a relationship to make them performance rewards, the usual contingency requirements reduce this perception even for these individuals.

Middle Management.   Whether or not *salary ranges* and movement through them provide performance motivation for middle management depends entirely on whether organization practice encourages the beliefs required by the model and whether or not the individuals involved want more pay and want their pay based on their performance. Fortunately for organizations, individuals who want more money based on their performance are probably able to select organizations that reward performance. Also, middle managers tend to want to hold the beliefs required by the model. But, unfortunately, organizations tend to do little to foster these beliefs and much to destroy them. So-called merit increase programs that provide increases based on pay history and pay comparisons within the organization and without, as well as performance, hide the performance-reward relationship. Programs that give all managers the same increase or provide automatic annual increases destroy it. Pay secrecy practices reinforce both.

On the other hand, an apparently growing number of organizations are publishing their compensation structure and increase guidelines. Also, more managers appear more willing to make conscientious appraisals and base compensation decisions on them. Finally, fast-track programs may have had the latent unintended consequence of telling managers that outstanding performance is rewarded in the organization. Some organizations, in fact, have started the practice of granting special awards that are neither salary nor bonus but one-time rewards based on performance.[67]

[66]Crystal, *Financial Motivation for Executives,* pp. 236–240.
[67]*Ibid.,* pp. 135–136.

As mentioned in the preceding section, organizations have also been systematically destroying the performance motivation values in *bonus plans* by including managers who can't influence profits in profit-based bonus plans and by paying all eligibles a bonus. Such practices destroy the beliefs that good performance leads to more pay and that managers' efforts lead to improved performance.

Fortunately, the growing complexity of organizations has encouraged the development of bonus plans for middle managers not based on organization profits but on variables that the managers do control— market position, productivity, product leadership, personnel development, and so on, as well as division or department profitability. Properly developed and administered, these standard accomplishment plans can meet the requirements of the model.

Professionals. With the exception of professionals who hold the values of middle management (engineers may be the best example),[68] there is a very real question of whether it is possible for organizations to obtain performance motivation from professional employees. Although they often want more money, they probably don't want their pay based on their performance, at least as performance is defined by the organization. As a result, the beliefs specified by the model seem especially difficult to obtain in the case of professionals.

Although most organizations use salary ranges for professional employees and virtually all organizations use performance ratings[69] as a basis of movement through ranges, these performance rankings and thus salary increases are highly correlated with age.[70] The result, of course, is that in spite of the terminology used by organizations, professionals find it hard to believe that good performance leads to more pay.

If organizations include professional employees in profit-based bonus plans and they receive bonuses along with everyone else, the result would seem to be to raise further questions concerning the belief that efforts do lead to improved performance. It is, of course, possible to develop standard accomplishment plans for professionals, especially if longer-term goals and progress toward them are used as standards. Some organizations have done so. But whether these plans work depends on whether or not the professionals want their pay based on their performance.

[68]R. R. Ritti, "Motivating Professional Employees: Fact and Fancy," *Proceedings of the 9th Annual Midwest Management Conference, Academy of Management* (Carbondale, Illinois: Business Research Bureau, Southern Illinois University, April 8–9, 1966), pp. 32–42.

[69]Lee, in *Personnel Journal* (January, 1969), pp. 33–38.

[70]Gene W. Dalton and Paul H. Thompson, "Accelerating Obsolescence of Older Engineers," *Harvard Business Review* (September–October, 1971), pp. 57–67.

Apparently, a growing number of organizations are using special awards for one-time contributions for professionals.[71] These rewards are not a part of salary and can meet the requirements of the performance motivation model even if professionals are more committed to their field than to the employing organization.

This analysis of economic performance rewards for professionals is based on the assumption, which seems to be supported, that professionals are more likely to be affiliated with their technical field than with particular employing organizations. This assumption may or may not be true of specific individuals. If professional employees do exhibit organization affiliation, the suggestions for middle-management performance rewards would seem to apply. But even here, organizations will want to determine whether efforts and resources should be spent on meeting the requirements of performance motivation or on removing the barriers to organization performance.

Supervisors.   Because supervisory salaries are keyed primarily to the pay of their subordinates, pay practices for supervisors are more similar to those for nonsupervisory employees than to those for managers. This means that although almost all organizations have *salary ranges* for supervisors and salary increases within them are called merit increases, whether or not they are actually performance rewards depends on the viability of merit philosophy at lower levels. Probably most so-called merit increases for supervisors are length of service or economic adjustment increases.

Actually, the requirements of the performance motivation model may be met for supervisors in most organizations. Supervisors usually want more money and want their pay based on performance. They probably also want to hold the other beliefs required by the model. But because organizations have probably done less in measuring supervisory work and setting standards of performance than in the case of middle management, it is difficult for supervisors to believe that their efforts lead to improved performance. More serious, in many organizations the supervisory job is designed so that the results produced by the supervisor's unit are largely beyond his control.

Some organizations include supervisors in profit-based *bonus plans.* Because supervisors are unlikely to have a direct effect on the profits of the organization, including supervisors in these plans may increase their status and enhance their membership motivation. But they are certainly not performance rewards.

[71]Jay R. Schuster and John B. Munson, "Toward a Direct Contribution-Reinforcement Pay System," *Management of Personnel Quarterly* (Spring, 1971), pp. 2–5.

Supervisory *incentive plans* exist in about 2 per cent of organizations.[72] In earlier practice, supervisory incentive plans were based on the incentive performance of subordinates. These plans are disappearing because they encourage improvements in the incentive earnings of subordinates whether legitimate or not and because subordinates must be on incentive.

More usual practice involves a standard accomplishment plan designed especially for supervisors. Such plans are typically based on labor costs, materials, quality, supplies, maintenance, and use of interdepartmental services.[73] Although such factors may encompass large parts of the supervisory job and encourage the belief that good performance leads to more pay, the last factor should remind us that unless these results are actually under the supervisor's control he is unlikely to believe that his efforts do result in improved performance. Also, because of the supervisor's dependence on his subordinates, his belief concerning the possibilities of negative consequences of good performance requires attention in supervisory incentive plans. Some organizations have programs that involve special awards for special achievements by supervisors.

ECONOMIC MEMBERSHIP REWARDS

Apparently, organizations have been intuitively aware of the importance of membership motivation of exempt employees and have provided them with many membership rewards. Because many employee groups within the exempt group want to expand their employment exchange when given the opportunity to do so, organizations have acquired additional contributions from these groups by providing additional membership rewards. Economic membership rewards for exempt employees include not only benefits but pay plans such as stock options and deferred compensation, which organizations often assume to be performance rewards.

Top Management. The primary economic membership reward provided to executives by organizations is the *stock option.* As explained previously, stock options are adjudged to be membership rewards rather than performance rewards because the market value of the stock can be influenced by only a few top executives, and only

[72]Sibson, *Wages and Salaries,* p. 199.

[73]"A Simple Incentive Plan for Your Factory Foremen," *Business Management* (September, 1966), pp. 75–77; H. K. von Kaas, *Making Wage Incentives Work* (New York: American Management Association, Inc., 1971), pp. 32–34.

partially by them. Also, in considerable measure, the value of stock options depends on the individual's skills as an investor.

Actually, the term "stock option" has become a generic term encompassing qualified stock options, unqualified stock options, and phantom stock plans. Often, restricted stock and dividend equivalents are included within the term. All of these devices are intended to yield increased income after income taxes to recipients and to tie the goals of executives to those of the owners by creating an ownership interest for executives. Other conscious or unconscious purposes are providing invisible compensation and a prime executive status symbol.

Qualified stock options are those that meet the requirements of the 1964 tax law: (1) approval by stockholders, (2) option must be exercised within five years, (3) minimum three-year holding period, (4) optionee must be an employee and may not own over 5 per cent of company stock, (5) older, higher-priced qualified options must be exercised first, (6) option price must be the fair market price on the date of the option grant. When these requirements are met, the individual need pay only capital gains income tax rates on the "spread"—the difference between the option price and the price obtaining when the option is exercised. But the organization cannot take a tax deduction for the spread.

Unqualified stock options do not meet these requirements and hence the gain is taxed at regular rates. But the corporation gets the tax deduction. Combination or tandem plans until outlawed by the IRS in 1973 offered the recipient a combination of qualified and unqualified options.

Phantom stock plans involve granting the recipient a number of units on which he receives the appreciation. Although the individual is taxed at regular rates, he does not have to make an investment. Dividend units are similar in that the individual receives dividends on the units when dividends on common stock are declared.

Restricted stock is acquired by the executive as a bonus or as an option. The stock cannot be resold except back to the organization for a number of years. Under the tax act of 1969, the recipient pays ordinary tax rates for the appreciation from date of grant to the date restrictions are lifted.

Stock options are a popular compensation device. A McKinsey survey of 565 large companies in 1969 found that 86 per cent of them had qualified stock option plans in effect.[74] Other types of stock option plans were usually in addition to qualified plans.

[74]*Current Trends in Executive Stock Plans* (New York: McKinsey and Company, Inc., 1970), p. 5.

The 1969 tax act, although widely predicted to reduce the number of such plans, has not done so. Although the proportion of qualified plans has been reduced, the proportion of other types of plans, with the exception of restricted stock, has increased. Apparently, even lower stock prices do not reduce the popularity of option plans.[75]

Stock option grant eligibility varies widely among organizations. Some organizations give them to all levels of exempt employees and even to nonexempt employees. Others restrict them to senior management. A study of 179 organizations[76] found that 10 per cent limit options to top management, but 12 per cent grant options down to the level of the first-line supervisor. Ten per cent of the organizations granted options to employees with salaries below $10,000 and 15 per cent restricted them to employees making above $25,000. The range of employee coverage was 0.01 per cent to .12.5 per cent.

The size of the option granted also varies, but is usually a function of job level. Surveys of organization practice have produced guides for granting options relating option size to salary. For example, one such guide[77] suggests an option of 1.5 times salary for an individual with a salary of $20,000, 3.0 times salary for $50,000, and 8.0 times salary at $200,000.

Obviously, during a period of rising stock prices, income from stock options can be sizable. For higher salaried managers it can easily double the income from bonus plans and be greater than salary. Stock option income of top executives accounts for between one-third and one-half of their after-tax compensation.[78]

The income purpose of stock options conflicts with the ownership purpose because to realize the income the executive must exercise the option and after the required holding period must sell the stock. The ownership purpose is emphasized to shareholders because stock options dilute their holdings. Hence, there may be pressure on executives to hold onto their stock. Although only 20 per cent of organizations admitted in one survey to exerting such pressure, over 40 per cent of executives reported feeling pressured.[79]

[75]"Stock Options: Hope Springs Eternal," *Forbes* (August 15, 1971), pp. 42–43; Bruce R. Ellig, "Qualified Stock Options: Alive and Well," *Compensation Review* (Second Quarter, 1971), pp. 17–24.

[76]Harland Fox, "The Executives Who Get Stock Options," *Conference Board Record* (March, 1968), pp. 42–46.

[77]Sibson, *Wages and Salaries,* p. 227.

[78]Wilbur G. Lewellen, "Executives Lose Out, Even with Options," *Harvard Business Review* (January–February, 1968), pp. 127–142; see also Wilbur G. Lewellen, *Executive Compensation in Large Industrial Corporations* (New York: National Bureau of Economic Research, 1968).

[79]Crystal, *Financial Motivation for Executives,* p. 214.

Another problem for the executive is financing the option. Obviously, large options can present a financing problem. Although not usual practice, some organizations make direct loans to executives to enable them to buy the stock.[80]

Although stock options obviously can increase after-tax income of executives, the cost to the organization has been a matter of some dispute. Answers to this question are available from the application of cost-benefit analysis to executive compensation plans.[81] Such analysis determines the cost to the organization of each dollar of compensation paid to executives through various compensation programs—cash, deferred compensation, various benefits, and stock option plans. As a result of the provisions of the 1969 tax law, such analyses show that qualified options are no longer cost-effective even for the highest-paid executive.[82] One result has been some tendency for organizations to shift to other types of options. But the fact that stock options largely provide invisible income to executives and represent a powerful status symbol may be expected to insure their continuance as an economic membership reward.

Another economic membership reward for executives is *deferred compensation,* which usually takes one of three forms: salary deferrals, bonus deferrals, or an employment agreement involving supplementary retirement payments. Short-term bonus deferrals typically pay the bonus in four or five annual installments. Long-term bonus deferrals typically pay the bonus in annual installments after retirement. Both arrangements seek to hold the individual in the organization. The long-term arrangement seeks also to increase the after-tax income of the individual by postponing the income until he is in a lower tax bracket. Deferred compensation contracts specify post-retirement payments and usually require that the executive refrain from joining a competitor, agree to serve as a consultant, or both. The purpose of these specifications is to avoid the possibility of tax authorities applying the doctrine of constructive receipt, which would make the deferred payment current income.

Organizations cannot take tax deductions on deferred payments until they are made. Nor can the deferred payments be formally funded. Tax consequences to individual executives depend on their

---

[80]John Perham, "New Executive Perk," *Compensation Review* (Fourth Quarter, 1971), p. 70.

[81]George W. Hettenhouse, "Cost-Benefit Analysis of Executive Compensation," *Harvard Business Review* (July–August, 1970), pp. 114–124; Gordon Wolf and Mario Leo, "A Systems Approach to Total Compensation," *Business Management* (February, 1970), pp. 44–48.

[82]Crystal, *Financial Motivation for Executives,* p. 231.

situation when the income is received. Forecasting the value of deferred income involves estimates of future income from investments, interest rates, and tax rates. This means that the longer the income is deferred, the more difficult such forecasts become. A compensation consultant suggests that executives within five years of retirement should earn at least $50,000 annually for deferred income to be advantageous and executives ten years from retirement should earn over $100,000 a year.[83] Hence, deferred compensation seems to be most advantageous to older, higher-paid executives.[84]

However, because the financial situation of individual executives varies widely, many organizations are permitting their executives to choose the amount of their income to be paid currently or deferred. To aid in such choices and in other choices permitted in the form of compensation, some organizations are providing executives with what has been called a new fringe benefit—financial counseling paid for by the organization.[85]

Executives, of course, receive benefits just as do other employees. But this form of economic membership reward is often extended for executives. For example, special insurance and pension plans for executives are common, as are longer vacations. Many organizations provide periodic physical examinations for executives. Other examples of benefits and perquisites are organization-owned resorts; the expense account; memberships in professional and social organizations; the organization-owned car or plane; executive dining rooms, parking lots, and washrooms; and office size, location, and furnishings.

A number of organizations have installed a cafeteria compensation plan for executives that permits them to choose the form in which they want their compensation to be paid.[86] Other organizations have developed individualized compensation plans that meet the financial and family situation of executives.[87] Obviously, the more executive

[83]Sibson, *Wages and Salaries,* p. 228.

[84]George H. Foote, "When Deferred Compensation Doesn't Pay," *Harvard Business Review* (May–June, 1964), pp. 99–106; Engel, in *Compensation Review* (First Quarter, 1969), pp. 16–21.

[85]Donald J. Petrie, "Executive Financial Planning—A New Fringe Benefit," *Personnel* (November–December, 1971), pp. 17–25; John Perham, "Financial Counseling: Worth the Price?" *Dun's Review* (August, 1971), pp. 29–31, 69–71.

[86]M. Brdlik, "Executive Salaries—Now It's Mix and Match," *Dun's Review* (March, 1969), pp. 57ff; George W. Hettenhouse, "Compensation Cafeteria for Top Executives," *Harvard Business Review* (September–October, 1971), pp. 113–119.

[87]Henry O. Golightly, "Personalized Executive Compensation: The Perfect Pay Package," *Business Management* (July, 1969), pp. 36, 57; George H. Foote, "Gearing Executive Compensation to Career Cycles," *Compensation Review* (Fourth Quarter, 1971), pp. 47–52.

compensation provides the rewards the individual values, the higher his membership motivation.

Middle Management.   Because organizations tend to extend stock options, some forms of deferred compensation, and executive fringe benefits to all levels of management, little more needs to be said about the economic membership rewards of middle management. It is useful to note, however, that because stock options are such powerful status symbols, middle managers are quite likely to value inclusion in the option eligibility list beyond its income potential. Also, although deferred compensation is likely to be less attractive than cash to middle management, there may be individuals within the group that would value it highly. Fringe benefits may also be highly valued by middle management because many of them offer huge income tax savings. But if our assumption that middle managers want to broaden and deepen the employment exchange is correct, the cafeteria compensation plan may provide the greatest amount of membership motivation. Because they want to increase their contributions in return for the rewards that they value, organizations may obtain not only more membership motivation but more performance motivation.[88]

Professionals.   Although some organizations grant stock options to professionals, it is doubtful that they represent membership rewards, except to those who consider themselves to be members of management. Although professionals value status symbols as highly as do others, they are more concerned with status in their field than in the organizations. Professionals are quite likely, however, to place a high value on benefits, especially if given an opportunity to choose those they want. They are likely also to place a high value on some benefits that are of less or no importance to managers. Some of these are technical libraries, paid attendance at professional meetings, education leaves and reimbursement, encouragement and support for publication in professional journals, paid membership in professional organizations, flexible working hours, patent rights, good laboratory facilities, more technical assistance, and suggestion awards.[89] Organizations would be wise to determine which of these economic membership rewards are important to professionals and to provide them.

Supervisors.   Although very few organizations extend stock option eligibility to supervisors, such practice provides a status symbol that serves as a membership reward. Typical organization practice appears

[88]Malcolm S. Salter, "What is 'Fair Pay' for the Executive?" *Harvard Business Review* (May–June, 1972), pp. 144–146.

[89]"Incentives Depend on Where you Sit," *Personnel* (May–June, 1965), pp. 6–7; George B. Strother, Michael S. Noling, and Klaus W. Hergel, "Attracting and Keeping Technical Personnel," *Personnel* (May–June, 1962), pp. 47–54.

to provide supervisors with the same benefits as nonsupervisory employees rather than including them in the management benefit package. Such practice serves to equate supervisors with their subordinates rather than with management and to reduce membership motivation.

On one benefit, however, organizations appear to be ambivalent in regard to whether supervisors are managers or not. Overtime pay for supervisors, although it appears to categorize supervisors with their subordinates, is considered essential by many organizations to maintain supervisor-subordinate pay differentials. Although organizations do expect managers to work extra hours when necessary, the issue is not so clear as stated because some organizations provide extra pay for overtime to employees paid as high as $20,000 per year.[90]

In practice, about one-half of organizations pay supervisors overtime when extended working hours are scheduled.[91] Straight-time and time-and-one-half are the most common methods. Other formulas include equal time off in lieu of overtime compensation, flat amounts, and percentages of base salaries. A growing practice is to pay time-and-one-half up to $700 per month, straight-time to $1,000, and no overtime above this figure for all employees. This arrangement removes the distinction among types of employees but provides extra rewards for extra time contributions.

Supervisory jobs seem sufficiently important to organizations to warrant additional attention to the employment exchange of supervisors. Unless organizations are certain that supervisors are receiving enough nonfinancial membership rewards to offset the lack of distinction between the economic membership rewards of supervisors and subordinates, additional attention to the latter seems called for.

NONFINANCIAL REWARDS

The complex nature of executive compensation programs and the frequent use of the word "incentive" in the executive compensation literature suggest that organizations believe that executives want only economic rewards from the employment exchange. Surveys of management opinion that show that managers want most of their compensation in cash[92] may suggest the same conclusion. The tentative listing of

[90]David A. Weeks, "Overtime Pay for Exempt Employees," *Personnel Policy Study No. 208* (New York: National Industrial Conference Board, 1967).

[91]Emil C. Beuttermuller, "Maintaining Supervisory Earnings Differentials," *Compensation Review* (Third Quarter, 1969), pp. 7–15.

[92]Thomas A. Mahoney, "Compensation Preferences of Managers," *Industrial Relations* (May, 1964), pp. 135–144.

nonfinancial rewards in Table 7, however, suggests otherwise, because many of them seem to be highly relevant to managers and professionals. Although as emphasized in Chapter 15, not much is known about which nonfinancial rewards are desired by which employee groups, even a cursory examination of the table suggests that many if not most of them apply to these groups. Although the importance that top management, middle management, professionals, and supervisors place on the different nonfinancial rewards obviously varies, nonfinancial rewards may be even more important to these groups than to lower-level employees. In fact, the variation among these groups in perceived importance may be partially explained by the relative availability of these rewards. Top management may place less importance on them because their identity with the organization has provided them with all these rewards that they want. Middle management, however, is likely to place a high importance on these rewards because they signify a broader and deeper employment exchange. Although professionals and middle management may not agree on the importance of the same nonfinancial rewards, the ones that they would seem to want may provide both more membership and performance motivation than appear possible from economic rewards. Supervisors must want and must be getting quite a number of these nonfinancial rewards, in spite of lack of attention by organizations. How, otherwise, can their continued job incumbency and organization membership, in spite of the small differentials in economic rewards between supervisors and their subordinates, be explained?

Chapter 15 points out that organizations have tended to ignore nonfinancial rewards and suggests some ways in which administration of nonfinancial rewards could be improved. Although these suggestions apply to all employee groups, they are especially pertinent for managers and professionals. The employment exchanges of these employee groups not only seem to be more important to organizations, but members of these groups expect their employment exchanges to include more rewards and more contributions than those of other employees. What seems even more important to organizations, the nonfinancial performance rewards (from Table 7) are undoubtedly more important to managers and professionals than to other employee groups. This means that proper administration of these rewards can yield more performance motivation and more membership motivation from managers and professionals.

Because solid knowledge of the importance of these nonfinancial rewards to various employee groups is quite meager, organizations are encouraged to match those their employee groups want with those the organization wishes to provide. For that reason and for reasons of space limitation, rather than detailing the rewards that the author believes are relevant to each group, this section is confined to highlighting what appear to be obvious group differences and similarities. For the specific rewards applicable to each group, the reader is encouraged to develop (and test) his own hypotheses by studying Table 7.

NONFINANCIAL JOB REWARDS

For managers and professionals, the most important nonfinancial job reward is the design of the job itself. Top managers, because they design their own jobs, are in a position to provide themselves with exactly the nonfinancial job rewards they want. Hence, nonfinancial job rewards that are provided to other employee groups by the organization, by supervisors, and by the employee himself are largely provided to top managers by themselves. Middle management, although given much leeway in designing their jobs, want more, and many organizations are increasing the rewards of middle management by encouraging their participation in designing their jobs. The leeway given professionals in the design of their jobs often largely depends on the amount of individual bargaining the labor market dictates, with the result that they often tend to feel that their jobs are too confining. More professional participation in job design, but not complete freedom, would increase their nonfinancial job rewards. Supervisors tend to have little to say about the design of their jobs. Although some of the restrictions are required by the technology of the organization, many of them are traditional and seem pointless.

Quality of supervision is another important nonfinancial job reward that is provided by the organization. Only very top management operates without an organization superior but, hopefully, top management supervision is colleagial rather than directive. Quality of supervision is especially important to middle management because of their extraordinary dependence on it. Although they tend to want colleagial supervision, there is some evidence that it is directive in many organizations.[93] Professionals also want colleagial supervision but organizations seem to have difficulty in providing it, largely because of differences in managerial and professional ideologies but also partly because organizations have not thought much about it. Supervisors expect and may welcome somewhat directive supervision, but if middle managers are becoming union-prone partially because of poor supervi-

[93]Alfred T. DeMaria, Dale Tarnowieski, and Richard Gurman, *Manager Unions?* (New York: American Management Association, 1972).

sion, it is hard to believe that supervisors get the kind of supervision they want.

Some nonfinancial job rewards are provided by the individual himself. For example, variety, dominance, power, sense of contribution, relative freedom of movement, and sense of pride in results may be available for all these employee groups. Although it seems true that the importance of these rewards varies more among individuals than among occupational groups, top management and middle management may get more opportunities to provide themselves with these rewards than professionals and supervisors.

NONFINANCIAL PERFORMANCE REWARDS

As mentioned previously, the nonfinancial performance rewards present exceptional opportunities to organizations because managers and professionals value them highly. But organizations have not taken full advantage of these opportunities.

Promotion, for example, the most well-known nonfinancial performance reward, in practice is often based on membership rather than performance. Status, which was mentioned frequently in connection with stock option eligibility, is often based on organization level rather than performance.

Although these and other nonfinancial rewards (recognition, power, influence, participation, goal-setting, variety, responsibility, autonomy, freedom, independence, using one's important skills and abilities, developing one's important skills and abilities) could be provided by the organization in return for better performance, there is evidence that organizations tend to provide them to all members of employee groups. Fortunately for organizations, individuals provide some of these and other rewards (personal growth, feeling of accomplishment, achievement, ego-involvement, self-fulfillment, commitment, challenge, interest, self-esteem, self-control, identification with organization goals) to themselves based on their performance, if given an opportunity to do so. Organizations tend to provide unlimited opportunities to top management to collect these intrinsic rewards, less opportunity to middle management, even less to professionals, and least of all to supervisors. If the organization does provide these opportunities, it does so primarily through job and organization design. Notice that all but the last reward listed are likely to be highly valued by managers and professionals alike.

NONFINANCIAL MEMBERSHIP REWARDS

Most nonfinancial rewards, even for managers or professionals, are rewards for membership. In part, this is a result of failure to tie some of the potential performance rewards to performance (promotion, for example). But it may also be due to the intuitive recognition by the organization of the importance of holding these members.

Nonfinancial rewards are provided primarily by the organization (often without its awareness that employees consider them to be rewards) and by the groups in which employees are members. Some of the rewards are characteristics of the organization—size, prestige, visibility, importance, profitability, even age. These rewards are equally available to all groups, but managers seem more likely to consider them relevant than professionals or supervisors. Other rewards associated with the way the organization is run (decentralization, delegation, authority system, communication system) are probably not considered rewards by top management, professionals, or supervisors. But middle management may consider them to be highly relevant rewards whether or not they perceive them to be high or low.

Security is a nonfinancial membership reward that varies greatly between organizations and perhaps just as greatly within organizations. Although all executives need and want security (pensions and deferred compensation provide evidence),[94] top executives often seem to deny that it is a reward, whereas middle management is often denied it[95] as are professionals. Supervisors, on the other hand, are usually assumed to value security and are provided with it to some degree.

A system of organization justice is likely to be considered unimportant by top management and often by professionals, of some importance by supervisors, and of extreme importance by middle management.[96] Organizations whose middle-management group has frequent external contacts may be forced to consider developing an explicit justice determination process as an important nonfinancial membership reward.

Management development programs are likely to be highly valued nonfinancial membership rewards for middle management and some professionals. Although it is possible that supervisory training programs are adjudged by supervisors to be rewards, this seems less certain.

---

[94]Robert Aaron Gordon, *Business Leadership in a Large Corporation* (Berkeley: University of California Press, 1961).
[95]DeMaria *et al., Manager Unions?*
[96]*Ibid.*

The opportunity to use one's knowledge and skills is likely to be a highly valued reward by middle management and professionals. Although casual observation suggests that this reward may be an acceptable substitute for economic rewards, organizations show little evidence of recognizing the fact.

The work group as a source of nonfinancial membership rewards for managers and professionals is especially likely to be unrecognized by organizations. Especially professionals, and many more members of middle management than organizations realize, consider the quality of associates and how well members work together to be important rewards.

Although organizations want middle management to identify with the organization and organization goals and to find membership in the organization compatible with their self-image, they are unlikely to consider these attitudes to be rewards. They seem even less likely to recognize that if professionals harbor these feelings they have not only rewarded themselves, but organizations may thereby secure membership motivation from professionals that seems impossible to obtain from economic rewards.

Because organizations have done so little thinking about nonfinancial rewards, it is surprising that reward systems work as well as they do. Undoubtedly the reason they work is that although organizations offer different rewards for different groups (often inadvertently), they become rewards only if the employee groups recognize them as such and consider them relevant. Better practice (as recommended in Chapter 15) would be to design reward systems for the different employee groups in terms of what the group wants and what the organization wants to provide to the group.

COMPARISON STANDARDS

Although executive compensation practice suggests that compensation of salesmen, professionals, and managers at all levels is becoming more alike, our analysis suggests that compensation programs should be separately designed for each employee group. Hopefully, it has been shown that the different employee groups want to receive different rewards and to make different contributions and that organizations want different contributions from these groups and want to reward them differently. It is also true that the different employee groups have different comparison standards, although information about the standards is less than complete.

The comparison standards of top management probably are primarily economic, as executive compensation practice implies. Because they tend to think of the organization as an extension of themselves and because economic organizations in our system are assumed to be in competition, they probably do compare both organization effectiveness and their contributions and rewards with organizations and top managements they consider to be competitors. Hence, the surveys of economic rewards by organization size and industry appear to provide relevant comparisons.

The comparison standards of middle management, however, seem much more complex. Although several studies have shown that higher salaried and more highly educated managers compare with managers outside the organization, reference group theory suggests that both anticipatory socialization and peer group comparisons are equally likely. Outside comparisons are likely to be made on economic grounds because economic information is most readily available. To the extent that anticipatory socialization involves comparisons with members of top management, comparisons are also likely to be economic because top management emphasizes economic rewards. Peer group comparisons are likely to be broader because more information on rewards and contributions is available within groups. But secrecy policies of organizations somewhat hamper peer group economic comparisons. Logically, members of middle management who interact frequently with outsiders are, like salesmen, likely to make outside comparisons. Managers are also likely to make comparisons with their own self-concept and to compare their present situation with a prior one.

This wide array of comparison standards employed by middle management suggests opportunities for organizations. If it is true that middle management wants to broaden and deepen the employment exchange, organizations can manipulate comparison standards in the organization's favor by providing middle management with information on how and why job, performance, and membership rewards, both economic and nonfinancial, are determined. Presumably part of this process involves informing middle management that the organization wants both continued membership and performance and that it expects to increase rewards as contributions increase. Management by objective programs probably help by signaling the kinds of performance contribution the organization values.

The comparison standards of professionals are probably largely external to the organization as organizations assume, except for professionals with middle-management orientations. But external comparisons are primarily economic because economic information is all that is available. This means that organizations that are willing to devote attention to tailoring the reward systems of professionals to the desires of professionals and to the organization's needs for continued membership and performance from professional employees, may be able to change comparison standards in the organization's favor. If, through the provision of other rewards that the professionals value, comparisons are shifted primarily to peer groups and the professional's own self-concept, membership motivation may be improved. But because comparisons within the organization are likely to also involve managers with whom professionals interface, organizations fostering such changes must be prepared to develop employment exchanges for professionals similar to those for middle management. Organizations that are not interested in long-term employment exchanges with professionals should probably encourage outside comparisons and primarily economic but short-term exchanges.

Supervisors under present arrangements appear to compare with subordinates and with other supervisors. Although organizations can probably change these comparisons, as suggested in the discussion of middle management, such changes require supervisors who want broader and deeper employment exchanges and organizations willing to make substantial changes in supervisory jobs and to devote as much attention to supervisors as to middle management. In the absence of these conditions, organizations may be wise to emphasize membership motivation for supervisors and to continue to build performance into the supervisory job.

Until more is known about the comparison standards of the separate employee groups, conclusions such as those reached in this section are somewhat tentative. But it does seem well established that organizations must develop distinctive employment exchanges for the top management, middle management, professional, and supervisory groups if they wish to optimize membership and performance motivation from these groups.

INTERNATIONAL EXECUTIVE COMPENSATION

International executive compensation, although even more complex than domestic executive compensation in details, involves application of the same model of the employment exchange used throughout this book. Although three different employee groups are involved (expatriate U.S. managers, third-country nationals, and locals) and the laws and customs of various countries are different, the major differences are in contributions, rewards, and comparison standards. Expatriates, for example, perceive themselves as making additional contributions by moving their families to new and strange localities and working under unfamiliar conditions and, hence, demand greater rewards. Third-country nationals are also working in countries different from their own and thus see themselves as making additional contributions. Customs and traditions in many countries call for recognition of personal contributions regardless of job assignment, and thus pay practices with respect to local managers reflect these differences.

As organizations acquire experience in multinational operations, pay practices with respect to expatriate managers and third-country nationals become more similar. Also, these organizations are either assigning U.S. executives for shorter periods of overseas service, at the end of which time the operation is turned over to local managers, or U.S. executives are divided into two categories: (1) those on temporary assignment, and (2) career internationals.[97] The latter are in effect identical to third-country nationals in following international careers. Organizations also adapt compensation practices for local managers to local conditions.[98]

This section analyzes international executive compensation in terms of differences from domestic executive compensation on contributions, rewards, and comparison standards. However, only the most obvious differences are examined.[99]

CONTRIBUTIONS

Interestingly, organizations assume that the job contributions of international executives are identical with those of domestic executives, as evidenced by the use of the same job evaluation plans. Although this practice is certainly understandable from the standpoint of administrative convenience; differences in laws, customs, and business infrastructure would seem to require different job contributions. Performance contributions are also assumed to be identical, as evidenced by the application of identical bonus arrangements.

Apparently, the contribution differences recognized by organizations are in personal contributions. Because expatriate executives must

[97]"The Career-Path Concept for Managers Overseas," *Compensation Review* (Second Quarter, 1971), pp. 50–52.

[98]Including using the term "remuneration" instead of "compensation," which in some countries refers to indemnification for damages or injury.

[99]For details, see Hans Schollhammer, "The Compensation of International Executives," *MSU Business Topics* (Winter, 1969), pp. 19–30; S. David Stoner, "The Problem of International Executive Compensation," in Moore, *Compensating Executive Worth,* pp. 207–224.

work under unfamiliar conditions, contend with different tax laws, and often spend more to achieve a similar standard of living, they are assumed to be making more personal contributions. The third-country national has also been assumed to be making additional personal contributions, but not so great as his U.S. counterpart. Many organizations apparently also recognize that local managers expect to be paid for personal contributions (education, age, length of service) rather than job and performance contributions and they have adjusted practices accordingly.

REWARDS

International executive compensation has emphasized economic rewards rather than nonfinancial rewards in part because domestic executive compensation does so and in part because organizations have believed this to be necessary to encourage executives to accept jobs overseas. Also, economic membership rewards have been stressed rather than economic job or performance rewards.

Organizations seek to pay expatriates the same base salary for foreign management positions as paid for the same job at home. Base salary of third-country nationals is often lower because it is keyed to going rates in their home country. Local managers' salaries are keyed to going rates. Salary surveys conducted by the American Management Association and consulting firms in several countries are increasingly used in salary determination. As expatriates are increasingly assumed to be international career executives, such surveys will probably be used to determine their salaries also.

About two-thirds of U.S. multinational companies have profit-based executive bonus plans.[100] This seems to be evidence that economic performance rewards are not differentiated in international executive compensation.

But it is in economic membership rewards that real differences exist in international and domestic executive compensation. Expatriate executives typically receive at least four types of allowances for service in foreign posts. Third-country nationals get some or all of them.

It has been observed that these allowances represent a holdover from colonial practice.[101] The apparently growing practice of using disappearing premiums and giving none or less in European countries may be evidence that if this were ever true, it is disappearing.[102]

---

[100]Arch Patton, "Upturn in Executive Compensation," *Harvard Business Review* (September–October, 1963), pp. 133–137.

[101]Stoner, in Moore, *Compensating Executive Worth,* pp. 207–224.

[102]Graef S. Crystal, "Paying U.S. Executives Abroad: The Role of Premiums," *Compensation Review* (Third Quarter, 1971), pp. 26–33.

At any rate, usual practice calls for foreign assignment allowances, cost-of-living allowances, housing allowances, and education allowances. In addition, currency and tax adjustments are often made. Foreign assignment allowances (overseas premiums) are assumed to provide an incentive to accept a foreign assignment and represent compensation for having to live and work in a foreign environment. Most such premiums are from 10 to 30 per cent of base salary and may vary with assignment and with expatriate or third-country national status.

Cost-of-living allowances are assumed to permit the executive to maintain the same standard of living he would have in his home country. Most U.S. based multinational firms use the local cost-of-living indexes computed by the State Department and published by the BLS.[103] Many organizations adjust cost-of-living allowances by applying the indexes only to the portion of salary spent in the foreign area.

Housing allowances are designed to compensate international executives for higher housing costs abroad. The State Department also collects information on housing costs, using 10 to 15 per cent of family income as a base. About three-quarters of organizations reimburse foreign service employees for housing costs in excess of a certain percentage of base salary.

Most organizations reimburse international executives for the extra costs of educating children. Most of them state expatriates' income in dollars and pay part in dollars and part in local currency. Third-country nationals are usually paid in local currency.

Tax considerations are extremely important in international executive compensation, in that most organizations have a policy that an executive should neither gain nor lose because of a foreign assignment. Most organizations reimburse executives for income taxes in excess of those they would have paid in the U.S. All organizations reimburse executives for relocation expenses.

Fringe benefits present special issues in international executive compensation. Although organizations attempt to equate the benefits of foreign and domestic executives, additional insurance, longer vacations and paid home leaves are often provided to expatriates. Benefits provided to third-country nationals[104] and local managers, and to some extent to expatriates, are greatly influenced by local customs and laws. To the extent that customs and laws affecting lower-level employees are applied to executives, benefits may range from 15 per cent to over 50 per cent of salary.

[103]"Cost-of-Living Indexes for U.S. Employees Abroad," *Monthly Labor Review* (April, 1972), pp. 46–47.
[104]John F. Hastings, "Benefits for Third-Country Nationals," *Compensation Review* (Fourth Quarter, 1971), pp. 52–56.

One result is that international executive compensation, just as domestic executive compensation, deals with a total package rather than treating salary and benefits separately. Even more interesting from the viewpoint of this book is the tendency to design international executive compensation in terms of the individual executive's needs and expectations as well as organization objectives and national laws and customs.[105]

Perhaps because the compensation of the U.S. executive working abroad is roughly twice as high as he would receive on a comparable job at home,[106] discussions of international executive compensation focus on economic rewards. But the same thing could be said about domestic executive compensation. Because it has been shown that there is a basic similarity around the world in employee goals (except when analyzed by occupation),[107] no basic differences are assumed in nonfinancial rewards for executives.

COMPARISON STANDARDS

Although organizations have apparently assumed that expatriates, third-country nationals, and locals employ different comparison standards, this may be becoming less true. The tendency for compensation practices for the three groups to become more similar and the tendency for some U.S. executives once abroad to become international career executives probably mean that differences in comparison standards accord more with organization level than with country of origin. To the extent that international executives fit the category designated as middle management, organizations can influence comparison standards.

[105]Stoner, in Moore, *Compensating Executive Worth,* pp. 222–223.
[106]Schollhammer, in *MSU Business Topics* (Winter, 1969), pp. 19–30.
[107]David Sirota and J. Michael Greenwood, "Understanding Your Overseas Work Forces," *Harvard Business Review* (January–February, 1971), pp. 53–60; Mason Haire, Edwin E. Ghiselli, and Lyman W. Porter, *Managerial Thinking: An International Study* (New York: John Wiley & Sons, Inc., 1966).

VI

System Integration
and Control

From the viewpoint of the organization, the purpose of the employment exchange is to achieve organization goals. Control is the process of seeking to ensure that these results are achieved—that actual results conform to desired results. Actually, the control process is synonymous with administration. Thus, because compensation administration has been the subject matter of this book, separate discussion of the control process is in a sense unnecessary.

But because organizations have limited resources with which to achieve their goals and because the control process is more complex than it is often assumed to be, separate discussion seems useful. Not the least of these complexities is the continual necessity of organizations to adjust to change. Because the environment, organizations, jobs, and employees are continuously changing, achieving desired results involves shooting at moving and partially unseen targets.

The phrase "system integration" in the title should remind us of the importance of correlating the numerous types of rewards with one another and with the equally numerous desired contributions in order to achieve organization and individual goals. Not only must organizations provide clear and unambiguous signals of the rewards available for achieving organization goals, but they must do so while providing different reward packages to different employee groups and somehow obtain both membership and performance from all of them.

22

Control and Integration
of the Compensation System

The primary purpose of compensation administration is control—channeling the energy of employees toward organization goals. In order to achieve organization goals, organizations require two quite different kinds of behavior from employees—membership and performance. However, the source of these two different kinds of behavior is different.

Membership is an unavoidable requirement if the organization is to survive. But the organization does not require long-term membership from all types of employees. Some, perhaps most, are considered permanent. From others, the organization requires only short-term membership. The requirements, however, for both long- and short-term membership are the same—the individual must perceive that the rewards at least equal and preferably exceed contributions and the organization must perceive that the individual's contributions are greater than his rewards.

To obtain this result, the organization must see that members get the rewards they want and are able to provide the contributions they want to make. These rewards and contributions should be expected to be different for different employee groups. Some groups may want only economic rewards and may want to provide only their time. Others, such as managers and professionals, will place strong emphasis on intrinsic rewards and want to make unlimited contributions.

Organizations that require continuing membership must ensure that employees perceive that rewards exceed contributions on a continuing basis. Because the employment exchange is perceptual, organizations must attend to changes in the environment that may affect the balance between rewards and contributions. Any change in the environment that changes the perceived reward-contribution balance can strengthen or weaken the employment exchange. An employee who perceives that his balance would be improved in another organization may leave. An employee who perceives that other jobs are not easily available may perceptually increase the value of his rewards and decrease the value of his contributions.

Because all employment exchanges have positive and negative elements and because they are perceptual, any change may result in re-evaluation of the balance. Also, a positive or negative change may have a cumulative effect.

A positive change in the balance strengthens the employment exchange, with the effect that the individual wants to continue it. A negative change produces efforts to change the situation in the individual's favor. These efforts involve actual and perceptual changes in rewards and contributions, changes in comparison standards, and finally, if the balance cannot be restored, leaving the organization. Actual changes in rewards (asking for a raise) or contributions (working less hard) are presumably tried first, then changes in attitudes and comparison standards, and finally, the individual terminates.

Thus if individuals perceive the employment exchange as fair, it is made or continued. Organizations get and keep members. Improvements in the balance exist in the eyes of the beholder and, if so, strengthen the exchange. Reductions in the balance weaken the exchange and may break it. Employee groups may be expected to differ in the rewards they want and the contributions they want to make. Organizations may not have the rewards that individuals want and may not be able to accept the contributions that individuals want to make. But if the organization is able to provide each employee group with a reward-contribution balance that each group considers fair, the organization reaps the results in the form of membership. But only membership is guaranteed.

Organizations also require performance from employees. But obtaining performance involves different requirements from organizations than does obtaining membership. The simplest method for organizations to follow is to build performance into jobs. This method involves specifying the contributions and rewards at the time the exchange is made. In this way membership achieves the performance the organization needs. This method is often the result of collective bargaining. Assembly lines and "white-collar factories" often have performance built into the jobs whether the organization is unionized or not.

Another method of obtaining performance is available to organizations if they can and wish to meet its rigorous requirements. This method involves (1) having available the rewards that individuals want and want more of, (2) tying these rewards to performance in such a way that individuals see that additional performance will result in more of the desired rewards, and (3) specifying appropriate contributions from employees.

From the viewpoint of the organization, using this method of obtaining performance implies an additional employment exchange beyond the original one achieving the result of membership. But this second employment exchange may be available only from certain employee groups. Some may not want more of the rewards the organization has to offer or the organization may not be able to offer more of the rewards that certain groups want. Some groups may find that the additional contributions required offset the desirability of the increased rewards.

But the most difficult part of this second employment exchange is convincing employees that additional performance does result in more rewards. In many jobs, measuring performance is difficult and employees may not accept the measurements. More important, employees may see that the organization requires contributions not measured or rewarded that must be reduced to achieve the rewarded contribution. Finally, employees may not believe that additional performance results in additional rewards and convincing them may be difficult and expensive for the organization.

Fortunately for the organization, however, individuals perceive only one employment exchange—the one resulting in membership. If they perceive the reward-contribution balance to be in their favor, they want to continue the employment exchange. Furthermore, in this situation, the individual expands his zone of indifference to organization demands.[1] Both he and the organization want to expand the employment exchange by exchanging more rewards and contributions.

But employee groups differ. Some groups want to continue the employment exchange with the same balance of rewards and contributions as in the initial one. Some groups want to expand the employment exchange and do so by providing more contributions in return for additional rewards (intrinsic) that they provide themselves. In this case the organization is achieving the second employment exchange without being consciously aware that it is providing additional rewards.

Attempts by the organization to obtain a second employment exchange from groups who prefer to maintain the original exchange

---

[1]C. I. Barnard, *The Functions of the Executive* (Cambridge, Massachusetts: Harvard University Press, 1938), Chapter I.

may be interpreted by these groups as an opportunity for continuous haggling over the terms of the agreement.[2] Attempts by the organization to obtain a second employment exchange from groups who wish to expand the employment exchange will be welcomed and result in commitment to organization goals.

Within limits, organizations can influence individuals to accept a broader employment exchange and individuals can influence organizations to offer them. Organizations can teach employees to value the rewards offered by the organization and that the contributions required by the organization are legitimate.[3] Individuals can influence organizations on the rewards to offer and the contributions to accept.

THE CONTROL PROCESS

To channel employee behavior toward organization goals, organizations make use of the control process. The formal control process in organizations involves (1) setting standards of satisfactory performance, (2) comparing actual performance to such standards, and (3) taking corrective action if performance does not meet standards. Although the formal control process is well-known, it is not the only control process operating in organizations. Because each individual is involved in an attempt to gain control over the major elements in his environment, individuals are attempting to control organizations just as organizations are trying to control individuals. It is useful to note that if either refuses to be controlled, the other loses the control he has. Actually, there are three major types of controls operating in organizations: (1) organization controls, (2) social control (by groups), and (3) self-control.[4] Unless these three types of control are operating in the same direction, the amount of actual control over behavior is considerably reduced. Resistance to controls in organizations can often be usefully explained by noting that these types of controls are working at cross-purposes.

Because organization controls are often deficient both in carefully developed standards and in measurement of performance, the control process in organizations is often referred to in less formal terms such as "administration" or "maintenance."

[2]Hilde Behrend, "The Effort Bargain," *Industrial and Labor Relations Review* (July, 1957), pp. 503–515.

[3]Sherman Krupp, *Pattern in Organization Analysis: A Critical Examination* (New York: Holt, Rinehart and Winston, Inc., 1961), p. 97.

[4]Gene W. Dalton and Paul R. Lawrence, *Motivation and Control in Organizations* (Homewood, Illinois: Richard D. Irwin, Inc., 1971), pp. 13–14.

Organization controls work better on some groups than on others, and in some types of organizations than others. For example, if tasks can be programmed, performed independently, and have a short-time cycle, organization controls can work very well. Similarly, they tend to work well if individuals both want and need control. But if the people involved have been trained for years to direct most of their own activities and if tasks cannot be prespecified, decisions are made jointly, and the time cycle is a long one, formal controls are more difficult to develop and apply. Fortunately, however, the latter situation is often one in which organization controls and self-control are working in the same direction, provided the individuals receive consistent signals about the direction in which the organization wishes to go and hold some commitment to organization goals. The individuals involved are those who wish to expand their employment exchange.

But it is useful to note that organization controls, although necessarily less precise in this latter situation, are still needed and still improve organization effectiveness. Measurements are in large part attention-centering devices.[5] The more precise the standards and measurements and the more rewards are tied to results of the measurement, the more attention is centered.

Thus, the control process, although more complex than usually assumed, is essential to the success of organizations in channeling employee behavior. Although measurement cannot always be precise, organizations can develop and communicate consistent signals that channel employee behavior toward organization goals.

CONTROL STANDARDS

Control standards, as mentioned, are only imperfectly developed in organizations. In part, this lack is due to problems of measurement. But more of it is probably due to insufficient attention by organizations to the employee behavior they want and need. It is also due to inconsistent signals resulting from fragmented responsibilities for different kinds of rewards.

Policy statements, if sufficiently specific, provide standards for control. For example, policies regarding preparation for bargaining, general pay increases, pay relationships among employee groups, merit and promotion increases, performance reviews, and incentive plans that appear in policy manuals and labor agreements represent control standards. Typically, labor agreements include policy statements on employee assignment, re-evaluation of jobs, pay progression, and wage

---

[5]Dalton and Lawrence, *Motivation and Control in Organizations*, p. 32.

grievances. Often, policies and procedures on hiring rates, amount and frequency of merit increases, employee classification, and job evaluation are furnished managers to aid them in pay decisions.

More specific control standards have been developed in some organizations. Examples are (1) indexes and ratios of payroll to sales, production, or other variables; (2) job, payroll, and expense budgets; (3) standard rates and ranges; (4) pay increase budgets; (5) overtime budgets; and (6) standard wage and salary distributions. Reports covering activities and results of compensation divisions can yield statistical control standards.

CONTROL MEASUREMENT AND ACTION

Comparing results to standards and taking appropriate action may be performed by top management or delegated to staff groups (for example, compensation, industrial engineering, labor relations) or to individual managers. Often, all three levels are employed in different areas of the compensation control process. Control of wage and salary levels and of benefits is largely retained by top management but may be delegated in part to compensation and labor relations. Control of wage and salary structures is usually delegated to compensation and, perhaps, to industrial engineering. Control of incentive plans is often delegated to industrial engineering but responsibility may be shared with compensation. Control of individual wage and salary rates may be delegated to compensation or to individual managers.

It is worth noting that in these arrangements attention to contributions is either fragmented or nonexistent, that pay and benefit decisions are likely to be uncoordinated, and that nonfinancial rewards are apparently no one's responsibility. Responsibility for measuring job contributions may be shared by compensation and industrial engineering, but usually responsibility for job design is assigned to individual managers. In some current practice, job design is coordinated by a separate unit within personnel, but not with compensation. Responsibility for measuring certain kinds of performance contributions (primarily effort on certain jobs) is assigned to industrial engineering, but developing standards and measuring other performance contributions are assigned to individual managers and are often uncoordinated. Even if performance contributions are coordinated by a successful program of management by objectives, the latter is seldom coordinated with compensation. Although our previous analysis showed that personal contributions are often recognized by organizations, they appear to be no one's responsibility.

Fragmentation in rewards exists when pay and benefit decisions are uncoordinated, as they are in many organizations. Nonfinancial rewards are at worst ignored and at best uncoordinated.

Top management, of course, retains ultimate responsibility in the control process. But the manner in which top management exercises control varies. This variation has been well described as control by (1) approval, (2) budget, (3) statistics, or (4) influence.[6]

Approval calls for assent to changes before they are made. For example, compensation decisions may call for advance approval by a member of top management or a compensation review committee as well as staff groups or individual managers. The chief advantage of this approach is the assurance that policy is complied with and that the advice and counsel of specialists are utilized. But approval is disadvantageous if employed to control the pay rates of individuals because higher managers have less knowledge of individuals than the immediate supervisor. In fact, if approval is used for other purposes than to ascertain that policy has been complied with, it can easily become an obstacle course.

Budgetary controls are widely used by organizations that delegate compensation decisions. Although budgets have little influence on the quality of compensation decisions, they do permit organizations to delegate these decisions. Budgetary controls provide for measurement against standard *before* decisions are made. Typically, organizations use a number of budgets for compensation control. Payroll budgets set limits on total payrolls of organization units. Pay increase budgets specify amounts allocated to organization units to cover individual pay increases during a time period.

Statistical controls are often developed from reports of compensation activities and results. Analysis of these reports can often develop standards. But even in the absence of standards, reports tend to suggest where problems exist and what action appears to be called for. Statistical reports are typically used by top management along with budgets to appraise the results of compensation decisions.

Influence involves helping individual managers make sound and consistent compensation decisions involving their subordinates. This approach requires carefully developed policies and procedures known and understood by managers. It also requires training managers in organization objectives in compensation administration. Furthermore, individual managers are provided the information they need to make compensation decisions, the time to make them, and help from staff specialists when needed. Finally, individual managers are held account-

[6]Robert E. Sibson, *Wages and Salaries: A Handbook for Line Managers,* rev. ed. (New York: American Management Association, 1967), pp. 132–137.

able for their compensation decisions. Obviously, control by influence is highly dependent on the extent to which these requirements are met.

The emphasis given by top management to each of these types of control varies widely by organization. Organizations primarily composed of individuals who want a broader employment exchange can probably successfully operate with control by influence. But even in these organizations, budgets and statistical controls will also be employed. Although inputs from individual managers to compensation decisions are indispensable, so is coordination. Whatever types of controls are employed by organizations, giving consistent signals to employees should be the major focus.

ORGANIZATION CONTROL METHODS

Discussion of control of compensation in organizations is complicated by the fact that control of compensation is intertwined with the general management control process and with controls assigned to selection, training, organization planning, and industrial engineering. This seems to be further evidence that the employment exchange is highly important to organizations but that administering it is fragmented. Because of these difficulties, the following discussion of compensation controls attempts to identify them wherever they may be found within the organization. The final section, however, makes some tentative suggestions about how they might be integrated.

Control of Contributions. Organizations have developed a somewhat elaborate control process for job contributions, much less for performance contributions, and none for personal contributions. Obviously, organizations do seek to control personal contributions but not in connection with compensation.

Job contributions—Organizations attempt to control contributions by controlling jobs and employee assignment to jobs. Thus job descriptions, job evaluation plans, and employee classification policies and procedures are control standards. In a dynamic world of changing jobs and employees, however, control of job contributions demands that (1) new jobs be recognized, described, and evaluated; (2) changed jobs be recognized, described, and re-evaluated; and (3) employees be classified according to the job they are actually performing.

In large organizations, a usual control standard for job changes is the job budget or manning table supplemented by a classification index. The job budget or manning table specifies the standard job complement for each department—that is, the number of each type of job authorized for the department. Some organizations have variable job budgets that specify standard complements at several levels of operation. The classification index is a listing of approved jobs in the organization. Use of the index permits the authorization of standard jobs in departments in which they did not exist without carrying out a new study.

A less common standard employed to control job changes is an expiration date on job descriptions. The most common standard is a policy calling for the evaluation of new jobs and the re-evaluation of changed jobs. Some organizations require supervisors to notify compensation of changes that affect jobs, and some organizations require approval from compensation or industrial engineering before jobs can be changed or new jobs added.

Standards for control of employee classification overlap with these standards. If manning tables or job budgets specify not only the jobs but the number of incumbents of each, they are also an employee classification standard. The most prevalent standards of employee classification, however, are policies requiring the supervisor to report all changes in employee assignment. Often, policy calls for clearing all new hires, transfers, promotions, and demotions through the compensation division.

Measurement and corrective action if job budgets are employed involve the preparation and analysis of reports of employees by job classification in each department. Comparing actual employees and job classifications to manning tables permits corrective action. Outdated job descriptions call for a new analysis and job evaluation.

If policy is the standard, the usual measurement is the audit. Regular audits of jobs and employee classification uncover changes that have been unreported. Policies calling for notifying the compensation division of all job and employee changes result in immediate action. Employee classification grievances also stimulate immediate corrective action.

Notice that control of job contributions relies on either advance approval by staff departments or reporting changes to staff departments. Job design is often assigned to industrial engineering for certain jobs, to individual managers for others, and in some cases to individual job incumbents. Job enlargement and job enrichment programs are typically administered separately from compensation and often from industrial engineering.

Because job design and redesign determine job contributions and, for at least certain employee groups, important intrinsic rewards, it would seem that these activities should be coordinated by some individual or group charged with total responsibility for coordinating employment exchanges. Although organization goals and technology and individual attributes are the important determinants of job design, organizations cannot afford to have job contributions determined in a manner unrelated to total rewards.

In unionized organizations job contributions are often specified (sometimes limited) by the labor agreement as a result of collective bargaining. If the labor relations division is assigned responsibility for decisions reached in collective bargaining, it seems important that these job design decisions be cleared in advance with some coordinating group.

Performance contributions—Standards for performance contributions are not well specified by organizations, except for those with wage incentive plans. Even in these organizations, industrial engineering is charged with setting standards for only certain kinds of performance contributions, whereas other performance contributions equally needed by the organization are ignored. Organizations with successful management by objective programs have developed performance standards, but MBO programs are typically not well coordinated with rewards. It is probably true that in most organizations, employees are not well informed of what the organization means by the term "performance."

Performance appraisal programs in most organizations operate without the aid of performance standards. Also, they are typically used for such a variety of purposes that they yield confused signals of the employment exchange.

Personal contributions—Standards for personal contributions are the responsibility of individual managers and those organization units charged with selection and employee development. Typically, the only specified relation of personal contributions to compensation control is policy on hiring rates, which usually states that applicants with minimum experience be hired at the bottom of the applicable range. One result of the myth that personal contributions have nothing to do with compensation is frequent conflict between managers and compensation administrators over the adequacy of the organization pay structure.

If this analysis is correct, organizations emphasize job contributions, assign much less importance to performance contributions, and largely ignore personal contributions. Because all organizations have limited resources with which to accomplish organization goals, it would seem wise for them to more carefully specify and measure the performance and personal contributions that they need.

Control of Rewards.   Organizations, not surprisingly, make stringent efforts to control economic rewards. They have devised methods of controlling total payroll, wage and salary levels and structures, individual pay increases, incentive plans, and benefits. The most elaborate array of control devices concentrates on individual pay increases, the least on benefits. On the other hand, organizations have made few conscious efforts to control nonfinancial rewards.

Most of these control devices appear to attempt to channel employee behavior toward the organization objective of employee membership (getting and keeping employees) rather than performance. For this reason the following discussion does not employ the previously used classification of job, performance, and membership rewards.

Total payroll—Standards for the control of total payroll are of two types—budgets and ratios. In most organizations the basic control standard is the budget. Wages and salaries are major items in the operating budget. Although there is some tendency for organizations to consider these items as investments in human resources, organizations treat them as expenses. In preparing the budget, department heads are asked to forecast wage and salary expenditures. Such forecasts, after some negotiation, enter the budget, which becomes the expense standard for each department and the total organization. Often, flexible or variable budgets are employed in which different budgets are made up for several levels of operation.

A few organizations prepare a separate payroll budget. This practice may serve to provide a more precise standard by forcing management to carefully think through both the number of employees and the wages and salaries to be paid.

Some organizations have developed one or more indexes or ratios relating certain organization variables to payroll to provide standards. Examples are ratio of payroll to sales or to units of output, ratio of direct labor payroll to sales payroll, indirect labor payroll, clerical payroll, inspection payroll, and so on. Again, the executive payroll or engineering and technical payroll may be compared to total payroll. These standards may emerge from organization experience or industry practice.

Measurement and corrective action in payroll control are shared by individual managers and top management. If budgets are used, individual managers provide the measurement and correction, which often consists of varying the number of employees. In organizations that employ ratios, the compensation division is often asked to prepare reports for top management that may result in top management decisions to adjust total payroll or the payroll of specific groups.

Wage and salary levels—Standards for control of wage and salary levels are less precise because pay levels are influenced by laws and regulations and collective bargaining as well as by economic conditions and organization policy. One standard about which very little is known is organization policy in preparing for collective bargaining.

A few organizations have developed standard wage and salary distributions that they wish to maintain. For example, the organization may attempt to maintain certain proportions of total employees in each pay grade. Such distributions could be developed around sensitive cost points for the organization or from global salary surveys. A few organizations employ ratios between the wage and salary levels of various employee groups as standards.

Some organizations have developed wage level standards tied to indexes of labor turnover. Although such standards have long been suggested because turnover tends to replace higher-paid with lower-paid employees,[7] they would seem to require careful development because high turnover may be a result of low wage levels.[8]

The wide use of wage and salary surveys suggests that relative position in labor markets is used as a wage level standard. Such a standard is now used as the wage level determinant for employees of the federal government. The evidence suggests that it is also the primary determinant in the case of professional employees. But although organization policy may specify a certain position in applicable labor markets for other employee groups, it often carries less weight than other considerations.

Some organizations have developed a wage level standard based on the success with which hiring rates secure acceptable employees. As in the case of standards tied to turnover, however, such standards require careful appraisal to ensure that applicant refusal was based on the pay offered.

Measurement and action in wage level control are typically shared by compensation, labor relations, a wage and salary review committee, and top management. Top management usually retains the responsibility for action with respect to wage and salary levels. Measurement involves (1) preparing and reviewing reports of present wage and salary levels of specific employee groups, (2) making and reviewing wage and salary surveys, (3) collecting other pertinent data as part of preparation for bargaining, and (4) preparing recommendations for top management.

[7]George R. Hulverson, *Personnel* (New York: Ronald Press, Co., Inc., 1927), pp. 243–257.

[8]See P. M. Oliver and W. K. Creelman, "An Econometric Approach to Understanding and Controlling Payroll Growth," *Personnel Journal* (October, 1963), pp. 446–452.

Action consists of negotiating a change in wage level in unionized organizations and a top management decision in others. In unionized organizations, wage level control is obviously only partially in the hands of the organization and within the organization, shared between labor relations and top management.

Wage and salary structures—Standards for the control of wage and salary structures overlap with wage level controls. Perhaps the ultimate standard for the control of wage and salary structures is employee acceptance of internal pay relationships. Such acceptance is fostered by formal and informal job evaluation and periodic wage and salary surveys. In unionized organizations it is backed up by the grievance procedure. Measurement and action are usually assigned to compensation, shared with labor relations in unionized organizations. Because pay is a powerful determinant of organization status, control of pay structures represents one attempt to control nonfinancial rewards.

Individual pay rates—The compensation control process has been more fully developed for individual wage and salary rates than for any other aspect of economic rewards. Not only have more standards been devised, but measurement and corrective action have been more carefully designed. The reasons for this are (1) this part of the control process is clearly distinct from general management controls, (2) uncontrolled individual rates have large cost implications, and (3) formal compensation programs employing standard rates and rate ranges provide rather obvious control standards. The control process applied to individual rates involves (1) insuring appropriate individual rates for new, transferred, promoted, and demoted employees; and (2) controlling wage and salary increases within ranges.

An example of a standard for the second part of the process is the "compa-ratio," which is a ratio of the actual pay rates in each grade to the midpoint. A composite ratio for the organization may be computed and separate ratios for departments as well as for each pay grade. A ratio of 1.0 signifies that the average individual pay rate is at the midpoint of the applicable range.

Organizations often establish control points within ranges and specify the proportion of employees that may be at or above these points. These control points are typically at the midpoint of the range but several, including the maximum of the range, may be used.

Many organizations employ pay increase budgets as standards for the control of individual wage and salary rates. Budgets for pay increases (usually called merit budgets) may be simply common percentage allocations to each department. Some large organizations, however, have developed conversion tables based on the compa-ratio and turn-over.[9] For example, the conversion table may be constructed on the principle that within the applicable ranges there should be fewer employees at each successive step so that departments with high turnover and low compa-ratios get larger proportions of the total budget.

Some organizations have compensation prepare reports comparing departments on number and amount of merit increases and promotion increases. In this practice, the averages tend to become standards.

Most organizations have developed quite specific ground rules for pay increases as standards. Such rules are designed to guide decisions on hiring rates, amount of merit increases, frequency of merit increases, promotion increases, demotions, and inequity adjustments. Typically, minimum increases are specified for various employee groups—3 per cent for production and office employees, 5 per cent for administrative supervisors and technical employees, and 7 per cent for management and professional employees.[10] Some organizations also specify maximum increases. Other common rules apply to the frequency of increases. Such rules assume that increases should come more slowly on higher-level jobs but that pay increases should be more frequent for new employees than for older ones, following the principle of the learning curve. For example, lower-level employees may be eligible for increases at three-month intervals during the first year, at six-months during the second and third, and yearly thereafter. Higher-level employees, however, may not be eligible for increases until the end of the first year, until after eighteen months during the second and third year, and after two or three years thereafter.

Many organizations have policies guiding promotion increases. Such rules may specify that a promotion increase should be larger than a pay increase, should raise the employee at least to the minimum of the range, and should be at least 5 per cent and at least 3 per cent for each pay grade advanced, but not more than 20 per cent. Many organizations also have ground rules for demotions. Common practice is to reduce the rate to the maximum of the new range, but some organizations place the employee in the same position in the new range as he was in the older one. Reasons for demotion are often accounted for in policy.

Measurement and corrective action in the control process involving pay increases typically involve several levels in the organization. If the compa-ratio and control points are used as standards, measurement

[9]Thomas H. Patten, Jr., "Funding Merit Increases for Salaried Employees," *MSU Business Topics* (Summer, 1968), pp. 7–18.

[10]Sibson, *Wages and Salaries,* p. 122.

and corrective action are usually assigned to compensation. Usual practice calls for preparation and analysis of reports followed by adjustments in department budgets.

The compensation unit is normally assigned responsibility for maintaining consistency in pay increases among departments. The preparation and analysis of reports that compare department pay-increase practice may be followed by action in the form of budget adjustment or management counseling.

If standards for pay increases are in the form of policy, organizations apparently intend to assign measurement and action to individual managers. Usual practice in the influence approach calls for compensation to provide the manager with the information he needs to make pay increase decisions and to provide counsel when required. Cases that are exceptions to policy call for approval by compensation and higher management. Many organizations, however, use the approval approach, which subjects the managers' decisions to review and approval at several levels. In both methods the compensation unit is typically assigned the responsibility for promoting consistency among departments in pay-increase practice. This is usually done by preparing and circulating comparative reports, followed by counseling managers.

Measurement and corrective action concerning pay rates of new, transferred, promoted, and demoted employees are usually assigned to compensation. Usually these rates must be approved by compensation before they take effect.

Although organizations appear to believe that individual pay increases are designed to provide performance motivation, a review of the control process for individual pay increases shows no evidence of channeling employee behavior toward increased performance. Although most organizations employ the term "merit" to describe pay increases, there is little in the control process to ensure that larger increases go to the superior performers and that these individuals perceive and believe that their pay increase is based on their performance. The one exception is the assignment of pay increase decisions to individual managers. But although these managers may have the information on the performance of their subordinates, there is nothing in the control process to assure that they will use it, and much to ensure that they will not. Some organizations do separate pay increases into merit, economic, and seniority portions, but even coupling this practice with delegation of pay increase decisions to individual managers only provides the opportunity of channeling employee behavior toward performance if not overwhelmed by other signals.

Incentive plans—The control process as applied to incentive plans, however, may serve to channel employee behavior toward organization performance. In most incentive plans, standards and the measurement process are carefully specified at the time of installation so that employees can see the relationship between their performance and their rewards. Furthermore, organizations typically develop other control standards in monitoring the effectiveness of incentive plans. Some examples of standards available for controlling wage incentive plans are production standards; quality standards; normal earnings rates; normal proportions of nonincentive time; normal relationships between earnings of incentive and nonincentive workers in the same pay grade; time paid for at average earnings; proportion of incentive employees who do not reach standard; and expected achievements in production, sales, or cost savings. Policies also provide standards for controlling incentive plans—especially for plantwide and executive incentive plans.

Measurement and corrective.action are shared by supervisors and staff groups. The immediate supervisor is constantly taking corrective action under wage incentive plans to ensure that results conform to standard. The industrial engineering department conducts continual audits of standards and prepares and analyzes reports to discover nonstandard conditions, earnings, rates, proportions of nonincentive time, proportions of average earnings paid, and proportions of employees who fail to reach standard. They are usually responsible for taking corrective action jointly with the supervisor. The compensation department may be assigned the measurement and action concerned with pay relationships between incentive and nonincentive employees. By preparing and analyzing reports they discover undesirable trends in these relationships. Corrective action is usually shared among supervisors, industrial engineering, and compensation. In wage incentive plans, the grievance procedure is an important part of the control process.

In plantwide, supervisory, and executive incentive plans, measurement and corrective action are usually performed by higher-level management. The measurement of results against policies suggests necessary action.

But although the control process as applied to incentive plans is partially designed to channel employee behavior toward performance, it is also designed to insure consistency in earnings opportunities for incentive employees and between incentive and nonincentive employees. To the extent that controls designed to provide equity (and thus membership motivation) conflict with controls designed to maintain the performance-reward relationship, performance motivation would seem to be reduced.

Benefits—The control process as applied to benefits is the least developed of controls of economic rewards. In part, this is because benefits, like wage and salary levels, are partially determined by competition, and decisions are reached through collective bargaining or through management judgment based on limited information. But it is also due to the complexity of the benefit package and the lack of information both inside and outside the organization on benefit costs and on employee desires.

Few control standards of benefits exist. Most organizations, of course, have standards for overhead expenditures. Cost standards for specific benefit programs have been determined in preparation for bargaining. Organizations with cafeteria compensation plans and those that have conducted organization benefit plan analyses have established cost figures for each benefit. A number of benefit consultants have aided organizations in analyzing benefit costs.

Broad surveys by such organizations as the national Chamber of Commerce provide rough industry standards of benefit costs. But attempts by organizations to use these broad surveys as standards encounter problems of work force composition, financing arrangements, and pay levels (many benefits are tied to pay). It seems that most organizations will have to develop their own standards, perhaps by determining what prevailing practice would cost the organization. Part of the process will presumably involve determining what benefits the organization's work force needs and wants.

Measurement and corrective action in the control process as applied to benefits in many organizations are shared by the benefits administrator, compensation, labor relations, and top management. Measurement of costs has usually been assigned to compensation. Corrective action has been assigned to labor relations and top management and takes the form of bargaining a revised benefit package or, in nonunion organizations, unilateral revisions. In the face of increasing benefit costs and increased employee interest in benefits, many organizations are conducting careful audits of the benefit package in terms of actual employee and organization need. As interest in and adoption of cafeteria compensation plans develop, organizations will be forced to measure costs of individual benefits and to control them.

Nonfinancial rewards—The control process as applied to nonfinancial rewards is at present so intertwined with organization activities of various types as to almost defy discussion. Part of the reason for this, of course, is the lack of recognition by the organization that they are rewards. Job design, for example, although increasingly recognized as a source of numerous nonfinancial rewards for many employee groups, has traditionally been assigned to individual managers and industrial engineering and handled as a matter of increasing organization output rather than as a source of nonfinancial rewards. Promotion, a potentially powerful nonfinancial and economic performance reward, has often been treated by organizations as a method of building the organization rather than as a reward.

As detailed in Chapter 15, organizations have a huge arsenal of nonfinancial rewards that are provided to various employee groups, often without the organization's knowledge that employees consider them to be rewards. Many of these rewards are consequences of organization design and functioning and exist because the organization is a dynamic people-resource, goal-seeking entity operating at specific locations in space and time at some level of effectiveness. The point is not that these variables are uncontrolled, although some of them may be because organizations have ignored them, but that rewards assumed to exist for other purposes and administered in separate parts of the organization are likely to conflict.

SYSTEM INTEGRATION

If compensation administration involves as broad an employment exchange as described in this book, the ultimate control seems to involve coordination of all the separate rewards and of rewards with contributions for each employee group. Both organizations and individuals seem to be demanding a broader employment exchange that includes more and more varied rewards and contributions. Furthermore, most organizations are including a greater variety of employee groups —more professionals, more women, more members of minority groups. The rewards that some of these groups expect and the contributions they want to make are quite different from the expectations of other groups. Organizations can be expected to respond with more differentiation among employee groups, both because of organization requirements and social pressures.

The differentiation of rewards for different employee groups creates a need for coordination of the reward process in organizations. If responsibility for the different rewards are assigned to separate organization units and some rewards are no one's responsibility, individuals receive contradictory signals. The logical solution for organizations is to assign the development of reward packages to one organization unit. The development of these packages should be based on the characteristics of the work force of the organization.

Coordination of rewards into an integrated whole is essential if the organization is to gain maximum value from the rewards. It is equally important that rewards be integrated with contributions. Organizations must focus more attention on the contributions required from each employee group and the relationship in each group between desired rewards and desired contributions. It thus appears essential that job and organization design, as well as the administration of other nonfinancial rewards (as suggested in Chapter 15), be integrated with economic rewards. Organization analysis of required contributions could usefully include an analysis of labor contracts in terms of the contributions they imply. Organizations would also be wise to more carefully spell out the expected contributions at the time of hiring. Also, MBO programs that spell out expected contributions need to be integrated with rewards.

Organizations have limited resources, and determining the optimum allocation of these resources is a crucial decision. Thus the organization must determine the contributions it needs from each employee group and how it can best distribute its available resources to attain them. This suggests that organizations should be willing to accept minimal performance and commitment from some employee groups while insisting on high performance and commitment from others. Some work can be highly programmed, requiring only that the individual maintain his membership at a minimum level of performance. For the groups involved, performance is built into the organization structure and the technology and rewards are primarily economic and defined explicitly.

Where, however, the organization requires that considerable discretion be exercised by the individual, more commitment is needed and this requires that the individual see a connection between his performance above the minimum level and additional rewards. These employment exchanges can probably never be completely specified, but they can be expanded through understanding of contributions relevant to both individual and organization and the availability of intrinsic rewards. Such employment exchanges imply future contributions by the individual and additional rewards for efforts to develop them.

Organizations obviously differ—in size, technology, organization climate, organization structure, and in other ways. Some may want to, and perhaps have to, limit the employment exchange to an economic transaction involving a simple exchange of money and time. But most organizations find themselves administering a number of different employment exchanges of varying complexity. Proper use of organization resources requires that these employment exchanges be designed and administered so as to give clear and consistent signals to each employee group. The alternative is too expensive in terms of organization resources and in terms of social goals. Because the employment exchange is perceptual on the part of both organizations and individuals, confusing signals can terminate it or seriously limit its results.

Name Index

Subject Index